Greece

P. De Wilde /HOA QUI

"Conversation taught me immediately that the Greeks are an enthusiastic, curious-minded, passionate people. *Passion*...Not only passion, but contradictoriness, confusion, chaos – all these sterling human qualities I rediscovered and cherished again ... *And generosity*... I was already enamoured of Greece, and the Greeks, before catching sight of the country."

Henry Miller
The Colossus of Maroussi

Travel Publications

38 Clarendon Road – WATFORD Herts WD1 1 SX - U.K.
Tel. (01923) 415 000
www.michelin-travel.com
TheGreenGuide-uk@uk.michelin.com

Manufacture française des pneumatiques Michelin
Société en commandite par actions au capital de 2 000 000 000 de francs
Place des Carmes-Déchaux – 63000 Clermont-Ferrand (France)
R.C.S. Clermont-Fd B 855 200 507

Dépôt légal février 2001 – ISBN 2-06-000885-9 – ISSN 0763-1383

Printed in France 02/2001/4.1

Compogravure : NORD COMPO, Villeneuve d'Ascq
Impression : I.M.E., Baume-les-Dames
Cover design : Carré Noir, Paris 17e arr.

THE GREEN GUIDE:
The Spirit of Discovery

The exhilaration of new horizons, the fun of seeing the world , the excitement of discovery: this is what we seek to share with you. To help you make the most of your travel experience, we offer first-hand knowledge and turn a discerning eye on places to visit.
This wealth of information gives you the expertise to plan your own enriching adventure. With THE GREEN GUIDE showing you the way, you can explore new destinations with confidence or rediscover old ones.
Leisure time spent with THE GREEN GUIDE is also a time for refreshing your spirit and enjoying yourself.
So turn the page and open a window on the world. Join THE GREEN GUIDE in the spirit of discovery.

Contents

H. Lewandowski/RMN

Alabaster perfume flacon

Caryatids of the Erechtheion

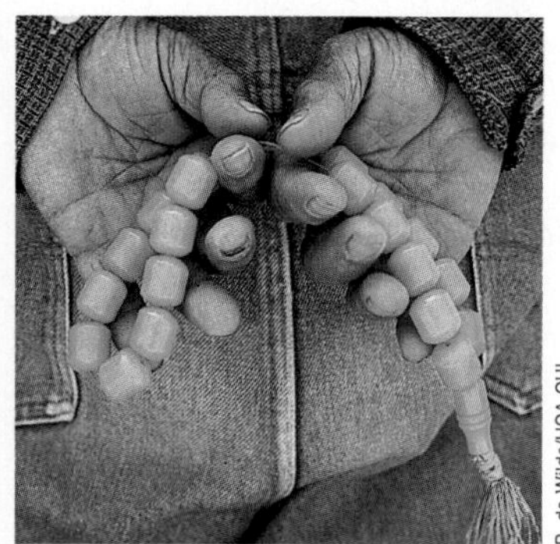

P. de Wilde/HOA QUI

Worry beads to pass the time

G. Simeone/DIAF

Byzantine church near Váthia

Maps and plans

COMPANION PUBLICATIONS

Map 980

– on a scale of 1:700 000, the whole Greek road network, islands and mainland (including Crete), with names indicated both in Greek letters and their transcription.

... and to travel to Greece

Road Atlas Europe

– with an index of place names, 74 town plans and maps of urban areas.

Michelin on the net: plan itineraries with the latest updates on road conditions, tolls, expected travel times; information on where to stay and where to eat and tourist attractions in the areas you are touring.

www.michelin-travel.com

Thematic maps and touring maps

Town plans

Museums, monuments and sites

Islands

Using this guide

- The summary maps are designed to assist at the planning stage: the **Map of principal sights** identifies the major attractions in the whole country and in more detail in the Peloponnese, and the **Map of touring programmes** outlines regional motoring itineraries.

- It is worth reading the **Introduction** before setting out as it gives background information on history, the arts – architecture, sculpture, painting, music and letters – also on traditional culture and food and wine.

- The main natural and cultural attractions are presented in alphabetical order, using the modern Greek place names, in the **Sights section**; excursions to places in the surrounding district are attached to many of the town chapters.
The chapter on **Athens** includes a number of typical and traditional cafés and restaurants, where the prices are reasonable.

- The clock symbol ⏲ placed after the name of a sight refers to the Admission times and charges chapter at the end of the guide.

- The **Practical Information section** is packed with useful travel advice, addresses, information on recreational facilities and a calendar of events.

- There is a **glossary** of Greek words and expressions at the end of the guide.

- To find a particular place, event, historic figure or practical information, consult the **Index**.

- We greatly appreciate comments and suggestions from our readers. Write to us at Michelin Travel Publications, 38 Clarendon Road – Watford Herts WD 1 SX – UK or send an e-mail to TheGreenGuide-uk@uk.michelin.com

P. De Wilde /HOA QUI

Key

★★★ **Worth a journey**

★★ **Worth a detour**

★ **Interesting**

Tourism

Admission Times and Charges listed at the end of the guide

Sightseeing route with departure point indicated

Ecclesiastical building

Synagogue – Mosque

Building (with main entrance)

Statue, small building

Wayside cross

Fountain

Fortified walls – Tower – Gate

Visit if time permits

AZ B — Map co-ordinates locating sights

Tourist information

Historic house, castle – Ruins

Dam – Factory or power station

Fort – Cave

Prehistoric site

Viewing table – View

Miscellaneous sight

Recreation

Racecourse

Skating rink

Outdoor, indoor swimming pool

Marina, moorings

Mountain refuge hut

Overhead cable-car

Tourist or steam railway

Waymarked footpath

Outdoor leisure park/centre

Theme/Amusement park

Wildlife/Safari park, zoo

Gardens, park, arboretum

Aviary, bird sanctuary

Additional symbols

Motorway (unclassified)

Junction: complete, limited

Pedestrian street

Unsuitable for traffic, street subject to restrictions

Steps – Footpath

Railway – Coach station

Funicular – Rack-railway

Tram – Metro, Underground

Bert (R.)... — Main shopping street

Post office – Telephone centre

Covered market

Barracks

Swing bridge

Quarry – Mine

B F — Ferry (river and lake crossings)

Ferry services: Passengers and cars

Foot passengers only

③ — Access route number common to MICHELIN maps and town plans

Abbreviations and special symbols

H — Town hall

M — Museum

T — Theatre

Hotel

Olympic Airways

ΕΛΠΑ ELPA — Greek Automobile Club

Ancient site

Ancient theatre

Christian cemetery

Muslim cemetery

Monastery

Windmill

Principal sights

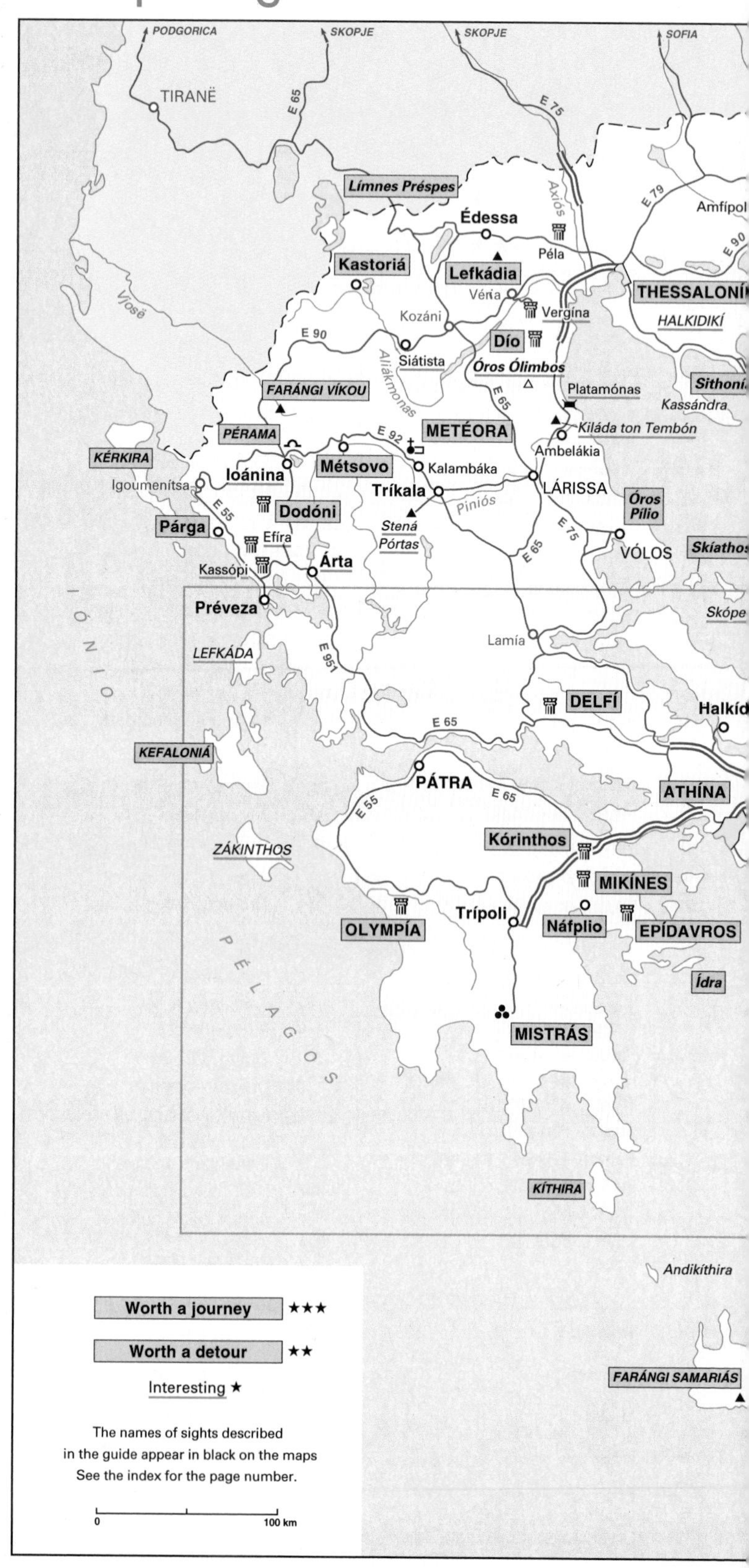

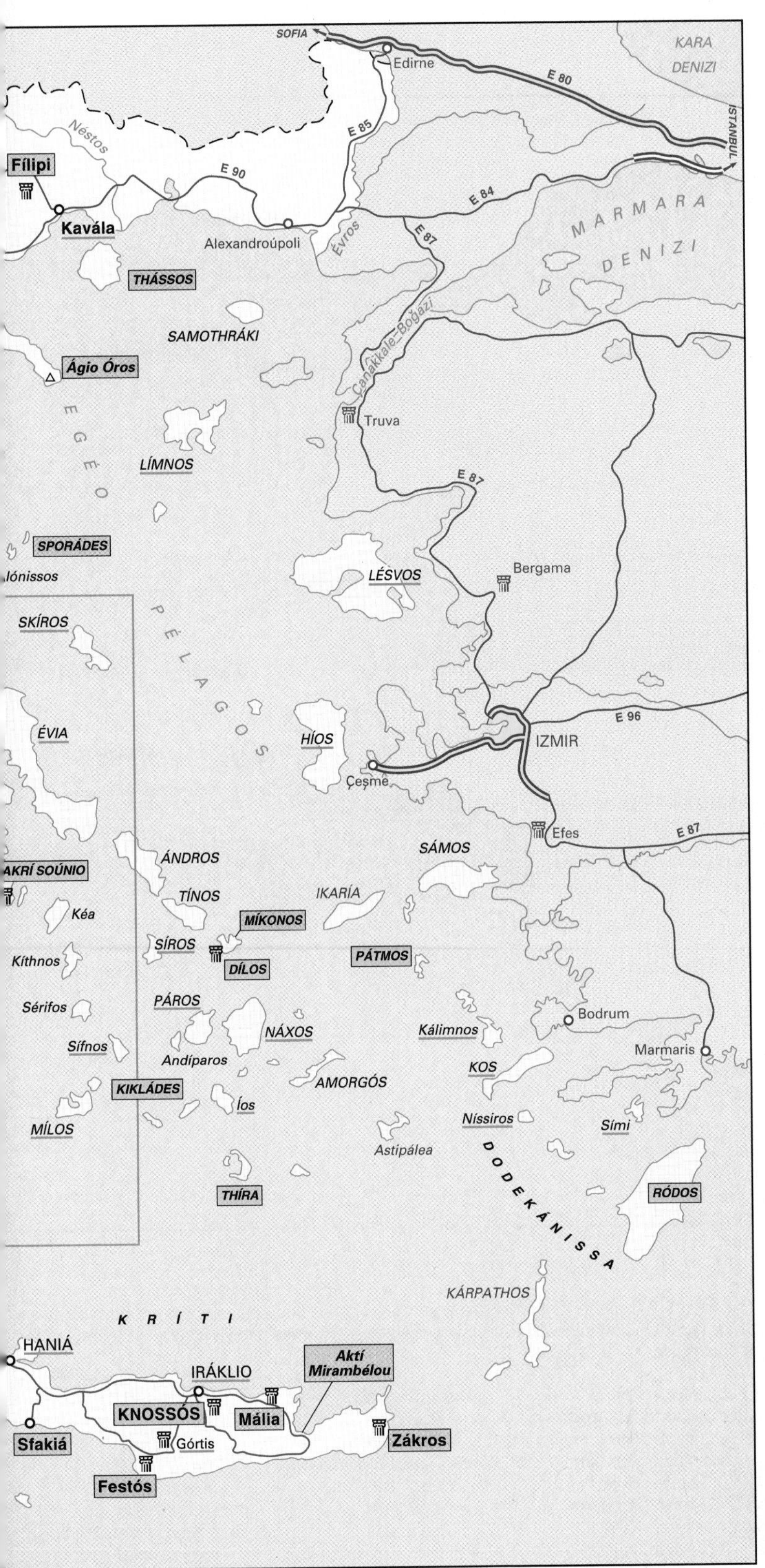
SOFIA
Edirne
KARA DENIZI
E 80
ISTANBUL
Néstos
E 85
Fílipi
E 90
E 84
MARMARA DENIZI
Kavála
Alexandroúpoli
Évros
E 87
THÁSSOS
SAMOTHRÁKI
Çanakkale-Boğazi
Ágio Óros
Truva
EGÉO PÉLAGOS
LÍMNOS
E 87
SPORÁDES
Bergama
LÉSVOS
SKÍROS
E 96
ÉVIA
HÍOS
IZMIR
Çeşme
Efes
E 87
SÁMOS
ÁNDROS
AKRÍ SOÚNIO
TÍNOS
IKARÍA
Kéa
MÍKONOS
SÍROS
PÁTMOS
Kíthnos
DÍLOS
Sérifos
PÁROS
Bodrum
NÁXOS
Kálimnos
Sífnos
Andíparos
Marmaris
KOS
AMORGÓS
KIKLÁDES
Íos
Níssiros
MÍLOS
Sími
Astipálea
DODEKÁNISSA
THÍRA
RÓDOS
KÁRPATHOS
KRÍTI
HANIÁ
IRÁKLIO
Aktí Mirambélou
KNOSSÓS
Mália
Sfakiá
Górtis
Zákros
Festós

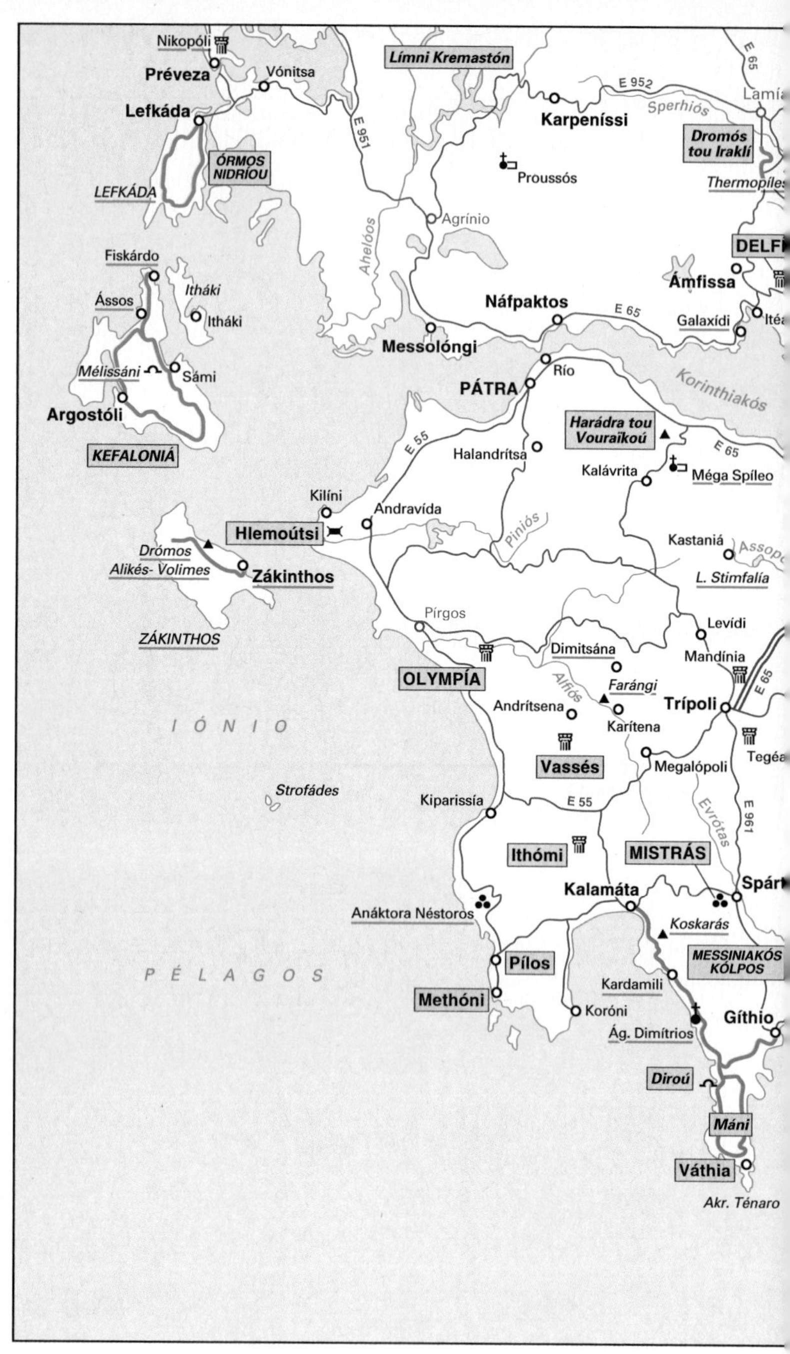

The PRINCIPAL SIGHTS MAP (see above and preceding pages) uses modern Greek place names, which are listed below opposite the names usually used in English and in this guide.

Aphaia	Aféa
Arcadian Coast	Aktí Arkadías
Athens	Athína
Mount Athos	Ágio Óros
Bassae	Vassés
Brauron	Vravróna
Chania	Haniá
Cephallonia	Kefalonía
Chaironeia	Herónia
Chios	Híos
Corfu	Kérkira
Corinth Canal	Dióriga Korínthou
Corinth	Kórinthos
Delos	Dílos
Delphi	Delfí
Eagles' Road	Drómos ton Aetón
Eleusis	Elefsína
Epidauros	Epídavros
Euboia	Évia
Gortyn	Górtina
Heraion	Akrotírio
Headland	Iréo
Herakles' Road	Drómos tou Iraklí
Heraklion	Iráklio

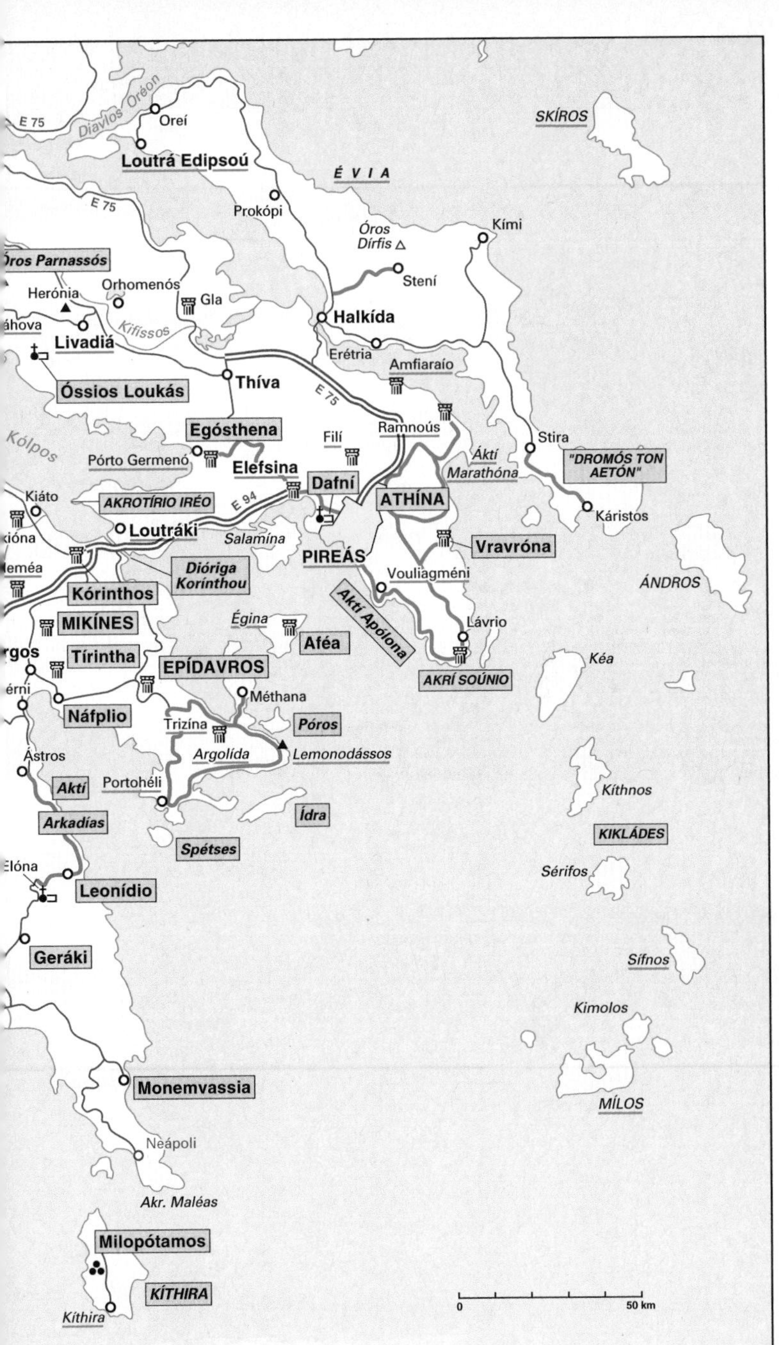

Kythera	Kíthira	Mount Olympus	Óros Ólimbos	Samos	Sámos
Leukas (Levkas)	Lefkáda	Mount Parnassos	Óros Parnassós	Santorini	Thíra
Mani	Máni	Mount Pelion	Óros Pílio	Siphnos	Sífnos
Melos	Mílos	Paros	Páros	Cape Sounion	Ákri Soúnio
Messene	Ithómi	Patras	Pátra	Spetsae	Spétses
Messenian Gulf	Messiniakós Kólpos	Pella	Péla	Syros	Síros
Mycenae	Mikínes	Phaistos	Festós	Taygetos	Taígetos
Mykonos	Míkonos	Poros	Póros	Tenos	Tínos
Nauplion	Náfplio	Rhodes	Ródos	Thebes	Thíva
Naxos	Náxos	Salonica	Thessaloníki	Thermopylae	Thermopíles
Nestor's Palace	Anáktora Néstoros	Samaria Gorge	Farángi Samariás	Zante, Zakynthos	Zákinthos

Touring programmes

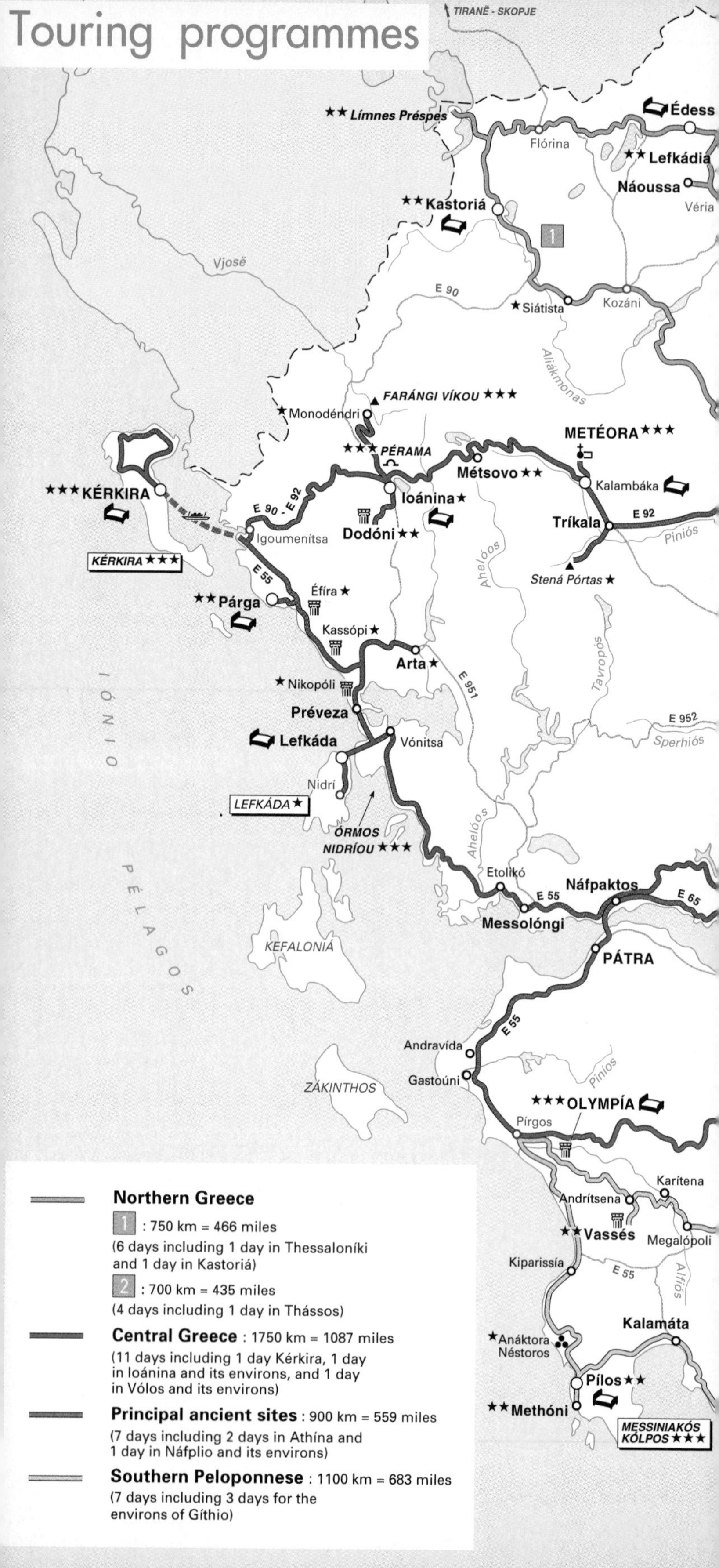

Northern Greece

1 : 750 km = 466 miles
(6 days including 1 day in Thessaloníki and 1 day in Kastoriá)

2 : 700 km = 435 miles
(4 days including 1 day in Thássos)

Central Greece : 1750 km = 1087 miles
(11 days including 1 day Kérkira, 1 day in Ioánina and its environs, and 1 day in Vólos and its environs)

Principal ancient sites : 900 km = 559 miles
(7 days including 2 days in Athína and 1 day in Náfplio and its environs)

Southern Peloponnese : 1100 km = 683 miles
(7 days including 3 days for the environs of Gíthio)

SKOPJE
SOFIA
E 90
ALEXANDROUPOLI
★★Fílipi
Kavála★
Néstos
E 79
Strimónas
Axiós
E 75
Amfípoli
Péla
86
E 90
1
2
E 90
THESSALONÍKI★★
Thássos★★
Vergína★
Palatítsia★
2
★★Dío
Vourvouroú
Litóhoro
Óros Ólimbos★
Platamónas★
Sithonía★★
Kiláda ton Tembón★
E G É O
LÍMNOS
LÁRISSA
P É L A G O S
E 75
VÓLOS
Óros Pílio★★
SPORÁDES
E 65
SKÍROS
Lamía
★ Thermopíles
E 75
Ámfissa
DELFÍ★★★
É V I A
Gla
Kifissos
Galaxídi★
Óssios Loukás★★
E 75
Eleftherés
Korinthiakós Kólpos
E 962
E 65
E 94
★★Kórinthos
★★Dafní
ATHÍNA★★★
Aktí Apólona★★
Assopós
MIKÍNES★★★
E 65
Égina
Árgos
Tírintha★★
AKRÍ SOÚNIO★★★
Mandínia
EPÍDAVROS★★★
Náfplio★★
Trípoli
Àstros
K I K L Á D E S
Ídra
Aktí Arkadías★★
Spétses
Leonídio★★
MISTRÁS★★★
Spárti
Elóna
E 961
Evrotas
Geráki★★
Overnight stop
Gíthio
Areópoli★
Monemvassía★★
Máni★★
Name under which a route is described. See the index for page number.
Diroú★★
Máni★★
0
50 km
Váthia★★
KÍTHIRA

Holy Trinity Monastery, Metéora

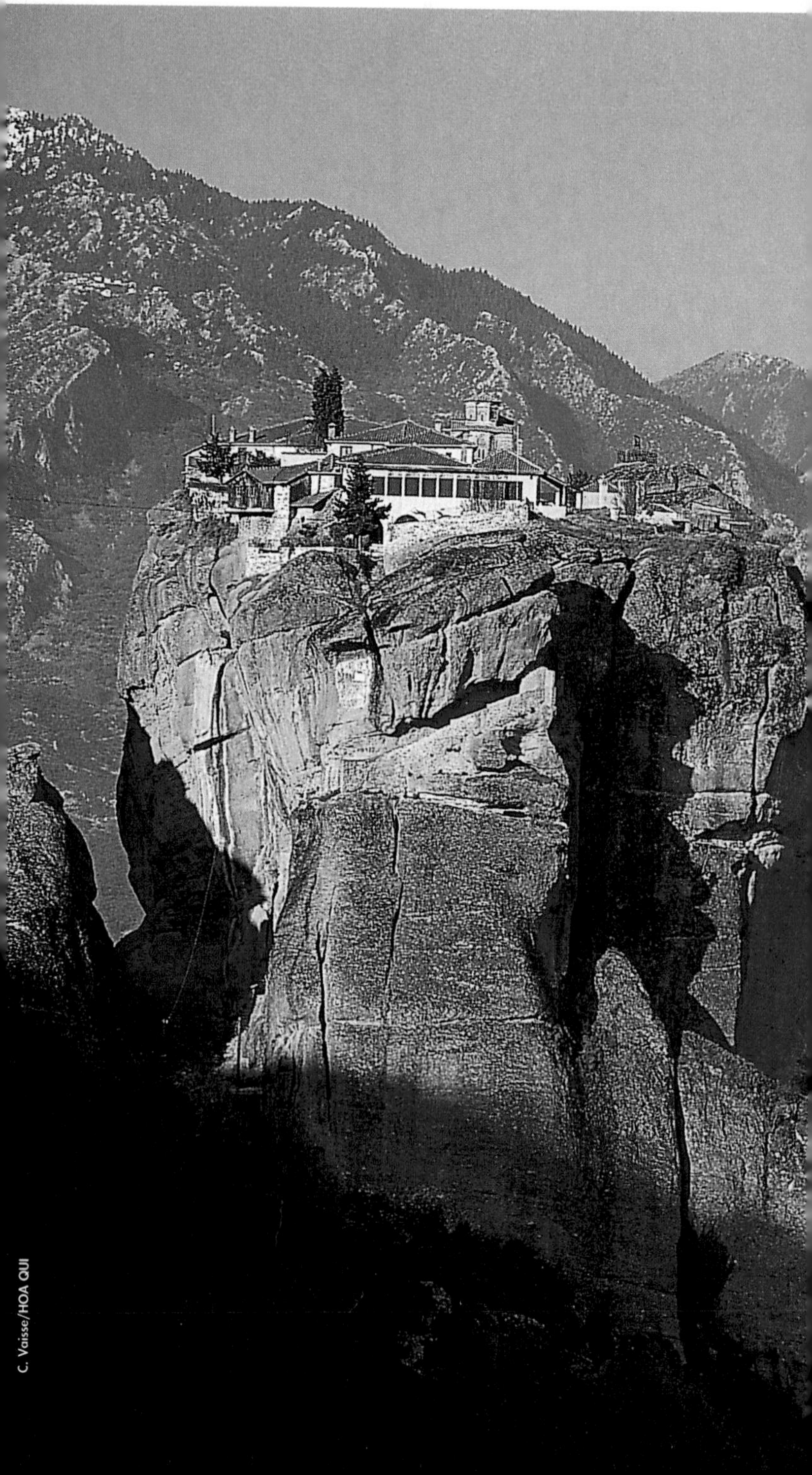

C. Vaisse/HOA QUI

Introduction

Landscape

Greece lies at the southern end of the Balkan peninsula. Its land mass (131 944km²/50 944sq miles) is punctuated by mountains, fragmented by the sea and skirted by a very long broken coastline (15 020km/9 332mi). The country's most distinctive characteristic is its many islands; between Thássos and Crete (600km/ 373mi) there are 427 islands, of which 134 are inhabited.
Greece is divided into nine regions *(for map see p 5)* which are sub-divided into departments *(nomí)*. The total population is about 10 259 900.

Topography – The country, which rises to its highest point in Mount Olympos (2 917m/9 577ft), presents a rugged but fragmented and complex topography, which can however be divided into two distinct zones.
In the east, an ancient primary substratum, consisting of crystalline metamorphic (granite, gneiss, marble...) rocks alternating with sedimentary limestone, has been raised by movements of the earth's crust: the mountain ranges of Thrace and Macedonia, the foothills of the Rodope massif in Bulgaria; Mount Olympos, its high peaks shaped by ice-age erosion, Mounts Óssa and Pelion extending into Euboia; the Aegean Islands, traces of a continent submerged at the end of the Tertiary Era by earthquakes which created troughs in the seabed (up to 4 850m/15 912ft deep) *(see p 316)*.
In the west, a tertiary chain, the Jugoslavian Dinaric Alps, continues south to form the spine of Greece, composed mainly of karst, a limestone rock eroded by running water to form caves, chasms and swallow holes *(katavóthres)* into which lakes and ponds drain away underground. This mountain range, which contains many small rounded sinkholes (doline) and runs mainly north-south despite many divergent minor chains, includes the peaks of the Pindos range (Mount Smólikas 2 637m/8 652ft) and the Ionian Islands, Mount Óthris and Mount Parnassos (2 457m/8 061ft), the mountains of the Peloponnese including Erímanthos (2 224m/7 297ft), Parnon and Taígetos (2 407m/7 897ft), ending in the mountain spine of Crete which rises to a peak in Mount Ida (2 456m/8 058ft).

CONTINENTAL GREECE

Central Greece and Euboia – Pop 1 260 495, excluding the Athens conurbation.

Attica, the heart of Greece, occupies a promontory consisting of low hills and plains covered in vineyards and olive groves. The city of Athens, which is bounded by several high peaks - Parnes, Pentelikon and Hymettos, extends its suburbs inland *(north)* and to the Bay of Eleusis *(west)*, to the port of Piraeus *(south)* and along the Apollo coast *(southeast)*, enveloping the plain where olive trees used to flourish. Between Mount Hymettos and the famous Laurion silver mines lies the Messógia *(see p 110 for map of ATHENS Region)*, once a marshy swamp but now parcelled out into orchards, fields and vineyards.
North of Mount Parnes and Mount Kithairon lies **Boeotia**; its main towns, Thebes and Livadiá, are agricultural markets. Wheat, corn and barley are grown in the Boeotian plain while the Tanágra basin is devoted to potatoes and tomatoes; the reclaimed land which was once flooded to form Lake Copaïs is now a huge cotton plantation. The island of **Euboia** (Évia) lies parallel to the east coast of the Attic peninsula to which it is linked by a bridge.

KAUFMAN /TOP

Mount Olympos under snow

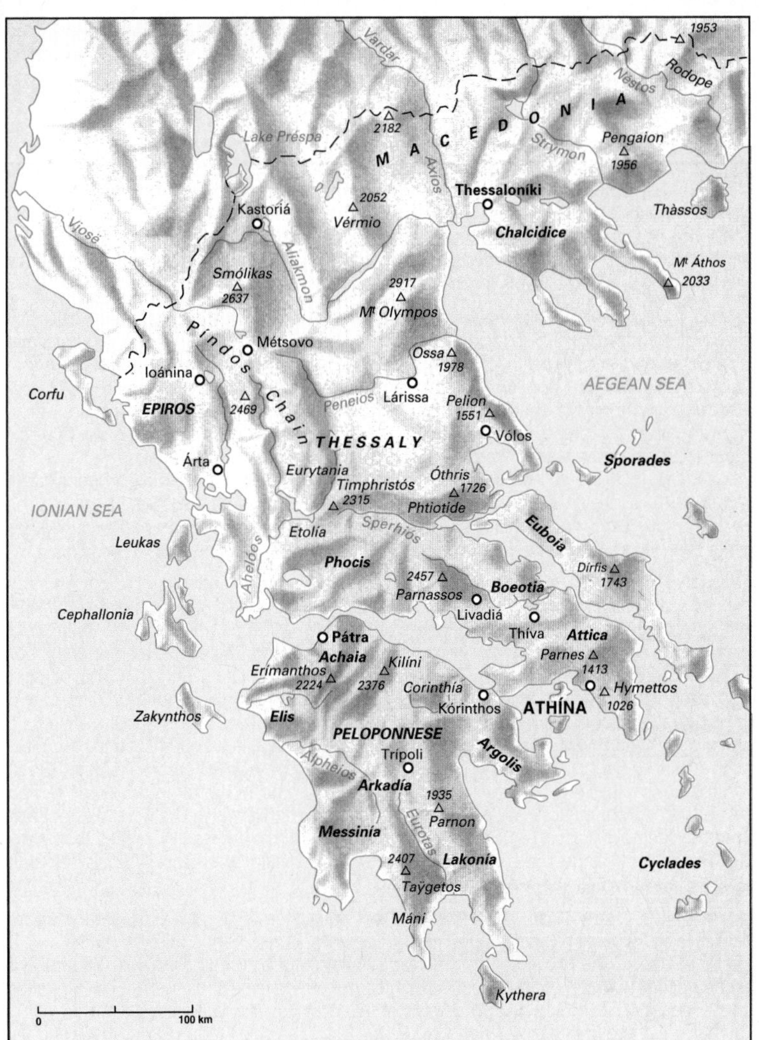

The western boundary with **Phocis** *(Fokída)* is marked by Mount Parnassos with its bauxite mines which have promoted the development of the important industrial complex of Andikíra for the production of aluminium; further west lies the lake formed by the dam on the Mórnos which supplies water to Athens. Phocis *(Fokída)* is particularly famous for the sanctuary at Delphi and the "sea of olive trees" which fills the Amphissa basin.

Etolía on the west coast comprises a cool mountainous district clothed with holm-oaks round the huge reservoir, Lake Trihonída, and the River Ahelóos expanding into the Agrínio basin where olives, tobacco and early vegetables are raised; the gleaming lagoon at Missolonghi (salt marshes) lies on the north coast of the Gulf of Patras.
The wooded highlands of **Eurytania** in the north of central Greece are still impenetrable in parts. Karpeníssi, dominated by Mount Timfristós (2 315m/7 595ft), is the main town in the region where forestry is the principal activity. On the western boundary with Etolía lies the vast Kremastá reservoir formed by the dammed waters of the River Ahelóos, which has a great energy production capacity. To the northeast the agricultural region (cotton, rice, cereals) of **Pthiotis** *(Fthiótida)* is bisected by the beautiful Sperhiós Valley. The only large town, Lamía, is an active business centre and an important road and rail junction. The Thermopylae Pass leads to the famous resort of Kaména Voúrla opposite Euboia.

Peloponnese – Pop 1 086 935. The Peloponnese, which is linked to Attica by the Isthmus of Corinth, now breached by the Corinth Canal, is a vast and mountainous peninsula also known in the Middle Ages as **Morea**. The landmass is made up of high peaks, inland basins caused by subsidence and irrigated coastal plains.
The eastern coastal plain, the **Argolid** *(Argolída)*, which is dominated by the citadels of Árgos and Mycenae, is devoted to cereals, as well as orchards and market gardens.
In the north lies a fertile coastal strip divided into **Corinth** *(east)* and **Achaia** *(west)*. The vines which are cultivated to produce wine and raisins often alternate with rows of vegetables or fruit trees (oranges). Patras, which is the third largest town in Greece and an important centre for wine merchants, is also a port where many tourists disembark.

Down the west coast extends the monotonous plain of **Elis** *(Ilía)*, partially composed of the alluvion deposited by the River Alfiós (Alpheios), which has been successively reclaimed since the Middle Ages. Small-scale enterprises are engaged in cereal cropping, market gardens, orchards and vineyards; their products are processed in local factories: canning plants, fruit juice extractors etc.

The southern coast is split into three promontories; the longest, an extension of the Taígetos massif, is **Máni**, a wild limestone region inhabited by people of spirit. Taígetos is flanked by alluvial plains, free from winter frost: **Lakonía** *(east)* round Sparta and **Messinía** *(west)* round Kalamáta. The fertile fields produce grain and early vegetables while the figs and olives of Kalamáta are well known for their quality.

At the centre of the Peloponnese, round Trípoli (between 600m and 800m/1 968ft and 2 625ft above sea level) lie the pasturelands of **Arcadia** (Arkadía).

Epiros – Pop 339 728. Between the Ionian Sea and the western border of Thessaly rise the mountains of Epiros, in particular the **Pindos** chain to the east; the landscape is majestic and harsh, deeply furrowed by valleys and gorges. Its severe climate and isolation allowed the people a certain autonomy under the Turks. Even today the Epirots retain many of their traditional customs in dress, dancing, crafts etc.

The mountain pastures round Métsovo are devoted to flocks of sheep tended by their shepherds while the thick forests still shelter a few bears and wolves.

The capital, Ioánina, is situated by a lake; round the shores are meadows where cattle and sheep are raised. Northeast rise the limestone heights of Zagória.

To the south extends the plain of Árta with its orange plantations and rice paddies while the plain of Préveza produces early vegetables (tomatoes and melons).

Thessaly – Pop 734 846. Thessaly, which has two main centres at Lárissa and the port of Vólos, is composed of a rich agricultural basin, watered by the River Piniós and surrounded by high peaks: Pindos to the west, Olympos to the north, Pelion and Óssa to the east and Timfristós in the south. Cold and damp in winter and very hot in summer, the country, which was formerly a marshy plain where buffalo roamed, now produces an abundance of cereals, sugar beet and cotton. Almond trees crowd the slopes of Óssa while apples and the famous Volos olives are grown on Pelion; a few picturesque towns boast traditional houses with balconies and flat stone roof tiles. At the foot of Pelion lies the port of Vólos providing maritime communications. Road and rail links with Macedonia to the northeast pass through the famous Vale of Tempe at the foot of Mount Óssa while the road to Ioánina and Epiros in the northwest climbs over the Métsovo Pass (1 705m/5 594ft), the highest road pass in Greece. As it rises into the Pindos range the road passes the curious pillars of rock created by erosion which are known as the Metéora.

Macedonia – Pop 2 236 019. The northern province with its continental climate stretches from west to east along the border with Albania and Bulgaria.

At the centre of the province lies the vast alluvial plain of the River Axiós, also known as the Vardar, with its characteristic rows of poplars, its canals, its ancient salt marshes converted into rice fields or cotton plantations and its simple houses.

Further west the crescent formed by Édessa, Náoussa and Véria on the lower slopes of Mount Vérmio – a large winter sports centre for all northern Greece – has for centuries been a very fertile area which enabled Philip and Alexander of Macedon to develop and extend their power – apples, cherries, apricots and particularly peaches, food crops, grain, barley for brewing, leguminous crops and fodder for cattle.

T.A.P.

Schwarz House, Ambelákia, Thessaly

Tobacco drying

East of the mouth of the Axiós, at the head of a small gulf *(Kólpos Thessaloníkes)*, lies the port of Thessaloníki (Salonica), the capital of Macedonia and the second largest town in Greece.

Chalcidice (Halkidikí), the region southeast of Thessaloníki consists of bare hills, where cereals are grown, ending in three wooded peninsulas; the most easterly shelters the famous monasteries of Mount Athos.

The country further east round Kavála is composed of broad valleys and inland depressions where tobacco and some cereals and sugar beet are grown overlooked by high plateaux and Mount Pangaion with its famous gold mines.

In the mountains of western Macedonia, round Kastoriá, there are some fine examples of typical Macedonian houses with balconies and shingle roofs. This region abounds in beautiful lakes particularly Préspa, a nature reserve on the northern border.

Thrace – Pop 338 005. Thrace is the most easterly province of mainland Greece, flanked by Bulgaria and Turkey; it became part of Greece after the First World War. Its dependent island, Samothrace, joined the Greek State in 1912.

The country consists of hills and plains devoted to growing tobacco, cereals and cotton. The planting of mulberry trees for feeding silk worms was a flourishing traditional activity in the past; it has suffered a considerable decline since the Second World War. The Greek Silk Museum at Souflí on the bank of the Evros near the Turkish border evokes the heyday of silk production in northern Greece. There is still a Turkish minority particularly round Komotiní, Álexandroúpoli and Souflí where Turkish is taught in primary schools. In the countryside the minarets, the country women wearing shawls on their heads and the ox-drawn farm carts are reminders of the Ottoman presence.

THE SEA AND THE ISLANDS

Thálassa, thálassa! – The sea, the sea! According to Xenophon this was the cry raised by the Greek mercenaries of Cyrus, the heroes of the Retreat of the Ten Thousand in 401 BC when they finally caught sight of the Black Sea after an exhausting march fighting a rearguard action over the mountains of Asia Minor.

The sea is never far distant in Greece; the long coastline is extended by countless bays and gulfs which are excellent for underwater fishing. There is no tide and the salinity reaches 3.8 per cent. The water is usually transparent and blue but it can get choppy; the absence of currents and the excellent visibility are favourable to navigation and fishing.

Fish and fishermen – Small-scale fishing still thrives in many of the little ports on the coast and on the islands. The major item of equipment is the boat, the wooden caïque *(kaíki)* which has almost no keel but sits well in the water, bobbing like a cork on the short, sharp, foam-flecked waves of the Mediterranean. The caïques, which are still built locally, no longer hoist their traditional double sails which have been replaced by a stout motor but they are often decorated in vivid colours, sometimes with a figure on the prow; the stern and the deck are finished with a balustrade.

The open boats *(venzínes)* propelled by a motor and crewed by only one or two men, usually carry lights, which are strung out at dusk to dazzle the fish which are caught in a net: red mullet, mackerel, sardines and whitebait *(marída)*. A typical catch includes squid *(kalamári)* and octopus *(oktapódi)*; the latter are beaten on a stone to make them tender and then hung on a line to dry.

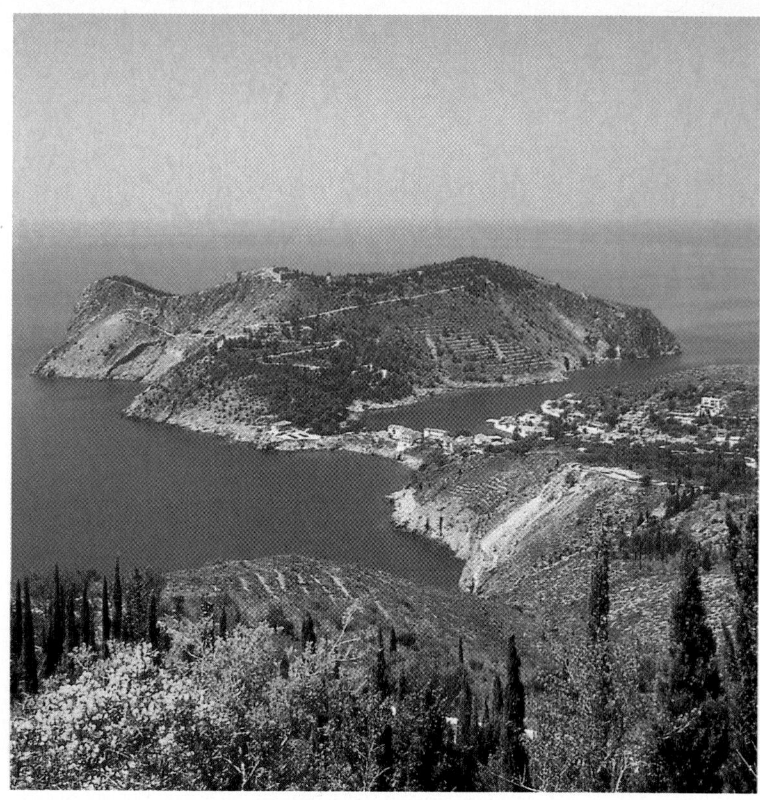
D. Boland/APPARENCE

Assos, Cephallonia

One sometimes sees flying fish and dolphins, which make a graceful escort for a boat but cause great damage to fishing nets.

Sponge diving, once common on many of the Aegean islands, now survives only on Hydra, Syme *(Sími)* and Kálimnos; the caïques set out in the spring round the coasts.

Aegean islands – Pop 456 712. Exposed to the wind, the sea and the sun, the Aegean islands are scattered between the Greek mainland and Turkey. The larger islands near the coast of Asia Minor – Lemnos, Lesbos, Chios and Sámos – are green and fertile and have not suffered much loss of population. In the Cyclades and the Dodecanese the cuboid houses under their dazzling whitewash contrast starkly with the barren rock-strewn land.

Under the brilliant light the islands are exposed to the prevailing wind which blows from the north. In winter it is known as te *voriás* but in spring and summer it becomes the *meltémi* which can blow for two or three days at a time, attaining a force of 6 to 8 (39-73kph/24-45mph); it makes the sea rough but refreshes the air.

Most of the Aegean islands have a port or a landing place called *skála* (steps) in a sheltered bay, a town called *hóra* (place) on a hill out of reach of pirates and a fortified site *(kástro)*, which may have begun as an ancient Greek acropolis, become a stronghold *(froúrio)* under the Byzantines and then a castle or citadel under the Venetians and the Turks.

Ionian islands – Pop 193 734. They are strung out in the Ionian Sea off the west coast of Greece; there are seven main islands running from north to south: Corfu, Paxí, Leukas, Cephallonia, Ithaca, Zakynthos, also known as Zante, and Kythera which is separate from the other six and lies off the southern tip of the Peloponnese.

They are pleasant and agreeable islands, slightly lacking in character compared with the Aegean islands but better suited to holidays owing to their mild climate and tourist facilities.

Their propinquity to Italy and their long occupation by the Venetians (15C-18C) have made them as much Latin as Greek. The architecture shows strong Venetian influence, particularly in Corfu which has not suffered from earthquakes.

The rainfall in the autumn and winter means that the islands are fertile, producing abundant supplies of cereals, olives, fruit and grapes.

Crete and the Dodecanese – *For description see pp 260 and 320.*

FLORA AND FAUNA

Flora – Over 6 000 species (about 600 are native to Greece including 130 in Crete alone) – will provide ample interest for the amateur botanist; it is at its best in the spring.

Trees – In antiquity the Greek countryside was well forested but the trees were gradually decimated by goats and by over-exploitation for ship building.
Cultivated trees are commonly to be found on farmland or in the plains and on the lower slopes of the hills, grown in plantations: olives more or less everywhere up to 600m/1 969ft, citrus fruits (oranges, lemons, citrons) on irrigated land, almonds in sheltered spots and mulberries, figs, pomegranates and jujubes on the outskirts of villages. Protective shade along the roads and in the towns and villages is provided by the stately plane tree, the aromatic eucalyptus and the pepper tree which resembles a weeping willow.
In open country and in scrubland the holm-oak predominates, growing singly or in clumps and providing shade for the shepherds and their flocks. The cypress, tamarisk and Aleppo pine trees are to be found along the coasts while in the mountains (over 1 000m/3 281ft) oaks, chestnuts, beeches, Corsican pines and fir trees thrive.

Olive tree

Almond tree

Olive tree: calcareous or siliceous soil: twisted trunk, silvery leaves.

Almond tree: plains and valleys; early pink flower; seed known as the almond.

Holm oak (or holly oak): calcareous soil, below 800m/2 625ft; evergreen leaves.

Aleppo pine: calcareous coastal slope; light foliage; twisted trunk and grey bark.

Shrubs – They are usually evergreen and grow on grazing land or scrubland together with thyme, lavender, rosemary, basil and above all marjoram (pink flowers); the roads and paths are more likely to be lined with bushes of scented broom, jasmin, mimosa, rhododendron and oleander; the latter are particularly common along water courses.

Arbutus: shiny leaves similar to bay leaves; whitish flowers and red fruit.

Lentisk: Pistachio species – dense foliage growing in groups of leaflets; small red fruit which darkens as it ripens; strong resin smell; sub-species – the famous lentisk which produces mastic gum and grows on Chios (Híos).

Myrtle: white scented flowers, blue-black berries; symbol of amorous passion.

Cistus: dark green leaves; pink or white flowers with separate petals.

Juniper: prickly leaves; purple berries attractive to birds (quails, blackbirds).

Plants – The common species, bulbs or succulents, grow in the open air.

Asphodel: long stems ending in white or yellow star-shaped flowers.

Bougainvillea: climbing plant with clusters of purplish leaves.

Hibiscus: Shrub with large vivid red flowers.

Acanthus: long, curved, denticulate leaves.

Cactus: strangely shaped succulent plant with spikes and cylindrical, annulate stems.

Agave: succulent plant with thick leaves ending in a black spike; yellow flowers.

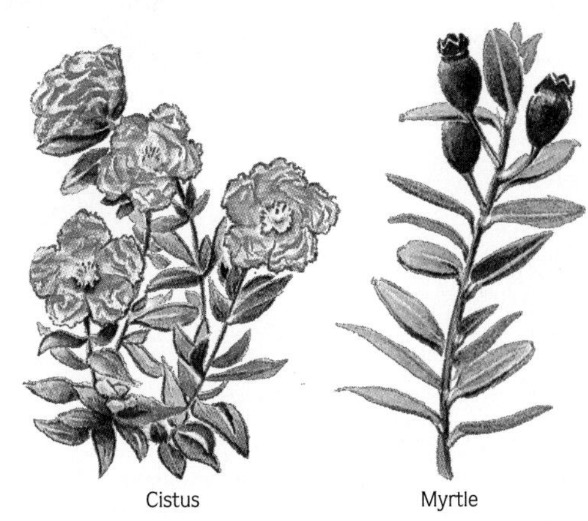

Cistus

Myrtle

Fauna – There may have been lions in Greece in antiquity since they appear frequently in Hellenistic art. During the Turkish occupation, there were jackals in the Peloponnese and caravans of camels plodding the paths of Macedonia, Thrace and central Greece. Nowadays a few species which are relatively rare in the rest of Europe are still to be found in Greece. The huge tortoises, which appear on the coins of certain ancient currencies, are sometimes seen in Attica and Boeotia. The forests on Mount Pindos still harbour brown bears and a few wolves; wild boars are more numerous.
Birds of prey – eagles, falcons, vultures – swoop over the mountain peaks and passes. In Epiros men breed "arrow" pigeons, which climb very high in the sky and then, in response to a whistle, plummet vertically towards the earth. A familiar bird in central and northern Greece is the stork searching for its food in the river deltas, the lakes and lagoons and marshy coastal plains: Missolonghi lagoon, the plains of Árta and Lárissa, the lakes at Ioánina and Kastoriá and in Macedonia and Thrace.

D. Hée /MICHELIN

The star ratings are allocated for various categories:

- *regions of scenic beauty with dramatic natural features*
- *cities with a cultural heritage*
- *elegant resorts and charming villages*
- *ancient monuments and fine architecture, museums and picture galleries.*

Antiquity

GREAT MEDITERRANEAN CIVILISATIONS

Below is a comparative table of the great periods of civilisation in the eastern Mediterranean.

	GREECE		ORIENT
	Historic facts	**Artistic eras**	
BC 3000	Early Helladic civilisation on the mainland, Cycladic in the Aegean Sea and Minoan on Crete	**Cycladic (3000-2000):** ceramics, idols, small useful objects	**Sumer** Egypt: Ancient Empire (2800-2100)
2500			*Pyramid of Cheops*
2000	Achaian and Ionian invasions	**Minoan (2000-1400):** frescoes, low relief sculptures, ceramics, statuettes	Egypt: Middle Empire (2100-1600) Abraham (2000)
1500	Linear B, early Greek script	**Mycenaean (1550-1100):** masks, golden vessels and funerary objects, ivory and rock crystal trinkets, arms, helmets	Babylon: First Empire (2000-1400)
1200	Capture of Troy by the Achaians (or Mycenaeans)		Anatolia: Hittites (2000-1300)
1150	Dorian invasions		Egypt: New Empire (1600-1200)
1100	Colonisation of Asia Minor by the Greeks (Ionians)	**Geometric (1100-700):** ceramics with linear decoration, small bronzes, implements, funerary objects	*Tutankhamun* (1450) *Ramesses II* (1250) *Moses* (1250)
1 000			Lebanon: the Phoenicians (1500-1000)
900	Homer		Assyrian Empire (1400-600)
700	Lycurgus (Sparta) Greek colonies in Syria, Italy, Sicily, Egypt, Euxine (Black Sea), Liguria (Marseilles)	**Archaic (700-500):** temples of tufa and sculptures in oriental style, kouroi and korai, Corinthian vases, black figure ceramics	*Kings of Judah: Saul, David and Solomon* (1000) Italy: Etruscans (750-500)
600	Solon (Athens) Peisistratos (Athens)		*Foundation of Rome* Egypt: Saitic Renaissance (650-500) *Assurbanipal (650)*
500	1st Persian War: Persians defeated at Marathon (490)		Babylon: Second Empire *Capture of Jerusalem by Nebuchadnezzar* (587)
480	2nd Persian War: Persians defeated at Salamis (480) Peloponnesian War won by Sparta	**Classical (500-300):** marble temples, marble, gold and ivory sculptures, great bronzes, red figure ceramics	
450	Age of Pericles (5C): Socrates and Plato in Athens		*Persian Empire* (500-300)
431-404	Peloponnesian War won by Sparta		*Cyrus, Darius, Xerxes (Ahasuerus)*

371-362	Theban hegemony		Rome: the Republic (500-100)
350	Philip of Macedon: Greeks defeated at Chaironeia (338)330 Alexander the Great		
		Hellenistic (300-100): Macedonian tombs and treasuries, stoas, great statues in marble and bronze, Tanágra figurines	Empire of Alexander the Great (300-200) Egypt: The Ptolemies (Ptolemy, Cleopatra)
200	First Roman incursions		
			Rome: the Empire
100	Greece a Roman province: capture of Athens by Sulla (86) battle of Actium (31)		*Capture of Jerusalem by Titus*
AD 50	St Paul the Apostle in Greece		
		Roman: urban complexes, administrative buildings, baths, arches, busts, portraits, mosaics	
130	The Emperor Hadrian and his favourite Antinoüs in Greece		
200	Barbarian invasions		

SOME FACTS FROM HISTORY

From the first settlements to the Roman Conquest

There are very few traces of settlements in Greece dating from before 3000 BC. They are however still sufficient to show that the area was already inhabited in the Neolithic period. The arrival of new inhabitants (it is thought from Asia Minor) made possible the establishment in the Bronze Age of the Helladic civilisation in Continental Greece, while a much more advanced civilisation was being developed on the Cyclades.
Around the beginning of the second millenium, the Achaians, an ethnic group from Thessaly, and the Ionians, an Indo-European people from the north, spread over the whole of the peninsula, while the Cycladic civilisation moved to Crete, where it blossomed into the Minoan civilisation. Half way through this millenium, a civilisation similar to that in Crete appeared in Continental Greece. This is known as the Mycenaean, from Mycenae, one of its main centres of development. Its rather sudden disappearance in the 12C BC may be connected with the invasion of Greece by the Dorians, another Indo-European people whose arrival caused part of the original Ionian population to leave and colonise Asia Minor.
The Dorian settlement saw the beginning of the so-called geometric period, during which the combined effects of population growth and contact with oriental civilisations led to profound changes. The most important of these was the appearance of a new form, the city state.

The Greek city states – The war-based structure of Dorian society was entirely compatible with the basic concept of the city, which seems to have originated in the tendency of tribes to cluster around a fortified point. Power was in the hands of a warrior class, and the citadel ruled over the surrounding countryside, extending its authority ever wider, to more and more distant territories. This form of oligarchy, of which Sparta was to remain an example, often developed into a tyranny where a single individual held power, while the need to expand led to the foundation of colonies throughout the Mediterranean. This first stage in the history of the Greek city states is known as the Archaic period, which ended with the **Persian Wars.**

The Persian Wars – Under a succession of three great kings, Cyrus II, Cambyses II and Darius I, the Persian Empire had spread in the 6C BC over western Asia, Macedonia and Egypt, and encircled the Greek cities of Asia Minor, which submitted to its domination. One of them, however, Miletus, started a rebellion and the colonies appealed to their mother cities for help. Darius then undertook the 1st Persian War, both to punish Athens for aiding the rebels and to strengthen his hold on the Aegean; it ended with the Athenian victory at the Battle of Marathon in 490 BC *(see p 109)*. Following in his father's footsteps, Xerxes I invaded Greece in 481 BC. At first the Greek city states failed to unite in sufficient force to face the danger. After a victory over the Spartans at Thermopylae, the Persians were none the less defeated in a sea battle at Salamis (480 BC) and on land at Plataea (479 BC) by the Athenian forces.

The Classical period – Boosted by the prestige gained through these victories, Athens assumed the leading role in the Greek alliance freeing the occupied territories and setting up the Delian Confederacy *(see DÍLOS)*, within which it gradually succeeded in getting its own way. At the same time political life became more democratic in Athens, initially at the instigation of **Kleisthenes** who reduced the powers of the Areopagos, the aristocratic judicial council, then under the rule of Pericles, who made the supreme magistrature accessible to all. Sparta however took a dim view of Athenian hegemony, and the two city states went to war for the first time in 446 BC. Owing to treaty obligations, a conflict between the Athenians and Corinthians started the **Peloponnesian War** in 431 BC, which embroiled the whole of Greece. In spite of the victories of Alcibiades, it culminated in 404 BC in the siege of Athens, whose fleet had suffered a crushing defeat the preceding year. Sparta, however, gained nothing from its victory, and went into an inexorable decline, while Athens was thwarted in its attempts to regain power by the ambitions of Thebes. The Greek city states were so impoverished by the war that none of them was in a position to oppose the Macedonian menace.

PICTOR

Odeon of Herod Atticus, Athens

The Hellenistic period – Philip II, King of Macedon (c 382-336 BC), having conquered Thrace and Chalcidice, had designs on Thessaly. After several attempts, Demosthenes succeeded in cementing an alliance between Athens and Thebes, who were none the less defeated at Chaironeia in 338 BC. At Corinth Philip imposed on the Greek cities the Hellenic League, which was designed to involve them in a war with the Persians, an aim which was taken up after his assassination in 336 BC by his son Alexander, but without success. When he in turn died in 323 BC and his empire was split up among his generals, Greece became a protectorate under the kings of Macedon, who destroyed Athenian democracy by imposing a reformed constitution. Cleomenes III, King of Sparta, tried to restore the independence of the Greek city states, but the Achaean League formed by 12 Peloponnesian cities feared a popular rebellion and appealed to the Macedonian king for help in fighting Cleomenes (222 BC).

The Roman conquest – After Philip V of Macedon (221-179 BC) had supported Hannibal in the 2nd Punic War, Rome began to take an interest in the Hellenic world inherited from the empire of Alexander. Having defeated Philip V at Cynoscephalae, Rome declared the freedom of Greece in 196 BC. In fact the Greeks recovered only part of their independence under Roman control. The continuing intervention of Rome in Greek affairs led in 146 BC to a rebellion by the Achaean League headed by Corinth, which was laid waste by the Roman legions. The various city leagues were then broken up and Greece came under Roman occupation, which subsequently spread to the rest of the Hellenic world; this was annexed completely after the triumph of Augustus at Actium in 30 BC. In 27 BC the Romans united the Greek lands to form a single province, the province of Achaia. Some cities were given the status of free cities (eg Byzantium), while others had federated or allied status.

Coming of the Byzantine Empire – Although the Greek city states lost power and prestige, **Hellenism** flourished and Greece retained its cultural, literary and artistic influence. No doubt this was largely due to the political and religious tolerance practised by Rome, which left administration in the hands of the local population and permitted the practice of the Greek religion. This relative autonomy granted by Rome gradually created two spheres of influence in the Roman Empire: on the one hand a Greek East combining the Greek world proper and the Hellenistic areas of Asia Minor, and on the other a Latin West.

From the 3C AD, Greece in common with the rest of the Empire had to face barbarian invasions, which were more successfully resisted by the eastern part of the Empire than the western part. These dangers made Rome's loss of influence more palpable and in 330 the Roman emperor, **Constantine**, made Byzantium *(Byzandion)*, a former Greek colony on the Bosphorus, the capital of the Empire. Initially called New Rome, the city was soon to bear the name Constantinople in his honour.
In 380 during the reign of **Theodosius the Great** Christianity became the official religion, pagan cults were banned, and in 393 the Olympic Games were abolished. In order to resist the barbarian invasions in its western part, he divided the Empire at his death in 395 between his two sons: Arcadius inherited the east and Honorius the west. Constantinople remained the capital of the Eastern Empire.

GREAT FIGURES IN ANTIQUITY

The dates given refer to the era BC unless otherwise indicated.

Alcibiades – c 450-404. An Athenian general and pupil of Socrates, who involved Athens in a risky Sicilian expedition and took refuge in Sparta after his disgrace. Reconciled with Athens, he had several victories during the Peloponnesian War, but was unable to stave off the final defeat and was exiled.

Alexander the Great – Philip of Macedon's son. A great conqueror *(see PÉLA)*.

Croesus – King of Lydia in the 6C. His wealth came from the gold bearing sands of the River Pactolus which ran through his capital; he was an ally of Greece and sent rich offerings to the sanctuary at Delphi.

Demosthenes – 384-322. Athenian orator and statesman. Famous for his tirades against Philip II of Macedon *(the Philippics)*, he took control of affairs and secured an alliance with Thebes against Macedon. Exiled after the defeat at Chaironaia, he encouraged the Greek rebellion and poisoned himself when this was put down.

Epaminóndas – General and statesman of Theban origin *(see ITHÓMI and THÍVA)*.

Hadrian – Roman Emperor and a great admirer of Greece *(see Kiláda ton TÉMBON)*.

Kleisthenes – Athenian statesman.

Leonidas – King of Sparta.

Mithridates – c 132-63. King of Pontus (a country in north-eastern Asia Minor), he tried to resist Roman expansion in the Hellenic world.

Peisistratos – He became Tyrant of Athens in the middle of the 6C and was an enlightened despot; he developed agriculture, implemented a sound economic policy and promoted public works (sewers, fountains etc); he encouraged art and literature – production of *kouroi* and *korai (see p 36)*, building of the Olympieion, founding of the first public library and publication of Homer's tales.

Pericles – c 495-429. Athenian statesman and leader of the democratic party. He was very influential in the political and economic spheres and also promoted writers and employed the best artists and architects. The Age of Pericles was one of the finest periods of Greek civilisation.

Philip II – c 382-c 336. King of Macedon *(see PÉLA)*.

Polycrates – A wise tyrant who ruled Sámos from 533 to 522.

Ptolemy – The son of Lagus and a Macedonian general in Alexander the Great's army. He founded the dynasty of the Ptolemies, who reigned over Egypt from 323 to 30 and included 15 Egyptian rulers; the last ruler was Ptolemy XV, Cleopatra's son. **Claudius Ptolemy** was a famous geographer who lived in the 2C AD.

Pyrrhus – A king of Epiros from 295 to 272 famous for his victories over the Romans (Heraklea and Pont Euxin) won with the help of elephants. The expression "Pyrrhic victory" means a victory won at too great a cost.

Solon – c 640-c 558. A poet and statesman of Athenian origin. His social and political reforms were at the root of Athens' rise to greatness.

Themistocles – c 528-c 462. An Athenian general and statesman. His reorganisation of the Athenian fleet was responsible for the victory at Salamis. He had to leave Athens because of intrigues against him, and took refuge with Artaxerxes, King of Persia.

Modern age

GREECE UNDER THE BYZANTINES

After the division of AD 395 the territory of the Eastern Roman Empire comprised the Balkans, present-day Greece, Asia Minor and Egypt. Although Latin was soon replaced as the official language by Greek, the language of the Church and the Near East, the inhabitants saw themselves as Romans *(Romaioi)* – "Romios" is still used today to mean Greek – and the entirely Hellenised Eastern Empire saw itself as the successor of the Roman Empire, especially after the fall of the Western Empire in 476.
The Byzantine Empire developed into a Greek Christian theocratic state, in which the Emperor and the Patriarch were interdependent (symbolised by the two-headed eagle, the emblem of the Empire); the former ensured the defence of the State and the latter preserved the Orthodox faith. The State was seen as the final order on earth and the people were acutely concerned with matters of doctrine since error could endanger not only their own souls but also the security of the State. Consequently religious issues had a crucial influence on the internal development of the Empire.

Historical notes

527-565 Reign of **Justinian I**, who recaptured Italy from the Ostrogoths, and part of Spain from the Visigoths.

610-641 Reign of **Heraclius**, who defeated the Persians but was unable to prevent the Arabs from conquering first Syria and then Egypt.

717-741 Reign of **Leo III** the Isaurian, who introduced iconoclasm and temporarily halted Arab expansion.

843 Re-establishment of Orthodox Christianity.

1204 Capture of Constantinople by the Crusaders and founding of the Latin Empire of Constantinople.

1261 The Nicaean Emperor Michael VIII Palaiologos destroyed the Latin Empire and restored the Byzantine Empire.

1453 Constantinople captured by the Turks.

Throughout its thousand years of existence the Byzantine Empire was under constant threat of invasion. Despite the great achievements of **Justinian** (527-565) and his wife **Theodora**, **Heraclius** (610-641) and **Basil II** (976-1025) in winning back lost territory (Justinian's empire included nearly all the territory around the Mediterranean basin, Asia Minor and the Balkans), the general pattern is of retrenchment until only Constantinople and its hinterland remained.
The threat came in the west from the barbarians, the Normans, Franks and Venetians in succession; in the north from the Slavs, who occupied the Greek mainland and the Peloponnese from the 6C to the 8C; in the east from the Persians, Arabs and finally the Turks. As the Empire diminished in size so did food supplies, recruits for the army and taxes to sustain the vast centralised bureaucracy which had grown up in Constantinople.
The Byzantines resisted their enemies not only by warfare – they invented the famous **Greek fire** (c 674) which gave them a great advantage particularly at sea – but also by intrigue and diplomacy; they bought off some enemies, received tribute from others and even converted their northern Slav neighbours to Christianity, hence the presence of the Orthodox faith in Bulgaria, Serbia and Russia.
The **Crusades** were launched in the west in the 11C and 12C by the Popes to help the Byzantines repulse the Muslims from the Holy Land but the Franks were more interested in the acquisition of land and the Venetians in commercial gain. In 1204 the Fourth Crusade was redirected against Constantinople itself, ostensibly to settle the disputed succession to the throne; the city was taken on 13 April, then sacked and the churches desecrated.
These events and the ensuing occupation *(see below)*, which was aggravated, in spite of various initiatives, by serious religious differences, led to great mistrust in relations between the Greeks and the western world. After a Latin emperor had been installed at Constantinople, the Byzantine Empire was reduced to three successor states: the despotate of Epiros (1205-1318) and the minor empires of Trebizond (1204-1461) and Nicaea (1204-61).
The Emperor of Nicaea, **Michael VIII Palaiologos**, recaptured Constantinople in 1261 and in the following years the Byzantines recovered some territory in the Peloponnese. In 1348 they established the **Despotate of Morea** at Mystra (Mistrás); it survived until 1460. From the 11C the **Turks** had gradually conquered the countries of Asia Minor, by the 14C they occupied the Balkans and in 1453 captured Constantinople from the last emperor **Constantine Palaiologos** who waited in vain for assistance from the western powers.

GREECE UNDER THE FRANKS (13C-15C)

The Fourth Crusade, initiated in the 12C, brought together the knights of Burgundy, Champagne, the Ile-de-France, Picardy and particularly Flanders as well as Lombards and Venetians from Italy. The religious arm was subordinated to commercial interests by the Venetians and Lombards who turned the army against Constantinople *(see above)*.

Latin Empire of Constantinople – A college of six Venetians and six French elected **Baldwin of Flanders** emperor. Greece, except for Epiros, was divided up between the Crusaders, according to the feudal system; the Venetians took the islands and the coastal sites to further their trading activities and the French and Lombards colonized the land.

As his personal fief Emperor Baldwin held Constantinople, which he shared with the Venetians, Thrace and the adjacent parts of Asia Minor until he was killed by the Bulgars at the battle of Adrianople in 1206. He was succeeded by his brother Henry of Flanders, then by Peter and Robert de Courtenay and finally by **Baldwin II de Courtenay** in 1261.

Two small states, the kingdom of Thessaloníki and the principality of Morea (the Peloponnese) were nominally dependent on the Emperor. When the kingdom of Thessaloníki was attached to the Despotate of Epiros in 1224, the principality of Morea, "where people spoke French like the Parisians", became the main area of Frank domination.

Principality of Morea – The princes, who took the title of Duke of Achaia, ruled through 12 vassal barons who bore the main responsibilities. The first princes were from Champagne, William de Champlitte and then the de Villehardouin *(see KALAMÁTA)* who were succeeded by the Anjou-Sicily dynasty in the person of Charles I of Anjou, brother of Louis IX of France. In 1261, however, the Byzantines recaptured Constantinople and then proceeded to reconquer the Peloponnese ending with the capture of Clarence *(see KILÍNI)* in 1428.

The princes of Morea, whose history is told in the Chronicle of Morea, also held sway over the Duchy of Thebes and Athens which had devolved to the La Roche who were succeeded by the Brienne: when Gautier de Brienne and his knights died in the battle of Kephisos *(see ORHOMENÓS)* in 1311, the duchy fell into the hands of the Catalans whence it passed in 1388 to the Acciaiuoli, Florentine allies of the Anjou-Sicily dynasty. Other territories dependent on the principality of Morea were: the county of La Sole, the marquisate of La Bondonice, the Duchy of Náxos including the Cyclades with the Venetian nobles, the county of Cephallonia including Zákinthos and Lefkáda which were controlled by the Venetians.

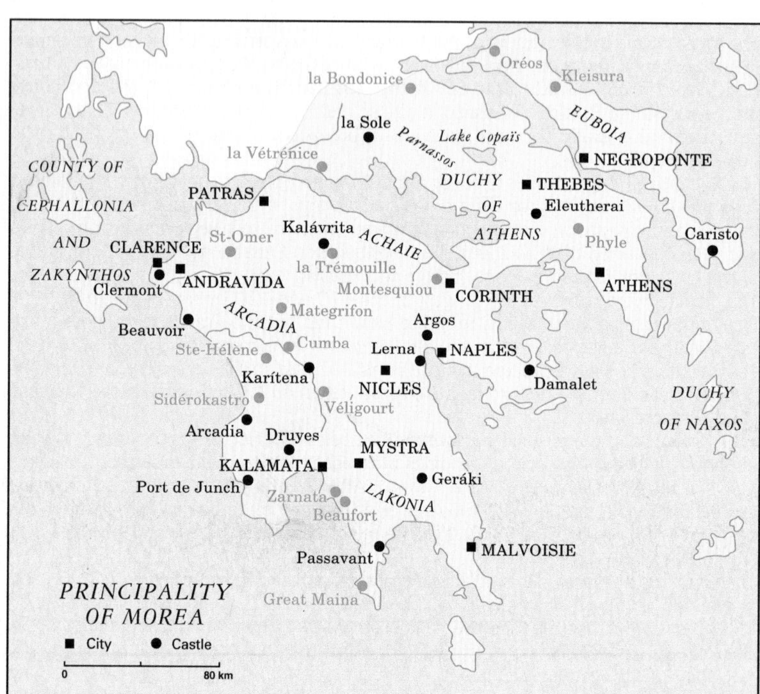

Towns and castles described in the text are marked in black on the map

GREECE UNDER THE TURKS (15C-19C)

The conquest of Greece by the Turks, which began with the capture of the Balkan territories followed by Constantinople, the capital of the Byzantine Empire, in 1453 by Sultan **Mehmet II**, was practically completed by the taking of Candia (Herakleion) from the Venetians in 1669.
In accordance with Muslim tradition the Turks practised religious tolerance in relation to the Christian and Jewish faiths, underpinned by the **Sultan**'s resolve to maintain these non-Muslim communities, known as *raïas*, in a subservient state in order to meet the empire's manpower requirements.
Large towns were administered by **pashas** while smaller towns and villages were ruled by **agas**. The government exacted heavy taxes from the Muslim and non-Muslim communities alike but the latter had to perform all sorts of additional duties imposed by the local rulers in the rich agricultural regions. The harshest aspect of the occupation especially during the first 200 years was the abduction of young boys; the strongest were chosen to serve as mercenary soldiers, **Janissaries**, the sultan's personal guard, the brightest were raised in the harem and became devoted government officials. Some Christians converted to the Islamic faith to escape poverty; many more took refuge in the harsh wild mountains where the Turks hardly ventured and they succeeded in forming prosperous and largely autonomous communities. From the 17C Phanariots, natives of the Phanar district in Constantinople, who were often descendants of the Byzantine imperial families, were appointed as governors *(hospodar)* of the Romanian provinces, and as interpreters *(dragoman)* for the sultan and often as ambassadors to the western powers.
From the start of the occupation the Sultan not only confirmed the authority of the **Patriarch of Constantinople** in religious matters but also appointed him as temporal chief *(ethnarches)*, the leader responsible for the internal affairs of all the orthodox communities throughout the empire; he was also answerable to the Turkish authorities for the loyalty and good behaviour of the Christian population. In spite of or perhaps because of this dual function, the Orthodox Church succeeded in maintaining the Greek religion, language and traditions in these difficult times. The monasteries, in particular those on Mount Athos, the Metéora and Patmós, were the principal centres of Greek culture.

Historical notes

1453	Constantinople captured by the Turks.
1444-1481	Reign of Mehmet II who completed the conquest of eastern Greece.
1480	Rhodes besieged by the Turks who forced the Knights of St John of Jerusalem to withdraw; Rhodes eventually fell to **Suleiman the Magnificent** in 1522.
1536	Signature of the **Capitulations**, an agreement between François I of France and Suleiman the Magnificent, by which France protected the Roman Catholics in the Levant and received certain commercial privileges.
1571	Turkish expansion curtailed by the Christians at the **Battle of Lepanto** *(see NÁFPAKTOS)*.
1669	Herakleion (Crete) captured by the Turks: end of Venetian control of Crete.
1687-1715	Reoccupation of the Peloponnese and Aigina by the Venetians, who retained control of Corfu and the other Ionian islands until the French Revolution.
Early 18C	Depopulation of Greece; Albanian settlers introduced by the Turks.
1822	Greek independence proclaimed by the Greek rebels at the Congress of Epidauros.

Struggle for Independence

There had been revolts in the 17C but it was in the 18C that a feeling of nationalism began to develop under the influence of the Orthodox Church which was teaching young Greeks in its "secret schools". In addition there were secret societies *(eteríes)*; the largest was the **Filikí Etería**, founded in Odessa in 1814 by Alexander Ypsilantis, aide-de-camp to the Tzar. These societies consisted of merchants and civil servants like the **Phanariots** (natives of the Phanar district in Constantinople), shipowners from the islands and businessmen, bankers and writers living in Greece or abroad where they were influenced by the ideals of the Age of Enlightenment and later of the French Revolution.
In the mountains bands of **klephts** (the word literally means robber in Greek) began to harass the Turks; they were joined by the militia *(armatoles)* composed of Greek citizens armed by the Turks in order to fight the rebels but who took up their cause.
The Patriarch **Germanós** raised the flag of revolt, a white cross on a sky blue ground, against Sultan Mahmoud II on 25 March 1821 at the Agía Lávra Monastery near Kalávrita. The revolt spread throughout the Peloponnese, into Epiros, ruled by Ali Pasha *(see IOÁNINA)*, and to the islands of the Saronic Gulf. This was the start of the War of Independence, also known as the **National Revolution**. By 1822 **Kolokotrónis** and his troops, **palikares**, were in control of the Peloponnese and Greek independence was proclaimed at Epidauros.

The next two years were marked by violent and sometimes bloody dissension among the Greeks. The Turks launched a counter attack led by Ibrahim Pasha, son of Mehmet Ali *(see KAVÁLA)*, viceroy of Egypt, against the Peloponnese and in 1826 he captured Missolonghi.
These tragic events and the subsequent repression gave rise in Western Europe to the **Philhellene Movement** which lasted into the 1850s and had its roots in the knowledge of Classical antiquity which resulted from the predominantly Classical studies of the educated classes. It consisted of altruistic liberals who campaigned for the Greek cause mainly through the work of writers, poets and artists.
Committees were set up in various countries to raise money. Eight shiploads of volunteers arrived in Greece from Europe and were formed into the Philhellene Battalion; there was a large contingent of Germans, many of whom died at Peta; the English and Americans numbered nearly 100. The Americans were particularly sympathetic towards a country struggling for independence and the war brought many travellers as well as volunteers: Mark Twain, Herman Melville and Julia Ward Howe, the author of the "Battle Hymn of the Republic".
Chief among these "friends of Greece" was **Lord Byron** who was persuaded by the London Greek Committee to carry arms and funds, raised in London in 1823, to the Greeks under Mavrokordatos. Two more substantial loans were raised in the City of London in 1824 and 1825. The siege and fall of Missolonghi in 1826 had a great impact in Europe. In 1827 General Sir Richard Church and Admiral Lord Cochrane were appointed to command the Greek forces by land and sea.
In the same year the United Kingdom, Russia and France decided to intervene to enforce an armistice "without however taking any part in the hostilities". The allied fleet went to parley with the Turkish fleet anchored off Pylos (Pílos) in Navarino Bay and ended up destroying it.
In October 1828 a French military expedition was dispatched under **General Maison**, which drove out the Turks while the Russians threatened Constantinople.
The Treaty of Adrianople in 1829 accorded autonomy to Greece; its independent status was recognised by the Great Powers in 1830 and by the Porte in 1832; Otto of Bavaria became king in 1834.

Heroes of the struggle for Independence

Lascarína Bouboulína (1771-1825) – Rich shipowner from Spétses, who fought the Turks at sea and in the Peloponnese.

Márkos Bótsaris (1790-1823) – Originally from Souli, he fought at Missolonghi *(MESSOLÓNGHI)* and was killed near Karpeníssi.

Germanós (1771-1826) – Archbishop of Patras. At Agía Lávra *(see KALÁVRITA)* he blessed the flag of Greek independence and preached the cause at Patras on 25 March 1821 (Greek national holiday).

Constantine Kanáris (1790-1877) – Sailor from Psará, specialist in fire ships *(see HÍOS)*, then a politician.

John Kapodístrias (originally Capo d'Istria) (1776-1831) – Born in Corfu; a diplomat in the Russian service. Head of the government in 1827, he organised the administration and founded the Bank of Greece. Assassinated in 1831.

Giorgos Karaïskakis (1770-1827) – Leader of the *palikares* on the mainland; he was killed at the battle of Phaleron near Athens.

Theodore Kolokotrónis (1770-1843) – A native of the Peloponnese. Military leader who first defeated the Turks in the Dervenáki Gorge in 1922. Equestrian statues in Nauplion, Tripolí and Athens.

John Makriánnis (1797-1864) – A native of Thessaly and a military leader. His *Memoirs* are a precious and picturesque testimony of the popular uprising.

Andréas Miaoúlis (1769-1835) – Sailor from Hydra (Ídra) who fought the Turkish fleet between 1822 and 1825.

INDEPENDENCE

1830	Independent Greek State established under the Treaty of London John Kapodístrias, the prime minister, assassinated in 1831.
1833-1862	Reign of Otto I of Bavaria, a Roman Catholic and centralist.
1863-1913	Reign of George I of Denmark, constitutional monarch.
1863	The Ionian islands, British possessions since 1814, became part of Greece.
1881	Greece recovered Thessaly from the Turks.
1882-1893	Building of the Corinth Canal.
1912-1913	Balkan War. Macedonia and Epiros liberated from the Turks by the Greek army under **Venizélos**. Crete became part of Greece.

John Kapodístrias, who was elected "governor" of the Greek State on the occasion of the 1827 National Assembly, was confirmed in his position by the Triple Alliance when Greek independence was recognised. Liberals within the country regarded him as too pro-Russian and a conspiracy resulted in his assassination in 1831 *(see NÁFPLIO)*, and the installation of an absolute monarch in the shape of a Bavarian prince, Otto I, who was not even 18 years old. Greece remained subject to the influence of Russia, Britain and France, and the administration was in the hands of Bavarian ministers until a coup on 3 September 1862 forced the King to grant a constitution and to appoint Greek ministers. Even so, as the King continued to intervene in political life, the wave of liberal opposition – secretly supported by the British who disliked the King's close relationship with Russia – culminated in a second coup and the deposition of King Otto.

The reign of George I (1863-1913) – On 6 June 1863 Prince William of Denmark (1845-1913), suggested by Britain as a possible candidate for the throne, accepted the crown and became king with the title of **George I**. For its part, Britain gave up its protectorate of the Ionian islands, which restored Greek territorial integrity. The role of the new dynasty was in fact to bring Greek policy into line with British in eastern Europe. Pressure from an increasingly influential middle class led the new King to grant a more liberal constitution in 1864, then to introduce parliamentary government in 1875.

The main problem, however, remained the territorial issue, as significant areas with Greek populations were still under Turkish occupation. In 1866 the King backed a Cretan rising against the island's Ottoman overlords but, lacking support from the big powers, he had to leave the island in the hands of the Sultan. When the Russo-Turkish war began in 1877-78, Greece invaded Thessaly but, although the Treaty of San Stefano recognised the independence of Serbia, Romania and Bulgaria, it maintained Turkish rule in Macedonia. It was not until 1881 and the Congress of Berlin that Thessaly became part of Greece. Public opinion in Greece favoured an agreement with the Balkan states in order to gain possession of Macedonia but the King intervened to put a stop to this initiative. In March 1896 Crete, with the support of Greek volunteers, again rebelled against the Sultan. The Greek government landed troops there in February 1897, while an army commanded by the Crown Prince Constantine invaded Macedonia, where it was defeated. The mediation of the big powers led to the signature in December of the Treaty of Constantinople, which granted Crete autonomy under the rule of the King's second son, Prince George.

Dissatisfied with the lack of territorial recovery, public opinion developed a lively discontent, which was aggravated by the Balkan crisis. The first sign of this potent nationalism occurred in 1908, when the Cretan **Elefthérios Venizélos** (1864-1936) proclaimed the unification of Crete with Greece. An army revolt in 1909 forced the King to call on Venizélos to form a government in 1910. The aim of Venizélos was to unite all territories with Greek populations and to reorganise the administration, army and economy. In 1911 he gained approval for a new constitution with better guarantees for individual freedoms. In 1912, together with Bulgaria, Serbia and Montenegro, he founded the **Balkan League**, which declared war on Turkey on 18 October. Greece invaded Macedonia, and in November took Thessaloníki where King George was assassinated in March 1913. The London Conference in May 1913 put an end to this first conflict but the arguments over the partition of Macedonia started a second one, with Bulgaria this time fighting its former allies. The Treaty of Bucharest in August 1913 sanctioned the annexation of southern Macedonia, southern Epiros and most of the Aegean islands by Greece, as well as her sovereignty over Crete, but gave northern Macedonia to Serbia.

1914-1919	**First World War**. Greece brought into the war by Venizélos on the side of the allies. Thrace and Smyrna awarded to Greece in 1919.
1919-1922	**Great Catastrophe**. New conflict with the Turks, resulting in 1 500 000 Greeks fleeing from Asia Minor to Europe.
1936-1941	Dictatorship of **General Metaxas**
1940	**Óhi (No) Day** when the Greeks repulsed the Italian invasion of Epiros.
1941-1944	**German occupation**. Greek resistance *(see p 101)*
1941-1949	**Civil War**.
1967-1974	Military dictatorship.
1974	Greece becomes a republic as the result of a referendum.
1981	Accession of Greece to the European Union.

The First and Second World Wars – When war broke out in 1914, the Greek government was split between the patriots with Venizélos at their head and the Germanophiles grouped around King Constantine I (1868-1923), brother-in-law of Kaiser Wilhelm II. Venizélos suggested that the King should align himself with the Allies but he was forced by the King to resign in March 1915. Returned to power by the electors, Venizélos tried to make a secret pact with the Allies but again the King demanded his resignation. The army then gave its backing to the prime minister and they together formed a republican government at Thessaloníki in September 1916. The King then started to form partisan battalions, so the French General Sarrail decided to occupy Thessaly and demanded the King's abdication. Meanwhile Venizélos entered Athens in June 1918. The new king, **Alexander I** (1893-1920), asked Venizélos to form a government and on 15 September aligned himself with the Allies. In the Treaties of Neuilly (1919) and Sèvres (1920), Greece gained eastern Thrace and the Smyrna region of Asia Minor came under its administration.

Then Britain, playing on Venizélos' imperialist ambitions, caused the Greek leader to start a new war with Turkey by annexing the Smyrna region. This proved very unpopular and brought about the downfall of Venizélos at the polls in November 1920, immediately after the death of the king. A plebiscite followed, recalling Constantine I.

Abandoned by its allies, Greece was unable to hold out for long against the Turks. Military failures led to Constantine's second abdication in September 1922, in favour of his son **George II** (1890-1947), and to the evacuation of Asia Minor and the tragic forced emigration of the Asian Hellenes.

This massive influx of new population could only aggravate an already difficult economic situation. The elections having returned the Venizélos party to power, the King preferred to abdicate (in December 1923) and a Republic was proclaimed on 25 March 1924 and confirmed by a plebiscite. It experienced numerous crises with a succession of alternating dictatorships and republican union governments. July 1928 saw the return of Venizélos as head of government until his resignation in 1932. Numerous domestic problems accentuated the political divide between the right and the Communist left. Consequently a further coup in March 1935, supported by Venizélos himself, abolished the Republic; a plebiscite soon restored the monarchy and reinstalled George II.

The King asked **General Metaxás** to form a government, although, to all intents and purposes, he acted as dictator until his death in 1941. With the King's agreement, Metaxás abolished the constitution, dissolved Parliament and adopted Fascist policies. Greece had, however, felt threatened by the annexation of Albania by Italy under Mussolini. When in October 1940 Italy demanded free passage for its troops, Greece rejected the ultimatum and came over to the British side. The Italians crossed the border into Greece but the Greek army succeeded in pushing them back towards Albania. German troops then came to Mussolini's aid. The King fled first to Crete and then, under British occupation, to Cairo; Greece was divided between the Italians, Germans and Bulgarians. Resistance groups, in particular the fiercely Marxist National Liberation Front (EAM), waged active guerrilla warfare against the occupiers with ever-increasing support among the population. The Russian offensive in Romania caused the Germans to evacuate Greece in October 1944. The King, George II, had meanwhile set up a government in exile under Papandréou, and promised not to return until there had been a plebiscite.

The contemporary period – As the Germans evacuated Greece to the north, the British army was disembarking at Piraeus. The British were particularly worried about the influence exerted by the EAM and asked in vain that their partisan army should be disarmed. In the elections of March 1946, massive abstentions on the part of the Republicans gave the victory to the royalists, who pressed forward with a plebiscite which came out in favour of the return of the King. When he died soon after, he was succeeded by his brother, **Paul I** (1901-64). While the Treaty of Paris of February 1947 gave the Dodecanese islands to Greece, the interior of the country faced an extremely critical situation since the left-wing parties refused to support the monarchy. In December 1947, with Soviet support, General Márkos formed a provisional government of Free Greece and took refuge in the mountains of the North; from there he waged a guerrilla campaign against the royalist government. The civil war lasted until October 1949 and was ended only by the capture, with the help of the United States, of the rebels' main stronghold in the Grámmos Mountains. The ensuing elections were a victory for the moderate parties but the governments which followed one another up to 1963 were in fact controlled by extreme right-wing forces, which formed in effect a parallel government. The emergency laws passed at the time of the civil war were never repealed and remained in force. When the elections of 1963 gave power to the democratic parties, **Giórgos Papandréou** (1888-1968) was asked to form a government; the positions he adopted were not however always in line with US policy, and the extreme right in Greece saw in his premiership a threat to their privileges. Badly advised, the young King **Constantine II** (b 1940) disagreed with his head of government, who resigned. This gave rise to a political crisis, in the course of which every attempt to form a legitimate government failed. When the elections held in 1967 failed to produce the parliamentary majority expected by the extreme right, a junta led by a number of colonels, who did not even represent a majority within the army, took power in the name of the King.

The colonels set up a regime based on terror; opponents were dragged before a military court and either imprisoned or deported. Constantine II tried to remove the colonels in a coup but failed; he left Greece on 13 December 1967. A new constitution restricted individual freedom and gave excessive powers to the army. The hostility of the majority of the population steadily increased and, in spite of some measures intended to give an illusion of liberalisation, such as the deposition of the king and proclamation of the Republic in July 1973, demonstrations against the regime grew in scale. The colonels responded by proclaiming martial law and setting up special courts but in 1974, owing to the Cyprus crisis and squabbles within the junta, those in power were obliged to call on **Konstandínos Karamanlís**, leader of the right-wing parties and an opponent of the regime.

Karamanlís abolished all the institutions of dictatorship and reintroduced the constitution of 1952, with the exception of the clauses relating to the monarchy. Fundamental liberties were restored, political parties legalised, and the main figures involved in the dictatorship brought to justice. The referendum of 8 December 1974 decided in favour of a **republic**, and a new constitution was promulgated in June 1975. Since then, the return to democracy has been clearly demonstrated by the alternation in power of right- and left-wing parties, and further reinforced by Greece's membership of the European Union, which it joined in 1981.

Greek political life continues however to be dominated by relations with its neighbours, especially Turkey, whose entry into the European Union it opposed, and Macedonia; in 1992 Greece refused to recognise the republic of this name formed from part of the former Yugoslavia, which also laid claim to part of the Greco-Macedonian heritage.

Greece today

ECONOMIC ACTIVITY

Agriculture – Almost 25 per cent of the active population is engaged in agriculture. Sufficient **wheat** (2 389 000t) is grown to meet domestic needs. High yields are obtained on the red soil of Boeotia and Thessaly.

Vines (173 000ha/427 310 acres) are tended to produce wine to which resin *(retsína)* is often added as a preservative. The major wine merchants congregate round Patras. Production of table grapes amounts to 248 000 tonnes and of raisins to 335 000t.
The **olive** (127 500 000 trees) reigns throughout central and southern Greece: the owners beat the trees to bring down the fruit which they press to extract as much oil as they need for their own use before sending the surplus to the refineries. Improved methods of cultivating **citrus fruits** in the coastal basins of the Peloponnese and Epiros mean that a quarter of the harvest can be used for juice extraction. The peach orchards in the Náoussa region in Macedonia provide large-scale exports to the USSR (one third of production) and to the European Union.
The plains of Boeotia, Thessaly, Macedonia and Thrace produce sugar beet, corn, barley, rice and **cotton**, of which Greece is the major European producer (420 000t). **Tobacco** grown in Macedonia and Thrace and Epiros is the main cash crop for export.

Industry and commerce – Greece lacks natural resources in minerals and energy. There are some hydroelectric installations and power stations. The only solid fuel is **lignite**; the oil discovered near Thassos meets only 10.3 per cent of the country's needs. The main product of the mining industry is **bauxite** (2 300 000t per annum) which is extracted from Mount Parnassos and converted into aluminium in Andikíra near Delphi. Production of cement, fertilisers, textiles and electric appliances is growing.
Half of Greece's external trade is with the other countries of the European Union; this produces a trade deficit: imports (oil, meat, manufactured goods) against exports (aluminium, textiles, tobacco, fruit and vegetables). The deficit is made up by "invisible earnings" from **merchant shipping** (Greek crews only) (3rd in the world and 1st in Europe), tourism (10 000 000 visitors in 1995) and money repatriated by Greeks abroad.

POPULATION

In 1991 Greece had 10 260 000 inhabitants, ie an average density of 69 inhabitants per square kilometre as opposed to 15 only in 1830. The population of Greece is fairly homogeneous, only 5 per cent being non-Greek. In Epiros there are a few **Vlachs**, nomadic shepherds from the north, speaking a language derived from Latin, while the Peloponnese, Attica and the Saronic islands contain small Albanian communities. There are Greeks of Turkish origin (100 000) in Thrace and in the Dodecanese; the gypsy people have no fixed abode. Of the 1.5 million Greeks who fled from Asia Minor in 1922 about one million have settled on the outskirts of large towns in the "**new**" *(néa)* communities named after their lost homes, such as New Smyrna *(Néa Smírni)* in Athens and on agricultural land made available by the government.

The legendary Greek shipowners

The fact that the Greek merchant fleet occupies such an important place in the modern world is due as much to the flexibility of government legislation as to the spirit of enterprise shown by certain shipowners.
The most famous of them is without any doubt **Aristotle Onassis**, who was born in 1906 in Izmir (Smyrna) and was one of the Greeks who fled from Turkey in 1922. In 1923 he emigrated to Argentina, where he launched himself in the export-import business. In 1929 he bought his first ship and profited from the economic crisis to enlarge his fleet. This was destroyed in the Second World War but he built it up again from 1945, making the construction of supertankers his priority. In 1957 he founded the airline Olympic Airways.
His private life was as turbulent as his business career. In 1946 he married Tina Livanos, the daughter of the richest Greek shipowner; he divorced her in 1960 in favour of another famous Greek, **Maria Callas**. When he married a third time in 1968, his bride was **Jacqueline Bouvier**, the widow of President Kennedy. In 1973 he lost his 24 year-old son in an air crash. He himself died in 1975 at Neuilly in France, leaving his fortune to his daughter Christina, who disappeared in 1988 in mysterious circumstances.
The fascination we still feel for Aristotle Onassis is due not only to his colourful lifestyle, but also to the dramatic context in which it took place. His legend is further enhanced by his rivalry with his brother-in-law, **Stavros Niarchos** (1909-96), another Greek shipowner who, after divorcing Eugenia Livanos (whose death also took place in suspicious circumstances) married first the heiress to the Ford car firm and then Tina Livanos, whose second husband had been the heir of the Duke of Marlborough.

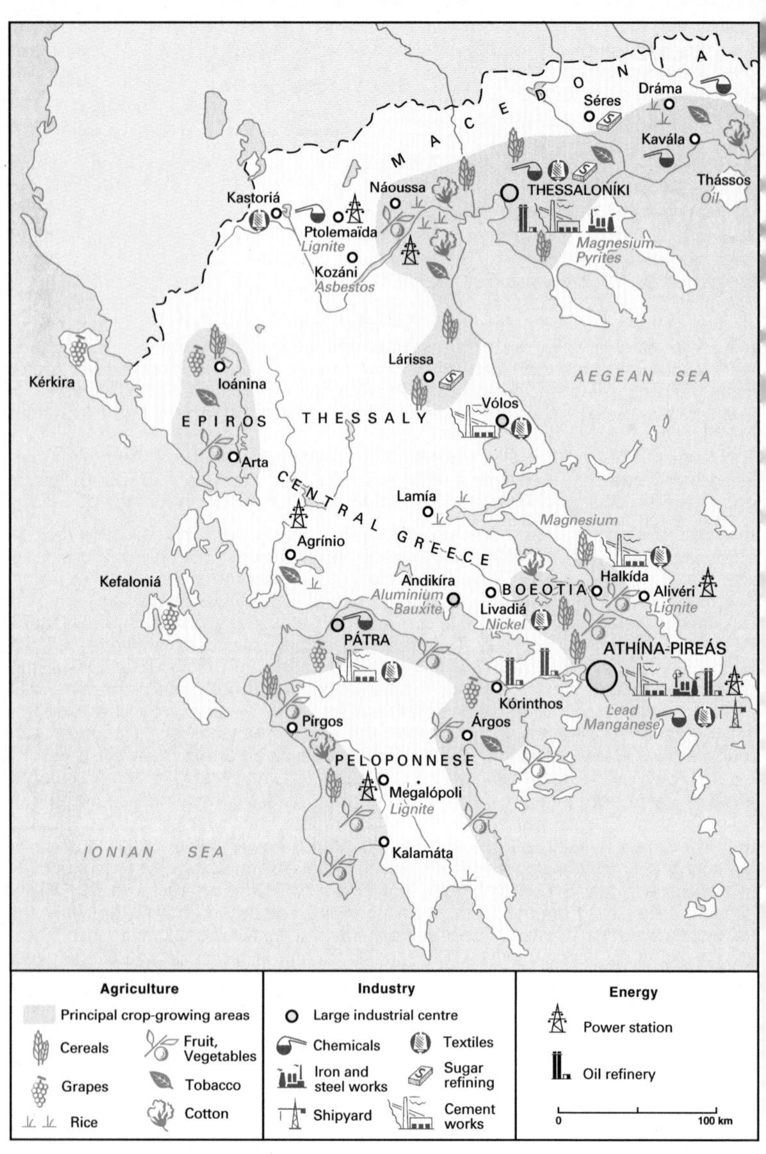

There is also a large and powerful Greek expatriate community. The greater number is made up of Greeks who emigrated in the 19C, establishing themselves in Egypt, the home of an influential group of businessmen *(Benáki)*, in Central Europe (*Sína* in banking in Vienna), on the Black Sea (Odessa), in the Middle East and particularly in the USA where their political weight is not to be ignored.

More recent emigrants were attracted by the high salaries of the industrial countries, such as Canada, Australia, South Africa and Federal Republic of Germany; they return to Greece after a few years or on retirement.

The number of expatriates is about 4 000 000, with 250 000 in Germany and 30 000 in France.

Education – The Greeks have a high regard for education since it is their chief means of promotion and 45 per cent of students come from average backgrounds. Primary and secondary education, public or private, is compulsory for 9 years. School parties are often to be seen on educational outings to the historic sights.

Higher education which involves 4.8 per cent of the active population is provided by the Universities of Thessaloníki, Komotiní, Ioánina, Patras, Crete (Herakleion and Rethymnon) and Athens which is also the home of the Polytechnic; many students go abroad to study. Graduates tend to enter the liberal professions (lawyers, doctors).

Daily Life – Although egocentric and individualistic in character, the Greeks are also hospitable and exuberant; they have a powerful need to talk and use their hands a great deal. To pass the time they often resort to worry beads (kombolóï), which resemble a rosary, endlessly clicking the beads of amber, box wood or plastic between their fingers. Their gaiety, however, hides a deep pessimism which is expressed in the melancholy strains of their popular songs and music. Time is of little importance to them and punctuality is not their forte. Although they enjoy drinking, there is little drunkenness. The Greeks combine a talent for business with a reputation for deep personal honesty. In the past women devoted themselves to working in the home and in the fields but nowadays they play an increasingly important role in the social and economic life of the country not only in the towns but also in the countryside. Greek women have had voting rights since 1952 and over 35 per cent of them work. Old people are highly respected. On rising the Greeks take a single cup of coffee before starting work but at mid-morning they pause for a snack of bread and cheese or a *koulouri*, a bread ring sprinkled with sesame seeds. Lunch, which is eaten between 1 and 2pm and sometimes at 3pm, consists of a light meal.

Then in summer comes the siesta until 4 or 5pm, when work sometimes resumes until 7 or 8pm.

The early evening is the best part of the Greek day when the men meet in the **café** *(kafenío)*, the centre of social life, and talk interminably over a glass of aniseed liqueur *(oúzo)* or a tiny cup of Greek coffee *(kafedáki)* with a simple glass of water; the main topics are football, politics and their fellow countrymen; some play cards or **backgammon** *(távli)*. In the provinces this is the time for the **evening promenade** *(perípato* or *vólta)* when people stroll in the main square.

Dinner, at home, is served about 10 o'clock or even later and is the heaviest meal of the day. People eat out frequently with the family or a group of friends. The evening ends at the café or the theatre (Athens and Thessaloníki) or out in the open air or watching television.

PUBLIC LIFE

The dominant features in social activity are the absence of rigid social classes and the passion for discussion; Athens retains her ancient reputation as the "town of gossips". The Greeks are fiercely individualistic and have inherited from their forebears, who invented democracy, a taste for argument and a propensity to dissension which has caused the country many political crises.

Political and administrative organisation – Since 1974, when the monarchy was abolished in a referendum, Greece has been a republic. Legislative power lies with the National Assembly which is composed of 300 members, elected by universal suffrage, who choose the President of the Republic by a two-thirds majority. The President is the guardian of the Constitution, which was approved in 1975, together with the Constitutional Council, but he does not preside over the Council of Ministers; he also has a representative role. Executive power is in the hands of the prime minister and his ministers but is also widely decentralised since many administrative responsibilities are exercised by the 9 regions *(see page 3)* and 52 departments *(nomí)* which are themselves divided into districts *(eparchies)*, large communes *(demes)* and parishes *(kinótites)*.

Press and information – The press, which is widely read, deals essentially with politics; about 130 daily papers are published in Greece: 18 in Athens and 2 in Thessaloníki which are distributed throughout the country; in addition there are about 10 financial and sports papers. Television has made rapid strides since 1975.

N. PESYLLAS

Art in antiquity

ARCHITECTURE

Quarries – The chief building material was stone: limestone tufa (often shell limestone), and marble from the quarries on Pentelikon, Thássos and Náxos. The stone blocks were quarried with a pickaxe and extracted with the aid of metal or wooden wedges – the latter were soaked to make them expand. Often the blocks were then shaped on the spot into architectural elements: columns, capitals, models of statues.

Transport – The blocks were removed from the quarry down a slipway constructed so as to have a regular gradient. Weighing on average 5t, the blocks were loaded on to wooden sledges which were lowered on ropes hitched round fixed bollards. The blocks were then transferred to carts or drays drawn by bullocks for transport to the building site.

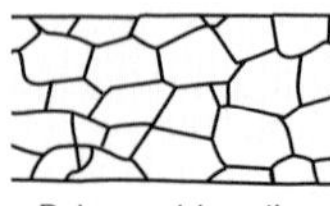
Polygonal bonding

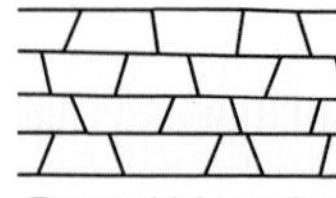
Trapezoidal bonding

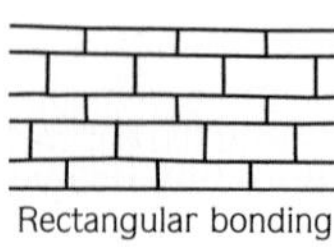
Rectangular bonding

Building sites – On the site the rough or prepared blocks were unloaded with the aid of levers or rollers and sent to the workshop to be dressed or decorated (fluting, moulding) or carved (capitals, pediments and metopes). The blocks were raised into position with a block and tackle and hoist or derrick. The dressed stones which were placed one upon another without mortar were held in place by H or N cramps. Wooden or metal pins were used to secure the piles of drums which made up a column: the holes which held them can still be seen. Stone columns received a coat of stucco.

Bonding – In large-scale constructions the blocks of stone were cut and placed in various ways according to the purpose and period of the building and the means and time available. No bonding material was used. This gives Greek stonework an almost unrivalled aesthetic and functional value. The Cyclopean style of construction, rough but sturdy, is to be found in some Mycenaean structures, especially at Tiryns. Polygonal bonding was used in all periods, often for foundations; at first the blocks were rough hewn, then came curved surfaces and finally flat ones. Trapezoidal bonding, with varying degrees of regularity, was widespread in the 4C BC. Rectangular bonding, which occurred in all periods, was used most frequently in the Classical period.

Palaces and Fortresses

Minoan Period – 2000-1450 BC. The Minoan dynasties which ruled the cities of Crete built complex fortified palaces which inspired the myth of the labyrinth *(see KNOSSÓS)*: blind external walls, symmetrical entrances, a cordon of storerooms and workrooms within the outer walls, at the centre a vast courtyard surrounded by the religious buildings and royal apartments grouped round light wells on several floors which were linked by a maze of stairs and corridors. Villas, such as Tylissos, show the same plan on a smaller scale. The best examples of Cretan palaces are Knossós, Mália, Phaistos and Zákros on Crete itself; other examples on Melos and particularly Thíra (Santoríni).

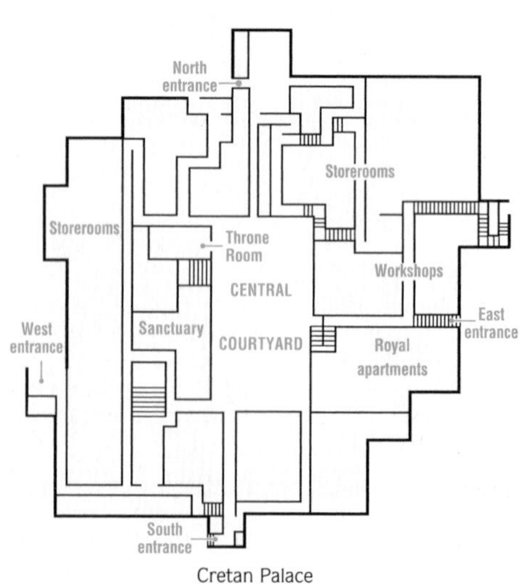

Cretan Palace

Mycenaean Period – 1550-1100 BC. The Mycenaean palace was less sophisticated than the Cretan and stood within a fortified city *(acropolis)* composed of Cyclopean walls, so called because legend said they had been built by giant masons, the Cyclops. The palace itself had a simple and logical plan: one entrance, a courtyard with the throne room on one side preceded by a vestibule and the main reception rooms on the other. The largest room was the *megaron* with four columns supporting the roof and surrounding the central hearth which served both domestic and religious purposes. Beyond lay the private apartments of the king and queen, usually furnished with baths.

The best examples of Mycenaean palaces are Mycenae, Tiryns, Pylos and Gla.

The dead were buried on the edge of the city in three different sorts of graves: a pit grave, a rock sepulchre or a circular domed chamber *(thólos)* with an entrance passage *(drómos)*. The skilled craftsmanship of the objects found in these tombs indicates that the princes who were buried in them were astonishingly rich; for many years the graves were known as "Treasuries". The best examples of Mycenaean graves are at Mycenae, Pylos, Vapheio, Peristéria in the Peloponnese and Orchomenos in Boeotia.

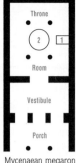

Mycenaean megaron
1 Throne 2 Hearth

Temples (from 700 BC)

The temple was the dwelling place of the god or goddess to whom it was dedicated and housed his or her statue; some temples were dedicated to more than one divinity.

Proportions – The temples, which were thought to represent the architectural ideal, are essentially a blend of structural simplicity and harmonious proportions. The proportions were governed by the module, the average radius of the column, which determined the height since the column was the basic element in the elevation of a building.

In some buildings the architects departed from rigid verticals and horizontals to correct optical distortion.

The horizontal entablatures were slightly bowed making the centre imperceptibly higher than the ends; each column was inclined towards its inner neighbour as it rose, the angle of incline increasing from the centre of the colonnade towards the outer corner.

Offset columns

Decoration – The sculpted figures, often didactic, were placed on the secondary architectural features: the tympanum (pediment) and the metopes (architrave).

The temples were painted; the background was generally red with the prominent features in blue to form a contrast. These brilliant colours made the stone or white marble sculptures stand out. A gilded bronze colour was used to pick out certain decorative motifs such as shields or acroteria.

Plan – There were three main types. The large peripteral temple consisted of a central oblong chamber *(naós)* containing the statue of the divinity and entered by a door, with a porch at either end screened by two columns; one porch *(prónaos)* led into the *naós*, the other *(opisthódomos)* contained the temple's most precious offerings. The roof of the *naós* might be supported on two rows of columns. Behind the *naós* there was occasionally an inner chamber *(adyton)* which only the priest might enter. This central section was surrounded by a colonnade (peristyle) and the temple was described in terms of the number of columns in the front and rear colonnades: hexastyle – six. The length of a temple was usually twice its width. The "in antis" temple consisted of a *naós* and *prónaos* screened by two columns between two pilasters (*antae* in Latin) at the ends of the extended walls of the *naós*. The *thólos* was a votive or commemorative circular building with a peristyle.

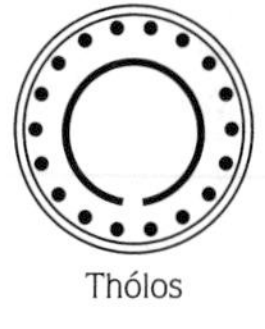

Thólos

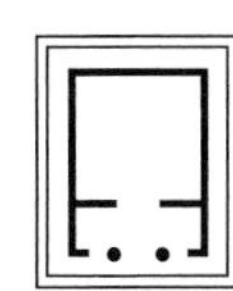

In antis

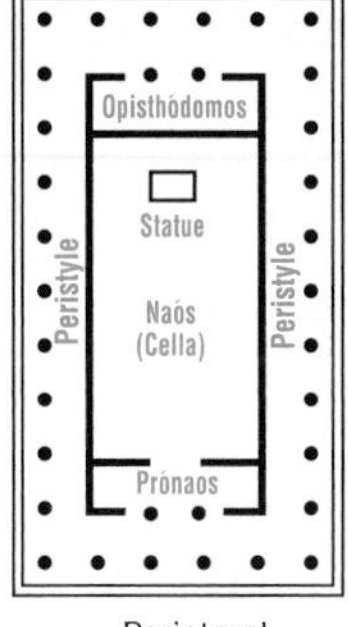

Peripteral

Elevation and orders – The main elements of a temple were the base (stylobate), the columns, the entablature supporting a wooden roof frame covered with tiles and a pediment at either end. The articulation of these elements gave rise to the orders.

Doric Order – It developed on the mainland among the Dorian people and was the most common style in Greece from the 7C onwards. The columns, which had 20 flutes, rested directly on the stylobate without bases; the capitals were plain. The entablature consisted of three parts one above the other: the architrave, the frieze and the cornice; the frieze was composed of metopes, panels often carved in high relief, alternating with triglyphs, stone slabs with two vertical grooves. The triangular pediments were sculpted with scenes in high relief and also adorned with decorative motifs *(acroteria)* at the angles. Along the sides above the cornice were sculpted ornaments *(antefixa)* which served as gargoyles.

Ionic Order – This style developed among the Ionians who had settled in Asia Minor in the 5C BC and was considered a feminine style; its delicate grace and rich ornament contrasted with the austere strength of the Doric order. Its main characteristics are tall slim columns with 24 flutes resting on moulded bases and crowned by capitals in the form of a double scroll; an entablature consisting of an architrave, a continuous sculpted frieze and a cornice decorated with egg and dart and leaf and dart moulding; a pediment with *acroteria* shaped like palm leaves at the angles. The best example is the Temple of Athena Nike in the Acropolis.

Corinthian Order – It was invented in Corinth in the 5C BC but did not spread until the 4C BC; it was very popular in the Roman period. It is a derivative of the Ionic order and its chief distinction is the scroll capital almost entirely covered in curled acanthus leaves. The best examples are the Olympieion and Hadrian's Arch in Athens and the Temple of Octavian in Corinth. The capital was invented by Kallimachos, a sculptor and contemporary of Pheidias; he is thought to have been inspired by a basket filled with flowers.

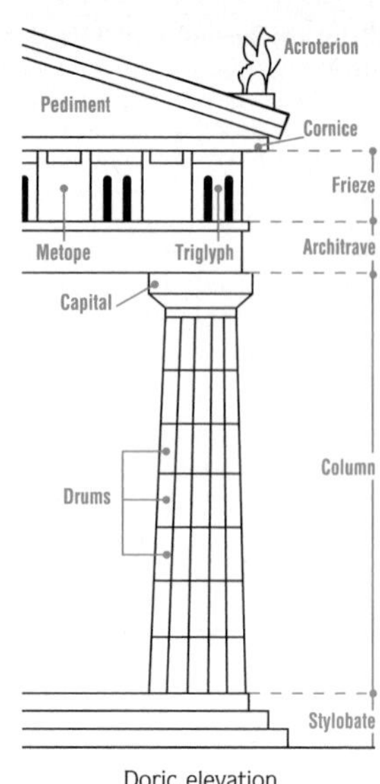

Doric elevation

Theatres

Nearly all religious sites in ancient Greece included a theatre which was originally designed for the Dionysiac festivals which included hymns or dithyrambs which later developed into tragedy.

The original wooden structures were later built of stone and from the 4C BC comprised:
– a central circular area *(orchestra)* where the chorus performed round the altar of the god and the actors wearing the appropriate masks acted their parts;
– tiers of seats *(koilon or theatron)* extending round more than half the orchestra to form the segment of a circle; the first row of seats was reserved for the priests and officials; a promenade *(diázoma)* ran round between the upper and lower tiers of seats. The audience reached their seats from above, from the *diázoma* or through passages *(parodos)* leading into the orchestra;
– a proscenium *(proskenion)*, a sort of portico forming a backdrop, and a stage *(skene)*, originally a store room. In the Hellenistic period the stage was incorporated into the performing area; the back wall improved the acoustics.

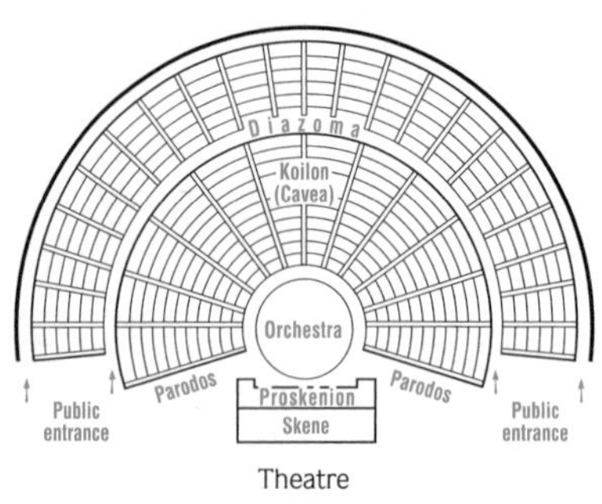

Theatre

Odeons were covered theatres which became very numerous in the Roman period.
The major theatres are in Athens, Delphi, Árgos and Epidauros and Dodona.

SCULPTURE

Archaic Period – 700-500 BC. In the 7C BC the Greek World began to produce its first full size statues, strange rigid figures with ecstatic expressions made of wood *(xoanon)* inspired by Asiatic, particularly Egyptian, models.

In the 6C BC two well-known and distinctive types of statue were produced: the *kouros*, a naked young man, and the *kore*, a young woman dressed in a tunic, Doric *peplos* or Ionian *chiton*. The figures, which were life size or larger, were sometimes made of bronze, like the Piraeus Apollo which was discovered in 1959, but more often of limestone *(poros)* or marble and then painted with vivid colours.

The high reliefs, carved in stone and also painted, mostly come from pediments and are impressive for their realistic and expressive appearance; the bronze sculptures are more stylised.

The Acropolis Museum in Athens has an important series of Archaic figures *(kouroi* and *korai*, high relief pedimental sculptures, *moscophoroi)* while the National Museum displays the Warrior of Marathon and several *kouroi* including the *kouros* of Sounion, the oldest known (600 BC), and the *kouros* of Anávissos; the Piraeus Apollo (late 6C BC) is to be found in the Piraeus Museum.

Other examples typical of Archaic art are the stone Gorgon from the temple of Artemis in Corcyra (Corfu Museum), the marble frieze from the Siphnian Treasury and two *kouroi* representing Cleobis and Biton (Delphi Museum).

Classical Period – 500-300 BC. There was a transition period, marked by the *Charioteer from Delphi* (475 BC: *illustration see p 122*), where the figure turns slightly to the right and takes his weight on one hip; Classical statuary then freed itself from the rigid frontal stance passing through two distinct phases.

In the idealistic phase (5C BC) Greek sculpture reached its height in the work of Polykleitos and Pheidias. The former established a standard model, the **canon**. The latter created an ideal standard of beauty composed of strength, majesty and serenity in the delicately carved lines of his marble figures: his genius is expressed in the Parthenon sculptures (Acropolis Museum, British Museum, Louvre); unfortunately the famous chryselephantine (gold and ivory) statue of Zeus at Olympia has been destroyed.

Other typical works of the period include *Athena Mourning* in the Acropolis Museum *(illustration see p 42)* and *Poseidon* from Artemision in the National Museum *(illustration see p 93)*.

During the "naturalist" phase (4C) majesty gave way to grace and the female nude made its appearance. Artists began to compose from nature giving their figures expressive faces; the best known are Skopas, Lysippos and Praxiteles who produced tall figures such as the Hermes of Olympia. The *Apollo Belvedere* (Vatican) also dates from this time as do the great bronzes in the Athens Museum: the *Ephebe* from Antikythera and the *Athena* and *Artemis* in the archeological museum in Piraeus.

Tanágra in Boeotia produced the famous funerary figurines in terracotta.

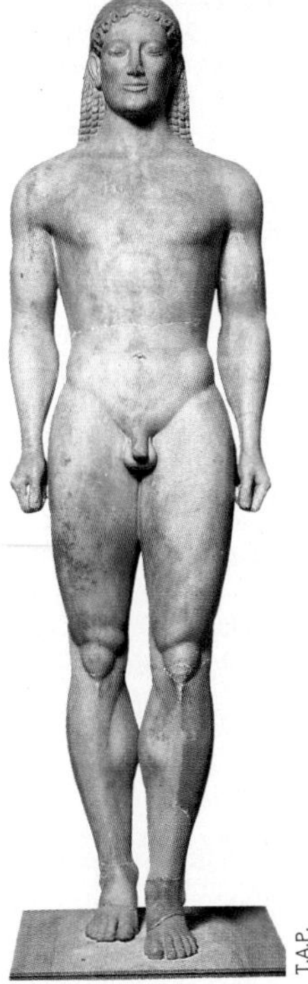

Kouros (National Archeological Museum)

Hellenistic Period – 300-100 BC. Sculpture began to be influenced by Expressionism and Orientalism. A realism, sometimes excessive, was used to express not only pain but also movement as in the *Laocoon* (Vatican) and the *Victory of Samothrace* (Louvre); at the same time it could produce the beautiful serenity of the *Melos Aphrodite (Venus de Milo)*. Artists took delight in representing old people and children, such as the bronze jockey from Artemision in the Athens Museum.

PAINTING AND CERAMICS

Except for the Minoan frescoes in Crete or Thíra (Santorini) and the Hellenistic funerary paintings in Macedonia *(see LEFKÁDIA-NÁOUSSA and VÉRIA)* few examples of ancient Greek painting have survived. In fact, although painting played a major role in the decoration of sculptures and monuments, it was less important as an art form in its own right and the works of the great painters of the 4C BC – Zeuxis and above all Apelles, Alexander the Great's favourite artist – have not survived the passage of time. For a knowledge of Greek painting one must study the decoration of pottery on the many vases which have come down to us.

Vases – The ornamentation painted on vases is one of the major sources of information about Greek religion and civilisation.

The *pithos* was used for storing grain, the *amphora* for the storing and transport of oil or wine. The *pelike*, *krater* and *hydria* were used as jars for oil, wine and water respectively. The *oinochoë* was used as a jug for pouring water or wine into a *kantharos*; the *kylix* was a drinking cup and the *rhyton* was a vessel shaped like a horn or an animal's head. The *lekythos* was a funerary vase.

Styles – The styles developed in step with the great artistic periods *(see p 21)*; there were several types.

Creto-Mycenaean vases (1700-1400 BC): scenes of flora and fauna treated with great freedom and decorative sense.
Typical examples: octopus *amphora*; Phaistos *krater* (Herakleion Museum); Santoríni vases (National Museum in Athens).

Archaic vases (1000-600 BC): **geometric style** in the Cyclades and Attica with large *kraters* or *amphorae* decorated with dotted lines, the key pattern, checks, lozenges and sometimes animals; **orientalising style** in Rhodes and Corinth where small vessels were decorated with oriental motifs: roses, lotus sprays, sphinxes and deer.
Typical examples: *amphorae* from the Kerameikos and the Dipylon (National Museum in Athens); perfume flasks (Corinth Museum).

Black figure vases (600-480 BC): subjects for decoration drawn from mythology or history: silhouettes in black painted on a red ochre ground.
Typical examples: *krater* showing Herakles and Nereus (National Museum in Athens).

Red figure vases (480-320 BC): subject for decoration not only mythological (so called "severe" style – 5C BC) but also familiar and more lighthearted: scenes and figures drawn in detail and accentuated by a black or white ground *(lekythoi)*.
Typical examples: *krater* from Kalyx and *lekythoi* from Er Ètria (National Museum in Athens).

Some famous names in Antiquity

Apelles – A native of Kos, and the finest 4C painter according to the Ancients.

Dioscourides – A mosaic artist from Sámos. Some of his works are to be found in the Naples Archeological Museum.

Hippodamos of Miletus – A great town planner.

Lysippos – 4C sculptor in bronze. Alexander the Great's official portraitist.

Pheidias – The most illustrious sculptor of the Classical period, who worked at Olympia.

Polykleitos – A sculptor in bronze.

Praxiteles – An Athenian sculptor.

Skopas – A sculptor and architect from Páros.

GLOSSARY OF SPECIALIST TERMS

Academy – The name of the gardens where stood the tomb of the hero Academos and where Plato founded his school of philosophy *(see p 113)*.

Achaians – The name of the first Greek-speaking Indo-European settlers, also known as Mycenaeans after their principal city, who arrived in Greece at the beginning of the 2nd millennium BC and drove away the Pelasgians. Homer and the ancient poets referred to all Greeks as Achaians.

Acropolis – The high ground, the Upper Town, where stood the citadel.

Aeolians – The descendants of the early Hellenic tribes and of the Minyans; they first occupied mainland Greece, then emigrated to the coastal lands of Asia Minor between Troy and the gulf of Smyrna.

Agora – The main square in a town, the centre of public life.

Altar – A small structure in the open, often in front of a temple, where offerings to the gods were placed.

Anastylosis – The total, or often partial, reconstruction of a monument using the original fragments found on the site and making up the missing parts with an easily distinguishable modern material.

Archon – A town's chief magistrate. It became an honorific title from the 5C BC.

Areopagos – A hill in Athens after which is named the council which met there.

Atlantes – Support in the form of a carved male figure.

Barbarians – A term referring to non-Greeks which did not necessarily have a pejorative connotation.

Bema – Rostrum for orators.

Boule – Senate or Council of State in ancient Athens. The Senate House was the *bouleuterion*.

Chiton – A tunic of Ionian origin, made from a flimsy fabric and worn next to the skin. It was worn knee-length by men and longer by women.

Chlamys – A short woollen mantle pinned at the shoulder.

Choregos – A wealthy citizen who was responsible for the organization of spectacles *(see p 83)*.

Chorus – A group of narrators or dancers, led by a *koryphaios*, who performed the lyrics of a play.

Chryselephantine – Made of gold and ivory.

Clepsydra – A water-clock used by the tribunal to limit the time allocated to speakers.

Dipteral – Term describing a monument with a double peristyle.

Dithyramb – A lyric poem sung in honour of a divinity, usually Dionysos.

Dorians – A Greek-speaking Indo-European tribe who settled in Greece between 1200 and 1100 BC, and were said to be descendants of Dorus, Hellen's son *(see p 44)*.

Doryphoros – Term describing a lance-bearer who guarded a tyrant *(see below)*.

Drachma – A weight and coin used in ancient Greece; also the modern currency unit.

Dromos – A passage or avenue, usually leading to a tomb.

Ephebe – A youth. The word also referred to young citizens of 18-20 enrolled for military training.

Exedra – Niche, usually semicircular, containing a ledge used as a seat or as a support for a statue.

Gymnasium – A derivative of the word *gymnos* – nude. It was a place comprising sports grounds and buildings (including baths) where athletes exercised naked. Gymnasia also had a social and cultural function as a meeting place for philosophers and their pupils.

Gynaeceum – Room or quarters reserved for women in a Greek house.

Herm (or Term) – A pillar topped by a human head representing a deity, sometimes with male organs at mid-height.

Heroon – A temple or funerary monument dedicated to a hero, the offspring of a god and a human.

Himation – A cloak, usually made of wool, worn over the *peplos* or the *chiton*.

Hoplite – A heavy-armed foot soldier, often wearing a plumed helmet.

Hypocaust – Underground heating installations in baths.

Hypostyle – A term describing a structure with the roof supported by rows of columns.

Ionians – Greek-speaking Indo-European people who settled in Greece in the 2nd millennium BC, shortly after the Achaians. After being driven out by the Dorians they settled in the Aegean islands and later on the coast of Asia Minor which became known as Ionia.

Key pattern – Ornament composed of combinations of straight lines, usually on a flat surface.

Lyceum – A school of philosophy founded by Aristotle.

Mausoleum – The tomb of Mausolus, King of Caria (4C BC) in Asia Minor. The name was later used to describe large-scale funerary monuments.

Metic – A resident alien in a Greek city.

Metope – A square space between the triglyphs on the frieze of the Greek Doric Order.

Minoans – Name derived from Minos, King of Crete, to describe the inhabitants of Crete in the 2nd and 3rd millennia BC.

Minyans – A prehellenic race who lived in Thessaly and Boeotia at the beginning of the 2nd millennium BC. They also settled in Lemnos and Lesbos.

Mycenaeans – Name given to the Achaians after their principal city, Mycenae *(see MIKÍNES)*.

Necropolis – The city of the dead. A large burial ground outside the city limits.

Nymphaeum – A small shrine near a fountain dedicated to the nymphs, nature deities who lived in rocks, trees, springs etc.

Obolos – A weight and currency unit worth 1/6 of a drachma.

Omphalos – "Navel". A conical block of marble marking the hub of the universe in Delphi *(see DELFÍ)*.

Oracle – An augury or a prophecy; the answer given by a deity (Zeus at Dodona, Apollo at Delphi) to the enquiries of those that consulted them through a **sibyl, pythia** (priestess) or priest.

Ostracism – An institution designed to safeguard democracy, introduced in Athens by **Kleisthenes**.

Paean – An invocation or a song of victory or thanksgiving.

Pelasgians – Name given by the ancient Greeks to the inhabitants of the Eastern Mediterranean seaboard before the arrival of the Hellenic people. Walls built of enormous blocks of stone in the prehellenic or Mycenaean periods are sometimes described as **pelasgic** or **cyclopean** walls.

Peplos – A long tunic, usually made of wool, worn by women.

Peripteral – A term describing a monument surrounded by a single row of columns.

Peristyle – A columned gallery surrounding a building, courtyard or garden.

Propylaia – A monumental portal with a gateway *(pylos)*.

Proxenus – The official representative of a state, chosen from the citizens of another state, to look after the interests of its citizens; a sort of consul.

Stadium – A vast open space where running, wrestling, jumping, discus and javelin throwing competitions took place. The stadium was lined on three sides by earthen, wooden or stone terraces. A stadium *(stadion)* was about 194yds/177m (variable according to the site) long and the word came to mean a measure of length. The main extant stadia are at Delphi and Olympia.

Stoa – A portico or gallery.

Strategos – A magistrate elected, in principle for one year, as army commander. Some, such as Pericles, had wider powers which were curtailed by democratic institutions.

Thermae – Public baths. From the Mycenaean period the Greeks used earthenware or stone tubs and large basins. Public baths with swimming pools opened in Athens in the 5C BC and the people came to keep warm in winter or to meet friends. The facilities were developed and perfected by the Romans.

Tyrant – In the 7C and 6C BC tyrants overthrew the rule of the aristocratic families and instituted dictatorship often with the support of popular uprisings. They styled themselves "demagogues", leaders of the people. Periander, the tyrant of Corinth, was a harsh ruler but enlightened tyrants such as Peisistratos and Polycrates ruled in Athens and Sámos.

Byzantine and modern art

After the Roman occupation, Greece passed through a long period of artistic inactivity. No doubt this should be seen as the result of its status as an occupied country, especially during the three centuries preceding independence when artistic expression was stifled to such an extent that talented people emigrated. The example of El Greco, born on Crete, is so well known as to hardly need mentioning. During this long period the only form of expression available was religious, and the only works of art remaining from it are the churches and their interiors. The sole exception to this rule were the Ionian islands belonging to Venice, where there was a small school of painters influenced by the Italian Renaissance.

BYZANTINE ART

Byzantine art, which came to be identified with oriental Christian art, was mystical and hieratical, a blend of the influences coming from Rome and Asia Minor.

Architecture

The main characteristics of Byzantine architecture are demonstrated in the religious buildings: symmetrical plan, dome symbolising the heavenly vault, use of brick either alternating with stone or on its own but arranged in a decorative pattern.

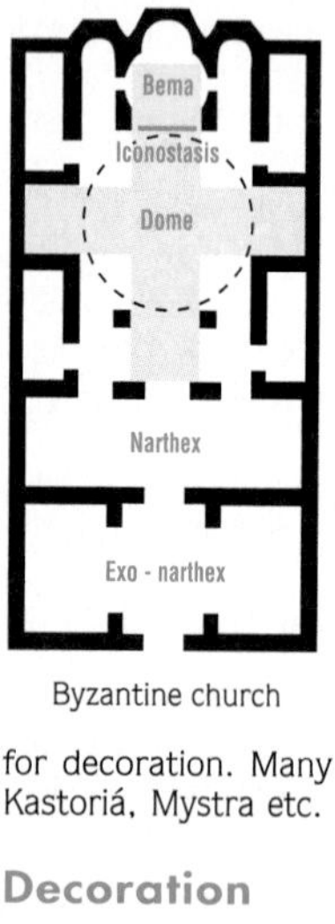

Bema
Iconostasis
Dome
Narthex
Exo - narthex

Byzantine church

First Golden Age: "Age of Justinian" 5C-6C – The church opened off a court *(atrium)*; it was built on the basilical plan (nave and two aisles) or the Greek cross plan, with a massive dome on pendentives and interior galleries for the women *(gynaecea)*. Typical examples: Agía Sophía in Constantinople; several churches in Thessaloníki and Philippi in Greece.

Second Golden Age: 9C-12C – The buildings were often small-scale but perfectly proportioned; they were built on the cross-in-square plan with the arms of the cross more evident on the exterior; a narthex preceded the main entrance and the dome was raised higher by the introduction of a "drum"; the walls were adorned with marble low relief sculptures decorated with coloured enamels. Typical examples in Greece: Old Metropolitan and St Theodore in Athens, Daphne, Óssios Loukás in Boeotia, Panagía Halkeón in Thessaloníki, Néa Moní in Chios and Agía Sophía in Monemvassía.

Third Golden Age: "Palaiologos Renaissance" 13C-16C – The buildings combine the basilical plan (ground floor) and the Greek cross plan: multiplicity of domes, widespread use of frescoes for decoration. Many examples in Thessaloníki (Holy Apostles, St Catherine's), Árta, Kastoriá, Mystra etc.

Decoration

The churches were richly decorated with multi-coloured marble floors, frescoes (from the 13C) and mosaics in warm colours embellished with gold that fired the imagination. The decorative scheme followed a well-defined liturgical and doctrinal arrangement: **Christ Pantocrator** (Ruler of All), in the dome, surrounded by Archangels, Apostles or Evangelists; the Virgin Theotókos (Virgin Mother) flanked by the Archangels Michael and Gabriel in the apse; scenes from the Life of Christ or the Virgin, not always in

Mosaic of the Resurrection, Óssios Loukás Monastery

chronological order but according to the calendar of feasts, in the nave and narthex. The icons, which were painted on wood, were hung on the **iconostasis**, a screen separating the nave from the sanctuary *(bema)* where the priest officiates.
The subjects of Orthodox iconography include: the **Preparation** *(Hetoimasia)* shown by an empty throne awaiting the return of the Lord to judge the world; the Descent of Christ into Hell; the Dormition of the Virgin and the Three Angels at Abraham's table. The most venerated saints are the Three Hierarchs or Doctors of the Church (John Chrysostom, Basil and Gregory of Nazianzus), John the Baptist (*Pródomos* meaning the Forerunner) represented with wings, St George on horseback piercing the dragon with his spear, St Andrew of Patras, St Demetrios of Thessaloniki, St Michael, St Nicholas, St Athanasios, St Cyril and St Pantaleon and the two Theodores; St Cosmas and St Damian together with St Pantaleon and Hermolaos known as the "holy penniless ones" as they practised medicine without charging fees.
The best collections of Byzantine mosaics are preserved in the monasteries at Daphne, Néa Moní in Chios and Óssios Loukás in Boeotia while the great series of frescoes on biblical themes can be seen in Mystra, in Patmos, in Kritsá in Crete and in the monasteries of Mount Athos.

19C TO THE PRESENT

The accession to the throne of Otto of Bavaria was followed by a temporary influx of painters from abroad who worked at the College of Fine Arts founded in 1843, where they taught some of the first fine Greek painters, while others went to study in Munich. The most important of them was **Nikifóros Lítras** (1832-1904), who concentrated on painting scenes from daily life and portraiture. Another famous name in Greek painting of this period was **Konstandínos Volonákis** (1839-1907), who made his name as a marine artist, although his *Munich Circus* exhibited at the National Gallery in Athens shows a move towards Impressionism. In all spheres of art, the second half of the 19C in Greece bore the stamp of officially approved Academicism.
At the turn of the century art in Greece underwent an important evolution under the influence, in painting, of **Konstandínos Parthénis** (1878-1967), who followed the path of Impressionism and Fauvism and taught at the College of Fine Arts, and of the sculptor **Konstandínos Dimitriádis** (1881-1943), who was inspired by Rodin. They opened the way for Greek art to embrace modern forms and the most advanced movements of the time, as seen in the work of the expressionist painter **Giórgos Bouziáni** (1885-1959), cubist **Níkos Gíka** (1906-94), and surrealist **Níkos Engonópoulos** (1910-85). Parallel to these was a stream taking its inspiration from popular Greek sources and traditions, represented by Spyros Vassilíou (1902-85) and Iánnis Tsaroúkis (1910-89), and in architecture by D Pikiónis.
After the Second World War, Greek art flourished again, following two principal directions. Together with the search for a true Greek spirit, of which the main exponent was Iánnis Morális (b 1916), there developed a strong movement concerned with contemporary forms. Its most notable members were the abstract painters **Aléxandros Kontópoulos** (1905-75), **Krístos Lefákis** (1906-68) and **Iánnis Spyrópoulos** (1912-90), and the sculptors Giórgos Zogolópoulos and Akilleús Apérgis. While on the one hand there is a clear return to representative art, notably with the painter Iánnis Gaitis (1923-84)

and the sculptor **Giórgos Giorgiádis** (b 1934), those Greek artists working in a contemporary vein are ever more closely linked with the various Western artistic movements, many of them working abroad.

In addition to figures such as George Candilis (b 1913), the architect who designed the urban development at Toulouse-le-Murail and also worked in Berlin, and Mario Prassinos (b 1916), well known for his pointillist works in black and white and the cartoons he produced for the Aubusson weavers, two names have gained international recognition. **Iánnis Kounellis** (b 1936) lives and works in Italy, where he has been active in the movement *Arte povera*; after offering performances and installations, he has taken a more minimalist line which purports to be close to poetry in its original form. Panayótis Vassilákis, known as **Takis** (b 1925), has been living in Paris since 1954. His name is associated with technology in art, with his research into magnetism using constructions of metal rods, winking indicators, and electromagnets, and making musical clocks.

Religion

GODS AND MYTHS OF ANTIQUITY

Religion enters every aspect of life for a Greek, who sees in all happenings, however insignificant, a possible manifestation of the divine presence.

The ancient religion, devoid of dogma or a sense of sin, had its roots in the past of the peoples who occupied Greece. It spawned a whole profusion of divinities, to which the Greeks were forever adding gods worshipped by other peoples (Apollo is a god of Lycian origin, from Asia Minor, while Aphrodite was a transformation of the Phoenician goddess Ashtart). Inheriting much from the Anatolian and Cretan religions as well as from Indo-European faiths introduced by the Ionians, the religion embraced both underworld (chthonian) and heavenly (uranian) divinities, born of a Great Mother who was the source of fertility. Personifying forces of nature or moral characterisics, the gods also had human traits attributed to them, both physical and psychological. It was immortality that distinguished them from men. Both individuals and whole communities looked to them for protection and for favours.

The divinities and their cults – The oldest divinities were Ge *(Gaïa)*, the Earth Mother, who begat and mated with Uranus *(Ouranos)*, the Sky; they produced Mnemosyne, Themis, the Cyclops and the Titans including Oceanus, the personification of water, and Kronos, Time. The latter mated with his sister Rhea and begat the first group of Olympian gods: Zeus, Hera, Hestia, Demeter and Poseidon. These divinities and other major gods and goddesses lived in majesty on Mount Olympos hidden in the clouds with Zeus the thunderer at their head. There was also a crowd of lesser divinities: local gods, Egyptian and Syrian gods, demi-gods born of the love affairs between the greater gods and mere mortals, and heroes; they all peopled an ever-growing pantheon where divinities from the Creto-Mycenean period gradually became confused with the great gods whose cult was reduced to catering for special needs.

T.A.P.

Athena Mourning

The celebration of the cult took various forms depending on the purpose of the ceremony, which could be adjusted for individual circumstances and used for initiation. The complex **mysteries** which made use of symbolic objects such as representations of sexual organs were supposed to bring eternal salvation and ensure an afterlife; the most famous were performed at Eleusis (Elefsína). Another purpose of the ceremonies was to foretell future events, and so the faithful also came to consult the **oracles**, replies which the gods sent through the medium of the priests. The sanctuary of Apollo at **Delphi** (Delfí) is famous for the predictions made there by the **Pythia**. The rites could of course involve the whole community, and the most important ceremonies took place on the occasion of particular festivals. They were accompanied by activities which for us today have no connection with religion, such as poetry competitions or games and sporting events. The athletic and horse-riding competitions also had an aspect of initiation in that the winner (for example at the **Panhellenic Games** held annually at Olympia) received a sacred olive branch brought by Herakles (Hercules). The cult of **Dionysos** was accompanied by choruses, originally not written down, which are considered to have been the origin of all forms of theatre, whether tragedy, comedy or satire (the Satyrs were the companions of Dionysos). The prayers were usually accompanied by an offering: libations of milk or wine, and cakes and fruit placed before the altar. In return for a favour from the god a commemorative stele or a small votive statue would sometimes be promised. For a more important request animal sacrifice was used, part of which was burnt on the altar and the rest divided between the priests and the faithful. There were also purification rites with the purpose of cleansing the persons or objects considered impure by sprinkling them with water.

The temple *(hieron)*, dedicated to the god or goddess, stood within a sacred precinct *(témenos)* which was entered by a grand gateway *(propylaia)*. Purified with lustral water, the worshippers entered the precinct and processed along the sacred way past the treasuries, small buildings for the reception of offerings, the semi circular bench seats *(exedra)* and the votive offerings (inscriptions, statues) which also surrounded the temple. The altar, where the libations were poured and the animals were sacrificed, stood in the open in front of the temple. After the sacrifice the people entered the temple vestibule to see the statue of the divinity through the open door of the inner chamber *(naós)* *(see p 35)*.

Major Gods *(Latin names in brackets)*

Names	Identity and Symbol	Attributes	Principal place of worship
Aphrodite (Venus)	Born from the sea. Mother of Eros. Love and beauty.	Doves, shell.	Kythera, Corinth, Rhodes.
Apollo (Apollo)	Physical beauty. Fine Arts.	Lyre, arrows, laurel, sun.	Delos, Delphi, Corinth, Bassae, Líndos.
Ares (Mars)	Aphrodite's lover. War.	Helmet, arms and armour.	
Artemis (Diana)	Chastity, hunting. Twin of Apollo.	Bow, quiver, crescent moon. Artemision.	Delos, Brauron, Corcyra, Delphi.
Asklepios (Aesculapius)	Apollo's son. Healing.	Serpent, rod.	Epidauros, Kos.
Athena (Minerva)	Wisdom. Arts and crafts. Victory in war.	Shield (aegis), helmet, owl, olive branch.	Athens (Parthenon).
Demeter (Ceres)	Agriculture, maternal love.	Ear of corn, sceptre, scythe.	Eleusis.
Dionysos (Bacchus)	Born from Zeus' thigh. Wine, joy.	Vine, thyrsus, panther.	Athens, Delos, Parnassos and Pangaion.
Hades (Pluto)	Kingdom of the dead.	Throne, beard.	Ephyra Nekromanteion.
Helios (Phoebus)	A Titan. Sun.	Sun's rays, chariot.	Rhodes.
Hephaistos (Vulcan)	Aphrodite's husband. Fire, metal.	Anvil, hammer.	Athens "Theseion", Lemnos.
Hera (Juno)	Zeus' wife. Marriage.	Peacock, diadem.	Árgos, Sámos, Perachora, Olympia.
Hermes (Mercury)	Messenger of the gods and souls. Commerce, eloquence.	Winged sandals and cap. Caduceus, ram.	
Hestia (Vesta)	Family hearth.	Fire.	
Leto (Latona)	Zeus' lover; gave birth to Apollo and Artemis on Delos.	Depicted with her children.	
Persephone or Kore (Proserpina)	Demeter's daughter. Death. Renewal.	Cock, plants.	Ephyra Nekromanteion.
Poseidon (Neptune)	Amphitrite's husband. Sea and storms.	Trident.	Athens, Cape Sounion, Isthmía.
Themis	Justice.	Sword, scales.	Ramnoús.
Zeus (Jupiter)	Lord of the gods and the world.	Eagle, sceptre, thunder.	Olympia, Dodona, Neméa.

Other mythological figures

Aegeus – King of Athens. He sent his son Theseus to Crete to kill the Minotaur *(see KNOSSÓS)*. Theseus on his return forgot to change the black sail which was meant to announce his defeat and Aegeus thinking his son was dead jumped into the Aegean Sea which now bears his name.

Aegis – A fabulous shield made for Zeus by Hephaïstos and presented to Athena.

Aeolus – The god of the winds which he secured in a leather bag and released on Zeus' orders.

Ajax – The son of the king of Salamis. He defended Achilles during the Trojan War.

Amazons – A nation of women-warriors supposed to have lived in the barbarian lands of the northeast. One of the labours of Herakles was to secure the girdle of their queen, Hippolyta, and Theseus captured Antiope who became his queen.

Antigone – Oedipus' daughter who suffered a tragic fate *(see THÕVA)*.

Ariadne – Daughter of Minos, King of Crete. With her help Theseus succeeded in killing the Minotaur *(see KNOSSÓS)*.

Atlas – One of the giants who was condemned by Zeus to support the heavens with his head and hands.

Atreids – *(see MIKÍNES)*.

Chimaera – A fabulous animal of oriental origin with the head of a lion, the body of a goat and the tail of a dragon. It was destroyed by Bellerophon with the help of the winged horse Pegasus.

Cyclops – One-eyed giants, the sons of Ouranos and Gaia and as the personifications of Thunder, Lightning and Thunderbolt, helped the gods conquer the Titans. In the *Odyssey* they were shepherds and cannibals and also built "Cyclopean" walls.

Daidalos – An Athenian architect and inventor. He was exiled for murder and took refuge in Crete where he built King Minos' palace in the form of a labyrinth *(see KNOSSÓS)*. He was Icarus' father.

Dioscuri (Castor and Pollux) – The twin sons of Zeus and Leda who were famous for their bravery.

Fates (Moirai, Parcae) – Three sisters personifying Fate: Clotho held the distaff, Lachesis drew off the thread and Atropos cut it short. The name "Moirai" is the origin of miroló-gia – funeral dirge *(see MÁNI)*.

Furies – Primitive goddesses also known as Erinyes or Eumenides, avengers of crime. Their names were Allecto, Megaera and Tisiphone.

Gorgons – Three monsters with serpents in their hair and glaring eyes which turned to stone anything that looked at them. Medusa alone of the three was mortal and was slain by Perseus.

Hellen – Prometheus' grandson; his parents repeopled the world after the flood and his descendants gave their names to the Hellenic races: Achaian, Dorian, Ionian and Aeolian.

Herakles (Hercules) – The son of Zeus and Alcmene, he performed the 12 Labours *(see TÍRINTHA)*.

Hesperides – Nymphs who lived far away in the west guarding a tree that produced golden apples, a present given by Gaia to Hera when the latter married Zeus.

Hypnos – The son of Night and the personification of Sleep. His twin brother was Thanatos, Death.

Minotaur – A bull with a human body which was kept in the labyrinth and was killed by Theseus *(see KNOSSÓS)*.

Mnemosyne – The mother of the Muses; she is also the personification of Memory *(see LIVADIÁ)*.

Muses – The daughters of Zeus and Mnemosyne *(see ARÁHOVA)*.

Nemesis – The daughter of Night, the personification of divine retribution, responsible for ensuring observance of the natural order and combatting excessiveness. A sanctu-ary at Ramnoús is dedicated to her.

Nereids – Fifty sea goddesses, the daughters of Nereus and Doris and grand-daughters of Oceanos. Amphritrite was Poseidon's wife; Thetis was Achilles' mother.

Nymphs – Nature deities who lived in rocks, trees, springs etc.

Odysseus – A king of Ithaca *(see ITHÁKI)* who took part in the Trojan War.

Pan – A nature god with a horned human head and a goat's body. The nymphs fled from his amorous advances. His attribute was the pipe of seven reeds *(see ARÁHOVA)*.

Pandora – The first woman created by the gods. Her curiosity made her open a sealed box given to her by Zeus from which escaped all the evils that afflict mankind. Hope alone remained at the bottom of the box.

Paris – Priam's son who was asked to judge a beauty contest including Hera, Athena and Aphrodite. He awarded the golden apple (of Discord) to Aphrodite who had promised that he would be loved by the fairest woman, Helen *(see MIKÍNES)*. Hector was his brother and Andromache his wife.

Pegasus – A winged horse sprung from the blood of Medusa when Perseus cut off her head. It was Bellerophon's faithful companion and helped him destroy the Chimaera.

Perseus – The son of Zeus and Danaë. With the help of winged sandals and a magic helmet he beheaded the gorgon Medusa and delivered Andromeda from the dragon. She became his wife.

Prometheus – The son of a Titan and the champion of mankind. He stole fire from the gods and gave it to man. In retribution Zeus had him chained to a rock in the Caucasus. He was released by Herakles.

Satyrs (Sileni) – Grotesque spirits of the woods and hills and the attendants of Dionysos.

Sirens – They are represented as birds with the heads of women. Their song lured men to death.

Tantalus – Pelops' father *(see OLIMBÍA)*. To atone for a mysterious sin he was condemned to look at but not touch food and drink set before him.

Thanatos – A winged deity representing Death. He was the son of Night and the brother of Hypnos, Sleep.

CHRISTIANITY

It is impossible to dissociate the Hellenisation of the Eastern Empire and its conversion to Christianity. Just as **Hellenism** *(see p 23)* was gaining ground, the Christian religion was spreading throughout the territory. In the early days of Christianity, its adherents were only united on a few articles of faith and worship. Its evolution was marked by the gradual growth of an internal hierarchy with the creation of bishops and archbishops. When in 380 Theodosius the Great made Christianity the official religion and outlawed pagan cults, his intention was to consolidate the temporal structure of the Empire by insisting on its spiritual unity. But the distance between Rome the religious capital and Constantinople the political capital made communication between the Emperor and the head of the Church difficult. So Constantinople was raised to the status of metropolis, the same title as Rome, by a Council of 381, a decision confirmed and reinforced by the Council of Chalcedon in 451 which gave Constantinople primacy throughout the East. While the link between the Emperor and the patriarchate in Constantinople and the dependence of the one on the other was confirmed, the Church of Rome maintained its supremacy over ever more vast territories beyond the control of the Eastern Emperor and insisted ever more firmly on its divine right to rule, inherited from its first bishop, St Peter.

Differences of interpretation between the two Churches also came to the surface. The **Monophysite heresy** (5C-6C), which emphasised Christ's divine nature at the expense of his humanity, was widespread in the eastern territories of the Empire. **Iconoclasm**, introduced by Emperor Leo III from 726 with the aim of bringing the eastern peoples back into the Christian fold, required the destruction of all images (icons and other representations of the godhead); the long internal conflict resulting from this also aggravated the divisions between the eastern and western churches. Iconoclasm was finally abandoned in 843, and icons have remained a prominent feature of Orthodox worship to this day.

In the temporal sphere, the crowning of Charlemagne as Emperor of the West by the Pope made him a usurper in the eyes of the Byzantines, who regarded their Emperor as the sole legitimate heir to the Roman Empire. In the religious field the main subject of dispute was the *Filioque* issue (the use in prayer of the doctrine that the Holy Ghost proceeds from the Father and the Son). Despite many attempts to restore unity, a gulf gradually opened up between East and West, between Orthodoxy and Roman Catholicism. The final break came in 1054 when the Patriarch of Constantinople, Michael Cerularius, and Pope Leo IX excommunicated one another.

Attempts at Oecumenism – Arrangements for the Crusades brought to Greece Roman Catholic monks, especially Cistercians, whose task it was to work towards oecumenism ("union"). At the same time, the critical situation in which the Empire found itself meant it had to seek a rapprochement with Rome, already indispensable in view of the capture of Constantinople by the Crusaders in 1204. The plan was to take on more concrete form with the **Council of Lyon** (1274) held by Pope Gregory X in the presence of the Latin emperor, Baldwin II de Courtenay, and the Byzantine emperor, Michael VIII Palaiologos, who accepted the conditions laid down by Rome. The plan failed owing to the opposition of the populations involved. There is still evidence of these efforts in curious churches with two naves, one for the Roman Catholic, and one for the Orthodox worshippers.

A second attempt to achieve oecumenism in Greece was made in 1438 at the **Council of Florence** which brought together Pope Eugenius IV, Emperor John VIII Palaiologos, Cardinal Bessarion and the philosopher Gemistos Plethon *(see MISTRÁS)*. After agreement had been reached on the *Filioque* clause, the condition of dead souls, the primacy of the Pope and the freedom of liturgical practices, the act of union was signed by the majority of the Orthodox priests present but this propitious project was wrecked by the Turkish invasion of Greece in 1461.

ORTHODOX CHRISTIANITY

This is the established church to which 97 per cent of the population belong; the remaining 3 per cent is divided among Muslims (100 000 in Thrace and the Dodecanese), Roman Catholics (35 000 in the Cyclades and the Ionian islands) and Jews (5 000).

During the struggle for Independence in the 19C the Orthodox church sided with the people. Under the nominal tutelage of the Patriarch of Constantinople, the church is administered by a Synod presided over by the Archbishop of Athens; the Metropolitans (bishops) are responsible for their dioceses; each parish is in the charge of a **pope** *(papás)* who is free to marry a wife *(papadiá)* while still a deacon.

There are over 200 monasteries *(moní)* inhabited by monks *(kalógeri)* or nuns; the most famous are at Metéora and on Mount Athos. Under the authority of a **superior** *(igoúmenos)* they follow a fairly relaxed rule apart from the obligation to attend services and provide hospitality.

Priests and monks can be recognised by their black robes (blue for informal occasions), their round high hats *(skoúfia)*, and their beards and long hair tied up in a bun in the Byzantine manner; bishops and abbots wear a pectoral cross.

The Byzantine rite has a liturgy rich in symbolism. The faithful receive communion in both kinds, bread and wine, make the sign of the cross from right to left (the opposite way to the Western church) and revere icons of Jesus, the **Virgin** *(Panagía)* and the saints. Their services are punctuated by magnificent unaccompanied chanting, with basses dominating. It is worth trying to see a baptism (by immersion) and a wedding with the crowning of the bride and bridegroom.

The most visible expression of Byzantine culture remains the churches, which are decorated with frescoes, mosaics and icons. The candles are always lit before the iconostasis, and incense is burning at the entrance to the sanctuary. The main saints are St Basil (Vassili), whose feast day is on the first day of the year, St Nicholas and St George. Epiphany takes precedence over Christmas, and on the Feast of the Annunciation there are important demonstrations as this is also the national holiday, but Easter is the great annual religious festival. Holy Week is celebrated with mourning – the icons veiled in black and the faithful making great lamentation before images of Christ painted on shrouds. The resurrection is symbolised by the appearance on the threshold of the church at midnight on Easter Saturday of the priest carrying a newly-kindled candle, from which all the waiting people light their own individual candles. On the Sunday, spit-roasted lambs are eaten.

PICTOR

Orthodox Church ceremony, Pátmos

Literature and language

GREAT FIGURES IN ANTIQUITY

The dates given refer to the era BC unless otherwise indicated.

Aeschylus – c 525-456. Dramatist and the founder of Greek tragedy. His plays deal with the themes of right and justice; the most famous are: *The Persians*, *Seven against Thebes*, the *Oresteia* trilogy and *Prometheus Vinctus*.

Aesop – A freed slave from Asia and a celebrated author of fables *(see DELFÍ)*.

Archimedes – c 287-212. A mathematician, physicist and engineer who was born and died in Syracuse in Sicily; he spent many years in Alexandria. He is famous for the Archimedes principle which he is said to have discovered in his bath; in his excitement he ran out naked into the street and exclaimed "Eureka! '(I have found it)"; he later wrote a treatise on relative volumes.

Aristophanes – Born c 445. Writer famous for his comedies in which he ridiculed contemporary traits. Eleven of his plays have survived including *The Clouds*, *The Wasps*, *Peace*, *The Birds*, *The Frogs*, *The Assembly of Women*.

Aristotle – 384-322. Plato's pupil. His philosophy is based on the observation of natural phenomena; he founded a school in Athens, the Lyceum, so called because it was near the temple dedicated to Apollo Lyceios. The school also came to be known as the Peripatetic School (*perípato* – to walk about) from his habit of walking up and down while conversing with his pupils. He was also Alexander the Great's tutor. The site of his school was identified by archeologists in 1996 during the construction of a Museum of Modern Art behind the War Museum.

Diogenes – Known as the "Cynic" who lived in a barrel in Corinth.

Epicurus – 341-270. A philosopher who advocated a wise and simple life. His school, which was located in a small house surrounded by gardens, was known as the Gardens.

Euclid – 3C. A mathematician. His principal work *Elements* deals with geometry and the theory of numbers and Euclid's propositions retained their authority until the 19C AD.

Euripides – 480-406. A dramatic author and friend of Socrates. He was Aeschylus' successor and was parodied and ridiculed by Aristophanes. His works include his masterpiece *Medea*, and *Andromache*, *The Trojans* and *Iphigenia in Tauris*.

Herodotos – c 484-c 420. A historian (the father of history according to Cicero) and great traveller. He was interested in local customs and geography.

Homer – The first and the greatest Greek poet who is thought to have lived during the early 8C and to be the author of the *Iliad* (story of the Trojan War) and the *Odyssey* (tale of Ulysses' return to his native land after the Trojan War and his adventures on the journey).

Pausanias – A travel writer who visited Greece in the 2C AD. His detailed descriptions are a useful source of information about ancient Greece.

Pindar – A lyric poet who was a native of Thebes *(Thíva)*.

Plato – He was born in Aegina in 429 and was a pupil of the Pythagorean and Sophist schools; he became a follower and friend of Socrates and presented Socrates' doctrines in the *Dialogues*. His philosophy is propounded in works such as *The Banquet*, *The Republic* and *The Laws* and his school was in the gardens of the Academy in Athens *(see p 113)*. Plato was Aristotle's tutor.

Sappho – A poetess born in Lesbos *(Lésvos)*.

Socrates – He was born in Athens in 470 and was the son of a midwife and a sculptor. He is among the three great philosophers of ancient Greece – the others are his pupil Plato, and Aristotle – who have shaped the philosophical doctrines of the western world. One of his maxims was "Know thyself" and he ironically stated that he was certain of one thing only: that he knew nothing. In 389 he was condemned to death on a charge of blasphemy and corrupting youth and died after drinking hemlock.

Sophocles – c 495-406. A dramatic author who was born at Colona near Athens and wrote 123 plays of which seven tragedies have survived: *Antigone*, *Oedipus Rex* and *Oedipus at Colona* are the best known.

Thales – Late 7C-early 6C. A philosopher, astronomer and mathematician who was a native of Miletus. He is said to have predicted a solar eclipse on 28 May 585; he propounded several geometrical theorems and held the theory that water was the prime element from which all things were derived.

MODERN GREEK LITERATURE

Poets and poetry

First signs of a Greek identity – Under the Turkish occupation a popular poetry had already begun to develop, which was both traditional and patriotic; extracts were translated into French in 1825 by C Fauriel *(Chants populaires de la Grèce)*. In the 17C in Crete, then under Venetian control, **Vinkéntios Kornáros** wrote a lyrical epic poem, the *Erotókritos* (published in English by the Bristol Classical Press 1991 ISBN 1-85399-123-6) *(see KRÍTI)*.

A double renaissance – The first took place in the Ionian Islands (1820-88), where the Greek uprising provoked the first neo-Hellenic poetry. **Andréas Kalvos** (1792-1867) holds an important place in the history of Greek literature owing to his publication of 20 odes in two volumes in Geneva and Paris in Greek and French – *La Lyre* (1824) and *Odes Nouvelles* (1826). The leader of this "Ionian School" was **Dionysos Solomós** (Zákinthos 1798-1857); he blended romantic feelings with classical rigour. Part of his *Hymn to Liberty*, translated into English by Rudyard Kipling, is now the Greek national anthem. The second renaissance occurred late in the same century in Athens (1888-1920).

Linguistic disputes – Fierce disputes arose between those in favour of the formal version of Greek *(katharévoussa)* and supporters of the popular language *(demotic)*. The former, taking a European view, were nostalgic for the perfection and glory of the Classical period, while the latter, taking a Romantic view, saw the future of the Greek identity in the popular form of speech.

The Romantic period –The Greek Romantic period, which was influenced by ideas from abroad, is characterised by nostalgia for the past, a melancholy, a sardonic humour and an emotional sadness. There are few works from this period. The unbridled romanticism of the **Athenian School** is full of a reactionary chauvinism mixed with foreign influences from writers such as Musset and Byron.
The most eminent interpreter of the Ionian and Athenian schools was **Aristotélis Valaorítis**. He took an active interest in politics and in national affairs. He devoted his literary talent almost exclusively to poetry. **Ioánnis Papadiamantópoulos** (1856-1910), who wrote in the French language under the pseudonym Jean Moréas, was a Symbolist poet/author and his themes were vanity, glory, solitude and old age.

Turn of the century – After 1880 the **Symbolist style** was dominant. **Kóstas Palamás** (1859-1943) was a leading light of the Athenian School, who revived the tradition and created new tendencies. **Koromikles Drossinis** (1859-1951) loved myths and stressed the folklore element. **Ángelos Sikelianós** (1884-1951) was a lyrical poet philosopher with a lively imagination (*Selected Poems*, translated into English by Edmund Keeley and Philip Sherard and published by George Allen & Unwin 1979 ISBN 0-04-889001-4 and by Denis Harvey 1996 (bilingual edition) ISBN 960-7120-12-4).

A brilliant generation – The remarkable poets of the **19C to 20C** brought to their work a tone which distanced them from symbolism.
The best known and most translated poet is **Constantine Caváfy**, an educated but private man, who was born in Alexandria in 1863, spent seven years in England in his youth and returned to Alexandria in 1885. His verse reflects two worlds – contemporary Alexandria and Greece (*Collected Poems* translated by Edmund Keeley and Philip Sherard and published by Chatto & Windus 1990/5 ISBN 0-7011-3662-6; *Collection of Poems* (bilingual edition) translated by Edmund Keeley and Philip Sherard and published by Loizou Publications ISBN 0-952124-6-29).
Some of the work of **Strátis Mirivílis** (1892-1969) is available in English. *(The Mermaid Madonna* translated by Abott Rick and published by the Efstathiadis Group ISBN 960-226-0874 and *The School Mistress with the Golden Eyes* ISBN 960-226-008-2). Other authors of this period are **Kóstas Kariotákis** (1856-1928), **Kóstas Hadzópoulos** (1868-1920), **Miltiádis Malakássis** (1869-1943), **Lorénzos Mavílis** (1860-1912), **Zakarias Papandoniou** (1877-1940), **Kóstas Ouranis** (1890-1953), **Nikos Kavadias** (1910-75), **Tákis Papatsónis** (1895-1976), **Ioánnis Gripáris** (1870-42), **Nekiforos Vrettácos** (1912-91).

The 1930s period – This was dominated by three writers. **Geórgios Seféris** (1900-71), influenced by Symbolism, expressed his anguish in confronting existence with poems imbued with an evocative power. He was awarded the Nobel Prize for literature in 1963. (*Complete Poems* translated by Edmund Keeley and Philip Sherard and published by Anvil Press Poetry 1995 ISBN 0-85-646-213-6). **Odysseus Elítis** (1911-96) reveals through his Surrealist poetry, the sacred feeling Greeks have for their natural environment – the land, the sea and above all the light. He was awarded the Nobel Prize in 1979. (*Selected Poems* translated by Edmund Keeley and Philip Sherard and published by Anvil Press 1991 ISBN 0-85646-2229-2). In his poems **Iánnis Rítsos** (1909-90) blends the commonplace with the imaginary, invoking memory, exile and death. (*The Lady of the Vineyards* published by Pella Publishing Co New York ISBN 0-918618-10-X and the *New Oresteia* published by Pella ISBN 0-918618-45-2).

Surrealism – First among the **Surrealist poets** were **Andréas Embiricos** (1901-75), who was a psychoanalyst, and **Níkos Engonópoulos**, who was also a painter (1920-85).

Land of poets – Two Nobel prizes awarded to Greek poets in 16 years shows that Greece is still a land of poets. Among contemporary poets can be mentioned **Titos Patrikios** (b 1928), **Tákis Sinopoulos** (1917-81), **Miltos Sahtouris** (b 1919), **Nikos Karouzos** (b 1926), **Héctor Kaknavátos** (b 1920).

Essayists and novelists

Compared with poetry, prose works were tardy in making an appearance but display greater freedom and originality.

The first chroniclers – Many works from the **early period** are an extension of the chronicles devoted to the wars of Independence and reflect the historical and traditional preoccupations of the period. **Adamántios Koraïs** (1748-1833) was a man of moderation, who adopted a simple and sober form of the educated language, enriched it and brought it up to date. He is a valuable example of evolution among Greek intellectuals. **Colonel Makriánnis** (1797-1864) was a great fighter, motivated by patriotic and political passion. His *Memoirs*, published in 1904, record a certain period in Greek culture. His manuscript, deciphered by Vlahoyannis, is a rare work owing to the language employed and the reflections on popular and political thought. **Emmanuel Roïdis** (1836-1904) was an anticonformist, author of a satirical novel, *Pope Joan* (1866), magnificently narrated in a simple but brilliant style, and some posthumous novels.

The 1880 generation – They took over the review *Hestia* and from 1881 Palamas and Drossinis were regular contributors. **John Psichári** (1854-1929), who lived in Paris for many years, contributed to the pre-eminence of the demotic language in Greek literature and also wrote several novels.
The principal figure in this group was **Nikólaos Politis** (1852-1921) who specialised in folklore and made an important contribution to the evolution of modern Greek culture.

Geórgios Vizyinós (1849-96) was one of the first writers to launch out into new fields. Most of his themes are connected with Thrace, his birthplace and with the study of contemporary manners. Initially he published collections of poetry (*My Mother's Sins and other stories* available in English).

Aléxandros Papadiamántis (1851-1911) was one of the great classical writers of Greek prose. His novels describe the humble and often tragic lives of fishermen and peasants in elegant but comprehensible language (*The Murderers* is translated into English).

Andréas Karkavitsas (1865-1922) was the author of several volumes of short stories, his best containing vivid descriptions of his period.

Constantinos Theotókis (1872-1923) was influenced by the great Russian novelists. He devoted himself to Greek politics. Most of his works, some of which appear in English, have a social orientation and some are very touching.

The 1930 generation – It was the authors of the **1930s generation** who revived prose works. This period was the most successful, particularly in prose, in modern Greek literature.

Níkos Kazantzákis (1883-1957), evoked the fierce heroism of the Cretans, particularly in *Zorba the Greek* (1946), *Christ Re-crucified* (1954), both of which were made into successful films and translated into English. His *Report to Greco* (1962) is a fascinating account of his own life (translated by P A Bien and published by Bruno Cassirer, Oxford). In 1938 he wrote a long philosophical poem *Odysseus*, translated by Kimon Friar and published by Secker & Warburg. He also published essays, plays and travel pieces.

Geórgios Theotokás (1905-66) combined a lively wit with Cartesian thought. His more recent works include travel writing and dramatic legend. (*Leonis* translated by D E Martin and published by Nostos 1985, *The Free Spirit* (1929), *Argo* and *The Game of Folly versus Wisdom*).

Pandelis Prevelákis (1909-86) described his native town, Rethymnon, in *Chronicle of a City* (1938) and his country in *The Cretan* (trilogy published from 1948-50).

Stratis Tsirkas (1911-80) is best known for two of his novels – *Lost Spring* (1947) and *Drifting Cities* (the latter translated by Kay Cicellis and published by Kedros ISBN 960-04-1141-7).
Other outstanding names in English translation include – **Kosmás Politis** (1888-1974), **Strátis Mirivílis** (1892-1969), **Iánnis Skaribas** (1893-1984) who wrote several works including a bitter and amusing novel set in the 1930s, **Thanássis Petsalis-Diomidis** (1904-95) who deserves a place in Greek literature, **Ilias Venézis** (1904-73), an imaginative writer and a humanist, who expressed his thoughts in clear and elegant phrases, **Ángelos Terzákis** (1907-61), the author of several remarkable works, **Mihális Karagátsis** (1908-60), a born storyteller, endowed with a great creative imagination, which is reflected in his vast output of stories and novels, **Níkos G Pentzikis** (1908-92), an exponent of the interior monologue, who believes in the power of speech.

Contemporary literature – Post-war writers whose work is available in English include **Vassilis Vassilikós** (b 1934) – *Dreams are Dreams* (translated by Mary Kitroëff, published by Seven Stories Press New York 1966 ISBN 1-888363-99-2); *The Coroner's Assistant* (translated by Peter Pappas, published by Pella 1990 ISBN 0-918618-41-X); **Kóstas Taktsis** (1927-88) (*The Third Wedding Wreath* translated by J Chioles, published by Hermes 1985).
Also available in English, published by Kedros, are **Margarita Liberáki** (b 1919) (*Three Summers* translated by Karen Van Dyck ISBN 960-04-0948-X); **Ménis Koumandaréas** (b 1933) (*Koula* translated by Kay Cicellis ISBN 960-04-0484-2); **Geórgios Cheimonás** (b 1938) (*The Builders* translated by Robert Crist ISBN 60-04-0485-2); **Aris Alexándrou** (*Mission Box* translated by Robert Crist ISBN 960-4-1183-2); **Máro Doúka** (*Fool's Gold* translated by Robert Beaton ISBN 960-04-0481-X); **Vangélis Raptópoulos** *(The Cicadas)*; **Aris Sfakianakis** *(The Emptiness Beyond)*; **Pétros Abatzóglou** *(What does Mrs Freeman Want)*; **Geórgios Ioánnou** *(Good Friday Vigil)*; **Christóforos Miliónis** *(Kalamas and Acheron)*; **Soritis Dimitriou** *(Woof Woof dear Lord)*; **Aléxis Danselinós** *(Betsy Lost)*.

For new and second-hand books in Greek or translated from the Greek – ZENO Booksellers and Publishers, 6 Denmark Street, London WC2H 8LP ☎/Fax 0171 836 2522.

Modern Greek

For a vocabulary of modern Greek words see p 373.

Modern Demotic Greek is a simplified version of ancient Classical Greek from which it has evolved. It is an inflected language and difficult to pronounce.
It is used in conversation, literature and education. A more formal and archaic version of the language *(katharévoussa)* which was officially abandoned in 1976, is still seen in certain official publications. This guide uses demotic Greek transcribed according to the system used on the road signs in Greece; the accent marks the stressed syllable.

Pronunciation – The equivalents given below are the nearest available in the English language.

vowels:	**a**	pronounced as in "hat"
	e	pronounced as in "wet" and never silent
	i	pronounced as in "meet"
	o	pronounced as in "hot"
consonants:	**d**	(transcription of Greek delta/thelta δ and Δ) is pronounced like th in "then"
	g	before e and i is pronounced as y in "yet" before a, o and ou is pronounced somewhat hard as in "gone" but also rolled in the back of the throat like a French "r"
	h	(transcription of Greek χ and X) before e and i is pronounced as in "hue" before a, o and ou is pronounced like the final ch in Scottish "loch"
	s	always soft as in "set" never as in wise or sugar
	th	pronounced as in "thing"
	x	pronounced ks as in "exit"
	z	pronounced as in "zone"

Greek Alphabet – transcription into Latin alphabet

alfa	Α	α	a	ni	Ν	ν	n
vita	Β	β	v	xsi	Ξ	ξ	x
gama	Γ	γ	g	omicron	Ο	ο	o
delta/thelta	Δ	δ	d	pi	Π	π	p
epsilon	Ε	ε	e	ro	Ρ	ρ	r
zita	Ζ	ζ	z	sigma	Σ	σ, ς	s or ss
ita	Η	η	i	taf	Τ	τ	t
thita	Θ	θ	th	ipsilon	Υ	υ	i
iota	Ι	ι	i	fi	Φ	φ	f
kapa	Κ	κ	K	hi	Χ	χ	h
lambda	Λ	λ	l	psi	Ψ	ψ	ps
mi	Μ	μ	m	omega	Ω	ω	o

ΑΙ	αι	e	ΓΧ	γχ	nh	ΝΤ	ντ	nd,d
ΑΥ	αυ	av, af	ΕΙ	ει	i	ΟΙ	οι	i
ΓΓ	γγ	ng	ΕΥ	ευ	ev, ef	ΟΥ, Ο	ου	ou
ΓΚ	γκ	ng, g	ΜΠ	μπ	mb, b	ΤΖ	τζ	dz

Cinema

It was in the period after the Second World War that Greek cinema began to develop. Although one trend runs into the next it is possible to identify the following distinct stages.
The theme of many of the films made between 1946 and 1949 was wartime resistance but as they were divorced from their social context they lack objective comment. There were also several comedies of which the most daring was *The Germans are back* by Alekos Sakellarios which pleaded for national unity at a time when the government was actively anti-Communist. The scenario used the return of the Germans to promote reconciliation among the Greeks who were divided.
The dominant influence during the 1950s was **Italian neo-Realism**. Two important directors made their appearance in 1954. **Mihális Kakoiánnis** with *Sunday awakening*, a neo-Realist comedy, with remarkable acting by Dimítris Horn and Elli Lambetti. At the same time appeared *Magic city* and *Serial killer* (1956), masterpieces by Níkos Koúndouros. In 1955 Geórgios Tavellas made his greatest film, *Counterfeit coin*. *Stella*, Kakoiánnis' best film, starred Melína Mercoúri, who played a cabaret singer, a liberated woman, who is stabbed by the man she loves and who loves her. The music, which incorporates traditional Greek elements, was by Mános Hatzidákis; the film was shown at the Cannes Film Festival.

The legendary couple of Greek cinema

Jules Dassin was born in the USA in Middletown, Connecticut in 1911. He began his careeer in New York and in barely three years achieved fame with four major films: *Brute Force* (1947), *The Naked City* (1948), *Night and the City* (1948) and *Thieves' Highway* (1949). At the time of the McCarthy tribunals, he was suspected of Communism and had to go into exile in Europe, where he again took up his promising career, although the films he made lacked punch. After making *Rififi* (1955), his first full-length feature in Europe, he met the Greek actress Melína Mercoúri and made her his lucky mascot, never making a film without her being present and giving her international star status in the justly famed *Never on Sunday* (1960). They married in 1966.

Melína Mercoúri (b 1923) began her career in the theatre and showed herself to be an excellent dramatic actress in Kakoiánnis' film *Stella*, before going on to achieve widespread popularity in *Phaedra* (1962), *Topkapi* (1964), *Promise at Dawn* (1970) and *A Dream of Passion* (1977), all directed by her husband. She also distinguished herself in other spheres, recording numerous songs and publishing her autobiography *I was born a Greek* (1972). In her last years she turned to politics, opposing the regime of the colonels. This stand earned her several years of exile, but also the post of Minister of Culture in the subsequent Socialist governments from 1981 to 1989 and from 1993 to 1994, the date of her death in New York.

Dassin and Mercoúri rapidly achieved legendary status for young Greeks, who were captivated by Melína's beauty and courage as well as by the charm of Jules Dassin, who never hesitated to give up his work (private in nature since 1978) in order to support his wife both in her artistic and her political careers.

The *foustanélla* genre is named after the traditional Greek dress for men. The themes are taken from sentimental rustic dramas, from folklore and from history, featuring brigands, shepherds and heroes of the War of Independence.

1956 is an important date as it was then that Mihális Kakoiánnis produced *Woman in black*, a love story set in the provinces, brilliantly played by Elli Lambetti and Dimitris Horn. In 1958 under the influence of neo-Realism, Georgios Zervos produced *The lake of lust*, which exposes the way of life of fishermen and their daily problems, with excellent performances by the actors, among whom was Tzeni Karezi.

Commercial films produced between 1950 and 1967 represented the four following genres – burlesque comedy, social melodrama, *foustanélla* films and musical comedies, which are the most highly rated.

In 1960 the efforts of Pávlos Zánnas resulted in the International Film Fair in Thessaloníki, the **first Greek cinema week**, now called the Thessaloníki Festival. The most interesting films of that decade are *The River* (1960) by Níkos Koúndouros, which won the prize for the best director at the first festival, and the comedy *Good Morning, Athens* (1960). *Never on Sunday* (1960) is the best cinematographic adaptation of Greek tragedy by Jules Dassin, excellently acted by Melína Mercoúri with music by Mános Hatzidákis.

CAT'S COLLECTION

Iphigenia (1978) a film by Michael Kakoyannis starring Irene Papas

In the 1970s Greek cinema reflected a social and political approach. Theo Angelópoulos produced a historical trilogy covering 1936 to 1977, *Alexander the Great* (1980) which won awards in Venice, *Voyage to Kythera* (1984), which won the prize for best scenario at the Cannes Festival in 1984, as well as *The Bee keeper* (1986) and *Foggy landscape* (1988), which won nine international prizes. More recently he made *The glance of Odysseus* (1995), for which he won the grand prix at the Cannes Festival, and then the palme d'or was awarded to him in 1998 for *Eternity and a day*, a deeply moving meditation on the passage of time, opportunities missed and vanished hopes. Other directors who have won prizes are Níkos Panayotópoulos (1978) at Locarno; Aléxis Damianós for *Evdokia* (1971); Tonia Marketaki for *John the violent* (1973), Pandélis Voúlgaris for *Anna's match-making* (1972), *Happy Day* which describes a place of exile and of man's fall from grace, and *The Stoney Years* (1985).

The ensuing period saw a return to classical forms; the following names are of note – Pávlos Tassios with *On request* (1980), *Knock-out* (1986), *Stigma* (1982), Geórgios Panoussópoulos with *Honeymoon* (1979), *The people opposite* (1981).

In his films Níkos Perákis combines political and social satire with commercial style – *Arpa-Kolla* (1982), *The easy way out* (1984) and *A chequered career* (1987).

The **current trend** of Greek cinema is not well defined. Christos Vakalopoulos and Stavros Tsiolis produced a comedy *Please, ladies, don't cry* (1993), Níkos Koúndouros directed *Byron, ballad for a demon* (1992) which won the grand prix at the Thessaloníki Festival. Among the younger directors are Sotiris Goritssas with *From the snow* (Thessaloníki Festival prize in 1993), Perikles Hoursoglou with *Lefteris*, Andonis Kokkinos with *Quartet in four movements* (Thessaloníki Festival prize in 1994), Dimitris Athanitis with *Goodbye Berlin*, Katerina Evangelatou with *Jaguar*. Greek cinema is however in crisis as the public prefers American films. Will these new hopefuls be able to revive its appeal?

Local arts and traditions

While for centuries the political situation in Greece ensured that a large number of traditions and practices with roots going back to Ancient Greece were preserved, rural folk traditions have now almost entirely disappeared owing to the combined effect of modernisation of agriculture and the revolution in means of communication, which has brought to an end the isolation of the villages.

CRAFTS

During the last decade a craft revival has been promoted by government organisations and private associations; schools and workshops have been set up throughout the country and about a 100 workshops produce **carpets** in beautiful designs, reviving the making of *flokáti* from shaggy wool which was formerly widespread in Thessaly. In the country practically all households had a loom in the past and **weaving** is still a common pursuit. The methods, materials (wool, silk or cotton) and designs (floral or geometric) vary from region to region; bags, cushions and bedspreads are the most common articles produced.

PICTOR

Young woman in Greek traditional costume

Embroidery, which enhances garments, curtains and bed valences, is highly decorative and red is usually the dominant colour; the floral designs denote the oriental influence of Greeks from Asia Minor; in Epiros, Skíros and Crete, scenes from everyday life are also included. Weavers and lacemakers are often seen at work on their doorstep.

Ceramics remain a male preserve except as regards decoration. Huge jars made in Crete, Attica and the western Peloponnese which were used in the past to store oil or cereals now serve as garden ornaments. The richly decorated glazed pottery found in the eastern Aegean islands and Rhodes recalls the influence on Greek art from Asia Minor. Skyros has beautiful decorative plates; Aegina and Siphnos have produced high-quality pottery for centuries.

Wood carving remains a special tradition in Epiros, Skyros, Thessaly and Crete (pews, iconostasis, wedding chests). Votive offerings and painted shop signs are popular forms of naive art.

TRADITIONAL DRESS

Traditional dress is hardly worn except for patronal festivals or feasts of the Virgin (processions), at weddings, during the carnival or, in a simpler form, on market day. The women are resplendent in embroidery and chased ornaments chiefly displayed on their bodices and skirts. A few men still wear the heavy pleated **kilt** *(foustanélla)*, which is the uniform of the soldiers *(évzoni)* of the Guard *(see p 96)*, as well as the **pompom shoes** *(tsaroúhia)*. Local costumes are most common at Métsovo in Epiros, on Leukás, in the northern Sporades, in the Peloponnese, on Kárpathos and Astipálea in the Dodecanese and also in Crete; women spinning are often to be seen in the country districts. Costumes are also displayed in the museums of traditional art such as those of Nauplion, Thessaloniki, Chios and Athens.

MUSIC AND DANCE

Musical instruments – **Popular music** is played at festivals and other ceremonies (weddings and funerals), in the cafés and squares. On these occasions the traditional instruments are used: the *bouzoúki*, a sort of lute with a very long neck, three or four pairs of strings, and a shrill tone imported from Asia Minor, the *baglamás*, which is a small bouzoúki, the Cretan lyre *(lyra)*, a three-stringed viol played with a bow *(see below)*, the *sandoúri* which is played by striking its steel strings with small hammers, and the Epirot *clarinet*. There are also various rustic wind instruments, such as the *floiéra*, a transverse flute from Epiros, the *dzamára*, a straight pipe, and the *pipiza*, a kind of high-pitched oboe.

Lucas Hapsis /ON LOCATION

Cretan lyre

Songs – Three or four of these instruments accompany the singers whose plaintive style owes much to oriental music: the *kléftikos* attributed to the **klephts** *(see p 27)* in the War of Independence and the famous *rebétika*, dramatic accounts of the terrible conditions in the urban slums or the search for an impossible love. The greatest exponent of *rebétika* was Vassilis Tsitsanis (1915-84), who succeeded in transcribing them in a very pure form.

Contemporary music – After 1945 Greek music was radically changed. Composers turned to the traditional forms for rhythm and melody and began to take an interest in *rebétika*. The leading lights in this musical renewal, who had different techniques but both exhibited the same attachment to popular Greek music, were Mános Hatzidákis (1925-94) – romantic, lyrical and elegant *(5 laîkos zografies, O megálos eroticós, I epochi tis Melissanthis)* – and Mìkis Theodorákis, with his passion for social problems *(Axion Esti*, a setting of extensive extracts from the verse work of this name by **Odysséas Elítis**, *Romiosini, Canto General*, film music for *Zorba the Greek* and *Z)*.

In mentioning this folk-inspired music, we must not forget that several composers working in a more experimental vein also did much to put Greek music on the map, notably Níkos Skalkóttas (1904-1949) and **Ioánnis Xenákis** (b 1922).

Dance – Some dances are of Oriental origin such as the *zembétiko*, improvised by a man on his own, or the *hassápiko*, the butchers' dance, performed by men who lay their hands on one another's shoulders. Others such as the Cretan *pendozáli* imitate war; a clarinet accompanies the *mirológia*, funeral dances and dirges, often improvised and danced in turn to the point of exhaustion by the women taking part in the wake (Máni and Crete). The national dance, *kalamatianós*, is danced in a ring and recalls the sacrifice of the Souliot women *(see p 152)*. The lively *sirtáki* devised for the film *Zorba the Greek* is aimed more at tourists (its name was even invented outside Greece); it was based on the *hassápiko*. The list would not be complete without the *anastenária*, a dance with a constantly accelerating rhythm performed in Macedonia and Thrace in May on St Constantine's day, in which the dancers achieve a trance-like state.

Food and wine

Greek dishes are simple but tasty; even in 4C BC they were being praised by a Sicilian Greek called Archestratos. Their main elements are Mediterranean: olive oil, tomatoes, lemons, herbs and aromatic spices (oregano, mint, sesame). The pastries and cakes, which are very sweet and flavoured with honey and cinnamon, evoke the orient. Authentic but inexpensive Greek dishes are to be found in the tavernas and some more modest restaurants *(estiatório)* in the towns and the country.

Eating in the Greek way – A Greek meal consists of a starter or a main dish or both accompanied by a vegetable or cheese or, most likely, a salad. A starter can be a small portion of a main dish. All the dishes will arrive together unless each course is ordered in turn. It is usual to order several starters and main dishes for all members of the party to share. Sometimes fruit is also available but usually dessert is eaten in a pastrycook's *(zaharoplastío)* and coffee drunk in a café *(kafenío)*.
A *psistariá* specialises in roast meat and a *psarótaverna* in fish. An *exohikó kéndro* is an open-air café-restaurant.

Aperitif – The national drink is a colourless aniseed spirit *(oúzo)*, served in tiny glasses accompanied by a glass of water or diluted in a glass of water which turns cloudy. Aperitifs are usually accompanied by *mezédes (see below: Snacks)*.

Soup – Fish soup *(psarósoupa)*; broth with rice and eggs beaten with lemon juice *(soúpa avgolémono)*.

Starters – Vine leaves stuffed with meat and rice *(dolmádes)*, offal sausages spit-roasted *(kokorétsi)*, aubergine purée with black olives *(melidzanosaláta)*, yoghurt with chopped cucumber and garlic *(tzatzíki)*, purée of fish roe and bread crumbs or potatoes *(taramosaláta)*, rice with tomatoes *(piláfi)*, stuffed tomatoes, peppers, aubergines *(gemistá)*.

PICTOR

Food shop in Pláka in Athens

Main dish – Aubergines and minced meat baked beneath bechamel sauce *(moussaká)* and macaroni and minced meat baked in bechamel sauce *(pastítsio)*.

Fish *(psári)* – lobster *(astakós)*; red mullet *(barboúni)*; prawns *(garídes)*; sole *(glóssa)*; mackerel *(koliós)*; swordfish *(ksifías)*; white bait *(marídes)*; squid *(kalamári)*; octopus *(oktapódia)*; John Dory *(tsipoúra)*; sardines *(sardéles)*; whiting *(sfirída)*.
Fish is boiled *(vrastó)*, fried *(tiganitó)* or grilled *(psitó)*; price according to weight.

Meat *(kréas)* – Lamb and mutton *(arnáki and arní)*; veal *(moshári)*; pork *(hirinó)*; chicken *(kotópoulo)*; cubes of beef, lamb or goat on a spit with tomatoes and onions *(souvláki or kebabs)*; minced meat balls *(soutzoukákia, keftédes* and *biftéki)*.
Meat is also served in cutlets *(brizóla)*, roasted, boiled or braised *(stifádo)* with a tomato and oil sauce seasoned with onions and herbs.
The words *tis óras* mean that the meat or fish is grilled to order whereas prepared dishes tend to be cooked in advance and served lukewarm.

Vegetables – Aubergines *(melidzánes)*; potatoes *(patátes)*; rice *(rísi)*; tomatoes stuffed with rice *(domátes gemistés)*; string beans *(fassolákia)*; tomato salad *(domatosaláta)*; country salad *(saláta horiátiki)* of tomato, cucumber, onion, green pepper and *féta* cheese.

Cheese *(tirí)* – Goat's or sheep's milk cheese *(féta)* which may be served with olive oil and olives; a sort of Gruyère *(graviéra)*; a mild, similar to Cheddar *(kasséri)*.

Fruit *(froúta)* – Olives *(eliés)*: those from Vólos, Kalamáta and Ámfissa are famous; strawberries *(fráoules)*; water melon *(karpoúzi)*; cherries *(kerássia)*; lemon *(lemóni)*; melon *(pepóni)*; orange *(portokáli)*; figs *(síka)*; grapes *(stafília)*; apricot *(veríkoko)*; peach *(rodákina)*.

Cakes and pastries *(gliká)* – Millefeuilles with walnuts or almonds and cinnamon *(baklavá)*; rolls of thread-like pastry with honey and walnuts or almonds *(kadaífi)*; cold custard pie *(galaktoboúreko)*; cold rice pudding *(rizógalo)*; mini doughnuts with honey and sesame or cinnamon *(loukoumádes)*; flaky pastry turnover with cream and cinnamon *(bougátsa)*; almond or sesame paste *(halva)*.

Snacks – Snacks are served in cafés, bars, dairies *(galaktopolío)* and at street stalls. The best snack for a group of people is an assortment of olives, almonds, shrimps, hard-boiled eggs, cheese, pieces of octopus or squid, known as *mezédes* or *pikilía* and served with drinks.
Others are cheese puffs *(tirópita)*; spinach puffs *(spanakópita)*; fried cheese *(saganáki)*; omelette *(omelétta)*; pieces of grilled meat wrapped in a pancake *(souvlakópita)*; yoghurt with honey *(yaoúrti me méli)* which is delicious at breakfast; macaroons *(amigdalotá)*; almond cakes *(kourabiédes)*; mini doughnuts with honey and sesame or cinnamon *(loukoumádes)*; Turkish delight *(loukoúmi)*.

Refreshments – Soda or fruit juice with lemon *(lemonáda)*; orangeade *(portokaláda)*; sorbet *(graníta)*; ice, ices *(pagotó, pagotá)*; iced coffee *(frapé)*. Tap water is safe.

Wine – With its dry warm climate and limestone or volcanic soil Greece is an excellent country for producing wine; the main wine regions are the northern Peloponnese, Attica, Crete, Rhodes and Sámos. Except in Sámos the business is not strictly controlled and the wine is sold under the name of the grower or a cooperative. It is worthwhile trying wine from the vat *(krassí híma)* served in carafes or copper pitchers. Greeks seldom get drunk and in antiquity they always diluted their wine with water.
The most well-known Greek wine is probably *retsína*, a white wine to which pine resin has been added as a preservative; this gives it an unusual taste, which is too suggestive of paraffin for some palates, but much appreciated by others. *Retsína* is not expensive and, served chilled as it usually is, it is very refreshing without being heavy.
Among the unresinated wines *(aretsínato)* some have earned a particular reputation: the full-bodied reds from Náoussa in Macedonia, the fruity reds from Neméa in the Argolid, the scented rosé from Aráhova near Delphi, the well-rounded dry white wines of Hymettos and Palíni in Attica, the sparkling dry white wine of Zítsa in Epiros, the white wines of Chalcidice, which preserve their quality well, and the popular white wines of Achaia (Demestica, Santa Laura, Santa Helena). In the islands there are the generous reds and rosés from Crete, dry whites from Lindos in Rhodes, the heady and scented wines from the Cyclades, particularly Náxos and Santoríni, and from the Ionian islands: Zakynthos (Verdéa, Delizia), Cephallonia (Róbola, fruity and musky) and Leukas (Santa Maura). Mavrodaphne from Patras and Samian muscat are dessert wines.

Coffee – Coffee, made in the Greek way *(elinikó)*, is strong and black and served in tiny cups, traditionally accompanied by a glass of cold water. The very finely-ground coffee is heated three times with or without sugar in a small pot and served unstrained; the grounds sink to the bottom of the cup and may add a granular texture to the last few sips of this very stimulating beverage. Coffee is ordered more or less sweet according to taste

very sweet *(glikó)* – medium sweet *(métrio)* – without sugar *(skéto)*.

Liqueurs – Samian wine can be drunk as a liqueur; *Métaxas* is the brand name of Greek brandy. There is also *oúzo (see above)*, Cretan *rakí*, a fruit brandy, and *mastíka*, a sweet liqueur flavoured with mastic gum.

The Acropolis, Athens

Sights

AMFIARAÍO

AMPHIARAEIO – Attica

Michelin map 980 east of fold 30

In a narrow peaceful valley, watered by a stream and shaded by pine trees, lie the ruins of a sanctuary dedicated to **Amphiaraos**, King of Árgos and warrior who took part in the expedition of the Seven against Thebes *(see THÍVA)*; he was also a seer and healer whose cult developed in these remote parts as did the cult of Asklepios in Epidauros.

The road from Kálamos down to the site affords fine **views** over the strait (Evrípos) to Euboia *(see EVÍA). Entrance on the right.*

Ruins ⌚ – The ruins were excavated by the Greek Archeological Society; the major part dates from the 4C BC.
To the right of the path was the temple of Amphiaraos with the base of the cult statue and the offering table in the centre; in front of the temple was a huge altar where a ram was sacrificed and the oracle was consulted; lower down under the trees is a fountain into which pieces of money were thrown by the pilgrims who had been cured.
On the other side of the path is the "Statue Terrace"; the pedestals date from the Roman period.
Beyond was the portico *(abaton)* where the sick lay down to sleep; Amphiaraos was thought to send his instructions for their treatment through the medium of their dreams which were interpreted by the priests. Note the feet of the supports for the marble bench which ran the whole length of the portico.
Further on was the theatre (3 000 seats) where the votive festival (Amphiaréa) took place every four years; the marble seats of the priests and dignitaries are well preserved.

For adjacent sights see ATHÍNA, DAFNÍ, ELEFSÍNA, ÉVIA, THÍVA.

AMFÍPOLI

AMPHIPOLIS – Séres, Macedonia

Michelin map 980 east of fold 6

The ancient city of Amphipolis lay in a favourable position not far from the mouth of the River Strymon and **Mount Pangaion** (Pangéo: 1 956m/6 417ft), known as the "holy mountain" to the ancients as much for the cult of Dionysos and his followers the Maenads as for its gold mines and thick forests.
Amphipolis was founded in the 5C BC and prospered under Philip and Alexander of Macedon (353-323 BC). It was a staging post on the Via Egnatia *(see THESSALONÍKI)* under the Romans and was still an important centre during the Byzantine period.

The Lion – On the left of the road from Thessaloníki, just before the bridge over the Strymon, stands a huge marble lion which was reconstructed in 1937 from Hellenistic fragments: it resembles the lion of Chaironeia *(see HERONÍA)* although it is later, dating from the end of the 4C BC.

Ruins – *After crossing the bridge over the Strymon, take the road to Séres (left); after 1.5km/1mi turn left to the modern village of Amfípoli and then left again towards the church; after 0.5km/547yd a path to the right leads to the ruins.*
On the plateau, not far from what was probably the *agora*, are traces of paleo-Christian basilicas: mosaics of birds *(partially covered)*.
The Hellenistic precinct of Amphipolis has recently been excavated; its wall was 7km/4mi long with a maximum height of 7m/23ft.

For adjacent sights see FÍLIPI, HALKIDIKÍ, KAVÁLA, THÁSSOS, THESSALONÍKI.

ANDRÍTSENA

Elis, Peloponnese – Population 881

Michelin map 980 fold 28 – Alt 765m/2 510ft

The red roofs of this typical mountain town stand out against the slopes of the peaks bordering Elis to the east. Among these mountains is the famous Mount Lykaion (Líkeo) (1 421m/4 662ft); it was a primitive sanctuary for the worship of Zeus, involving human sacrifice and ritual cannibalism.
Andrítsena is a market town and an excursion centre *(hotels)*. It has many old wooden houses with projecting upper storeys and craft workshops (blacksmiths, wood turners, weavers...) lining the streets where goats, donkeys and pigs roam at will. A fountain in the shade of a plane tree lends charm to the main square.
Andrítsena possesses a library of some 25 000 volumes which was started with a nucleus of 6 250 works presented in 1840 by **Agathófros Nikolópoulos** (1786-1841), a scholar and philologist, who died in Paris after twenty years at the Bibliothèque de l'Institut: many incunabula; plays by d'Alembert with comments by J-J Rousseau.

EXCURSION

★★ **Temple at Vassés** **(Bassae)** ⏱ – *14km/8mi south.* Access by a fine modern road up the side of the Andrítsena Basin.

The temple of Apollo at Bassae stands alone on a lofty cheerless **site★★** (1 130m/3 707ft) on the southern face of Mount Paliovlátiza (Kotilion) surrounded by ravines *(bassai)*; on the distant horizon rise the mountains of Lakonía *(south-east)* and Messinía *(southwest). As the mountain climate is severe the temple is under cover in order to facilitate the restoration work which is likely to last several years.*

It was built from c 450 to 420 BC by the inhabitants of ancient Phigaleia *(Áno Figália southwest)* in honour of Apollo who had preserved them from the plague. According to Pausanias (2C AD) the architect was Iktínos, one of the designers of the Parthenon in Athens. Forgotten for many centuries it was discovered in 1765 by a French architect, Joachim Bocher, who was working for the Venetians. In 1811 C R Cockerell and Haller von Hallerstein visited the temple and the latter together with Baron Stackelberg made a record of the architecture in 1812. The internal frieze and other fragments were auctioned in Zakynthos and acquired by the British Museum where they are now displayed. It is one of the best preserved of Greek temples but was in imminent danger of collapse when restoration work began in 1975.

It is built of greyish limestone in the Doric style and is completely surrounded by a colonnade. It is not outstanding but its merit lies in its pleasant proportions and its harmony with the landscape. The building has several unusual characteristics:

– exceptional length in relation to its width (15 columns by 6);
– north-south orientation as opposed to east-west, with the entrance facing north *(uphill)*;
– opening in the long east side to shed light on the statue of Apollo in the *naós*;
– Ionic half-columns in the *naós* linked to the walls by buttresses.

At the southern end of the *naós* stands a Corinthian column, the first known in this style; the base is extant but the capital which was decorated with acanthus leaves is missing; the two flanking columns may also have been Corinthian.

The architrave was surmounted by a frieze of sculpted metopes while the walls of the *naós* were decorated on the inside with another frieze of low-reliefs representing the battles between the Greeks and Amazons on the one hand and the Centaurs and Lapiths on the other; this is the earliest example of a sculptured frieze decorating the interior of a Greek building.

There is an overall view of the site from above the keeper's house.

For adjacent sights see KARÍTENA, KIPARISSÍA, MEGALÓPOLI, OLIMBÍA, Aarahova.

J.-P. Charbonnier/TOP

Temple of Bassae

ARÁHOVA★

Boeotia, Central Greece – Population 3 084
Michelin map 980 north of fold 29 – Alt 905m/2 969ft

Once over the **Aráhova Pass** (940m/3 084ft) on the traditional road from Livadiá to Delphi, the traveller is greeted by a very fine **view★★** down on to the site of Aráhova, a small mountain town on the southern face of Mount Parnassos above the Pleistos ravine. It is a winter resort for skiers who come to enjoy the slopes of Mount Parnassos.
The climate is fairly harsh with snow in winter and rain in spring and autumn which feeds the many fountains in the town; in summer the temperature stays quite cool. In spring on St George's Day *(23 April)* the town attracts the people from the country round who come dressed in their traditional costume to take part in the folk dancing while the old men compete in a race in which the winner receives a lamb presented by the shepherds of Parnassos.

Main Street – The narrow street winds its way between tavernas and workshops. In the tavernas one can savour a dish of soft fried cheese – *formaéla* – and the mountain cheeses together with a delicious red wine which tastes of redcurrants. The workshops sell shoulder bags, carpets and long haired rugs *(flokatí)* in bright colours.

St George's Church – Picturesque streets lead up to the terrace which offers a **view★** of the Pleistos ravine and Mount Kírphis.

EXCURSIONS

★★**Corycian Cave and Mount Parnassos** – *45k/27mi, about 2hr 30min. From Aráhova take the road towards Delphi; turn right towards Lílea. After 11km/7mi, just beyond Kalívia, turn left (sign "Chat Tours") into a narrow stony track which winds uphill for 5km/3mi; as the last 3km/2mi are particularly difficult, it is advisable to turn off after the first 2km/1.25mi onto the side road leading to a car park; 5min on foot to the cave.*

★★**Koríkio Ándro** (Corycian Cave) – In antiquity the cave was devoted to "the god **Pan** and the Nymphs"; on the neighbouring slopes orgies in honour of Dionysos were organised by his attendant Thyiads.
The cave is high above sea level (1 300m/4 265ft) and very extensive. It was already in use in the Neolithic and Mycenaean periods as excavations made in 1970 by the French School of Archeology have shown. Subsequently it was used as a refuge. One can penetrate right into the cave which receives good natural light; there are a few stalactites.
From the threshold there are **views** towards Parnassos, the Pleistos Valley and the Bay of Itéa.

Return to the road north to Lílea.

★★**Óros Parnassós** (Mount Parnassos) ⌚ – The road follows the hanging valley of **Kalívia** where sheep are pastured. After about 15km/9mi turn right into a good road which climbs through a mountain landscape of pine trees to a chalet belonging to the Athens Ski Club (1 900m/6 234ft). From here one can make the ascent of **Mount Liákoura** (2 457m/8 061ft), the highest peak of Parnassos *(about 1hr 30min on foot there and back)*. On a clear day, which is rare, there is a superb panorama of a large part of Greece from the Peloponnese to Mount Athos *(east)*.
Parnassos, which is often under snow or enveloped in clouds, was thought to be the home of Apollo, whose main sanctuary was nearby, and of the nine **Muses:** Clio (History), Euterpe (Music), Melpomene (Tragedy), Thalia (Comedy), Terpsichore (Dancing), Urania (Astronomy), Erato (Elegy), Polyhymnia (Lyric poetry) and Calliope (Epic poetry).
The Parnassos range, which is not easy of access and still harbours a few wolves, was the base of the local *klephts* during the Greek War of Independence and served again after the Second World War as the stronghold of the ELAS resistance movement which survived there until 1949. There are many bauxite mines.

For adjacent sights see DELFÍ, HERÓNIA, Drómos tou IRAKLÍ, LIVADIÁ, ORHOMENÓS, ÓSSIOS LOUKÁS Monastery.

*Consult the Places to stay map at the beginning of this guide to select an overnight stop or holiday destination. The map offers various categories of resort.
Depending on the region, this map also shows marinas, ski resorts, spas, centres for mountain expeditions etc*

ARGOLÍDA★

ARGOLID PENINSULA – Peloponnese

Michelin map 980 folds 29 and 30

This peninsula, which separates the Saronic and Argolic gulfs, is composed of limestone hills, often covered with pine woods and olive groves, while the coastal plains are planted with citrus orchards.
The little ports and sheltered creeks for bathing which are dotted along the shore were formerly accessible only by sea but now there is a coast road serving the modern hotels and resorts and offering attractive views of the islands of Póros, Hydra and Dokós.

★ROUND TOUR FROM PORTOHÉLI *About 186km/116mi – 1 day*

★**Portohéli** – Well sheltered in its attractive bay, Portohéli (Eel Port) is a fishing village and port for Spetsae and an excellent mooring for caïques and yachts. In recent years a seaside resort with modern hotels has developed which is linked to Zéa (Piraeus) by hydrofoil *(see SPÉTSES)*.

Take the road up to Kranídi.

Beyond **Foúrni** a vast **crater** appears in the mountain side on the left of the road. According to local tradition it was formed by a meteorite and dates from the 19C. A dirt road suitable for cars *(sign "pros spilia")* leads to a larger **crater** (500m/545yd further) which is not visible from the road because of its orientation. Steps lead down a tunnel to a little chapel half-way down the side of the crater; it was built by the people of a neighbouring village in thanksgiving for a narrow escape.

Continue towards Ligourió. Just before Trahiá turn right to Fanári.

Beyond **Fanári**, clinging to the steep hillside, a corniche road descends the cliff face providing spectacular **views**★ of the Saronic shoreline and the Méthana peninsula which ends in Mount Helóni (743m/2 438ft), an extinct volcano. *7km/4.5mi beyond Kaloní turn left towards Méthana.* The road crosses the neck of land leading to the former volcanic island of Méthana, jagged and mountainous. In 1820 Colonel Fabvier *(see ATHÍNA: Historical Notes)* pitched camp on the island before going to relieve the Acropolis in Athens and the place is still known as Favićpoli. Just before Méthana there is an attractive view of the town and the harbour.

Méthana – There is a boat service from Piraeus to Méthana which has a small harbour protected by a wooded promontory where traces of a 4C BC fortress have been found. It is a seaside resort and also a spa; its warm sulphurous waters are used in the treatment of rheumatism and skin diseases.

Return to the crossroads on the mainland and turn left towards Galatás; after 2km/1.25mi turn right (sign) into a minor road leading to Trizína (formerly Damalas).

★**Trizína (Troizen)** – The third Greek National Assembly at which John Kapodístrias *(see KÉRKIRA: Historical Notes)* was elected head of the new state took place in the village in 1827.
A few traces of the ancient city have been excavated by the French School of Archeology. It was the birthplace of Theseus *(see ATHÍNA: Historical Notes and KNOSSÓS)* and the scene of dramatic events which form the theme of famous tragedies by Euripides and Racine. **Phaedra**, Theseus' wife, fell in love with her stepson Hippolytus who rejected her; she denounced him falsely as her seducer to Theseus who delivered his son to the fury of Poseidon; in despair Phaedra took her own life.

Go through the village and follow the signs "Acropolis of Trizína"; turn right into a minor road (sign "Diavologéfira" and "Antiquities"). At a junction near a Roman bridge bear right and continue for 1.5km/1mi along a track past two churches (after the second church the track is in poor condition for 700m/765yd). Sign "Sanctuary of Hippolytos, Asclepieion, Episkopi".

On the left of the road are the scanty remains of the shrine of Hippolytus with on the left those of an asklepieion, a sanctuary to Asklepios the god of healing *(see EPÍDAVROS)* who brought Hippolytus back to life. A short distance away stand the ruins of a Byzantine church and a bishop's palace. *Return to the junction and turn right at the Roman bridge.* A Hellenistic tower *(300m/330yd further up the road)* was part of an ancient fortress; the upper section dates from the Middle Ages. *Continue to the end of the road 500m/545yd further.* A walk *(5min)* leads to the lower end of the **Devil's** Gorgea and to the Devil's Bridge, "Diavologéfira", a natural rock formation linking both sides of the gorge; it is overshadowed by thick plane trees in a wild site which is refreshingly cool in summer. The path runs west to the top of the cliffs where stood an ancient acropolis, a sanctuary to Pan and the fort of Damalet, the seat of a 13C Frankish barony.

Return to the road to Galatás.

The fertile coastal plain is a sea of orchards growing oranges, lemons, citrons, figs and carobbeans, dotted with the occasional dark plume of a cypress tree.

Galatás – *Ferries and hire boats to Póros.* Magnificent **views★★** of the straits and Póros Island.

★★Póros – *Description see PÓROS.*

Continue along the coast south to Ermióni.

★Lemonodássos – On the coast opposite Póros Island there is a huge lemon grove of about 30 000 trees covering a gentle slope above Alíki beach. These delicate trees die if the temperature drops below -3°C (26.6°F) but bear flowers and fruit throughout the year.

Park the car beside the road near the sign by a chapel. From there one walks up the hill *(30min on foot there and back)* through the scented lemon grove which is irrigated by narrow channels of running water. The path *(sign "Pros Kéntron Cardássi" or "Restaurant Cardássi")* soon reaches the Cardássi taverna surrounded by oleanders, bougainvilleas and banana palms near a cool spring; attractive view of Póros Island *(see PÓROS)*.
The coast road to Ermióni is a recent construction opening up views of Hydra and Dokós through the ubiquitous olive groves.

★Hydra Beach (Plepí) – New resort with a pleasant aspect: villas and flats attractively sited, harbour for leisure craft. *Motor launches from Plepí.*

Ermióni – Former Byzantine see; now a resort and sheltered fishing port. *Regular services to Hydra (see ÍDRA).*

Continue along the coast road bearing left at the fork to Kósta.

Kósta – Modern resort. *Ferry to Spétses (see SPÉTSES) and coastal vessels to Hydra.*

For adjacent sights see ÁRGOS, EPÍDAVROS, ÍDRA, LERNÍ, MIKÍNES, NÁFPLIO, SPÉTSES, TÍRINTHA.

ÁRGOS

Argolis, Peloponnese – Population 21 901
Michelin map 980 fold 29

From afar a spit of rock crowned by a citadel indicates Árgos, capital of ancient Árgolis (Argolída), whose population equalled that of Athens.
The town was burned by Ibrahim Pasha during the War of Independence and rebuilt on a grid plan so that it is now a featureless overgrown village, which acts as a communications centre and a market for the agricultural produce of the coastal plain: cattle, tobacco, cereals, fruit and vegetables (particularly tomatoes, artichokes and melons).

Oldest town in Greece – The Ancients believed that Árgos was the oldest town in Greece, having been founded by an Egyptian, Danaos, father of the famous **Danaids** who killed their husbands and threw their heads into the Lerna marshes *(see LERNÍ)*; they were condemned by the god of the underworld to fill a leaking vessel with water. Later the city of the Argives, like Mycenae, came under the control of Perseus and his descendants among whom was Diomedes, the faithful companion of Odysseus in the Trojan War.
Árgos grew to prominence in the 8C. Throughout the Archaic period the city with its twin citadels, Lárissa and Aspís, dominated the northeast of the Peloponnese in rivalry with Sparta. Although it began to decline at the end of the 6C, during the Classical period it supported a brilliant civilisation which produced a school of sculptors in bronze including **Polykleitos**, second only to Pheidias.
In 272 BC during the Hellenistic period, **Pyrrhus**, King of Epiros, was killed in Árgos in street fighting, hit by a tile which an old woman threw down from the roof of a house. Under the Roman occupation Árgos again enjoyed a period of prosperity but, despite having the strength to hold out for seven years against the Franks, the city was subsequently supplanted by Náfplio in importance not only under the Franks but also during the later occupations by the Venetians and Turks. The city did however feature in the Greek War of Independence: in 1822 Kolokotrónis and D Ypsilántis (1793-1832) held out against the Turks from the citadel *(kástro)* and the Greek National Assembly held sittings in the ancient theatre in 1822 and 1829.

★Arheótites (Ancient ruins) ⏲ – *Southwest along the road to Trípoli.*
Excavations being carried out by the French School of Archeology on a site at the foot of the hill below the citadel *(kástro)* have uncovered Greek and Roman remains.
By the western entrance to the site is an ancient road leading to a theatre to the left of which are the remains of a large building comprising a vaulted chamber with a crypt and an apse and three rooms opening into a courtyard surrounded with porticoes. Roman **baths (B)** were built here in the 2C, surrounded by their hypocausts

for the heating; the porticoes in the western section have been converted into a room; next comes the frigidarium with its three pools and the three *caldaria* which were decorated with numerous statues now in the museum. There are traces of mural paintings and mosaics (partly covered up).

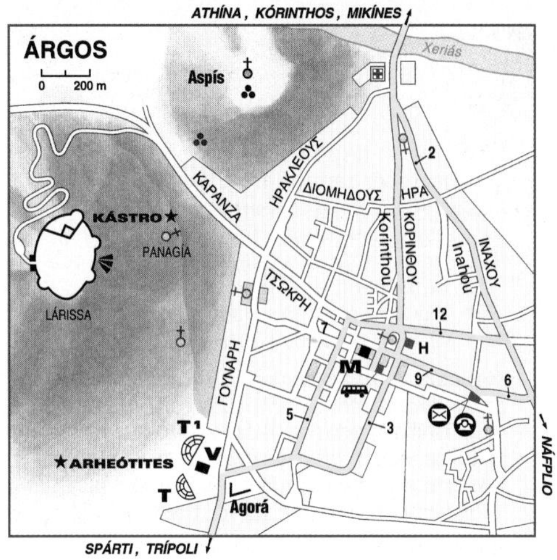

The **theatre** (**T**), which dates from the 4C BC, was altered by the Romans who converted the orchestra into a *naumachía* for staging mock sea-fights.

Together with the one at Dodona, this theatre was one of the largest in Greece: the terraces, which were either hewn out of the rock or supported by an embankment, could accommodate 20 000 spectators. The central terraces (81 rows), the orchestra and the entrances and exits are well preserved. On the wall in the south corridor there is a low-relief sculpture of the Dióscuri on horseback *(left in the direction of the theatre)*.

Bouboulinas	ΜΠΟΥΜΠΟΥΛΙΝΑΣ	2
Danaou	ΔΑΝΑΟΥ	3
Fidonos	ΦΕΙΔΩΝΟΣ	5
Makariou	ΜΑΚΑΡΙΟΥ	6
Metaxa	ΜΕΤΑΞΑ	7
Nikitara	ΝΙΚΗΤΑΡΑ	9
Vas. Sofias	ΒΑΣ. ΣΟΦΙΑΣ	12

Moussío..... **M** Odío ....**T** Théatro ......**T'** Thérmes .....**V**

South of the theatre are the remains of an **odeon** (**T'**) (2C-3C AD), a small indoor theatre, of which the curved terraces, the entrances and the stage remain.

On the opposite side of the road are the remains of the *agorá* (**A**), which dates from the 4C BC: traces of a meeting room followed by a double doorway and two *nymphaea* (2C BC) - the second is linked to the city sewer. Recent excavations have uncovered new buildings which have not yet been identified.

Museum ⏱ (**M**) – Built and organised by the French School of Archeology, the museum displays the finds excavated at Árgos and Lerna *(see LERNÍ)*.

They are attractively presented in chronological order: in the righth-and room a superb suit of armour (8C BC) including a crested helmet such as Homer's heroes wore and a fragment of painted pottery (7C BC) showing Odysseus and his companions putting out the eye of the Cyclops, Polyphemus.

Under a portico in the garden there are Roman mosaics evoking Bacchus, the Seasons and hunting scenes.

★**Lárissa Citadel** – The Deirás Gap separates **Aspís Hill** (traces of a sanctuary to Apollo and a fortress – *café-restaurant* – fine view of the citadel) from Lárissa Hill. *Bear left at the crossroads into the road which winds round the back of the hill to the top* (290m/951ft).

The citadel on this wild and isolated but very beautiful site was built by Byzantines and completed by the Franks of the house of Enghien in the 13C-14C on the foundations of an ancient acropolis from which a few huge blocks of masonry remain; Gautier de Foucherolles from Burgundy was the governor early in the 14C.

The building was altered by the Venetians and the Turks and now consists of an outer wall with towers and the castle itself. The water cisterns are impressive. There is a fine **view**★★ of the fertile plain of Argolis stretching from the barren mountains to the gulf of Náfplio.

★**Iréo (Argive Heraion)** ⏱ – *8km/5mi northeast. From the centre of Árgos take the road to Corinth (Kórinthos); bear right after the river bed (sign Inahos, Prósimna). In Inahos continue straight ahead (sign "Ireon"); in Hónikas* (11C Byzantine church) *take the road to Mycenae (Mikínes) and then continue for 2km/1.5mi along a minor road (sign "Ancient Ireo")*.

The sanctuary, which was consecrated to **Hera**, the tutelary goddess of fertile Argolis, was already in existence in the Mycenaean period and the Greek chiefs may have sworn their oath of loyalty to Agamemnon here before setting out for the Trojan War. The ruins which were discovered in 1831 occupy three terraces cut into the mountain side, a magnificent solitary **site**★★ above the plain of Árgos. On the first terrace stand the bases of the columns which formed a 5C BC portico *(stoa)*; at the back, built of limestone blocks, is the retaining wall of the second terrace, which is reached by steps at the righthand end of the portico.

On the second terrace stood a Classical temple (late 5C BC) containing a huge statue, overlaid with gold and ivory, of Hera. The extant foundations reveal the design of the building which measured about 40m/131ft by 20m/66ft; the sculptures are on display in the Athens Museum.
On the upper terrace are the massive lower courses of an Archaic Doric temple (early 7C BC) which burned down in 423 BC owing to the negligence of the priestess Chryseis, who fell asleep while her lamp was still burning.
The cult of Hera was still celebrated on this spot in Roman times; Roman baths have been found on the west slope; Nero is known to have presented the goddess with a purple robe and Hadrian made a gift of a peacock (Hera's symbol), gilded and set with precious stones.

Kefalári – *9km/5.5mi southwest. Take the road to Trípoli. After 5km/3mi turn right into a track which leads to the Erássinos spring.*
The river gushes from a cave consecrated in antiquity to Pan and Dionysos; a sanctuary stands on the terrace above. The ancients thought that the water flowed beneath the mountain from Lake Stymphalos (Stimfalía) *(northwest)*.
In summer the cool shade of the huge plane trees and the tall poplars is particularly welcome *(open air cafés)*.

Agía Triáda – *10km/6mi east. Take the road to Náfplio and then turn left. Description see NÁFPLIO.*

For adjacent sights see ARGOLÍDA, AKTÍ ARKADÍAS, EPÍDAVROS, ÍDRA, LERNÍ, MIKÍNES, NÁFPLIO, SPÉTSES, TÍRINTHA, TRÍPOLI.

AKTÍ ARKADÍAS★★

ARCADIAN COAST – Arkadía

Michelin map 980 south of fold 29

The east coast of the Peloponnese from Ástros to Leonídio, which forms part of Arkadía, has long been overlooked by tourists as it was accessible only by sea. Since 1976 however a new sometimes corniche road has been built which follows the course of the lonely winding coastline overlooking the Argolic Gulf. It is still not much used and offers a succession of views across the gulf to the Argolid peninsula and Spetsae Island.
The Arcadian coast is formed by the foothills of the **Mount Párnonas** (Parnon) range which rises to 1 935m/6 348ft; its limestone slopes are mostly barren except at altitude where a few wolves inhabit the forests. Life is still traditional: many peasants go to work in their fields riding on a donkey or a mule, the women spin by hand and the fishermen pull their boats up on the shore... Extended villages of white houses topped by pantile roofs appear in the distance clustered in coastal depressions amid orchards fed by irrigation channels.

★★FROM ÁSTROS TO LEONÍDIO

50km/3mi by car, about 2hr; petrol stations are rare.

Ástros – Ástros is an agricultural centre specialising in the cultivation of fruit trees (olives, citrus fruits and particularly peaches); there is a small seaside resort (Paralía Ástros) down on the coast at the foot of a promontory below the remains of an ancient citadel refurbished by the Franks. In 1823 Ástros was host to the Second National Assembly of Greece which met to revise the 1821 Constitution.
Beyond Ágios Andréas the road passes above several inlets which are suitable for bathing.

★**Tirós** – An old town which spreads out like a fan among terraced olive groves, which is bypassed by the new road running along the coast below through the little resort of **Paralía Tiroú**, which has a beach and several hotels.
Beyond Tirós a corniche road offers beautiful views across the sea to Spetsae.

★**Sambatikí** – Attractive site in a curving bay protected by a watch tower; beach and fishing boats.

The road runs high up above Leonídio Bay and the fertile coastal strip which produces olives, citrus fruit and vegetables. The river mouth is flanked by two small beaches – Lékos and Pláka *(tavernas; guest houses; hydrofoil landing point)*.

Fast craft ...

The **hydrofoil** from Piraeus to Kíthera calls at Pláka, the port for Leonídio, giving quicker access than by road and the possibility of a brief excursion to Spétses. For details contact the Ceres Group ☎ (01) 42 80 001 in Piraeus, (0757) 22 206 in Leonídio.

★★ Leonídio – Timeless and peaceful *(at least out of season)* the little town of Leonídio extends from the bank of its river to a high red cliff. It has a certain old-world charm: a 12C fortified house *(recently restored)*, old rough-cast houses with balconies and Saracen chimneys, the workshops of craftsmen and tradesmen (baker's oven), old wood-panelled cafés with marble-topped tables.
Walk to the far end of the town for a view (near the ruined tower) over the site and the coastal basin down to the sea.
Further inland *(32km/20mi return)* along the road lies the **Elóna Monastery** huddled against the rocks on a wild **site★** overlooking a narrow valley.
The road beyond the monastery is magnificent but very rough in places, as it continues to Kosmás and Geráki *(see GERÁKI)*, from where one can reach Sparta or Githio.

For adjacent sights see ARGOLÍDA, ÁRGOS, AKTÍ ARKADÍAS, EPÍDAVROS, ÍDRA, LERNÍ, MIKÍNES, NÁFPLIO, SPÉTSES, TÍRINTHA, TRÍPOLI.

ÁRTA★

Árta, Epiros – Population 19 087
Michelin map 980 fold 15

Árta, which was known in antiquity as Ambracia, is situated in a bend in the River Árahthos and dominated by a 13C **citadel** built on ancient foundations.
It was a thriving city which Pyrrhus, King of Epiros in the 3C BC who died in 272 BC in Árgos *(see ÁRGOS)*, and the despots of the Comnenos dynasty in the 13C-14C chose as their capital; in 1259 Anna Comnena was married here to William de Villehardouin *(see p 26 and KALAMÁTA)*. Nowadays the town is above all a market for the citrus fruits which are grown in the neighbourhood and also a craft centre: embroidery, long-haired rugs *(flokáti)*.

★ Bridge – The 17C hump-backed bridge over the Árahthos on the edge of Árta (Ioánina road) is celebrated for its elegant curve and its wide arches alternating with smaller ones which ease the flow of water when the river is in spate. The bridge has inspired several legends; one recounts that the architect used his wife's body to reinforce the foundations.

★ Panagía Parigorítissa ⌚ – The great church of the Virgin Comforter near Skoufá Square was built at the end of the 13C by Anna Palaiologos, wife of the Despot Nikephoros I. With its six domes it was inspired by the churches in Constantinople and was restored after the Second World War.
From the outside it looks like a huge square palace and is constructed of bricks and stones forming a decorative pattern.
The interior is surrounded by galleries for women *(gynaecea)*. The central dome is raised on three stages of projecting columns (some of them ancient). The base of the dome is supported on squinches of such an unusual type that the only other example is St Theodore's Church in Mystra *(see MISTRÁS)*.
The mosaics (Christ Pantocrator; the Prophets) are of the same date as the church itself; so too are the original Italian sculptures which decorate the vaulting and the bases and capitals of the columns of the third stage.
There is an **Archeological Museum** (icons, sculptures etc) in a neighbouring building.

Agía Theodóra (St Theodora's Church) ⌚ – *Northwest of the main street going towards the citadel.* The church was originally attached to a convent, which has since disappeared, to which Theodora, wife of Michael II, Despot of Epiros, withdrew in the 13C. On the left of the entrance is Theodora's tomb, set up by her son Nikephoros I and reconstructed from 13C pieces found in the last century. The massive capitals in the sanctuary probably came from one of the first Christian churches in Nikopolis *(see PRÉVEZA)*.

EXCURSIONS

Vlahérna ⌚ – *2km/1.25mi northeast of Árta.* The **monastery** stands on the top of a hill in the country. The church, which was built in the 13C on the basilical plan, has retained some of its original decoration (mosaic floor, frescoes) and contains two marble tombs which are thought to belong to Despot Michael II and his sons.

Rogoús Fortress – *15km/9.5mi west, near the village of Néa Kerassoús on the Préveza road.* Above a bend in the River Loúros stand the ruins of this ancient fortress; it is impressive for its size and state of preservation. It was built late in the 5C BC on older foundations, partially destroyed by the Romans and then restored by the Byzantines. Fine polygonal stonework. The frescoes in the little church are somewhat spoiled.

For adjacent sights see EFÍRA, IOÁNINA, KASSÓPI, LEFKÁDA, PÁRGA, PRÉVEZA.

ATHÍNA★★★

ATHENS – Attica – Population 772 072 (Greater Athens: 3 072 922)
Michelin map 980 fold 30

The attractive site, the brilliant light (sometimes hazy with pollution), the beauty of the ancient monuments and the quality of the museums all contribute to the pleasure of visiting Athens, the city of Athena, the cradle of European civilisation.
Athens also has many Roman, Byzantine and neo-Classical souvenirs and certain districts, such as the old Bazaar, have a strong and enticing oriental flavour. It is remarkable that, although Athens numbered less than 10 000 inhabitants in the 19C, as the capital of modern Greece it has now become a huge conurbation, lively and cosmopolitan, extending from Piraeus on the coast to Kifissiá in the north (15km/over 9mi).

OUT AND ABOUT IN ATHENS

Transport

Arriving by air – There are three air terminals, which are linked by Express bus no 19, which also goes to Piraeus (in summer, every hour – every 90min from midnight to 6am; the journey time is 15min to 30min). Only the East Terminal has a left luggage facility (to the south of the building).

Elinikó West (West Terminal) for Olympic Airways services (international and domestic flights), ☎ 93 63 363, reservations 96 66 666;
Elinikó East (East Terminal) for services by foreign airlines;
New terminal which handles charter flights, ☎ 96 94 466/7.
Olympic Airways – Timetables ☎ 144.
96 Leofóros Singrou, 11741 Athens ☎ 92 67 251/4;
15 Odós Fillelinon (Síndagma) ☎ 92 67 444.

Express airport bus service

To the town centre – From the east terminal (foreign airlines) and the west terminal (Olympic Airways): Express bus no 091 stops at Stiles (by the Olympeion at the top of Leofóros Singrou), Síndagma Square and Omónia Square.

To Pireás/Piraeus (Dockside) - Express bus no 19 runs – every hour – from the east terminal (foreign airlines), to the new terminal for charter flights, to the west terminal (Olympic Airways) and then on to Neo Fáliro and Piraeus (domestic services at Akti Tzepeli and international port, Akti Miaoúli *(plan Pireás, see p 104)*.

Taxis – Metered taxis can be hired at a taxi rank or will stop on request. Other passengers going in the same direction may share the taxi but rarely the cost. It is advisable to make sure that the right change is given in exchange for high value bank notes.

Flag falling charge	200Dr
Fare per kilometre	62Dr
Fare per km after midnight	120Dr
Surcharge from ports and airports	300Dr
Surcharge from long-distance bus terminals	150Dr
Surcharge for each piece of luggage	50Dr
Radio-taxi call	150Dr
Surcharge at Christmas and Easter	150Dr

Traffic – Driving in Athens is extremely difficult: crowded narrow streets which are usually one-way; lack of discipline among drivers who tend to rely on their horns.
The greater part of the old town (**Pláka**) *(plan Pláka see p 86)* is a **pedestrian precinct** but pedestrians should take great care when crossing the road elsewhere.

Parking – It is almost impossible to park in the town centre despite the construction of several car parks, including an underground one at Klathmónos Square. Sometimes there are spaces near Zápio Park or the Pedío Areos *(plan Athens Central see p 81)*. The number plates of cars parked illegally may be removed by the police; they can be reclaimed at the police station after the driver has paid a fine.

Greek Automobile Touring Club (ELPA) – 69 Odós Evrou Ambelokipi, 115 27 Athens; ☎ 777 46 65 or 777 96 98.

Athens by bus and underground

There is a flat rate fare (100DR for buses; 100DR or 150Dr for the metro), regardless of the length of the journey, on the blue buses, yellow trolleybuses and the metro (HSAP), which operate between 5am and midnight. Buses and trolleybuses are reliable and inexpensive. For information on the different routes ☎ 185; also ☎ (01) 324 8311.
The metro central station is Omónia Square. At the moment there is only one metro line *(north-south)* running between Piraeus and Kifissiá via Omonia Square; a second line *(east-west)* is currently under construction.

There are ticket machines for the metro. Bus tickets, which must be bought before boarding, are sold at:

- special kiosks in the main square
- the ticket offices at the terminus
- kiosks near the bus stops
- certain bus stops
- newspaper kiosks *(períptera)*.

Public Transport outside Athens

There is an extensive **bus network** covering the whole country; the buses operate between 6.30am and 8.30pm (later on some routes). Information ☎ 142.
For **bus services south** to the Peloponnese, and to the islands of Zakynthos, Cephallonia, Ithaca, Leukas, Corfu and to the main towns of central Greece, Thessaly, Epiros, Macedonia and Thrace.
- **KTEL Bus Station (A)** – 100 Odós Kifissiou *(plan Greater Athens, see p 105)*, ☎ 51 24 910 (or 911).
For **bus services north** to Euboia (Chalkis and Edipsos) and to the towns of Thebes, Livadiá, Delphi, Amfissa, Kaména Voúrla (near the port of Agios Konstandínos), Lamiá, Lárissa and Tríkala (for the Méteora).
- **KTEL Bus Station (B)** – 260 Odós Liossion *(plan Greater Athens, see p 105)*, ☎ 83 17 163.

The **railway network** is less extensive.
- **OSE (Greek Railways)** – ☎ 52 22 491, 36 24 402/6; 52 40 519. Ticket sales 32 36 747.
For railway services to Northern Greece and to destinations outside Greece (OSE trains and buses).
- **Larissa Station** – *Plan Central Athens, see p 81.* Access by trolleybus no 1.
For railway services to the Peloponnese (OSE trains and buses).
- **Peloponnese Station (Pelopónissos)** – *Plan Central Athens, see p 81.* Access by trolleybus no 1.

Tourist offices

Greek National Tourist Office (GNTO/EOT) – Information offices: 2 Odós Karagiórgi Servias (ground floor of National Bank of Greece) ☎ 32 22 545 (this office faces Síndagma Square); and at the Eliniko East Terminals (foreign airlines). Head Office, 4 Odós Amerikis, 10 564 Athens (*plan Central Athens, see p 81*), ☎ 33 10 437 and 32 41 081. 545.

Tourist offices – 125-127 Leofóros Kifissias; ☎ 64 82 496 and 10 Odós Stadiou; ☎ 32 40 237 (8am to 2pm).

Tourist Police – 77 Odós N Dimitrakopoulou (Koukaki), ☎ 171. Information kiosk in Sindagma Square on the corner of Odós Ermou.

Services

Post – The central post office at 100 Odós Eólou (near Omónia Square, on plan) and the post offices in Monastiráki, Síndagma and Kodzia Squares are open from 7.30am to 8pm (2pm Saturdays and 9am to 2pm Sundays). Poste Restante mail is sent to the central post office but letters can also be addressed to the two other offices.

Telephone (OTE) – The OTE head office at 15 Odós Stadiou (near Omónia Square) is open until midnight every day *(see also p 367)*.
Telephone number for emergencies – 171.

Banking – Opening times are Mondays to Fridays, 8am to 1.30pm. The National Bank of Greece in Síndagma Square is also open in summer in the afternoons and evenings and also on Saturdays and Sunday mornings. Other banks in the same area also open longer hours.
The banks at Athens' airports are open all round the clock.
Foreign currency can also be changed at post offices (but not on credit cards), and also at the numerous foreign exchange offices in and around Síndagma Square (open usually 9am to 9pm).

Useful telephone numbers

171	Tourist Police
100	Police (immediate action)
108	Port Police (immediate action)
102, 107	Information about pharmacies
105	Information about doctors
106	Hospitals for emergencies
166	Ambulance
148, 149	Information about the weather
642 1616	Lost property service
523 0111	Traffic police

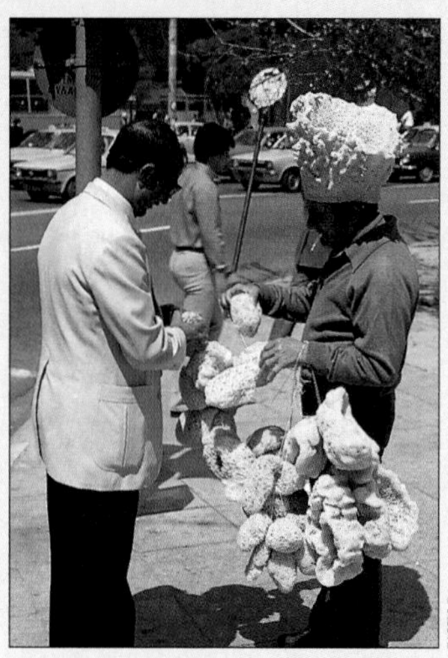

Sponges for sale

Embassies

– **United Kingdom**, 1 Odós Ploutarhou, 10675; ☎ 72 36 211.
– **United States of America**, 91 Leofóros Vas Sofias, 10160; ☎ 72 12 951.
– Visa section 9 Leofóros Venizélou.
– **Australia**, 37 Odós D Soutsou and 24 Odós A N Tsocha, 11521; ☎ 64 47 303.
– **Canada**, 4 Odós Gennadíou, 11521; ☎ 72 39 511-9.

Shopping *See p 74.*

Entertainment

The **Athens Festival** is held from May to September at the foot of the Acropolis in the **Odeon of Herod Atticus**. International and national groups and companies perform plays, operas, concerts, ballets, traditional dancing and classical tragedies. Tickets are obtainable from the ticket office at 4 Odós Stadiou (at the end of the arcade) and at the door just before the performance.

Concerts of jazz, rock music and Greek music are given at the **Lycabettos Theatre**, also as part of the Athens Festival. Information and ticket booking at 4 Odós Stadiou (at the end of the arcade), ☎ 32 21 459 and 32 23 111-9 (ext 240).

Concerts are given (except in summer) in the **Athens Concert Hall** (Mégaron Mousikís Athinón), Odós Vasilisis and Odós Kokali. Tickets on the spot or from the GNTO office (access from Odós Voukourestia or 4 Odós Stadiou), ☎ 72 82 333.

Traditional dancing is performed at the **Philopappos Theatre** by the Dóra Strátou Company from May to September every evening at 10.15pm (additional performances on Wednesdays and Sundays at 8.15pm). Tickets on sale at the theatre before the performance, which lasts 1hr 30min. ☎ 22 44 395 (from 9am to 1.30pm) and ☎ 92 14 650 (from 7.30pm).

Restaurants in and around Athens

In addition to the establishments suggested below, there is a range of hotels and restaurants listed in the **Michelin Red Guide: Europe.**

FOR LUNCH AND DINNER

Kallisti, *137 Odós Asklipiou ☎ 64 53 179 and 64 45 476.* Fine Greek cuisine, with Cypriot specialities on Mondays and Tuesdays and Calabrian Greek dishes on Thursdays and Fridays. Closed on Sundays.

Tavérna Strofi, *25 Odós Rovertou Gali and Odós Propileon, 11742 Akropoli ☎ 92 14 130.* Booking essential. Attractive terrace and beautiful view of the Acropolis. Closed on Sundays.

Gerofinikas, *10 Odós Pindarou, Kolonáki ☎ 36 22 719.* Pleasant setting and good food, frequented by quite a number of tourists but spick and span.

Rodia, *44 Odós Aristidou, Lycabettos ☎ 72 29 883.* Singing and guitar music. Open evenings only, closed on Sundays.

Xanthipi, *14 Odós Arhimidous, Pangráti ☎ 72 24 489.* Terrace open in the summer. Open evenings only.

Filippou, *19 Odós Xenokratous, Kolonáki ☎ 72 16 390.* Open from 12 to 5.30pm and 8 to 12.30pm. Closed Saturday and Sunday evening. Good value and good food.

Kentrikón, *3 Odós Kolokotroni, close to Síndagma Square ☎ 32 32 482.* Local and international cuisine. Excellent quality for the money. Closed evenings and Sundays.

Kafenion, *26 Odós Loukianou, Kolonáki ☎ 72 29 056.* Traditional Greek cooking. Open midday and evenings. Closed on Sundays.

Avinissia Café, *Avinissias Square, Monastiraki ☎ 32 17 047.* Saturdays and especially on Sundays, lively ambiance with accordion music from 3 to 6pm (7pm on Sundays). Closed on Mondays.

Xinou, *4 Odós Angelou Geronda, Pláka ☎ 32 21 065.* Good food, very pleasant setting in a courtyard, with singing and guitar music giving a congenial atmosphere. Closed on Sundays. Open in August.

47 Maritsa's, *47 Odós Voukourestiou (corner of Odós Fokilidou), Kolonáki ☎ 36 30 132.* Fine Greek cuisine served until 1.30am. Closed on 15 August.

Ideal, *46 Odós Panepistimiou ☎ 33 03 000*. Greek and international cuisine. Open midday and evenings, serving until 1am. Closed on Sundays.

Apagio, *8 Odós Megistis, Kalamaki ☎ 98 39 093 and 98 81 329*. Open until 1am. Closed on Mondays. Very good regional food and plenty of it. Worth making the detour.

Ippokrátous, *166 Odós Ippokrátous ☎ 64 26 305*. Very good local food and value for money. Closed on Sundays.

Dimokritos, *23 Odós Dimokritou, Kolonáki ☎ 36 13 588*. Local dishes. Good value for money. Closed Sunday evenings in August.

Chryssa, *81 Odós Dimophondos, Ano Petrálona ☎ 34 12 515*. Greek specialities served until 2am. Closed on Sundays.

Mandio, *4 Odós Delphon, Kolonáki ☎ 36 19 682*. Good, well-prepared food served until 2am. Closed on Sundays. Trendy.

Electra Palace Hotel, *18 Odós Nikodimou, Pláka ☎ 32 41 401*. Greek food. Good value for money. View of the Acropolis from the terrace.

G.B. Corner, *Hôtel de Grande-Bretagne, Sindagma Square ☎ 33 30 000*. Excellent Greek and international cuisine. Setting has period charm.

Mamacas, *41 Odós Persephonis ☎ 34 64 984*. Carefully prepared small dishes. Open midday and evenings. Closed on Tuesdays.

Filistron, *23 Odós Vassoléos Pavlou, Thissio ☎ 34 22 897 and 34 67 554*. Good Greek food and, in summer, a superb view from the terrace of the Acropolis and Lycabettos.

Tavérna tou Kosta, *64 Athinéon Efivon, Ambélokipi ☎ 72 21 489 and 72 29 394*. Fish specialities. Closed Sunday evenings and in August.

Terpsi, *70 Odós S. Venizélou, Halandri ☎ 68 42 585*. Good local food, attractive setting. Open all year. Closed on Sundays.

Stoa Cooper, *101 Odós Patission and Kodrigktonos (inside the arcade) ☎ 82 53 932*. Very congenial, trendy and lively, a restaurant, café and bar rolled into one. Open from 12pm.

Panorama, *4 Odós Iliou, Kavouri ☎ 89 51 298 and 96 58 401*. Istanbul specialities. View of the sea. Closed 1 January, Easter Sunday and Christmas Day.

Tavérna Antonópoulos, *55 Odós Diadahou Pavlou, Glyfada ☎ 89 48 521*. Fish specialities. Open from 12pm to midnight.

Athinaikon, *2 Odós Themistokleous, Kolonós ☎ 38 36 485*. Good value and good local food. Open from 11.30am to 1am. Closed on Sundays.

Thalassinos, *36a Odós Tsakalof, Kolonáki ☎ 36 14 695*. Excellent well-prepared Greek cuisine. Open from 1pm to 1am. Closed on Sundays.
A second establishment is open in summer daily except Sunday evenings and Mondays at 32 Odós Lissikratous and Irakleous, Dzidzifies (at Kalithea, north-east of the Hippodrome). ☎ 93 04 518.

Trendy places

BARS AND RESTAURANTS

Mezzo-Mezzo, *58 Odós Syngrou ☎ 92 42 444*. Greek and international cuisine. Excellent wine bar with a large selection of wines of different qualities. Meals served in the restaurant from 8pm to 1am. Closed Sunday evenings. In summer (from June to the end of September) transfers to the coast in the premises of *La* **Playa**, *18 Odós Alkionydes, Voula. ☎ 96 59 939 and 940*.

Pritanio, *7 Odós Milioni, Kolonáki ☎ 36 43 353-4*. In a very pleasant pedestrianised passage, lined with cafés and restaurants. Closed on 15 August.

Taki 13, *13 Odós Taki, Psiri ☎ 32 54 707*. Very congenial, with good food and atmospheric music on Saturdays and Sundays. Open daily midday and evenings.

Aiolis, *23 Odós Aiolou and Odós Agias Irinis (city centre) ☎ 33 12 839*. Art café and restaurant. Good, well-prepared Greek food served midday and in the evening. Closed in August for two weeks (around 15 August).

O Stávlos, *10 Odós Iraklidon, Thissio ☎ 34 67 206 and 34 52 502*. Bar, restaurant and café. Good atmosphere and lively.

Methystanes, *26 Odós Lepeniotou and Ogigou, Psiri ☎ 33 14 298*. In a fashionable area. Good food and live Greek music on Tuesday evenings, Saturday, and Sunday afternoons. Closed on Mondays.

Multi-Culti, 8 *Odós Agias Théklas, Psiri ☎ 32 44 643*. Good Greek food, some more sophisticated dishes. Stylish with a good atmosphere and excellent music. Record shop on the first floor. Food served until 2am.

Bee, *corner of Odós Miauli and Thémidos, Monastiraki ☎ 32 12 624*. Bar and restaurant open from the morning until very late in the evening.

Táde Éfi Dína, *72 Odós Ermou ☎ 32 13 652*. Good small regional dishes, served midday and evening. Closed on Mondays.

BARS – Most of these move to the coast during the summer.

Memphis, *5 Odós Vendiri (behind the Hilton)* ☎ *72 24 104*. Central and has an attractive terrace and rock music. Trendy. Open from 10pm until daybreak.

Balthazar, *27 Odós Tsoha, Ambelokipi* ☎ *64 41 215*. Attractive and spacious courtyard. International food. Open every day from 9.30pm until daybreak. The restaurant closes at 1.30am. Only the bar is open on Sundays.

City, *43 Odós Haritos* ☎ *72 28 910*. Very lively pedestrianised street lined with cafés and restaurants.

"REBÉTIKA" MUSIC

Stoa ton athanaton, *19 Odós Sofokleous and Stoa Athanaton* ☎ *32 14 362*. Open every day from 3.30pm to 6am. Closed on Sundays, and from June to the end of September. Booking essential.

SOUVLAKI

Pitta pam, *Omonia Square* ☎ *52 41 248* and Odós Elpidos, Victoria Square ☎ 82 53 041. Definitely one of the best!

Thanassis, *69 Odós Mitropoléos, Monastiraki* ☎ *32 44 705*. Good small popular restaurant, good atmosphere. Open midday and evening.

VEGETARIAN

Eden, *12 Odós Lyssiou, corner Odós Mnisikléous, Plaka* ☎ *32 48 858*. Good natural food. Open from midday to midnight.

CAFÉ-BARS

Skoufáki, *47-49 Odós Skoufa, Kolonáki* ☎ *36 45 888*. Very congenial bistro, good light food (at lunchtime), with a wide choice of coffees. Open from 10am to 2am. Closed in August.

Ciao, *2 Odós Tsakalof*, Kolonáki. Lively, with Italian and Greek specialities at midday, and excellent Italian coffee.

Zonars, *at the corner of Odós Voukourestiou and Panepistimiou*, Kolonáki. The oldest café in Athens, which refuses to be modernised. Good ices.

Brazilian, *1B Odós Voukourestiou, Kolonáki* ☎ *32 45 225*. Open from 7am to 8.30pm, on Saturdays from 8am to 4pm. Closed on Sundays.

Filion, *34 Odós Skoufa, Kolonáki* ☎ *36 12 850*. A stylish café open from 7am to midnight, in the summer from 8am to 5pm on Saturdays and Sundays.

Exotic Restaurants

JAPANESE

Sushi Bar, *Varnava Square, Pangrati* ☎ *75 24 354 and 75 64 964*. Well-prepared food, speciality raw fish, served until 1am.

Kiku, *12 Odós Dimokritou, Kolonáki* ☎ *36 47 033*. Sushi bar. Minimalist setting, refined modern decor. High prices. Food served until 1am. Closed on Sundays.

Kyoto, *5 Odós Garibaldi, Akropolis* ☎ *92 41 406*. Traditional food served until 12.30am. Closed on Sundays.

Furin Kazan, *2 Odós Apollonos, Syndagma* ☎ *32 29 170*. Japanese fast food restaurant. Only open at lunchtime. Closed on Saturdays and Sundays.

Mitsiko, *27 Odós Kydathinéon, Plaka* ☎ *32 20 980*. Sushi bar. Food served until 11.30pm. Closed on Sundays.

CHINESE AND OTHERS

Far East, *7 Odós Stadiou, Syndagma* ☎ *32 34 996*. Also at Odós Lazaraki and Odós Pandoras, Glyfada ☎ 89 40 500. Good food served until 1.30am.

Kina, *72 Odós Efroniou, Ilissia* ☎ *72 33 200 and 72 45 746*. The oldest restaurant, with good Chinese cuisine. Open midday and evening, except Sundays. Food served until 12.30am.

Mekong, *60 Odós Agias Varvaras, Paléo Faliro* ☎ *98 52 474 and 98 89 688*. Korean cuisine served until 1am.

Won ton, *57 Odós El. Venizélou, Néa Smirni* ☎ *93 16 997*. Good food; eat as much as you like buffet at lunchtime. Open from 12pm until 1am.

Loon Fung Tien, *143 Odós Alkyonidon, Voula* ☎ *89 58 083 and 89 53 360*. Good Cantonese cuisine.

Dragon Palace, *3 Odós Antinoros and Odós Risari, Pangrati* ☎ *72 42 795*. Chinese food served from 12pm to 3pm and 8pm to 1am.

I Kilia tou Vouda, *28 Odós Froklou, Varnava Square, Pangrati* ☎ *75 25 73 and 70 10 048*. Chinese food served until 1am.

Folia tou Tchang, *15 Odós Doiranis and Athidon (level with 192 Odós Syngrou)*, Kallithéa. Chinese food. Open from 12pm to 12.30am.

HISTORICAL NOTES

Ancient Athens

Birth of Athens – The Acropolis was built on a natural defensive site consisting of a hill (about 156m/512ft high) with steep sides, not far from the sea, the approaches protected by two rivers – Kifissós *(west)* and Ilissós *(east)* – and a circle of hills forming outposts. Athens is thought to have been founded by **Cecrops**, the king of a prehistoric race; he was deified in the form of a serpent with a human torso and believed to have introduced the cult of the owl.

In all the mythical accounts **Poseidon**, the bellicose god of the Sea, and **Athena**, the goddess of Wisdom, are said to have rivalled one another in the performance of miracles for the good of the first inhabitants; one produced a spring and a horse, the other the olive tree, symbol of peace and harmony.

Erechtheos, a descendant of Cecrops, established the cult of Athena, the goddess who was associated with the olive and the owl: the cult was practised in the king's palace itself, on the site where the Erechtheion now stands. There are fragments of a wall dating from this period near the Propylaia.

Aigeus' son, **Theseus** (12C or 11C BC), made Athens the capital of a coherent state covering present-day Attica and afforded great importance to the processions in honour of Athena, called the Panathenaia. He was the Athenian national hero throughout antiquity. In his reign the area covered by the city was scarcely larger than the Acropolis which contained the royal palace and the houses of the patricians *(Eupatrides)*. A few shrines were built however on the banks of the Ilissós, near the Kallirhoë fountain; an *agora* was created and the first graves were dug at the roadsides.

Athens in her glory – **6C-5C BC**. After the great urban reforms introduced by **Solon** and the enlightened dictators, Peisistratos and his sons (561-510), the city developed extensively. A new circuit wall was built enclosing the Areopagos hill northwest of the Acropolis, where certain assemblies were held, as well as the two *agoras* of Theseus and Solon, which became the political centre of the city. At the same time various

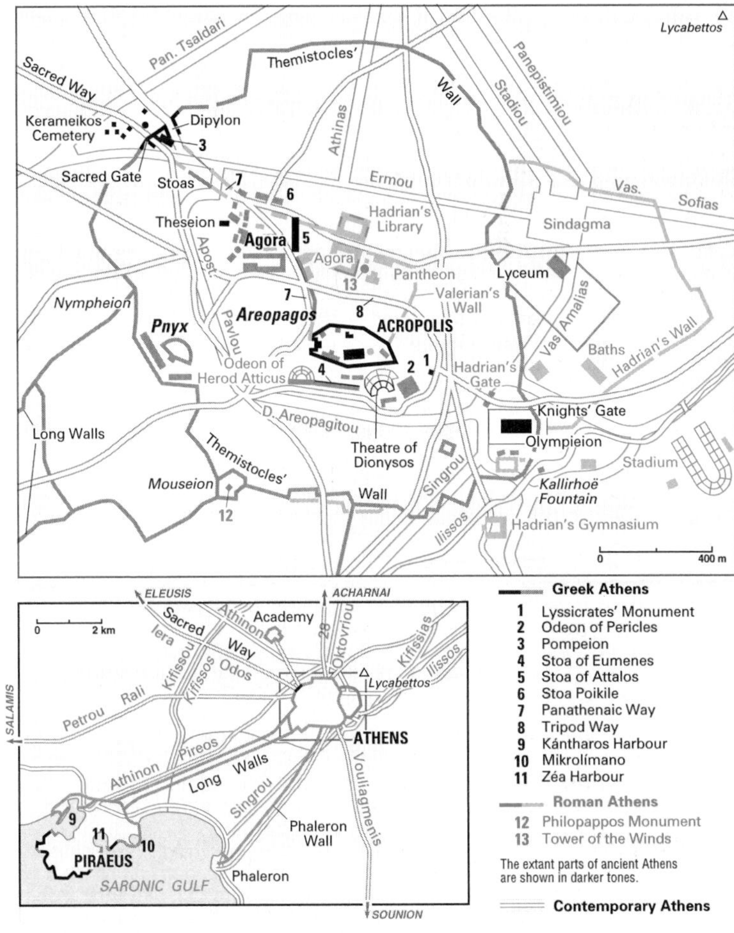

municipal undertakings were being carried out in the lower town: public buildings constructed of tufa, provision of water, sewers and roads. The first coins were struck bearing the effigy of Athena and the owl; the Lyceum and the Academy, famous gymnasia surrounded by gardens, were established.

When **Kleisthenes** rose to power in 508 BC he organized Athens into a direct democracy and introduced **ostracism** so that any individual who was a danger to the State could be excluded from public affairs for 10 years after a vote had been taken.

Legislative power was exercised by an assembly of the people *(Ecclesia)* which met three or four times a month on the Pnyx *(see below)*, a Senate *(Boule)* of 500 members which was subordinated to the Assembly and a tribunal *(Heliaia)* comprising elected magistrates and juries chosen by lot.

Executive power was exercised by the *archons* and the *strategi*; the latter were in command of the army.

Following the damage caused by the enemy in 479 BC at the end of the Persian wars, Themistocles, the victor of the battle of Salamis, gave orders for the construction of the wall which bears his name and of which a few traces remain; he also built the "Long Walls", a sort of fortified corridor linking Athens and Piraeus.

In the Age of **Pericles**, that great Athenian statesman devoted himself to the reconstruction of Athens with the advice of the sculptor Pheidias. An overall plan was drawn up for the Acropolis; various buildings in white Pentelic marble rose against the blue sky: the Propylaia, the Parthenon, the Erechtheion and the temple of Athena Nike surrounded by votive monuments and statues. In the lower town the *agora* was restored and enlarged. Almost the whole area within the walls was covered by brick houses, usually built round a central courtyard; they were particularly dense on two hills near the beginning of the Long Walls west and southwest of the Acropolis, the Mouseion and the Nympheion. The Kerameikos cemetery, beside the road leading to Plato's Academy, was the largest in the city where the most important citizens were buried.

Athens in decline – **4C–2C BC**. The Peloponnesian War (431–404), in which Athens was defeated by Sparta, marked the beginning of a decline in the moral sphere which is illustrated by the death of the philosopher **Socrates** who was unjustly condemned to drink hemlock (399 BC) in the presence of his pupil Plato.

Despite the exhortations of the great orator **Demosthenes**, the Greeks failed to agree on a concerted policy and after the Battle of Chaironeia (338 BC) Athens became subject to Philip of Macedon who was succeeded by Alexander the Great.

Secure under the Macedonian "protection" which lasted until the end of the 3C BC, the Athenian municipal authorities embarked on public works of embellishment particularly under the orator Lycurgus (338-326 BC): the theatre of Dionysos and the choregic monument of Lysicrates.

The Hellenistic period which began with the death of Alexander (323 BC) was marked by the division of the Macedonian Empire into several kingdoms. Athens vegetated; only the building of a few porticos and gymnasia, in the reigns of the kings of Antioch and Pergamon, reveal the city's continuing intellectual power.

Conquered by Rome, Athens conquers Rome – **1C BC–4C AD** The political independence of Athens came to an end in 86 BC when the city was captured by Sulla and the walls were razed.

Nonetheless the "Roman peace" enabled Athens to retain its leadership in cultural affairs in the Mediterranean world; the Romans carried away or copied her works of art, imitated her citizens' way of life and sent their sons to Athens to complete their education. In the 1C BC a temple to Rome and Augustus (Naós Rómis ke Avgoústou) was built on the Acropolis hill and a Roman forum and a hydraulic clock, known later as the "Tower of the Winds", were built at the foot; a covered theatre (Odeon) was built on the old *agora*.

In AD 53 Christianity was brought to Athens by **St Paul** who preached the gospel, without much success it is true, and exalted the "unknown god" on the Areopagos; Paul did however convert one member of the famous tribunal, Dionysius the Areopagite, who was the first bishop and martyr of the new community.

Later, in the 2C AD, **Emperor Hadrian**, who cherished all things Greek, was very generous in his embellishment of Athens: he completed the temple of Zeus (Olympieion) begun by Peisistratos, built a library and aqueducts and a new district east of the Acropolis protected by a wall. Herod Atticus, a wealthy Athenian, contributed to these public works by constructing a theatre (Odeon), which still bears his name, on the southern slope of the Acropolis and a splendid white marble stadium, which has been restored in recent years, on the east bank of the Ilissós.

Byzantine and Medieval Athens

Byzantium and the rise of Christianity – **5C–13C**. Following the Germanic invasions in the middle of the 3C the division of the Roman Empire in 395 attributed Athens to the emperor residing in Byzantium (Constantinople).

The Edict of Milan in 313 allowed Christians to practise their religion legally and their proliferation in Athens from the 5C to the 7C led to the suppression of the schools of philosophy and the establishment of Christian basilicas in the Parthenon, the Erechtheion, the Hephaisteion, the theatre of Dionysos, Hadrian's library etc.

The majority of the Byzantine churches date from the 9C and often incorporated fragments of ancient buildings. They were small but well proportioned and carefully decorated and many have survived: the Holy Apostles (late 10C) in the Greek *agora*, St Theodore (11C), the Kapnikaréa (11C) and the Old Metropolitan (12C).
Until the late 12C when Athens was sacked by the Saracens, it was a flourishing city with a stable population protected by the castle on the Acropolis.

Dukes of Athens – 13C–15C. The Fourth Crusade which captured Constantinople in 1204 *(see p 25)* caused Athens to fall into the hands of the Frankish knights who also held Thebes. Athens passed to a family of Burgundian origin, **de la Roche**, who had a castle in Thebes: during their tenure Athens was raised to a Duchy by Louis IX of France (1260).
They were succeeded by Gautier de Brienne but he was killed by the Catalans at the Battle of Kephisos (1311) near Lake Copais in Boeotia *(see ORHOMENÓS)* and the Frankish domination of Athens came to an end. The Franks fortified the Acropolis and altered the Propylaia to form a palace guarded by a keep, known as the Frankish Tower, which was 28m/92ft high and stood until it was demolished in 1875.
The Catalans then occupied the region but established their stronghold in Thebes rather than Athens so that in 1387 Nerio Acciaiuoli, a member of a Florentine family involved in banking and arms manufacture, broke out of Corinth where his family ruled and captured Athens after a long siege. After a brief Venetian interlude from 1394 to 1403 the Acciaiuoli reigned over Athens until 1456 when they were obliged to submit to the Turks who had captured Constantinople three years earlier.

Athens under the Turks

Athens asleep – 1456–1687. Sultan Mahomet II, who captured Constantinople, granted a certain degree of autonomy to Athens and the Turks allowed several churches to be built; in the 17C they even permitted the Jesuits and Capuchins to found monasteries. The Acropolis was fortified to form the kernel of the Turkish fortress; in 1466 the Parthenon was converted into a mosque with an adjoining minaret; the Propylaia was used as a powder magazine and the Erechtheion housed a harem.
Athens was simply a small provincial town which was thought in the west to have degenerated into the fishing village of Porto Leone (in fact Piraeus) since in the 16C most knowledge of Greece was acquired from merchants and chaplains in the British Levant Company and as there was no trade with Athens few people went there. A few intrepid travellers however did visit the ancient city. In 1675 Sir George Wheler described the Parthenon as "absolutely both for matter and art the most beautiful piece of antiquity remaining in the world".

Athens at its lowest ebb – 1687–1821. After reconquering the Peloponnese, the Venetian troops led by the **Doge Francesco Morosini** and by Koenigsmark laid siege to Athens in 1687; during the bombardment a powder magazine on the Acropolis exploded causing grave damage to the Parthenon. The Turks surrendered but recaptured the town a year later. In the meanwhile, however, the Venetians had removed the great white marble lions (now at the Venice Arsenal) and drawn up a plan of the town.
From then until independence Athens was just a small town of about 10 to 15 000 inhabitants living in the narrow streets crowded on the northern slopes of the Acropolis hill. There were about 1 500 Greek families as opposed to 400 Turkish ones who, together with the garrison, lived in the citadel on the Acropolis and in the Bazaar district near the Roman forum; their cemetery lay west of the Acropolis.
Although only a backwater in the Ottoman Empire, Athens began to attract many visitors from western Europe who, having been introduced to Greek architecture in southern Italy, desired to visit the source of such excellence. From 1751-53 "Athenian" Stuart and Revett were at work in Athens preparing "an accurate description of the antiquities of Athens"; the first volume was published in 1762. Richard Chandler, who visited Athens some 10 years later, remarked that it was "to be regretted that so much admirable sculpture as is still extant... should be all likely to perish... Numerous carved stones have disappeared; and many, lying in the ruinous heaps, moved our indignation at the barbarism daily exercised in defacing them". Lord **Elgin**, British Ambassador in Constantinople at this period, is famous for his acquisitive activities which incidentally protected the marble sculptures from further deterioration. His chief rival in the collection of antiquities was Fauvel, who had acted as agent for the French Ambassador, Choiseul Gouffier, and remained in Athens, adding to his collection and acting as guide to all important visitors.

Athens, capital of Greece

Athens resurrected – Independence – 1821–34. On 25 April 1821 the Athenians rose in rebellion and occupied the town except for the Acropolis which held out until 10 June. A counter-attack launched by Ibrahim Pasha in 1826 enabled the Turks to capture Missolonghi *(see MESSOLÓNGI)* and to lay siege to Athens. Although 500 volunteers under Colonel **Fabvier**, a Frenchman, managed to breach the blockade and enter the Acropolis, the Greek troops were forced to surrender on 24 May 1827. Eleven months of fighting and bombardment had devastated the town from which the inhabitants had fled and the great olive grove of 150 000 trees to the west of the town had been almost totally destroyed by fire. Despite the War of Independence ending in 1829, the Acropolis remained in Turkish hands until 1834 when Otto of Bavaria made his triumphal entry into Athens which succeeded Náfplio as the capital of the new state of Greece; the population numbered barely 4 000.

Athens transformed: first neo-Classical era – 1834–1900. In 1832 the Great Powers imposed on Greece a German king, the young **Otto of Bavaria**, son of Ludwig I of Bavaria, who had a passion for both Greece and Lola Montes, the dancer.
In the reign of Otto and Queen Amalia, a policy of great works was inaugurated under the aegis of the Bavarian architect, Leo von Klenze. A new town with straight streets was traced out in a triangular area based on Odós Ermoú with Odós Pireós (Panagí Tsaldári) and Odós Stadíou forming the two sides and meeting in Omónia Square. After 1860 new districts were developed: to the east of Síndagma Square, the foreign embassy district, and to the north round the axes formed by Odós Patissíon and Odós Sólonos. In 1861 the population of Athens had reached 41 298.
Many of the buildings from this period were in the neo-Classical style: imposing and severe public monuments, modest houses with cornices and *acroteria*; the latter have unfortunately almost all been pulled down. The main German contributions were the Royal Palace, the University, the Academy and the Observatory. The Parliament building, however, was designed by a French architect, Boulanger, and another Frenchman, Daniel, was responsible for public works (roads, sewers etc). **Kleanthes**, a Greek architect, worked more on houses for private clients: the Duchess of Plaisance' residence in Ilissia and his own house in Pláka.

Athens' expansion – After 1900. When the Greeks from Smyrna in Asia Minor were expelled by the Turks in 1922, known as the Catastrophe *(see p 29)*, a wave of refugees settled in Athens, mainly in the district north of Piraeus, as can be seen from the suburb of New Smyrna **(Néa Smírni)** where the population rose from 292 991 in 1920 to 452 919 in 1928.
The city has continued to expand: the old-fashioned cornice houses have been replaced with concrete blocks of flats. The lower slopes of Lycabettos have been covered by the elegant Kolonáki district; the Ilissós now runs underground beneath a broad highway; the outer districts of detached houses now extend from Kifissiá in the north to Fáliro (Phaleron) in the south. After the Second World War new buildings were concentrated along Leofóros Venizélou: the Hilton Hotel and the American Embassy by Gropius, the Athens Tower at Ambelókipi, and the more recent Olympic stadium at Maroússi are the most striking constructions.

ATHENIAN WAY OF LIFE

For tourists the centre of Athens is Síndagma Square with its large hotels, its travel agencies and airline companies, its banks and famous open-air cafés. Bars and night-clubs crowd the side streets. Women's dress shops line Odós Ermoú which extends the axial perspective from the main square towards Piraeus.
Southwest of Síndagma Square lies Pláka, an old district of narrow streets and little squares with terraces perched on the lower slopes of the Acropolis hill; it is very lively in the evenings when tourists throng the souvenir shops (in Odós Adrianou to the east and Odós Pandrassou to the west) and the tavernas resound with *bouzoúki* music interspersed with the exploits of *sirtáki* dancers. Lysikrates Square (Platía Lissikrátous) was until recently the home of the shadow theatre *Karagiósis (see p 100)*.
Pláka merges into Monastiráki *(northwest)*, an old Turkish bazaar which has become a sort of flea market *(particularly on Sunday mornings)*.
Northeast of Síndagma Square lies Kolonáki, an elegant district where the wealthy Athenians live. Beyond Kolonáki Square the streets run straight up the slopes of Lycabettos; some are so steep they end in flights of steps and cars are excluded. Here are the luxury shops: fashion, antiques, art galleries, restaurants, high class groceries and pastrycooks.
Síndagma Square is joined to Omónia Square *(northwest)* by two busy shopping streets, Odós Stadíou and Odós Venizélou, which is better known to Athenians as Odós Panepistimíou, lined by smart hotels and restaurants and shops overflowing onto the pavement.
Omónia Square is a very lively and crowded place in the less expensive part of town which has retained some of its oriental atmosphere. The streets are full of small shops and businesses belonging to tradesmen and artisans. Running south from Omónia Square Odós Athinas passes through the Central Market (Kendrikí Agorá), a huge covered market which sells a fascinating and astonishing variety of foodstuffs.
On fine evenings Athenians stroll in Síndagma or Omónia Square, in the Kolonáki district or in the Zapio Garden where they dine at the restaurants or attend the popular musical entertainment. Lycabettos *(café-restaurant)* has a magnificent view south over Athens while Pedío Áreos is known for its open-air cinemas. Well worthwhile are the open-air productions at the Herod Atticus Odeon (Athens Festival of music and theatre), at the Philopappos Theatre (traditional national dancing) and at the new Lycabettos Theatre. The son et lumière spectacle at the Pnyx is also to be recommended.

SITE OF ATHENS

★★★ **Likavitós (Lycabettos)** – *Access: Bus no 23 from Káningos Square or Kolonáki Square stops in Odós Kleomenous below the funicular. It is also possible to drive up by car to the terrace between the summit and the Lycabettos Theatre.* Lycabettos (Wolves' Hill) rises to 227m/909ft and is crowned by a chapel dedicated to St George. The terraces next to the chapel offer an admirable **panorama**★★★ embracing the city of Athens, the Acropolis, the sea coast at Piraeus and the major mountain peaks: Hymettos to the southeast, the Pentelikon *(east)* riddled with marble quarries and Parnes with its massive bulk to the north. *A path leads down to the Hotel St George-Lykabettos.*

★★★ **Lófos Filopápou (Philopappos Hill)** – *Access: Bus no 230 then continue on foot along paths which start near the Dionysos Restaurant.* In antiquity Philopappos Hill (alt 147m/482ft) was dedicated to the Muses and bore the name **Mouseion**. The path climbs up through groves of pine trees past ancient troglodyte cave-dwellings; one was long thought to be **Socrates' prison**. The hill is dominated by the **Philopappos monument** (AD 116) which was raised by the Athenians in memory of a prince of Syrian origin, who became a Roman consul and a citizen and benefactor of Athens. There are spectacular **views**★★★, particularly at sunset, of the Acropolis, Athens, Hymettos and the plain of Attica extending south to the Saronic Gulf. The **Philipappos Theatre** on the west face of the hill presents performances of traditional dances by the Dóra Strátou company.

ACROPOLIS AND ITS ENVIRONS *4hr 30min*

★★★ **Akrópoli (Acropolis)** – *Main entrance in Leofóros Dionissou Areopagitou which passes the Theatre of Dionysos and the Odeon of Herod Atticus. Parking is not allowed near the Acropolis. Take a bus (no 230 from Síndagma Square) or trolleybus (no 1, 5 or 9, "Makrigiáni" stop) or a taxi to the Acropolis and walk down the Panathenaic Way and the Agora or through Pláka back to town. In summer avoid the midday heat.*

An extensive programme of restoration or conservation work which will last several years is in progress or scheduled. Some areas may be temporarily closed.

The artistic climax of Greek architecture, the Acropolis, meaning the upper town, stands on the summit of a steep rock platform. It measures 270m/885ft long by 156m/512ft wide and covers an area of 4ha/just under 10 acres. It reaches a height of 156m/512ft and dominates the lower town by 100m/329ft.

The Acropolis comprises traces of construction from various periods dating back to the second millennium BC (Mycenaean period) but the principal buildings – the Propylaia, the Temple of Athena Nike, the Erechtheion and the Parthenon – are all in white Pentelic marble and belong to the Age of Pericles (5C BC). The air pollution in recent years has made it necessary to take steps to protect the stone and to replace the remaining sculptures with copies. The Acropolis Interpretation Centre gives a clear picture of the conservation work in progress.

The entrance to the Acropolis is known as the **Píli Beulé** (Beulé Gate) since it was discovered in 1853 beneath the Turkish bastion by a French archeologist Ernest Beulé. The gate, which was flanked by two towers, is late Roman. Beyond is a flight of steps, also Roman, which is flanked by the Temple of Athena Nike *(south)* and a pedestal of grey Hymettos marble *(north)* (12m/39ft), the **Mnimío Agrípa**, which in about 15 BC supported the quadriga of Agrippa, Augustus' son-in-law. Before the Roman period the entrance to the Acropolis was below the Temple of Athena Nike; it consisted of a steep ramp continuing the Sacred Way (Ierá Odós) along which the Panathenaic processions made their way up to the temple.

A projecting terrace north of the Agrippa Monument gives a good view of the three hills to the west: Philopappos, the Pnyx and the Areopagos; in the Middle Ages steps led down from the terrace to the Clepsydra Spring which was discovered in 1873.

★ **Propílea** – *The steps are very slippery.* The monumental gates to the Acropolis, the **Propylaia**, were built by the architect Mnesikles using a combination of blue Eleusinian marble and Pentelic marble. They consist of a central section flanked by two asymmetrical returning wings.

From the 12C to the 15C they were adapted to create a palace for the bishops and dukes of Athens; a square defensive tower, the **"Frankish Tower"**, was erected on the south wing. The Turks reinforced the fortifications by the addition of bastions and it was not until 1836 that the Propylaia were stripped of their military accretions; the Frankish Tower was demolished by Schliemann in 1875.

The central section was preceded by a portico with a triangular pediment; it was supported on fluted Doric columns without capitals of which six remain. The vestibule in the central section consisted of three parallel passages divided by two rows of three Ionic columns; part of the coffered ceiling has been reconstructed. Part of the east wall of the vestibule still exists; it contained five wooden doors of which the one in the centre opened into a Doric portico similar to the western porch and giving access to the Sacred Way within the Acropolis.

The north wing was divided into a portico and a gallery (Pinakothíki) for exhibiting paintings, the Pinakotheke; the south wing consisted simply of a portico.
On passing through the Propylaia, one comes face to face with the graceful silhouette of the Erechtheion *(left)* and the majestic golden pile of the Parthenon *(right)*; the intervening space is scattered with blocks of marble (the blocks are to be re-erected in their original position as far as possible), fragments of monuments or votive offerings long gone. Opposite the Propylaia stood the **Prómahos Athiná** (9m/30ft high), an impressive warrior figure of Athene, designed in bronze by **Pheidias** to commemorate the Athenian victory over the Persians.

The Sacred Way skirts the north side of the Parthenon to reach the entrance.

★★★ **Parthenónas** – The Doric temple known as the **Parthenon** was built by Iktínos under the direction of Pheidias in the Age of Pericles and dedicated to Athena whose statue in gold and ivory, designed by Pheidias, adorned the sanctuary. Pheidias was also responsible for the sculptures decorating the pediments, friezes and metopes, all of which were painted in vivid colours.
The statue of Athena was removed to Constantinople in the Byzantine period and destroyed by the inhabitants in 1203 when the city was besieged by the Crusaders. The Parthenon was then converted into a church dedicated to the Holy Wisdom and richly decorated with frescoes and mosaics; the entrance was moved to the west end. After eight centuries of Orthodox worship the church was plundered by the Franks who converted it to the Roman rite under the title of St Mary of Athens. The Turks converted the Parthenon into a mosque and built a minaret at the southwest corner. The building still retained the majority of its sculptures which were recorded by J Carrey, a painter employed by the Marquis de Nointel, before the explosion of the powder magazine in 1687 destroyed many of them and brought down the Parian marble roof slabs, the walls of the *naós* and 28 columns.

Elgin Marbles

When **Lord Elgin** arrived in Constantinople as British Ambassador to the Porte (the central office of the Ottoman government in Constantinople) he obtained a firman from the Sultan granting him permission to make copies and models of ancient buildings, to erect scaffolding, to dig down to the foundations and to remove any interesting pieces. His agents in Athens induced the local Turkish authorities to allow pieces of sculpture to be removed from the temple itself. About eighteen months later he obtained further written documents saying that the Turkish government approved all that the local authorities in Athens had done to assist him in his acquisitions. Elgin's purpose in acquiring his collection of antiquities had been to improve artistic taste and design in Britain. His expenses, which he had hoped to recover from the government, made him bankrupt and he was finally forced to sell his collection to the British Museum at half the cost of obtaining it.

Since 1834 efforts have been made to restore the structure, particularly the re-erection of the colonnades, a difficult operation known as anastylosis, which was carried out by Greek archeologists after the First World War. The iron clamps used in this early work have since rusted causing the marble to crack and are now being replaced by titanium clamps. The current programme also involves protecting the stone from atmospheric pollution and the rock floor from erosion.

Exterior – The Parthenon rests on a marble stylobate and is surrounded by a peristyle of 46 fluted columns (8 at the ends and 17 down each side) which measures 10.43m/34ft 3in high, 1.90m/6ft 3in across at the base and 1.45m/4ft 9in across at the height of the capitals. The columns incline slightly inwards to correct an optical distortion which would make them appear further apart at the top than at ground level.
The pediments were decorated with painted sculptures against a blue background. The east pediment showed the Birth of Athena, fully armed, from the head of Zeus in the presence of the Sun (Helios) and the Moon (Selene) who are driving their chariots; this description of the scene is taken from the mouldings of the originals now kept in the British Museum. The west pediment represented the Quarrel between Athena and Poseidon for possession of Attica; two very damaged pieces have survived.
The Doric frieze consisted of the usual triglyphs alternating with 92 metopes showing sculpted battle scenes against a red ground: the Battle between the Giants and the Olympian Gods *(east)*, the Battle between the Lapiths and the Centaurs *(south)*, the Battle between the Greeks and the Amazons *(west)* and the Siege of Troy *(north)*. Only a few of the original metopes still exist; there are 15 in the British Museum, one in the Louvre in Paris and several others in the Acropolis Museum.

The shields which were presented by Alexander the Great *(see PÉLA)* were attached to the architrave.

Interior – *Closed to the public.* The east portico *(prónaos)* where the offerings were placed led into the sanctuary through a door 10m/33ft high.
The inner chamber *(naós)* contained a gigantic statue of Athena (12m/39ft high); it was made of a wooden frame covered with ivory and gold (more than a tonne of gold was used); a few base blocks show where it stood.
Behind the *naós* there was another chamber, the Parthenon itself, which housed the treasure of the Delian League which was under the leadership of Athens; four Ionic columns supported the ceiling.
The wall enclosing the *naós* and the Parthenon was decorated on the outside with the **frieze of the Panathenaia**; it was 160m/525ft long and started at the southwest corner extending round both sides towards the entrance. This famous band of sculpture, which contained 400 human figures and 200 animals, showed the procession which took place every four years at the end of the festival in honour of Athena; it consisted of the young girls bearing gifts and baskets *(kanephoroi)* and the magistrates, musicians and men on horseback coming to offer the goddess the tunic which had been woven and embroidered by the young Athenian women. About 50 pieces, the best preserved, are displayed in the British Museum; a few others can be seen in the Acropolis Museum.
The west portico *(opisthódomos)* was a symmetrical counterpart of the *prónaos*; there are traces of a Turkish minaret near the southwest corner.
There are casts of the majority of the Parthenon sculptures at the Acropolis Interpretation Centre.

Cross the area between the Parthenon and the Erechtheion: foundations of the earlier temple of Athena (Arhéos Naós Athinás) built in the early 6C BC and destroyed 100 years later to make room for the Erechtheion.

★★★ **Eréhthio** – The **Erechtheion** is the first of the buildings of the Acropolis to have been fully restored.
The design of this little Doric and Ionic temple, which was completed in 407 BC, is unexpectedly complicated because of the sloping ground and because several existing shrines had to be incorporated in it; the most important of these were the shrines of Athena, Poseidon and of Erechtheos and Cecrops, kings of Athens, to which the Panathenaic procession made its way. During the following centuries the building was used as a church, a palace, a harem and a military powder magazine. After Greece had gained her independence it was restored under the auspices of Piscatory, the French Ambassador in Athens.
The famous southern portico faces the Parthenon. It is known as the **Kariátides**, the **Porch of the Caryatids** because it is supported by six statues of young women, over 2m/6ft 6ins high; their expressions are calm and noble and their garments fall in vertical parallel folds resembling the fluting on the columns which they replace. In fact the present figures are copies; one of the originals was removed by Elgin and is in the British Museum; the others were removed in 1977 to protect them from further decay and are on display in the Acropolis Museum.
The eastern portico, supported on six Ionic columns, opens into the sanctuary which contained the oldest statue of Athena which was made of olive wood.

PICTOR

Caryatids of the Erechtheion, Athens

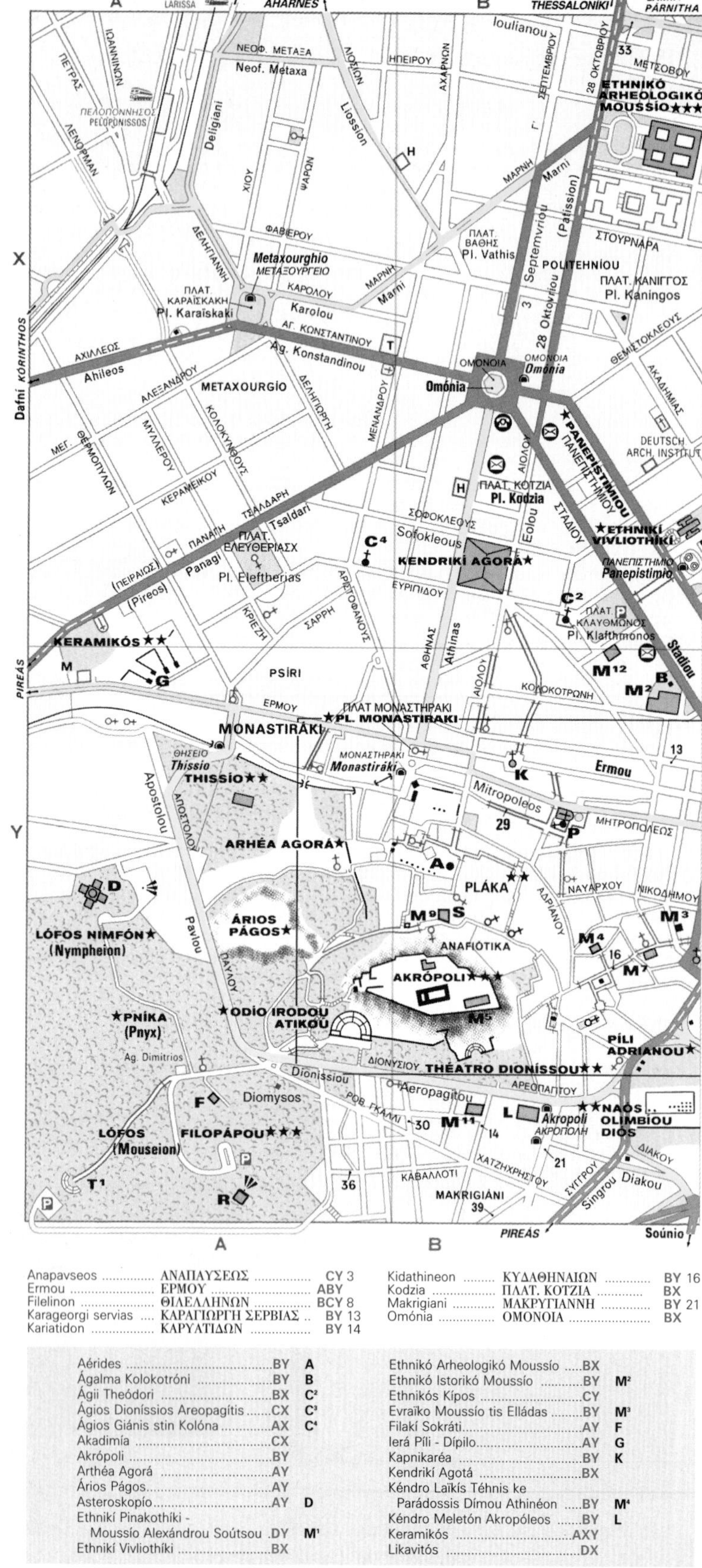

Anapavseos	ΑΝΑΠΑΥΣΕΩΣ	CY 3
Ermou	ΕΡΜΟΥ	ABY
Filelinon	ΦΙΛΕΛΛΗΝΩΝ	BCY 8
Karageorgi servias	ΚΑΡΑΓΙΩΡΓΗ ΣΕΡΒΙΑΣ	BY 13
Kariatidon	ΚΑΡΥΑΤΙΔΩΝ	BY 14
Kidathineon	ΚΥΔΑΘΗΝΑΙΩΝ	BY 16
Kodzia	ΠΛΑΤ. ΚΟΤΖΙΑ	BX
Makrigiani	ΜΑΚΡΥΓΙΑΝΝΗ	BY 21
Omónia	ΟΜΟΝΟΙΑ	BX

Aérides	BY	A
Ágalma Kolokotróni	BY	B
Ágii Theódori	BX	C²
Ágios Dioníssios Areopagítis	CX	C³
Ágios Giánis stin Kolóna	AX	C⁴
Akadimía	CX	
Akrópoli	BY	
Arthéa Agorá	AY	
Ários Págos	AY	
Asteroskopío	AY	D
Ethnikí Pinakothíki - Moussío Alexándrou Soútsou	DY	M¹
Ethnikí Vivliothíki	BX	
Ethnikó Arheologikó Moussío	BX	
Ethnikó Istorikó Moussío	BY	M²
Ethnikós Kípos	CY	
Evraïko Moussío tis Elládas	BY	M³
Filakí Sokráti	AY	F
Ierá Píli - Dípilo	AY	G
Kapnikaréa	BY	K
Kendrikí Agotá	BX	
Kéndro Laïkís Téhnis ke Parádossis Dímou Athinéon	BY	M⁴
Kéndro Meletón Akropóleos	BY	L
Keramikós	AXY	
Likavitós	DX	

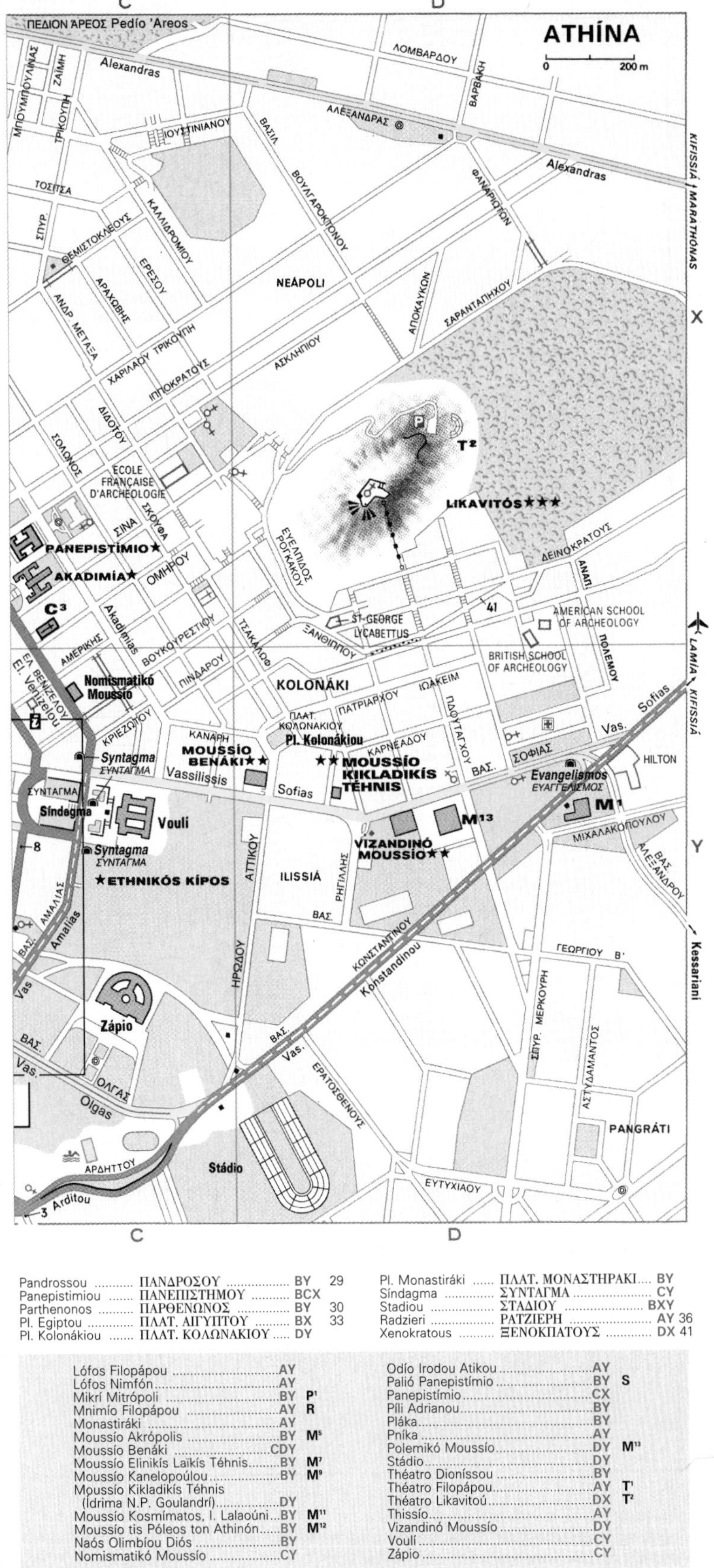

Pandrossou	ΠΑΝΔΡΟΣΟΥ	BY	29
Panepistimiou	ΠΑΝΕΠΙΣΤΗΜΟΥ	BCX	
Parthenonos	ΠΑΡΘΕΝΩΝΟΣ	BY	30
Pl. Egiptou	ΠΛΑΤ. ΑΙΓΥΠΤΟΥ	BX	33
Pl. Kolonákiou	ΠΛΑΤ. ΚΟΛΩΝΑΚΙΟΥ	DY	
Pl. Monastiráki	ΠΛΑΤ. ΜΟΝΑΣΤΗΡΑΚΙ	BY	
Síndagma	ΣΥΝΤΑΓΜΑ	CY	
Stadiou	ΣΤΑΔΙΟΥ	BXY	
Radzieri	ΡΑΤΖΙΕΡΗ	AY	36
Xenokratous	ΞΕΝΟΚΠΑΤΟΥΣ	DX	41

Lófos Filopápou	AY	
Lófos Nimfón	AY	
Mikrí Mitrópoli	BY	P¹
Mnimío Filopápou	AY	R
Monastiráki	AY	
Moussío Akrópolis	BY	M⁵
Moussío Benáki	CDY	
Moussío Elinikís Laïkís Téhnis	BY	M⁷
Moussío Kanelopoúlou	BY	M⁹
Moussío Kikladikís Téhnis (Ídrima N.P. Goulandrí)	DY	
Moussío Kosmímatos, I. Lalaoúni	BY	M¹¹
Moussío tis Póleos ton Athinón	BY	M¹²
Naós Olimbíou Diós	BY	
Nomismatikó Moussío	CY	
Odío Irodou Atikou	AY	
Palió Panepistímio	BY	S
Panepistímio	CX	
Píli Adrianou	BY	
Pláka	BY	
Pníka	AY	
Polemikó Moussío	DY	M¹³
Stádio	DY	
Théatro Dioníssou	BY	
Théatro Filopápou	AY	T¹
Théatro Likavitoú	DX	T²
Thissío	AY	
Vizandinó Moussío	DY	
Voulí	CY	
Zápio	CY	

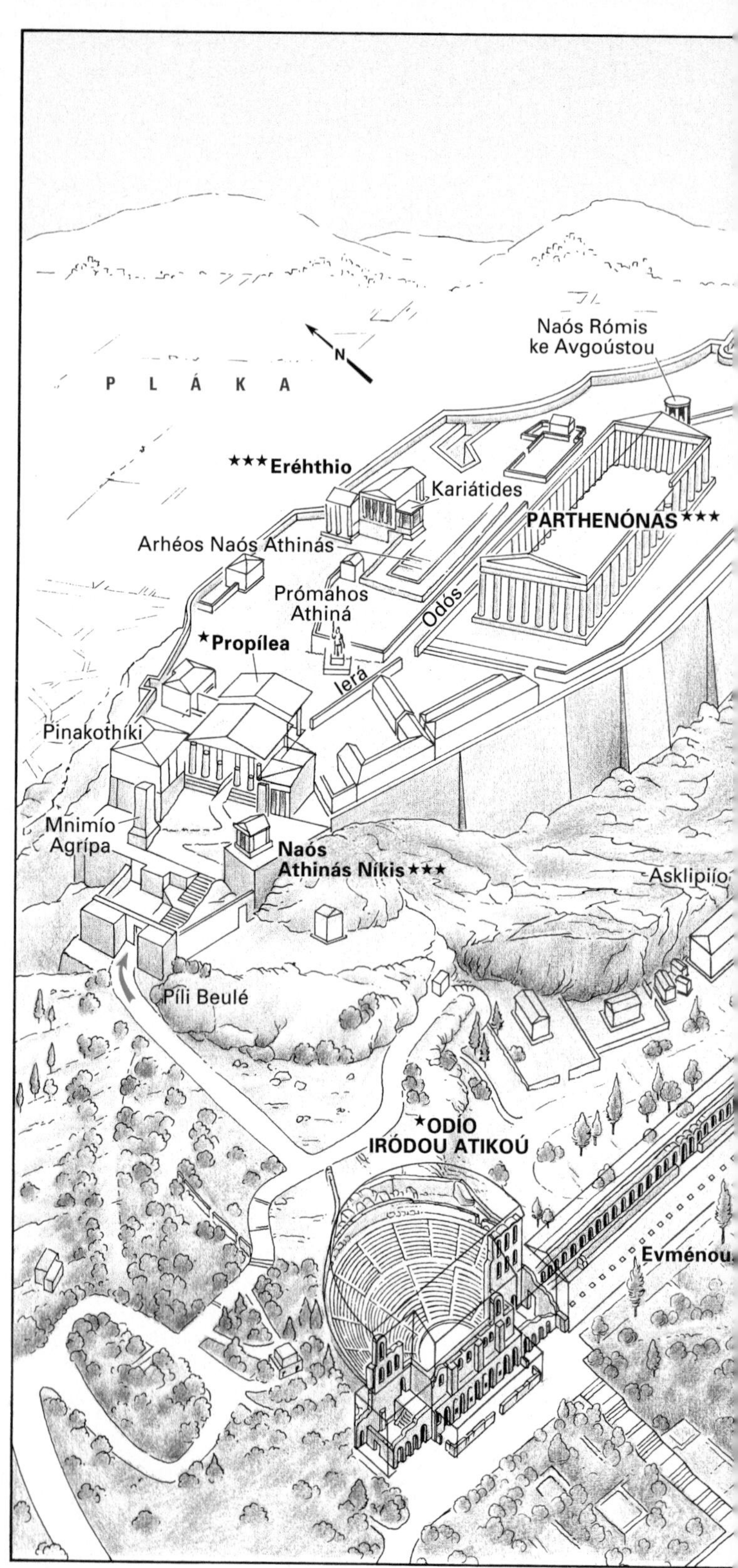

In summer it is advisable to avoid visiting archeological sites in the middle of the day owing to the intense heat and reflection

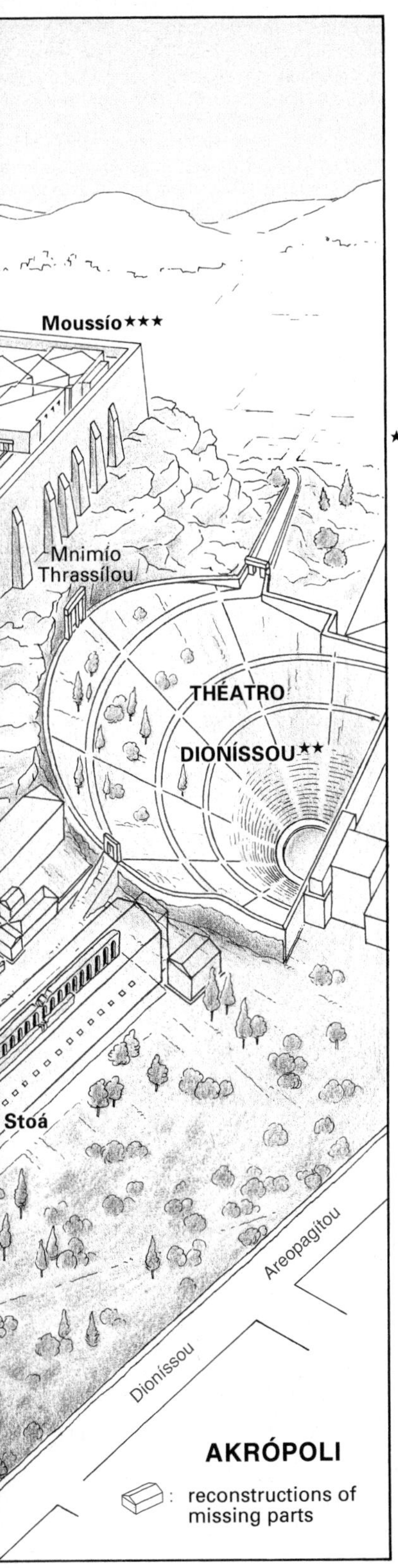

The western façade was altered in the Roman period. The olive tree in the adjoining courtyard was planted as a reminder that the sacred olive tree of Athena was venerated in this temple. From the belvedere in the northeast corner of the site there are dramatic **views★★** over the Roman town *(east)* (Hadrian's Arch, temple of Zeus), down into the old district of Pláka *(north)* and over the suburbs to the northeast of Athens surrounded by the Parnes, Pentelikon and Hymettos ranges.

Make for the Acropolis Museum skilfully recessed in a hollow in the rock.

★★★ **Moussío** ⓥ (**Pláka**) – The Acropolis Museum is due to be transferred to a site near the Acropolis Interpretation Centre at the foot of the hill.
It contains the sculptures and other objects found during the excavation of the Acropolis, in particular a remarkable series of Archaic works. By the entrance is an owl in marble (beginning of 5C BC), the bird associated with Athena and the symbol of wisdom. The entrance hall contains a bust of Alexander the Great as a young man *(no 1331)* from the end of 4C BC; a statue of Procne *(no 1358)* preparing to kill her son Itys to take revenge on her husband Tireos, King of Thrace (first half of 5C BC); and the head of a philosopher *(no 1313)* (end of the first half of 5C BC). Rooms 1 *(entrance)* and 2 *(left)* display the pediments or fragments of pediments, carved and painted, which date from the 7C and 6C BC; these pieces are often in tufa rather than the marble of the Classical period. The subject of the sculptures is often the legend of Hercules (Herakles in Greek): Hercules and the capture of the many headed Hydra of Lerna *(no 1) (Room 1)*, the Apotheosis of Hercules by the Gods of Olympos from the old temple of Athena *(no 9) (Room 2)*, Hercules' struggle with Triton and a three headed monster *(no 35) (Room 2)*. Also in Room 2: a beautiful fragment (the forequarters) of a marble quadriga *(no 577)*, the Pediment of the Olive Tree or of Troilus *(no 52)* in tufa, showing the son of Priam killed by Achilles at the fountain with Athena's olive tree on the left, and above all the **Moscophoros** (no 624), a young man carrying a sacrificial calf, a painted marble statue with eyes originally of glass paste, a votive statue of about 570 BC; and a headless *kore (no 593)* in white marble, the oldest of the ones from the Acropolis (between 580 and 570 BC).

Room 3 presents a Bull being attacked by two lions *(no 3)* (between 570 and 560 BC) and a sphinx-like *acroterion (no 632)* dating from 540 to 530 BC; two *korai (no 619 and no 677)* from Náxos (first half of 6C BC); and two statues of seated women (lower body parts) dating from 520 BC. In Room 4 a seated figure of Athena *(no 625)* is surrounded by an important collection of statues of young women (**kore** in the singular, **korai** in the plural, in coloured marble (6C BC) with slight malicious smiles: early *korai* standing erect like columns *(no 679, 682, 684)*, Ionian *korai* richly ornamented *(no 682, 594, 670, 673, 675)*, Attic *korai* showing Ionian influence *(no 685, 683, 672)*, a dignified *kore* with almond eyes *(no 674)*, Attic *korai* more austere *(no 671, 669)*. The peplos *kore (no 679)* is attributed to Phaidimos, the oldest Attic sculptor to have been identified; also by him are an extraordinary life-like Dog *(no 143)*, a Lion's Head *(no 65)* and a smiling Horseman *(no 590* – the head is a copy); the original known as the Rampin Horseman is in the Louvre.

Room 5 contains four statues from the pediment (c 525 BC) from the old temple of Athena, which were part of a scene illustrating the Battle between the Gods and the Giants: Athena brandishing a lance. Among other remarkable works on show are the *kore* by Antenor *(no 681)* of 500 BC, a *kore (no 1360)* of great refinement from the end of 6C BC, the statue of Nike (Victory) in flight *(no 691)*, dating from about 500 BC, and the *kore* with the dove *(no 683)* of 510 BC.

Near the entrance *(left)* to Room 6 is the famous **Athena mourning** (no 695), a 5C votive relief; nearby is the "Fair Head" *(no 689)* of a young man in marble which was formerly coloured yellow (early 5C BC). Also in this room: young man's head in marble *(no 699)* from Pheidias' studio; the forequarters of a horse *(no 697)* (5C BC); headless torso of a young man *(no 692)* (490 BC) and the "Kritios Boy", an ephebe by Kritios (c 480 BC), also the Euthydikos *kore* (c 490 BC) *(no 686 and 609)*.

Room 7 is devoted to reconstructions of the Parthenon pediments: Birth of Athena, Quarrel between Athena and Poseidon. There is one original metope from the Doric frieze showing a Centaur abducting a Lapith woman *(no 705)*.

Room 8 contains sculptures removed from the temples: the Panathenaic procession from the Parthenon *(south frieze no 856, 857, 860, 862, 864, 865; north frieze nos 863, 872, 874, 871, 859, 868)*, and items from the temple of Athena Nike *(nos 972, 989, 994)* including the figure of **Nike** (Victory) *(no 973)* undoing her sandal before offering a sacrifice, a marvellously balanced and fluid figure.

In the last room the famous **caryatids** from the Erechtheion are displayed behind a protective glass screen.

On leaving the museum walk along the southern edge of the Acropolis hill: interesting views down over the theatres of Dionysos and Herod Atticus *(see below)*.

★★★ **Naós Athinás Níkis** – The **Temple of Athena Nike**, which was formerly but incorrectly known as the **temple of Nike Apteros** (Wingless Victory), stands on a projecting bastion west of the Propylaia overlooking the Sacred Way. According to legend, Theseus' father, old Aigeus, threw himself down from here believing his son to be dead, when he saw the black sail hoisted instead of the white on the vessel in which his son was returning from Crete after defeating the Minotaur *(see KNOSSÓS)*.

It was a small (8.27m x 5.44m/27ft x 18ft) but graceful Ionic temple (late 5C BC) which was reconstructed by the Bavarian archeologists of King Otto. It consisted of a chamber *(naós)* between two porticoes supported on monolithic columns. The *naós* contained a statue of Athena Nike (bringer of victory) which was later confused with the figure of Victory which was usually represented without wings *(apteros)*. The exterior frieze, which is badly damaged, comprises a few original pieces *(east and south sides)*; the rest is made up of copies.

From the temple there are extensive views south over the Attic plain, the coast at Piraeus and the Saronic Gulf.

Leave the Acropolis by the Beulé Gate and bear north to the Areopagos.

★ **Ários Págos (Areopagos)** – Theseus' enemies, the Amazons, camped on this limestone hill (115m/377ft high) and consecrated it to Ares, god of War. Another legend says that **Orestes**, who was being pursued by the Furies *(see KIPARISSÍA)*, the avenging divinities, for murdering his mother Clytemnestra, was judged here by the forerunner of the Council of the Areopagos which originally was a judicial tribunal and political assembly but later reduced to safeguarding laws and customs. In 375 BC the courtesan Phryne, friend and model of the sculptor Praxiteles, appeared before this open-air court on a charge of impiety and was acquitted; appealing to the jury in her defence Hyperides bared her bosom saying "Can such beauty be guilty?".

It was here too that **St Paul** is thought to have preached when he converted the senator who was to become **St Dionysius the Areopagite**, the first bishop of Athens; he was later confused with Dionysius, the Pseudo-Areopagite who invented the celestial hierarchy with nine choirs of angels.

Fine view of the Acropolis and of the Greek *agora* and Roman forum below.

★★ **Théatro Dioníssou (Theatre of Dionysos)** ⏲ – *Access: By trolleybus (nos 1, 5 or 9, "Makrigiani" stop) from Omónia or Síndagma Square.*

The first stage to be built on this spot was set up in the 6C BC within the sacred precinct dedicated to Dionysos Eleutherios where the Dionysiac Festivals consisting of mime, the chorus and the dancing of satyrs and maenads took place.

Early in the following century these rather basic facilities were improved by the addition of a real theatre equipped with wooden terraces where the great classical dramas were played: *The Persians* by Aeschylus, *Oedipus Rex* by Sophocles, *Medea* by Euripides and the *Wasps* by Aristophanes.
The present stone structure which dates from the time of Lycurgus (4C BC) provided 17 000 seats and was also used for the popular assemblies which had formerly been held on the Hill of the Pnyx.
Extensive alterations were carried out by the Romans. Following the barbarian invasions the theatre was abandoned and used for raising crops. It was restored by the German Archeological Society early in the 19C.
Beyond the remains of a temple to Dionysos and a portico lies the stage of the theatre; its foundations date from the 4C BC but it was rebuilt under Nero (1C AD): the front of the stage facing the orchestra is decorated with sculptures dating from this period which evoke the legend of Dionysos including a crouching Silenus. The marble paving of the orchestra describes a lozenge shape; at the centre stood the altar to Dionysos round which the chorus was grouped during the performances.
The terraces (4C BC) are partially preserved; they rose as high as the monument to Thrasyllos, 30m/98ft *(below)*. In the first row were the seats reserved for individuals bearing the names of the officials, priests and dignitaries who occupied them in the 2C AD; the one in the centre belonged to the priest of Dionysos and is decorated with lions, griffons, satyrs and grapes.
From the top there is a good view of the site; on the left are traces of the **Odeon of Pericles**, a covered theatre which was mostly used for rehearsals and music competitions.

Mnimío Thrassílou (Choregic monument of Thrasyllos) – There is nothing left but the pedestal of this votive monument, set up by Thrasyllos, a chorus-leader *(choregós)* in 4C BC, in honour of Dionysos, who was worshipped in the cave *(below)*, later converted into a chapel (Panagía Spiliotissa) for Christian worship. The two Corinthian columns above, which date from the Roman period, bore two choregic tripods.

Asklipiío (Asklepieion) – A long terrace west of the upper part of the theatre of Dionysos bears the remains of two sanctuaries to Asklepios (Aesculapius); one dates from the 4C BC *(east)* and the other *(west)* from the 5C BC. Each consisted of a small temple, a sacred spring where the sick were purified and a portico where they slept.

Stoá Evménous – Below the Asklepieion, facing south, is the *stoa* of Eumenes II, King of Pergamon, who had it built in the 2C BC. It was 163m/535ft long and comprised two storeys of colonnades; the column bases are clearly visible. The *stoa* was used as a shelter and promenade for the theatre of Dionysos and later for the Odeon of Herod Atticus.

★**Odío Iródou Atikoú (Odeon of Herod Atticus)** – *Access: By the same buses as for the Theatre of Dionysos. The Odeon is not open except for performances but there is a good view from the south path up to the Acropolis.*
The Odeon was built in memory of his wife, Annia Regilla by Herod Atticus, a Greek patron of Roman origin, who became an archon, consul and senator; it was completed in 161 BC and would then have had a cedarwood roof.
The **façade**★ is fairly well preserved; it is typically Roman with its round-headed doors and arches; there were three entrances. Inside it has been completely restored to provide a setting for the dramatic and lyric performances of the Athens Summer Festival: it can accommodate from 5 000 to 6 000 spectators.
It was through the ruins of the Odeon that help arrived for the besieged Greeks on the Acropolis on 17 December 1826 when Colonel Fabvier, a famous French Philhellene, accompanied by 500 volunteers broke through the Turkish blockade.

★★**Thissío ke Agorá** ⏱ – *Entrances in Leofóros Apostólou Pávlou (west), Odós Adrianóu (north) and the Panathenaic Way (southeast). From the Acropolis one can walk down the Sacred Way. Visitors are advised to begin with the Theseion (Hephaisteion).*

★★**Thisío** (Theseion) – This 5C BC Doric temple, one of the best preserved in the Greek world, stands on a mound (66m/217ft) dominating the *agora*, the centre of Athenian public life in antiquity.
Known since the Middle Ages as the **Theseion** (temple of Theseus), it is in fact the **Hephaisteion** mentioned by Pausanias, the temple of Hephaistos, god of smiths and metal workers who were as numerous then as they are today in the neighbouring district (Odós Iféstou).
In the Byzantine period the temple was converted into a church dedicated to St George and the entrance was moved to the west end. Under the Turks it became the burial place of Englishmen and other Protestants; some of the memorial plaques have been transferred to St Paul's Anglican Church *(see p 102)*. Even in the last century it was still out in the country and on Easter Sunday people would come from Athens dressed in their best to dance nearby. The last service was held

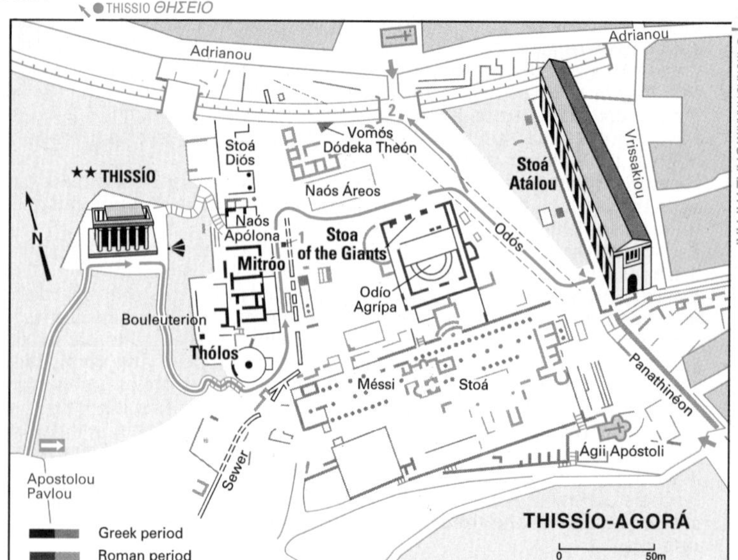

in 1834 when the building was used to house the first collections of the National Museum. Pomegranates and myrtle trees have been planted round the temple to recall the trees which covered the slopes in antiquity.

The Hephaisteion, which is older and smaller than the Parthenon, is built of stone rather than marble but it is well proportioned and was originally painted. It measures 31.77m x 13.72m/104ft x 45ft and has 26 columns down each side and 12 at each end which narrow towards the top and incline slightly inwards. The sculptures of the external frieze, which are badly damaged and difficult to discern, recall the exploits of Herakles (Hercules) and Theseus.

The east portico with its marble coffered ceiling still in place leads into the *naós*, which resembles the nave of a church with its doorways and barrel vaulting (5C AD); one of the funerary plaques on the north wall in memory of George Watson, who died in Athens in 1810, bears a Latin inscription by Byron.

The temple terrace offers fine views of the *agora*, the Monastiráki district and the Acropolis.

★**Arhéa Agorá** (Agora) – The *agora* which is now a confused jumble of ruins was originally a rectangular open space covering about 2.5ha/6 acres and divided diagonally by the Panathenaic Way which ran past the Altar of the Twelve Olympian Gods from which the distances to other Greek cities were measured. Large trees,

PICTOR

Church of the Holy Apostles and the Agorá, Athens

fountains, statues and votive offerings dotted the ground which was enclosed within administrative buildings, temples and shops, arranged in a long portico *(stoá)* where the idlers gathered to hear the news and listen to the orators.
The Romans encroached on the open space with buildings such as the Odeon of Agrippa and the temple of Ares. In AD 267 the *agora* was destroyed by barbarians. Under the Byzantines a district grew up around **Ágii Apóstoli** (the Church of the Holy Apostles – late 10C AD). Here in the late 18C to the early 19C lived Fauvel, French Consul during the Napoleonic Wars, who produced a plan of Athens and acted as guide. His house was more like a museum owing to the huge collection of antiquities he was amassing on behalf of Choiseul Gouffier, the French Ambassador in Constantinople. In 1931 the buildings were expropriated and demolished to clear the site for excavations by the American School of Archeology.
The **thólos**, which dates from about 470 BC, was a round building where the 50 senators *(prytaneis)*, responsible by turn for the government of the state, met to take their meals; the standard weights and measures were also kept here.
To the north of the *thólos* stood the **Metroon** (Mitróo), the temple of the Mother of the gods, behind which stood the Bouleuterion, the Senate house; beyond the Metroon stood the temple of Apollo Patroos and the Stoa of Zeus. Only the foundations of these buildings remain but there are also traces of a great drain which passed to the east of them and of pedestals for statues: one of them bears the likeness of Emperor Hadrian (1).
Turning east one sees the **Stoa of the Giants**, named in modern times after the Giant and two Tritons which originally decorated the Odeon of Agrippa, a covered chamber for 1 000 people which was built by the son-in-law of Emperor Augustus, destroyed by the barbarians and converted into a gymnasium in about 400 AD; there is little left.
The **Stoá Atálou**, which was built in the 2C BC by **Attalos**, King of Pergamon, has been reconstructed. It is a long (116m x 19.5m/380ft x 64ft), two-storey building which displays the articles found during the excavations in the *agora*. The external gallery displays the Apollo Patroos (4C BC), which is headless, and the interior gallery contains objects from everyday life in antiquity, an *amphora* with a seated sphinx (7C BC) and a Spartan shield in bronze (5C BC) *(centre)*.

Near the entrance in Odós Adrianóu there is a mosaic reconstruction (2) *showing the Agorá as it was in antiquity.*

OLD ATHENS *2hr 30min*

On the northern slopes of the Acropolis old Athens still survives in the Pláka and Monastiráki, the only districts in the capital which can evoke the atmosphere of Athens in the Middle Ages or during the Turkish occupation. The conservation of the old buildings and the exclusion of traffic have greatly enhanced the charm of the area.

★★Pláka

Particularly in the steeper part Pláka consists of picturesque and peaceful narrow streets and alleys opening out into tiny squares and terraces linked by steps. There are a few Byzantine churches tucked in between the old houses with their pantile roofs and wooden balconies; sometimes the plume of a cypress or pine tree or the straggling branches of a fig betray the existence of a hidden garden. Here and there one catches a glimpse of the city or the Acropolis. The broader streets below the slope are thronged with shops and inexpensive guest-houses.
After dark Pláka comes alive. The tavernas with their cavernous rooms decorated with barrels and their trellis covered terraces are illuminated with multicoloured lights: crowds of Athenians and tourists tarry late into the night, savouring the Greek cuisine with glasses of *retsína*, listening to the *bouzoúki* (electric guitar) music and the latest singers and dancing the modern *sirtáki*. As well as the tavernas there are nightclubs where food and drink are offered together with a show which is well done when it is based on traditional music.

From the southwest corner of Síndagma Square take Odós Mitropóleos.

On the left under the arcade of a modern building is the tiny chapel of Agía Dínami (17C). The street opens into a square, Platía Mitropóleos: the Orthodox cathedral, which is known as the **Megáli Mitrópoli** (Great Metropolitan) and dates from the 19C, dwarfs its neighbour the Small (or Old) Metropolitan.

★★**Mikrí Mitrópoli** – The **Small Metropolitan**, which is dedicated to the Virgin who answers prayers swiftly (Panagía Gorgoepíkoos), is a charming 12C Byzantine church built on the Greek cross plan with a dome; its modest proportions reflect the general height of houses in Athens at that period.
Incorporated in the external walls are many decorative pieces from an earlier age: between the two Corinthian capitals flanking the façade stretches an unusual ancient frieze (4C BC) showing the months and the signs of the Zodiac together

with their corresponding festivals or activities. There are also several 9C-10C AD low reliefs of symbolic Christian motifs: lions flanking a cross *(door lintel)*; griffins feeding on the eucharistic grape and peacocks drinking at the source of eternal life. On the other hand the cross with a double bar and the arms of the La Roche and de Villehardouin families *(pediment)* were added in the Frankish period (13C). Other sculpted marbles, both ancient and Byzantine, decorate the side walls and the chevet: low relief from the Archaic period showing some dancing girls.

Take the streets going south and west, Odós Paleologou Venizélou, Odós Erehthéos and Odós Kirístou, to reach the Tower of the Winds.

★**Aérides** ⓥ – This **Tower of the Winds** is an octagonal building (12.8m/42ft high) in white marble which dates from the reign of Julius Caesar (1C BC) and was then part of the Roman forum. It takes its name from the carved winged figures (one

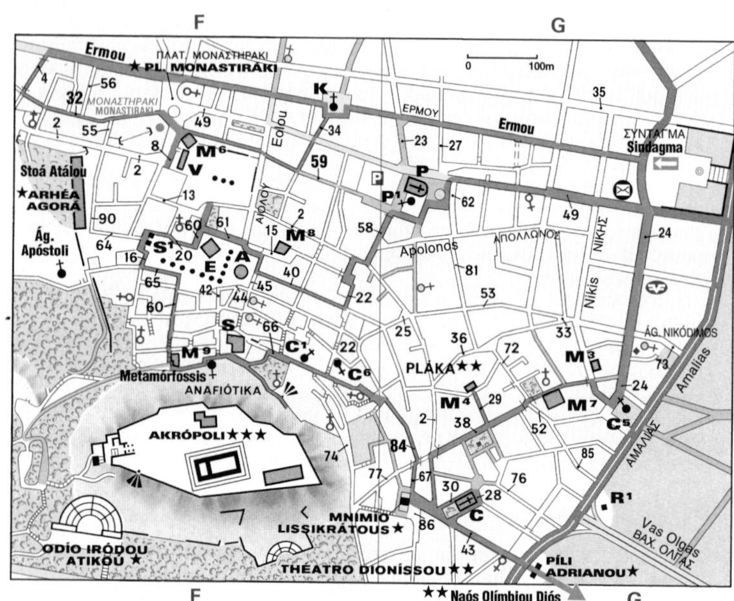

PLÁKA

Adrianou	ΑΔΡΙΑΝΟΥ	F 2
Ag. Filipou	ΑΓ. ΦΙΛΙΠΠΟΥ	F 4
Areos	ΑΡΕΩΣ	FG 8
Dexipou	ΔΕΞΙΠΠΟΥ	F 13
Diogenous	ΔΙΟΓΕΝΟΥΣ	F 15
Dioskouron	ΔΙΟΣΚΟΥΡΩΝ	F 16
Epaminonda	ΕΠΑΜΕΙΝΩΝΔΑ	F 20
Erehtheos	ΕΡΕΧΘΕΩΣ	F 22
Ermou	ΕΡΜΟΥ	F
Evangelistrias	ΕΥΑΓΓΕΛΙΣΤΡΙΑΣ	G 23
Filelinon	ΦΙΛΕΛΛΗΝΩΝ	G 24
Flessa	ΦΛΕΣΣΑ	G 25
Fokionos	ΦΩΚΙΩΝΟΣ	G 27
Galanou	ΓΑΛΑΝΟΥ	G 28
Geronda	ΓΕΡΟΝΤΑ	G 29
Herefondos	ΧΑΙΡΕΦΩΝΤΟΣ	G 30
Ifestou	ΗΦΑΙΣΤΟΥ	F 32
Iperidou	ΥΠΕΡΕΙΔΟΥ	G 33
Kapnikareas	ΚΑΠΝΙΚΑΡΕΑΣ	F 34
Kar. Servias	ΚΑΡ. ΣΕΡΒΙΑΣ	G 35
Kekropos	ΚΕΚΡΟΠΟΣ	G 36
Kidathineon	ΚΥΔΑΘΗΝΑΙΩΝ	G 38
Kiristou	ΚΥΡΡΗΣΤΟΥ	F 40
Klepsidras	ΚΛΕΨΥΔΡΑΣ	F 42
Lissikratous	ΛΥΣΙΚΡΑΤΟΥΣ	G 43
Lissiou	ΛΥΣΙΟΥ	F 44
Markou Avriliou	ΜΑΡΚΟΥ ΑΥΡΗΛΙΟΥ	F 45
Mitropoleos	ΜΗΤΡΟΠΟΛΕΩΣ	F 49
Monis Asteriou	ΜΟΝΗΣ ΑΣΤΕΡΙΟΥ	G 52
Navarhou Nikodimou	ΝΑΥΑΡΧΟΥ ΝΙΚΟΔΗΜΟΥ	G 53
Nissou	ΝΙΣΟΥ	F 55
Normanou	ΝΟΡΜΑΝΟΥ	F 56
Paleologou Benizelou	ΠΑΛΑΙΟΛΟΓΟΥ ΜΠΕΝΙΖΕΛΟΥ	FG 58
Pandrossou	ΠΑΝΔΡΟΣΟΥ	F 59
Panos	ΠΑΝΟΣ	F 60
Pelopida	ΠΕΛΟΠΙΔΑ	F 61
Pl. Mitropoleos	ΠΛΑΤ. ΜΗΤΡΟΠΟΛΕΩΣ	G 62
Pl. Monastiráki	ΠΛΑΤ. ΜΟΝΑΣΤΗΡΑΚΙ	F
Pikilis	ΠΟΙΚΙΛΗΣ	F 64
Polignotou	ΠΟΛΥΓΝΩΤΟΥ	F 65
Pritaniou	ΠΡΥΤΑΝΕΙΟΥ	F 66
Selei	ΣΕΛΛΕΥ	G 67
Síndagma	ΣΥΝΤΑΓΜΑ	G
Sotiros	ΣΩΤΗΡΟΣ	G 72
Souri	ΣΟΥΡΗ	G 73
Stratonos	ΣΤΡΑΤΩΝΟΣ	F 74
Thalou	ΘΑΛΟΥ	G 76
Thespidos	ΘΕΣΠΙΔΟΣ	FG 77
Thoukididou	ΘΟΥΚΥΔΙΔΟΥ	G 81
Tripodon	ΤΡΙΠΟΔΩΝ	G 84
Tsangari	ΤΣΑΓΚΑΡΗ	G 85
Vironos	ΒΥΡΩΝΟΣ	G 86
Vrissakiou	ΒΡΥΣΑΚΙΟΥ	F 90

Aérides	F	A
Agía Ekateríni	G	C
Agii Anárgiri	F	C[1]
Ágios Pávlos (Anglikanikí Eklissía)	G	C[5]
Ágios Ioánis o Theológos	F	C[6]
Dzamí Fetiye	F	E
Evraïkó Moussío tis Elládas	G	M[3]
Kapnikaréa	F	K
Kéndro Laïkís Téhnis ke Parádossis Dímou Athinéon	G	M[4]
Megáli Mitrópoli	G	P
Metamórfossis	F	
Mikrí Mitrópoli	G	P[1]
Mnimío Lissikrátous	G	
Mnimío Lórdou Vírona	G	R[1]
Moussío Akrópolis	F	M[5]
Moussío Elinikís Laikis Keramikis (Palió Dzamí Dzistaráki)	F	M[6]
Moussío Elinikís Laïkis Téhnis	G	M[7]
Moussío Elinikón Moussikón Orgánon	F	M[8]
Moussío Kanelopoúlou	F	M[9]
Naós Olímbiou Diós	G	
Palío Panepistímio	F	S
Píli Adrianou	G	
Romaïkí Agorá	F	S[1]
Vivliothíki Adrianoú	F	V

on each face) which are identified by inscriptions and represent the winds which blow in Athens.
On the north side, facing Odós Eólou, is **Boreas**, the cold north wind, shown as a bearded man blowing into a conch shell; on the west the gentle **Zephyr** strews flowers from her lap.
In fact the tower was built to house a hydraulic clock invented by Andronikos of Kyrrhos in Syria or Macedonia. The water supply came from the **Klepsídra spring** on the north slope of the Acropolis hill whence came the word *clepsydra* meaning a water clock. The semicircular tower attached to the south face was the reservoir from which the water flowed in a steady stream into a cylinder in the main tower; the time was indicated by the level of the water in the cylinder; the northwest door of the tower stood open so that people could consult the clock.

T.A.P.

Tower of the Winds, Athens

In the 6C the tower was converted into a chapel; under the Turkish occupation it became a Muslim convent *(tekké)*, and in the 18C it was occupied by whirling dervishes. At that period it was thought to have been the tomb of Socrates.
North of the tower by Odós Eólou are the remains of an 18C Muslim seminary *(medréssa)*.

Romaikí Agorá (Roman Forum) – Walk round in an anti-clockwise direction *(Odós Diogénous and Odós Pelopida)* passing an old 16C mosque, the **Fetihie Cami**, with domes and an attractive columned porch. Take a few steps in Odós Panos to the right to enjoy a view of Hadrian's Library. Then walk back down to Odós Epaminonda for an interesting view of the Acropolis and the north side of the Erechtheion. Architectural elements from ancient monuments have been reused in the rock's supporting wall.
On the west side stands the monumental Forum gateway completed by the Romans in the 2C AD with funds provided first by Julius Caesar and then by Augustus. The gateway consists of four columns supporting a pediment and gave access to the forum proper; the interior court, which was paved with marble and surrounded by a peristyle, has been excavated.

Walk south down Odós Dioskoúron, turn left into Odós Polignotou and right into Odós Panos; towards the end of the street on the corner by the Kanellopoulos Museum (see p 101) turn left.

A little way along on the right stands the small **Church of the Transfiguration** (Metamórfossis) which dates from the 12C-14C; its dome of semicircular tiles rises above the houses of the semi-rural district of Anafiótika which was founded by refugees from Anaphe in the Cyclades.
Below and to the north of the church lies the **"old university"** (Palió Panepistímio) (19C) which was originally the house of the architect **Kleanthes**. It housed the first university founded by the new Greek State in 1837 which later moved to its present site. The building is now used for exhibitions.

Turn right and continue for 100m/110yd up an alleyway which climbs above the Anafiótika quarter.

A fine **view★★**, especially beautiful at sunset, unfolds over the roofs of the old quarters, beyond to the town centre dominated by Lycabettos, southeast to Hymettos and the white stadium set amid the greenery, south to the columns of the Olympieion at the far end of the National Garden (Ethnikós Kípos), and north, left of Lycabettos, to the suburbs spreading up the slope of Pentelikon while to the east the town stretches to the foot of Mount Parnes.

Continue east along Odós Pritaniou.

The **Church of Ágii Anárgirii** *(left)*, a 17C building, stands near two tall cypress trees in the courtyard of the convent of the Holy Sepulchre. Further on stands the 12C **Chapel of St John the Evangelist** (Ágios Ioánnis o Theológos).

Bear round to the south.

Odós Tripódon – The **Street of the Tripods** is a very ancient street, linking the theatre of Dionysos *(see above)* to the *Agorá*, where the winners in the Dionysiac Games used to erect choregic monuments supporting the bronze tripods which they received as prizes.

★**Mnimío Lissikrátous (Lysicrates' Monument)** – The only survivor of the votive monuments in Odós Tripódon was erected in 334 BC. Subsequently in 1669 it was incorporated in the French Capuchin convent where many Christian travellers, such as Sir George Wheler, Richard Chandler and Lord Byron, used to stay during the Turkish occupation. The monument was used by the holy fathers as a library and was known as the **Lantern of Demosthenes** since tradition wrongly asserted that the great orator had worked there on his speeches.
The monument of Lysicrates escaped the turmoil of the War of Independence, which destroyed the convent, and was restored in 1845 by the French School of Archeology in Athens; it is still French property.
The monument is in the form of a rotunda, 10.20m/about 33.5ft high; its six columns with their remarkable Corinthian capitals are linked by white marble plaques. Above runs the dedicatory inscription together with a carved frieze showing Dionysos changing pirates into dolphins, which is presumed to be the subject of the drama competition which Lysicrates won. The roof consists of a single marble plaque topped by several acanthus leaves which supported the tripod, now disappeared. Recent excavations have uncovered the bases of other similar monuments.
Further east on the far side of a shady square stands **St Catherine's Church** (Agía Ekateríni) ; it was built in the 13C but has been altered several times since.

Proceed along Odós Lissikratous to Leofóros Amalias.

★**Píli Adrianoú (Hadrian's Arch)** – It dates from c 131 BC. An inscription in the frieze indicates that the arch divided the Greek city from Hadrian's new Roman city (Hadrianopolis) which extended from the present-day Leofóros Amalias as far as the River Ilissós *(east)* which is now covered. A short distance from the gate stands a monument to Lord Byron *(see p 28)*.

★★**Naós Olímbiou Diós (Olympieion)** ⌚ – There are only few traces beyond Hadrian's Arch of the temple to Olympian Zeus which was one of the largest in the Greek world (107.45m x 41m/352ft x 134ft). As early as the 6C BC the Peisistratids *(see p 71)* had chosen this site for a colossal temple; a few drums have been found but the work was interrupted when they fell from power and not resumed until the 2C BC but construction was again halted some time later. The temple was not completed until AD 132 under Emperor Hadrian who also erected a colossal statue of Zeus. The barbarians wrecked the temple which was used as a stone quarry in the Middle Ages. Of the 84 original marble columns only 15 remain. Even today the Corinthian columns are impressive owing to their width and height; Chateaubriand compared them to Egyptian palm trees.

Make for Odós Kidathinéon; turn left to reach Odós A Hatzimiháli and the Centre for Popular Art and Traditions (see p 101); return to Odós Kidathinéon which contains the Museum of Greek Folk Art (see p 99); at the next corner turn right into Odós Nikis to visit St Paul's Anglican Church.

Turn north into Odós Filelínon to visit the **Russian Church of St Nicodemus** (Ágios Nikódimos), an 11C building with a dome, which was altered in the last century.

★Monastiráki

This was the centre of the Turkish town with the bazaar and the souks as well as the main mosques and administrative buildings. Now it is a popular commercial district incorporating the Athens flea market.

Start from Síndagma Square. Go west down **Odós Ermoú**, a busy shopping street lined with boutiques selling feminine apparel, dress materials and ready-to-wear clothes, furs and shoes, leather goods and jewellery.

Kapnikaréa – The church, which stands in the middle of the street at road level, is attached to the University of Athens and probably takes its name from one of its founders. In fact it is a double church consisting of two adjoining chapels, one *(right)* dates from 11C and is built on the Greek cross plan, the other dates from the 13C and is roofed with a dome. The narthex joining the two was also built in the 13C. Although in the Byzantine style, the paintings are in fact modern.

Walk south down Odós Kapnikaréas and turn right into Odós Pandróssou.

★**Odós Pandróssou** – This is a narrow street, thronged with busy crowds; it resembles a market with awnings and pavement stalls where the proprietors stand touting for custom. There is an amazing range of articles for sale: Turkish slippers, shoes with pompoms *(tsaroúhias)*, carpets and embroidery, *palikares'* belts, gold and copper work, incised or embossed, icons and ceramics etc.
On the left was the entrance to the bazaar, a market set up in the ruins of Hadrian's Library which burned down in 1885.

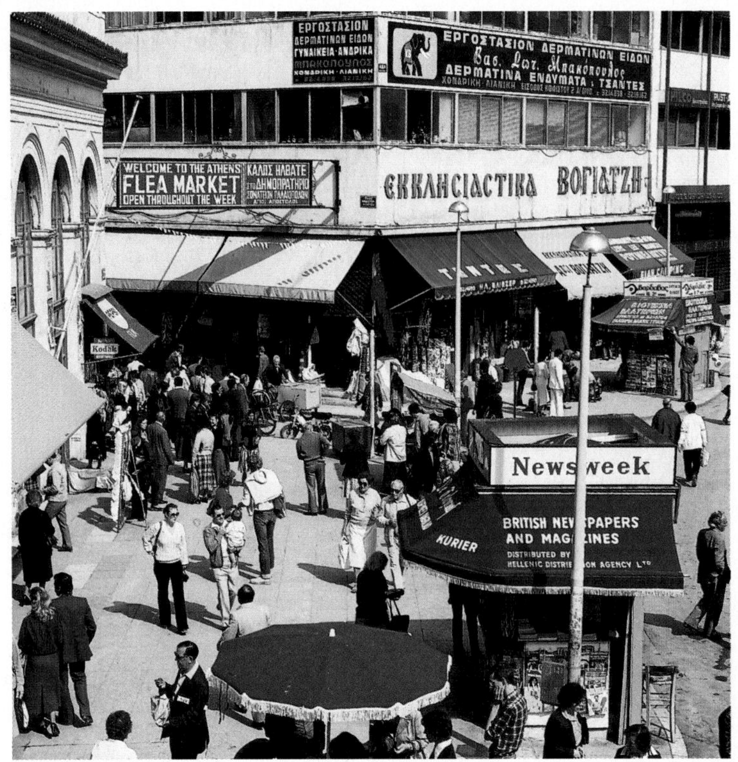

PICTOR

Monastiráki, Athens

★**Platia Monastiráki** – This square, with its frippery goods displayed on open-air stalls, is one of the attractions of Athens; it is always very lively, particularly in the morning. The church, **Pandánassa**, is a 17C building heavily restored, which originally belonged to the convent from which the square takes its name.
At the junction of Odós Pandróssou with Odós Áreos stands the former **Dzistaráki Mosque** (1759); it has lost its minaret but it was skilfully restored in 1975 to house the **Moussío Elinikís Laikís Keramikís** (Museum of Traditional Greek Ceramics) ⓥ: pottery and porcelain from the different regions are pleasantly displayed in the setting of a Muslim place of worship with its *mihrab* (recess facing Mecca) and its galleries.

Vivliothíki Adrianoú (Hadrian's Library) – The destruction by fire of the bazaar in 1885 made it possible to investigate the remains of **Hadrian's Library** built by the Emperor in 132 BC and described by Pausanias.
It was an impressive rectangular building, 122m x 82m/400ft x 269ft, with a peristyle of 100 columns, which was devastated by the barbarians and restored in the 5C AD when a quatrefoil building was constructed in the library courtyard; this building was subsequently replaced by two churches, one in the 7C, the other in 11C-12C; the remaining columns belonged to the 7C church.
The façade containing the entrance (Odós Áreos) is quite well preserved, particularly the Corinthian colonnade which is made of Euboian marble. It is about half the length of the original façade which preceded the courtyard where the foundations of the Byzantine church are visible. The Library proper, where the books were housed, stood on the far side of the courtyard. *Excavations in progress by Odós Eolou.*

Return to Monastiráki Square and continue westwards along **Odós Iféstou**, the street which is named after Hephaistos, the god to whom the nearby temple, the Hephaisteion (Theseion) is dedicated. Nowadays as in antiquity it is devoted to metal workers, particularly coppersmiths.

★★★MUSEUMS

Ethnikó Arheologikó Moussío ⓥ – *Access by trolleybus – nos 2, 4, 5, 11 – from outside the National Garden (Ethnikós Kípos) near Síndagma Square.*
The **National Archeological Museum**, which is one of the richest in the world, is devoted to ancient art from the Neolithic period to the Roman era and displays the major works of art from the Greek archeological sites, except for Macedonia, Delphi,

Olympia and Crete. It was founded in 1834 in the Hephaisteion (Theseion) and transferred in 1874 to the present neo-Classical buildings which were later enlarged. Sculpture is displayed on the ground floor, ceramics on the first floor as well as frescoes and ceramics from Santoríni.
It is easier to envisage the exhibits in their original setting and period and therefore more worthwhile to visit the Museum after seeing the main archeological sites on the mainland and the islands.

Neolithic (8000-3000 BC) **and Cycladic** (3000-2000 BC) **antiquities:**

Room 5. Idols, notably the idol of the Goddess with child *(kourotrophos, no 5937)* and a seated male idol *(no 5894)*, and ceramics originating in Thessaly in particular, and jewellery (earrings) from Polióhni *(see LÍMNOS)* similar in style to finds made at Troy.

Room 6. Vases and stylised marble idols with rounded contours originating in the Cyclades *(see KIKLÁDES)*: near the entrance a female figure of the earth-mother goddess from Amorgós *(no 3978)* and the celebrated harp player *(no 3908)* and flute player *(no 3910)*. The shape and decoration of the vases, especially the examples from Filakopí (Melos), recall the Santoríni ceramics.

Mycenaean antiquities (16C-11C BC):

Room 4. This room, the most famous in the museum, is mainly devoted to the finds from the excavations conducted at Mycenae since 1876 by Schliemann and his successors. There are also objects from the same period found on other sites in the Peloponnese such as Tiryns, Árgos and Pylos:
1 – in the case *(no 3)* left of the entrance, the **"mask of Agamemnon"** *(no 624)*, the famous funerary mask of an Achaian king discovered by Schliemann in the Mycenae acropolis (5th tomb in the 1st circle) and believed by him to be the mask of Agamemnon; in the same case, bronze daggers *(no 8839)* with blades encrusted with gold, silver and enamel (Mycenae, same tomb); in a neighbouring case, hexagonal wooden box covered with embossed gold plate showing lions pursuing deer (same tomb) *(no 811)*
2 – a flask *(rhyton)* used for libations in the shape of a **bull's head** *(no 2947, second case on the right)*, in silver with gold horns and muzzle and a gold rosette (Mycenae, 4th tomb in 1st circle)
3 – a shallow vessel, like a sauceboat, in the shape of a duck *(no 8638, fourth case on the left)* made of rock crystal (tomb in 2nd circle)
4 – a woman's or sphinx's head *(no 4575, fifth case on the left)* in limestone painted so as to pick out the features in vivid colours (Mycenae: house on the acropolis)
5 – two admirable **Vapheio Cups** in embossed gold *(no 1758 and 1759)*, discovered at Vafió near Sparta and decorated with scenes showing (on one) the capture of a bull and (on the other) the animal's domestication by man; in the last case in the centre, a seal ring in gold: spirits with lions' heads offer libations to a goddess holding a cup (Tiryns Treasury).

Room 3. Finds from the Mycenean period discovered at sites in central Greece, in Thessaly and on Skópelos.

Return to the entrance hall and turn right into Room 7.

Geometric and Archaic art (10C-6C BC):

Room 7. The main attraction is the huge geometric *amphora* (6) *(no 804)* dating from the mid 8C which had been placed on a tomb in the Kerameikos cemetery: the key pattern decoration frames a funeral cortège.

Room 8. The "Dipylon Head" *(no 3372)* which was found near the gate of the same name *(see below)* is beautifully sculpted, particularly the hair; it belonged to a funerary *kouros* standing on a tomb. The huge votive *kouros* from Sounion (7) *(no 2720)* once stood in front of the first temple to Poseidon erected on Cape Sounion.

Room 9. Several *kouroi* or *korai* from the Cyclades and Attica including at the far end on the left the crowned *kore* Phrasikleia *(no 4889)* clad in a dress decorated with flowers. Also the statue of Winged Victory from Delos *(no 21)*.

Room 10. In the middle stands a very fine *kouros (no 1906)* found at Volomandra in Attica at the same time as the *kore* Phrasikleia. Funerary *steles.*

Return to Room 8 and walk through to Room 11.

Room 11. The most remarkable exhibit here is the funerary *stele* of Aristion, the **"warrior of Marathon"** (8), sculpted by Aristokles *(no 25)* who signed his name at the bottom. There is also a painted female head *(no 62)* in the case opposite.

Room 12. An unusual tombstone shows a "running hoplite" or a Pyrrhic dancer *(no 1959)*.

Room 13. It contains a superb funerary *kouros* (9) *(no 3851)* from Anávissos in Attica: an inscription states that the statue used to decorate the tomb of Kroisos. The statue of Aristodikos *(no 3938)*, one of the later *kouroi*, shows the transition from Archaic to Classical art. Two bases of statues *(no 3476 and 3477)* discovered in Themistocles' wall *(see above: Historical Notes)* are decorated with low reliefs showing youth's *(ephebes)* practising physical exercises: wrestling, throwing, hockey and chariot racing, and a cat and dog fight.

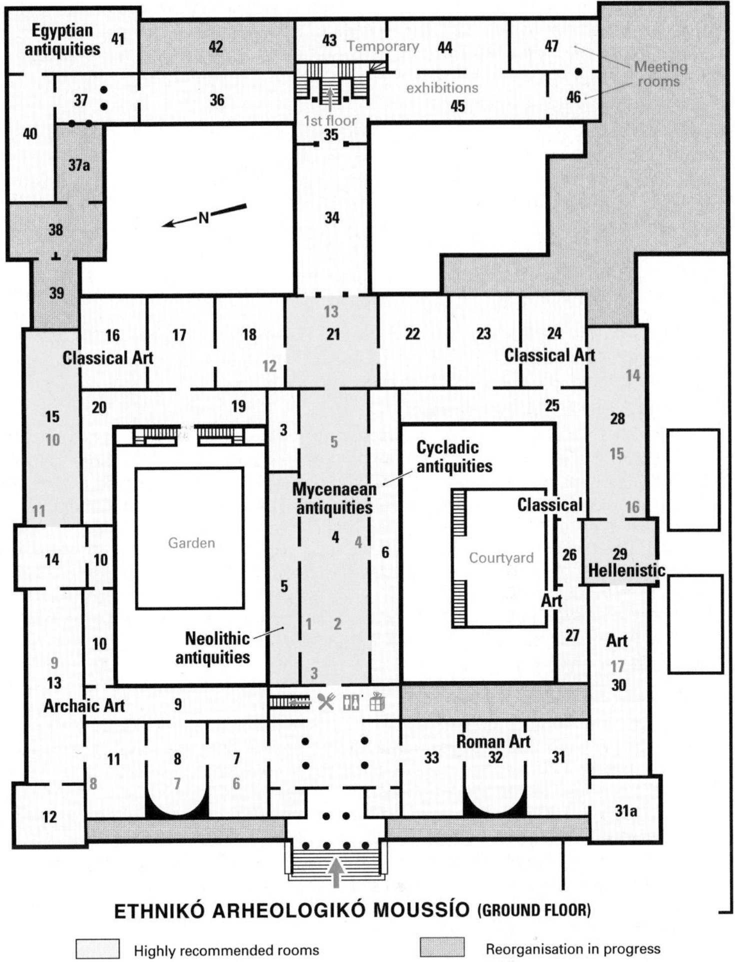

ETHNIKÓ ARHEOLOGIKÓ MOUSSÍO (GROUND FLOOR)

Room 14. Among the tombstones and votive tablets there is a votive relief in honour of a girl named Amphotto *(no 739)* holding an apple (c 44 BC); also the Attic relief of the ephebe crowning himself *(no 3344)* found at Cape Sounion.

Classical art (5C-4C-3C BC):

Room 15. Two of the museum's masterpieces are exhibited here:

(10) The extraordinary **Artemision Poseidon** *(no 15161)*, a bronze statue c 460-450 BC which was salvaged from the sea off Cape Artemision at the northern end of Euboia. The Sea god held the symbolic trident in his right hand; the figure is superbly posed with a delicate and noble head, although the ivory eyeballs are missing from the sockets.

(11) The **Eleusinian Relief** *(no 126)* (c 440-430 BC) is admirable for its solemnity and the composition of the figures; Demeter *(left)*, the goddess of fertility and protector of agriculture, accompanied by her daughter Persephone, is presenting an ear of corn to Triptolemos, son of the king of Eleusis, who has been entrusted with teaching agriculture to the human race.

Room 16. The great Myrrhine *lekythos (no 4485)* found in Síndagma Square stands out in the midst of the funerary *steles*. Hermes in the centre leads the young woman to the Acheron; on the left relatives bid her farewell.

Room 17. This contains Classical sculptures and votive reliefs; worth seeing are the relief dedicated to Hermes and the Nymphs *(no 1738)* and a second dedicated to Dionysos *(no 1500)*.

Rooms 19 and 20. Classical sculpture: copies of the original Classical 5C and 4C BC statues, in particular the Parthenon Athena, a lost work by Pheidias.

Room 18. Hegeso's tombstone (12) *(no 3624)*, formerly in the Kerameikos, shows a young girl sitting on an unusually elegant seat: she is studying a piece of jewellery taken from a coffer presented by her servant. It is dated c 410 BC and is attributed to Kallimachos, a pupil of Pheidias.

Room 21. The astonishing Horse and **Jockey of Artemision** (13) *(no 15177)* is a 2C BC Hellenistic bronze which, like the Poseidon, was salvaged from the sea off Cape Artemision; the galloping horse and the spirited rider are vigorously sculpted.

Rooms 34 and 35. Sculptures of various periods and votive reliefs are exhibited here.

Turn left at the end of the hall.

Room 36. The Karapános collection consists of figurines and various small bronze items from 8C BC to 3C BC. The most remarkable are those from the sanctuary of Zeus at Dodona (Epiros). Note the little statue of Zeus *(no 16546)*, a horse *(no 16547)* and a statuette of an armed man *(no 16727)*.

Room 37. This room houses objects from various sources on the islands, in Thessaly and northwest Greece, in Olympia, on Crete and in the Peloponnese from the 8C BC to 4C BC. Note the Athena Promachos from the Acropolis *(no 6447)*.

Return to the hall (Room 34) and Room 21.

Room 22. Interesting series of 4C BC sculptures from the temple of Asklepios (Aesculapius) at Epidauros; attractive *acroteria*.

Rooms 23 and 24. Funerary monuments of 4C BC.

Rooms 25 to 27. Votive reliefs of 4C BC.

Room 28. Four remarkable works attract attention. A high relief (14) *(no 4464)* of a spirited horse held by a black slave comes from a 2C BC funerary monument found in Athens in 1948 near Lárissa station; this lively and realistic work shows the transition from Classical to Hellenistic art. The Ephebe of Antikythera (15), a statue in bronze of 4C BC *(no 13396)* which was found in the sea off the isle of Antikíthera, shows Paris offering the apple *(missing)* to Aphrodite. A stone head of Hygeia (16) *(no 3602)* with soft lines and an introspective expression is attributed to Skopas. The bronze Ephebe of Marathon *(no 15118)* was retrieved from the Bay of Marathon; it is a 4C Classical work of such plasticity and elegance that it may have come from the school of Praxiteles.

Hellenistic art (3C-2C BC):

Room 29. Hellenistic sculptures.

Room 30. This room is dominated by the colossal and dramatic statue of Poseidon of Melos (17) *(no 235)* (2C BC) and by two bronze portraits which are decidedly individualistic and astonishingly expressive: a philosopher's head *(no 13400)* (3C BC) salvaged at the same time as the Ephebe of Antikythera and a man's head *(no 14162)* (c 100 BC) excavated on Delos. A small stone statue of a child wearing a cape with a hood and holding a dog *(no 3485)* is known as "the little refugee" as it was found at Smyrna in 1922 and brought back to Athens at the same time as refugees from Asia Minor were arriving in Greece. Note the group with Aphrodite, Eros and Pan *(no 3355)* (c 100 BC) and a marble statue of the goddess Artemis *(no 1829)*, both found on Delos.

Roman Art

Room 31. Works from various Greek schools of the Roman period (1C BC).

Room 31a. Portraits, honorary inscriptions, *steles* and reliefs (2 and 3C AD).

Rooms 32 and 33. Greek works from the Roman period (2 and 3C AD).

Continue to Room 40.

Collection of Egyptian Antiquities

Rooms 40 and 41. This fine collection (the **Dimitriou Collection**) of Egyptian antiquities from the pre-dynastic period to the Ptolemaic period (5000 BC-1C BC) is the fourth most important in Europe, consisting of 7 000 items, of which only 311 are currently on display.
There are notable statues (in wood, granite, clay, alabaster and bronze), jars, vases, *amphorae*, fragments of knives, votive reliefs (some of them double-sided), scarabs, tablets covered in hieroglyphics, sarcophagi, funerary masks and statuettes and jewellery.

Helene Stathátos Collection

At present this collection is not on view. It is proposed to accommodate it alongside the rooms in which the collection of Egyptian antiquities is displayed.
An impressive collection of ancient and Byzantine gold jewellery mostly from Macedonia and particularly Thessaly: bracelets representing serpents or finished with bulls' heads, pendant earrings, brooches, necklaces, diadems etc.

Ceramics

First floor: access by the stairs in Room 35. The collections are exhibited in chronological order; turn right at the top of the stairs into Room 49.

Rooms 52, 53, 54, 55 are closed to the public for an indefinite period.

Rooms 49, 50, 51 and 56. Although the exhibits in the ceramics department are less arresting than those in the sculpture galleries, a careful study of the scenes depicted on the pieces will yield many curious details about the adventures of the gods and mythological heroes *(see p 42)* as well as about daily life in ancient Greece.

Kore with almond-shaped eyes

Artemision Poseidon

Mask of Agamemnon

The Fisherman (Santorini)

Red-figure *kantharos*

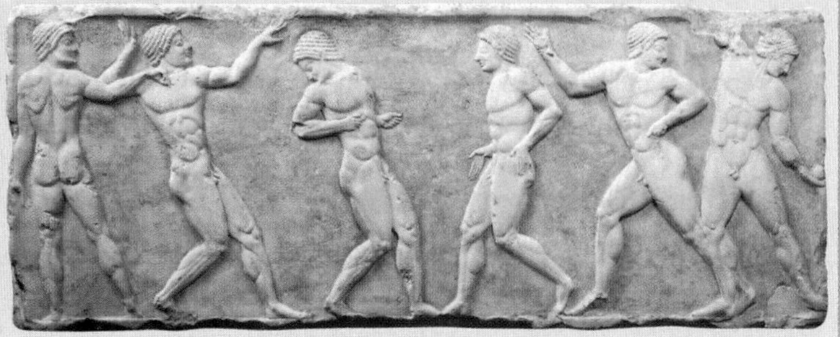

Athletes exercising *(low relief)*

Photos T.A.P.

A distinction is to be made between early ceramics with Geometric decoration and Archaic ceramics (7C-6C BC) decorated with plants or fantastic animals. Ceramics from the Classical period are decorated with black figures on a light ground in the 6C BC and with red figures on a black ground in the 5C-4C BC *(on ceramics see also p 34)*. Among the most precious pieces are the funerary *krater* of the Dipylon type found near the Kerameikos cemetery *(Room 55)*, the Nessos Amphora and the four *kraters* from Melos *(Room 51)*, a *krater* showing Herakles (Hercules) struggling with Nereus *(Room 52)* and white-ground funerary *lekithoi (Room 55)*.

Santoríni Frescoes and Ceramics *(display in Room 48 on 1st floor – upper level)*
The magnificent frescoes discovered in the 1970s by Professor Marinatos on Santoríni together with ceramics from the same site are a most valuable source of information about life on the island in the 16C BC. They are very lively descriptive murals reflecting the influence of Minoan Crete but executed with great elegance and grace. They have survived without much damage although some areas have been reconstructed. They depict various aspects of Cycladic civilisation: two boys engaged in fisticuffs, a fisherman with his catch, springtime, antelopes, young women and a long panel showing a "naval expedition".
The ceramics found on Santoríni include some highly original pots of local manufacture: graceful pitchers, sometimes nippled, with beaked spouts. The purpose of the oblong vessels, known as "kymbes", decorated with goats, dolphins and swallows is not known. A display case contains kitchen utensils and burnt food remains (millet, beans); next to these are the present-day foodstuffs.

★★ **Moussío Benáki (Benáki Museum)** ⓥ – *Snack bar on top floor; attractive view of National Garden and the Acropolis.*
Closed to the public since 1995 for reorganisation.
This museum, which is devoted mainly to Greek and oriental art, houses the collection of Antonis Benáki (1873-1954), a patron of the arts who founded a dynasty in Egypt and made a fortune in cotton. The exhibits which have been augmented by later bequests are appropriately displayed in the setting of an early 20C patrician mansion in Benaki's own house.

Ground floor – The rooms on the left of the entrance hall, where the collection of Greek art is displayed, contain an exceptional series of golden artefacts and jewellery, ancient workmanship such as some cups from Euboia (3000-2800 BC), a 7C BC funerary frieze from Kos, 3C and 1C BC earrings and necklaces, a 3C BC brooch representing Aphrodite, gold wreaths from Thessaly from the 3C to the 2C BC. Examples of Coptic art include two portraits from Fayyum (2C-3C AD) and glass, ivory and wooden objects dating from the 2C to the 6C AD.
The rooms of Byzantine and post-Byzantine art display in particular a remarkable series of icons on subjects such as the *Hospitality of Abraham* which is very well drawn (late 14C), *St Demetrios* (15C), a fine *Transfiguration* (16C) and an extraordinary composition by Th Poulakis (Crete, 17C), a pictorial synthesis of the *Hymn to the Virgin and the Last Judgement*. There is also a superb representation of St James and two youthful works by El Greco: the *Adoration of the Magi* (1560-65) and *St Luke* (1560).

18C Cretan cushion (Benáki Museum, Athens)

The room at the rear contains a rare collection of porcelain, said to be from Rhodes but in fact made in Isnik (Nicaea) in Asia Minor from the 16C to the 18C, the 11C-12C decorated Fatimid ceramics and a reconstructed room with 17C mosaics and fountain.

Basement – Large collection of regional costumes and traditional jewellery. The late 18C reception room from a house in Kozáni in Macedonia is not to be missed; the room, which was reconstructed by Helene Stathátos and is decorated with fine wood carvings, is the setting for a display of the goldsmith's art containing both religious and secular pieces (jewellery): famous pectoral cross from Patmos in the shape of a caravel (17C).

First Floor – There are several rooms devoted to the War of Independence including arms, portraits and souvenirs of Lord Byron but visitors may be more interested in the gallery devoted to the history of Athens from the 17C to the 19C as depicted in paintings, water colours, drawings, engravings and models made by English (Sir Charles Eastlake, J Stuart, W Gell and Edward Lear), French (David Leroy, J-B Hilaire, Cassas etc) and German artists.
There are additional collections of traditional embroidery and Islamic art: ceramics, textiles, glasses... beautiful 18C bed hangings for a tester bed from Rhodes; the traditional costumes from the Dodecanese are some of the best in the museum. The museum possesses also a rich collection of works of art from the Far East – particularly Chinese porcelain.

★★**Vizandinó Moussío (Byzantine Museum)** ⓥ – The museum is being enlarged, and a new building is in the course of construction in the courtyard. It is the only museum in Europe which concentrates exclusively on Byzantine art and it is particularly rich in icons. It is housed in a former residence of the **Duchess of Plaisance** which was built between 1840 and 1848 by the famous Greek architect, **Kleanthes** (1802-61), in the Italian Renaissance style.

Ground floor of the house – For the display of religious sculpture the rooms have been arranged to resemble churches. The room on the right of the entrance recalls a small paleo-Christian basilica: 4C-5C AD gravestone depicting Orpheus charming the animals with his music. The second room contains the Byzantine sculptures properly speaking (low reliefs from the 9C to the 13C). The third room represents a small Greek cross church with a dome such as is frequently seen in Athens. The fourth room represents a church at the time of the Turkish occupation (15C-19C): richly sculpted iconostasis (17C-18C).

T.A.P.

14C icon of the Archangel Michael (Byzantine Museum, Athens)

First Floor – *Start in the first room on the right of the entrance.* The collection of icons covers the 9C to the 15C (in particular note a Virgin and Child and a Crucifixion both from the 14C); there are also fragments of frescoes, liturgical objects and embroideries, a 6C parchment with a biblical text from Cappadocia, and frescoes from churches in Laconia (14C) and Náxos (13C). Note the icon in mosaic from Asia Minor (14C).

Outbuildings – *Being restored, closed to the public for an indefinite period.* Rich collection of icons, grouped chronologically and according to subject. There is also an astonishing version of the Evangelistary (1765) composed of small plaques of silver incised and inset with precious stones; scenes from the Old and New Testaments, figures of saints.
In an adjoining building is the Loverdos collection of 8C to 17C frescoes arranged in chronological order.

★★ **Moussío Kikladikís Téhnis** ⌚ – The private collection of N P Goulandris provides the major part of the exhibits in the **Museum of Cycladic Art**, which illustrates the development of Greek art over a period of 3 000 years. The quality of the exhibits is matched by their superb presentation.

First floor – 230 objects produced by the Cycladic island civilisation – Ancient Cycladic I (3 300 – 2 700 BC), Ancient Cycladic II (2 800 – 2 300 BC) and Ancient Cycladic III (2 400 – 2 200 BC) – *(see KIKLÁDES)* which traded with mainland communities: marble and pottery vessels, some with herring bone decoration; magnificent collection of Cycladic marble **idols**: idols from Ancient Cycladic I, in the shape of a violin *(nos 19, 20, 21)*, female figures mostly with folded arms *(nos 178, 161)* from Ancient Cycladic II, and lyre or almond shaped heads where only the nose was in relief, the other features being painted; these figurines are remarkable for their austere style and clarity of line. A seated male figure proposing a toast is an outstanding work. Note also a dish with doves *(no 164)* and a bird *(no 160)*, also an idol in the form of a statue 1.4m/4ft 7in in height *(no 724)*.

Second floor – Among the 300 works illustrating ancient Greek art are: Minoan and Mycenaean artefacts; a fine collection of vases with red and black figure decoration; in particular an Attic bell *krater* (430 BC) showing a girl flautist and two male dancers and a *lekythos* showing horse racing (560-550 BC); the Lambros Evtaxias Collection of cult and household **bronze vessels** (8C BC–1C AD) including a bronze *kados* from Thessaly with two handles and elaborate plant decoration; gold and bronze jewellery and clay vases from Skyros (1000-700 BC); South Italian fish plates (4C BC); glass perfume flasks; fine collection of Boeotian terracotta and female idols with bird faces from the same area (590-550 BC); marble sculpture and funerary reliefs.

Third floor – *Reserved for temporary exhibitions.*

New wing – *Pass through the glass door on the ground floor into the garden.*
There are temporary exhibitions in the house occupied by Othon and Athena Stathatou, built in the neo-Classical style in 1895 to the design of the architect Ernst Ziller.

Nomismatikó Moussío ⌚ – The **Numismatic Museum**, which is displayed in a house built for Heinrich Schliemann *(see p 98)*, possesses 600 000 coins and medals, 2 000 of which are gold and 4 000 silver. Some Greek coins were among the first in the world, being minted as early as the 7C BC. One can admire rare items from Greek and Roman antiquity, the Byzantine era, the Middle Ages and modern times. Also remarkable are a collection of lead seals from the Byzantine period, a number of antique and Byzantine weights, jewellery from various periods, ancient lead and bronze tokens, as well as casts of coins.

Room 1. This houses Heinrich Schliemann's personal collection.

Room 2. The visitor can follow the development of coinage from the first examples to the Byzantine period. The various minting techniques are explained, and a series of treasure trove finds from different periods discovered in Corinth, Dramas, Karditsa etc can be seen, which are of interest as much from the point of view of iconography as from that of art or history.

Room 3. A collection of coins struck by the Mint in Athens and by Greek towns in southern Italy and Sicily. Some of the items are masterpieces of the minter's art.

Room 4. Coins and engravings of monuments.

Room 5. History of Athens Numismatic Museum (1829-1964).

Room 6. This contains mainly remarkable items donated by famous collectors such as A Mourouzis, A Soutzos, J Vassileiou, G Embédoklis and L Riancourt.

The second floor is being prepared to receive further collections from the Roman and Byzantine periods in the near future.

ADDITIONAL SIGHTS

★ **Platía Sindágmatos** – **Síndagma Square** (Constitution Square) is in the elegant part of Athens which attracts the tourists. The east side is filled by the former royal palace, built for Otto I of Bavaria, which became the **Parliament (Voulí)** in 1935.
In front of the palace, before the monument to the Unknown Soldier, two **soldiers** *(évzoni)* stand guard; they are dressed in the distinctive kilt *(fustanélla)* and pompom shoes *(tsaroúhias)*. From time to time they emerge from their boxes to perform a sort of military ballet, very graceful but precise, before retreating into their boxes. The spectacle is particularly grand on Sundays *(11am)* when the ceremony is conducted with additional military personnel, dressed in smarter uniforms.
On the north side of the square stands the famous Hotel Grande Bretagne, which began life in 1843 as a private house, was occupied from 1856 to 1874 by the French School of Archeology (now at the junction of Odós Didotou and Odós Sina)

PICTOR

Changing the guard

and then converted into a hotel (remodelled in 1958). It was occupied successively by Greek, German and British forces during the Second World War; an attempt to blow it up on Christmas Eve 1944 when Churchill was visiting Athens was fortunately foiled.

★**Panepistimíou** – This is University Avenue which is lined at first by luxury hotels, large terraced cafés, restaurants, cake shops and smart boutiques. **Schliemann's House** is a large private house known as the "palace of Troy" (Iliou Mélanthron) which the brilliant German archeologist had built in 1879 to designs by the architect Ernst Ziller (1837-1923) in the style of a Venetian Renaissance palace; it now houses the **Numismatic Museum** *(see above)*.

A little further on stands the Roman Catholic cathedral of **St Dionysius the Areopagite** (Ágios Dionisis Areopagitis).

★**Panepistímio, Akadimía, Ethnikí Vivliothíki** – The **University, Academy** and **National Library** – three 19C buildings in white Pentelic marble – compose an architectural group in the elegant but slightly arid neo-Classical style.
The **University** in the centre is the oldest of the three buildings; it was designed by Christian von Hansen, the Danish architect, and built between 1837 and 1864; the pure design of the façade is outstanding. Near the pavement stands a statue of Gladstone *(see KÉRKIRA)* who is also remembered in the name of a nearby street.
The **Academy** *(right)* was paid for by Baron Sina, a Greek banker in Vienna, and designed by Theophilos von Hansen (1813-91), Christian's brother, in the style of an Ionic temple; it is flanked by two tall columns surmounted by statues of Apollo and Athena.
The **National Library** *(left)*, which is reminiscent of a Doric temple, contains 500 000 volumes and 3 000 manuscripts.

Platía Omónia – **Omónia Square** (Concord Square) with its noise, crowds and hawkers, is in complete contrast with Síndagma Square; this is even more marked in the evening.
In Platía Kaningos, northeast of Omónia Square, stands a statue of **George Canning**, who as Foreign Secretary in 1823 reversed the previous British indifference to the Greeks' struggle for independence and subsequently supported their aim through a policy of "peaceful interference". The other Canning is a relative who was killed in Greece in the Second World War.

Return to Síndagma Square by Odós Stadíou (southeast corner), parallel to Odós Panepistimíou.

Odós Stadíou – At its start this is a shopping street; half way along on the south side is **Platía Klafthmónos** (Wailing Square), named after the civil servants of the neighbouring ministries who came there to bewail their lot when they were dismissed. In the west corner stands the **Church of the Sts Theodore** (Ágii Theódori) (11C), the oldest in Athens; the dome rests on the walls instead of columns. The small neo-classical mansion (1834) designed by the architect Leo von Klenze south-east of the square was the residence of the Greek royal family from 1836 to 1842; it now houses the City of Athens Museum.

Moussío tis Póleos ton Athinón ⌚ – The exhibits in the **City of Athens Museum** illustrate daily life and social customs during the reign of King Otto. On the first floor the rooms have been arranged as they were in the 19C: pictures are from the Kosma Stathi collection, with paintings by visiting European artists including Edward Lear, Dodwell and Gasparini. Plans to illustrate the history of Athens since the conquest of the Franks have been adopted.

Beyond **Platía Klafthmónos** *(east)*, in **Platía Kolokotrónis**, there is an equestrian statue of **Kolokotrónis** (**S**), a hero of the War of Independence; it stands front of the **old Parliament** which was built by Florimond Boulanger from 1858 to 1871 and vacated in 1935; the chamber has been preserved and the attendant rooms now house the National Historical Museum.

★**Ethnikó Istorikó Moussío** ⌚ – The **National Historical Museum** should be visited by those who are interested in modern Greece and more especially in the period from the fall of Byzantium (1453) to the end of the Second World War.

For a good understanding of the historical context of the exhibitions, visitors should refer to the Introduction – The Modern Age – and to the descriptions of the places mentioned.

Engravings and watercolours by 19C travellers are displayed in rooms opening off the main passage along which portraits and busts of the heroes of the War of Independence are on view, including a modern statue of Constantine Palaiologos, the last emperor of Byzantium.

Beyond it *(right)* are Rooms A and B, devoted to Greece under Venetian and Ottoman rule: a painting of the Battle of Lepanto (1571) probably by an eye-witness; portraits of Greek dragomans and governors *(hospodars)* including Ali Pasha of Ioánina and a section on the **Filikí Etería** (Greek Liberation Movement). Rooms C to F evoke the War of Independence: portraits, fine arms, clothes belonging to the heroic participants (Kolokotrónis, Karaïskákis, Mavromihális, Nikitarás and other insurgents).

In Room E is the moving *Girl weeping for the death of Botzaris* by David d'Angers *(see MESSOLÓNGI)*. Room F presents naval battles, in particular the Battle of Navarino, and famous commanders (Kanáris, Bouboulina).

An adjoining room traces the history of the Philhellene movement, in particular in France and in Britain.

The final rooms describe the eventful progress of Greece since independence to the present day: the reigns of Otto I *(Rooms G and J)* and George I *(Rooms H and J)* (costumes *Room M*), great statesmen such as Kapodístrias, "the first governor of Greece" *(Room G)*, and Venizélos, the Balkan Wars and the conflict in Asia Minor *(Room I)*.

In Rooms K and L attractive national and regional costumes are displayed, as well as fine embroidery and pottery. It is also possible to see the room where the old Parliament met until 1934.

★**Kendrikí Agorá** – Athens' **Central Market** presents a marked oriental atmosphere to this day. The meat market is a spectacular sight, so too are the egg vendors and the goldsmiths and money changers with their scales on the north side (Odós Sofokléous).

From the south side of the market go west along Odós Evripidou to no 72 where at the back of a small square stands the **Chapel of St John of the Column** (Ágios Ioánnis stin Kólon), which was built round a Corinthian column; the chapel is much sought after for curing fevers.

Platía Kodziá, to the north of the market, was the centre of Athens in the second half of the 19C; the square was planted with palm trees and lined with private mansions, many of which remain. The National Bank of Greece (Ethnikí Trápeza tis Eládos) on the east side was founded in 1842. About 5 000 ancient tombs have been found in the centre of the square, just outside the city walls. The cemetery was abandoned and the area was taken over by potters in the Roman era; ovens and workshops have been uncovered.

★**Keramikós Cemetery and Dípilo** – *148 Odós Ermou. Access by bus no 025 from Síndagma Square-Odós Mitropoleos. By metro: Thissío station.*

★★**Keramikós** ⌚ – The Kerameikos, the largest cemetery in Athens, was situated outside the city wall; it takes its name from the clay (kéramos) used by potters to make funerary vases. From the 6C BC the graves were marked with gravestones and statues which were most flamboyant in the age of Pericles. The site was first excavated in 1863 and has yielded some handsome finds which are now displayed in the National Museum; a few statues and stones have been left in place.

Leaving the museum on the left descend the path (South Way) which leads to the best preserved part of the cemetery: tombs dating from the 4C BC to the 1C AD. Turn left into the West Way which is lined by tombs erected in the 4C BC by rich Athenian families; on the corner there is a family tomb with a low relief (moulding) of a cavalry man fighting; this is Dexileos who was killed in 393 BC in the war against the Corinthians. Further on there is a group of three monuments belonging to a family from Heraklia in the Euxine near the Black Sea. The tomb of Dionysos, the treasurer, is recognisable by the bull standing on a pillar while the monument to Lysimachides, the archon, and his family, is crowned by a dog. On the other side of the West Way stands the famous grave stone of Hegeso (moulding); the original is in the National Museum. On the south side are the gravestone of Antidosis which was painted and the vase *(lekythos)* of Aristomachos.

★**Ierá Píli ke Dípilo** – The **Sacred Gate** was built at the same time as Themistocles' wall (5C BC) and marks the beginning of the Sacred Way to Eleusis *(see ELEFSÍNA)*. The **Dipylon**, which dates from the same period, was a double gate with a square tower at each corner, and the main entrance to Athens. The road from the *agora* to the Academy passed through it. The **Pompeion** was a building used to store the things required for the Panathenaic processions *(see p 82)*, which started from here.

★**National Garden (Ethnikós Kípos) and Zappeion (Zápio)** – The former royal garden which was designed for Queen Amalia was remodelled in 1840. It is pleasant to stroll in the shade of its abundant vegetation, past its pools and flower beds, its fine palm trees, orange trees, cypresses and Aleppo pines. There are some 500 species of trees and plants, a botanical museum (charming neo-Classical building) and a small zoo. Adjoining the National Garden to the south is the Zappeion Park, which is named after the Záppas brothers who gave the land. It is very popular, particularly in the evenings, with the Athenians. The **Zappeion Hall** (Zápio) is a pleasant neo-Classical building (1888) which is now used for exhibitions. The agreement admitting Greece to the European Community was signed here in 1989.

★**Pnyx and Nympheion** – *Access by bus no 230 and then on foot.*

★**Pníka** ⊙ – *Son et lumière about the Acropolis.* The **Pnyx** (literally a place where people are squashed close together) forms a sort of amphitheatre, where the Assembly of the people *(Ecclisía)* met between the 6C and the 4C BC. The assembly was a democratic meeting of citizens to discuss proposed legislation. Each man was entitled to speak once and many famous orators, such as Themistocles, Pericles and Demosthenes, addressed the Assembly. In the early days attendance at the Assembly was good but gradually, despite the indemnity paid to those who attended, apathy grew so that in the 4C archers had to be sent out to compel the Athenians to perform their civic duties: the quorum was 5 000. From the terrace where the citizens gathered there is a splendid **view**★★★ of the Acropolis.

★**Lófos Nimfón** – The **Nympheion**, the Hill of the Nymphs, is scattered with traces of dwellings. Its modern name is derived from an inscription in the rock. View of the Parthenon. The hill (104m/341ft) is crowned by an **observatory**, a neo-Classical building which was completed in 1957 with the addition of a seismology station.

★**Kéndro Meletón Akropóleos** ⊙ – *Dionissiou Areopagitou.* The **Acropolis Interpretation Centre** which is devoted to conservation, restoration and research, traces the history of the Acropolis and its monuments and explains the work in progress. The Acropolis Museum is scheduled to be transferred nearby.

On the ground floor are copies of the Parthenon friezes including the sculptures still decorating the monument, the ones in the Acropolis Museum and those in the British Museum (the "Elgin Marbles"); copies of the latter were presented to Greece in 1846 by the British Government. In total there are copies of 110m/330ft of the frieze which was originally 160m/525ft long. Copies of sculptures from the Erechtheion and from the temple of Athena Nike will be displayed in other rooms. On the first floor photographs, models and tools trace the history of the Acropolis and the dilapidation of the monuments. In the past the damage was caused by earthquakes and explosions, but today atmospheric pollution erodes the marble and earlier restoration work has brought about further deterioration. The current programme includes a minute examination of the stonework of all the Acropolis monuments and replacement of the iron clamps used earlier by titanium clamps to prevent rusting and expansion. The stones scattered near the monuments have been identified and replaced in their original position; new blocks have been added where necessary to make the buildings stable. Work to consolidate the rock itself is in progress and urgent measures have been adopted to reduce pollution in the area around the Acropolis.

★**Moussío Elinikís Laïkís Téhnis** ⊙ – *Kidathinéon (see plan p 87).* Most of the exhibits in the **Museum of Greek Folk Art** date from the 18C and the 19C. On the ground floor the domestic and religious articles are accompanied by a large collection of embroidery from the Dodecanese, Epiros, Crete and Skyros, richly

coloured or delicately decorated with motifs which are often of Byzantine origin. On the first floor there is a display of objects in carved wood for domestic use (utensils and furniture) or for use in connection with a trade (needles, boat figureheads, shepherds' crooks), as well as printed fabrics. Also striking are the figurines in leather or cardboard of *Karagiósis*, an important character in the Greek shadow theatre.
On the second floor there is a reconstruction of a village interior with wood panels decorated (between 1924 and 1930) by the naive painter **Theophilos**, 1873-1934 *(see LÉSVOS)*. The upper floors display a great variety of traditional costumes: the sober and hard wearing woollen dress of the Sarakatsani who are nomadic shepherds, the cheerful colours of the clothes worn by the Balkan Greeks, the sumptuous embroidery of ceremonial dress, heavy with silver ornaments, and the elegant costumes of Central Greece and the Peloponnese.

Shadow theatre

Oriental in origin, this is one of the earliest forms of popular Greek theatre. The plays take their inspiration from history, myth, legend and everyday life. **Karagiósis** ("Evil eye") is one of its most representative figures, a shrewd character expressing the gently mocking spirit of the typical Greek. His adventures often evoke the days of the Turkish occupation as well as modern everyday and political life.

Moussio Elinikón Moussikón Orgánon ⓥ *Diogenous (see plan p 87)*. This **Museum of Popular Musical Instruments**, a collection of traditional Greek instruments, is housed in a residential building (of 1842) together with the Fivos Anoyanakis Centre for Musicology.
The 600 instruments (from the 18C to the present) are displayed in glass cases on four levels, headphones being provided to give an idea of what they sound like. The exhibits are divided according to the four main categories of instruments: on the ground floor are the **wind instruments** *(flogéres, sourávlia, mandoúres* – flutes – and *tsaboúnes, gáides* and *zournádes)* and **percussion instruments** (*toumbelékia* and *daoúlia* – drums – and *défia* – tambourines). On the first floor are assembled the **stringed instruments**: *tambourádes* and *lagoúta* (lutes), *oútia*, guitars, *mandolináta, sandoúri, kanonáki* and *líres*. The **idiophones** are to be found in the basement: *koudoúnia* (handbells), *zilia* (cymbals), *koutália* (spoons), *trigono* (triangle) and the *sémandro*, still used in some monasteries to call the faithful to prayer.

★**Evraikó Moussío tis Elládas** ⓥ – *39 Odós Nikis(see plan p 87)*. The **Jewish Museum of Greece**, founded in 1977, traces the history of the Jews in Greece whose origins date back over 2 000 years. The first Jewish community was founded in Thessaloníki in the early 3C BC; other settlements followed shortly after in Corinth and Sparta. These communities, while keeping their own tradition, were soon influenced by the Hellenic culture. The Jews within the Byzantine Empire were known as Romaniotes as the empire and its people saw themselves as successors of the Roman Empire.
Under the Turks, Jewish communities spread to the large cities of the Ottoman Empire. Sultan Bayazid II invited the Sephardic Jews expelled from Spain and Portugal in 1492 to settle in Thessaloníki, Constantinople, Edirne and Smyrna in the midst of the Romaniote communities. The Sephardim brought with them the refinement of the great Hispano-Moorish cities and the progressive ideas of the Renaissance; they retained their Hispanic dialect (Ladino) and customs and built their own synagogues. These distinctions between the Romaniote and Sephardic Jews continued into the 20C. At the beginning of the Second World War, the Jews fought with great heroism at the battle of Epiros. During the German occupation, 87 per cent of the Jewish population were eliminated, thus causing the decline of a 2 000 year-old tradition. Today the Jewish community of Greece numbers about 5 000.
The long history of the Jews in Greece is presented by periods and themes. Maps and other documents trace Jewish settlement in the Roman and Byzantine empires, and the routes taken in the 15C by the Jews expelled from Spain and Portugal. Models and watercolours show Jewish costumes worn under the Turkish empire from the 16C to the 19C. There are also religious objects: carved wooden boxes *(tik)* containing the Torah. One room is dedicated to the Holocaust. One room is a reconstruction of the 19C Romaniote synagogue of Patras.

★**Ethnikí Pinakothíki – Moussío Alexándrou Soútsou** ⓥ – *Leofóros Vas Konstandinou. The rooms containing the permanent collections are being restored and are therefore closed to the public for an indefinite period. It is still worth seeing the temporary exhibitions, which are equally remarkable.* The **National Gallery and Alexander Soutzos Museum** is devoted to painting. Pride of place in the collection goes to three remarkable works *(upper level)* by Domenico Theotocopoulos **(El Greco)** who was born in Crete, near Herakleion *(see p 281)* including his famous *Concert of the Angels*, and to a selection of post-Byzantine icons (17C).

The upper floor, which is devoted to the different periods in Hellenic art since its inception, presents a number of 18C works from the Ionian islands and a collection of 19C canvases illustrative of the Munich School (Gysis, Lítras, Iacovidès, Volanakis etc); one room is devoted entirely to K Parthenis (1878-1967) whose influence has been decisive in the development of 20C Hellenic art. Between the floors are displayed a dozen frescoes and canvases by the naive painter **Theophilos** *(see LÉSVOS)*. The first floor is devoted to contemporary Hellenic painting particularly from the 1930s. The collection of sculpture, including works by the great Greek sculptor Yiannoulis Halepás, is displayed in two rooms and the garden.

★ **Moussío Kanelopoúlou** – The collections in the **Kanellopoulos Museum** are presented in a 19C mansion: remarkable series of ancient ceramics, Tanágra figurines, busts of Sophocles and Alexander, jewellery, Byzantine icons, popular works of art etc.

Polemikó Moussío ⓥ – *Leofóros Vas. Sofias.* On the ground floor of the **War Museum** there is a gallery of ancient weapons and splendid military uniforms. The first floor presents Greece's military history from antiquity to the present day: models of Byzantine and Frankish citadels, displays on the War of Independence, the "Great Catastrophe" of Asia Minor, and the Second World War, in particular the battle of Epiros and the Resistance Movement.

Platia Koloniakíou – **Kolonáki Square**, which is named after the column at its centre and ringed with luxury shops, cafés and restaurants, is at the centre of the Kolonáki district, a modern and elegant part of town on the slopes of Lycabettos. The streets are lined with the smartest shops in Athens: fashion, jewellers, bookshops, art galleries etc.

Stádio – *By trolleybus nos 2, 4, 11.* The **stadium** stands on the site of the ancient stadium laid out under Lycurgus in the 4C BC and rebuilt by Herod Atticus in AD 144. It fell into ruin and was turned into a wheat field. In 1896 it was rebuilt on its original plan for the modern Olympic Games. From the top of the white marble terraces which can accommodate 70 000 spectators, there is a view of the National Garden and the Acropolis.

Kéndro Laikís Téhnis ke Parádossis Dimou Athinéon ⓥ (**Pláka**) – This handsome mansion, once the house of Angelika Hatzimihali (1895-1965), who made a detailed study of traditional Greek culture, now houses the **City of Athens Centre for Popular Arts and Traditions** exhibiting collections of woven cloth and embroidery (coloured lace and embroidery), regional costumes, musical instruments, old agricultural implements etc. A reconstruction of a typical beehive hut of the nomadic Sarakatsani has been erected on the first floor.

Moussío Kosmímatos I Lalaoúnis ⓥ – *Corner of Odós Kariatidon and Kalispe.* This private **jewellery museum** houses the superb creations of the world-famous jeweller, Ilías Lalaoúnis.
As one passes among the 3 000 exhibits (in 45 collections) one can follow the evolution of Greek jewellery. The artist takes his inspiration from the past, while remaining true to his own time. He is influenced above all by the subjects, the motifs and the art of all the different periods: paleolithic, neolithic, Minoan, Mycenaean, Cycladic, Archaic, neo-Geometric, Classical, Hellenistic and Byzantine. There is a fine view of the Acropolis from the terrace. Films on the art and the making of jewellery are shown on the top floor.

Archeology in Greece

The first serious archeological work in Greece dates from the 19C. Schliemann discovered the site of Troy in Asia Minor in 1874 and then of Mycenae in Greece in 1876. French archeologists worked at Delos in 1872 and at Delphi in 1892. In 1900 Sir Arthur Evans began excavations at Knossós in Crete.
The **French School in Athens** on the slopes of Lycabettos was founded in 1846 by Louis-Philippe. As well as promoting Hellenic culture, both ancient and modern, it has done much impressive archeological work at sites in Greece and Turkey, in particular making extremely important discoveries at Delphi. It uses the latest technology to continue research not only at the old sites but at new sites in Greece, Cyprus and Albania, as well as assisting in the excavations at Alexandria.
Also in Kolonáki on the slopes of Lycabettos is the **British School of Archeology at Athens** *(52 Odós Souidías)*, founded in 1886, which houses a chemical analysis laboratory and the Penrose Library, named after a Classical scholar and containing 30 000 volumes, providing for both Classical and Byzantine studies. There is an out station at Knossós.
Next door is the **American School of Classical Studies**, founded in 1882 for the study of Greek archeology; it also promotes research into other aspects of Greek culture and history.

They died in Athens ...

In the 1830s the Protestant graves in the Theseion cemetery were moved to a new burial ground by the River Ilissós, purchased jointly by several Protestant governments – United Kingdom, the Netherlands, Denmark, Sweden, Prussia and Bavaria. When Queen Amalia required the land for her palace garden, the bodies were transferred to the Protestant corner of Athens **First Cemetery (Próto [1°] Nekrotafión Athinón)** *Odós Anapáfseos (southwest of the Stadio).*

Here are memorials to Sir Richard Church *(obelisk)*; George Finlay, the historian of medieval and modern Greece, whose library forms part of the British Archeological School; Carl Blegen (1887-1971), an American from Minneapolis who came to Greece in 1910 and devoted his life to Mycenaean archeology: he excavated at Pylos *(see PÍLOS)* and at Troy.

Other interesting memorials are to be found at **St Paul's Church (Pláka).** Outside the church *(east of the door)* are monuments to **Lusieri**, an Italian landscape painter who acted as Lord Elgin's agent for 20 years helping to record and preserve the Parthenon sculptures, and to **John Tweddell**, an exceptional scholar and Fellow of Trinity College Cambridge, who spent four years on a grand tour collecting a mass of material before dying of fever in Athens in 1799. The victims of the Dílessi Murders *(see p 114)* are commemorated in the east window. Three other foreigners may be remembered in connection with the construction (1838-43) of this simple 19C Gothic church – **Sir W Henry Acland**, who was travelling in Greece at the time and drew up the original plans; **C R Cockerell**, the English architect who had been excavating at Bassae *(see ANDRÍTSENA)* and on Égina *(see below)* and made modifications to the design; **C von Hansen**, the Danish architect *(see above: University)*, who also made modifications and acted as consultant.

SUBURBS

★Pireás (Piraeus)

10km/6mi southwest of the centre of Athens. Access by underground, by bus (no 049 from Omónia Square or no 40 from Síndagma Square), by Express bus no 19 from the airport, by car along Odós Piréos or Leofóros Singroú (the latter is less direct but quicker).

Access to Piraeus

From Athens airport – The express bus no 19 operates only in summer, every hour (90min at night). Route: West Terminal (Olympic Airways) direct to Piraeus or first to East Terminal (foreign airlines), back to the West Terminal and then via Neo Fáliro to Piraeus. Stops at: the international harbour *(Kendrikó Limenarhío)*, Akti Miaouli, the harbour at Akti Tzepeli (domestic services).

By train and metro – The Larissa and Peloponnese railway services (OSE) each have a station in Piraeus *(for destinations see above: Practical Information)*. The metro terminus is at the Peloponnese station close to the north basin of the harbour *(see plan PIREÁS)*.

Piraeus (pop 476 304) is a typically Mediterranean port, lively and cosmopolitan. Together with the capital it forms one huge conurbation. It is the first port of Greece and the country's major industrial centre. Even in antiquity it was chosen as the port of Athens owing to its exceptional situation: it consists of a peninsula *(aktí)* which forms a deep inlet on the west side and is favoured with two well protected natural round harbours, Zéa and Mikrolímano, on the east coast. It is the point of embarkation for the islands and the roadstead has often been used as an anchorage by Mediterranean fleets.

Piraeus is a modern town with a noisy vibrant population, tavernas serving fish and seafood and popular cabarets which attract sailors from every corner of the world.

The port in antiquity – *See local map.* It was **Themistocles** in c 493 BC who decided to move Athens' harbour to Piraeus from Phaleron *(see below)*, which was further east and too exposed to the wind. The new town was protected and linked to Athens by the Long Walls, nicknamed the Long Legs by the Athenians, which formed a fortified corridor.

In the age of Pericles the town was rebuilt according to a grid plan designed by **Hippodamos of Miletus**, a philosopher and geometer. For several hundred years the inhabitants enjoyed great commercial prosperity produced by the "display of samples" in the great porticoes *(stoas)*.

In 85 BC however the Romans under Sulla sacked Piraeus and set it on fire; three bronze statues *(displayed in museum)*, then lying in the basement of a warehouse waiting to be shipped to Rome, were discovered by chance in 1959 in Leofóros Georgiou-A.

In the Middle Ages Piraeus came to be known as **Porto Leone** after the ancient lion at the harbour entrance which served as a leading mark and was carried away by the Venetians and set up in front of the Arsenal in Venice in 1687.

Later the island of Syros *(see SÍROS)* in the Cyclades developed as the main port of Greece and when Otto of Bavaria arrived in Piraeus in 1834 after the overthrow of the Turks the population had fallen to about 50 but the designation of Athens as the capital of Greece and the opening of the Corinth Canal in 1893 marked the beginning of a commercial revival.

The modern port – The modern port complex consists of Piraeus harbour, Herakles harbour, the Eleusinian Gulf (Kólpos Elefsínas) and the two small harbours, Zéa and Mikrolímano, which accommodate pleasure craft and fishing boats.

The main Piraeus harbour comprises: the central harbour (Kendrikó Limáni) for goods but more particularly for domestic and international passenger liners; for the latter there is a large maritime station; Alón harbour, the northern section of the central harbour, is used by coasting vessels; the outer port deals in wood and containers. Herakles harbour *(west)* is reserved for freighters fitted with hatches in the bow or stern or sides of the ship opening directly from the hold on to the quay. The ship builders and ship repair yards are to be found in the Eleusinian Gulf.

Traffic in the port rose in 1996 to 9 800 000t of goods and nearly 6 000 000 passengers. From Piraeus to Eleusis the coast is lined with petrol refineries, metal works, food processing plants, cement works and tobacco factories; this is the largest industrial complex in Greece.

★ **Zéa** – *Access by metro and from the Port of Piraeus to the Naval Museum by bus nos 904 and 905.* In antiquity this round bay which is almost completely enclosed was a large port for triremes: the ship-sheds which sheltered these warships spread round the bay; traces of them are still visible.

Zéa harbour and its outer roads can now accommodate up to 400 pleasure craft. The waterfront is lined with fish restaurants and tavernas which are usually crowded.

Zéa harbour is the embarkation point for the hydrofoils of the Ceres Flying Dolphins company.

★ **Arheologikó Moussío** ⏱ – The colossal lion at the entrance of the **Archeological Museum** and the seated figure of Cybele further away adorned a 4C BC tomb found in Mosháto. On the ground floor there is a collection of sculptures made in an Attica workshop in the 2C AD (some in several copies) and intended to decorate the monuments of Rome; they were rescued in 1930 from an ancient shipwreck in Piraeus harbour. A room (left of entrance hall) contains a 4C monument dedicated to Polyxena, daughter of King Priam of Troy, who was sacrificed by the Greeks. The most remarkable sculptures (found in 1959) are displayed on the first floor: the Piraeus Apollo (c 525 BC), a splendid Archaic *kouros* which is probably the oldest known Greek statue in bronze and the Piraeus Athena (c 340 BC) wearing a *peplos* and a crested helmet and holding a statuette or a cup in the right hand and a shield or lance in the left. Two other bronze statues represent Artemis with her quiver.

Behind the museum are the remains of a 4C BC theatre.

Naftikó Moussío ⏱ – The **Naval Museum** contains 12 rooms illustrating the history of navigation in Greece from antiquity to the Second World War: models of ships including examples from Santoríni based on a fresco in the National Museum, a trireme from the Peloponnesian War, a Hellenistic merchant ship and Byzantine war ship; maps tracing Ulysses' travels, the Trojan War, Greek expeditions to the North Sea and to the Orient; reconstructions of naval battles (Salamis, 480 BC; Navarino, 1827; the Dardanelles, 1912); arms and portraits of great leaders of the War of Independence. In the hall stands a beacon from a lighthouse which was in use in Istanbul until the Balkan War.

From a café terrace near the museum, there is a pleasant **view** of the outer harbour and Phaleron Bay.

Restaurants specialising in sea food

Value for money is very good in spite of the crowds of tourists.

Zefyros, *48 Akti Koumoundourou, Mikrolímano ☎ 412 79 19 and 417 51 52.*

Zorbas, *14 Akti Koumoundourou, Mikrolímano ☎ 411 16 63.* Guitar and bouzoúki music.

El Greco, *20 Akti Koumoundourou, Mikrolímano ☎ 412 73 24.*

Diasimos, *306 Akti Themistokleous, Piraeus ☎ 451 48 87.*

Kritikos, *324 Akti Themistokleous, Piraïki ☎ 451 12 31.* Excellent value for money.

Ioirochti, *3 Odós Epidavrou, Kastéla ☎ 413 04 37.* Garden open in summer.

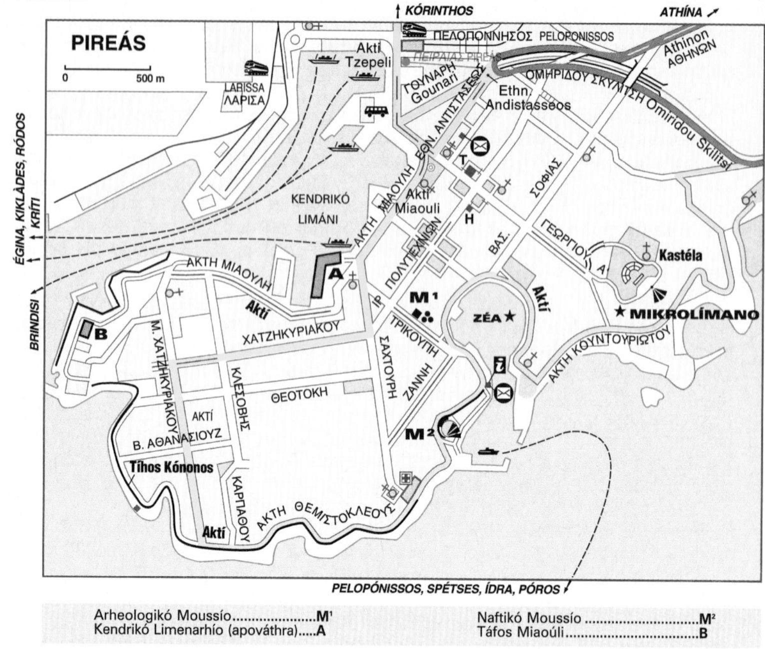

The battleship **Averoff** ⓥ is moored in Trocadero Harbour in Phaleron Bay *(see plan p 105)*. This 10 000t cruiser, launched in 1910, took part in all the Balkan wars; it was withdrawn from service in 1946.

★**Mikrolímano** – Like Zéa, Mikrolímano was a harbour for triremes in antiquity and is now lined by fish tavernas. The harbour lies at the foot of **Mounychia Hill** (Kastéla), 87m/285ft high, which was crowned by an acropolis and a sanctuary to Artemis. From the neighbourhood of the open-air theatre there is a fine view of Piraeus, the coast and the Saronic Gulf.
Further east, in the Néo Fáliro district, is the saddle-shaped **Stádio Irínis & Filías** (Peace and Friendship Stadium) which was inaugurated in 1965.

Aktí – The **coast road** round the peninsula gives attractive views of the port and the coast. There are traces of the sea wall (Tíhos Kónonos) built by Konon in the 4C BC. Near the public garden at the western end of the peninsula stands the tomb of Miaoúlis, a famous Hydriot admiral *(see ÍDRA)*.

★Kifissiá *2hr 30min*

14km/9mi northeast of Athens. Access by underground (30min from Omónia Square) or by road (leave by Leofóros El Venizélou).

Kifissiá is an elegant residential town which is pleasantly cool and fresh in summer owing to its altitude (276m/906ft), its water and its trees: even in antiquity the Athenians came up to Kifissiá for refreshment.
Kifissiá comprises: the lower town near the underground station and the public park; its shops and tavernas give it a relaxed atmosphere; the elegant upper town with avenues of plane trees, 19C villas and luxury hotels and restaurants.

★**Moussío Goulandrí Fissikís Istorías** ⓥ – *13 Odós Levidou (plan p 105)*. The **Goulandris Museum of Natural History** which is housed in an elegant 19C villa, presents attractive displays: stuffed animals, botanical and mineralogical specimens. The **herbarium** contains 200 000 different varieties of plants from the Mediterranean basin.

★★Kessariani Monastery and Mount Hymettos

9km/5.5mi east of Athens. Access by bus 224 (bus stop behind the Archeological Museum, Odós Akadimías and Leofóros El Venizélou) plus 45min on foot.

Beyond the suburb of Kessarianí *(bus terminus)* the road climbs in leisurely bends up the verdant slopes through fragrant groves of pine and eucalyptus trees. After 3km/2mi the Kessarianí Monastery appears on the right.

★★**Moní Kessarianí (Kessarianí Monastery)** ⓥ – The fresh water of the springs, the shade of the plane trees, pines and solemn cypresses and the silence, which is barely broken by the murmuring of the bees on Mount Hymettos, all add to the charm of a visit to this monastery. It was founded in the 11C and dedicated to the Presentation of the Virgin. Formerly it was famous for the wisdom of its superiors and for the richness of its library but it was destroyed during the War of Independence and is now deconsecrated.

A recess in the outer wall of the monastery on the east side of the first courtyard contains the famous **Ram's Head Fountain**, a sacred spring in antiquity which was celebrated by the Latin poet Ovid in his *Ars Amatoria*.

The inner courtyard is cooled by running water and scattered with ancient fragments. In the Middle Ages the 11C building *(left)* was the monks' bath house: the main room is roofed with a dome. The building was later converted into cellars with a press. The adjoining wing has a gallery at first floor level serving the monks' cells.

The **church**, *katholikon (right)*, on the Greek cross plan dates from the 11C but the domed narthex and the side chapel with its belfry were added in the 17C. The interior is decorated with murals: those in the narthex date from 1682; those in the church itself are probably 18C and show Christ Pantocrator in the dome, the Virgin in majesty between the Archangels Michael and Gabriel in the top of the apse and the Life of Jesus around the transept. Four ancient columns support the dome and the choir screen comes from a paleo-Christian basilica *(see below)*.

Leave the monastery on this side and take the path up through the olive trees and cypresses (15min on foot there and back) to a sanctuary southeast of the monastery. Here there are traces of a 10C church with a nave and two aisles built on the foundations of a paleo-Christian basilica; adjoining the basilica was a 13C vaulted Frankish church dedicated to St Mark; there is also a later chapel dedicated to the Archangels. All these buildings incorporate ancient fragments. Fine **views** of Athens, Attica and the Saronic Gulf.

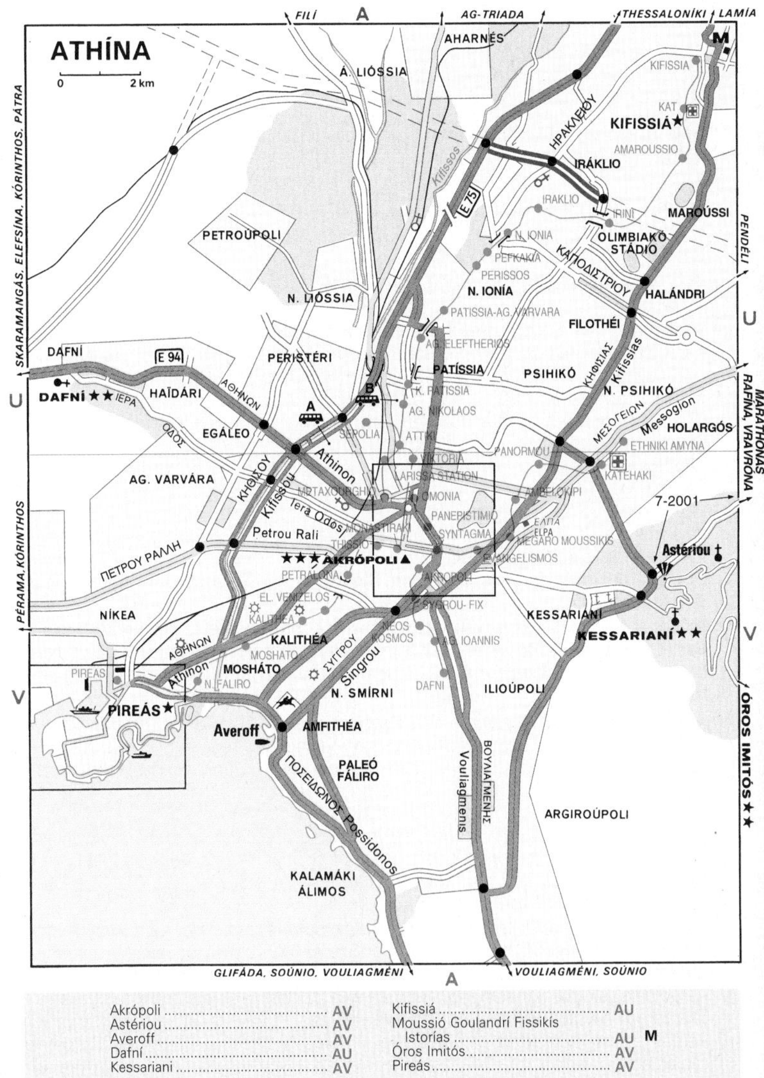

Akrópoli	AV	Kifissiá	AU
Astériou	AV	Moussió Goulandrí Fissikís Istorías	AU M
Averoff	AV	Óros Imitós	AV
Dafní	AU	Pireás	AV
Kessariani	AV		

★★ **Óros Imitós (Mount Hymettos)** – Continue up the road which climbs Mount Hymettos through the pine trees; soon the 11C **Asteri Monastery** appears on the left; then the road emerges from the woods into scrub. There are views of Athens and the Saronic Gulf as far as the Peloponnese to the west and of the Attic peninsula (Mesógia), its eastern shore and Euboia to the east. The summit is prohibited *(military zone)* but in antiquity it was crowned by a statue of Zeus.

The Hymettos range, which rises to 1 026m/3 366ft, extends north-south for about 20km/12.5mi. Hymettos was already famous for its honey in antiquity. It also boasts a vineyard *(see p 54)* and its grey blue marble is still quarried.

EXCURSIONS

★★★ Akrí Soúnio (Cape Sounion) *Itinerary* 1 *Round trip of 143km/89mi*

It is traditional to visit Cape Sounion at sunset and return to Athens in the evening twilight but for a better appreciation of the region it is advisable to make a whole day excursion: spending the morning exploring the Apollo Coast by the new coast road, lunching at Cape Sounion and returning to Athens by the old inland road via Laurion and Markópoulo.

Access

Apollo Coast and Peanía – By blue bus from Leofóros Vas Olgas (south of Zápio) *(plan p 79)*.

Cape Sounion – By orange bus (2hr) every hour from 14 Odós Mavromateon (Pedio Áreos Park) *(plan p 79)*.

From Athens take Leofóros Singróu; in Fáliro turn left into the new "expressway" which, after skirting the south side of the Elenikó Airport, follows the coast of the Saronic Gulf which is called the Apollo Coast.

★★ **Aktí Apólona** – The **Apollo Coast** road from Fáliro (Phaleron) to Soúnio (Sounion) offers frequent views of the Saronic Gulf and the islands. Unfortunately it has been spoiled in places by unattractive modern developments.

Glifáda – This is a sizeable resort just south of the Elinikó Airport which comprises a beach with facilities, a marina and an 18 hole golf course. *Numerous hotels, bungalows, fish restaurants, nightclubs.*

The road passes through Voúla (beach with facilities) and Kavoúri skirting many small bays.

★ **Vouliagméni** – An elegant resort, Vouliagméni is pleasantly situated at the head of a deep inlet flanked by two promontories indented by many small creeks. The fragrant pine trees, one huge beach with facilities and several smaller beaches, a safe mooring and several hotels add to the attractiveness of the resort.

From the southern headland beyond the harbour there is a **view** of the bay and the coast extending south towards Cape Sounion.

The road continues to **Várkiza** and then to **Lagoníssi**, another summer resort which has a sandy beach in an attractive bay partially enclosed by a reef.

The broken rocky coastline becomes more dramatic with views of the Saronic Gulf and the isle of Patroclos which is named after one of Ptolemy II's admirals who fortified the island in 260 BC.

One of the most famous *kouroi* in the Athens Museum was found in **Anávissos** (seaside resort).

Sounion – A small seaside resort has grown up on the site of the ancient town and port of Sounion. In an inlet near the headland dry dock facilities for two triremes have been found. **View**★ of Cape Sounion, crowned by the columns of an ancient temple.

★★★ **Ákri Soúnio (Cape Sounion)** – The "sacred headland" (Homer) is the outpost of Attica; it occupies a commanding position facing the Aegean Sea and the Cyclades at the entrance to the Saronic Gulf. The situation is enhanced by the ruins of a **temple to Poseidon**, the sea god invoked by sailors rounding the cape, which crowns the precipitous headland some 60m/197ft above sea level.

Known formerly as Cape Colonna, the headland was celebrated by romantic writers such as Byron and the sailor-poet, William Falconer, whose once popular work *The Shipwreck* was inspired by his own experience in a storm in 1750. The site now attracts busloads of tourists.

Temple ⏱ – The path leading up to the temple crosses the wall, which enclosed the ancient acropolis and is fairly well preserved (traces of square towers), and then enters the sacred precinct *(peribolos)* at the point where the original gate *(propylaia)* stood, flanked *(right)* by a large portico where the pilgrims assembled.

The temple, which was built of marble between 444 and 440 BC on the orders of Pericles, was dedicated to Poseidon. It was a Doric building with a peristyle replacing an earlier 6C BC sanctuary of tufa which had been destroyed in the

Temple of Poseidon, Sounion

second Persian War. Abandoned for many years to the ravages of the weather and treasure seekers, it was restored in the 19C: during the excavations two colossal Archaic *kouroi* were found which are now in the Athens Museum; several columns have been re-erected.

The entrance façade *(facing east)* consisted of a portico leading into the *naós* of which the corner pillars have been preserved: the one on the right is covered with "graffiti" including the name of Byron, although not perhaps in his own hand, who visited the temple in 1810.

The 16 columns of the peristyle which remain of the 34 originals which supported the architrave seem very tall although they are only 6.10m/20ft high; they have no entasis and the diameter is only 1m/3.25ft at the base and 0.79m/just over 2ft 6in at the top.

A tour of the ruin reveals the variation in thickness of the podium which was built for the original Archaic temple to provide a level base: it is several metres deep at the northwest corner.

The temple steps, where the votive *stele* were placed, give a beautiful **view**★★★ of the sea, which is often quite choppy, the islands (Makronísi to the east with Kéa beyond) and the Saronic Gulf.

From Sounion to Laurion (Lávrio) the road winds its way along the east coast of Cape Sounion. The landscape is more verdant than on the western side; villas and hotels are dispersed among the pine and olive trees above little beaches nestling in the creeks.

Lávrio – This small industrial town (foundries) and mineral port is surrounded by a desolate landscape of spoil heaps at the foot of Mount Lavreotíki; the mines were well known even in antiquity.

Recent excavations by Belgian archeologists suggest that the mines at **Laurion** were already being worked early in 3000 BC but it was early in the 5C BC that the deposits of silver bearing sulphides began to be systematically exploited bringing wealth and power to Athens. Shafts were sunk up to 100m/328ft deep leading to radial galleries, no more than 1m/3ft 6in high, where the mineral was extracted; it was then crushed and smelted. At its peak activity up to 20 000 slaves worked in the mine. In the 2C BC the lodes became exhausted and extraction had to cease.

In 1864 a new process for treating the mineral made it possible for mining to be restarted and a French company founded in 1876 was responsible for almost the whole output not only of silver but also of zinc until 1981.

From Lávrio there is a narrow road along the coast to Thorikó: bear right (sign "Théâtre antique").

Thorikó – Thorikó was a large fortified city with two ports where wood was imported from Euboia for the metal foundries in Laurion. It was inhabited from 2 000 BC until the Roman period. The site is being excavated and comprises a **theatre** capable of seating 5 000 spectators on its unusual elliptical terraces facing a rectangular orchestra, and a residential district below an acropolis.

Views of Mount Laurion and its mining installations.

Return towards Lávrio to rejoin the road to Athens. Beyond Keratéa the road enters the **Messógia** (inland), a sparsely inhabited plain caused by subsidence which was formerly marshy but has since been drained and now produces cereals, olives and vines.

Peanía – The birthplace of Demosthenes. The **Vorrés Museum** ⏱ (modern and popular art) presents over 300 paintings and 40 sculptures by Greek artists in the post-war years: paintings by Fassianos, Moralis, Gaitis, Tsarouchis, Vassiliou etc. A good road leads to the **Koutoúki Cave★** ⏱ (Spileo Koutoúki) 500m/1 640ft up the slope of Mount Hymettos; it has recently been arranged to show off the beautiful stalactites, stalagmites and variously coloured curtains.

Return to Athens by the road which passes over the saddle between Hymettos and Pentelikon.

★★Vravróna (Brauron)

Itinerary 2 *Round trip of 81km/50mi*

Access

By orange bus from 14 Odós Mavromateon (Pedio Áreos Park) *(plan p 79)*.

Peanía – *See above (Itinerary 1).*

From Athens take the road to Rafína bearing right to Markópoulo. The route crosses the Messógia Plain past wheat fields, olive groves, orchards and vineyards. In Markópoulo turn left (northeast) into the road which descends towards Vravróna and Pórto Raftí. After 8km/5mi one reaches the Brauron archeological site.

★★Vravróna – The **Brauron** sanctuary was set among hills not far from the Aegean shore *(beach)*; anciently it was a place of pilgrimage dedicated to Artemis Brauronia. According to a legend referred to by Euripides in his *Iphigenia in Tauris* Agamemnon's daughter, Iphigenia, who had escaped being sacrificed and fled to the land of the Tauris in the Crimea, returned with the sacred statue of Artemis, to live out her days in Brauron. To atone for the sacrifice of a bear protected by Artemis – the goddess had a special association with the bear – Iphigenia founded the sanctuary of Artemis Brauronia which was served by young priestesses, known as "bears", who were dressed in saffron robes and dedicated to the goddess at the age of seven.

"Bear" with a hare, Brauron

T.A.P.

Sanctuary ⏱ – Beyond a 6C AD paleo-Christian basilica *(left)* is the sacred fountain which flowed into a stream spanned by a 5C BC bridge.

On the right, below St George's Chapel (15C) are the foundations of the temple of Artemis (5C BC); behind in a crack in the rock is the "Tomb of Iphigenia". Opposite was the grand peristyle courtyard which was flanked on three sides by the "parthenon" where the "bears" lived; the rooms were furnished with wooden beds and stone tables. Part of the colonnade has been re-erected.

Moussío ⏱ – The **museum** displays geometric vases (9C-8C BC), a low relief votive sculpture showing the figures of Zeus (seated), Leto, Apollo and Artemis (5C BC) and particularly a series of ravishing statuettes or marble heads of little "bears" (4C BC) with unusually delicate expressions: the **"Bear with a bird"** and the **"Bear with a hare"** are masterpieces.

Return to Markópoulo via **Pórto Ráfti**, a seaside resort and the port of the Messógia (Limáni Messogéas). At the mouth of the bay there is an island crowned by a colossal Roman marble figure of a man sitting cross-legged; it is popularly called the tailor *(ráftis)* and was probably used as a leading mark.

Return to Athens by the same road as for the outward journey.

★Aktí Marathóna (Marathon Coast)

Itinerary 3 *Round trip of 108km/67mi*

From Athens take the road to Rafína which passes between Hymettos and Pentelikon and through the village of Pikérmi.

Rafína – The ferries for Euboia and the eastern Cyclades leave from Rafína which is a commercial and fishing port. Fish tavernas line the waterfront and the beach.

Dílessi Murders

The fatal incident, also known as the Marathon Massacres, took place in 1870. On 11 April a party of eight consisting of Lord and Lady Muncaster, Edward Lloyd, an English barrister, and his wife and daughter (aged 6), Edward Herbert, third Secretary at the British Legation in Athens, Frederick Vyner, a young Englishman, and Count Alberto de Boïl, a Piedmontese nobleman from the Italian Legation, made an excursion to the battlefield at Marathon.
On the return journey their coach outstripped the escort of infantry and just before the bridge at Pikérmi (known subsequently as "the bridge of the Lords" but demolished in 1954 in a road improvement scheme) they were abducted by brigands.
The women and child were released immediately and Lord Muncaster followed soon after to raise the ransom. The brigand leader, who was led to believe his prisoners were "kings", altered the terms for their release almost daily. The authorities mishandled the matter and sent troops to block the road. On 21 April the soldiers caught up with the brigands, who were moving from Skála Oroupoú on the north coast of Attica to Dílessi, and opened fire. The brigands, true to their code, promptly murdered their four captives.
The bodies of Herbert and Vyner were sent home after first being buried in the Protestant Cemetery in Athens. The victims are commemorated in the east window in St Paul's Anglican Church in Athens.
This incident inspired the film *Megaléxandros* made by Angelopoulos in 1981.

Take the road north along the coast past a series of beaches where the Athenians flock on Sundays and then rejoin the main road at Néa Mákri; after 5km/3mi there is a right-hand turning leading to the Marathon battlefield.

★**Marathon Battlefield** – The stretch of coastal plain south of Marathónas was the scene of the famous battle which took place in 490 BC and was described by Herodotos.

Warriors of Marathon – The Persian fleet set sail from Asia Minor to punish the Athenians and Eretrians (Euboia) for supporting the revolt of Miletus in 499 BC. The archers and cavalry were landed in the Bay of Marathon to march on Athens. The Athenian hoplites had however taken up their position on the lower slopes of Mount Agrilíki at the southern end of the plain. They probably numbered about 7 000 assisted by 1 000 Plataians whereas the Persians numbered about 20 000.

Access

Rafína – By orange bus (1hr) every 30min or 45min from 29 Odós Mavromateon (Pedio Áreos) *(plan p 79)*.

Marathon Barrow – By the same orange bus, getting off at the stop for Marathónas and Néa Mákri.

Ramnoús – By orange bus from 14 Odós Mavromateon (Pedio Áreos) *(plan p 79)*.

For eight days the two armies faced each other. Then the Persians re-embarked some of their troops and the Athenians, commanded by **Miltiades**, attacked the remainder and overwhelmed them so that they fled to their ships across the marsh to the north. According to tradition there were 6 400 Persian dead while the Greeks lost only 192 men.
The victory won, Miltiades sent a messenger to Athens to announce the good news. The runner is supposed to have made the journey from Marathon to Athens without pausing for breath. On arrival he announced the victory and dropped dead of exhaustion.
This feat inspired the Marathon race which is part of the modern Olympic Games and has recently become a popular mass event among amateur runners in many major cities. The official distance (42.195km/26mi 385yd) was established in 1908 when the Games were held in England and the Marathon was run from Windsor Great Park to the White City Stadium. At the first modern Games in 1896 the distance was shorter (40km/24.9mi) which more nearly corresponds to the distance from Marathon to Athens.

Timvos Marathóna ⓥ – Isolated in the plain, the **Marathon Barrow** which was raised over the Athenian hoplites who died at Marathon is 9m/30ft high. At the foot is a reproduction of the gravestone of Aristion, the so-called Soldier of Marathon; it is a low relief showing a hoplite like those who fought on the battlefield (original in the National Museum in Athens).

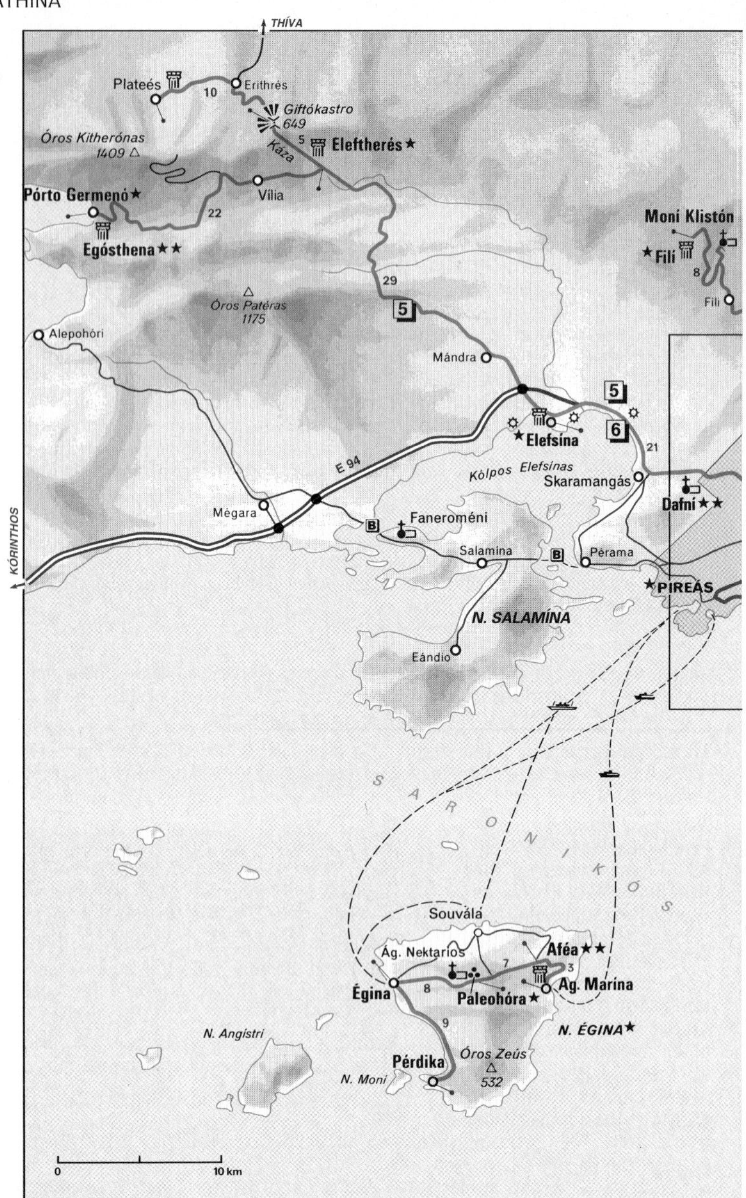

Originally gravestones bearing the names of those who died were set round the sides of the barrow. From the top there is a fine view of the plain, formerly uncultivated but now used for crops, and the surrounding mountains.

Return to the main road and 1km/0.5mi further north turn left to the Barrow of the Plataians. Immediately on the right stands a hangar covering a cemetery.

Eladikó Nekrotafío – This **Helladic cemetery** is proof of very ancient human occupation of the plain of Marathon where, according to mythology, Theseus killed the bull, brought by Herakles from Crete, which was devastating the countryside. The tombs which have been excavated date from 2000 BC and contain perfectly preserved skeletons.

Timvos Plateéon ⓥ – The **Barrow of the Plataians** covers the graves in which were buried the remains of the soldiers of the Boeotian city of Plataia *(see below)* who died in the Battle of Marathon.

Moussío – The **museum** contains an interesting collection of primitive objects from the Helladic and Mycenaean periods which were found during recent excavations: funerary urns, one of which, for a child, is most unusually shaped like a cocoon; statuettes; helmets and weapons; mirrors etc.

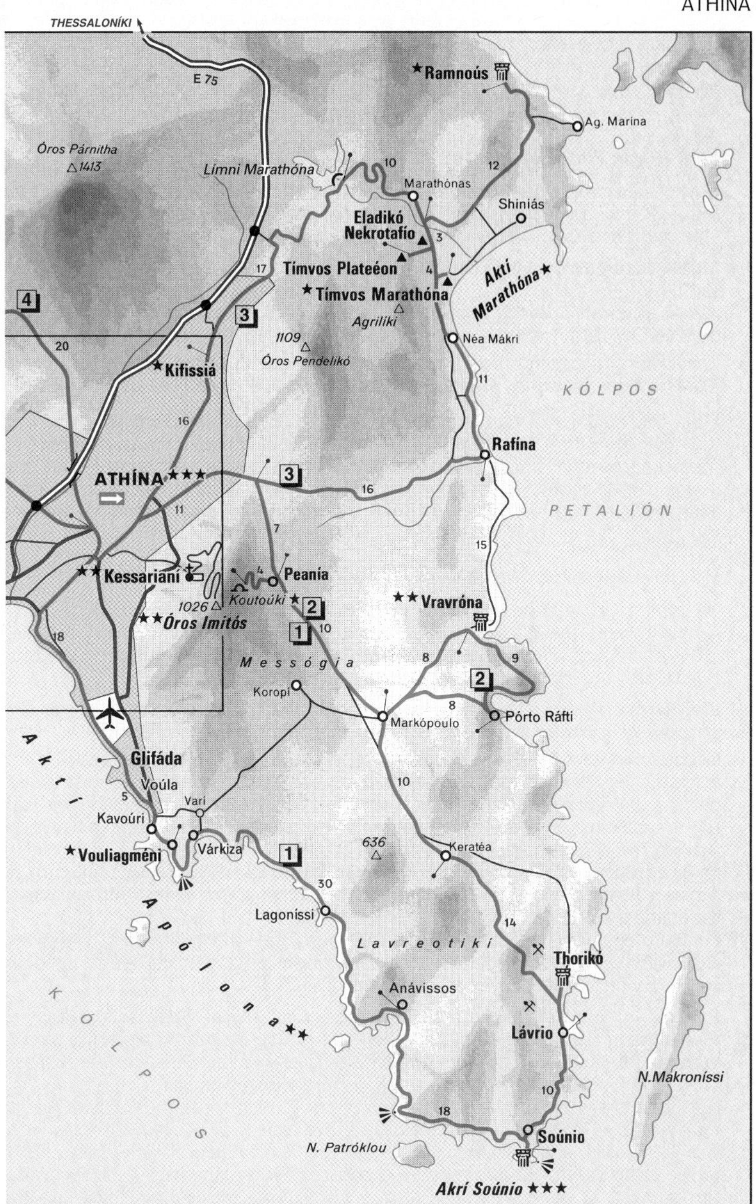

Near the museum is a Helladic and Mycenaean cemetery; one of the graves contains the skeleton of a horse.

Return to the main road continuing north; just before Marathon turn right to the pleasant beach at Shiniás (beautiful pine grove) and Ramnoús.

★**Ramnoús** ⓥ – The ruins of ancient Ramnoús lie in a remote valley running down to the sea opposite Euboia. Its name is thought to derive from a thorny shrub *(rámnos)* which still grows in the area and is classified by botanists in the same family as the buckthorn under the name *rhamnaceae*.

The first ruins to greet the visitor are a platform bearing the foundations of two Doric temples built side by side. The smaller (6C BC) was dedicated to Themis, goddess of Justice (statue in the National Museum in Athens); the larger (5C BC) contained a famous effigy of Nemesis, goddess of Punishment and divine Retribution, whose head is now displayed in the British Museum in London.

Continue down the path to the headland where the acropolis stood; the ruined fortress dates from the 5C-4C BC. There are traces of the enclosing wall, which had one gate flanked by square towers, of a small theatre, of various buildings and of a citadel which stood on the top of the hill.

There are fine views of the wild and rocky coast; the position of the ancient lower town can be surmised as well as the harbour at the mouth of the stream.

Return to the Marathon road. On leaving Marathon turn left into the new road which passes Lake Marathon. Return to Athens by the motorway via Kifissiá.

★Filí (Phyle Fortress) *Itinerary 4 56km/35mi there and back*

From Athens take Odós Liossíon which follows the railway to Néa Lióssia and then Áno Liόssia. Beyond the village of Phyle the road starts to climb Mount Parnes. Turn right at one of the bends into a road (sign "Moní Klistón").

Moní Klistón (Convent of the Gorge) – Alt 500m/1 640ft. The convent of nuns known as The Virgin of the Gorge (Panagía ton Kleistón) takes its name from its spectacular **position★** above a deep gorge riddled with caves, some of which were occupied by hermits. Some of the buildings date from the 14C.

The road continues upwards (beehives on the slopes) past the track (right) to the Plátani Kriopigí taverna; soon after turn left to reach Phyle Fortress.

★**Filí** – 683m/2 241ft. In an empty landscape the ruins of **Phyle Fortress** merge with the rock escarpment on which they stand commanding one of the passes between Attica and Boeotia. Considerable sections of the enclosing wall are still standing; it was built in the 4C BC of huge rectangular blocks up to 2.70m/over 8ft thick and reinforced with several square towers of which two remain standing, and one round one.

★Pórto Germanó *Itinerary 5 174km/109mi there and back*

On leaving Elefsína (Eleusis) bear right into the Thebes (Thíva) road which climbs gently towards the Kithairon mountain range which forms the border between Attica and Boeotia. *Continue past the turning (left) to Vília;* the ruins of Eleutherai (Eleftherés) are soon visible on a rock spur *(right).*

★**Eleftherés** – *Park near a disused petrol station and taverna and return to the path (left) which leads up to the fortress (30min on foot there and back).*

Eleutherai Fortress stands on a desolate site, exposed to the wind, commanding the way over the Kithairon range at the southern end of the Káza Pass. The walls were built by the Athenians in the 4C BC with gates and posterns, reinforced with high towers and provided with a parapet walk which is quite well preserved particularly on the north side; views of Attica.
At first the city of Eleutherai was Boeotian but in the 6C BC it was attached to Athens when the wooden statue of Dionysos Eleutheros was taken to Athens where it became a cult object.
Continue by car to the **Giftókastro Pass** (649m/2 129ft) where there is a magnificent view westwards over Mount Kithairon and northwards over the fertile Boeotian plain. A short distance away are the ruins of Plataia.

Plateés – Only a few traces remain of the ancient city of **Plataia**, whose hoplites fought bravely at the battle of Marathon *(see p 71)*; they lie on a sloping terrace in a majestic situation at the foot of the north face of Mount Kithairon (Kitherónas). There is a fine **view** of the red earth of the fertile Boeotian plain.
Northeast of the site on the level ground by the River Assopós the Battle of Plataia took place in 479 BC when the Greeks beat the Persians whose general, Mardonios, was killed. This victory, coming in the year after the battle of Salamis *(see p 114)*, forced the troops of Xerxes to leave Greece and so terminated the Persian Wars. On the right of the road from Erithrés, just outside the modern town, are the ancient ruins, in particular traces of the 5C-4C BC circular walls reinforced by towers which were open on the inside.

Return downhill to the turning (right) to Vília.

The road runs through the pleasant little town of **Vília** *(hotels, restaurants)*, past the military road *(right)* which leads to the summit of **Mount Kithairon** (Óros Kitherónas) which reaches 1 409m/4 623ft *(military zone)* and winds down through stands of Aleppo pines to the bay of Pórto Germenó.

★**Pórto Germenó** – This quiet seaside resort is a modern development with a huge beach. It is pleasantly sited in a bay at the eastern end of the Gulf of Corinth. The white houses are scattered among the pines and olives which cover the lower slopes of Kithairon.

★★**Egósthena** – *Access by the narrow coast road.* Above the olive groves stands a very well preserved acropolis which is a good example of Greek military architecture in the late 4C BC; the enclosing wall (180m/590ft long) is built of rough blocks of stone and strengthened with posterns, huge lintels and high towers; the most handsome tower *(on the right going up)* rises 9m/30ft above the curtain wall.
In the 13C **Aigosthena Fortress** ⓥ was restored by the Franks – there are traces of a monastery – and linked to the seashore by two fortified walls enclosing the lower town; part of the northern wall is still extant.

★★Dafní – Elefsína (Daphne – Eleusis)

Itinerary 6 *42km/26mi there and back*

On the right beyond the junction of Leofóros Athinón with the road to Thessaloníki is the site of the garden of the **Academy**, the famous school of philosophy founded by Plato near the town of **Colona** (Kolonós) where Sophocles was born in 496 BC. On the left just before the beginning of the motorway to Corinth, at the foot of a wooded hill, stands the Daphne Monastery. A famous **wine festival** takes place in the adjoining park; the price of entry includes free tasting of the major Greek wines.

★★**Dafní (Daphne Monastery)** – *See DAFNÍ.*

West of Dafní the road skirts the **Bay of Eleusis** which is guarded by the island of Salamis *(see below)* and cluttered with unchartered ships. **Skaramangás** is the home of the national shipyards which were formerly the property of the shipping magnate **Stavros Niarchos**. **Elefsína** (Eleusis) is now an industrial town on the edge of a fertile plain. The sanctuary of Eleusis is on the west side of the town *(sign)*.

★**Sanctuary of Eleusis** – *See ELEFSÍNA.*

Salamína (Salamis) *96km²/37sq mi – Pop 23 061*

The island, which almost blocks the entrance to the Bay of Eleusis, has few interesting sights except for the beautiful 18C frescoes (Last Judgement) in the church of the **Faneroméni Monastery** ⌚ (17C) but many Athenians have a holiday house on the island.

Access

By ferry and launches from Piraeus, Pérama and the coast near Mégara.

Battle of Salamis (480 BC) – The name of Salamis survives in the annals of the second Persian War because of the famous naval engagement described by Aeschylus in his play *The Persians*. The Persians had overrun Athens and Attica and assembled their fleet in the Bay of Phaleron while the Greek triremes had withdrawn into the Bay of Eleusis. By a ruse Themistocles induced the Persian fleet to launch an attack off Pérama to confine and destroy the Greek ships but it was unable to manoeuvre in the narrow channel and was dispersed and mostly destroyed under the eyes of Xerxes, the "king of kings", who was following the battle from a vantage point high up on the cliffs.

★Égina (Aigina) – *83km²/32sq mi – Pop 11 639*

The isle of Égina comprises a series of volcanic heights in the centre and the south which culminate in Mount Zeus (532m/1 745ft), now known as Mount Profítis Ilías; its pyramidal silhouette, formerly crowned by a temple to Zeus, acted as a landmark for sailors. To the north and west the island consists of a coastal plain and low hills covered by plantations of pistachio nuts, almonds and olives and a few vineyards.

In Greek mythology the island was known as the kingdom of **Aiakos**, Achilles' grandfather, who, together with Minos and Rhadamanthos, was made judge of the underworld.

In the Archaic era (7C-6C BC) Égina was a powerful maritime State, minting its own coins, marked with a tortoise, exporting its ceramics and bronzes and establishing colonies round the Mediterranean. Its rivalry with Athens, however, proved fatal and in 455 BC the islanders were defeated and had to emigrate.

Égina Town – Pop 6 373. The low, pink and white houses of the town cluster round the little harbour of coastal and fishing vessels protected by a charming chapel dedicated to St Nicholas, the patron of sailors. The shops along the waterfront sell the local specialities: pottery, pistachio nuts and marzipan; some of the boats act as floating shops dealing in fish, fruit and vegetables.

Égina enjoyed a brief moment of glory during the struggle for independence from 1827 to 1829 when it was the capital of the new

Access and accommodation

Access – By **hydrofoil** (40min) from Piraeus (main harbour) to Égina Town. Information from Ceres Flying Dolphins Group: Piraeus ☎ (01) 42 80 001.

Accommodation – In Égina Town, about 20 hotels (cat A to E); in Agía Marína, about 50 hotels (cat A to E); some hotels at Souvála, Vaía and Pérdika; on Angístri Island, about 20 hotels (cat C to E). **Camp site** on Moní Island.

Transport – Horse-drawn carriages, bicycle hire.

Greek State and Kapodístrias, who is buried on Corfu, set up his government on the island. Printing presses produced the first books and newspapers of free Greece and the first national money was minted bearing a phoenix, symbol of rebirth.
On **Cape Kolóna** (Colonna), north of the town, stands a fluted column crowned with a capital (8m/23ft high), once part of a temple to Apollo erected in the 5C BC; **excavations** ⊙ in the neighbourhood have uncovered the remains of a theatre and a stadium, as well as a prehistoric dwelling (museum). From the beach one can see remains of the quays of the ancient harbour below the surface of the sea.

★**Paleohóra** ⊙ – *8km/5mi east by the road to Agía Marína.* The road climbs slowly through pistachio orchards before reaching the **sanctuary of St Nectarios** (Ágios Nektários), a popular place of pilgrimage. *A track leads to Paleohóra.*
Paleohóra was the capital of the island under the Venetians and the Turks when the coast was vulnerable to piracy. In the 18C the town counted 400 houses and about 20 religious establishments; it was abandoned by its inhabitants early in the 19C. The houses were demolished but the cathedral, a basilical building, and the churches and chapels, most of which are 13C, have been restored; some are adorned with interesting frescoes and iconostases. The Venetian castle on the hilltop provides a good view of Mount Zeus and the northwest coastline.

★★**Aféa** – *14km/8mi east by the road to Agía Marína.* The **Temple of Aphaia** ⊙ stands on a magnificent site on the summit (199m/653ft) of a wooded hill overlooking the bay of Agía Marína and the rocky coast where sponge divers used to operate *(east)* and Athens and Mount Hymettos, Salamis and the Peloponnese *(north and west).*

Temple of Aphaia, Égina

The temple, which is quite well preserved, was built in the Doric style; some of the 22 limestone columns (5.27m/17ft 3in high) are monolithic. The scale is modest but well proportioned. The temple dates from the beginning of the 5C BC and was dedicated to Aphaia, a local divinity. The pediments of sculpted marble depicted Athena presiding over a battle between Greeks and Trojans. These carvings, known as the Aigina Marbles, were bought in 1812 by Prince Ludwig of Bavaria, later King Ludwig I, and displayed in Munich.
The temple is approached by a ramp from the east near the sacrificial altars. The position of the *naós*, containing the statue of Aphaia, is clearly visible in the interior. South of the temple are traces of an entrance gate *(propylaia)* and the priest's lodgings.
The site was first excavated in April 1811 by C R Cockerell and von Hallerstein and again in 1901-03 by Bavarian archeologists under Furtwängler. Traces of an Archaic temple were discovered in 1969.

Agía Marína – *3km/2mi below.* The place is a popular seaside resort.

Pérdika – *10km/6mi south.* There is a fine beach on the way to Pérdika. The charming fishing harbour lined by fish tavernas, affords a good **view**★ of Moní Island. Excursions by boat can be made to the island (old monastery, beach, camping site) in summer.

For adjacent sights see AMFIARAÍO, DAFNÍ, ELEFSÍNA, ÉVIA, KÓRINTHOS, Dióriga KORÍNTHOU, LOUTRÁKI, PÓROS.

DAFNÍ Monastery★★

DAPHNE – Attica

Michelin map 980 fold 30 – Local map of ATHENS Region see p 78

The monastery, which is tucked between the Athens-Corinth road *(north)* and a sweet-scented pine-clad hill *(south)*, is known to art enthusiasts for its church and its Byzantine mosaics.

Duke of Athens' Burial Place – The monastery stands on the site of a temple to Apollo which was originally surrounded by laurel trees *(dáfni)*, Apollo's favourite trees because they reminded him of the nymph Daphne whom he had loved. The monastery was founded in the 5C AD and dedicated to the Dormition of the Virgin; it was reduced to ruins by the barbarian invasions and rebuilt in the late 11C.

When the crusaders arrived in 1205 Attica passed under the domination of the French. The new lords of Athens, who were natives of Burgundy or Champagne, took the monastery under their protection and the first of them, Otho de la Roche, gave it to the Cistercians. The monks of St Bernard restored it and under the name of Dalphinet it became the chosen burial place of the dukes of Athens in imitation of Citeaux in France where the Capetian dukes of Burgundy were buried; Guy I de la Roche was buried at Daphne in 1263 and Gautier de Brienne in 1311 but the Turkish invasion in 1458 forced the Cistercians to leave.

Access

By bus every 40min from Athens (Odós Deligiorgi, west of Omonia Square, between Platía Karaïskaki and Odós Panagi Tsaldari-Pireos, plan of Athens).

TOUR ⊘

Overall view – From the slope of the hill south of the precinct one can see – the cloister and the church in the foreground, the original entrance *(west side of site)* and the rectangular precinct with a well-preserved section of the 5C to 6C wall complete with sentry walk and square towers *(north side parallel with the main road)*.

Cloister – The peaceful paved court with its solemn cypress trees is flanked on the east side by a typically Cistercian arcade with double arcatures; the cells were added in the 16C. Under the western arcade are ducal sarcophagi; one is decorated with fleurs-de-lys and heraldic serpents (guivres). Fragments of stonework discovered in the crypt.

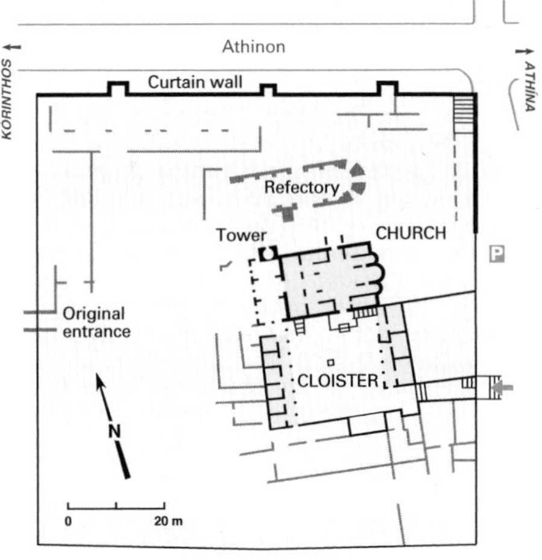

Church – The domed Byzantine church was built over the crypt in the 11C and enlarged and refurbished in the 13C by the Cistercians who were responsible for a certain number of windows including the triple ones, the exo-narthex and the creation within of a number of chapels for the monks whose rule required them to celebrate mass daily and simultaneously.

Exterior – There is a fine view from the cloister of the south front of the church with its brick window frames. The entrance to the **exo-narthex** is composed of twin arches supported on a central antique column. This narthex, which is crenellated, must have been built on the model of Citeaux for the use of the lay brothers whose accommodation is likely to have been nearby; the tombs of the dukes of Athens were placed here. The pointed arches of the west front and traces of a groined vault suggest the inspiration of Burgundian architecture.

On the north side of the church, beyond the square tower which protected the church on this side, are the remains of the 11C refectory. The elevation of the church and the dome can be admired; the small windows date from the 11C; the others are probably 13C.

Interior – The church is magnificently decorated with late 11C **mosaics**★★ against a gold background which are remarkable for their delicacy of line and colouring. The most beautiful scenes, which are arranged according to the theological concepts of those days, include:

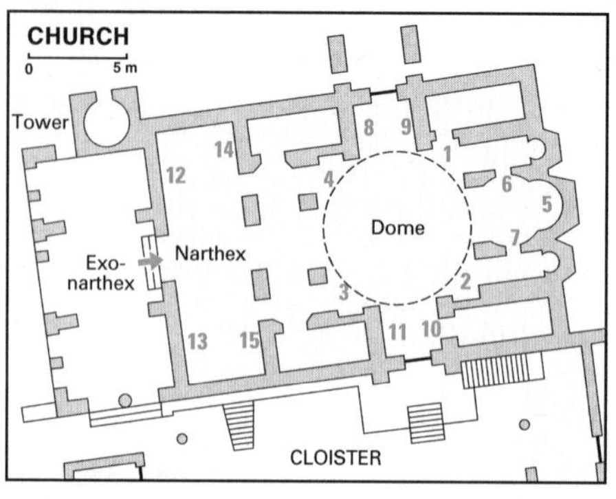

– in the dome, Christ Pantocrator, surrounded by the 16 prophets; in the squinches, the Annunciation (1), the Nativity (2), the Baptism (3) and the Ascension (4) of Christ;
– in the apse, the Virgin Mary (5) flanked by the Archangels Michael (6) and Gabriel (7);
– in the transept arms, gospel scenes including the Birth of the Virgin, the Entry of Christ into Jerusalem (8) and the Crucifixion (9) *(north transept)*, the Adoration of the Magi, Christ rising from the dead (10), doubting Thomas (11) *(south transept)*;
– in the narthex, the Betrayal by Judas (12) and a scene from the legend of Joachim and Anne (13) are opposite the Last Supper (14) and the Presentation of the Virgin in the Temple (15).

For adjacent sights see AMFIARAÍO, ATHÍNA, ELEFSÍNA, ÉVIA, KÓRINTHOS, Dióriga KORÍNTHOU, LOUTRÁKI, PÓROS, THÍVA.

DELFÍ★★★

DELPHI – Fokída, Central Greece – Population 2 426
Michelin map 980 fold 29 – Alt 573m/1 880ft

In antiquity Delphi was one of the most important religious centres; the sanctuary of Apollo, which is situated above the River Pleistos gorge against the backdrop of Mount Parnassos, attracted a host of pilgrims who came to consult the oracle. Even now an aura of mystery invests the sparse ruins exposed on the rocky slope where the trees – olive, pine, cypress and lentisk – struggle for a toehold. A visit to Delphi tends to be a more impressive experience than any other in Greece.

★★★**The site** – The road from Athens runs east to west through the archeological site to the modern town.
Beneath the silent watch of birds of prey the ancient ruins range down the mountain side below two roseate rock faces, the Phaidriades (250m–300m/820–984ft high). Between them is a deep cleft from which emerges the Kastalian Spring. This awesome and majestic landscape is subject to occasional earthquakes and violent thunderstorms. The view to the south, on the other hand, at the foot of the mountain presents a contrasting and pleasant spectacle. The deep valley of the River Pleistos, silver-grey with olive groves, winds west and south round the foot of Mount Kírphis towards the coastal basin, forming the famous "sea of olive trees" which extends to the shore where the waters of the Bay of Itéa gleam in the pearly light.
The European Cultural Centre, founded in 1977, works in collaboration with the "Save Delphi" committee and other associations for the preservation of the site. It organises an art festival in the stadium in summer.

PRACTICAL INFORMATION

Access – **By bus:** from Athens (3hr) from bus station B (near 260 Odós Liossion) 5 services daily *(see ATHÍNA: Practical Information)*; from Patras via Itéa.

Cultural events – In summer the European Cultural Centre (headquarters in Delphi) organises cultural and artistic events in the Angelos House and in Eva Sikelianos, a museum presenting the festivities of Delphi.

Accommodation – About 30 hotels (cat A to D); some guest-houses and rooms in private houses; youth hostel; 2 camping sites in Delphi, 1 in Hrissá on the Itéa road. Also possible to stay in Aráhova *(see ARÁHOVA)* 12 km east; in Itéa 18 km southwest (5 to 6 hotels, 3 camping sites); also at pretty Galaxídi harbour (7 to 8 small hotels and guest-houses; rooms in private houses; camping site).

Tour – Visitors who are pressed for time can visit the Apollo sanctuary and the museum in half a day. Those interested in archeology can take a day and a half to visit the site following the path of the pilgrims of old (Marmaria, Kastalian Spring, sanctuary of Apollo, stadium) with half a day reserved for the museum and the views.

LEGEND AND HISTORY

The primitive earth goddess Ge or Gaia – According to legend, Delphi was founded by Zeus. The historians of antiquity, who thought that the world was shaped like a flat disc, recounted how the leader of the gods wanted to know the position of the centre of the earth over which he reigned and sent two eagles out to reconnoitre. The two birds met above Mount Parnassos and identified the **omphalos** *(see below)* which was to make Delphi the hub of the universe.
In fact, the sanctuary's origins go far back into the past. In the 2nd millennium BC Delphi was already a place of worship dedicated to the earth goddess (Ge or Gaia) and her daughter Themis, one of the Titans, who expressed themselves in the booming of earth tremors, the rustle of vegetation and particularly the murmuring of water flowing from faults in the rock. The goddess hid at the bottom of one of these faults, guarded by her son, the snake Python; the divine pronouncements were already being interpreted by an oracle.

An archer takes the stage – It was at the end of the Mycenaean period that **Apollo**, Olympian God and guarantor of universal harmony, is supposed to have overcome the old underworld deities. A hymn attributed to Homer tells how, after his birth on Delos *(see DÍLOS)* Zeus' son came to Delphi, killed the snake **Python** with his bow and arrow and in accordance with divine law, he went into exile for eight years to atone for the killing of the snake and on his return, he took his place, becoming the god Python, who gave oracles through the intermediary of the Pythia. A festival consisting of lyrical contests to be held every eight years was instituted and named the Pythian Games in honour of the snake.
The cult of Apollo, which was inaugurated by the Cretans, was joined by the cult of Dionysos and Athena. Early in the 6C BC, when the Athenians were the major power in central Greece, they reorganised the Pythian Games at Delphi at which sports and poetic contests were held. This was the heyday of Delphi as a panhellenic sanctuary attracting pilgrims from all over the Greek world, from Spain to the Black Sea.
The sanctuary was maintained by the dues paid by those who consulted the oracle and enriched by offerings from both Greeks and barbarians. Despite the depredations of war and earthquakes and the pillaging of Sulla and Nero, Delphi was still thriving under Emperor Hadrian in the 2C AD.
When **Julian the Apostate** (361-363), the last pagan emperor of Rome, sent his quaestor, Oribasius, to consult the Pythian oracle, its utterance was worthy to be its own epitaph:

> "Go tell the king – the carven hall is felled;
> Apollo has no cell, prophetic bay
> Nor talking spring; his cadenced well is stilled."

It was finally closed in 381 by the Byzantine emperor Theodosius the Great.

The oracle – Originally the priestess of the sanctuary was chosen from among the local virgins but later she had to be a woman of over 50 whose life was beyond reproach. Known as the **Pythia** and later as the Delphic Sibyl, she delivered replies inspired by Apollo in answer to the questions put by the pilgrims. First she drank from the Cassotis fountain near the temple which was supposed to bestow the gift of prophecy; then she entered the temple crypt where she breathed the fumes of burning laurel leaves (Apollo's tree) and barley meal. Finally she took her seat on the famous tripod, a sort of three-footed cauldron, near to the *omphalos* and Dionysos' tomb.

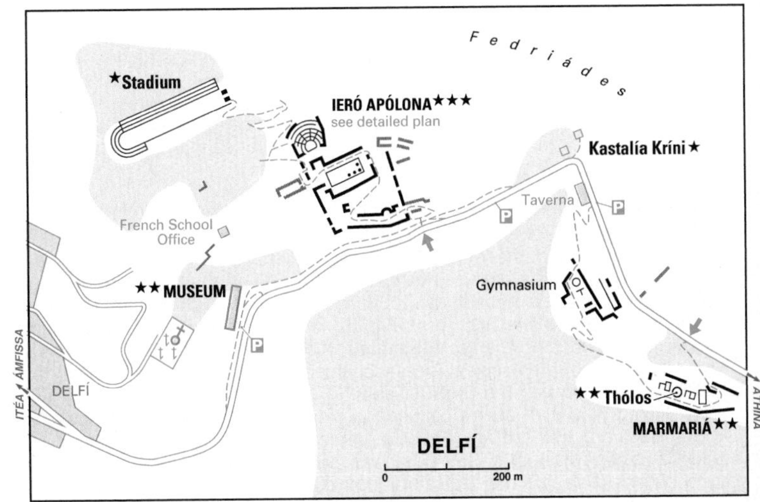

The pilgrims (men only) were admitted to the neighbouring room where they gave their questions to the priests who passed them on to the Pythia. She went into a trance; the sounds that she uttered, her posture and her convulsive movements were interpreted by the priests who delivered the oracle couched in ambiguous phrases in hexameter verse. The replies took the form of advice rather than predictions. The Pythia seems to have been well informed in politics; in turn she favoured Xerxes during the Persian invasions, then Athens, Sparta and Thebes in the 4C BC, then Philip of Macedon and Alexander the Great whom she proclaimed invincible and finally Rome.

The Pilgrim Way – Having come overland or disembarked at Kirra near to Itéa, the pilgrims climbed the northern slope of the Pleistos Valley and approached the temple past present-day Marmaria where they made their devotions to Athena. Then they proceeded to the Kastalian spring for ritual ablutions before crossing the *agora* and entering the sacred precinct. Once within they started up the Sacred Way, stopping at their national **Treasury** *(see below)* to deposit their offerings. Finally, after making the ritual propitiatory libations and sacrifices, they reached the temple.
As well as the sanctuary itself, the religious territory of Delphi included the Pleistos Valley and the coastal plain. This sacred domain was administered by a sort of Greek Society of Nations, the **Amphictyony**, in which each of the 12 Greek "peoples" was represented by two deputies. Nonetheless there were rivalries and in 339 BC the Thessalians and Boeotians, who were members, invited the intervention of Philip of Macedon. The sanctuary itself was served by two high priests, a steward, a treasurer, five priests, of whom Plutarch was once one, and several acolytes, who attended the Pythia.

Excavations and restoration – Although a village grew up over the sanctuary, the site of the Delphic oracle was never completely forgotten; it was visited by Cyriacus of Ancona in the 15C, George Wheler and Dr Spon in the 17C and by Byron and other 19C travellers. The credit for its excavation, however, goes to the French School at Athens.
- 1838: Laurent, an architect, studied the site and the visible traces;
- 1880: B Haussoulier, an archeologist, made confirmatory trials;
- 1892: the French Parliament voted a sum of 750 000FF to demolish the village and rebuild it away from the archeological site;
- 1892-1902: excavations directed by **T Homolle**, Director of the French School and E Bourguet; 400 workmen uncovered the temple and the theatre from under a layer of earth up to 20m/66ft thick in places; the spoil was evacuated by narrow gauge railway using 75 wagons over 3km/2mi; inauguration of the first museum;
- 1903-52: further excavation and reconstructions by anastylosis – discovery in 1939 of a cache of precious objects beneath the Sacred Way;
- since 1950: investigations in the direction of the Kastalian spring; display of the paleo-Christian mosaics in the modern town and excavation of the stadium; reorganisation of the museum.

★★★ IERÓ APÓLONA (SANCTUARY OF APOLLO) ⓥ

It is a short walk uphill to the *agora* which precedes the sanctuary of Apollo.

Agora – The Romans remodelled the *agora* and added some houses and baths built of brick; traces of these buildings are visible above the *agora* and road.
Down one side of the *agora* ran an Ionic portico with shops for the pilgrims; a few of the columns have been re-erected. There are fragments from a paleo-Christian church displayed (1) in the far corner.
Four steps lead up to the main entrance, one of nine, to the sacred precinct **(témenos)**. The wall is 4C BC except in places; the polygonal construction *(west side)* is 6C BC; it encloses a trapezoidal area 200m/656ft by about 130m/427ft, of which the lower part contains the votive offerings (statues, inscriptions etc) and the Treasuries, small temples erected by the Greek city states to receive the offerings made by their citizens; the whole area is thickly studded with monuments.

Walk up the Sacred Way.

Sacred Way – No vehicles were allowed on the Sacred Way which leads up to the temple of Apollo; the paving dates from the Roman period.

Votive offerings – On the right, as one enters, stands the base of the bull of Corcyra (2), a bronze animal offered in the 5C BC by the city of Corcyra (now Corfu). Again on the right is the votive monument of the Arcadians (3) next to that of the Lakedaimonians *(see SPÁRTI)*; on the left the votive monument of Marathon, which the Athenians decorated with statues by Pheidias, is followed by the monument of the Argives. These monuments, what little is left of them, testify to the rivalry between the Greek cities.
The Sacred Way then passes between the foundations of two semicircular structures erected by the Argives. The best preserved *(right)* was the monument of the king of Árgos (4), built in 369 BC; it was decorated with 20 statues of the kings and queens of Árgos; the dedicatory inscriptions were written from right to left.

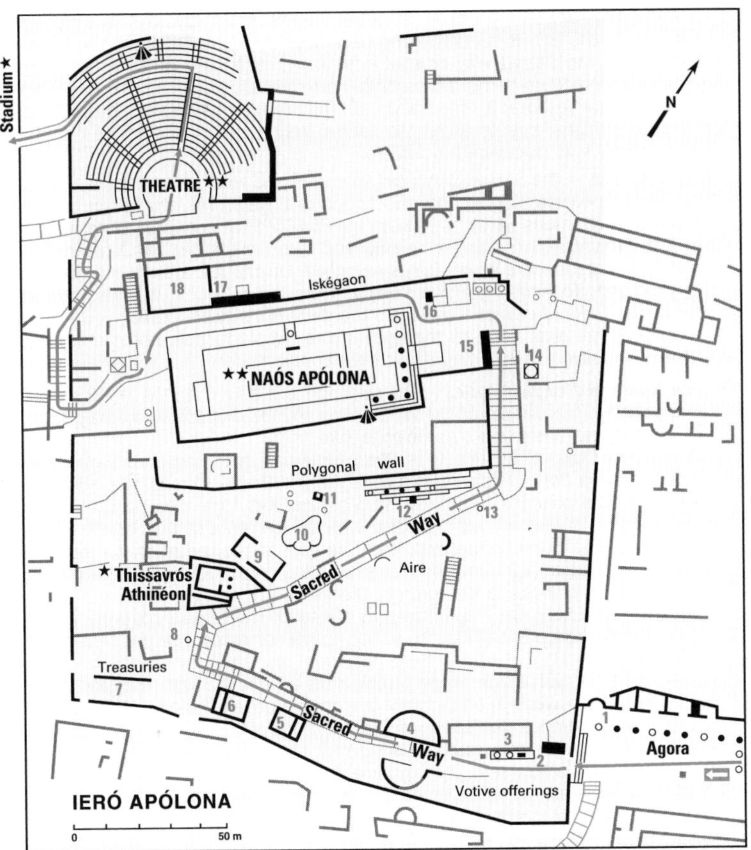

Treasuries – The first is the treasury of Sikyon (5), northwest of Corinth; the bases remain; it was built of tufa to a rectangular plan with two columns at the entrance (6C BC).

Beyond stands the wall of the Treasury of Siphnos (6), which was built in about 525 BC by the inhabitants of this Cycladic island out of the proceeds of its gold mines. It was an Ionic building in marble with a sculpted pediment supported by two caryatids and a beautiful sculpted frieze *(in the museum)*.

In the southwest corner of the precinct stood the Treasury of Thebes (7); the tufa foundations are visible; it contrasted with its neighbour by the austerity of its grey limestone architecture. Nearby on the outside of the bend in the Sacred Way are the foundations of the Treasury of the Boeotians and a limestone version of the *omphalos* (8).

The **Treasury of the Athenians★** *(Thisssavrós Athinéon)*, which has been reconstructed by anastylosis, is a Doric building (490-480 BC) in white Parian marble, paid for with part of the booty captured from the Persians at Marathon. It was decorated with sculptures illustrating the Athenians' favourite themes: the battle between the Greeks and the Amazons, the legends about Theseus and Herakles *(in the museum)*. The Treasury was built on a mound and preceded by a triangular terrace. The south wall of the terrace bears a dedication inscribed in huge letters: "The Athenians to Apollo, after their victory over the Persians, as an offering to commemorate the battle of Marathon". The base and walls of the Treasury bear other inscriptions accompanied by crowns of laurel: for the most part the inscriptions are in honour of the Athenians.

After the Treasury come the sparse ruins of the Senate of Delphi (9) *(bouleuterion)*, followed by a pile of rocks (10) (the sacred rock of the Sibyl) marking the site of the early Delphic oracle, which was guarded by the snake Python; behind the rocks stood the sanctuary of the Earth goddess, Ge or Gaia. Further on are the fallen drums of an Ionic marble column (11), 10m/33ft high, a gift from the Naxiots to Apollo in about 570 BC; the column was surmounted by a sphinx *(in the museum)*.

Polygonal wall – The famous polygonal wall retaining the terrace on which the temple of Apollo is built is 83m/272ft long; it was built in the 6C BC of huge blocks of random-shaped limestone. The wall is inscribed with more than 800 acts granting slaves their freedom during the Hellenistic and Roman periods.

Three columns of Pentelic marble mark the Stoa of the Athenians (12) which dates from about 480 BC; it contained the naval trophies captured from the Persians. At this point the Sacred Way crosses a circular area *(halos)* where processions to the temple formed up before proceeding; note the handsome Ionic capital (13) and the curved seat *(exedra)* for the priests. On the edge of this area stood the Treasury of the Corinthians; nearby under the Sacred Way a cache of precious objects *(in the museum)* was discovered in 1939.

Temple approach – The Sacred Way rises steeply to the level of the temple of Apollo. The circular pedestal *(right)* bore the Tripod of Plataia (14), erected in commemoration of the famous Battle of Plataia *(see PLATEÉS)*; it consisted of three bronze serpents intertwined forming a column and was transferred by Constantine the Great to Constantinople where it has remained. On the left are the foundations of the great altar to Apollo (15) which dates from the 5C BC; it was also called the altar of the Chiots because they wrote the dedicatory inscriptions.

The huge stone pillar (16), to the right of the temple façade, bore an equestrian statue of Prusias (2C BC) King of Bithynia in Asia Minor.

★★ **Naós Apólona (Temple of Apollo)** – The existing ruins date from the 4C BC; the previous building, the temple of the Alcmeonids (6C BC), which was partly financed by Croesus, was destroyed by an earthquake.

The outline of the 4C BC temple is clear; some half dozen columns have been re-erected. It was a Doric building with a peristyle, 60.30m/198ft long by 23.80m/781ft wide, with tufa columns faced with stucco 12m/39ft high. The portico, in which stood a statue of Homer, was inscribed with the precepts of the Sages of Greece: "Know thyself", "Nothing in excess" etc. The *naós* at the centre of the temple was furnished with altars and statues; beyond was the crypt *(adyton)* where the Pythia sat near the *omphalos* and the tomb of Dionysos.

The views from here are magnificent; to the south the temple columns stand out against the backdrop of the Pleistos Valley; to the northwest rise the perfect curves of the theatre.

Parallel with the uphill side of the temple runs a retaining wall **"Iskégaon"**, built in the 4C BC; at the western end, on the site of the votive offering of Polyzalos (17), was found the famous Charioteer of Delphi *(in the museum)*.

The rectangular base of a votive offering (18) has preserved the dedicatory stone on the back wall on the left. The monument was set up c 315 BC by one Krateros *(see PÉLA Museum)* who had saved the life of Alexander the Great in a lion hunt; a bronze group by Lysippos recalls the scene.

Steps lead up to the theatre.

★★ **Theatre** – The original theatre dates from the 4C BC but it was remodelled 200 years later by the Romans who refurbished the orchestra and the stage. The 35 terraces of seats could accommodate 5 000 spectators who came to watch the "mysteries" re-enacting the struggle between Apollo and the Python as well as to hear recitals in honour of the god; in the first row are the seats for the priest and other officials.

From the top row there is a marvellous **view**★★★ down over the sanctuary ruins, across the Pleistos Valley with its carpet of olives to the silent mass of Mount Kírphis.

Schneider /CAMPAGNE CAMPAGNE

Delphi Theatre

The gangway *(diázoma)* running round the theatre half way up continues westwards as a path winding up the hillside to the Stadium; very fine views of the site of Delphi *(30min on foot there and back)*.

To reach the stadium, take the path to the left of the theatre. It is a steep climb, but it is worth it for the superb views over the site.

★**Stadium** – It is surrounded by the silent conifers which clothe the hillside. Before the first stone seating was built in the 3C BC the stadium was surrounded by earth terraces buttressed along the south side by a polygonal wall. In the 2C AD it was altered by Herod Atticus who built the present terraces, which can hold 6 500 people, and erected a monumental **gateway** of which the columns have been partially rebuilt at the east end of the track.
The southern terraces were buttressed by a rampart which has half collapsed; those on the north side are built into the rock; at the centre is the presidential enclosure. The starting and finishing lines are still in place, 178m/584ft (600 Roman feet) apart. In summer during the Festival of Delphi plays are performed in the stadium.

★★MUSEUM ⏲

Work on the enlargement of the building is in progress. The refurbishment of the whole museum and the new arrangement of the exhibits is scheduled to be completed during 1999.

The museum displays the works of art excavated at Delphi by the French School in a clear and pleasant presentation. At the top of the steps stands a conical block of marble covered by a sculpted lattice effect, representing the *agrenon*; it is a Hellenistic copy of the famous **omphalos**★ (navel) which was kept in the crypt of the temple of Apollo and supposed to mark the centre of the world. Note on the left some fragments illustrating the exploits of Herakles (Hercules), which probably came from the frieze on the theatre's proscenium.

Enter the Hall of Shields and turn right into the Hall of the Siphnians.

★**Hall of the Siphnian Treasury** – Devoted to Archaic sculpture (6C BC).
In the middle stands the winged Sphinx of the Naxiots mounted on its column. It is flanked by two caryatids from the Treasuries of Knidos and Siphnos.
Around the walls are pieces of the marble frieze from the Siphnian Treasury; the sculptured decoration was painted in bright colours, traces of which survive in places. The scenes depict: the Trojan War showing Aeneas and Hector in combat with Menelaos and Ajax (fine horses) under the interested gaze of the gods of Olympos; a beautifully composed Gigantomachy, the war between the giants and the gods.

★**Hall of the Kouroi** – The two *kouroi*, which were part of votive offerings, are huge Archaic statues from the 6C BC, representing Cleobis and Biton, twins from Árgos, who died of exhaustion after pulling their mother's chariot for 45 *stadia* (just under 5mi); she was a priestess of Hera hurrying to the Argive Heraion *(see ÁRGOS)* to perform a sacrifice.

★**Hall of the Bull** – Assembled here are the cult objects found in 1939 beneath the Sacred Way where they had been buried in two pits, probably because they were no longer in use, in accordance with an ancient custom which persisted in western Christian tradition.
The principal item is an Archaic bull dating from the 6C BC which was made of silver plates attached to copper strips fixed to a wooden framework. Dating from the same period are several gold panels, engraved or embossed, which probably adorned a statue and a statuette in ivory of a god taming a fawn. The bronzes include an incense burner held by a young girl dressed in a *peplos* (5C BC).

Retrace your steps and cross the Hall of the Kouroi and Hall of Shields, then enter the Hall of the Athenian Treasury on the right.

Hall of the Athenian Treasury – The sculpted metopes *(damaged)* which date from the Archaic period, belonged to the Athenian Treasury. They illustrate the legends of Herakles and Theseus; some of the heads, particularly the head of Theseus *(left)*, are very fine.

★**Halls of the Temple of Apollo** – These contain the sculptures from the west pediment (showing the battle of the giants) and the east pediment (showing the epiphany of Apollo), as well as other items from the Archaic temple of Apollo (called "of the Alcmaeonids"; end of the 6C BC).

Hall of the Funerary Stelae – Funerary stelae from the 5C BC. Note the altar with a decorative frieze of young girls as a base (second half of the 2C BC), found on the Marmaria site.

★**Hall of the Thólos** – Architectural fragments and sculptures from the decoration of the metopes of the Thólos are assembled here. At the end of the hall four metopes from the frieze have been reassembled. Note also on the left in a glass case some fragments of sculptures, including torsos of Amazons and Greek warriors.

The Hall of the Antinoüs is closed to the public. Most of the exhibits have been moved temporarily to the Hall of the Monument of Daochos, awaiting the completion of the refurbishment of the museum.

★★**Hall of the Monument of Daochos** – A magnificent group of three dancers (**Thyiads**) (4C BC) in Pentelic marble stands on an acanthus column; the dancers are bacchantes or Thyiads, priestesses of Dionysos. The column was a votive offering erected by the Athenians in front of the Monument of Daochos, which stood above the open space before the temple of Apollo.

Against the wall *(right)* are the statues from the monument (4C BC) of Daochos II, who represented Thessaly in the Amphictyonic league. Note the figure of the athlete Agias *(second from the right)* who won the *pancration* (a contest involving boxing and wrestling) in the Olympic and Delphic Games. It is probably a copy of a bronze by Lysippos.

★**Hall of the Antinoüs** – The marble statue (2C BC) of Antinoüs is one of the best representations of the favourite of Emperor Hadrian, who deified him after his death. There is a fine marble **head** thought to represent the Roman general T Q Flaminius. The showcases contain votive figurines offered to Pan in the Corycian cave *(see p 123)*.

★★★**Hall of the Charioteer** – The Charioteer of Delphi, which is wonderfully well preserved, is one of the most beautiful Greek statues from the late Archaic period (478 BC); it was discovered in 1896 not far from the theatre. The figure was part of a bronze votive offering representing the winning quadriga (four horse chariot) in the Olympic Games of 473 and 474; it was presented by Polyzalos, Tyrant of Gela in Sicily.

The noble, life-size figure (1.80m/5ft 11in) is facing slightly to the right (Polyzalos is thought to have been at his side) and holding the horses' reins in his hands. He is wearing the victor's headband. The great beauty of the modelling of the head is enhanced by the original eyes composed of enamel and coloured stones. The feet are so realistic that they seem to have been moulded from nature.

A showcase in the same room displays another work of art, a white libation cup (5C BC) showing Apollo seated, wearing a crown of laurel and holding a tortoise-shell lyre; he is pouring a libation in the presence of his sacred bird, the crow.

By the exit are displayed paleo-Christian mosaics, discovered recently near the modern town.

T.A.P.

The Charioteer, Delphi

ADDITIONAL SIGHTS

★★**Marmariá** – *South of the road to Aráhova; main entrance to the east (sign "Temple of Athena Pronaia").*

The **Sanctuary of Athena Pronaia** which the pilgrims visited before going on to the sanctuary of Apollo, stood on a beautiful site looking across the Pleistos Valley to Mount Kírphis. Now in ruins, the sanctuary has been known as Marmariá since it was used as a quarry for marble.

Old Temple of Athena – All that remains of this Archaic Doric temple, built of tufa in the 6C BC, are the bases of some columns and some sections of wall. The building was damaged by rock falls and eventually abandoned in the 4C BC. It incorporated elements of an earlier 7C BC temple, particularly some capitals which can be seen resting on the ground or on the remains of columns.

Between this temple and the rotunda *(thólos)* are the remains of two treasuries; the second probably belonged to Massalia, present-day Marseilles.

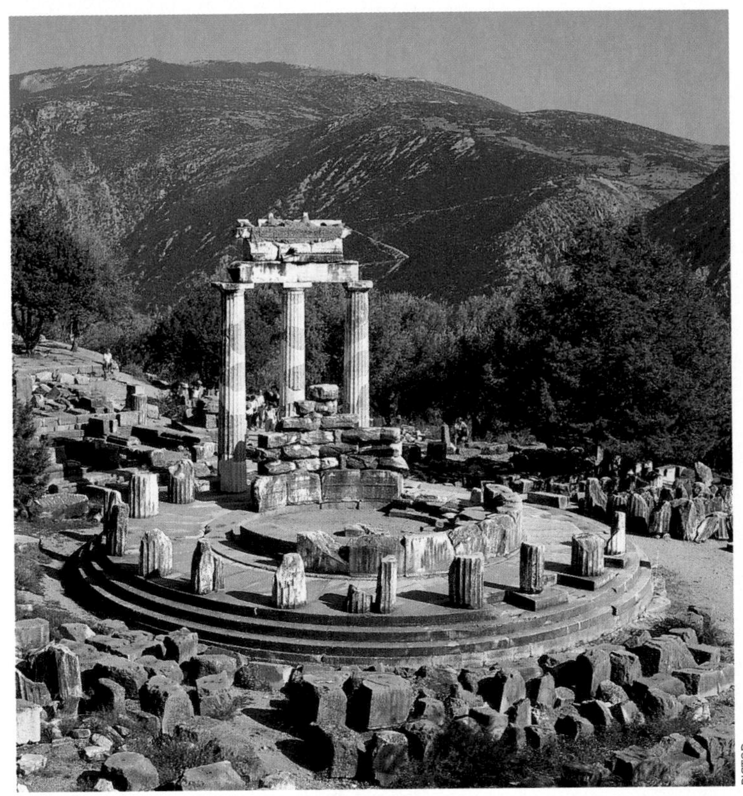

Thólos, Delphi

★★**Thólos** – This elegant peristyle rotunda *(illustration below)*, built of marble in the 4C BC, probably as a shrine of the earth goddess (Ge or Gaia), is picturesquely recalled by what remains: a stylobate, drums of fluted columns, lower courses of a circular wall and three Doric columns (re-erected) supporting an entablature with triglyphs and metopes bearing reliefs of a battle of the Amazons.

New Temple of Athena – The old tufa building was replaced in the 4C BC by a smaller temple built of limestone without a peristyle. The foundations are visible.

A steep path leads to the upper terraces where a **gymnasium**, built in the 4C BC and remodelled by the Romans, extended over two levels *(closed to the public for restoration)*; on the lower level, there are traces of a peristyle court which served as the *palestra* and of a circular pool; on the upper level traces of the covered track *(xystos)* are visible: part of the end wall and colonnade dating from the Roman era.

★**Kastalía Kríni** – *Closed to the public for restoration.* The **Kastalian Spring** where the nymph Kastalia is said to have drowned herself to escape from the attentions of Apollo wells up at the end of the wild ravine which divides the Phaidriades Rocks. Here the pilgrims of old performed ritual ablutions to purify themselves before entering Apollo's sanctuary; the water is now channelled to irrigate the olive groves.

Part of the ancient arrangements are still visible: a huge Archaic paved basin excavated in 1958, a longer basin hewn out of the rock at the base of the cliff with steps leading down into it and above it part of the side of the reservoir which supplied the basin below through openings which are still visible.

It is from the top of the Phaidriades Rocks *(Fedriádes)* that **Aesop** (6C BC), who composed the fables, is supposed to have been hurled for mocking the Delphians.

EXCURSIONS

Itéa – *17km/11mi to the southwest.* The road descends in long loops down the slopes of the Pleistos Valley into the olive groves in the coastal plain which belonged to the sanctuary of Apollo and was the setting of the ancient racecourse.

The famous olive groves, aptly referred to as a **sea of olives**★, are tended and watered with care. Together with the more recent plantations on the slopes of the Pleistos Valley, they number some 400 000 olive trees; harvesting begins in September.

The mills in which the olives are pressed are powered by the waters of the Pleistos. Itéa is a bathing resort and port at the head of Itéa Bay. It was chosen by the Allies in 1917 as the base town on the supply route which ran via Amphissa, Brálos, and Lamía to the eastern front. To the east of Itéa lay the ancient port of Delphi, **Kirra**; there are traces of an ancient jetty.

Ámfissa – *20km/12mi northwest.* The rival of Delphi in antiquity, Amphissa is built against the curved slope at the head of the valley planted with olive groves. Known as Salona in the 13C, it was the seat of a Frankish domain which was taken by the Turks in 1394. Its fortress, formerly called Chateau de la Sole, was erected on the site of the old acropolis which can still be traced in the occasional massive blocks of stones. There are remains of the keep, the living quarters and a 13C round tower. Fine views of the town and of the valley.

★**Galaxídi** – *33km/21mi southwest via Itéa and the coast road.* Fine view of the Bay of Itéa. Galaxídi is a charming old town with a sheltered harbour, which until early this century was a rival to Syros *(see SÍROS)*. The fine stone houses with their balconies suggest former days of wealth; in the 19C Galaxídi traded throughout the Mediterranean; there were 50 shipping magnates out of a population of 6 000. A small **Maritime Museum** ⏱ evokes the port's past glories. The cathedral at the top of the town contains a beautiful 19C carved wood iconostasis.

For adjacent sights see KÓRINTHOS, Dióriga KORÍNTHOU, LOUTRÁKI, MIKÍNES, ÓSSIOS LOUKÁS, THÍVA.

DÍO★★

DION – Pieriá, Macedonia

Michelin map 980 fold 17 – 16km/10mi south of Kateríni

At the foot of Mount Olympos in the fertile Pieriá plain lies the sacred town of ancient Macedon; its name declares its link with Zeus (Días).
It was famous in the past for its athletic and dramatic festival which was known as the **Olympic Games of Dion** and instituted by Archelaos in the 5C BC in honour of the Muses. At the height of its prosperity the town numbered 15 000 inhabitants. The site lies on the bank of a navigable river and was served by a river port. The fortifications were built in the reign of Alexander the Great who had a particular liking for the town.

Access

By train from Athens, Vólos and Thessaloníki via Liktóhoro and Kateríni; then by bus or taxi.

Excavations ⏱ – Excavations to date have revealed three sections of interest: the town, the sanctuary and the cemetery. The **town**, which was laid out according to the custom of that time, had a complete network of streets (22 have been excavated so far). Administrative buildings, warehouses, houses, baths, public latrines etc have been uncovered. A mosaic of the Triumph of Dionysos depicting the god in his chariot drawn by marine panthers and flanked by centaurs was uncovered in 1987 in the banqueting hall of a house. A Hellenistic **theatre**, two Roman **odeons and** a stadium bear witness to the cultural activities which took place in Dion and which put the town on a level with the thriving cities of southern Greece. The largest of the **sanctuaries** discovered was dedicated to the Egyptian divinities, Isis, Serapis and Anubis and consisted of several temples.

Moussío ⏱ – The **museum** contains the objects found during the excavations at Dion and neighbouring sites. The ground floor is devoted to the sanctuaries and the upper floor to objects found in the town and on neighbouring sites.

For adjacent sights see LEFKÁDIA-NÁOUSSA, Óros ÓLIMBOS, PÉLA, PLATAMÓNAS, THESSALONÍKI, VÉRIA.

Spílea DIROÚ★★

DIRÓS CAVES – Lakonía, Peloponnese

Michelin map 980 fold 41 – Local map see p 184

Part way down the west coast of Máni, opening into Dirós Bay are two caves which were explored after the Second World War. The largest, Glifáda, is one of the most spectacular natural sights in Greece. *Bathing from the seashore.*

Glifáda Cave ⏱ – The cave consists of chambers and a gallery created by an underground river forcing its way through the limestone of Máni to reach the sea below the actual entrance.
The cave is well organised for visitors with floating lights and coloured light projectors. The guided tour consists of a boat trip *(about 2km/1.25mi)* along both arms of the river which splits in two in the cave. All along the route are white or

W. Louvet /VISA

Glifáda Cave

coloured concretions: pillars, curtains, stalactites and stalagmites which can appear like human silhouettes, fabulous beasts, fantastic flowers or surrealist buildings (the Dragon's Cave, the Cathedral, the Pavillion...).
The water is up to 15m/50ft deep in places with a temperature of 12°C/54°F. The air temperature varies from 16°C–20°C/62°F–70°F.

Alepótripa Cave ⓥ – Traces of prehistoric occupation, now exhibited in the museum, have been found in this cave, which is called the fox hole. It is being excavated by archeologists *(closed to the public)*.

Moussío (**Museum**) – Alepótripa Cave was used for habitation, for storage, for religious rites, and also for burial. Items from the Neolithic period found here are on display in the museum: a fine collection of weapons, tools made of stone and bone, earthenware jars and other vessels, utensils and other domestic items (such as needles), as well as human skulls and skeletons. The cave was abandoned when an earthquake blocked the entrance.

For adjacent sights see GERÁKI, GÍTHIO, KALAMÁTA, KÍTHIRA, KORÓNI, MÁNI, MESSINIAKÓS Kólpos, MISTRÁS, SPÁRTI.

Drómos tou IRAKLÍ★

HERAKLES' ROAD – Fthiótida, Central Greece

Michelin map 980 south of fold 17

This is a superb mountain road running between Brálos and Iráklia *(21km/13mi – about 1hr)* over the Fournatáki Pass (590m/1 935ft) between Mount Íti and Mount Kalídromo; before the motorway was built along the coast it was the main road north from central Greece into Thessaly.

Death of a hero – When Herakles fell in love with Iole, his jealous wife, Deïaneira, sent him a tunic impregnated with what she thought was a love philtre but was in fact a poison given her by the centaur Nessos whom Herakles had mortally wounded for coveting his wife. As the cloth touched his skin, Herakles was in agony as if his body was on fire. When he could bear the torment no longer, he built himself a pyre on Mount Íti and his companion Philoctetes set it alight. A shaft of lightning struck the earth and Herakles was carried into the next world.

The road – It winds steeply through an impressive landscape with extensive views of Mount Kalídromo (1 375m/4 511ft) *(east)*, Mount Íti (2 152m/7 060ft) *(west)* and Parnassos (2 457m/8 061ft) *(south)*.
The road descends into the Lamía basin near Iráklia revealing the unusual **sight** of the railway line from Athens to Thessaloníki traversing the steep east face of Mount Íti through a series of tunnels linked by viaducts which span the river valleys.
The line played a part in the course of the Second World War: on 25 and 26 November 1942, British commandoes and the Greek resistance blew up the railway viaduct spanning the **Gorgopótamos**, a tributary of the Sperhiós, east of

Iráklia. This incident caused a three month delay in the supply line to Rommel's army in North Africa. A few months later, on 20 and 21 June 1943, another British commando unit destroyed the Assopós viaduct (near Íti) again disrupting the line while earlier the Greek partisans had blown up a tunnel.

For adjacent sights see ARÁHOVA, ÉVIA, DELFÍ, HERÓNIA, KARPENÍSSI, LIVADIÁ, ORHOMENÓS, ÓSSIOS LOUKÁS Monastery, THERMOPÍLES, THÍVA, VÓLOS.

ÉDESSA

Péla, Macedonia – Population 17 128

Michelin map 980 folds 4 and 5

Édessa was built on the edge of a plateau overlooking the Macedonian plain. In antiquity it was one of the main strongholds in Macedon, not far from the site of the assassination of Philip II *(see VÉRIA)* in 336 BC. The town is known for its situation and the waters of the River Vódas which make it an agreeable summer resort.

★**Waterfalls** – *East of the town (sign "Waterfalls" and "Pros Katarâktes").* A public garden shaded by huge plane trees *(restaurant)* leads down to the point where the various streams which flow through the town meet in an impressive waterfall; the water tumbles 25m/82ft down a rock face covered by luxuriant vegetation.

Old town ⏱ – *Below the modern town, north of the Thessaloníki road.* Excavations in the Longos area have revealed the remains of a Macedonian fortress and its surrounding wall built in the 4C BC and restored by the Romans, as well as ruins of early Christian basilicas.

For adjacent sights see KASTORIÁ, LEFKÁDIA-NÁOUSSA, PÉLA, THESSALONÍKI, VÉRIA.

EFÍRA★

EPHYRA NEKROMANTEION – Préveza, Epiros

Michelin map 980 centre of fold 15 – southeast of Párg

Near the village of **Messopótamo** stood a sanctuary dedicated to the Oracle of the Dead (Nekromanteion) on the banks of the River Ahérondas (Acheron), the ancient "river of the underworld". Gradually the estuary was filled and drained to form the present Fanári Plain which supports the cultivation of corn and rice and the raising of buffalo.

Entrance to the kingdom of the Dead – In antiquity the **Acheron** (Ahérondas) emerged from a wild ravine and spread out to form an inaccessible and mysterious lagoon, Lake Acheroussia. The ancient people used to tell how the shades of the Dead had to cross this marshy lake to reach the infernal kingdom of **Hades** and his wife Persephone (Kore). The Dead who had not been buried according to the ritual were condemned to wander endlessly in the reed beds which lined its banks. The others gave **Charon** the ritual coin and embarked in his boat; the fierce ferryman steered his craft into the sinister gorge which led to the bowels of the earth where **Cerberus**, a monstrous many-headed dog, kept guard.

Only two living souls managed to penetrate the kingdom of the Dead, Herakles (Hercules) and **Orpheus** whose lyre enabled him to snatch the nymph Eurydice from the infernal deities but he lost her again because he turned to look at her before they had emerged from Hades.

Charon often appears as a symbol of death in the popular songs of modern Greece.

Souliot Country – The Acheron flows through a wild and desolate mountainous region, where in the 15C Christians took refuge from the Turks. Albanian in origin, the people were named after their major settlement, Souli, which consisted of a few villages on a plateau 2 000ft up in the Acheron Gorge. They kept flocks of goats and sheep and survived on brigandage and tribute from their subject villages in the plains (Parasouli). Although few in number (about 5 000), the **Souliots** were brave and indomitable. Divided into clans and protected by the inaccessibility of their mountain fortresses, they maintained their autonomy for a long time.

Eventually they were defeated in battle at Nikopolis and in 1803 at Zálongo *(see KASSÓPI)* by the troops of Ali Pasha but he could not destroy them. They rose again in revolt against the Turks in 1820-23, taking part in the defence of Missolonghi under the orders of one of their own leaders, the famous **Bótsaris**.

Since then the Souliots have been dispersed; many of them live in Leukas, Cephallonia and Naupaktos.

★**Sanctuary** ⏱ – A chapel on a rocky hillock near the Acheron and the site of Lake Acheroussia marks the position of the **Nekromanteion** which was a sanctuary dedicated to Hades and Persephone at the entrance to the underworld, where the people came to consult the spirits of the Dead through the oracle.

The Nekromanteion was already in existence in the Mycenaean period but the traces of the building which are now visible are Hellenistic (3C BC). It was constructed of fine polygonal stonework and comprised a series of corridors and rooms culminating in the sanctuary itself, a huge chamber where the priests wreathed in sulphureous vapours pronounced the oracle to the pilgrims who had previously been through a propitiatory rite and taken hallucinogenic drugs. The oracle was located in a crypt, hollowed out of the rock beneath the central chamber, which was thought to communicate with the abode of Hades.

The items found during the excavations are on display in the **museum** in Ioánina.

For adjacent sights see ÁRTA, IOÁNINA, KASSÓPI, KÉRKIRA, LEFKÁDA, PÁRGA, PRÉVEZA.

ELEFSÍNA★

ELEUSIS – Attica

Michelin map 980 fold 30 – Local map see p 105

The sanctuary at Eleusis, where the cult of the "great goddesses", Demeter and Persephone, was celebrated, was one of the great shrines of antiquity. It was linked to Athens by the Sacred Way and was the setting for the initiation ceremonies which could not be divulged on pain of death; death was also the punishment for non-initiates who penetrated the sanctuary.

The sanctuary was built against a low hill topped by an acropolis overlooking Eleusis Bay and Salamis Island. The ruins were first discovered in 1815 by the Society of the Dilettanti and excavated in a series of digs, the first by French archeologists in the 19C. The topography is confused as the ruins are part Greek and part Roman.

Statue of Demeter – The statue of a woman with a basket on her head at the entrance to the village was already well known to 18C travellers when **Edward Clarke**, an Englishman who acted as travelling tutor to young noblemen, visited Eleusis early in the 19C and decided to acquire the statue. The goddess stood "in a dunghill buried to her ears"; the statue was worshipped by the villagers who placed lighted lamps before it in the belief that it protected the fertility of their corn fields. With the gift of a telescope Clarke obtained a permit *(firman)* from Athens for the purchase of the statue and after two days of delay and dispute with the villagers he succeeded in removing his treasure. The Eleusinians predicted disaster; the ship which carried the statue to England went down off Beachy Head. Demeter was however rescued and now stands in the Fitzwilliam Museum in Cambridge.

The Eleusinian mysteries – In mythology it was at Eleusis that Demeter found her daughter, Persephone, who had been abducted by Hades, king of the underworld, near Lake Pergusa in Sicily. Keleos, King of Eleusis, gave the goddess hospitality and in return she gave **Triptolemos**, the king's son, the first grain of wheat and showed him how to make it bear fruit. At the same time she is supposed to have entrusted Eumolpos with the ritual of the fertility cult.

The secret rites, known as the "Eleusinian mysteries", were celebrated until the 4C BC. Initiation, which was open to all, took place during the great Eleusinian festival in the autumn and consisted of two stages. In the second year those partially initiated *(mystai)* met on the third day of the festival in the Stoa Poecile in Athens where they had to prove that they had not committed murder and were Greek-speaking. On the following day they were conducted to Phaleron Bay *(see p 105)* where they plunged into the water (purification rite) together with a young pig destined to be sacrificed. The following days were devoted to retreat, fasting, sacrifices and a solemn procession which brought back to Eleusis along the Sacred Way the sacred objects *(ierá)* which had been taken to Athens at the beginning of the festival.

During the last three days the priests proceeded with the last part of the initiation in the heart of the sanctuary. This is thought to have consisted of revelations, a sort of sacred pageant on various themes: the union of Zeus and Demeter – a sign of fertility; the legend of Persephone detained in the world of the dead for six months – symbol of Nature being dormant during the winter and reawakening in the spring; the journey to the underworld – evocation of man's final destiny. At the end of the ceremony the sacred objects were revealed to the initiates.

The dramatist Aeschylus was born at Eleusis in c 525 BC.

★TOUR *about 1hr*

Great Forecourt – 2C AD. The square, which is paved with marble, was laid out in the Roman era. Near the site of a temple to Artemis *(Naós Artémidos)* is the colossal medallion bust of the Roman emperor Antoninus Pius (1) from the pediment of the Great Propylaia.

Great Propylaia – 2C AD. This was the entrance to the sanctuary, which the Romans rebuilt on the model of the *propylaia* in Athens. Traces of steps and the bases of columns mark the two Doric outer doors and the three passages divided by Ionic columns.

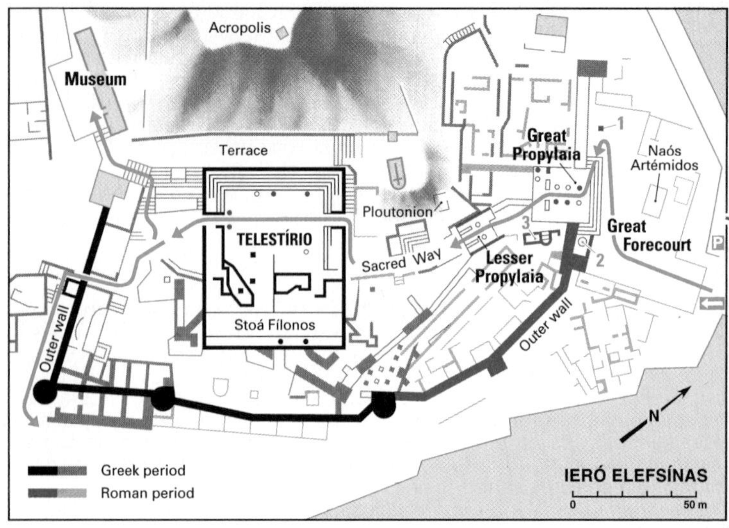

To the left of the entrance *(outside)* is the **Kallichoron well** (2) (6C BC) round which the sacred dances were performed in honour of Demeter. Again on the left but inside are traces of the Roman sewer *(cloaca)* (3).

Lesser Propylaia – 1C BC. To the right are parts of the architrave decorated with symbolic ears of corn.

The Sacred Way, which was paved by the Romans, leads *(right)* past caves hollowed out of the hillside to symbolise the entrance to the underworld; at the base on a triangular terrace stands a little temple, the **Ploutonion**, which was dedicated to Hades.

Telestírio – The Telesterion at the heart of the sanctuary was a majestic building in which the mysteries were revealed. It was almost square, measuring 54m x 52m/177ft x 170ft and the ground floor consisted of a huge room divided by six rows of columns and surrounded by raked seating which could accommodate about 3 000 people; another room *(megaron)* on the first floor under the wooden roof held the sacred objects. A paved portico, the **portico of Philo** (Stoá Fílonos), runs along the southeast front.

The building has been refashioned many times and retains traces of every period, from the Mycenaean to the Roman via Peisistratos (6C BC), Pericles (5C BC), Philo (4C BC) and Antoninus Pius (2C AD), which are very difficult to disentangle. The overall plan is, however, easily traced as well as the bases of votive statues.

Beyond the Telesterion it is possible to go outside the precinct and look at the Classical Greek walls surrounding the site.

Then climb the steps of a terrace which gave access to the upper floor of the Telesterion to reach the Museum which overlooks the Bay of Eleusis and Salamis Island (laid-up ships).

Museum – The courtyard displays a horse's head dating from the Hellenistic period, which once decorated the base of a statue, and a sarcophagus from the Roman era with sculptures of Meleager hunting the boar which was ravaging the Calydon region (near Missolonghi).

The museum contains sculptures found during the excavations: low reliefs of Demeter, Persephone, Triptolemos and a curious caryatid (2C AD) from the Lesser Propylaia. There is also a reconstruction of the sanctuary in its heyday.

For adjacent sights see AMFIARAÍO, ATHÍNA, DAFNÍ, KÓRINTHOS, Dióriga KORÍNTHOU, MIKÍNES, PÓROS.

Arhéa EPÍDAVROS★★★

Ancient EPIDAUROS – Argolis, Peloponnese

Michelin map 980 folds 29 and 30

At the heart of the gentle Argolid hills set about with pine trees and oleanders, lie the ruins of the famous sanctuary of the hero Asklepios, the god of medicine, where people from all over ancient Greece would come to consult the oracle. Modern crowds congregate here to admire the perfect proportions of the theatre, one of the marvels of Greece and very well preserved.

LEGENDARY AND HISTORICAL NOTES

Beneath the Caduceus – **Asklepios** (Aesculapius in Latin) was the son of Apollo and Koronis, a Boeotian princess; he was suckled by a nanny goat and educated by **Cheiron**, the wise centaur *(see Óros PÍLIO)*, who taught him surgery and the art of healing with plants. Owing to Cheiron's teaching and his own innate supernatural gifts, Asklepios became so knowledgeable that he was able to resuscitate the dead; this attracted the ill will of Hades and Zeus, jealous of a power reserved for the gods alone. So Zeus sent a thunderbolt to strike Asklepios dead and his body was buried at Epidauros. However that may be, from the 6C BC Asklepios became the object of a cult which reached its greatest intensity in the 4C BC and even extended to the persons of his children including his two daughters, Hygieia and Panaceia. The great Greek doctors *(archontes)*, even the famous Hippocrates of Kos *(see KOS)*, claimed authority from him. Asklepios is generally represented as a bearded figure leaning on an augur's wand accompanied by the magic serpent; these elements later came to be included in the caduceus, the doctor's emblem.

The Epidauros treatment – The sick, who came from Árgos, Troizen or from the town of Epidauros itself which was a few miles away on the east coast, would first make a sacrifice to the gods and accomplish a ritual purification and then spend the night in the sacred dormitory *(abaton)* where they lay on the skin of the animals which had been offered in propitiation. During their sleep they might be cured instantly or Asklepios might appear to them in dreams which the priests would translate into treatment accompanied, according to the different cases, by physical exercises or relaxation or baths or intellectual pursuits. This explains the importance given to the theatre and the sports facilities (stadium, gymnasium, palestra) and to the Asklepian Games which were held every four years and consisted of sporting contests and poetic or musical competitions. The people expressed their gratitude with the sacrifice of a cock and votive offerings in the shape of the part of the body which had been cured.

Under the Romans thaumaturgy gradually yielded to a more scientific form of medicine. Late in the 5C AD a Christian basilica was built on the site of the ancient sanctuary.

Nothing more was heard of Epidauros until the beginning of the 19C when an English traveller and topographer, Sir William Gell, made a plan of the ruins. In 1822 the independence of Greece was proclaimed in the theatre. In 1881 Greek archeologists, assisted by the French School in Athens, began to work on the site.

PRACTICAL INFORMATION

Three localities bear the name Epídavros: Néa Epídavros (New Epidauros) and Paléa Epidavros (Old Epidauros by the sea) and Arhéa Epídavros (Ancient Epidauros) also called Asklípio.

Access by bus – from Náfplio numerous services daily; from Athens station A (2hr 30min) 2 services daily *(see ATHÍNA: Practical Information)*.

Accommodation – Small Xenia hotel (cat B) near Arhéa Epídavros.

Epidauros Festival – In summer (late June to late August) the plays of the great Greek dramatists are performed in the theatre. For timetable (evening) and programme see the brochure issued by the GNTO/EOT. Organised excursions from Athens, Náfplio, Portohéli and the Saronic Gulf islands.

From the huge car park (beside the road from Náfplio) a path leads through the trees past the hotel-restaurant Xénia to the archeological site.

TOUR

★★★Theatre *1hr*

Set apart from the sanctuary *(southwest)* is the theatre, the most outstanding in the ancient world owing to the beauty of its setting, its magnificent lines and harmonious proportions. It was built in the 4C by the Argive architect, Polykleitos the Younger and is set into the north slope of Mount Harani (then Kynortion) facing the valley sacred to Asklepios. In 1954 it was restored to take modern productions of the ancient repertory as well as musical recitals at which Dimitri Mitropoulos (1896-1960) and Maria Callas have performed.

Epidauros Theatre

The **theatre**, which can accommodate 14 000 spectators, forms a section of a circle slightly larger than a semicircle. It consists of 55 rows of seats divided by a promenade *(diázoma)* into an upper and a lower section. The seats of honour, reserved for the magistrates and the priests, were situated in the first row of the upper section and in the back and first row of the lower section; the spectators in the rest of the lower section probably had cushions to sit on. The performance could be heard and seen perfectly from every seat in the theatre as can be demonstrated today by whispering or rustling a piece of paper in the centre of the orchestra; the sound carries without distortion to the top back corner of the huge spread of terraces some 22.50m/74ft from the ground.

There were two entrances at ground level on either side of the orchestra and steps up between the rows of seats in both sections; the upper section was also served by two ramps on either side of the seats.

The circular **orchestra** (20.28m/21yd in diameter), where the chorus performed, is marked at the centre by the base of the altar to Dionysos. Between the edge of the orchestra and the first row of seats there is a channel to take the rain water. On the north side of the orchestra are the foundations of the stage and the proscenium incorporating a sort of arch which supported the scenery.

It is worth climbing the steps between the rows of seats to appreciate the contours and proportions of the theatre which are regulated by the "golden mean" (c 8:13), particularly in the ratio between the lower and upper sections of seats. The view from the top is very fine, particularly in the early evening when the sacred valley of Asklepios lies peacefully in the shelter of the surrounding hills.

Additional sights

Leave the theatre, passing the museum *(see below)* to reach the **gymnasium**; the central part of it was converted into an odeon by the Romans. Descend the ramp, which led up to the main entrance to the gymnasium, passing the remains of the **palestra** *(right)* on the way to the sanctuary.

To the northwest are the foundations of the Temple of Artemis, **Naós Artémidos** (late 4C BC), which has been partially reconstructed in the museum.

★**Asklipiío (Sanctuary of Asklepios)** – *Excavations in progress.* The main monuments are to be found here surrounded by a wall within which the sacred serpents were confined. It flourished from the 6C and 5C BC until 86 BC, when it was sacked by Sulla. In the 2C AD it experienced a new flowering before being finally closed by Emperor Theodosius.

Naós Asklipioú – An outline of rectangular foundations marks the site of the small Doric temple with a raised peristyle which was designed by the architect Theodotos (4C BC) who also assisted in the construction of the Mausoleum of Halikarnassos. The temple contained a statue in gold and ivory of Asklepios seated on a throne, a baton in his right hand and his left resting on the head of a serpent. South of the temple are the remains of the altar where the sacrifices were made *(partial reconstruction in the museum)*.

Thólos or **Thymele** – More foundations *(west)* belong to the famous rotunda *(thólos)* which was built in the 4C BC by the architect of the theatre, Polykleitos the Younger, as a mausoleum for the hero Asklepios.
The building consisted of two concentric colonnades – the outer one of tufa in the Doric order and the inner of marble in the Corinthian order. At the centre was a maze; its purpose has been the subject of many hypotheses: Asklepios' tomb, a pen for the sacred serpents, a ritual labyrinth like those in medieval cathedrals, a symbolic representation of a molehill since the god's name, Asklepios, is similar to the Greek word for a mole.
The rotunda was sumptuously decorated: different coloured marbles, paintings of Love and Inebriety and finely sculpted motifs. Sculptures of Nereids and Nikes from the east and west pediments and acroters (4C BC) are on display in the National Archeological Museum in Athens (Room 22).

Abaton – To the north of the rotunda and the temple are the foundations of a portico which dates from the same period but was enlarged by the Romans. It was the dormitory where the sick slept in the hope that the god would appear to them in a dream.

Propílea – Traces of the foundations of the monumental entry *(propylaia)* to the sanctuary built in 4C BC.

Return towards the museum. On the north side are traces of a huge 4C BC hotel **(katagógeion)** comprising 160 rooms arranged round four courtyards.

Museum ⓥ – Although the chief sculptural finds on the site have been taken to the museum in Athens, the Epidauros museum contains several items of interest including some unusual *stele* bearing inscriptions (the accounts for the construction of the rotunda, descriptions of miraculous cures) and a collection of Roman medical instruments. There is a partial reconstruction of the rotunda using authentic elements: finely carved capitals and ceiling coffers, and also sculpted architectural fragments from the Temple of Artemis and the Propylaia.

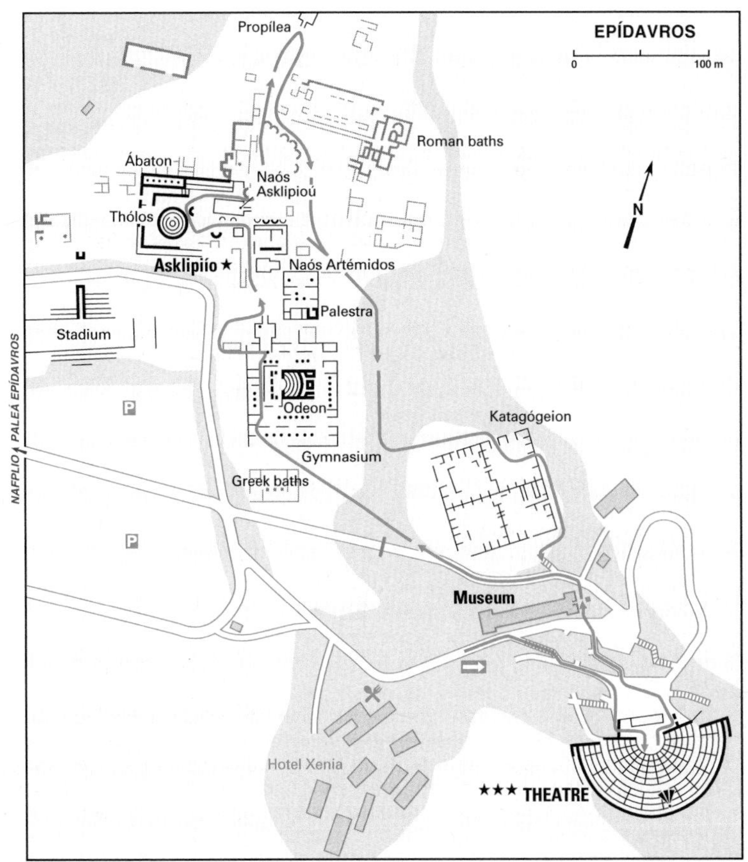

Stadium – It was built in the 5C BC in a hollow in the ground. The starting and finishing lines are extant, 181.30m/594ft apart. Stone seats were provided for the important people only.

Sanctuary of Apollo Maleatas – *3km/2mi from the theatre (30min on foot). Take the road above the theatre, behind the Hotel Xenia. The sanctuary is currently closed to the public, as excavations are in progress.* Discovered in 1928, the building dates from the 4C BC; there are ruins of a supporting wall, and some 2C AD Roman structures including a cistern and baths. There is a fine view of the surrounding area.

EXCURSIONS

Agnountos Monastery – *7km/4.5mi northeast, before the village of Néa Epídavros (on the right when coming from Arhéa Epídavros).* A fortified building of the 6C and 8C, it consists of an interior courtyard and a charming 11C church, remodelled in the 14C. Earlier decorative elements have been reused on the façade. The Byzantine form with a plan in the shape of the Greek cross is here combined with a basilica plan with an octagonal dome. Inside there are 13C frescoes (scenes from the Old and New Testament and the Last Judgement), icons dating from 1759, and an iconostasis in exquisitely decorated carved wood of 1713 (copy on show for security reasons). The monastery has been inhabited since 1980 and the nuns are tackling its restoration stage by stage.

Paleá Epídavros – *9km/5.5mi northeast.* Small fishing village and resort with several fish tavernas at the end of a picturesque valley planted with olive and citrus fruit trees.
At the end of the road running along the seashore, a path passing through the orchard of citrus fruit trees leads to the recently discovered small theatre from the time of Alexander the Great *(10min on foot, turn right at the junction).*

For adjacent sights see ARGOLÍDA, ÁRGOS, AKTÍ ARKADÍAS, ÍDRA, KÓRINTHOS, Dióriga KORÍNTHOU, LERNÍ, LOUTRÁKI, MIKÍNES, NÁFPLIO, NEMÉA, SIKIÓNA, SPÉTSES, TÍRINTHA.

ÉVIA★

EUBOIA – Central Greece – Population 205 507
Michelin map 980 folds 18, 30 and 31 – 3 654km²/1 410sq mi

Évia runs parallel to the east coast of Attica and Boeotia and is linked to the mainland at Halkída (Chalkis), the capital, by a bridge spanning the Evrípos, a narrow sea channel, which at this point is only 40m/130ft wide. It is the second largest Greek island after Crete, being 150km/93mi long and 10–50km/6–31mi wide.
It is well populated and fertile (beehives) with a varied landscape: cultivated plains and basins, verdant valleys, mountains partially clothed in forests of pine, chestnut and plane trees with the waters of the Aegean in the background.

PRACTICAL INFORMATION

Access – In addition to the bridge at Chalkis, several ferries and hydrofoils per day link Continental Greece and Euboia:
Rafína-Marmari and Rafína-Káristos: South Evía Consortium ☎ (0294) 24 713 (in Rafína).
Agia Marina-Stíra and Agia Marina-Port Almiropótamos: ☎ (0224) 41 266 (in Stíra).
Skála Oropoú-Erétria: ☎ (0295) 32 270 (in Oropós).
Arkítsa-Loutrá Edipsoú: ☎ (0233) 91 275 and 91 418 (in Arkítsa).
Glifa-Agiókambos: ☎ (0238) 61 288 (in Glifa).

Accommodation – There are many seaside resorts or holiday villages particularly on the southwest coast facing the mainland: (from south to north) Káristos, Marmári, Néa Stíra, Amárinthos, Ágios Minás, Erétria, Malakónda and Gregolímano.

Touring – Follow the road which runs the length of the island from Káristos *(south)* to Loutrá Edipsoú *(north)* making two detours to Kími and Mount Dírfis; this itinerary takes about two days. Tourists with less time to spare are advised to visit the southern half between Káristos and Chalkis which includes a particularly spectacular stretch from Káristos to Stíra, called the "Road of the Eagles" (Drómos ton Aetón).

HALKÍDA (CHALKIS) *Population 51 646*

Halkída, the capital of Évia, is built on the edge of a fertile plain; it is a port, a market for agricultural produce and an industrial centre (cement works, textiles, food processing). The ramparts built by the Venetians to protect the town have been demolished, leaving a modern seafront composed of hotels, fish restaurants and cafés; the beaches lie along the coast north of the town.

Venetians and Turks – From the 13C to the 15C the Venetians held a commanding position in Chalkis which they developed into an important commercial centre exporting the products of Euboia and controlling the maritime trade in the north of Greece. Italian and Greek merchants traded in competition with the Jews whose cemetery still exists.
The Venetians fortified both Halkída and the bridge over the Evrípos. They knew the town (and also of the whole island) as **Negroponte**, a name derived from a corruption of Evripo (Egripo – Negripo) which they rationalised into Negroponte (black bridge). Despite its defences Negroponte was attacked several times in the 14C both by the Catalans and by the Genoese.
In 1470 the town was captured by Sultan Mahomet II himself but nonetheless remained a lively trading centre with many commercial companies. In 1658 even the Jesuits succeeded in establishing themselves and one of them, Father Coronelli, who was a geographer, sketched a profile of the town.
In 1688 15 000 Venetian soldiers tried to recapture the town by laying siege to it but they were decimated by malaria which carried off their leader, Koenigsmark, and were forced to retire.

Karababá Fort – It was built on the mainland on the site of a Venetian fortress in 1686 by the Turks to serve as a bridgehead and was in use until 1856.
From the west bastion, there is a fine **view★** of Halkída, the Evrípos and the **Bay of Aulis** *(south)* where the Greek fleet mustered before setting out for Troy and where, so it is said, Agamemnon sacrificed his daughter **Iphigenia** to obtain a favourable wind.

Evrípos Bridge – A variety of bridges has served since the first in 411 BC. The present bridge (1962), consisting of two half spans decked with wood, which drop down and then roll back on rails beneath the approaches, replaces the famous fortified bridge with its central bastion which dated from medieval times and can be seen in many old prints; it was longer than the present structure since one of the arms of the Evrípos has been filled in. The bridge is opened from time to time to allow the passage of leisure craft and coastal shipping moving with the flow of the current.
This current can attain 7 or 8 knots and it changes direction from north-south to south-north at least six and as many as 14 times a day. This natural phenomenon can easily be observed; it is caused by the variation and the combination of the tides in the bays on either side of the canal, the prevailing winds and the atmospheric pressure. **Aristotle** is supposed to have drowned himself in the Evrípos because he could not explain the enigma; in fact he did die in Halkída in 322 BC but of natural causes.

Archeological Museum ⏲ – It contains some beautiful Archaic sculptures (early 5C BC) from the Temple of Apollo in Erétria *(see below)*: a group showing Theseus abducting Antiope (Hippolyta) and a bust of Athena holding a shield *(aegis)* bearing a Gorgon's head; also a 2C Roman work of Antinoüs disguised as Bacchus. Beyond the museum there is a picturesque market with an oriental atmosphere.

Agía Paraskeví Basilica – *Second street on the left coming from the bridge.* The church, which is situated in the old town, is Byzantine in origin and rests on ancient columns of cipolin marble; in the 13C-14C it was converted into a Gothic cathedral: Latin cross plan, rib vaulting in the chapels flanking the square chancel, rose window in the façade.
Not far away in the small square *(Platía Kóskou)* there is a disused mosque and a Turkish fountain; at the beginning of the 19C there were 1 600 Turkish families living in Chalkis.
Before the Second World War there was also a large Jewish community which had its own cemetery to the east of the town centre.

NORTH OF HALKÍDA (CHALKIS)

Kími – This little town, which is also known locally as Koúmi, is the main centre of a fertile region which produces olives, fruit, grapes and honey **(baklavá)**. It has developed from the ancient town of Kyme whose inhabitants founded Cumae near Naples in Italy. The town stands on a beautiful site on a rocky plateau about 260m/850ft above the Aegean Sea looking out towards the island of Skyros.
A fine old house has been turned into a **Museum of Popular Art** (**Laografikó Moussio**) ⏲: crafts, costumes and furniture.

The ferry to Skìros leaves from the little port of Paralía Kímis *(sandy beach)* down on the coast *(4km/2.5mi; bus)*.

Mount Dírfis – From Néa Artáki there is a good road which passes through a region devoted to cereal and chicken farming and then climbs the lower slopes of Mount Dírfis.

Stení is a cool and shady mountain resort; its chalets are built on either side of a mountain torrent. There are many walks in the forests of chestnut and conifer trees which cover the slopes of Mount Dírfis (1 743m/5 718ft); very varied flora.

Prokópi – South of Mandoúdi, deep in the picturesque **Klissoúra Valley** lies Prokópi, formerly known as Achmet Aga. The banks of the stream which runs through the valley are covered by luxuriant vegetation: planes, poplars, walnuts and oleanders. In the Middle Ages the valley was commanded by a famous fortress on an almost inaccessible peak. More recently the area has been the estate of the Noel-Baker family, who have been careful but not uncontroversial landlords.

★**Loutrá Edipsoú** – Its pleasant position by the sea made this important spa very fashionable in antiquity. Sulla, Augustus and Hadrian came to take the waters, which contain sulphur and are used to treat rheumatism and gynecological complaints.

Beyond the neo-Classical pump room on the east side of the town are the hot springs with their sulphureous vapour; some of the water tumbles into the sea by a little beach in a smoking cascade.

An attractive excursion can be made by car along the coast from Loutrá Edipsoú. It follows a spectacular corniche road southeast to **Ílía**, a fishing village *(9km/5.5mi)*, to Roviés *(29km/18mi)* and thence to **Límni** *(13km/8mi)*, a fishing village well known to artists. From Límni a road rejoins the northern road.

Oreí – This is an ancient barony where the Venetians built a castle using materials from ancient structures. From the port there are fine views across the Oreí Channel to Mount Óthris on the mainland and the entrance to the Vólos Gulf (north).

SOUTH OF HALKÍDA (CHALKIS)

Erétria – *Ferry to Skála Oropoú on the mainland; sandy beaches.* Erétria was for many years the rival of Chalkis for possession of the rich Lelantine (Lefkandí) Plain. More recently it has also been known as **Néa Psará** since refugees from the island of Psará settled there in 1821 but the name Erétria is now re-established.

There are several traces of the **ancient city** ⏲ which was extensive and prosperous; the main ones lie to the north: a fairly well preserved theatre (3C BC) at the foot of the acropolis with the foundations of a shrine to Dionysos and a house decorated with mosaics (4C BC) nearby.

In the centre of the modern town are the ruins of a Temple to Apollo where the fine Archaic sculptures now in the Halkída Museum were found.

Dístos (Ruins) – *Access from the Káristos-Halkída road by an earth track.* Isolated on flat open ground, by a little lake, lie the ruins of ancient Dystos which the Venetians converted into a fortress. The 5C BC walls are of polygonal construction with strengthened square towers.

Stíra – Pop 473. The village on the slopes of Mount Klióssi is known for its marble quarries and its beach at Néa Stíra down below on the coast; to the east stood the mighty Frankish castle of Lármena.

★★★**"Drómos ton Aetón"** – Between Stíra and Káristos (about 30km/18.5mi) the **Eagles' Road** runs along a ledge 700–800m/2 300–2 600ft above sea level on the southwest coast of Euboia. Birds of prey hover over the bare and empty hillsides which offer splendid views down over Marmári, across the bay to the Petalií islands and into the cove at Pórto Láfia, a resort which is reached by a steep winding road.

Káristos – Pop 4 081. This is a summer resort with a port used by fishing boats and ferries (from Rafína) surrounded by olive groves and vineyards. **Mount Óhi** (1 398m/4 587ft) which rises behind the town was already being quarried in antiquity for its green cipolin marble. Under the Venetians the town was one of the three great baronies of Euboia.

On the top of Mount Folí stand the ruins of a huge castle with a double bailey which was built in the 13C by Ravano delle Carceri and called **Castel Rosso** (Red Castle) owing to the colour of the stone. When Emperor Baldwin II de Courtenay fled from Constantinople, he took refuge here in 1261 with **Otho de Cicon**, son of Sibylle de la Roche; in return for this hospitality Baldwin gave Otho a chased silver coffer containing St George's arm; two years later Otho himself offered this reliquary to the Abbey of Citeaux in Burgundy.

For adjacent sights see HERÓNIA, LIVADIÁ, ORHOMENÓS, ÓSSIOS LOUKÁS Monastery, THERMOPÍLES, THÍVA.

FÍLIPI★★

PHILIPPI – Kavála, Macedonia

Michelin map 980 centre of fold 7

The road from Kavála to Dráma runs through the Macedonian plain where tobacco, wheat and corn grow on the well-drained land; it bisects the site of the ancient **city of Philippi** which was named after Philip II of Macedon; the ruins now visible are, however, more evocative of the Romans and the early Christians than of the Macedonians.

Roman and Christian Philippi – After the assassination of Julius Caesar in 44 BC, his murderers, Brutus and Cassius, fled east with their forces and occupied the country east of the Adriatic.

Antony and Caesar's nephew, Octavian, marched against the Republican partisans and met them west of Philippi in October 42 BC. After various inconclusive engagements Antony and Octavian gained the advantage; Cassius and Brutus committed suicide. The victors then shared power until the Battle of Actium *(see PRÉVEZA)*.

Later veterans of the victorious army were settled in Philippi which was granted the status of a Roman colony which meant that the inhabitants had the same rights as the Romans in Italy. The city quickly grew prosperous owing to its position on the Via Egnatia *(see THESSALONÍKI)*, its proximity to the gold mines of Mount Pangaion and the fertility of the surrounding countryside.

In AD 49 **St Paul** arrived from Neapolis and preached for the first time in Philippi; he was denounced and imprisoned for a period together with his companion Silas. Christianity spread rapidly as Paul was able to see when he returned to Philippi six years later. St Paul's Epistle to the Philippians was probably sent from Rome in AD 64.

TOUR

East Section

Píli Neápolis (Neapolis Gate) – The entrance to Philippi from Kavála was part of the Byzantine walls which still exist in places and were reinforced with towers and redoubts. The section running north climbs up to the Greek acropolis where three towers were built in the Middle Ages.

The area between the walls and the forum is still being excavated. The French School in Athens has discovered traces of a large **paleo-Christian basilica** *(no access)* which, an exception from usual, was built on an octagonal plan similar to St Vitale in Ravenna, a baptistry and a bishop's palace both of which were reached by a gateway on the Via Egnatia.

★★SOUTH SECTION *Access by steps from the modern road*

Egnatía Odós – The **Via Egnatia**, which is the first level below the modern road, formed the main street *(decumanus maximus)* of Roman Philippi; on the left of the steps are the ruts worn by the wagons which plied the road.

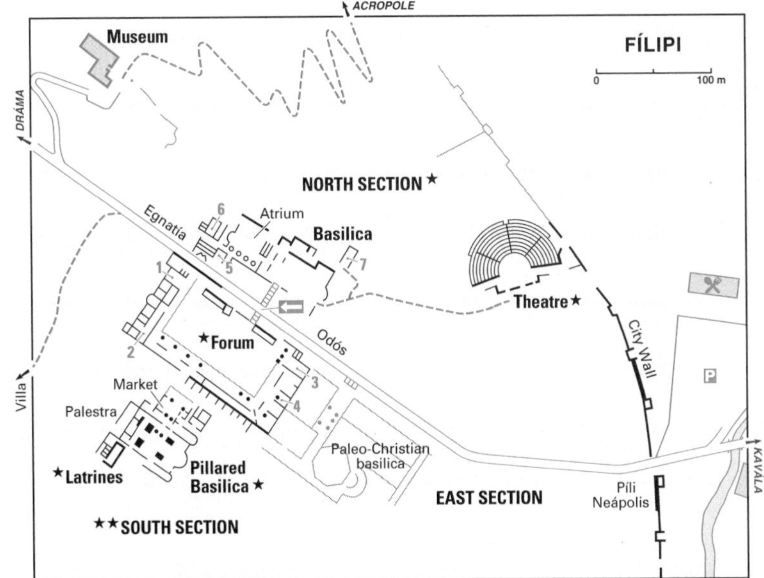

★**Forum** – At the centre is a large marble-paved court (some 100m/328ft by 50m/164ft). Most of the forum was built in the reign of Emperor Marcus Aurelius (AD 161-180). The plan is clearly recognisable: down the north side runs the Via Egnatia; the other three sides were bordered by steps and porticoes leading to the main municipal buildings which can be identified by their foundations.
Parallel with the Via Egnatia were fountains, a rostrum for speeches and commemorative monuments.
The west side is bordered by traces of a temple (1) and administrative buildings; in the southwest corner stands an unusual upturned **marble table** (2): the different-sized cavities in it are thought to have been used for measuring; further on at the foot of the second column of the south portico there are holes in the ground for the game of marbles.
The east side was bordered by another temple (3) incorporating the fluted columns and a library (4).

Market – On the far side of the street which runs parallel with the south side of the forum lay the market composed of shops and a hall supported on columns, some of which have been re-erected. Between them on the paving stones are the marks of various games. The southern section of the market was levelled in the 6C for the construction of the Pillared Basilica.

★**Pillared Basilica** – Also known as the Direkler, which means pillars in Turkish, the basilica was begun in the 6C but, so it seems, never finished because it proved impossible to construct a dome to cover such a large building. The huge pillars still in place, which are composed of ancient drums, and their Byzantine capitals, which are delicately carved with acanthus leaves, point to the ambitious nature of the building which had a narthex, a nave and aisles and a rounded apse. On the north side, towards the forum, are traces of a baptistry and a chapel which housed the bishop's throne.

Roman Palestra – There are a few traces of the *palestra* (2C AD) beyond the narthex of the basilica.

★**Latrines** – Contemporary with the *palestra* and situated below the southwest corner is a huge Public Latrine, almost perfectly preserved. Most of the original marble seats and water ducts are still extant, as are the entrance steps.

Villa or Schola – Further south in the fields *(15min on foot there and back)* are traces of a building (3C AD) consisting of numerous rooms arranged round a peristyle courtyard; it was probably an elegant villa or a sort of farmers' guild.

★North Section

Terrace – From the entrance climb up to the terrace which provides an extensive view southwest to Mount Pangaion.

Basilica with atrium – It was built in the 6C but was probably destroyed by an earthquake soon afterwards. From east to west it consisted of an apse, a nave and two aisles, a narthex and an atrium as in St Demetrios' in Thessaloníki. There are still traces of the steps which descended into the confessio which housed the relics beneath the high altar.
Below the basilica, at road level, is the **Roman crypt** (5) which by the 5C had come to be considered as the prison where St Paul and Silas were detained.
Higher up rear the massive blocks of the foundations of a Hellenistic temple (6); the Byzantines converted them into a cistern.
The path to the theatre passes at the foot of some little **rock sanctuaries** (7), recesses hollowed out of the rock.

★**Theatre** – The shell-shaped hollow, in the lower slopes of the Acropolis hill contained a great theatre which dated back to the 4C BC but was refurbished by the Romans in the 2C AD and then remodelled in the 3C when the stage was converted into an arena for gladiatorial and animal combats. The carvings on the entrance pillar are 3C; they show Mars and Victory, the divinities of circus games, and a splendid bucrane.
The theatre was modernised in 1959 for the summer drama festival.

Museum – It contains the finds excavated by French archeologists on the prehistoric site of **Dikili Tash**, near Philippi, the *acroteria* from the west temple in the forum and capitals from the Pillared Basilica.

For adjacent sights see AMFÍPOLI, HALKIDIKÍ, KAVÁLA, THÁSSOS, THESSALONÍKI.

GERÁKI★★

Lakonía, Peloponnese – Population 1 381
Michelin map 980 fold 41

The ruins of Geráki Castle and of a medieval town *(kastró)* lie on an outlying spur of Mount Parnon, on the northern edge of the Lakonian Plain, not far *(about 4km/2.5mi)* from the little medieval town of Geráki with its many old houses and Byzantine churches which are decorated with 15C and 16C murals.

Tour of the castle ⓥ – *Ask for the keeper in the village. If the keeper is not available to open the churches, the tour (1hr) is worthwhile for the architecture of the buildings and the views.*

Take the road below the village towards Ágios Dimítrios passing a school and a cemetery near several Byzantine churches (see below). Turn left 600m/660yd after the cemetery towards the kastró and continue for 2.5km/1.5mi to the car park.

Early in the 13C William de Champlitte divided the Peloponnese, which he had just conquered, into 12 baronies and gave Lakonía, which contains Geráki, to Guy de Nivelet, a knight from the Franche Comté. His successor, **John de Nivelet** built the present fortress in 1254 in imitation of the castle being built by William de Villehardouin in Mystra. The Franks did not hold Geráki for long; it passed to the Byzantines at the end of the 13C.

The castle is shaped like an irregular quadrilateral formed by ramparts reinforced by strong towers; huge cisterns enabled it to withstand long sieges.

The tour includes several Gothic and Byzantine chapels, set on the slope, which are decorated with painted murals. **St George's Church** (13C), within the castle wall, has a nave and side aisles and is also decorated with paintings; a great Gothic tomb in a recess *(left)* bears the heraldic emblems of the Franks.

The parapet walk offers extensive **views**★★ of Mount Parnon *(north)*, the Eurotas Valley running south to the sea and Mount Taígetos *(west)* with Sparta in the foreground.

Byzantine Churches ⓥ – Down in the village, by the road to the castle *(kástro)*, the early 13C domed church of **Ágios Athanássios** decorated with large, brightly-coloured frescoes, stands near the cemetery.

A short distance away, a by-road on the other side of the main road leads down through the olive groves to the finely proportioned, domed **Ágios Sósson** (12C) and further down to **Ágios Nikólaos** (13C) with its barrel vaulted twin aisles and a fresco depicting St Mary the Egyptian in the chancel. The tiny church of Ágii Theodori stands in the middle of a field near the road.

Above the cemetery, walk up in the village to the 12C church of the **Evangelístria**; the frescoes were probably painted by an artist from Constantinople.

For adjacent sights see Aktí ARKADÍAS, Spílea DIROÚ, GÍTHIO, MÁNI, MEGALÓPOLI, MESSINIAKÓS Kólpos, MISTRÁS, MONEMVASSÍA, SPÁRTI.

GÍTHIO

Lakonía, Peloponnese – Population 4 054
Michelin map 980 fold 41 – Local map see p 182

Gíthio boasts an attractive **site**, just west of the mouth of the River Evrótas (Eurotas), overlooking the graceful curves of the Lakonian Gulf and the outline of the island of Kythera which can be seen to the south on a clear day. Gíthio is both a quiet seaside resort *(hotels and camping sites)* and a port exporting the produce of Lakonía: olives, oil, rice, cotton, citrus fruits.

In antiquity it played a role as the arsenal of Sparta. When Paris carried off Helen, the unfaithful wife of Menelaos, king of Sparta, they are said to have spent their first night together on the island of Kranai (now Marathónissi) before embarking for Kythera and thence for Troy and provoking the Trojan War which Homer described in the *Iliad.*

The town – The harbour area consists of picturesque narrow streets below the ruins of a medieval castle; the street parallel to the quayside is lined by attractive Turkish houses with balconies. There is a small but well-preserved ancient theatre next to the barracks northwest of the town.

On the island of Marathónissi stands one of the typical towers of Máni.

Tzanetáki Tower ⓥ – The **Historical and Ethnological Museum** contains an attractive permanent exhibition, which traces the history of Máni by means of texts, drawings, photographs and sketches of its localities by the numerous travellers who passed through the region from the 16C to the 20C, including the French man of letters François Pouqueville (1770-1838), author of *Travels in Morea.*

For adjacent sights see Spílea DIROÚ, GERÁKI, KÍTHIRA, MÁNI, MESSINIAKÓS Kólpos, MISTRÁS, SPÁRTI.

HALKIDIKÍ★

CHALCIDICE – Macedonia

Michelin map 980 folds 6, 7, 18 and 19

The peninsula of Chalcidice extends like a three-fingered hand from the coast of north eastern Greece into the Aegean Sea. Its northern limit is marked by two lakes – Korónia and Vólvi – lying in a depression between the Strymon Gulf *(east)* and the Gulf of Thessaloníki *(west)*. It is a region of gently rolling hills where grain is grown.
The fingers are three mountainous wooded promontories: Kassándra, Sithonía and Mount Athos which is known for its unique monastic life.

ACCESS

No female creature of any kind has been allowed on the peninsula since 1060. Only men over 21 are permitted to enter. About 170 permits are issued daily, 10 for foreigners and 100 for Greek nationals; the number of permits applied for annually is estimated at about 350 000. It is essential to book well in advance – at least two months in advance for a summer visit and more than six months in advance for important religious holidays, such Easter. Access is by boat from Ouranópoli or Trípití to Dáfni.
An entry permit, valid for a three-night stay, costs 8 000Dr. (foreigners) and 4 000Dr. (Greek nationals) and can be obtained from the Pilgrims Office, 9 Odós Engnatia, Thessaliníki; ☎ (031) 861 611 (foreigners), 833 733 (Greek nationals); Fax 861 811. Bookings must be confirmed at least two weeks prior to departure. Food and accommodation is free of charge.
In the summer season there are boat excursions – from Ouranópóli, from Órmos Panagías on the Sithonía peninsula and from Thássos –, which skirt the coast of the Mount Athos but must remain at least 500m/550yd from the shore. The people in the boats must be decently clothed.

★★ÁGIO ÓROS (the HOLY MOUNTAIN – Mount ATHOS) ⓥ

The most easterly of the three peninsulas, the **Holy Mountain** (Ágio Óros) (45km/27mi long x 5km/3mi) is covered with forests (oaks, chestnuts and pines) culminating at the southern tip in Mount Athos, 2 033m/6 670ft high. The steep slopes drop sheer into the sea which is often turbulent. Since the 10C the peninsula has been a sort of monastic Orthodox republic with **Kariés** as the capital; the Greek State is represented by a governor.

Unique Theocratic State – The first community *(lávra)* of monks dates from 963 when **St Athanasius of Trebizond** was encouraged by Emperor Nikephoros Phokas to found the monastery of the Grand Lavra. Other communities were established from the 13C onwards and by the 16C there were 30 000 monks in about 30 monasteries. Before the First World War the monks numbered 9 000.
At the last census in 1981 there were 1 472 monks (309 more than in 1971), in about 20 monasteries; the majority are Greek but a few monasteries receive other nationalities, eg Russians (Ágiou Panteleímonos), Bulgarians (Zográfou) and Serbs (Hiliandaríou). Most of the monks are old and they all wear beards. There are several different life styles; the idiorrhythmic rule, which the larger monasteries follow, relies on individual discipline; the coenobitic communities live a communal life with a very strict diet; smaller groups of monks live in ascetics' dwellings *(skétes)*, while there are anchorites living in remote huts or isolated caves and also a few peripatetic monks.
Mount Athos is administered by four supervisors *(epistátis)* based in Kariés. Each monastery is governed by a superior or abbot *(igoúmenos)* who is in charge of the novices *(rasophori)*, the professed monks *(kalógeri)* and the lay brothers *(parámikri)*; visitors are received by the head of the guest-house *(arhondáris)*. The church services are announced by beating on a piece of wood (**símandro**) with a mallet.
The major monasteries, which are immense and decorated in brilliant colours, were usually arranged round a courtyard and fortified with towers, the highest of which acted as the keep, to protect them from pirates in earlier centuries. The buildings round the courtyard accommodate the guest-house, the monks' cells giving on to external balconies and the refectory *(trápeza)* in front of which stands the washing place *(fiáli)*. In the centre of the court stands the church *(katholikon)*, a cross-in-square building roofed with one or several domes. The walls of the churches and refectories are decorated with frescoes; the most beautiful were painted by artists such as M Panselinos (14C), **Theophanes the Cretan**, Zorzio or Frango Kastellanos (16C). The libraries, which are often housed in the keep, contain upwards of 10 000 ancient manuscripts, some of which are unfortunately badly damaged.

The monasteries mentioned here are the most famous or the most easily visited. They all close at sunset.

Megístis Lávras (**Grand Lavra**) – The oldest (AD 963) and the largest (104 monks) of the monasteries on the Holy Mountain is situated near the end of the peninsula at the foot of cloud-capped Mount Athos. Commanding the sea and its own natural harbour, the monastery looks like a fortified city and contains over 100 relics.

Athanasius, the founder, is buried in the 10C-11C church beneath the huge dome. Outside the immense 16C refectory stands a handsome *fiáli* (16C) with a porphyry basin; within the chairs and tables are of stone and the walls are covered with famous frescoes also 16C by Theophanes the Cretan. The library contains 5 000 volumes, about half of which are manuscripts.

Further south lies a stony waste known as the **Hermits' Desert** because a number of anchorites have established themselves in the cavities in the rugged cliff.

Vatopedíou – This huge monastery was established in 980 in an idyllic site overlooking a bay and a little port. It was fortified early in the 15C. The maze of buildings includes some 15 chapels as well as the church, a red building dating from the late 11C. The 15C bronze entrance doors came from Agía Sophía in Thessaloníki; the mosaic is a remarkable piece of 11C work. Within are some interesting 13C to 16C icons.

The Treasury boasts some rare gold reliquaries and a 15C jasper cup on an enamelled silver base belonging to Manuel Palaiologos. The Library is well stocked with ancient manuscripts (about 600) including a 12C copy of Ptolemy's Geography.

Ivíron – This 10C monastery, which was originally dedicated to St John the Baptist, is hidden in a hanging valley overlooking the sea and surrounded by olive and pine trees. The church is 11C; a chapel contains the miraculous icon of the Mother of God of the Gate (Panagía Portaítissa) (10C). The library possesses many illuminated manuscripts (11C to 13C).

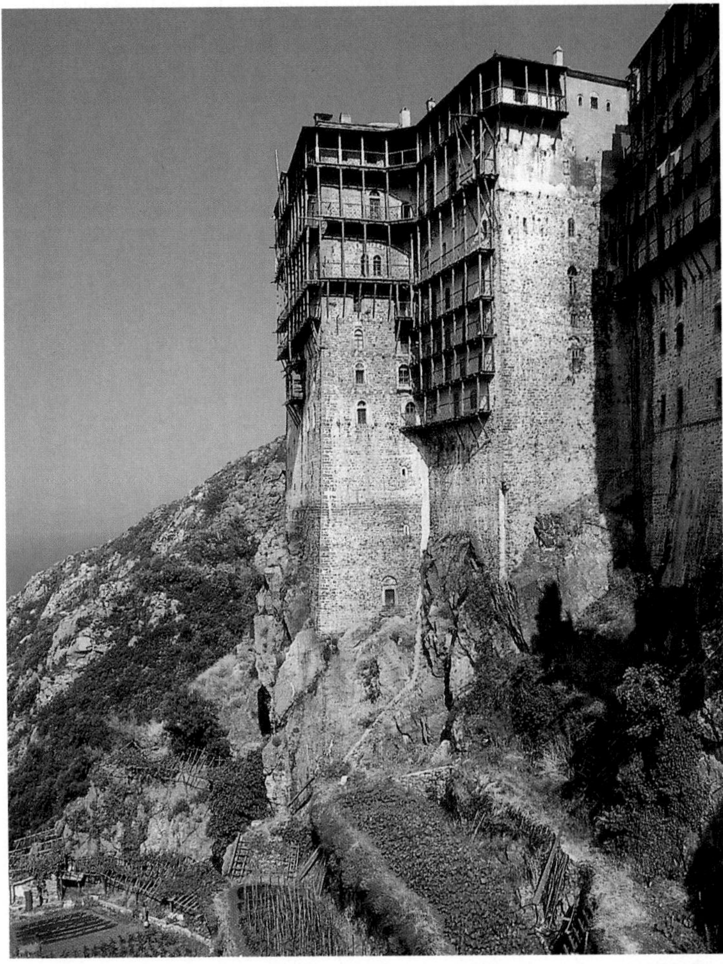

Y. Cavaille /EXPLORER

Símonos Pétras Monastery, Mount Athos

Símonos Pétras – The lofty 14C coenobitic monastery with its row upon row of wooden balconies occupies a spectacular site atop a rock barely attached to the western face of the mountain.

Ágiou Dionissíou – This monastery was founded in the 16C on a rocky site overlooking an inlet on the west coast. The church and refectory are decorated with remarkable frescoes dating from the 16C by Zorzio the Cretan and from the 17C. The library contains a 7C evangelistary.

★★SITHONÍA PENINSULA

Round tour of 109km/68mi – about 3hr 30min

Sithonía boasts many natural beauty spots: forests of sea and umbrella pines, fine sandy beaches in secluded bays and inlets, deep fjords with sheer rock walls penetrating the rugged coastline and providing under-water fishing.
The coast road runs past many beautiful sites, becomes a corniche road along the cliffs and opens up extensive views particularly east to Mount Athos although the summit is often shrouded in clouds.

Órmos Panagías – Picturesque hamlet in a rocky bay.

Sárti – Small cultivated coastal plain running down to a sandy bay.

★**Cape Drépano** – Rocky promontory deeply indented with many inlets extending into fjords particularly at **Koufós** and round Kalamítsi.

★**Toróni Bay** – The long sandy beach of this idyllic bay curves gently south into a tiny peninsula which bears the remains of an ancient fortress mentioned by Thucydides and of paleo-Christian basilicas *(excavations in progress)*.

Pórto Carrás – Seaside resort masterminded by the oil tycoon, John C Carras. It is a spectacular undertaking centred on two hotels of imposing design, a charming seaside village with a harbour, a golf course, tennis courts, a casino, a riding stable etc. Nearby John Carras established a model farm with lemon and olive groves, almond orchards and vineyards producing an excellent wine.

KASSÁNDRA PENINSULA

60km/37mi south of Thessaloníki, then a round trip of 118km/73mi to make a complete tour of the peninsula.

Petrálona ⓥ – *12km/8mi to the east off the road from Thessaloníki to the peninsula.* A detour can be made on the way to the Kassándra Peninsula to view the **cave of Kókines Pétres** ⓥ (the Red Stones) which is known to paleontologists for the discovery of a Neanderthal skull and fossils of prehistoric animals. The cave stretches over 10 400m²/12 438sq yd but only 2km/1mi may be visited for the fine concretions. There is a small museum.

The **Kassándra** peninsula is less wooded and less attractive than Sithonía but it is more fertile (wheat, olives) and more densely populated.
The isthmus has been breached by a canal at Néa Potídea, the site of ancient Poteidaia. The peninsula offers pleasant beaches and a number of hotels especially at Saní, Kalithéa, Agía Paraskeví and **Palioúri**★ which lies at the southern end looking across a bay to the Sithonía peninsula.

For adjacent sights see AMFÍPOLI, FÍLIPI, KAVÁLA, PÉLA, THÁSSOS, THESSALONÍKI.

HERÓNIA

CHAIRONEIA – Boeotia

Michelin map 980 fold 29 – 14km/9mi north of Livadiá

The Kifíssos Valley, traditionally the route for invasions from the north, is now the route south for the road and railway. Beside the road stands a monumental marble lion recalling the battle and the ancient town of Chaironeia.

North versus South – At the battle of Chaironeia in 338 BC the phalanxes of **Philip of Macedon** (30 000 infantry armed with the Macedonian spear *(sárissa)*, 2 000 cavalry) were ranged against the slightly less numerous forces of the Greek cities who had come to the aid of Thebes owing to the exhortations of Demosthenes who took part in the fighting. The southern Greeks were overwhelmed by the heavy infantry and the Macedonian cavalry in which Alexander, then 18 years of age, was making his debut in battle. The famous **Theban Sacred Band** *(see THÍVA)* fought to the death and Greece fell into the control of Philip of Macedon.
The biographer **Plutarch** (c AD 50-127), who wrote the *Lives of Eminent Men*, was born and died in Chaironeia.

The Lion – A clump of cypresses marks the position of the colossal lion (5.50m/18ft high) which gazes down from its pedestal at the passing cars. It was set up after the Battle of Chaironeia on the ossuary containing the remains of the soldiers of the Sacred Band who were killed on that fatal day: when the mausoleum was excavated 254 skeletons were discovered.
The lion was discovered by a party of English travellers in 1818 half buried in the ground. It was smashed to pieces in the War of Independence because it sounded hollow and was supposed to contain treasure. Nothing was found and it was restored early this century.
The **museum** contains the bones, weapons and vases excavated from the tumulus of the Macedonian dead *(4km/2.5mi northeast near the railway line)*.

For adjacent sights see ARÁHOVA, ÉVIA, DELFÍ, Drómos tou IRAKLÍ, LIVADIÁ, ORHOMENÓS, ÓSSIOS LOUKÁS Monastery, THERMOPÍLES, THÍVA.

HLEMOÚTSI★★

CHLEMOUTSI CASTLE – Elis, Peloponnese
Michelin map 980 fold 27

Chlemoutsi Castle, the watchtower of Frankish Morea and a masterpiece of medieval military art, reigns proudly over the Kyllene (Kilíni) peninsula from its position on top of Cape Chelonátas (alt 256m/840ft) overlooking the Ionian Sea to Zakynthos.

From Geoffrey to Ibrahim – This fortress, which was the most powerful in Morea, was built between 1220 and 1223 by **Geoffrey II de Villehardouin**, who called it Clermont, from which the Greek Chlemoutsi is derived. Late in the 13C it passed to the Angevins of Naples *(see KILÍNI)* who held Marguerite de Villehardouin captive in the castle until she died in 1315; she was the daughter and only descendant of William de Villehardouin.
Subsequently it was dubbed **Castel Tornese** by the Italians probably because of the coins, called *tournois*, produced by the local mint which bore the façade of St Martin's Church *(destroyed)* in Tours in France on one face. The castle passed into the possession of the Palaiologi, the despots of Mystra and other places in the Peloponnese, in 1427; in 1460 it was captured by the Turks who adapted it for the use of artillery, added a bastion and then abandoned it. It was damaged again in 1827 by the forces of Ibrahim Pasha.

CASTLE ⓥ

Access from the village. The fortress consists of an outer court and the castle proper, which is built on a polygonal plan according to a formula apparently inherited from the crusader castles.

Outer court – The entrance, a mini fort in itself, leads into the outer court, which was the domain of the servants; it is enclosed by a curtain wall, which dates back to the 13C but was extensively altered by the Turks. The buildings which backed up against the curtain wall have almost all been destroyed leaving only their fireplaces and foundations.
There is a fine view of the walls of the castle; originally the round towers were some 6m/20ft higher than the walls.

Rafik /CAMPAGNE CAMPAGNE

Interior of Chlemoutsi Castle

Castle – A plaque placed at the entrance on 29 May 1953 recalls that **Constantine XII Palaiologos**, the last Byzantine emperor, lived for five years in the castle and died in the battle for Constantinople which was taken by the Turks on 29 May 1453. The impressively large vaulted entrance is flanked *(left)* by the chapel which is on two floors, the lower one for the servants and the upper one for the owner and his suite, and *(right)* by a vast structure (70m/230ft long) also with two floors, the lower one being a guard room and the upper being a hall where the assemblies of the Frankish barons of Morea were probably held.

At the centre of the castle is a hexagonal court (53m x 30m/174ft x 98ft) where jousts and other entertainments were held. Surrounding it are vast halls built against the outer curtain wall which is in places up to 8m/26ft thick. These chambers, which originally had an intermediate floor, have vaulted ceilings supporting a terrace above. From the terraces there is a splendid **panorama★★** of Zakynthos *(west)* and the other Ionian islands *(northwest)*; the coast by Missolonghi *(north)*; the plain of Elis *(east)*, which is bordered to the north by Mount Skólis and Sandoméri, named after a castle built in the 14C by Nicolas II de St Omer; and the valley of the River Piniós *(east)*, the mountains of Arcadia *(southeast)* and Cape Katákolo *(south)*.

For adjacent sights see KALÁVRITA, KILÍNI, MÉGA SPÍLEO, OLIMBÍA, PÁTRA, Harádra tou VOURAÏKOÚ, ZÁKINTHOS.

ÍDRA

HYDRA – Attica – Population 2 837

Michelin map 980 south of fold 30 – 50km²/19sq mi

An arm of the sea forming a strait (Kólpos Ídras) separates Hydra from the Argolid peninsula. The island consists of an impressive ridge of barren rock 18km/11mi long and rising to 590m/1 936ft. The town of Hydra, which lies midway along the coast facing the mainland, is invisible from the sea until one arrives opposite the narrow gap in the sheer cliffs which leads into the natural harbour.

Water supply – It seems that Hydra was once greener and more abundantly supplied with water than it is now. Pine woods covered the mountain and the lower slopes were terraced and cultivated. Huge underground cisterns, many of which are still in existence, collected the rain water which was then channelled to the gardens. The cisterns also made good hiding places for gold and other goods.

Gradually the surface water grew rarer, the pine forests were over-exploited for ship building and the cultivated terraces were abandoned. Since 1960 water has been imported from the mainland by tanker.

Thriving maritime power – In the 15C Hydra began a quasi-autonomous existence; the inhabitants came to terms with the Turks and were protected against attack from abroad by the island's inhospitable coastline and their sailors' vigilance.

The first Hydriot ship was launched in 1657 but it was not until the middle of the following century that the ship yards began to produce in quantity; the ships which ranged from 100 to 400t traded throughout the Mediterranean and even across to America; the island made its fortune.

During the wars of the French Revolution and the Napoleonic Empire the Hydriots turned pirate when it suited them. Their two-masted, square-rigged brigs and swift and elegant *polaccas* slipped through the English blockade, sometimes with the aid of their cannon, in order to bring wheat from the Peloponnese to Marseilles where there was a large and prosperous Greek colony. Profits from these ventures which sometimes showed a 400 % return on the capital invested were shared between the captain and crew and the ship owners who built themselves elegant mansions.

Cool and calculating and with a highly developed political sense, these ship owners constituted one of the forces in the War of Independence, not only supplying funds but also planning naval operations. In 1821 the Greek fleet was equipped by four Hydriot families: Koundouriótis, Tombázis, Voúlgaris and Miaóulis; it included the famous "fire ships" of **Andréas Miaoúlis** (1769-1835), old vessels packed with explosive which were launched into the wind against the Turkish fleet and exploded on contact. After independence part of the Hydriot fleet went back to sponge fishing in which it still engages in summer in the Aegean Sea.

PRACTICAL INFORMATION

Access – Daily services from Pireás/Piraeus (with or without ports of call), from Ermióni and from Portohéli. Information from Ceres Group: Piraeus ☎ (01) 42 80 001, Ídra (0298) 54 053, Ermióni ☎ (0754) 31 170 and 31 970. Portohéli ☎ (0754) 51 543 and 51 544.

Accommodation – About a dozen small hotels (cat A to D); guest-houses, rooms in private houses; very popular destination in summer.

Transport – On foot; no cars allowed on the island; donkeys and mules carry the luggage; in season boat-taxis to villages, beaches and coves.

PICTOR

Hydra harbour and town

★★ÍDRA (HYDRA TOWN)

★★★**The site** – Defended by a few cannon for 100 years and more, the little port of Hydra, which is packed with yachts in the season, is hidden in a rounded inlet, bordered by old houses which fan out up the dry and rocky hillside towards the monastery.

There is usually a lively crowd strolling on the large smooth paving stones of the waterfront past the modest sailors' houses which have mostly been converted into cafés, tavernas, restaurants and pastry cooks' (speciality: almond cakes – *amigdalotá*) or into craft shops selling carpets and rush mats, jewellery and enamels, pots and ceramics; set back behind the houses on the quay is the 17C bell-tower belonging to the church of the monastery of the Virgin (Panagía). The heat and bustle of the waterfront is counterbalanced by the cool peacefulness of the upper town where the shipowners had their elegant houses. The narrow but scrupulously clean streets slope steeply uphill; there are occasional glimpses down into the harbour; from time to time a file of donkeys or mules clatters by.

★**Shipowners' houses** – Most of them were built early in the 19C, often in imitation of Venetian palaces (loggias, internal courtyards) and have retained their state rooms decorated with carved wood mouldings and furnished in the style of the period. Many of these noble residences belonging to the leading citizens of the day have remained in the family; it is worth mentioning three which are on the west side of the harbour: the Voúlgaris house *(at the far end of the waterfront)*, the Tombázis house *(further up)* which is now a School of Fine Arts and the Koundouriótis house *(half-way up the hillside)*.

Fort-Belvedere – A shady promenade to the west of the harbour affords a good view of the mainland and of Dokós. 19C cannons guard the roadstead. Down among the rocks bathing platforms have been constructed. *(Continue as far as Kamínia if desired)*.

EXCURSIONS

★**Monasteries** ⓥ **of Profítis Ilías (Prophet Elijah)** and **Agía Efpraxía (St Euphrasia)** – *2hr 30min on foot there and back (1hr 45min ascent; 45min descent) by Odós Miaoúli and the valley*. These two convents, one for men, the other for women, were built near a pine wood 500m/1 640ft up; fine **views** of Hydra, the coast and the other Saronic islands.

Kamínia – *45min on foot there and back following the harbour quay round to the west.* Beyond the fort *(see above)* the coast path continues to **Kamínia**, a quiet fishing hamlet with a shingle beach and several tavernas. Return to Hydra by the quiet inland lanes.

Mandráki – *1hr on foot there and back or by taxi-boat or caïque.* Follow the quayside round to the east past the Merchant Navy Captains' School which occupies an old shipowner's house. The road continues to Mandráki Bay *(sandy beach)* formerly protected by two forts; this was the site of the 19C ship yards; the major part of the Hydriot fleet, which at its height numbered some 125 vessels and 10 000 sailors, used to anchor in the bay.

For adjacent sights see ARGOLÍDA, ÁRGOS, Aktí ARKADÍAS, EPÍDAVROS, LERNÍ, MIKÍNES, NÁFPLIO, SPÉTSES, TÍRINTHA.

IOÁNINA*

Ioánina, Epiros – Population 56 699
Michelin map 980 fold 15 – Alt 520m/1 706ft – Airport

Ioánina, also known as Janena or Yannina, is the capital of Epiros, an administrative and commercial centre, the seat of a university and a tourist excursion centre. It is a modern town except for the old district near the lake which has an Islamic air owing to a bazaar and several mosques and minarets which date from the Turkish occupation.

Ali Pasha's city stands on the edge of an immense lake in a broad green valley, rich in pastureland and fields of tobacco, vines and cereals, against a backdrop of majestic mountains rising to 2 000m/6 561ft. A good view of the **site**** can be obtained by climbing up to the Tourist Pavilion (Touristikó Períptero) built in the regional style on a rise to the west of the town.

Local craftsmanship produces embroidery and silverwork; there are shops in Odós Avéroff. **Gastronomic specialities** include eels, frogs, trout and crayfish from the lake, cheese from Dodóni/Dodona and a sparkling white wine from the region of **Zítsa**.

"The Lion of Ioánina" – A Norman possession in the 11C, capital of the despotate of Epiros early in the 13C, dependence of the Serbian kingdom from 1345 to 1431, Ioánina then became Turkish until 1913 and had its hour of glory under the rule of **Ali Pasha**. Ali Pasha, who was born in 1744 in Tepelene in Albania, was made pasha of Ioánina by the Sultan in 1788. For more than 30 years, during which he expelled Napoleon's troops and the Souliots *(see p 126)*, he exercised almost sovereign power over his territory which was known in western Europe as Albania and extended from the Ionian Sea to Árta on the Ambracian Gulf in the south, to the Pindus range of mountains *(east)* and to Valona or even Durazzo in the north.

B.N., Paris

Ali Pasha of Ioánina

In his day Ioánina was like a capital city and developed into an important centre for Greek culture. Consuls were appointed by the major European nations and the British and French representatives vied with one another to exert influence over the pasha. Ali, however, cultivated both sides and also made sure of the support of the Greek partisans in the mountains, the **klephts** *(see p 27)*, to assist him in his effort to become independent of the Sultan.

The Turkish government became alarmed at the growing power of Ali and in 1820 it sent an army of 50 000 men who besieged the citadel of Ioánina for 15 months. In the hope of negotiations Ali was lured to the island in the lake where he was surprised and killed by the Turks on 22 February 1822. His head was exposed in Ioánina. This cunning tyrant had a harem of 500 women and was surrounded by a guard of assassins. In 1797 while Ali was allied to the French his daughter married General Roze but when the truce was broken Ali captured his son-in-law and sent him to Constantinople where the unfortunate man soon died. Acting on information from his daughter-in-law Ali also caused his son's favourite mistress, Euphrosine (Frosini), together with 16 other women to be drowned in the lake for being unfaithful to their husbands.

Byron visits Ali Pasha – On his first visit to Greece in 1809 Byron and his companion Hobhouse arrived in Ioánina in September and Ali, who was cultivating the support of the British against the French then in possession of the Ionian islands, sent for them to Tepelene where he was staying. Byron described the scene: "I was dressed in a full suit of staff uniform with a very magnificent sabre. The Vizier (Ali) received me in a large room paved with marble; a fountain was playing in the centre; the apartment was surrounded by scarlet ottomans. He received me standing, a wonderful compliment from a Mussulman, and made me sit down on his right hand...".
Other Englishmen who visited Ioánina at the time included Col William Leake, who was sent on a mission to Ali to make a military survey of the country, Henry Holland, Queen Victoria's physician, whom Ali consulted about his health, and C R Cockerell who was "struck with the easy familiarity and perfect good humour of his (Ali's) manners"; he and his party were entertained to a dinner consisting of 86 dishes, all of which had to be tasted at least.

★★ Límni Ioanínon – A shady walk beneath the walls of the citadel along the edge of **Lake Ioánina**, still known as Lake Pamvótis, provides a pleasant **view** across the waters to the island where storks can be seen on the wing.
The lake is contained in a depression lined with alluvium. It collects the waters flowing down from Mount Mitsikéli *(north)* and its level varies according to the seasons and the outflow of the **swallow holes** *(katavóthres)* worn through the soft limestone round the shore. It is marshy in the northern part but in the south it reaches 12m/40ft in depth; it is liable to sudden storms.

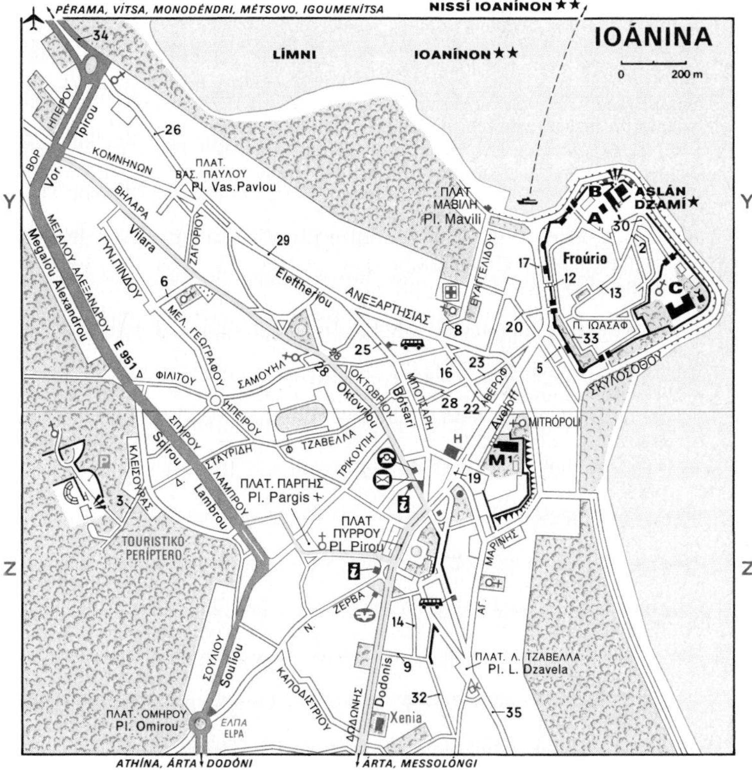

A. Paleologou	Α. ΠΑΛΑΙΟΛΟΓΟΥ	Y 2	Koundouriotou	ΚΟΥΝΤΟΥΡΙΩΤΟΥ	Y 20
Dim. Evangelidou	ΔΗΜ. ΕΥΑΓΓΕΛΙΔΟΥ	Z 3	Kristali	ΚΡΥΣΤΑΛΛΗ	Y 22
Ethn. Andistasseos	ΕΘΝ. ΑΝΤΙΣΤΑΣΕΩΣ	Y 5	L. Vironos	Λ. ΒΥΡΩΝΟΣ	Y 23
Evergeton	ΕΥΕΡΓΕΤΩΝ	Y 6	Pan. Dagli	ΠΑΝ. ΔΑΓΚΛΗ	Y 25
Hadzikosta	ΧΑΤΖΗΚΩΣΤΑ	Y 8	Pan. Mavrogiani	ΠΑΝ. ΜΑΥΡΟΓΙΑΝΝΗ	Y 26
H. Peleren	Χ. ΠΕΛΛΕΡΕΝ	Z 9	Papazoglou	ΠΑΠΑΖΟΓΛΟΥ	Y 28
Ioustinianou	ΙΟΥΣΤΙΝΙΑΝΟΥ	Y 12	Pavlou Mela	ΠΑΥΛΟΥ ΜΕΛΑ	Y 29
I. Paleologou	Ι. ΠΑΛΑΙΟΛΟΓΟΥ	Y 13	Pl. Katsandoni	ΠΛΑΤ. ΚΑΤΣΑΝΤΩΝΗ	Y 30
Kaloudi	ΚΑΛΟΥΔΗ	Z 14	Roma-Garivaldinou	ΡΩΜΑ-ΓΑΡΙΒΑΛΔΙΝΟΥ	Z 32
Kaningos	ΚΑΝΙΓΓΟΣ	Y 16	Thoma Paleologou	ΘΩΜΑ ΠΑΛΑΙΟΛΟΓΟΥ	Y 33
Karamanli	ΚΑΡΑΜΑΝΛΗ	Y 17	VIII Merarhias	VIII ΜΕΡΑΡΧΙΑΣ	Y 34
Kons. Eleftherotou	ΚΩΝΣ. ΕΛΕΥΘΕΡΩΤΟΥ	Z 19	21 Fevrouariou	21 ΦΕΒΡΟΥΑΡΙΟΥ	Z 35

Arheologikó Moussío	Z	M¹	Nissí Ioanínon	Y	
Aslán Dzamí	Y		Paliá Sinagogí	Y	A
Froúrio	Y		Paliá Toúrkiki Vivliothíki	Y	B
Límni Ioanínon	Y		Táfos Ali Pasa	Y	C

★★**Nissí Ioanínon** ⓥ – *Access by boat (15min) from the landing-stage in Mavíli Square about every 30min. Visitors are advised to check the opening times of monasteries with the EOT. The island restaurants are some of the best in Ioánina.*
This charming little wooded island *(restaurants, tavernas)* is surrounded by reed beds cut through by backwaters in which the residents moor their boats. It has a pretty lakeside village and five monasteries decorated with interesting frescoes.
The 16C **Monastery of Pandeleímonas** ⓥ secluded among enormous plane trees *(turn left at the end of the street coming from the landing-stage)* is the best known: here can be seen the house with its wooden balcony (now a museum) where Ali Pasha was killed by the Turks. Beyond is the **Monastery of St John the Baptist** (Ágios Ioánnis Pródromos) ⓥ with its 16C church and a cave which contained an ancient hermitage.
The **Monastery of the Philanthropiní** ⓥ – also known as Nikólaos Spanós – *(turn right at the end of the street coming from the landing-stage)* was built on a hill in the 13C, but altered in the 16C. The church is decorated with remarkable 17C **frescoes**★: in the narthex, the Annunciation, portraits of the founders of the monastery kneeling before St Nicholas, effigies of the ancient philosophers; in the sanctuary, the Life of Christ on the walls, the Communion of Saints in the apse.
The **Monastery of Stratigópoulos** ⓥ – also known as Nikólaos Dílios – dates from the 11C; the church is decorated with beautiful 16C **frescoes**★ showing the Last Judgement and the Life of the Virgin (narthex) and the Life of Christ with the Betrayal by Judas (sanctuary).

Froúrio – The huge **fortress** dominating the lake is surrounded by a wall which was built during the despotate of Epiros (13C) and restored by Ali Pasha.
It was inhabited by the Turks and then from the 17C by Jews but is now almost deserted; it has retained an Islamic appearance provided by the narrow streets, the overhanging roofs of the houses and the former mosques; Ali Pasha had his palace here on the top of the rock.

★**Aslán Dzamí** – The **Aslan Aga Mosque** was founded in 1619 on the site of an orthodox monastery; its slim pointed minaret still stands.
The building, which is composed of a vestibule, containing a recess for the worshippers' shoes, and a prayer chamber, has been converted into a little **Folk Art Museum** (Moussío Laikis Téhnis) ⓥ: handsome Epirot costumes and arms.
From the terrace there are very fine **views**★★ of the lake and mountains.
Below the mosque stands the former **Turkish Library** roofed with several little domes; further west is the **Old Synagogue**, a reminder that in the 19C there were nearly 6 000 Jews in Ioánina.

Inner Citadel – It contains the tomb of Ali Pasha, a mosque and the former palace of "the Lion of Ioánina" which has recently been restored and now houses the **Byzantine Museum** (Vizandino Moussío).

Arheologikó Moussío ⓥ – The **Archeological Museum** contains well-presented collections of objects found in the Ephyra Nekromanteion *(see EFÍRA)* (votive figurines in terracotta) and at Dodona *(see below)* (bronze votive offerings); Hellenistic sarcophagi, Byzantine capitals, icons.

EXCURSIONS

★★★**Pérama Cave** ⓥ – *6km/3.75mi to the north.* The cave was discovered by chance during the Second World War when people were looking for shelter from aerial bombardment. It extends for about 1km/0.5mi and covers an area of 14 800m²/5714sq mi; the walls continuously stream with water.
Most of the caverns are very high and artistically lit to show off the splendid limestone concretions which occur in many hues (red, orange and even green) in the form of stalagmites and stalactites including excentrics, curtains, low walls and pools. The bones and teeth of cave bears have been found in the cave.
The exit, as opposed to the entrance, is the natural opening into the cave: superb **views**★★ over Ioánina.
For those with time to spare it is worth continuing east along the road to Métsovo for several miles: extensive **views**★★ from the overhanging road down over the valley, the lake and the town of Ioánina in its attractive mountain setting.

★★**The Zagória country** – *79km/49mi there and back – about 2hr 30min – plus 1hr walking or sightseeing.*
Take the road north which continues past the airport up a broad valley cut off to the east by the barrier of Mount Mitsikéli which rises to 1 810m/5 938ft. After 19km/12mi turn right into a narrow tarred road which climbs towards Vítsa, overhanging the valley and producing beautiful views. This is the approach to the **Zagória country**, the "land beyond the mountains", which follows the renowned trout stream, the River Voidomátis, as it flows north into Albania. It is a region of forests (conifers, oaks, chestnuts) and pasture; the traditional habitat has not been disturbed; there

are many houses of beautiful grey stone, with projecting upper storeys and wooden balconies, roofed with stone, churches with painted interiors and old "Turkish bridges". In these wild mountains, where bears and wolves still roam, Greek troops defied the advancing Italian forces when they invaded from Albania in November 1940.

10km/6.25mi after turning off the main road, there is a narrow tarred road to the right leading to a very unusual bridge *(géfira)* with three arches downstream from **Kípi** which is the administrative centre of the Zagória country.

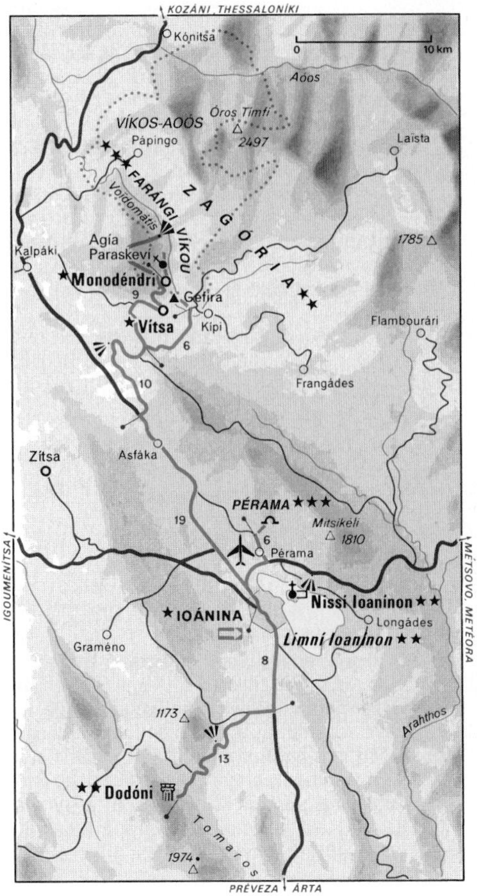

★**Vítsa** – Pop 140. The town is built on a picturesque site; most of the houses are in the traditional style.

★**Monodéndri** – Pop 136. *Taverna (speciality "tirópita" – cheese puffs). Accommodation available in restored traditional houses.*

Together with Kípi this is the main regional centre; many mountain style houses built of stone with shingle roofs and fine church with an external gallery typical of the Zagória region.

Take the narrow road (600m/660yd long) on the far side of the village which leads to the Monastery of Agía Paraskeví and the Víkos Gorge.

★★★**Farángi (or Harádra) Víkou** (Víkos Gorge) – The grey stone buildings of the Monastery of Agía Paraskeví cling to the rocks directly above a precipitous drop into the bottom of the gorge 1 000m/3 281ft below, which the River Voidomátis has created.

A path starting from the monastery winds down the face of the cliff past some terraces once cultivated by the monks and some caves which provided shelter for klephts *(see above)* and hermits; it reaches a platform overlooking the confluence of the Voidomátis and a neighbouring mountain stream; the atmosphere is oppressive and wild.

The gorge continues downstream towards Kónitsa.

There is another magnificent **view**★★★ of the gorge from the hamlet of Osía which can be reached by a narrow forest road *(7.3km/4.5mi)* from Monodéndri.

★★**Dodóni** (**Dodona**) – *21km/13mi south. From Ioánina take the road to Árta, after 8km/5mi turn right.* A good tarred road climbs a mountain chain (magnificent **views**★★ back over the Ioánina basin) to reach the ancient site of Dodona (630m/2 067ft) in a high fertile valley; to the southwest Mount Tómaros rises to 1 974m/6 476ft.

Ancient Dodona grew out of a sanctuary dedicated to Zeus where a famous oracle flourished from the second millennium BC until the 4C BC. This oracle made known its pronouncements through the whispering of the breeze in the leaves of a sacred oak tree. The message was interpreted by the priests, known as *Helloi* or *Selloi*, who were accustomed to sleep on the ground the better to be in tune with the god's manifestations. Later, however, the oracle was interpreted by priestesses. Dodona was destroyed by barbarians in the 6C AD but has been excavated by Greek archeologists from 1873 to the present day.

Dodona Ruins ⓥ – *Drama festival in summer. Tourist Pavilion.* Dodona was dominated by an acropolis; part of the walls still exists. The first ruins to be seen after the entrance are the remains of the stadium (late 3C BC) indicated by traces of the terraces of seats.

The **theatre★★** on the left is one of the largest (130m/427ft broad by 22m/72ft high) and one of the best preserved of ancient Greece. It was originally constructed in the late 3C BC, destroyed in 219 BC and rebuilt in the reign of Philip V of Macedon (221-179 BC). Under the Romans it was transformed into an arena for gladiatorial and animal combats; at this time the arena was separated from the public by a wall which is still in place and by a channel for the evacuation of water. The outer wall of the structure is composed of massive blocks of grey stone; there is a fine view of the theatre from the top of the terraces of seats.

Beyond the theatre are the foundations of an assembly hall *(bouleuterion)* and a little temple to Aphrodite. Next come the remains of the **sanctuary to Zeus Naios** which included the precinct of the oracle of Zeus enclosing the sacred oak, the area devoted to the cult of Zeus, Dione (a primitive earth goddess) and Herakles (Hercules).

Finally, traces of a basilica with a nave and two aisles dating from the 6C AD are a reminder that in the Byzantine period Dodona was the seat of a bishop.

For adjacent sights see ÁRTA, EFÍRA, KASSÓPI, KÉRKIRA, MÉTSOVO, PÁRGA, PRÉVEZA.

ITHÁKI

ITHACA – Ionian Islands – Population 3 082

Michelin map 980 fold 27 – 96km²/37sq mi

The smallest (after Paxí) of the Ionian islands is composed of two mountains joined by an isthmus. The steep west coast contrasts with the eastern shoreline which is less stark and more welcoming.

Ithaca is famous as the island of **Odysseus** and corresponds closely to the descriptions in Homer's *Odyssey*. Schliemann *(see p 193)* began his archeological career on Ithaca in 1860 by digging on what he judged to be the sites described in the *Odyssey*. Subsequent research by scholars and excavations carried out in 1930 by the British School at Athens have confirmed the Homeric story and identified the places where Odysseus, his father Laertes, his wife Penelope and their son Telemachos lived. When **Byron** visited the island in August 1823 *(commemorative plaque in Vathí)* he found it so beautiful that he considered buying it and living there permanently.

Practical Information

Access – Daily ferry services from Astakós on the mainland *(east)* – ☎ (0646) 41 052); from Patras on the mainland *(south-east)* ☎ (061) 62 26 02); from Vassilikí or Nidrí on Lefkáda *(north)* ☎ (0645) 31 520 (Vassilikí), (0645) 95 258 (Nidrí).

Accommodation – 4-5 hotels in Vathí and Fríkes; rooms in private houses.
Music and Theatre **Festival** in July and August.

Itháki – Pop 1 714. Itháki, which is also known as Vathí, is the capital of the island, a port and a resort. It occupies a charming **site★** at the head of a deep and narrow inlet; the green slopes on either side are covered with smart white houses built after the earthquake in 1953.

It was here that the Phaeacians (Corfiots) set down the sleeping Odysseus. The road from Itháki to Stavrós and then a path to the left lead to the **Nymphs' Cave**, 190m/623ft up, with a clump of cypresses at the entrance *(1hr 30min on foot there and back)* ; here Odysseus is supposed to have hidden the treasure given him by the Phaeacians before making himself known to his swineherd Eumaeos.

Stavrós – The village *(tavernas)* is reached from Itháki by a fine road built high on the cliff face; it is the starting point for two walks.

One walk climbs to the top of Pelikáta *(30min on foot there and back)* where excavations have uncovered Mycenaean remains which may have been the palace where Odysseus presented himself to Penelope disguised as a beggar.

The other walk *(1hr 30min on foot there and back)* goes down into Pólis Bay where the port is thought to have been in Odysseus' day; bronze tripods contemporary with the King of Ithaca have been found in a cave sanctuary to the north.

For adjacent sights see HLEMOÚTSI, KEFALONÍA, KILÍNI, LEFKÁDA, MESSOLÓNGI, NÁFPAKTOS, PÁTRA, ZÁKINTHOS.

Use the Map of Principal Sights to plan an itinerary.

ITHÓMI★★

Ruins of MESSENE – Messinia, Peloponnese

Michelin map 980 south of fold 28

The ruins of ancient Messene lie against a majestic backdrop of mountains dominated by Mount Ithómi; at the centre stands the modern village of **Mavromáti**.
Messene, the capital of Messenia, was for a long time a rebellious subject of Sparta which eventually destroyed the town; it was rebuilt by **Epaminóndas** *(see p 248)* who defeated the Spartans at Leuktra (371 BC) and in an effort to contain them constructed a defensive cordon consisting of Messene, Megalopolis, Mantineia and Argos.

TOUR

Excavations are currently in progress on the site and new finds are constantly being made. It is planned eventually to restore some of the buildings.

★★ **Circuit Wall** – The circuit wall (over 9km/5.5mi long), which dates from the 4C BC and was well known in antiquity, had four gates and turned the town into a sort of fortress. It was reinforced at regular intervals by towers and reached up to 2.50m/8ft thick in some places; although only 4-5m/13-16ft high it was protected by the escarpment below.
The best preserved section is on the north side of the site around the **Arkadia Gate** and forms a perfect system of defence. In fact the gateway consists of two sets of gates separated by an unusual round courtyard enclosed by strong walls constructed without mortar of rusticated stone blocks; the niches contained statues of the divinities who protected the city. The inner gate comprises an enormous monolithic lintel; the outer gate is flanked by two projecting square towers from which it could be protected by volleys of arrows and javelins.
Follow the ancient road (wheel ruts) out beyond the gate for a view of the ramparts; several tombs have been found in this area: handsome sarcophagus near to the Arkadia Gate.

★ **Asklepieion** ⏱ – A path leading off the road northwest of Mavromáti descends to the remains of a small theatre, the fountain of Arsinoë and a sanctuary dedicated to Asklepios (Aesculapius) which was formerly thought to be an *agora (sign "Ithómi, Archeological site"; about 30min on foot there and back).*
The excavations have uncovered the foundations of a temple to Asklepios from the Hellenistic period (71.9m/237ft x 66.67m/220ft) together with a sacrificial altar. The temple stood in the centre of a courtyard surrounded by porticoes; the bases of the colonnades have been revealed; in the corners are traces of semicircular benches *(exedrae)*. As at Epidauros, next to the sanctuary there is a theatre *(ecclesiasterion)* which was also used as a meeting place for ritual ceremonies; adjoining this are the council chamber *(bouleuterion)* and the Propylaia.
To the west, the Temple of Artemis Orthia (10.3m/34ft x 5.8m/19ft) was divided into three parts: the cella which housed the statue of the goddess, attributed to the famous sculptor Damophon, around which stood in a semicircle the statues of the priestesses (in the museum). To the north, the Sebasteion was dedicated to the cult of Augustus and the Roman emperors, while to the south of the Asklepieion the Hellenistic public baths included a swimming bath fed by pipes of terracotta. The Hierothysion was a temple containing not only the statues of the 12 Olympian gods, but also one in bronze of Epaminóndas, the founder of the city. Further south are the remains of a stadium with 19 rows of seats and of its palaestra, also vestiges of a large funerary monument in the Doric style, the Heroon, modelled on the mausolea of Asia Minor.

Moussío arheologikó ⏱ – *Situated between the Arkadia Gate and the village of Mavromáti. Occasionally open but mostly closed for reorganisation.* The **Archeological Museum** displays architectural fragments and fine sculptures, including the marble statue of the goddess Artemis Lafrias found in pieces but restored, and also the six statues of the priestesses from the temple of Artemis Orthia; small bronze objects; and the model of the Asklepieion.

Lakonia Gate – From Mavromáti drive up to the Lakonia Gate which provides a fine view of Mount Éva where there used to be a sanctuary to Dionysos; below lies the new Voulkáno Convent.

Mount Ithómi – 798m/2 618ft. From the Lakonia Gate a steep path *(1hr 30min on foot there and back)* climbs up past the remains of a temple to Artemis to the ancient **citadel of Ithómi**.
At the summit is the old **Voulkáno Convent**, which was founded in the 8C on the site of a temple to Zeus and abandoned in 1950. Under the Franks it housed a Templar commandery which later passed to the Knights of St John of Jerusalem. Magnificent **views**★★ of Messene, the region of Messenia and the southern Peloponnese.

For adjacent sights see ANDRÍTSENA, KALAMÁTA, KARÍTENA, KIPARISSÍA, KORÓNI, MEGALÓPOLI, METHÓNI, Anáktora NÉSTOROS, PÍLOS.

KALAMÁTA

Messinía, Peloponnese – Population 43 625

Michelin map 980 folds 40 and 41 – Airport

Kalamáta is not only the capital of the fertile region of Messenia (Messinía) but also an agricultural market and an administrative and commercial centre. The town, which was rebuilt on a grid plan in the 19C, stretches from the castle, at the foot of which part of the old town still survives, to the port which is huge but not much used; it opens into a broad roadstead. A holiday resort is developing to the east along the coast.

The town, which was nearly destroyed by an earthquake in 1986, had been partly rebuilt two years later on the same grid plan; the old quarter at the foot of the castle survived although badly damaged. The bazaar area and the seafront are once again bustling with activity.

Local specialities: fresh and preserved olives, figs, bananas, honey and sesame cakes, *rakí*.

Access

By air – From Athína/Athens (1 service daily).

By train – From Pireás/Piraeus and Athína/Athens several services daily via Árgos and Trípoli (about 8hr), also via Pátra/Patras and Pírgos (about 10hr 15min).

By bus – From Athína/Athens 11 services daily (4hr 30min).

Calamate, a Frankish city – The Franks worked their way down the west coast of the Peloponnese from Patras and settled in Kalamáta and the Messenian delta, known to them as Calamate and Val de Calamy, in 1206; they remained for over 200 years. William de Champlitte gave the fief of Kalamáta to Geoffrey I de Villehardouin who succeeded him in 1210 as Prince of Morea and built a castle. The de Villehardouin used to spend the winter in Kalamáta, enjoying the gentle climate free from the cold north wind; the surrounding country with its plains and rivers, its hills and meadows, was also to their taste.

William de Villehardouin was particularly attached to the castle where he was born in 1218 and where he died in 1278. Fluent in both Greek and French and keen on tournaments and courtly literature, he held court in a sumptuous manner together with his Greek wife Anna Comnena who was said to be as beautiful as Helen of Troy. In 1248 he assembled in Kalamáta the 400 French knights of Morea who were to join the Seventh Crusade led by Louis IX.

When William died without a male heir his position passed to his nephew, Guy II de la Roche, Duke of Athens. In the 14C the town was in the hands of the Angevins of Naples and their Florentine allies and was not captured by the Byzantine despots of Mystra until 1425. Thereafter, except for two Venetian interludes from 1463-79 and 1685-1718, it was under Turkish occupation.

Kástro ⏲ – *Proceed via Odós Faron, passing through Ipapandis Square with its church, and continue as far as Odós de Villeardouin, where the entrance is to be found.* The castle built by the de Villehardouin stands on a rocky eminence overlooking the coastal plain on the site of the ancient acropolis; it incorporated an earlier church and houses. All that remain are traces of the 13C keep and the circuit walls which were repaired by the Venetians.

From the terrace there is a view of Kalamáta and the Gulf of Messenia.

Next to the kástro, a small modern open-air theatre is the venue in July and August for an **international dance festival** *(information from the Tourist Police)*.

Bazaar – Lively and teeming, the shops of the bazaar are grouped around a morning vegetable market in the old town between the museum and the double church of the **Holy Apostles** (chancel originally a 10C Byzantine chapel).

Museum ⏲ – Two handsome old houses near the bazaar now house the museum's collections: funerary stelae and reliefs, icons, various architectural elements, an ancient statue of Hermes, Roman mosaics (Dionysos); souvenirs of the War of Independence: helmet belonging to the Maniot hero Mavromichalis (1765-1848) *(see MÁNI)*. Some of the architectural items are displayed in an attractive small courtyard behind the museum.

For adjacent sights see Spílea DIROÚ, GÍTHIO, ITHÓMI, KORÓNI, MÁNI, MEGALÓPOLI, MESSINIAKÓS Kólpos, METHÓNI, MISTRÁS, Anáktora NÉSTOROS, PÍLOS, SPÁRTI.

Consult the suggested Touring Programmes at the beginning of the guide
Plan a trip with the help of the Map of Principal Sights.

KALÁVRITA

Achaia, Peloponnese – Population 2 111

Michelin map 980 east of fold 28

Kalávrita (beautiful springs) is a pleasant cool summer resort *(hotels)* at 750m/2 461ft above sea level ringed by mountain peaks rising to over 2 000m/6 562ft and linked to the coast of Achaia on the Gulf of Corinth by a spectacular panoramic road and a famous narrow-gauge rack railway *(see p 254)*.

From 1205 to 1230 the town was a Frankish seigneury first held by Otto de Tournai and then by the **La Trémouille** family, barons of Chalandritsa, early in the 14C.

On 13 December 1943 the Nazis destroyed the town, which was a centre for the Resistance, and massacred 1 436 male inhabitants over 15 years of age *(memorial)*.

EXCURSIONS

★★**Vouraïkós Gorge** – *11km/6.75mi northeast by the Trápeza road or the railway to Diakoftó. See Harádra tou VOURAÏKOÚ.*

★**Monastery of Méga Spíleo** – *Same access route. See MÉGA SPÍLEO.*

Monastery of Agía Lávra ⏱ – *7km/4.5mi southwest.* Despite its remote position in the mountains where it was founded in 961, the monastery has earned its place in history. On 25 March 1821 **Germanós**, Archbishop of Patras, raised the standard of revolt against the Turks in the 17C conventual church which one can see before entering the present-day monastery.

Outside there is a terrace shaded by an enormous plane tree beneath which Germanós used to stand when he addressed the crowd. The monastery buildings *(guest-house)*, which were burnt by the Turks in 1821 and again by the Nazis in 1943, now house an interesting **museum**: manuscripts, icons, gold and silver ware, souvenirs of the War of Independence (the famous standard).

Above the monastery a path leads off the road *(sign "Paleón Monastírion"; 30min on foot there and back)* to the original **hermitage** where the monks lived until 1689: at the foot of the rock there is a chapel decorated with barely visible murals.

A hillock near the monastery bears the modern **Independence Monument**.

For adjacent sights see HLEMOÚTSI, KILÍNI, MÉGA SPÍLEO, PÁTRA, Harádra tou VOURAÏKOÚ.

KARÍTENA

Arkadía, Peloponnese – Population 248

Michelin map 980 south of fold 28

The road running northwest from Megalopolis to Andrítsena is carried over the River Alfiós by a modern bridge which overshadows its 15C predecessor. From the bridge there is a spectacular view of the **site**★★ of Karítena, a picturesque medieval town built into the curve of a hillside below a powerful Frankish castle commanding the mouth of the Alfiós Gorge.

Drive up to the square at the top of the town. Just below are the Church of Our Lady (Panagía) with a square stone belfry (17C) in the western style and St Nicholas', a small post-Byzantine church marked by a clump of cypress trees.

★**Castle** – The first-class defensive site boasts a feudal castle, the stronghold of the barony of Karítena, which was created by the Franks in 1209 for the de Bruyères family; it was one of the strongest in the Frankish principality of Morea and consisted of 22 fiefs. The lord of Karítena, who was one of the "peers" of Morea, had the power to administer justice.

The castle was built in 1254 for Hugues de Bruyères and then passed to his son, **Geoffrey de Bruyères**, the famous "Sire de Caritène", a model of chivalry, whose exploits were told in the *Chronicle of the Morea*. Karítena castle was sold in 1320 to the Byzantine emperor Andronikos II Palaiologos; during the War of Independence Kolokotrónis defied Ibrahim Pasha from the security of its stout walls.

The triangular precinct, reinforced by towers, has only one entrance. Only the ruins of the residence of the lord of the castle remain against the south wall but several cisterns, some vaulted, some underground, have been preserved *(danger of falling)*. From the top (alt 583m/1 913ft) there are extensive **views**★★ of the Alfiós Gorge *(west)*, the Megalópoli basin *(east)* and Mount Líkeo (Lykaion) *(south)*.

EXCURSIONS

★**Alfiós Gorge** – *Follow the road to Andrítsena for about 15km/9.25mi.* There are views back towards Karítena and down into the gorge created by the River Alfiós between the Megalópoli basin and Ilía (Elis). This succession of narrow passes, which was known in the Middle Ages as the **Escorta**, was guarded by the castles at Karítena, St Helena, Cumba...

Dimitsána – *25km/15mi north on the road to Tripoli.* Buried at the heart of the Peloponnese is the old medieval city of Dimitsána which is built on a spectacular **site★★** (850m/2 789ft) on a ridge overlooking the narrow and rugged Loússios Valley.
In the 18C its remote position and inaccessibility made it a good centre for the national revival with its secret schools which were attended by several patriots who later became leaders in the independence movement, such as the Patriarch Germanós *(see p 151)*; owing to its arsenal and powder magazine, it took on a military role at the outbreak of war against the Turks.
For adjacent sights see ANDRÍTSENA, ITHÓMI, KILÍNI, KIPARISSÍA, MEGALÓPOLI, OLIMBÍA, TRÍPOLI.

KARPENÍSSI

Evritanía, Central Greece – Population 5 868
Michelin map 980 south of fold 16

Karpeníssi is a winter sports resort majestically situated in a high "alpine" valley (alt 960m/3 150ft) south of the Timfristós range (alt 2 315m/7 595ft). It is a very good centre for walks and excursions into the Evritanian pine forests.
It was near Karpeníssi that **Márkos Bótsaris** (1790-1823) was killed; he was a hero of the War of Independence who fought at Missolonghi *(see MESSOLÓNGI)* where he is buried.

EXCURSIONS

Proussós Monastery ⏱ – *30km/18.5mi southwest by a good earth road.* The monastery, which stands in an isolated **site★** in the mountains near Proussós *(taverna)*, houses an icon of the Virgin said to have been painted by St Luke. The walls of the church are decorated with beautiful Byzantine and post-Byzantine mosaics. There is a small museum of religious art.
The track to the pass *(suitable for cars)* affords views over the Timfristós peaks. *The drive down to Thérmo and Trihonida Lake is long and tiring (poor road surface).*

★★ **Límni Kremastón** – *55km/34mi west by the road to Agrínio.* The road west of Karpeníssi to **Kremastá Lake** passes through very wild and beautiful scenery. The lake is a reservoir, the largest in Greece, which was created in the 1960s by the construction of a hydroelectric dam at the confluence of two rivers, the Ahelóos and the Tavropós; two villages are submerged beneath its glaucous waters, which spread on all sides like tentacles between the steep hillsides *(tavernas)*.
There are spectacular views of the reservoir from the Karpeníssi to Agrínio road which overlooks the lake from a great height except where it drops down to cross an arm of water by an elegant concrete bridge.
For adjacent sights see ÉVIA, Drómos tou IRAKLÍ, LÁRISSA, THERMOPÍLES, TRÍKALA, VÓLOS.

KASSÓPI★

KASSOPE – Préveza, Epiros
Michelin map 980 fold 15 – 25km/15mi north of Préveza

A turning *(sign "Ancient Kassopi")* on the inland road from Préveza to Igoumenítsa climbs the lower slopes of **Mount Zálongo** and offers glimpses of the colossal sculpted effigies of the "Souliot Women" *(see below)*.

After about 6km/3.75mi a path, on a bend to the left, leads to the ruins.

Ruins ⏱ – **Kassope**, which was founded in the 4C BC and later destroyed by the Romans, stood on the slopes of Mount Zálongo on a terrace which offers extensive **views★** south over Préveza to Leukas and east over the Ambracian Gulf south of Árta. Excavations have uncovered the *agora* and the remains of a portico, an odeon and a square structure built round a courtyard with a peristyle which may have been the *prytaneion* where the city magistrates met. Further off is the site of a theatre.

Zálongo Monastery – *4km/2.5mi north.* In 1803 the **Souliots** *(see p 126)* who were fleeing from the troops of Ali Pasha took refuge in the monastery. To escape a worse fate 60 women climbed on to the bluff above the convent, where they performed their national dance *(see p 54)*, and then threw themselves together with their children over the precipice.
The line of impressive cement figures recalling their sacrifice was sculpted by Zongolopoulos and set up in 1954. Their desperate courage was also celebrated in a painting by **Theophilos** *(see LÉSVOS: Variá)* and in verse by Byron in *Don Juan* and by Mrs Felicia Hemans in *The Suliote Mother.*
For adjacent sights see ÁRTA, EFÍRA, IOÁNINA, KÉRKIRA, LEFKÁDA, PÁRGA, PRÉVEZA.

KASTORIÁ★★

Kastoriá, Macedonia – Population 14 775
Michelin map 980 fold 4 – Alt 690m/2 263ft – Airport

Kastoriá, the city of furriers, lies on the neck of a peninsula jutting out into the picturesque waters of a lake. The charm of the old houses and numerous little Byzantine churches has not been overwhelmed by its modern buildings.

Fur capital – Kastoriá, which legend says was founded by Orestes, has prided itself for 500 to 600 years on being involved in the furriery business, an activity probably started by Jewish settlers who traded with the Balkans and Central Europe. According to a different tradition the industry dates back to the Byzantine period when furriers and merchants from Kastoriá who had settled in Constantinople and sold furs from Russia to the rich families in the capital, sent back to their relatives in Kastoriá rejected skins to be made up into garments. Exemption from import tax on the pelts, a concession granted during the Turkish occupation (which started in 1385), and particular skill in making up rejected skins enabled the local workshops to produce coats and wraps for export to Constantinople and to the capitals of Central Europe, Vienna, Budapest and Leipzig. The goods are now exported directly to western cities where furriers originally from Kastoriá have set up workshops. The local furriers buy pelts mainly from America and Scandinavia but nowadays there are mink and wolf farms on the outskirts of the town. The fur shops and the chamber of commerce are in the main street, **Odós Mitropoleos**; the workshops are dotted about the town and skins stretched out on frames and drying in the sun are to be seen on the pavements.

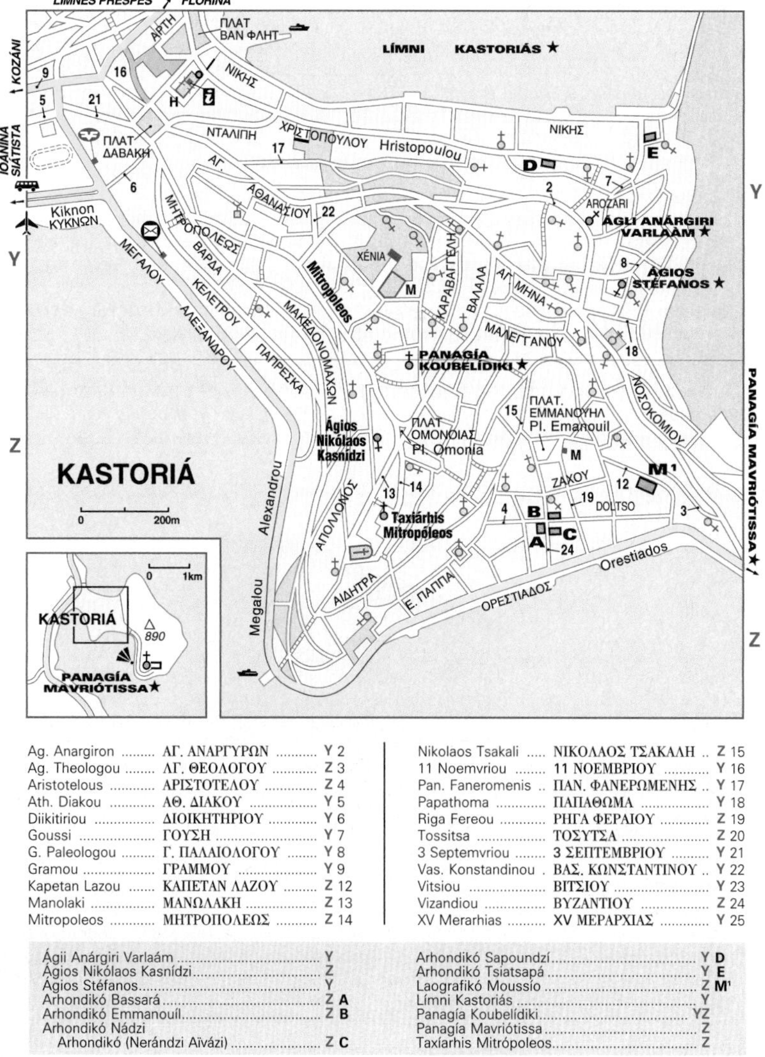

Ag. Anargiron	ΑΓ. ΑΝΑΡΓΥΡΩΝ	Y 2
Ag. Theologou	ΑΓ. ΘΕΟΛΟΓΟΥ	Z 3
Aristotelous	ΑΡΙΣΤΟΤΕΛΟΥ	Z 4
Ath. Diakou	ΑΘ. ΔΙΑΚΟΥ	Y 5
Diikitiriou	ΔΙΟΙΚΗΤΗΡΙΟΥ	Y 6
Goussi	ΓΟΥΣΗ	Y 7
G. Paleologou	Γ. ΠΑΛΑΙΟΛΟΓΟΥ	Y 8
Gramou	ΓΡΑΜΜΟΥ	Y 9
Kapetan Lazou	ΚΑΠΕΤΑΝ ΛΑΖΟΥ	Z 12
Manolaki	ΜΑΝΩΛΑΚΗ	Z 13
Mitropoleos	ΜΗΤΡΟΠΟΛΕΩΣ	Z 14
Nikolaos Tsakali	ΝΙΚΟΛΑΟΣ ΤΣΑΚΑΛΗ	Z 15
11 Noemvriou	11 ΝΟΕΜΒΡΙΟΥ	Y 16
Pan. Faneromenis	ΠΑΝ. ΦΑΝΕΡΩΜΕΝΗΣ	Y 17
Papathoma	ΠΑΠΑΘΩΜΑ	Y 18
Riga Fereou	ΡΗΓΑ ΦΕΡΑΙΟΥ	Z 19
Tossitsa	ΤΟΣΙΤΣΑ	Z 20
3 Septemvriou	3 ΣΕΠΤΕΜΒΡΙΟΥ	Y 21
Vas. Konstandinou	ΒΑΣ. ΚΩΝΣΤΑΝΤΙΝΟΥ	Y 22
Vitsiou	ΒΙΤΣΙΟΥ	Y 23
Vizandiou	ΒΥΖΑΝΤΙΟΥ	Z 24
XV Merarhias	XV ΜΕΡΑΡΧΙΑΣ	Y 25

Ágii Anárgiri Varlaám	Y
Ágios Nikólaos Kasnídzi	Z
Ágios Stéfanos	Y
Arhondikó Bassará	Z **A**
Arhondikó Emmanouíl	Z **B**
Arhondikó Nádzi Arhondikó (Nerándzi Aïvázi)	Z **C**
Arhondikó Sapoundzí	Y **D**
Arhondikó Tsiatsapá	Y **E**
Laografikó Moussío	Z **M¹**
Límni Kastoriás	Y
Panagía Koubelídiki	YZ
Panagía Mavriótissa	Z
Taxíarhis Mitrópoleos	Z

★★BYZANTINE CHURCHES ⓥ

Once Kastoriá boasted 75 churches; now about fifty survive, some of which date from the 10C. The churches – some are tiny – which are beautifully decorated with frescoes and sculptures were built by rich local families, by officials exiled from Constantinople or by trade guilds.
A **Byzantine museum** (Vizandinó Moussío) ⓥ which will display works of art from the churches of the region, is planned near the Zenia Hotel in the upper town.

★**Panagía Koubelídiki** – *Near the school.* Built in the mid 19C near the castle and dedicated to the Virgin, it is the only domed church in Kastoriá with a tall drum, hence its name after a Turkish word *(kouben)* meaning drum. The frescoes (Herod's Feast, Virgin of Sorrows) in the porch date from 1496; those in the cross-plan interior are 13C except for the ones in the apse which are 17C. The narthex vaulting bears the Holy Trinity which is rarely represented in the Byzantine tradition. In the nave, above the narthex door the Dormition of the Virgin includes a seated figure of Christ (he is usually shown standing) holding a child representing the Virgin's soul.

Ágios Nikólaos Kasnídzis (**St Nicholas of Kasnitsis**) – *Below Platía Omonia.* The exterior of this small 12C church was partly decorated with frescoes; traces are visible above the apse. Inside, in the narthex are depicted the donors, Nicephoros Kasnidzis and his wife Anna, and the miracles of St Nicholas. The nave is decorated with 12C frescoes: the Dormition of the Virgin and figures of warrior saints.

Taxiárhis Mitropóleos – The 9C **Metropolitan church of the Taxiarchs** (leaders of the heveanly host), the Archangels Michael and Gabriel, contains capitals from an early-Christian basilica which previously stood on the site. It was probably used as a funerary chapel for local dignitaries who are represented together with religious themes on the south and west external walls. Inside, the east walls of the aisles and the narthex still bear traces of 9C frescoes whereas in the rest of the church these have been painted over in the 17C. In the apse the Interceding Virgin is framed by the archangels Michael and Gabriel and on the upper wall in the nave the figures in the Passion Scenes are particularly expressive.

★**Ágios Stéfanos** (**St Stephen's**) – *Northeast, on the hillside.* The closed porch on two sides is a late addition to the 9C church which was probably a bishop's church on the evidence of the throne base in the apse. The vaulting of the lofty nave is painted with 12C frescoes: the Nativity and Purification on the south wall. In the rest of the church and in the upper sections of the narthex, the 9C frescoes have been preserved: the Last Judgement on the south wall and ceiling. A stairway leads to a women's gallery, a unique feature in Kastoriá (St Ann's Chapel).

★**Ágii Anárgiri Varlaám** – *Northeast on the hillside.* High up above the lake, the church, which was probably built in the 10C, is among the largest in Kastoriá and is dedicated to the "holy penniless ones", the physicians who practised medicine without charging fees *(anárgiris).* The title is usually given to St Cosmas and

Agií Anárgiri Varlaám Church, Kastoriá

St Damian but also applies to St Pantaléon and St Hermolaos. The saints are portrayed in the porch. Inside the majority of the frescoes are 11C or 12C but an earlier 10C layer is visible in some parts of the church: on the arches of the south wall in the narthex the heads of St Basil and St Nicholas are out of proportion with their bodies; at the far end near the door leading to the north aisle are St Constantine and St Helena dressed in imperial robes. In the north aisle three layers of frescoes are to be seen to the left of the door to the narthex. On the south wall near the nave, the Virgin is portrayed with the founders: Theodore Limniotis and his son *(right)* and his wife Anna clad in a gorgeous cloak *(left)*. In the tall nave, St George and St Demetrios in armour are depicted on the arches of the north wall; above is a moving Entombment. At the east end of the south aisle, the majestic archangels Michael and Gabriel stand on either side of the Virgin with St Cosmas and St Damian above.

OTHER SIGHTS

★**Old houses** – A few handsome houses *(arhondiká)* in the typical Macedonian style, built in the main in the 17C and 18C for the rich local furriers, add to the charm of the quarters near the peninsula. These tower-like houses are usually three-storeyed: the first two had ashlar walls with cross-beams. In the houses built in the 18C and 19C, the projecting top floor, built in wood and limewashed, was supported on curved beams. The ground floor which was used as a storeroom had few openings apart from the large main door. The middle floor with its wooden openings protected by grilles was the living and working area (the wooden shutters have been replaced by glass panels). The upper floor, used for receptions and as summer quarters, was well lit by two rows of windows, one composed of wooden shutters traditionally without glass and a second row above decorated with coloured glass in the manner of stained glass. There was sometimes a covered wooden balcony between the projecting floors.

There are two of these old houses in the north Arozari quarter near the lake: the **Sapoundzís mansion** (Odós Hristopoulou) and **Tsiatsapás mansion**. Most are situated in the Doltso district south of the town and in particular in Odós Vizandiou south of Platía A Emanouíl: the **Nadzis**, **Emanouil** and **Bassarás mansions**. Further along, near the peninsula, the restored Nerándzis Aïvázis mansion is now the Folklore Museum.

★**Museum of Folk Traditions** ⌚ – *Odós Kapetan Lazou.* The architecture of the 17C **Nerándzis Aïvázis mansion** is simpler and its decoration less ornate than later mansions but the interior evokes the life of a rich Macedonian family in earlier times. On the ground floor, around the paved hall are storerooms for wood, wine, foodstuffs and the kneading-trough; in the courtyard are the kitchens and ovens as well as a shed for boat and fishing-tackle and also a well. The summer living room now houses a furrier's workshop. A platform leads to the winter living room with its chimney; the decorations have not survived. In the middle of the upper floor, the reception room with its painted walls and ceilings was also used for dancing. The dignitaries were received in the parlour or "kiosk" which was hived off the reception room by a balustrade while the ladies were entertained in a smaller room to the southeast. The summer and winter quarters where young girls could watch the parties were on the north side of the house.

★**Límni Kastoriás (Kastoriá Lake)** – *Tour of the peninsula: 9.2km/5.5mi. From the Folklore Museum to the monastery: 5km/3mi there and back.*

At the start of the tour, the road skirting the peninsula offers lovely **views**★ of the southern part of the town stretched out on the hillside. On the lake typical flat-bottomed boats with raised prows are still to be seen under the plane and willow trees. Not far from the monastery of the Virgin *(2.5km/1.5mi)* the road widens and is lined by tall plane trees *(café-restaurant)*. Fine view of the lake.

★**Panagía Mavriótissa** ⌚ – The monastery built in Macedonian style has twin churches. The exterior south wall of the main **Church of the Virgin** (Panagía), which dates from c 1000, is decorated with 13C frescoes *(under cover)*: the Tree of Jesse showing the Virgin framed by the Apostles on the branches and probably Emperor Michael VII Palaiologos and his brother John on the trunk. The Last Judgement is depicted on the east wall above the door in the narthex: on the right the angels rebuke the long-toothed damned; on the south wall another group of the damned. 12C frescoes on the east and west walls of the nave evoke the Passion *(above the door)*, Pentecost *(beyond)* and the Dormition of the Virgin *(below)*. **The Chapel of Ágios Ioánnis Theológos** (John the Evangelist) was built in the 16C on the southeast side of the church.

Return to Kastoriá by the same route *(drive carefully as on the return journey cars do not have priority)* or continue round the peninsula *(one-way road from the monastery)* to the north side of the town and the small harbour.

EXCURSIONS

★★ **Límnes Préspes (Préspa Lakes)** – *64km/40mi. The road is unsurfaced for 20km/12mi half-way along. From Kastoriá take the Flórina road north.* Beyond the town *(about 5km/3mi)* a fine **view**★★ unfolds over Kastoriá, the peninsula and the lake in its mountain setting. Beyond a pass the road skirts the wooded valley of the Ladopótamos, a tributary of the Aliákmonas. *After 35km/21.5mi turn off the Flórina road and bear left towards the lakes and Lemós.* After a saddle the road affords a splendid **view**★★ of the Little Préspa lake.

★ **Mikrí Préspa** (Little Préspa Lake) – The lake (43km²/16.5sq mi) which extends southwest into Albania, was designated as a national park in 1974 together with the Greek section of the Great Préspa Lake; both lakes lie at an altitude of 853m/2 795ft. An abundant fauna thrives in the reed beds around Little Préspa including pelicans (also the white species), cormorants, egrets, herons and cranes.

There are two islands: on the larger, Ágios Ahílios, are several Byzantine churches including the 11C Church of St Achilles. There are boat trips to the islands and to bird watching posts from Makrolímni *(4km/2.5mi from the junction)*. The main road skirts the little lake and at the junction at the far end a road on the right leads to the village of **Ágios Germanós** with its 11C domed church, at the foot of Mount Varnóus (Peristéri – 2 156m/7 074ft).

Lodgings in traditional houses in Ágios Germanos organised by the Country Women's Tourist Cooperative (see p 366) or in Flórina ☎ (0385) 51 320, 51 470.

★ **Megáli Préspa** (Great Préspa Lake) – *Left at the junction.* The lake (288km²/111sq mi) belongs to Albania, Yugoslavia and Greece which owns 38km²/15sq mi. The road runs along the long sand bar dividing the two lakes; at its west end there is a small beach on the shore of the great lake where the temperature of water reaches 24° C in summer.

The village of **Psarádes** with its traditional houses with wooden balconies *(hotel, guest-houses)* overlooks a deep bay on the other side of the peninsula *(9.5km/6mi further on)*. The tavernas in this fishing village (Psarádes means fishermen) offer fish specialities.

On the Greek side excursions by motor launch take visitors to the rugged cliffs and caves (in particular the cave of the Panagía Eleoússa) painted by hermits in the 14C and the 15C. Good **views**★ of the Albanian shore and mountains.

★ **Siátista** – *59km/36.75mi southeast of Kastoriá; 30km/18.5mi west of Kozáni.* From the 16C to the 18C Siátista was famous for its trade in wine and leather. As the vines suffered from phylloxera, the town changed over to fur manufacture and trade at the beginning of the 20C. Its two quarters are dominated by a tall bell-tower. In the upper town, Hóra, most of the 18C mansions *(arhondiká)*, built in the Macedonian style as in Kastoriá, are in the care of the archeological department housed in the **Neranzópoulou Mansion** ⏲ which has painted ceilings and stained glass windows. Further down the street are **Manoúsi Mansion**★ and **Poulkídi Mansion**, splendidly decorated with painted walls and ceilings. The **Hatzimiháli Kanatsoúli Mansion** ⏲ at 430, Odós Mitropoleos, near the bell-tower, is still lived in.

For adjacent sights see ÉDESSA, LEFKÁDIA-NÁOUSSA, PÉLA, THESSALONÍKI, VÉRIA.

KAVÁLA★

Kavála, Macedonia – Population 56 577

Michelin map 980 fold 7 – Airport

Kavála, which was under Turkish domination from 1380 to 1913, still has an oriental air. It is the centre of the Macedonian tobacco industry, a bustling, lively town built on the shores of a broad and shining bay. The old district is huddled on a rocky promontory crowned by a citadel while the modern town extends westwards along the harbour.

Twixt east and west – Kavála, which was originally a colony founded by Thássos *(see THÁSSOS)* and then became the port of Philippi *(see FÍLIPI)* under the name of Neapolis, was a port of call throughout the Classical period; St Paul passed through with Silas on his way from Asia Minor to Philippi.

In the Middle Ages the town changed its name again to Christoupolis; in 1306 bands of Catalans from Gallipoli landed in the port and then went on to defeat the Franks at the Battle of Kephisos *(see ORHOMENÓS)* and to take possession of the Duchy of Athens. In the 16C the French traveller **Pierre Belon** reported that the town housed many Jews and was called Bucephalos, after Alexander the Great's horse; this is probably the origin of its present name Kavála.

Kavála was the birthplace of the famous **Mehmet Ali** (1769-1849), viceroy of Egypt and reviver of its fortunes; as the father of Ibrahim Pasha *(see PÍLOS)* Mehmet Ali founded the dynasty which ruled in Egypt until the time of King Farouk.

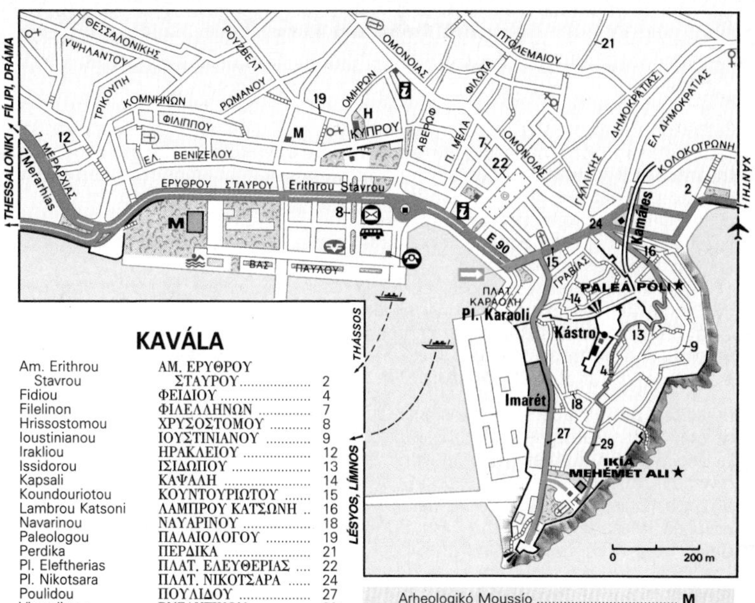

Am. Erithrou Stavrou	ΑΜ. ΕΡΥΘΡΟΥ ΣΤΑΥΡΟΥ	2
Fidiou	ΦΕΙΔΙΟΥ	4
Filelinon	ΦΙΛΕΛΛΗΝΩΝ	7
Hrissostomou	ΧΡΥΣΟΣΤΟΜΟΥ	8
Ioustinianou	ΙΟΥΣΤΙΝΙΑΝΟΥ	9
Irakliou	ΗΡΑΚΛΕΙΟΥ	12
Issidorou	ΙΣΙΔΩΡΟΥ	13
Kapsali	ΚΑΨΑΛΗ	14
Koundouriotou	ΚΟΥΝΤΟΥΡΙΩΤΟΥ	15
Lambrou Katsoni	ΛΑΜΠΡΟΥ ΚΑΤΣΩΝΗ	16
Navarinou	ΝΑΥΑΡΙΝΟΥ	18
Paleologou	ΠΑΛΑΙΟΛΟΓΟΥ	19
Perdika	ΠΕΡΔΙΚΑ	21
Pl. Eleftherias	ΠΛΑΤ. ΕΛΕΥΘΕΡΙΑΣ	22
Pl. Nikotsara	ΠΛΑΤ. ΝΙΚΟΤΣΑΡΑ	24
Poulidou	ΠΟΥΛΙΔΟΥ	27
Vizandinou	ΒΥΖΑΝΤΙΝΟΥ	29

Arheologikó Moussío .... M

★**Paleá Póli** – Within the ramparts lies the picturesque old town; its narrow streets and steps wind between the Turkish houses with tiny courtyards and flowering balconies.

Starting from **Platía Karaolí**, a charming shady square lined by restaurants with outdoor terraces *(fish specialities)*, walk up the narrow street, Odós Poulídou, which passes the Imarét *(right)*.

Imarét – This is a huge and unusual collection of buildings, designed in the Muslim style with many little domes, which is unfortunately derelict. The Imarét was founded by Mehmet Ali as a sort of alms house, run by Islamic monks (dervishes) for 300 poor men.

Higher up the hill the street opens into a small square where an equestrian statue of Mehmet Ali stands in front of his birthplace.

★**Ikía Mehémet Áli** ⓥ – This 18C house was the birthplace of Mehmet Ali, the son of a rich tobacco merchant of Albanian origin. It is now owned by the Egyptian government.

There is a magnificent view from the thick-set garden which surrounds the house; the wooden partitions and the layout are typical of a Turkish dwelling: stable and kitchen on the ground floor; on the first floor the householder's apartments and the harem which is fitted with moucharabies, wooden lattices which enable one to see out without being seen.

Walk out to the belvedere on the very tip of the promontory: extensive **view**★★ of the harbour, the town and the bay as far as Thássos Island; immediately below berths for shipping have been hewn out of the rock.

Walk through the old Turkish quarter, Odós Vizandinóu and Odós Fidíou, past a mosque and up to the Kástro.

Kástro – The citadel stands on the site of an ancient acropolis and is surrounded by Byzantine ramparts, reinforced with towers; **views**★ of Kavála. The 16C aqueduct supplied the old town with water. Within the ramparts there are prisons and a cistern.

Kamáres – The **aqueduct** which spans the depression between the modern town and the old town was built in the 16C by Suleiman the Magnificent to supply the Kástro with water from local springs.

Arheologikó Moussío ⓥ – The **Archeological Museum's** collections are well presented in a modern building.

Room 1. Devoted to the excavations at Neapolis. The colossal Ionic capitals came from the sanctuary of Parthenos (6C-5C BC) excavated near the Imarét.

Room 2. The items displayed here come from the necropolis at Amphipolis *(see AMFÍPOLI)*: carved stele, glass and gold Hellenistic jewellery.

For adjacent sights see AMFÍPOLI, FÍLIPI, HALKIDIKÍ, SAMOTHRÁKI, THÁSSOS, THESSALONÍKI.

KEFALONÍA★★

CEPHALLONIA – Ionian Islands – Population 32 474

Michelin map 980 fold 27 – 735km²/284sq mi

Cephallonia is formed of jagged hilly limestone. It is the largest of the Ionian islands (50km/31mi long). The landscape is varied; fertile terraces by the sea contrast with the more arid mountain slopes which nonetheless support clumps of cypresses among the olives. **Mount Énos** (Ainos), the highest point (1 628m/5 941ft), is covered by a particular kind of spruce peculiar to the island.

Local specialities include the delicious **Robóla** wine, dishes composed of meat and rice and thyme-flavoured honey.

The Cephallonians are reputed to be a spirited people whose patriotism was praised by Byron. The island has not only produced soldiers, sailors and enterprising emigrants, but has also fostered an aristocratic and cultivated society which produced scholars and politicians such as Metaxas (1871-1941) who rejected the Italian ultimatum on 28 October 1940 *(see p 29)*.

Invasions and invaders – Cephallonia did not play a major role in antiquity although several Mycenaean tombs have been discovered.

During the Middle Ages the island first belonged to the Norman kings of Sicily, one of whom, Robert Guiscard, died on Cephallonia in 1085. Then it became the County of Cephallonia, one of the great fiefs of the Frankish principality of the Morea, and included Ithaca and Zakynthos. For 300 years it was ruled by Italian overlords: the Orsini from 1155 to 1356 and the Tocchi until 1478.

The Turks held the island for only 20 years; by 1500 the Venetians, assisted by the Spanish troops of **Gonzales of Cordoba**, the Great Captain, had recaptured the island and they held it until 1797. After 1808 Cephallonia was occupied by the British, who promoted many improvements under the Residency of **Sir Charles Napier**. In 1823 Byron spent four months in a rented house in Metaxáta near Argostóli before sailing to Missolonghi. The island was finally returned to Greek control in 1864.

When Marshal Badoglio signed an armistice with the Allies in 1943, 9 000 Italians belonging to the "Acqui" Alpine division held out for nine days against the German air and land attack. When they finally surrendered, the survivors – 341 officers and 4 750 soldiers – were shot en masse on Hitler's orders; only 34 escaped.

In 1953 an earthquake caused severe damage throughout the island.

PRACTICAL INFORMATION

Access by air: from Athens 2 to 3 daily flights.

Access by boat: regular ferry services from Vassilikí or Nidrí (Leukas) to Fiskárdo (information ☎ (0645) 31 520 for Vassilikí, (0645) 95 258 for Nidrí and (0674) 41 315 for Fiskárdo), from Kilíni to Póros or Argostóli depending on the season (information: ☎ (0623) 92 351 for Kilíni, (0674) 72 484 for Póros and (0674) 25 151 for Argostóli), from Astakós to Sámi (information: ☎ (0646) 41 052 for Astakós and (0674) 22 456 for Sámi); also services in season from Patras to Sámi (information: ☎ (061) 62 26 02 for Patras and (0674) 22 055 for Sámi).

Accommodation – At Argostóli, about 20 hotels, cat B to D; more hotels throughout the island in particular in Sámi, Fiskárdo and Póros; rooms in private houses all over the island; camping sites.

Transport – Car and moped hire service.

Sámi – The port of Sámi nestles in a gently curving bay *(beaches)* where the fleet of the Holy League assembled on the eve of the battle of Lepanto *(see NÁFPAKTOS)*. There is a fine view of the narrow entry to the bay and of the stark coast of Ithaca.

★ **Melissáni Cave** ⏲ – *3km/2mi northwest; take the road to Agía Efimía, turn left into the track which leads to the cave.* The underground lake which receives its water via subterranean passages from the swallow holes *(katavóthres)* near Argostóli *(see below)*, is explored by boat. The roof has fallen in places but the intensity and variety of the colours of the water, the contrast of light and shadow and the resonance and echo produce a fantastic effect.

Drongaráti Cave ⏲ – *2km/1.25mi southwest; take the road to Argostóli and after 2km/1.25mi turn right into a track.* A flight of steps leads down into this cave, which is easy to explore. Among the beautiful concretions are some enormous stalagmites.

Argostóli – Pop 6 815. The road from Sámi crosses the **Agrapídies Pass** which gives a magnificent view of the **site**★★ of Argostóli, stretching away below along a promontory towards the Lixoúri peninsula.

The main approach to Argostóli is over a bridge (650m/711yd long) which crosses the Koútavos Lagoon and was built between 1810 and 1814 by Bosset, a Swiss working for the British.

After the earthquake in 1953 the capital of the island had to be rebuilt and has unfortunately lost its Greco-Venetian atmosphere. That can however be recaptured by visiting the **Korgialénios Museum**★ ⓥ: remarkable collection of old costumes, documents relating to Argostóli in the past, reconstructions of the interiors of aristocrats' houses and craftsmen's workshops.

Swallow-holes *(katavóthres)* – Near the end of the promontory, level with a restaurant, the sea water flows into a fissure and disappears underground before reappearing on the other side of the island in the Melissáni cave using the principle of communicating vessels.

The hydraulic power thus created was used to turn the mills of which one example with its paddle wheel can be seen. View of the sea and the Lixoúri peninsula.

★★**Tour of the Island** – *From Argostóli (167km/104mi by car, plus 1hr 30min of walking and sightseeing).* Leave Argostóli by the English Bridge and turn left into the coast road which climbs up the mountain side with extended views of the Argostóli Gulf and the Lixoúri peninsula. After crossing the isthmus, the road runs high up in a corniche providing spectacular **views**★★ of the Mirtos Gulf and the empty Ionian Sea and then winds downhill towards the Ássos peninsula.

★**Ássos** – This is a fishing village *(guest-houses, tavernas)* on an enchanting **site**★★ on the neck of a hilly peninsula which is crowned with a Venetian fortress (16C); the road up offers attractive views of the harbour below. The combination of the sea and the mountain, the scent of the pine trees, the sense of peace emanating from the little port and its shady square surrounded by flower-bedecked houses, make Ássos one of the most charming places in Cephallonia. The reconstruction of "Paris Square" after the earthquake in 1953 was financed by the city of Paris in France. The corniche road, where eagles are often sighted, continues north overlooking the many creeks which punctuate the coastline. Just before Fiskárdo there is a remarkable **view point**★★ over the straits which separate Cephallonia and Ithaca from the cliffs of Leukas (Lefkas) *(see LEFKÁDA)* and the coast of Akarnanía.

★**Fiskárdo** – This charming sheltered port was spared by the earthquake in 1953 and has therefore kept its character. Its name derives from **Robert Guiscard**, the Norman king of Sicily, who died on Cephallonia in 1085; he may have been buried in the ruined church with its two Norman towers, visible on the other side of the bay.

Return to Divaráta and bear left at the T-junction.

The road crosses the mountains and skirts Sámi Bay: fine views of the bare mountainous coast of Ithaca.

Sámi – *See above.*

The road from Sámi to Póros, which is picturesque but very circuitous and sometimes in a poor state of repair, passes through several inland valleys where olive and cypress trees grow.

PICTOR

Island of Cephallonia

Póros – A little seaside resort in a rocky inlet.

The road climbs back up the ravine from the sea and then continues to the south coast through gorges studded with slim cypresses.

Markópoulo – On 15 August, the feast of the Assumption, so it is said, serpents with black crosses on their skins appear for the day only to be gone next morning. Beyond Markópoulo there are attractive views across the sea to Zakynthos *(see ZÁKINTHOS)*. Below the road on the left lie the ruins of the Franciscan convent of Sissíon, named after St Francis of Assisi.
The olive groves in the fertile plain of Livathó are over 100 years old.

★**Ágios Geórgios** ⏱ – The curtain wall (600m/656yd long) of **St George's Castle** is reinforced with three bastions and encloses a 13C keep. Until 1757 the kastró was the capital of the island with 15 000 inhabitants, but was severely damaged by an earthquake in 1636. Among the ruins beneath the pine trees are traces of St George's Collegiate Church with the arms of the Orsini over the door.
The castle stands on a height (320m/1 050ft) overlooking the Livathó Plain *(south-east)*, the Lixoúri Peninsula *(northwest)* and Zakynthos *(south)*.

For adjacent sights see ITHÁKI, LEFKÁDA, MESSOLÓNGI, NÁFPAKTOS, ZÁKINTHOS.

KÉRKIRA★★★

CORFU – Ionian Islands – Population 105 115
Michelin map 980 fold 14 – 593km²/229sq mi

Corfu, which lies just off the coast of Albania (Shqipëria) and Epiros, is the most attractive of the Ionian islands. Its charm derives from its very varied coastline washed by the violet-blue sea, its rolling hills and luxuriant gardens, its gentle climate and the smiling welcome of its inhabitants. Greek by language and tradition, the island spent many years under foreign domination – British and French but mainly Venetian – and is now a most attractive summer and winter resort with a cosmopolitan atmosphere.
Main beaches (sand): Ágios Spirídonas and Róda *(north coast)*; **Ágios Geórgios**, Mirtiótissa, Glifáda and Ágios Górdis *(west coast)*; Kávos *(southern promontory)*.
Specialities: fish including crayfish, *sofritó* (beef or veal cooked in a sauce of garlic, vinegar and black pepper), *graviéra* (type of gruyère cheese), honey, *dzinzerbíra* (ginger-beer), kumkwat (mini oranges in alcohol); white "Paloúmbi" wine.
Folk dances are held on the feast of St Spyridon and other festivals, in particular on 21 May, the anniversary of the union of the Ionian islands with Greece.

GEOGRAPHICAL AND HISTORICAL NOTES

Corfu is 60km/37 mi long and culminates in the north in Mount Pandokrátor (906m/2 972ft). It is formed of limestone rock, very worn by erosion: fissures, caves, inland valleys lined with deposits of marl and clay.
The climate, which is warm and damp in winter and hot in summer, favours the growth of vegetation which is further encouraged by the depth of soil: a forest of age-old olive trees, citrus fruits, vineyards, maize, semi-tropical trees such as magnolias, palms, jujubes, succulents and myrtle clothe the island in a green mantle which contrasts sharply with the barrenness of the mainland.

Isle of the Phaeacians – In the *Odyssey* Homer tells how Odysseus lingers on the Isle of Ogygia for love of the nymph Calypso, is set free by the intervention of Hermes and is on course for Ithaca when a storm throws him up on the coast of the isle of Scheria, identified as Corfu.
There he is discovered by the gracious **Nausicaa**, "of the white arms", who is playing ball with her companions, and she conducts him to her father, Alcinoüs, king of the Phaeacians. He receives Odysseus in his palace, which is surrounded by enchanting gardens, lays on a banquet in honour of Laertes' son who recounts his adventures, offers him rich presents and finally provides him with a ship to return to Ithaca, one of the Ionian islands *(see ITHÁKI)*.
In the 8C BC the Corinthians founded a colony on the island which became known as **Corcyra** (Kérkira) until the Middle Ages.

The mark of the Lion (1386-1797) – From 1267 to 1386 the Angevin kings of Naples, following in the train of Charles I of Anjou, brother of Louis IX (St Louis), controlled Corfu but then the Venetians took command and made the island the main port of call for their **galleys** (merchant ships) on the route to the Levant.
During the Venetian occupation Corfu had to face attacks by the Turks on several occasions. They ravaged the island in 1537 under Suleiman the Magnificent (1494-1566) but failed to take the citadel. In 1571 a force of 1 500 Corfiot sailors took part in the naval battle of Lepanto *(see NÁFPAKTOS)*. Finally in 1716 an army of 30 000 Turks invaded the island but the fierce resistance of the garrison, a mixed force of Greeks, Slavs, Italians and Germans, under the command of a Saxon mercenary, Count von der Schulemburg, beat them back.

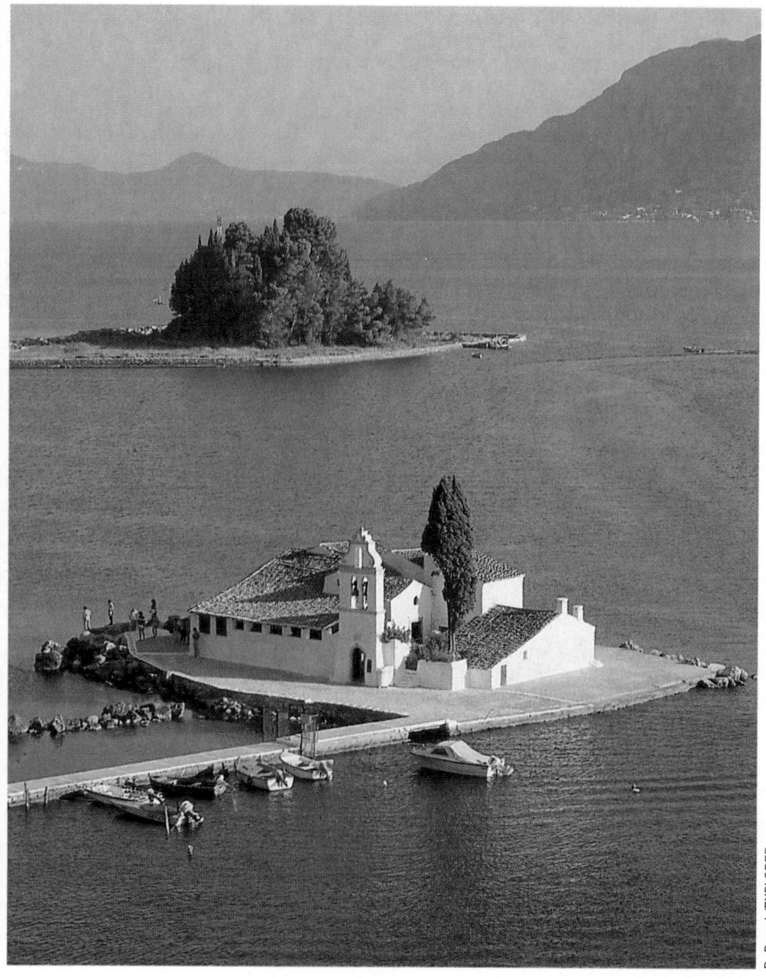

Vlahérna and Ponddikoníssi, Corfu

Through their representative, *provveditore*, the Venetians imposed their rule on Corfu, which became an arsenal and warehouse, with the assistance of the local nobility who were inscribed in a Golden Book as in Venice. Italian became the official language, Roman Catholicism held a privileged position and the Venetian government paid a sequin for every new olive tree planted, since Venice lacked oil.
This period of Venetian domination saw the building of rectangular churches with flat ceilings and detached bell-towers, of tall narrow houses some with loggias, of wells with sculpted surrounds and arcaded Italian farmhouses *(fattorias)*; many of the icons are the work of artists who were driven out of Crete by the Turks in the 17C; the most famous is Emmanuel **Tzanés** (1610-90).

Napoleonic Occupation – When French Republican troops occupied Venice in June 1797, several thousand men were sent to Corfu under General Gentili, a Corsican, who was welcomed with shouts of enthusiasm. Trees of Liberty were planted, the Golden Book was burned and Greek was reinstated as the official language. But the French incurred the anger of the Corfiots by their lack of respect for the relics of St Spyridon, patron saint of the island. Two years later they were driven out by the Russians and the Turks who set up the Septinsular Republic covering all the Ionian islands including Kythera.
In 1807, under the Treaty of Tilsit, France regained Corfu which Napoleon considered the key to the Adriatic. During seven years of enlightened government under General Donzelot 500 cannons were mounted on the fortifications, the appearance of Corfu Town was improved (arcades on the Spianáda) and agriculture was encouraged by extending the use of the plough. The use of the press which had been created in 1797 was extended and in 1808 the first Ionian Academy was founded consisting of 26 members including Ugo Foscolo *(see ZÁKINTHOS)*, Fauvel *(see ATHÍNA: Agora)*, and the famous Greek philosopher **Adamántios Koraïs** *(see HÍOS)* who at that time lived in Paris.

British Protectorate (1814-64) – Under the Treaty of Paris the Ionian islands were granted independent status under the protection of the British government. In reality, although the constitution was drawn up in favour of the islanders, the British High Commissioner held the effective power.
Nonetheless, Sir Thomas Maitland and Sir Frederick Adam, whose wife was a Corfiot, a member of the Palatianos family, provided the island with a solid infrastructure: public buildings, a road network, water supplies etc.
In 1824 Lord Guilford (1766-1827), a Philhellene who dreamed of reviving the spirit of ancient Greece and adopted the Orthodox religion, founded a second Ionian Academy with four faculties – theology, law, medicine and philosophy – and presented it with an extensive library. Originally he had intended to site his university on Ithaca.
In 1856 Edward Lear, who called Corfu a paradise and spent long periods on the island between 1848 and 1863 and painted many views of it, was offered the post of Director to the new Art Department in the University but he declined.
Corfu developed as an intellectual centre attracting the poets Andreas Kalvos, who lectured at the Academy, and **Dionysos Solomós**, who composed the Greek National anthem.
Although the Corfiots were prevented from playing an official part in the Greek War of Independence, they supplied money and volunteers and the first head of the new Greek state, **John Kapodístrias** (1776-1831), who came of an ancient line of Istrian origin and was buried in the Platitera Monastery on Corfu.
In 1861 Gladstone, who had served as Lord High Commissioner Extraordinary in the islands in 1858-59 and was then Chancellor of the Exchequer, declared that "it would be nothing less than a crime against the safety of Europe" to cede the islands to Greece but a year later in December 1862 the decision to cede was made and the islands joined the new independent Greek State on the accession of George I to the throne (1863).

PRACTICAL INFORMATION

Access by air: from Athens 3 to 4 flights daily; from Thessaloníki/Salonica 3 services a week.

Access by boat: night ferry service from Pátra/Patras (☎ (061) 62 26 02 in Pátra/Patras).

Access by bus: direct services from Athína/Athens (9hr 30min, KTEL bus station); *see ATHÍNA: Practical Information.*

Accommodation – Many hotels of all categories, apartments and villas to let, rooms in private houses and camping sites all over the island.

Transport – Car, motorcycle and bicycle hire services.

★★KÉRKIRA (CORFU TOWN) – Pop 31 359

The old town of Corfu between the old and new citadels has retained its Greco-Venetian atmosphere while the Spianáda, where Corfiot and tourist meet, supplies a touch of British dignity. Barouches drawn by horses sporting plumes and pompoms provide an agreeable means of transport.

★**Spianáda** – Once an open space for drilling soldiers and now a popular place for walking, the Spianáda (or Platía) was planted with gardens, palm and eucalyptus trees during the Napoleonic occupation.
It is liberally adorned with commemorative monuments and statues: neo-Classical rotunda in memory of Maitland the High Commissioner, statues of Schulemburg (18C near the entrance to the citadel), of Lord Guilford and of Kapodistrias (near the former Academy to the south).
The west side of the Spianáda is lined by the **"Liston"**, an arcaded terrace housing restaurants, tea rooms and bookshops; the building which was designed by Mathieu de Lesseps, father of the builder of the Suez Canal, dates from the French Empire Period (1804-14) and was inspired by Rue de Rivoli in Paris.
The Spianáda also incorporates the famous Corfu **cricket pitch** ⌚. The Corfiots were introduced to the game under the British Protectorate and have played with enthusiasm ever since.

Paleó Froúrio ⌚ – A promontory, consisting of two hills linked by a saddle and separated from the Spianáda by a canal, the site of the **Ancient Citadel** was also the site of the early township of Corfu. By the Middle Ages fortifications already covered the twin peaks, the "sea fort" and the "land fort", protecting the houses which huddled round the Cathedral of St Peter and St Paul. The citadel is now occupied by a Military Academy.

Cricket in Greece

The first game of cricket in Greece was played on Corfu in April 1823 between officers of the Royal Navy and officers of the garrison, who were stationed there under the British Protectorate of the Ionian islands (1814-63). Twelve years later there were two Corfiot teams to challenge the British visitors. Two local clubs – Gongakis and Cambissis – survived after the British had left but in 1893 they merged into one – Gymnastikos. In 1923 it was joined by the Ergatikos Club which later took the name Byron CC. In 1932 the cricket festival was attended by the Prince of Wales.

After the Second World War the cricket season developed owing to the interest shown by the British media and British Airways. Many amateur teams began to make regular tours to Corfu, following the tradition established by the annual visits of the Mediterranean fleet before the Second World War, which is now maintained through the Anglo-Corfiot Cricket Association (founded in 1970-71). The season runs from April or May, depending on the weather, to the end of October; during those months there is a daily game; matches against visiting teams are usually played on Monday, Wednesday, Saturday and Sunday between 3pm and 8pm (2pm and 7pm in April and October). There are now 15 cricket clubs in Greece – 13 on Corfu, one in Athens and one in Thessaloníki. Since 1966, when the Greek national team first visited Great Britain, Greek cricketers have competed successfully in the Mediterranean Cricket Festival, the European Clubs Champions Cup, European Nations Cup and European Indoor Championship.

In the 16C the Venetians repaired the fortifications; they dug the canal and built the two bastions which flank the bridge linking the promontory to the Spianáda. The interior is much changed; **Ágios Geórgios** (St George's Church) was built in the form of a Doric temple for the British garrison in 1830 and the former Venetian barracks dominate the little port of Mandráki where the Venetian galleys rode at anchor. Fine views of the town and the roadstead.

Palace of St Michael and St George – It was built from 1818 to 1823 as an official residence for the British High Commissioner and designed by Colonel George Whitmore. It is a neo-Classical building preceded by a Doric colonnade containing 32 columns. In 1864 it became a royal residence for the Greek monarch. The statue of Sir Frederick Adam in front of the façade is by the Corfiot sculptor Pavlos Prosalentis.

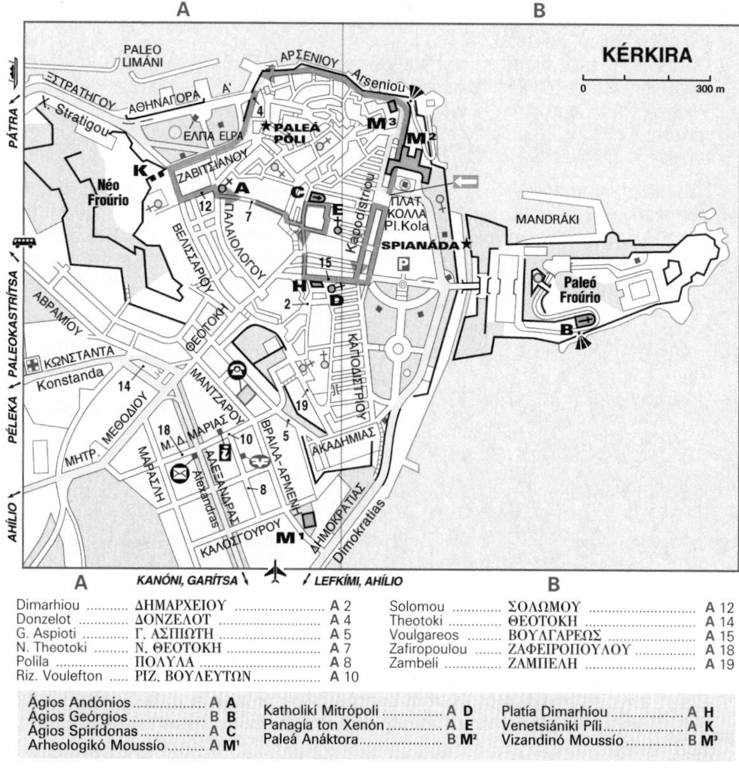

Dimarhiou	ΔΗΜΑΡΧΕΙΟΥ	A 2
Donzelot	ΔΟΝΖΕΛΟΤ	A 4
G. Aspioti	Γ. ΑΣΠΙΩΤΗ	A 5
N. Theotoki	Ν. ΘΕΟΤΟΚΗ	A 7
Polila	ΠΟΛΥΛΑ	A 8
Riz. Voulefton	ΡΙΖ. ΒΟΥΛΕΥΤΩΝ	A 10
Solomou	ΣΟΛΩΜΟΥ	A 12
Theotoki	ΘΕΟΤΟΚΗ	A 14
Voulgareos	ΒΟΥΛΓΑΡΕΩΣ	A 15
Zafiropoulou	ΖΑΦΕΙΡΟΠΟΥΛΟΥ	A 18
Zambeli	ΖΑΜΠΕΛΗ	A 19

Ágios Andónios	A	A
Ágios Geórgios	B	B
Ágios Spirídonas	A	C
Arheologikó Moussío	A	M[1]
Katholikí Mitrópoli	A	D
Panagía ton Xenón	A	E
Paleá Anáktora	B	M[2]
Platía Dimarhíou	A	H
Venetsiániki Píli	A	K
Vizandinó Moussío	B	M[3]

The palace now houses the tourist office and an interesting **Museum of Asiatic Art**★ ⏲ containing 10 000 items: funerary urns and Chinese bronzes, incense flasks, rare lacquers, ceramics and engravings, Japanese screens richly decorated; also beautiful 17C and 18C icons by the Creto-Venetian School.

★**Paleá Póli (Old Town)** – A walk *(about 1hr 30min)* takes in the narrow streets where the washing is hung out to dry, the little paved squares resembling theatre sets, the elegant church façades and the high arcaded houses which made old Corfu so picturesque during the Venetian period.
Leave the Spianáda by the northwest corner, pass the left side of the palace to emerge on the corniche which is lined by old houses, some with Venetian loggias, overlooking the Corfiot roadstead and the Epirot coast. Here stands a small **Byzantine Museum** (Vizandinó Moussío) ⏲ displaying mainly icons.
Just offshore is the **Islet of Vídos** which was so densely covered with olive trees in the 17C that it was described as "a forest swimming on the waves". It was denuded by 3 hours of heavy shelling in an allied attack on the French in 1798 when only 50 of the original 700 defenders survived.
Odós Donzelot, bordered by handsome houses belonging to shipping magnates, leads down to the quays of the Old Port *(fish tavernas)* where the ferries from Igoumenítsa and the mail boats from Paxí dock.

Néo Froúrio – *Not open to the public.* The **New Citadel** was built in the 16C and the 17C but altered in the 19C; the Venetian Gate bears the winged lion of St Mark.
Odós Solomoú leads into the upper town. At the beginning of Odós Nikifórou Theotokí stands St Antony's Church, a 14C building with an 18C Baroque iconostasis. Halfway up this street, which has many shops and was the main artery of Venetian Corfu, turn left to St Spyridon's Church.

Ágios Spiridónas – This 16C church with its tall detached bell-tower was dedicated to **St Spyridon**, a 4C Cypriot bishop whose relics were transferred from Constantinople in 1456 and who became the patron saint of Corfu. A chapel houses the silver coffin which contains the mummified body of the saint. From time to time it is solemnly paraded round the town, particularly on the Orthodox feasts of Palm Sunday, Holy Saturday, 11 August and the first Sunday in November.
Southeast of St Spyridon's Church is a charming little square flanked by the church of Our Lady of Strangers (Panagía ton Xénon). *Continue to the town hall.*

Dimarhío – Since 1903 the **town hall** has occupied the low building in the square decorated with medallions which was built as a loggia in 1693 and converted into a theatre in 1720; at one end is a monument to Morosini who expelled the Turks from the Peloponnese in 1691.
On the east side of the square stands the Roman Catholic cathedral which dates from the 17C and was restored after the last war; it contains a delicate 15C Venetian painting of the Madonna *(third chapel on the right).*
Return by Odós Voulgáreos (attractive arcades) and Odós Kapodistríou (busy shops) to the starting point.

★**Arheologikó Moussío** ⏲ – This modern style **Archeological Museum** displays three Archaic works from ancient Corcyra *(south of Garítsa Bay):*
– the Gorgon pediment (6C BC) which belonged to the temple of Artemis and consists of a colossal figure of the Gorgon Medusa scowling with two serpents entwined about her waist; it is flanked by two feline creatures; anyone who gazed upon this Gorgon was supposed to turn to stone;
– a curious high relief sculpture of a Dionysiac banquet;
– the Archaic "lion of Menecrates" (7C BC) which covered a warrior's tomb.
There is also a collection of terracotta votive offerings and a head of the Athenian poet Menander (342-292 BC).

EXCURSIONS

★★**Walk to Kanóni** – *4km/2.5mi south.* Follow the attractive curve of Garítsa Bay as far as the suburb of Anemómilos where the villas are surrounded by gardens, and then bear right into Odós Iássonou Sossípatrou which leads to a 12C Byzantine church, **Ágios Iássonas-Sossípatros**. In the narthex are four fine 17C icons by Emmanuel Tzanes: St Jason and St Sossipater, disciples of St Paul who brought the Gospel to Corfu, and St John of Damascus and St Gregory Palamas.
The road which is narrow and congested skirts the villa known as **Mon Repos** *(not open)* which is surrounded by a beautiful park and stands on the site of the ancient acropolis of Corcyra. It was designed as a summer residence for Adam, the British Commissioner, in 1824 by Colonel George Whitmore, an engineer officer. Later it was given to the Greek royal family and Prince Philip, Duke of Edinburgh, was born there in 1921.

★★**Kanóni** *(hotels and restaurants)* – The platform at the end of the peninsula was built by Napoleon's soldiers as a battery for a single cannon to command the entrance to the Halkiópoulos Lagoon which is now bisected by the airport runway. From the gun emplacement there is a **view**★★ down on to the monastery of Vlahérna (17C) *(accessible on foot)* and beyond it to circular Mouse Island (Pondikoníssi) which also has a monastery *(accessible by boat from Vlahérna) (illustration above)*. According to a local legend, Pondikoníssi is said to be the ship of Odysseus turned to stone by Poseidon. Another candidate for this honour is Kolóvri Rock in the Bay of Paleokastrítsa.

★★**Ahílio** – *11km/7mi south; from Corfu Town take the road to the airport and continue through Gastoúri.*

On a wooded hillside rising to 145m/476ft stands the **Achilleion**. It was designed in 1890 by an Italian architect for the Empress **Elisabeth of Austria** (1837-98) who greatly admired the Greek hero Achilles and named her palace after him. After her assassination by an anarchist in Geneva, the villa stood empty and was then bought in 1907 by Kaiser Wilhelm II who came for a month each spring until 1914, when it was confiscated by the Greek government. In 1916 the French turned it into a hospital and it served in this capacity during the Second World War. In between it became a museum and now it has been restored and converted into a casino.

The villa is built in the neo-Classical style and divided into large rooms decorated with frescoes and ancient motifs; there are souvenirs of Elisabeth (portrait by Winterhalter) and Wilhelm (his desk).

The Italian terraced gardens are planted with flowers and Mediterranean trees and adorned with statues including *The Dying Achilles* (1884) by the German sculptor Herter opposite which Wilhelm II set up a huge bronze of *Achilles the Victor*.

From the end of the upper terrace there are extended **views**★★ of the northern end of the island and of the Albanian coast.

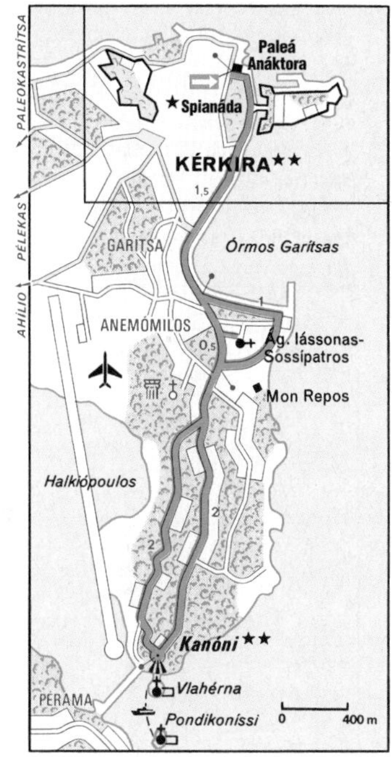

★★**Pélekas** – *13km/8mi west.* The "Kaiser's Throne" *(sign "restaurant")* is an alternative name for this viewpoint where Kaiser Wilhelm II often used to stop to admire the superb panoramic **view**★★ of the countryside in the centre of the island; below on the coast is the huge and popular beach at Glifáda.

Órmos Gouvión – *9km/5.5mi north.* Sheltered and gently curving, **Gouviá Bay** is very popular. On the shore are the remains of an 18C Venetian arsenal. During the First World War the bay was used as a naval base by the French fleet.

Daniliá ("The Village") *(2km/1.25mi southwest of Gouviá)* evokes the traditional Corfiot way of life; reconstructions of interiors and workshops, museum of arts and crafts and folklore. Traditional festivals are organised in the season.

Benítses – *13km/8mi south.* Typical fishing village and seaside resort at the end of a valley thick with olive groves.

In an orange grove a few traces (mosaics) survive of some Roman baths.

There is also the beginning of an aqueduct built by the British to supply water to Corfu Town.

DISTANT SIGHTS

★★★**Paleokastrítsa** – Very popular seaside resort.

★★**The Bay** – At the foot of a steep hillside cloaked in holm oaks, olive and cypress trees, the ochre rocks of the coastline are broken up into half a dozen sandy creeks, one of which provides a harbour.

The road runs to the end of the promontory where the monastery of Paleokastrítsa was founded in the 13C; the present buildings date from the 18C; the church contains some precious icons.

This may be the site of Scheria, the city of Alcinoüs, king of the Phaeacians, who gave hospitality to Odysseus. The Ermónes creek *(southeast)* may be the spot where Nausicaa was approached by Odysseus.

★★★ **View of the site** – Excellent bird's-eye views of the site can be obtained from Lákones and Angelókastro *(20km/12.5mi return by car plus 1hr 30min walking).*

Lákones – **A terrace** *(about 800m/0.5mi beyond the village of Lákones; sign "parking")* provides an extraordinary **view**★★ of the many rocky inlets in Paleokastrítsa Bay.

Continue towards Kríni. Before entering the village bear left into a narrow road to Angelókastro *(sign)* which leads to a hamlet and then to a restaurant. *Park the car nearby and take the path to Angelókastro (1hr on foot there and back).*

Angelókastro – The ruins of Angelókastro on their hilltop recall an Angevin citadel mentioned in the 13C in the Neapolitan archives and named Sant'Angelo in honour of the Archangel Michael. From near St Michael's Chapel there are splendid **views**★★★ of the coast.

★★ **Sidári** – This little resort at the northern end of the island commands a view of a curious **rock formation**★★ towards Cape Drástis where the sea has eaten away the parallel strata of tertiary sediment forming rocky inlets, some with little beaches, islets and promontories resembling piles of ruins, caves and caverns where the sea rushes in. About 15km/9mi south lies **St George's Bay** (Ágios Geórgios: *tavernas*) with its magnificent beach.

★ **Ípsos** – This pleasant resort is situated on the edge of a huge sandy bay which is ideal for all water sports: bathing, sailing, water skiing etc. At the other end of the bay is **Pirgí**, also a popular resort.

★ **Spartílas** (424m/1 391ft) – *9km/5.5mi north.* The road loops its way up through the olive groves providing beautiful glimpses of the coast south to Corfu Town and of Albania on the mainland.

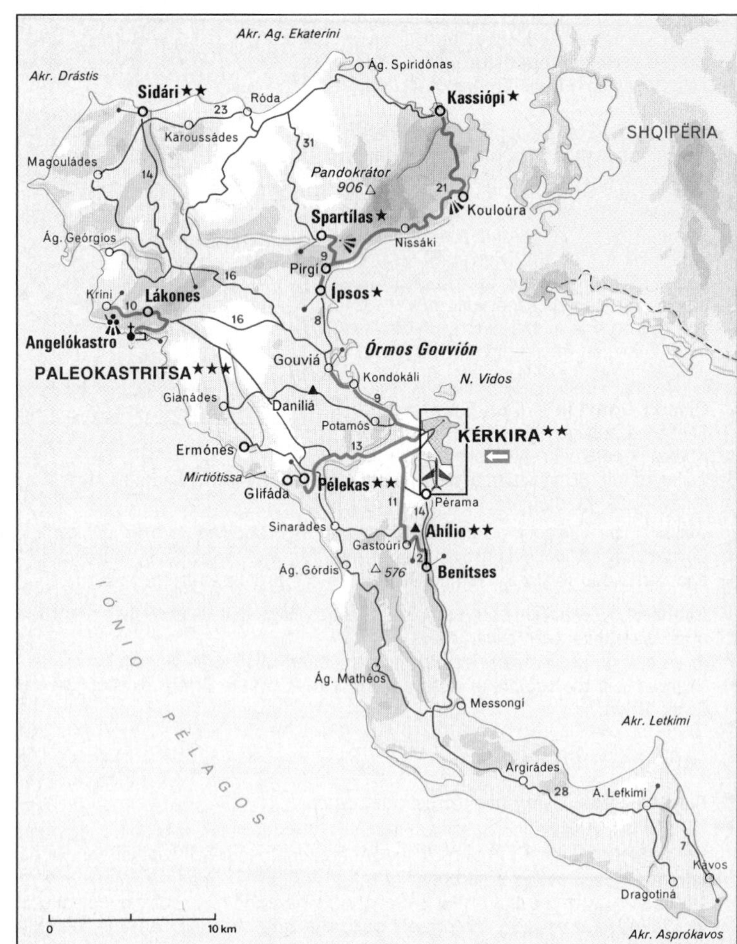

G. Grigoriou /FOTOGRAM-STONE

Paleokastrítsa Beach, Corfu

★**Kassiópi** – *21km/13mi northeast.* This charming fishing port and resort is approached by a spectacular **corniche road**★★ which goes to **Koloúra** where the writer Lawrence Durrell lived with his wife before the Second World War. He had first come to live on Corfu in the 1930s with his mother and sister and brothers; his younger brother Gerald has written several accounts of his idyllic boyhood. Remarkable views of the Albanian coast.
Kassiópi is dominated by the remains of a 13C feudal Angevin fortress. The 16C church contains 17C icons and frescoes.

For adjacent sights see EFÍRA, IOÁNINA, PÁRGA.

KILÍNI

KYLLENE – Elis, Peloponnese – Population 952

Michelin map 980 fold 27

A seaside resort (Olympic Beach) and a small harbour sheltered by the **Kyllene headland** make up the modern town of Kilíni (Kyllene) which has replaced the older town of Clarence, famous in the Middle Ages and now reduced to a few stones. *(Ferries to the island of Zákinthos/Zante).*

Proud Clarence – Clarence was founded in the 13C by the Crusaders on the shores of a sheltered bay and for two centuries was the major port of Morea under the de Villehardouin, the Angevins of Naples and the Venetians who called it Glarentza or Chiarenza. Late in the 13C and in the 14C Clarence was one of the privileged possessions of the Angevin princes of Naples who would from time to time hold court there on a sumptuous scale. In those days, there was a great deal of traffic with their territories in Italy through the ports of Naples, Amalfi, Taranto, Bari and Manfredonia; the last being one of the main crusader ports.
Being a port of call where Genoese ships and Venetian galleys *(see KÉRKIRA)* frequently put in, Clarence grew rich and populous, crowded with merchants, sailors, monks, knights, artists etc. The great European banks opened branches there including the Acciaiuoli who held first place. **Nicolo Acciaiuoli**, who was the chief adviser of Catherine de Valois and the princes of Taranto and came from a Florentine family which was in the service of the Angevins of Naples, became Prince of Cephallonia and Lord of Corinth; he was the patron of Boccaccio who set one of the stories in his *Decameron* in Clarence.
In the 13C the city had also obtained the privilege of issuing money and minted gold and silver coins of good quality which were highly valued on the money markets.
In about 1428 Constantine Palaiologos, the future despot of Mystra *(see MISTRÁS)* defeated Carlo Tocchi, Lord of Clarence, who gave his niece Theodora in marriage to the victor with all his Peloponnese lands as dowry. Clarence, which came under

Byzantine control, was superseded by Mystra, the capital of the Palaiologos in Morea, before falling into oblivion. The name survived in Great Britain into the 20C: the title of Duke of Clarence was brought to the British throne by Phillipa, a great-niece of William de Villehardouin, who married Edward III of England.

City Ruins – *From the town 1.5km/1mi by car along the coast to the northwest then 10min on foot from a farm up to a bluff marked by a concrete post.* A few traces of the citadel are all that remain of Clarence: one can make out the footings of the curtain wall, a keep which was blown up during the Second World War, and a huge church similar to the cathedral at Andravída. The **view** of the coast *(beach below)* and of the islands is particularly attractive.

EXCURSIONS

Moní Vlahernón ⓥ – *On leaving Kilíni, turn right in the hamlet of Káto Panagía into a narrow road (sign).* After 2km/1.25mi the road enters a verdant but deserted valley containing the **Vlacherna Monastery** which takes its name from a famous church in Constantinople dedicated to the Virgin. The monastery was built in the 12C in the Byzantine era but was altered under the de Villehardouin when it was most probably served by a community of Cistercians.
Although the brick walls of the **abbey church** suggest Byzantine influence, the corbelled cornice is in the western style and the external porch is Burgundian. In the interior too, certain architectural and decorative elements suggest French Gothic: nave and side aisles separated by columns, pointed arches over certain openings and early ogival arches in the narthex decorated with a lamb and a dove.

★**Kilíni Peninsula** – From the 13C to the 15C the region between Kyllene and Andravída was the main base of the Frankish rulers of Morea *(see p 26)* and was open to western influence. There are many monuments and other reminders of their occupation both on the promontory, the site of the famous Clermont Castle *(see p 141)*, and on the banks of the River Piniós which flows through the fertile plain of Elis; under the Turks the land deteriorated into its original state of marshland but in the last hundred years it has again been reclaimed.

Andravída – The modern city is an unremarkable market town but in the Middle Ages, known as Andréville under the patronage of St Andrew, Andravída was the capital of Achaia, the seat of a Roman Catholic bishop and the principal residence of the **de Villehardouin**, a family from Champagne in France, who ruled Morea for almost the whole of the 13C. They founded a famous "school of chivalry" and often called their barons together in an assembly.
The Templars had a church in Andréville, St James's, where Geoffrey I, Geoffrey II (1218-40) and William I de Villehardouin were buried. It also contained the tomb of Agnes of Achaia, who died in 1286; her tombstone has been found with an epitaph in French but the church has disappeared as has the monastery of St Nicholas of Carmel (13C).
Only part of the former church (13C) of the Dominicans remains *(on the outskirts of the town on the west side of the Pátra road)*: a large square chancel with early ogival vaulting and square chevet flanked by two chapels; traces of the nave and aisles are visible.

Gastoúni – *South of Andravída.* Known as Gastogne in the Middle Ages, Gastoúni was another residence belonging to the princes of Morea. There remains an 11C Byzantine church which was altered in the 13C (Gothic north door); the interior contains some Byzantine paintings and some naive icons *(bear right in the square where the road divides on the south side of the town).*

For adjacent sights see HLEMOÚTSI, KALÁVRITA, MÉGA SPÍLEO, OLIMBÍA, PÁTRA, Harádra tou VOURAÏKOÚ.

KIPARISSÍA

KYPARISSIA – Messinía, Peloponnese – Population 4 520
Michelin map 980 south of fold 28

Kyparissia, the town of cypresses, is set just back from the coastline; in the Middle Ages it was called **Arkadia** after the people who were driven there from the neighbouring region to the east by the Slav invasions and was the personal fief of William de Villehardouin. After being destroyed in 1825 by Ibrahim Pasha *(see KAVÁLA)*, it is now a modern city, dominated by the ruins of a Frankish castle which had been built where an ancient and then a Byzantine acropolis had once stood. From the top there is a fine **view**★ across the Ionian Sea to Zakynthos *(northwest).*
Due west lie the **Strofádes Islands**, in antiquity the home of the **Harpies** (Snatchers), also called the **Furies**; they were tempestuous divinities represented as birds with women's faces. They are also to be found among the symbols of medieval Christianity.

Peristéria Tombs ⓥ – *8km/5mi northeast; take the Pírgos road for 5km/3mi; turn right (sign) and continue for 5.5km/3.25mi (very bad road).* Among the green hills looking down into the narrow valley of the Peristéria, excavations have revealed some domed royal tombs dating from the Mycenaean period.
A fine collection of jewellery, seals and vases found in one of the tombs is currently on display in Hóra museum.

For adjacent sights see ANDRÍTSENA, ITHÓMI, KALAMÁTA, KARÍTENA, KORÓNI, MEGALÓPOLI, METHÓNI, Anáktora NÉSTOROS, OLIMBÍA, PÍLOS.

KÍTHIRA

KYTHERA – Ionian Islands – Population 3 091
Michelin map 980 folds 41 and 42 – 280km²/108sq mi

Kythera lies just off **Cape Malea** (Ákri Maléas), the southwest tip of the Peloponnese which creates a dangerous passage for sailors. Going by its portrayal by famous artists, one would expect Aphrodite's island to resemble the Garden of Eden; in reality the landscape is rather arid, recalling the Cyclades more than the Ionian islands, although it is to the latter group that Kythera has been joined throughout their history of occupation by the Turks, the Venetians (18C), the French (Revolution and Empire), and the British until 1864.
The island is rimmed by fine beaches.

Aphrodite's Isle – Aphrodite, who is supposed to have sprung from the foam, was blown by the Zephyrs to Kythera which some legends cite as her birthplace (others name it as Cyprus). Then **Paris**, who had judged her to be more beautiful than Hera and Athena, built the first sanctuary to Aphrodite here on his way from the island of Kranai *(see GÍTHIO)* to Troy. In fact the cult of the goddess of love seems to have been imported from Asia by the Phoenicians, who came to these shores to collect the murex, a shellfish which yields a purple dye.
Whatever the origins of the cult, several temples to Aphrodite were built but almost nothing remains. The largest contained a statue of the goddess made of myrtle which the Romans carried off to Rome. Kythera has been a rich source of inspiration for numerous artists and poets, including Watteau, Baudelaire and Gérard de Nerval.
To the south, in the waters off the island of **Antikythera**, in 1900 a sponge diver discovered an ancient wreck loaded with marbles and bronzes including the famous Ephebe of Antikythera (4C BC) which may be a likeness of Paris *(Athens Museum)*. More recent excavations by the British School of Archeology at Athens have explored various Minoan sites producing much valuable information.

PRACTICAL INFORMATION

Access by air: from Athens 3 services daily in season.

Access by boat: 2 or 3 hydrofoil services a week from Piraeus to Agia Pelagía (boarding also possible when calling at Portohéli, Leonídio, Monemvassía and Neápoli): Ceres Group ☎ (01) 42 80 001 in Piraeus, (0735) 31 390 in Hóra. Ferry from Gíthio on the line continuing to Kastéli (Crete).

Accommodation – 14 small hotels (cat A to D) in Agia Pelagía, Diakófti, Kapsáli, Kythera (Hóra) and Manitohóri; rooms to let mainly in Agia Pelagía, Kapsáli and Livádi.

★ **Hóra** or **Kíthira Town** – Pop 226. The capital of the island occupies a very beautiful **site**★★ overlooking a magnificent roadstead and next to a rocky peak crowned by a Venetian citadel with a panoramic view; an **Archeological Museum** (Arheologikó Moussío) ⓥ has been set up. To the southeast lies the little port of Kapsáli and two magnificent, matching bays separated by a promontory.

At **Livádi** are to be found the church of Agios Andréas (12C) and the largest bridge (150m/164yd long) on the island, which was built by the British and has 13 bays.

On the southeast coast at **Poúrko** is the church of Agios Dimítrios, decorated with 12C frescoes; further north the **Monastery of Agía Eléssa** ⓥ stands on top of a hill (433m/1 420ft high), a most attractive **site**★, overlooking the Bay of Melidóni.

The 17C **Monastery of Mirthidión** ⓥ (near Kalokairinés) contains a fine icon of the Virgin and Child with miraculous powers.

At **Milopótamos** lie the **ruins**★★ of a Byzantine and Venetian town with the lion of St Mark over the fortified gateway.

★★Agía Sofía ⓥ – The **Cave of St Sophia** (2 000m²/7 176sq ft), whose chambers were used as chapels (traces of flooring and frescoes), has recently been restored; it contains passages with concretions (stalactites and stalagmites) and underground lakes. At Fónissa there is a **fine waterfall★**, and north of Milopótamos is the monastery of Orfanís.

On the east coast of the island near Kastrí is Paleópolis, the ancient city of Skándia, of which some tombs remain. At **Avlémonas**, a picturesque fishing village, an attractive small Venetian citadel guards the harbour entrance. Above **Diakófti**, the road to Friligiánika leads to the abandoned **Monastery of Agía Moní** (1840).

The commercial centre of the island is **Potamós**, with the church of Agios Theódoros.

At **Paleohóra★★** *(uneven approach road)* there are the remains of the Byzantine fortress built after the 12C and destroyed in 1536 by a Turkish pirate called Barbarossa; it is on a very beautiful mountain site perched high over the gorge of Langáda (reached from the coast road).

The island's second port of disembarkation, **Agía Pelagía**, is a tourist village.

For adjacent sights see GERÁKI, GÍTHIO, KALAMÁTA, MÁNI, MESSINIAKÓS Kólpos, MISTRÁS, MONEMVASSÍA, SPÁRTI.

KÓRINTHOS★★

CORINTH – Korinthía, Peloponnese – Population 22 658

Michelin map 980 fold 29

An impressive acropolis and the remains of many buildings recall "wealthy Corinth", one of the busiest trading cities in antiquity, a cosmopolitan and dissolute city which comprised an acropolis on its hill, the town proper on a lower plateau and Lechaion the port on the coast, all of which was protected by walls (up to 20km/12.5mi long). The modern town was built in 1858 at the head of the gulf after the old town, which was further inland, was wrecked by an earthquake. It is both a port and an agricultural market dealing particularly in sultanas which have been exported since the 14C. The local *souvláki (see p 55)* are particularly good.

HISTORICAL NOTES

Corinth, the metropolis – Corinth occupied an eminently favourable position at the crossroads of the land and sea routes linking Attica and the Peloponnese, the Ionian and the Aegean seas; its almost impregnable acropolis, Acrocorinth, high on its hill controlled movement in all directions on the isthmus of Corinth. Moreover the hinterland was well watered with springs and fertile with olives and grapes.

According to legend, the city was founded by Korinthos, grandson of the sun god, Helios; one of the early kings was **Sisyphos**, who was considered to be the most cunning of mortals, and whom Zeus in a jealous rage condemned to carry a rock up a slope in Hades, which constantly fell to the bottom again. In the Mycenaean period Corinth was dependent on Árgos.

In the Archaic era Corinth became very prosperous. The city was governed by a local oligarchy or by tyrants, such as the cruel Periander, who was yet considered one of the Seven Sages of Greece, and imposed considerable taxes on the passage of goods across the isthmus. The warehouses were filled with wheat from Sicily, papyrus from Egypt, ivory from Libya, leather from Cyrenaica, incense from Arabia, dates from Phoenicia, apples and pears from Euboia, carpets from Carthage and slaves from Phrygia.

The Corinthians also used the coastal clay to make the ceramic vases, often very tiny (perfume flasks), which they exported throughout the Mediterranean basin; in addition they developed the production of bronze (cuirasses, statues), glass and purple-dyed cloth; their naval shipyards launched the first triremes. They facilitated their trade by establishing colonies, in particular in Leukas, Corcyra (Corfu) and above all in Syracuse (734 BC). After a partial eclipse by Athens in the 5C BC Corinth regained its lustre in the following century when she took her place at the head of the Greek cities in the **League of Corinth** under Philip of Macedon and Alexander the Great.

The **Corinthian capital** is thought to have been invented in the 5C BC by the sculptor **Kallimachos**.

Their great wealth led the Corinthians astray into the paths of luxury and sensual pleasure. Corinth became known throughout the ancient world for her courtesans; at times they numbered over 1 000: priestesses *(hierodules)* engaged in sacred prostitution in the precincts of the Temple of Aphrodite; dancers and flautists and oboists *(hetairai)* who attended the banquets. These servants of Aphrodite included the famous Lais whose tomb in the pine woods by the Kraneion on the outskirts of Corinth was described by Pausanias the historian as being "crowned with a ram in the clutches of a lioness".

In the following century, however, Corinth became famous for the presence of the austere philosopher **Diogenes** the Cynic who lived in a barrel, in fact a large earthenware jar. When Alexander asked him if he wanted anything he replied "Yes, don't keep the sun off me".

Corinth, a Roman colony – In 146 BC the Consul Mummius captured the city which was then pillaged and burned by his legions: the bronze, as well as the gold and silver, on the statues was removed to be used for the roof of the Pantheon in Rome whence it was later removed by Pope Alexander VII to make the baldaquin in St Peter's.
In 44 BC Julius Caesar founded a new town, Colonia Julia Corinthiensis, on the ruins of ancient Corinth. It became the capital of Roman Greece and was mainly populated by freedmen and Jews, who were Latin speakers. During the next two centuries Corinth developed into a rich city devoted to business and pleasure which attracted merchants, ship owners, and tourists in large numbers. Everyone dreamed of going to Corinth despite the high cost of the entertainment available.
Between AD 51 and 52 however **St Paul** spent 18 months in the city; in his Epistle to the Corinthians he castigated the shameless behaviour of the citizens. He preached Christianity equally to the pagans and the Jews and the Jewish priests dragged him before the Proconsul Gallion in the *agora* but he was acquitted.
Nero visited Corinth in AD 67 to announce the independence of the Greek cities and to take part in the Isthmian games. Hadrian in his turn erected many buildings, refurbished the baths and built an aqueduct to bring water from Lake Stymphalos *(see Límni STIMFALÍA)*. Under the combined effect of barbarian invasions and earthquakes Corinth was brought low; only Acrocorinth retained a certain importance as a military stronghold.
During the Turkish occupation ancient Corinth disappeared under urban development except for the Temple of Apollo which was described by the majority of travellers. The earthquake which destroyed the town in 1858 did however assist the Americans in their excavations which began in 1896 and uncovered a jumble of ruins, mostly Roman; the large number of small shops bears witness to the commercial importance of ancient Corinth.

MODERN TOWN

Moussio Vassou Petropoulou – Pan Gartaganis ⓥ – *Close to Eleftério Venizélou Square on the harbour.* This **Historical and Folk Museum** came into being in 1988 as a private venture on the part of Alkmene Pétropoulos. It contains a fine collection of a variety of **traditional costumes** coming from different regions and Greek islands, beautiful embroidery (from Skyros, Crete and Epiros), wonderfully rich in motifs, as well as finely worked jewellery and silver. On the second floor there is a reconstruction of a room in a village house, with carved wooden furniture.

**ARHÉA KÓRINTHOS (ANCIENT CORINTH)

7km/4.5mi southwest of the modern town. Take the road for Árgos, turn right and go straight on at the junction; at the next crossroads go left and follow the signs to the ancient site. Park in the car park; the main entrance is on the west side of the archeological site. It is also possible to reach the site from the Lechaion road.

TOUR ⓥ *about 2hr; follow the route shown on the plan*

First move south to the **Naós Oktavías**, the **Temple of Octavian**, a Roman building from which three fine Corinthian capitals found in the 18C by the French architect Foucherot have been re-erected.

Museum ⓥ – The collections consist of most of the pieces produced by the excavations. The gallery of Hellenistic antiquities (vestibule – *right*) houses several examples of the beautiful Archaic ceramics with oriental decoration (vases with plant motifs painted in black and a reddish colour) which Corinth exported in large quantities in the 8C-7C BC. At the back there are sphinx statues (6C BC). The gallery of Roman antiquities (vestibule – *left*) contains a statue of Augustus and a head of Nero; mosaics and, at the far end of the room, huge statues of captives from the *agorá*.
An internal courtyard has a collection of various architectural fragments and statues.
Make for the upper level of the *agorá* with its rows of shops and then bear left round **Naós Íras**, an old sanctuary to Hera, to reach the adjoining **Gláfki Kríni**; this **fountain** is named after Glauke (also known as Creusa), the second wife of Jason, who threw herself into the water to cool the burning caused by the poisoned robe which Medea the witch had given her.

★**Naós Apólona** – The highest point on the site of ancient Corinth is still marked relics of the **Temple of Apollo** (6C BC) – 7 out of 38 monolithic Doric columns, made of tufa and originally covered with white stucco. According to the description given by Dr Spon in the 17C and the drawings made by the architects Leroy and Stuart in the 18C, it was surrounded by a peristyle. The high ground affords spectacular **views** of the Gulf of Corinth and of Acrocorinth.
A grand flight of steps built in the 5C BC leads down to the lower level of the *agorá*. The façade (1) of a Roman **basilica**, which stood in the centre of the north side, was adorned with four huge statues of captives, of which two are displayed in the museum.

Ierá Kríni – A wall surmounted by tripods and statues marked the eastern side of the **sacred fountain**; the base with its rhythmic frieze of triglyphs is still recognisable. Steps lead down to the underground spring which was linked by a secret passage, with the **sanctuary of the Oracle** (2); its position nearby *(northwest)* is marked by the foundations. A priest hidden beneath the altar answered the petitioners who were thus led to think they were in direct communication with the god.

Temple of Apollo, Corinth

Agorá – This huge open space, which provides remarkable views up to Acrocorinth, comprises a rectangle on two levels (measuring 150m x 90m/492ft x 295ft).
Along the north side, below the terrace supporting the great Temple of Apollo, are the remains of 15 Roman shops; the one in the centre (3) is still roofed.
The west side of the *agorá* is marked by the foundations of six small Roman temples.

South Stoa – The south side of the *agorá*, on the upper level, is filled by the South Stoa, an immense building which was used by the Greeks as a guest-house and converted by the Romans into an administrative centre. The bases of the colonnade are still extant and at the west end one can still trace the arrangement of each "compartment" with its courtyard and well; in the Greek period they were probably places of refreshment.
In front of the *stoa*, separating the upper and lower sections of the *agora*, are the remains of a row of Roman shops. In the centre stood the **Bema** (4), a sort of platform from which the governor Gallio passed judgment on St Paul (there was a church on the site in the Middle Ages).
To the east lie the remains of the **Julian Basilica** (Ioulía Vassilikí), a former law court and meeting room dating from the Roman era. Excavations in front of it have revealed earlier Greek paving with the starting line of a race track (5).

Propílea – Only the base of the monumental entrance *(propylaia)* to the *agora* remains. In the Roman era it was surmounted by two great gold chariots belonging to Helios and his son Phaeton.

★★**Piríni Kríni** – The **Peirene Fountain** dates originally from the 6C BC but has been remodelled many times. The original Greek part is at the back of the atrium *(south side)*: six stone arches preceding a row of underground reservoirs.
The colonnade in front of the arches, the rectangular basin and the three niches creating a *nymphaeum* were added under the Romans.

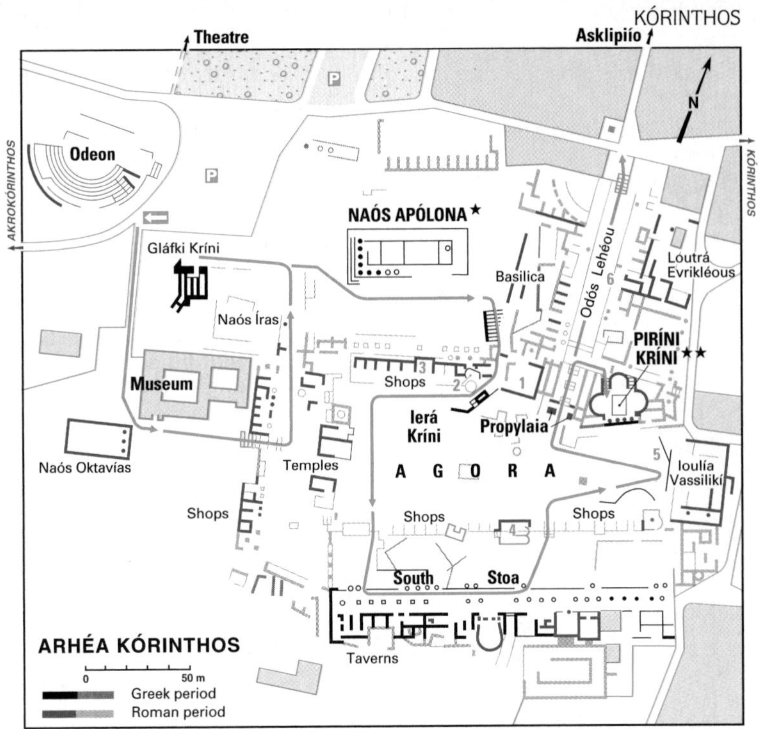

Leave the ancient city by the **Lechaion Way** (Odós Lehéou), the beginning of a road running from the agora to the harbour at Lechaion. In the Roman period it became a ceremonial way leading to the Propylaia and bordered by porticoes housing the **Baths of Eurykles** (Loutrá Evrikléous) with their public latrines (6) which are well preserved.

Odeon – Excavations have revealed a small Roman theatre dating from the 1C AD; its semicircular plan is clearly visible. The banks of seats, most of which are hewn out of the rock, could accommodate about 3 000 spectators.
In the reign of Herod Atticus the Odeon was linked to the theatre by a colonnaded court which can be traced in places.

Theatre – Begun in the 5C BC it was remodelled several times particularly in the 3C AD when the stage was enlarged to accommodate gladiatorial combats and nautical spectacles. It held about 18 000 people.
A little further north are the remains of a brick-built Roman bath house.

Asklipiío – The plan of the temple dedicated to Asklepios, the god of Medicine set in a colonnaded rectangular courtyard can be clearly traced on the ground. Near the entrance *(east)* is an unusual stone offertory. West of the temple is the Fountain of Lerna which supplied the hydrotherapy facilities.

★★★AKROKÓRINTHOS (ACROCORINTH) ⌚ *about 2hr on foot*

Take the road on the left going uphill *(7km/4.5mi by car there and back, tarred road)* which passes the Hotel Xenia and the old potters' district on the right, bears left in front of a Turkish fountain not far from the excavated remains of a temple to Demeter and then climbs in a succession of bends up to the citadel entrance *(taverna)*.
Poised between heaven and earth and almost indistinguishable from the rock, the ruins of Acrocorinth are some of the most impressive in the world owing to their extent, the desolate grandeur of their elevated site and the immense panorama which they command.
Acrocorinth was first a Greek acropolis, then a Roman citadel and then a Byzantine fortress. It was captured by the Franks in 1210 after a five year siege, became a fief of the de Villehardouin and then in c 1325 came under Philip of Tarentum, of the Angevin dynasty, who ruled Naples. In 1358 it passed to the Florentines when Robert II of Tarentum gave the seigneury of Corinth to Nicolo Acciaiuoli *(see KILÍNI)*, an arms manufacturer and banker, who had been adviser to his mother Catherine of Valois, Princess of Morea. Subsequently Acrocorinth was held by the Palaiologi of Mystra (1394), by the knights of Rhodes and from the 15C by the Turks except for a Venetian interlude from 1687 to 1715.

The access ramp from the car park to the fortress offers spectacular views of the three lines of defence and the three gates which protect the citadel on the western approach.

First Gate – It dates from the 14C and is defended by a moat hewn out of the rock.

Second Gate – It too dates from the 14C but was almost entirely rebuilt by the Venetians; it is flanked by a tower.

Third Gate – It is flanked by two powerful rectangular towers; the one on the right is mainly ancient (4C BC); the one on the left is Byzantine. The curtain walls, which are reinforced with rectangular towers, date principally from the Byzantine era.
A steep path leads up the slope among the ruins through the old Turkish district (remains of mosque – *left*) to the rampart and the northern postern. Return to the decapitated minaret and pass a fine brick-vaulted cistern to reach the medieval keep.

Keep – It dominates the remains of the Frankish castle of the de Villehardouin, princes of Morea in the 13C and the 14C; in 1305 Isabelle de Villehardouin and her husband Philip of Savoy commanded the Frankish barons of Morea and Attica to gather at the castle to take part in a tournament which assembled over 1 000 knights in passages of arms. Fine view of the Byzantine ramparts with their rectangular towers, the surrounding heights and the Gulf of Corinth. From the keep return along the south ramparts and continue eastwards (view of the mountains of the Peloponnese) to the Peirene Spring which is to be found near a bend in the wall next to a ruined Turkish barracks.

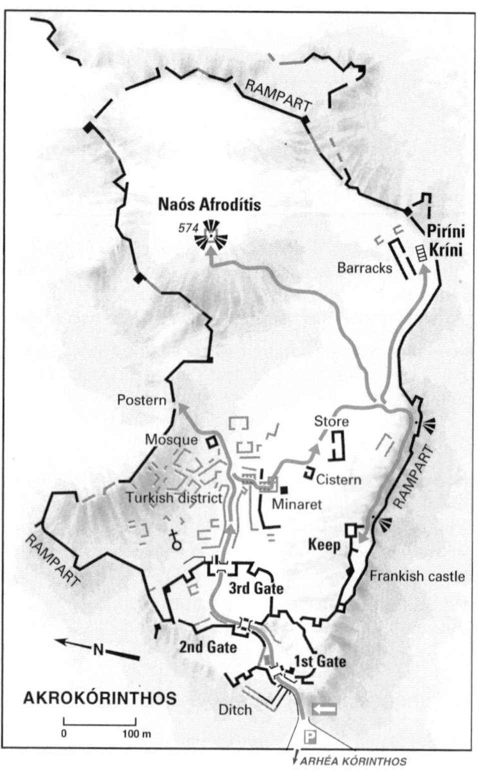

Piríni Kríni – Modern steps lead down into a Hellenistic underground chamber (ancient graffiti) which was reroofed by the Romans. More steps led down into another chamber which has since flooded with water. Some authors say that the **Peirene Spring** was created by the winged horse Pegasus stamping its foot; Pegasus was then captured by Bellerophon while drinking at the spring.

Retrace your steps and take the path on the right to the top of the hill.

Naós Afrodítis – The site of the famous **Temple of Aphrodite** on the highest point of Acrocorinth (574m/1 883ft) is now marked by a column. There is a splendid **panorama★★★** extending beyond the isthmus of Corinth to Mount Parnassos *(north)*, across Attica *(east)* and to the mountains of the Peloponnese *(south)*. To the south-west, perched on a rocky peak, are the medieval ruins of the Frankish castle of Montesquiou, built according to the *Chronicle of the Morea* under Geoffrey de Villehardouin and now known as Pendeskoúfi, possibly a corruption of the original French name.

For adjacent sights see ARGOLÍDA, ÁRGOS, Aktí ARKADÍAS, EPÍDAVROS, Dióriga KORÍNTHOU, LERNÍ, LOUTRÁKI, MIKÍNES, NÁFPLIO, NEMÉA, SIKIÓNA, STIMFALÍA, TÍRINTHA.

Dióriga KORÍNTHOU★★

CORINTH CANAL – Korinthía, Peloponnese

Michelin map 980 folds 20 and 30

The Corinth Canal, which provides a maritime short cut between the Gulf of Corinth (Korinthiakós Kólpos) and the Saronic Gulf (Saronikós Kólpos) , traces a straight line across the isthmus, the narrow neck of land joining the Peloponnese to mainland Greece.

A superb strategic position – Since the isthmus is narrow (only 6km/4mi wide) and of easy passage, attempts to defend it have been made since the Mycenaean period. Recent excavations near Isthmía have uncovered several sections of a Cyclopean wall dating from the 13C BC. Another wall, built in 480 BC to contain the Persian invasion, spanned the isthmus; it was reinforced with towers and kept in good repair until the Venetian period.

The ancient Greeks also sought to cut a channel through the isthmus to avoid ships having to circumnavigate the Peloponnese or be hauled over the *diolkós (see below)*. Both Periander and Alexander the Great had considered the question but it was Nero who inaugurated the digging in AD 67 with a golden shovel: 6 000 prisoners were employed on the work. The site was abandoned after about 3 or 4 months when Nero returned to Rome.

In those days the isthmus was more densely inhabited than it is now: there were two ports on the east coast at Schoinous and Kenchreai and one on the west at Lechaion. Every two years the Isthmian Games, second only to the Olympic Games in the whole of Greece, were held at the local religious sanctuary and the roads were thronged with chariots.

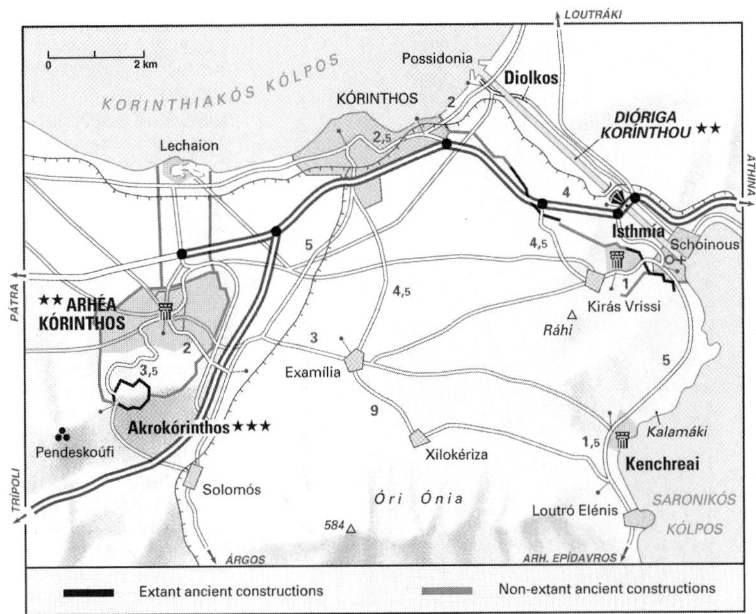

★★THE CANAL

The canal was begun in 1882 by a French company, the Société Internationale du Canal Maritime de Corinthe, inspired by a proposal made in 1829 by Virlet d'Aoust, a member of the Morean Commission. Work stopped in 1889 when the company went bankrupt but the canal was completed by the Greeks in 1893. This spectacular undertaking permanently altered the shipping routes and Piraeus took the place of Syros *(see SÍROS)* in the Cyclades as the major port of Greece.

The canal is 6.343km/nearly 4mi long, 8m/26ft deep and 24.60m/27yd wide at water level. The walls rise to 79.50m/260ft at the highest point. The channel is so narrow that it is not used regularly except by a few coastal traders and cruising ships drawn by tugs.

★★ **View** – *To admire the view it is advisable to park the car on the south bank of the canal.* The two one-way bridges which carry the expressway (E 94) over the canal offer impressive views of the almost vertical walls of the dead straight channel which broadens slightly at the centre to form a dock. People with a geological bent can analyse the different strata: alluvium and marine sand at the top, then clay and limestone. Most photographers are keen to catch that rare moment when a train crossing the viaduct coincides with the passage of a ship beneath.

ADDITIONAL SIGHTS

"Diolkós" – On the road from the canal to the outskirts of Corinth there is a right-hand turning which leads after 2km/1.25mi to Possidonía bridge at the west end of the canal. The central section of the bridge sinks on to the canal bed to let the shipping pass.

Near the bridge on either side of the modern road one can see the *diolkós*, an ancient portage way paved with stone along which the ships were dragged on chariots or on wooden rollers across the lowest and narrowest part of the isthmus *(shown on the map above)*. On the side near the Gulf of Corinth the paving stones are marked with letters of the Corinthian alphabet but their purpose is unknown; on the other side can be seen the ruts worn by the chariots.

This stone slipway was probably built in the 6C BC and was still in use in the 12C AD.

R. Cuzin /MICHELIN

Corinth Canal

Isthmía (**Isthmian Sanctuary** ⌚) – *Coming from Athens, leave the expressway at the interchange just after Corinth Canal and proceed as for Arhéa Epídavros; on leaving the village of Kirás Vrissi turn right at the junction, then immediately left into the first uphill road. The museum marks the entrance to the excavations of the Isthmian sanctuary.*

Museum and excavations – The museum contains a clear presentation of the objects found during the excavations of the Isthmian sanctuary and the port of Kenchreai. Apart from the usual finds there are some unusual glass mosaics (decorated with plant and bird motifs, human figures and landscapes) found in submerged packing cases at Kenchreai; they were probably imported from Egypt for the internal decoration of houses. Amphoras, gymnastic apparatus and ceramics are also on view.

The excavations carried out from 1952 to 1960 by the Americans have revealed the foundations of a temple to Poseidon (5C BC) and a stadium where from 582 BC the Isthmian Games took place every two years: note the 16 grooves made in the stone which diverge near the starting line. At the southern end of the stadium was the Palémonion (1C BC) of which only slight traces have been found. Beyond are the ruins of a Roman theatre as well as the remains of the defensive wall and the Roman fortress: the latter was probably rebuilt *c* AD 400 using Greek material.

Port of Kenchreai – In antiquity, this was the port for Corinth on the Saronic Gulf. Traces, mainly Roman, of harbour installations extend beneath the water. To the south are the foundations of a Christian basilica (4C) which replaced a temple to Isis.

St Paul the Apostle disembarked at Kenchreai in AD 51 and founded a Christian community.

For adjacent sights see ARGOLÍDA, ÁRGOS, Aktí ARKADÍAS, EPÍDAVROS, KÓRINTHOS, LERNÍ, LOUTRÁKI, MIKÍNES, NÁFPLIO, NEMÉA, SIKIÓNA, STIMFALÍA, TÍRINTHA.

To find the description of a sight, a historical event, a monument ... consult the index at the end of the guide.

KORÓNI

KORONE – Messinia, Peloponnese – Population 1 794

Michelin map 980 fold 40

The white houses of Korone with their pink tiled roofs are scattered over the slope of a promontory which protects a charming little port. A castle surmounts the high point at the end of the promontory while a long beach skirts the southern shore.
Korone, called Coron by the Franks, was conceded to the Venetians in 1206 and they used it for nearly three centuries as a port of call and trading port on the route to the Dardanelles; together with Methone *(on the west coast)* it was known as one of the "eyes of Venice" surveying the Mediterranean. It was taken by the Turks and then recaptured by the Venetians after a siege in 1685.

Citadel – *Leave the car in the village and climb a steep street and steps (out of season it is possible to go by car as far as the small square in front of the Byzantine monastery in the citadel).*
The entrance to the very extensive citadel is an imposing Gothic gate built by the Venetians. The original circuit wall, which was reinforced with square towers, was strengthened in the 15C and 16C by the Venetians and the Turks with bastions designed for the use of artillery. Views of Korone and the Messenian Gulf.
The citadel encloses a few houses, former storehouses, the Byzantine monastery of St John the Baptist (Timiou Prodromou) and the remains of the basilica of St Sophia; part of the apse has been converted into a chapel.

EXCURSION

Finikoúndas – *25km/15.5mi to the west. From Koróni take the road for Kalamáta; in Harokopio turn left into a small road signed to Finikoúndas and Methóni.* Situated at the end of an elegant bay, this pleasant seaside resort has a fine sandy beach much frequented in July and August. But in spite of the crowds and the numerous tavernas and hotels, the natural beauty of the place has been successfuly preserved.

For adjacent sights see ITHÓMI, KALAMÁTA, KIPARISSÍA, MÁNI, MESSINIAKÓS Kólpos, METHÓNI, MISTRÁS, Anáktora NÉSTOROS, PÍLOS.

LÁRISSA

Lárissa, Thessaly – Population 112 777

Michelin map 980 fold 17 – Airport

Lárissa is a modern-looking town, the capital of Thessaly and an important junction on the south bank of the River Piniós; there are shady squares and pedestrian streets. From 1389 to 1881 the town was occupied by the Turks who maintained a strong garrison. Now it is a market for agricultural produce and a food processing centre.

Arheologikó Moussío ⓥ – *2 Odós 31 Avgoustou.* The Archeological Museum is housed in an old mosque in the town centre; large collection of Greek, Roman and Byzantine funerary *stele.*

The river area – In **Odós Venizélou**, the main street in the old part of town, the low houses with awnings and the open-air street stalls are a lingering reminder of the Turkish occupation. The ruins of a Hellenistic **theatre** are visible from the corner of Odós Papanastasiou and on the right as the street climbs up to the site of an ancient acropolis where stands a **medieval castle**. Excavations *(in progress)* in front of the castle have revealed an early-Christian **basilica** ⓥ with mosaics and a painted tomb, probably that of St Achileos. At the end of Odós Venizélou the River Piniós flows at the foot of the hill. Further on is **Alkazar Park**, a favourite place for a stroll for the local people.

For adjacent sights see Kiláda ton TÉMBON, Óros ÓLIMBOS, METÉORA, TRÍKALA, Óros PÍLIO, VÓLOS.

LEFKÁDA★

LEUKAS – Ionian Islands – Population 19 346

Michelin map 980 south of fold 15 – 303km²/117sq mi

Lefkáda, also known as Leukas or Levkas and by the Latins as **Santa Maura**, is almost linked to the mainland by a narrow strip of land forming a lagoon.
It is a mountainous island – rising to a peak in Mount Eláti (1 158m/3 799ft) – with several fertile valleys where wheat, olives and citrus fruits are cultivated; the vineyards produce an excellent red wine called **Santa Maura**.
After coming under Franco-Venetian domination during the Middle Ages, the island was occupied by the Turks from 1467 to 1684 when it was reconquered by the Venetians who held it until 1797.

Lefkáda has preserved a fair number of its old houses with balconies and projecting wooden superstructures; some of the women still wear traditional costume consisting of a green or brown skirt and a black shawl. The Lefkáda International Festival in August presents traditional dances both local and foreign, plays and concerts.
Lefkáda was the birthplace of two great poets: **Aristotéles Valaorítis** (1824-74) and **Ángelos Sikelianós** (1884-1951) who restored the "Delphic Games" *(see p 47)*.

Practical Information

Access – In addition to the road bridge built in 1987, there is one daily flight linking the island with Athína/Athens.

Accommodation – About 30 hotels (cat A to E) mainly in Lefkáda Town; many rooms to let in town and in the villages; about 6 camping sites on the east coast.

Transport – Bicycle and motorcycle hire services; in season launches to the beaches and islets.

Santa Maura Fort – The fort was begun in the 14C by the Orsini, lords of the Ionian islands, passed to Gautier de Brienne, the Duke of Athens, in 1331 and then to the Tocchi, courtiers from the Angevin kingdom of Naples. Its present appearance, however, with its low curtain walls which are less easily attacked by cannon and its massive bastions, owes most to the Venetians and the Turks. It was originally surrounded by the waters of the lagoon and reached by two bridges.
Inside the curtain wall are traces of the town of Santa Maura which was the capital of the island until 1684 and contained the famous collegiate church of Santa Maura, which the Turks converted into a mosque. The parade ground is still visible; from the ramparts there is an attractive view of Lefkáda and the lagoon. Opposite, on the mainland, Grivas Castle, built during the War of Independence, stands sentinel.

Lefkáda (Lefkáda Town) – Pop 6 344. Lefkáda, the island capital, is a peaceful port on the lagoon with a Venetian atmosphere owing to the network of paved streets lined by low houses. Venetian influence is also responsible for the many little **churches** ⏲ built by the great local families, with Classical façades, single naves and painted ceilings; Ágios Minás, at the end of the main street, has a very fine ceiling painted by Nicholas Doxarás in the middle of the 18C.
Behind the cathedral in the main street is the tomb of the poet Valaorítis (1824-74). Faneroméni monastery *(3km/2mi southwest)* provides **views★** of Lefkáda and the lagoon.

Lagoon – It is fairly shallow (only 1–2m/4–6ft deep) and therefore suitable for fish farming or the extraction of salt. The fishing includes eels and grey mullet. It is possible to drive round the north branch of the lagoon: huge beaches, windmills, view of Lefkáda which seems to float on the water.

★★**Tour of the Island** – *88km/55mi – about 4hr – plus 2hr sightseeing.* The road from Lefkáda first skirts the west side of the lagoon, with a view across the water of Fort St George, which was built by the Venetians in the late 17C; then it follows the east coast of the island which faces Etolía. On reaching Nidrí turn left to visit the harbour.

★★★**Órmos Nidríou** – **Nidrí Bay** is sheltered by a screen of little islands covered with cypress and olive trees; an enchanting prospect is created by the natural contours of the site, the balmy air and the limpid light.
From the resort of Nidrí there are boat trips round the bay *(1 to 1hr 30min)* which include:
- Madourí Island where Valaorítis' Italian villa nestles in an idyllic setting; after the union with Greece he retired here to write, having served in the local Parliament under the British Protectorate;
- **Skorpiós Island**, owned by the shipping magnate, **Aristotle Onassis**, who was married on the island to Jacqueline Kennedy in 1968 and was buried there in 1976 (his two children are also buried there); the neighbouring island is a hunting reserve;
- Agía Kiriakí peninsula which contains the house and tomb of Dörpfeld (1853-1940), a German archeologist and follower of Schliemann, who tried to identify Lefkáda as Odysseus' Ithaca;
- Meganíssi Island (pop 1 346) which has many inlets.

The road beyond Nidrí looks down on **Vlihó Bay** which is joined to Nidrí Bay by a narrow passage.

Póros – Picturesque inlet below the village *(beach, taverna)*.

Vassilikí – Charming fishing village on the edge of a fertile plain *(beach)*. There are boat trips from Vassilikí to the famous **Lefkáda Leap** (known locally as Sappho's Leap), a high cliff 72m/236ft above sea level *(lighthouse)* from which the poetess **Sappho** (6C BC – *see LÉSVOS*) who had been deceived in love by the handsome Phaon, is supposed to have jumped to her death.
The headland (Ákri Doukáto) bears faint traces of a temple to Apollo whose priests used to jump off the cliff landing without harm owing to nets spread on the surface of the water to break their fall and to wearing something like wings.
The return journey up the west side of the island offers a direct view of Mount Eláti. In Komilió there is a junction with the rough road which leads to the Lefkáda Leap.

For adjacent sights see ÁRTA, EFÍRA, KASSÓPI, KÉRKIRA, MESSOLÓNGI, NÁFPAKTOS, PÁRGA, PRÉVEZA.

LEFKÁDIA-NÁOUSSA★★

Imathía, Macedonia

Michelin map 980 folds 4 and 5

The region of **Náoussa** *(which can be reached by train: Náoussa station is on the Thessaloníki-Florína line)*, well known for its fruit (peaches, apricots, apples, strawberries etc) and wine, is also famous for three unusual Macedonian *hypogea* (3C-2C BC), huge temple-like underground tombs situated out in the country near the little village of Lefkádia on the Véria to Édessa road.

Great Tomb ⓥ – *Sign "Great Macedonian Tomb".* The tomb, which was excavated in 1954, is built of conchitic limestone. A flight of steps leads down to the two-storey façade; the lower section is Doric, the upper Ionic. It was decorated with paintings; those remaining show a warrior (probably Death), the god Hermes (leader of souls to the underworld), Aiakos and Rhadamanthos (Judges of Hades) and battle scenes.
The interior comprises a vestibule and a chamber which still contains a sarcophagus.

Second Tomb – *150m/492ft beyond the Great Tomb, on the left of the path.* Majestic steps descend to the superb columned façade of this *hypogeum* which is very well preserved both in its architecture and in its paintings.

Lyson-Kalliklés Tomb ⓥ – This tomb is most unusual; it is in fact a burial vault for three families furnished with 22 funerary recesses inscribed with the names of the dead; ornamental paintings in an excellent state of preservation.

For adjacent sights see DÍO, ÉDESSA, KASTORIÁ, PÉLA, THESSALONÍKI, VÉRIA.

LERNÍ

LERNA – Argolis, Peloponnese

Michelin map 980 fold 29 – south of Argos

On the northwest shore of the Argolic Gulf near the modern village of **Míli** lies the site of ancient Lerna. The narrow tract of land between the road and the seashore contains the Hydra Springs and the Lerna Marshes, now much reduced in size but still inhabited by huge eels; both evoke souvenirs of ancient legends.
This was the scene for one of the Labours of Hercules. He had to kill the many-headed **Hydra**, a water snake that lived in the marsh; when one of its heads was cut off, others grew in its place. The legend may symbolise an unsuccessful struggle to drain the marsh.
The ancient Greeks thought that the Lerna marshes were bottomless and an entrance to the underworld. After killing their husbands, the Danaïds *(see ÁRGOS)* threw their heads in the marshes.

Prehistoric remains ⓥ – *On leaving Míli going south bear left after a church into a path which leads to the excavations (200m/220yd).*

The **House of the Tiles**, which is protected by a roof, takes its name from the great quantities of tiles which were found among the foundations. The internal arrangement of this ancient palace, which dates from about 2200 BC, is perfectly visible. It is the only great building from the early Bronze Age to come down to us in such good condition; in fact it was destroyed by fire in 2100 BC and then covered by a protective layer of earth to form a tumulus.

For adjacent sights see ARGOLÍDA, ÁRGOS, Aktí ARKADÍAS, EPÍDAVROS, KÓRINTHOS, Dióriga KORÍNTHOU, MIKÍNES, NÁFPLIO, NEMÉA, SIKIÓNA, SPÉTSES, STIMFALÍA, TÍRINTHA, TRÍPOLI.

LIVADIÁ★

Boeotia, Central Greece – Population 18 437

Michelin map 980 north of fold 29

Livadiá, the capital of Boeotia, spreads out at the mouth of the gloomy Erkínas (Hercyna) Gorge which was thought in antiquity to be the entrance to the underworld. It changed hands many times during the Middle Ages but under the Turkish occupation it became the second most important city in Greece after Thessaloníki. It is a lively town, an important junction in the road network and an industrial centre; the textile mills treat the cotton grown in the Copaïc Basin *(see ORHOMENÓS)*. The upper town is graced by white houses with jutting wooden balconies dating from the 18C and the 19C, little shops shaded by broad Turkish awnings and tavernas where mini-kebabs *(souvláki)* and cherry conserve, the local specialities, are served.

SIGHTS

Park the car in the square in the centre of the modern lower town and take one of the streets which lead to the upper town. They follow the valley of the River Erkínas as far as a square which gives access to the Turkish bridge, the old houses and the fulling mills beside the stream.

★★ **Erkínas Gorge** – Walk upstream leaving the great square tower to the right. An old hump-backed stone bridge spans the river. On the east bank the **spring of Mnemosyne** (Remembrance) flows into a pool where niches for votive offerings have been carved out of the cliff face. A passage not far away leads to what is thought to be the **spring of Lethe** (Oblivion); its waters bestow forgetfulness of the past. Beneath the shade of the maple trees a hotel (restaurant, swimming pool) has been built.

Continue up the gorge, deep into the rocky mountain where a few oleanders brighten the gloom. Only the cries of falcons break the silence of the canyon. There are fine views of the fortress and the Jerusalem hermitage.

Return to the square tower, which is at one end of the fortress' outer wall, and turn left into a path which follows the line of the wall past a beautiful Byzantine church with an apse and a dome.

★ **Kástro** – The fortress which stands on the top of Mount Elijah (Ágios Ilías) (402m/1 319ft) controls the approaches to Thessaly. The position was first fortified in the 13C by the Franks, who held Thebes, but the present fortress dates from the 14C when the Catalans ruled the land. They had in their possession a remarkable relic, the head of St George, which eventually turned up in Venice.

The former outer bailey of the castle precedes the main gate which leads to the keep. Near it stands a chapel built on the site of a temple to Zeus. From the ramparts there are spectacular **views**★★ of the Erkínas Gorge, the Jerusalem hermitage, the town and the mountains.

At the highest point there is a cave in which the oracle of an infernal divinity, Trophonios, was thought to operate: the oracle was consulted by **Pausanias**, who travelled in Greece in the 2C AD and described the ritual and trials required at that time.

For adjacent sights see ARÁHOVA, ÉVIA, DELFÍ, HERÓNIA, Drómos tou IRAKLÍ, ORHOMENÓS, ÓSSIOS LOUKÁS Monastery, THERMOPÍLES, THÍVA.

LOUTRÁKI★

Korinthía – Population 9 388

Michelin map 980 folds 29 and 30

Loutráki, which combines the old fashioned charm of a traditional spa with the more modern attractions of a seaside resort, is tucked into the crook of the Bay of Corinth at the foot of the Mount Geránia chain which rises to 1 351m/4 432ft. Luxury hotels, a palm tree walk and a luxuriant public garden with oleanders, pine and eucalyptus trees bordering a little harbour all add to the visitor's pleasure.

Loutráki is the largest spa in Greece; its warm water which is radioactive is used in the treatment of renal infections and rheumatism. Loutráki water, which is alkaline and contains traces of magnesia, is sold in bottles throughout Greece.

★★★ **Akrotírio Iréo (Heraion Headland)** – *46km/29mi return – about 2hr.*

At first a corniche road runs north from Loutráki offering admirable views *(left)* down on to the coast and the Bay of Corinth; then by a taverna (view north towards the headland crowned by a lighthouse) it bears right inland. On the outskirts of **Perahóra** (350m/1 148ft; small archeological museum) turn left into a narrow road *(sign "Limni Heraion")* which passes through olive groves and then skirts **Lake Vouliagméni** *(hotels, tavernas, camping)* which is linked by a channel to the sea. At the junction marked by a chapel bear right into an earth road which skirts the few traces of ancient Perahora which are scattered in an olive grove (ancient cistern on the left of the road) before reaching a car park.

The **Heraion** (a sanctuary dedicated to Hera) is to be found on the rocky slopes of the headland which separates the Bay of Corinth from the Gulf. Its remote and wild **site★** is hidden in the bottom of a narrow valley which slopes down to the transparent waters of a sheltered cove below an acropolis. From the car park walk down into the heart of the valley. Near a house are the ruins of a Hellenistic cistern; it is oblong in shape with a row of internal pillars. Higher up are the foundations of a temple to Hera Limenia (6C BC) and of an apsidal temple to Hera Akraia (8C BC). The path from the car park to the lighthouse *(30min on foot there and back)* provides a splendid **panorama★★★**, particularly at sunset, of the ancient site, the coast and mountains of the Peloponnese *(southwest)*, the Gulf of Corinth stretching northwest, the Halcyonic Gulf *(Kólpos Alkionídon)* on the north side of the headland and on the skyline to the north the Parnassos massif towering over Delphi. The site, a rich deposit of Archaic Corinthian pottery, was excavated between 1930 and 1933 under Humfry Payne, Director of the British School at Athens, whose wife Dilys Powell mentions the dig in her book *An Affair of the Heart.*

For adjacent sights see ARGOLÍDA, ÁRGOS, Aktí ARKADÍAS, ATHÍNA, EPÍDAVROS, KÓRINTHOS, Dióriga KORÍNTHOU, LERNÍ, MIKÍNES, NÁFPLIO, NEMÉA, SIKIÓNA, STIMFALÍA, THÍVA, TÍRINTHA.

MÁNI★★

Lakonía, Peloponnese

Michelin map 980 fold 41

The southern spur of Mount Taígetos, which rises to 1 214m/3 970ft, extends south between the Messenian and Lakonian gulfs to form a promontory which ends in Cape Matapan (Akrí Ténaro), the southernmost point of continental Greece. This is the Máni peninsula, a wild and sparsely inhabited region, as remote and timeless as it was in feudal days. The barren windswept landscape and the grey villages with their abandoned towers create an unusual and even oppressive impression.

For a description of the area to the north, known as Messenian Máni, see MESSINIAKÓS KÓLPOS.

A proud and courageous people – The Maniots, who are thought to be descended from the ancient Spartans, originally came from the north of Lakonía from which they were expelled in the 7C by invading Slavs. In the following centuries they managed to maintain a de facto autonomy from the succession of occupying forces – the Franks in the 13C, the Byzantines, the Venetians and particularly the Turks against whom they rose in revolt in 1769 and 1821; **Petrobey Mavromichális** (1765-1848) was one of the leaders in the War of Independence *(see NÁFPLIO)*.

Exclusive and bellicose, the Maniots lived in tribal villages under the rule of the local chiefs, sometimes confronting one another in vendettas; these disputes which could go on for generations explain their distinctive villages where the houses and even the fields were fortified. Sir George Wheler, writing in the 17C, described the Maniots as "famous as pirates by sea and pestilent robbers by land".

The Maniots also had a spirit of adventure. Some settled in Corsica in the 17C, under the protection of the Republic of Genoa, forming communities in Paomia and later in Cargese *(see Michelin Green Guide Corsica)*. Others took up piracy, particularly in the Cyclades. Few in number, the Maniots still live in their steep villages dotted with olive trees on the mountain slopes preserving the cult of honour and hospitality. The women still wear the long black dress and veil of the mourners in antiquity and perpetuate their tradition of singing funeral dirges **(mirológia)**.

The towers – There are about 800 towers, isolated or grouped in villages; the oldest go back to the 15C; their height increased with the power of the family that built them. They were constructed of irregularly shaped blocks of stone, about 15m–25m/50ft–80ft high and square in shape; they comprised three or four rooms, one above the other, linked by ladders and trap doors. Windows were small and few in number and the top floor was crenellated so that the tower looked like a castle keep. The greatest concentration of towers is to be found in Kíta and Váthia in the south.

The churches – Máni was probably converted to Christianity in the 9C and the 10C and many of the churches and chapels date from the 11C and the 12C. They are small buildings in the traditional Byzantine style of a Greek cross plan surmounted by a dome; the walls are a mixture of stone with bands of brick. Some have gable-end belfries, a feature which may have been introduced by the Franks. Fragments of ancient or paleo-Christian marble have often been incorporated in the structure. The walls of the interior are decorated with charming 12C-13C and 14C frescoes which are naive in treatment but very lively and illustrate the usual Byzantine themes; Frankish influence can sometimes be traced in the representation of knights and horses.

Unfortunately many of these churches are difficult to reach being isolated in the countryside; the keys are often kept at a neighbouring house. Here and there in the fields stands a lonely tombstone.

The sites of interesting Byzantine churches are underlined in red on the map of Máni.

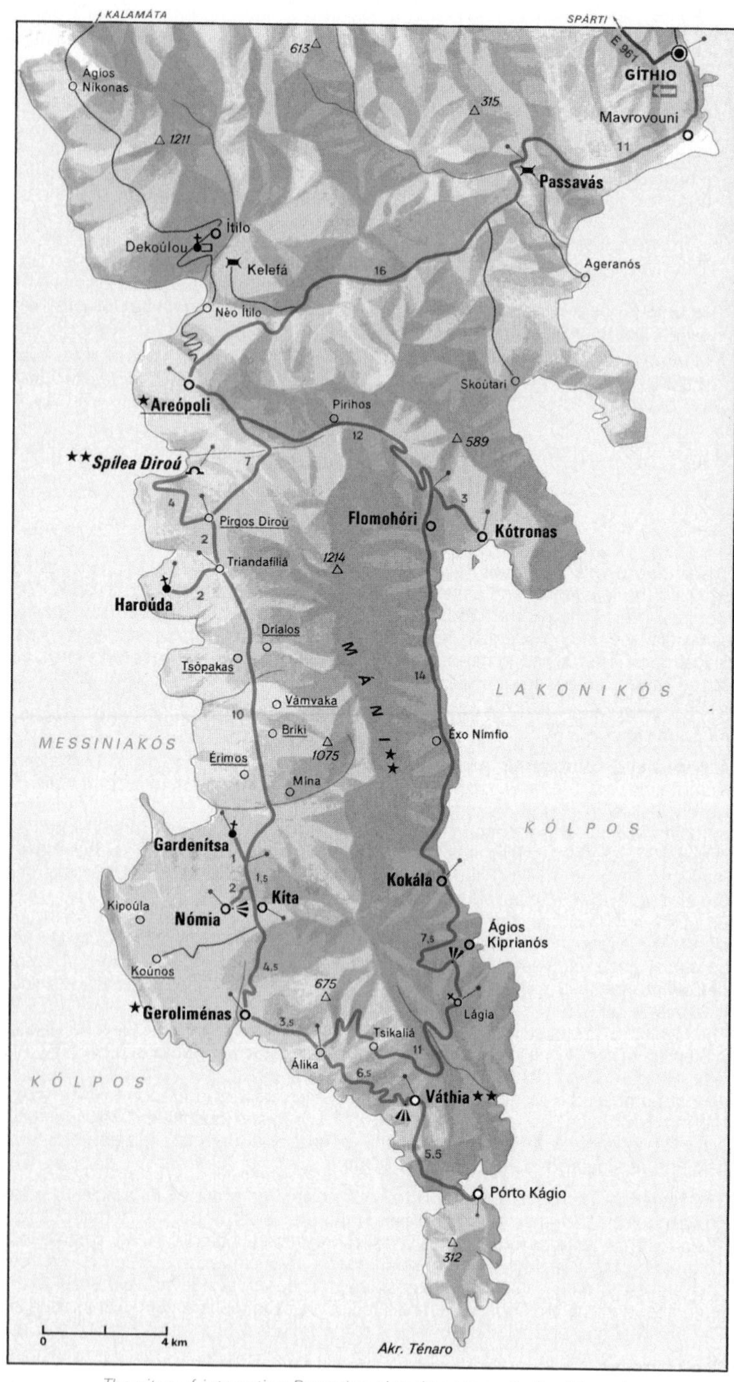

The sites of interesting Byzantine churches are underlined in red

TOUR STARTING FROM GÍTHIO

160km/100mi, about 6hr, plus 1hr 30min walking or visiting. Can be completed in a day but for a leisurely pace, stopping to look at a few churches, it is better to take two days spending the night at Geroliménas.

Gíthio – *See GÍTHIO.*

From Gíthio take the Areópoli road.

Mavrovoúni is a village *(3km/2mi from Gíthio)* with tavernas and a fine beach. The road climbs into the mountains through a gorge *(11km/7mi from Gíthio)* guarded at its northern end by Passavant Castle.

Passavás – The Frankish **Passavant Castle** with its merlons and crenellations *(restored)* appears briefly on a bluff on the east side of the road. Its name recalls the medieval motto of the Neuilly family – *passe-avant* – which means "Go forward". It was built by Jean de Neuilly, lord of the barony who held the military title of Marshal of Morea.
Continue along the Areópoli road which crosses the mountain chain; the western approach is guarded by **Kelefá Castle**, a huge Turkish fortress (16C-17C) which appears on the north side of the road.

★**Areópoli** – This is a large village (with *tavernas*) in the typical Maniot style with tradesmen's workshops (bakery), tower houses and churches. The Taxiarchs' Church (18C), at the centre of the village, is unusual owing to the decoration sculpted on the apse (signs of the Zodiac) and the side doors (escutcheons, angels and martial saints); **St John's Church** (Ágios Ioánis) ⏲, in a neighbouring street, is decorated with naive frescoes (18C).

At the junction with the road to Kótronas (left), bear right down to the Dirós Caves.

★★**Dirós Caves** – *See Spílea DIROÚ.*

Return to the Geroliménas road which runs along a sort of limestone terrace (caves) between the mountain and the sea, dotted with villages of tower houses, such as Drίalos, and olive groves or Barbary fig trees. Below the road *(west)* lies Haroúda.

Haroúda – Pop 31. The **church** ⏲, which dates from the 11C and 12C, is decorated with some interesting and well preserved frescoes.

Gardenítsa – 1km/0.5mi west of the road *(sign)* stands St Saviour's Church (Ágios Sotírios) which dates from the 11C and 12C. It has a porch and an interesting apse with a sculpted decoration in Kufic script; within are 13C-14C frescoes revealing Frankish influences (knights, horses).

Nómia – This village is scattered on the west side of the road with unusual **views**★★ of the towers of Kíta.
Below and to the left of the road leading to the village stands the white **Taxiarchs' Church** ⏲ which is decorated with a fine series of **frescoes** (13C-14C) illustrating the Life of Jesus.

Kíta – The village is set in an olive grove to the east of the road. Despite the great number of towers it seems to be abandoned. In the hamlet of Tourlotí, St Sergius' Church (Ágios Sérgios – 12C) is well proportioned.
Northwest of Kipoúla overlooking the Messenian Gulf rises a rocky bluff on which the famous **castle of the Great Maina** (Kástro tis Oriás, *difficult access*) was built in 1248 by William de Villehardouin; it was surrendered to the Byzantines in 1263.

★**Gerolimėnas** – This is a simple resort and fishing village, tucked into a rocky inlet in remote and wild **surroundings**★.
Take the road to Álika and bear right into a mediocre road leading to Váthia which rises proudly on its rocky site on the horizon.

★★**Váthia** – Forsaken by almost all its inhabitants, Váthia is the most impressive of the tower communities which are characteristic of the Máni. Stony paths wind between the silent towers and the empty houses mount to the top of the hill: **view**★★ of Cape Matapan (Akrotírio Ténaro).
From Váthia the road continues south to **Pórto Kágio** (Quail Port) situated on the neck of a precipitous peninsula, where game is abundant, and ends in **Cape Matapan** (Akrotírio Ténaro) once crowned by a temple to Poseidon, which was replaced by the Church of the Assumption, of which traces remain. On 28 March 1941 a naval engagement took place off Cape Matapan between the British and the Italians; the latter lost three cruisers.
Return to Álika and bear right into the road to Lágia over the ridge of the Máni. Beyond Lágia (towers) it descends down rock-strewn slopes past old marble quarries offering magnificent and precipitous **views**★★ of the Maniot coast. Beyond **Ágios Kiprianós** it skirts the east coast of the Máni which is less inhospitable and windswept than the western seaboard. The corniche road provides spectacular views of the coastline with its lonely bays and of the occasional villages and feudal ruins on the mountain slopes.

Kokála – An attractive sheltered inlet with a church at the water's edge.

Váthia

Flomohóri – Typical village of tall towers dotted with cypress trees.

About a mile beyond Flomohóri, turn right to Kótronas.

Kótronas – Small seaside resort set on the edge of a bay; fishing port.

For adjacent sights see GERÁKI, GÍTHIO, KALAMÁTA, KÍTHIRA, KORÓNI, MESSINIAKÓS Kólpos, MISTRÁS, MONEMVASSÍA, SPÁRTI.

MEGALÓPOLI

MEGALOPOLIS – Arkadía, Peloponnese – Population 4 646

Michelin map 980 folds 28 and 29

Megalópoli lies in the upper Alfiós Valley; it is known for its power station fuelled by lignite from the neighbouring mines and for an ancient ruined city.

Ruins of Megalopolis ⊙ – *1km/0.5mi north on the Karítena road on the left (sign).* The ancient city of Megalopolis was built between 371 and 368 BC by Epaminóndas so that Sparta could be kept under surveillance and contained. As the headquarters of the Arcadian League it played an important role in the Hellenistic and Roman periods. It was the native city of **Philopoimen** (253-183 BC), the "last of the Greeks", who sought to maintain Greek unity in the face of the Roman expansion, and of **Polybios** (204-122 BC), the historian, who described the Roman conquest of Greece in his *Histories*. Ancient Megalopolis was sacked several times and disappeared with the barbarian invasions.

Thersilion – The huge size of this assembly hall, which was designed to hold the "Ten Thousand", the representatives of the Arcadian people, can be judged from the foundations of the rectangular precinct and the many bases of columns within it. The hall was named after its founder; it measured 66x53m/217x174ft and the 67 pillars were placed so that almost all those present could see the speaker who stood in the centre of the side next to the theatre.

Theatre – A fringe of shrubs makes a rustic crown for the theatre which is the largest in Greece (145m/476ft in diameter) and could accommodate about 20 000 spectators on the 59 rows of seats; the acoustics were excellent. The lower rows, reserved for officials and members of the religious orders *(inscriptions)*, are well preserved.

For adjacent sights see ANDRÍTSENA, ITHÓMI, KALAMÁTA, KARÍTENA, KIPARISSÍA, MISTRÁS, OLIMBÍA, SPARTÍ, TRÍPOLI.

MÉGA SPÍLEO★

Achaia, Peloponnese

Michelin map 980 fold 29 – Alt 924m/3 031ft

Access either by car by the new road between Trápeza on the coast and Kalávrita (southwest) or on foot or a donkey (summer only) (45min) by the path from Zahlorоú in the Vouraïkós Gorge (see Harádra tou VOURAÏKOÚ); taverna.

The monastery of Méga Spíleo ("great cave"), which attracts many pilgrims, appears at the foot of a bare rockface on a wild **site★★** deep in the magnificent landscape of the Vouraïkós Valley. It was founded in the 8C by two hermits, Simeon and Theodore, following the discovery of a miraculous image of the Virgin which was found by Euphrosyne, a shepherdess, in a cleft in the rocks.
The monastery reached its apogee in the Middle Ages under the Palaeologi, the despots of Mystra *(see MISTRÁS)* who sometimes used to stay there. The conventual buildings which were burnt down in 1934, have been rebuilt in a style which does not meet with unanimous approval. In 1981 there were 12 monks in residence.

Monastery ⓥ – The rock church (17C) occupies the great cave from which the monastery takes its name. There is a beautiful door of embossed copper (early 19C); at the base is the Prophet Jesse beneath two scenes of the legend of the icon and effigies of archangels and the Virgin and Child. A recess harbours the miraculous image of the Virgin which was found by Euphrosyne and is attributed to St Luke. The oratory consecrated to the founding saints is next to the cave where Euphrosyne is supposed to have discovered the miraculous Virgin. The "Treasury" is full of reliquaries, icons and Byzantine manuscripts, some of which date from the 9C.
The guests' refectory and the household rooms (bakery, cellar) are also open.

For adjacent sights see HLEMOÚTSI, KALÁVRITA, KILÍNI, KÓRINTHOS, Dióriga KORÍNTHOU, NEMÉA, PÁTRA, SIKIÓNA, STIMFALÍA, Harádra tou VOURAÏKOÚ.

MESSINIAKÓS Kólpos★★★

MESSENIAN GULF – Messinia, Peloponnese

Michelin map 980 folds 40 and 41

The whole perimeter of the Messenian Gulf offers numerous places with excellent bathing, varying from the lonely coves dotting the eastern coastline to the fine beaches stretching along the western coast between **Petalídi** and Koróni *(see KORÓNI)*. The magnificent road between Kalamáta and Areópoli, which often climbs high into the western foothills of the Taígetos chain, provides frequent views of the indented eastern shoreline of the gulf where the empty waves sparkle into the distance.
The road passes through a varied landscape: fairly austere in the south on the edge of the **Máni** *(see MÁNI)* where the ravines and slopes are partially covered by scrub and untended olive groves; more hospitable further north where cultivated basins alternate with terraced hillsides dotted with dark rows of cypress trees and clumps of pine trees. The villages are very charming; their houses cluster on the hillsides round the main square with its fountain and giant plane tree in the shade of which a café is often to be found; there are many Byzantine and post-Byzantine **churches** ⓥ.
For description of the coast from Areópoli round to Gíthio see MÁNI: Tour starting from Gíthio.

FROM KALAMÁTA TO AREÓPOLI

80km/50mi – about 2hr (not including the excursion to Viros Gorge) plus 2 to 3hr for visiting

Kalamáta – *See KALAMÁTA.*

★**Koskarás Defile** – The river has created a gorge which is spanned by a bold modern bridge. Park the car and climb down a short way to admire the design and the site. Leaving the Kámbos basin, presided over by the medieval ruins of **Zarnáta Castle**, the road climbs only to drop down again to Kardamíli, giving bird's-eye **views★★** over the Kardamíli basin and the coast.

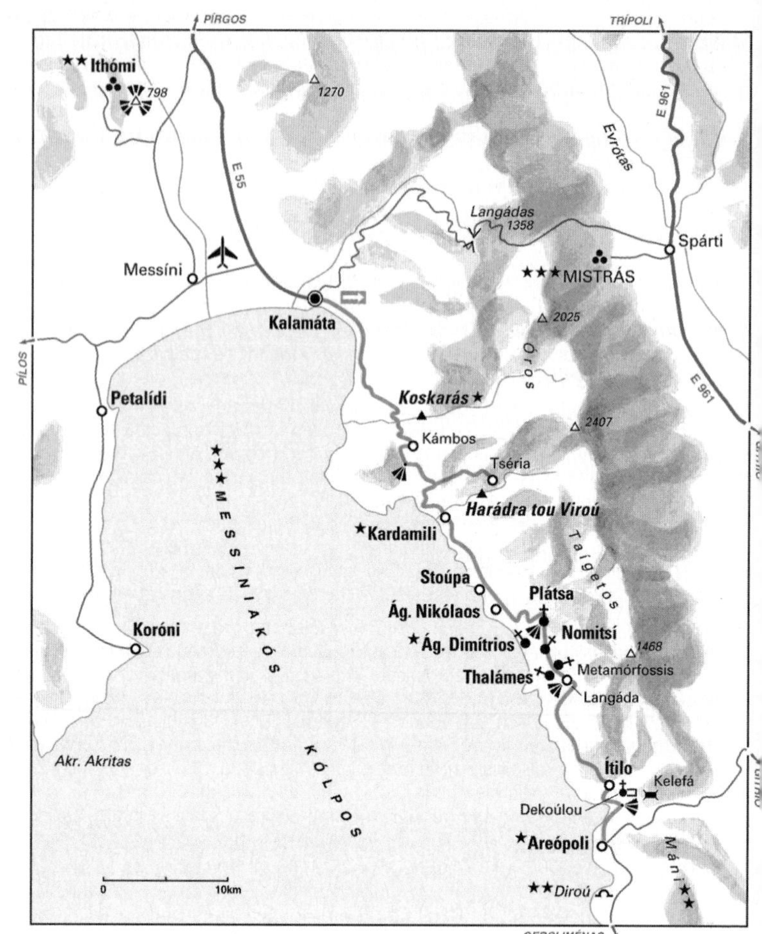

★**Kardamíli** – Kardamíli is a simple holiday resort and fishing port protected by a fortified islet offshore; its old houses and churches cluster on the banks of a mountain stream. The best-known church is St Spiridon's (13C) in the old quarter of Kardamíli (Ano-Kardamíli), with its low relief carvings and fine pointed belfry with four storeys of arcading.

The land behind Kardamíli, now planted with olive trees, was once guarded by **Beaufort Castle** which was built by the Franks on a withdrawn site.

From Kardamíli it is possible to make an excursion on foot to the Viros Gorge. Allow 6hr extra and take good shoes and a supply of water.

Harádra tou Viroú – *The excursion is easier starting from Tséria (6km/4mi north-east of Kardamíli), taking a track on the right from there.* The splendid **Virós Gorge** excursion involves first descending to its bottom and then climbing out again up a track leading to Exohóri. Continue along the same path, which again descends, and after reaching the monasteries of Sotíras and Likaki return to Ano-Kardomíli.

Resume the itinerary from Kardamíli.

Stoúra – Fine beach, good for swimming.

Ágios Nikólaos – Little fishing village with small tavernas by the sea.

Plátsa – Several Byzantine churches worth visiting, superb view of the gulf.
Just before a cluster of pine trees an admirable **view**★★★ opens out over the whole of the Messenian Gulf. About 100m/110yd further on is **St Demetrios' Chapel.**

★**Ágios Dimítrios** – *About 1km/0.5mi before Nomitsí on the right.* This little chapel (13C) stands among the olives and cypresses on the terraced hillside facing Koróni across the Messenian Gulf.

Nomitsí – Beside the road through the village stands the chapel of St Cosmas and St Damian (Anárgiri); it takes the rare form of a cruciform plan within a square; it has a rooftop belfry and the interior is decorated with frescoes.

In an enclosure on the left side of the road between Nomitsí and Thalámas stands the **church of the Transfiguration** (Metamórfossis) which dates from the 11C; unusual capitals carved with Byzantine motifs (peacocks, cockerels etc); traces of frescoes.

Thalámas – 13C church of St Sophia.

At **Langáda** with its church and towers there are superb views looking down over the gulf.

Ítilo – *Map see p 182.* The ancient capital of the Máni, now a wine-producing centre, stands on a hill facing the Turkish castle of Kelefá (16C and 17C) inland and a sheltered bay on the coast (Néo Útilo) where Napoleon's fleet anchored in 1798 en route for Egypt. In the 17C it was the port of embarkation for those Maniots who settled in Corsica *(see MÁNI)*. On the slope below the road lies the **Dekoúlou Monastery** (18C); the church is decorated with frescoes and wood carvings (iconostasis, baldaquin).
As one approaches Areópoli there are views of **Kelefá Castle** on the left.

Areópoli – *See MÁNI.*

For adjacent sights see Spílea DIROÚ, GÍTHIO, ITHÓMI, KALAMÁTA, KIPARISSÍA, KÍTHIRA, KORÓNI, MÁNI, METHÓNI, MISTRÁS, MONEMVASSÍA, Anáktora NÉSTOROS, PÍLOS, SPÁRTI.

MESSOLÓNGI

MISSOLONGHI – Akarnanía, Central Greece – Population 10 916
Michelin map 980 north of fold 28

Missolonghi is famous for the death of Lord Byron and for a heroic siege. It lies on the edge of a lagoon, surrounded by salt marshes and fish ponds. Here one can taste botargo *(avgotáraho)*, a relish made of salt fish roe from the tunny or the grey mullet. 10km/6.5mi east stood the ancient city of **Calydon**; the king had failed to sacrifice to Artemis who therefore sent a monstrous boar to ravage the whole region. The hunting and killing of the beast by **Meleager** and his companion Atalanta was a favourite scene with artists.

Missolonghi and the War of Independence – The first Turkish attack was launched in 1822; the following year Missolonghi was again threatened. It was defended by **Márkos Bótsaris**, a Souliot *(see EFÍRA)*.

Siege of Missolonghi – The final siege began in April 1825 when Reshid Pasha (known to the Greeks as Kiutahi) arrived at the head of 15 000 men; the besieged behind their feeble defences numbered only 5 000 but they fought furiously and made many sorties so that a year later they were still holding out when Ibrahim Pasha arrived with 10 000 Egyptian reinforcements.
The Greeks had run out of food and decided to make a mass sortie *(éxodos)* during the night of 22 to 23 April 1826. 9 000 set out including many women and children but they were massacred by the Turks who had been alerted by a traitor and only 1 800 reached Ámfissa (80km about 50mi east). Chrístos Kapsális and the last defenders blew up the powder store burying themselves and their attackers under the ruins.
This historic gesture had a particular impact in France where it was magnified by the writings of Chateaubriand and Victor Hugo and the paintings of Eugène Delacroix *(Greece on the Ruins of Missolonghi)* and Ary Scheffer; David d'Angers created a marble sculpture, *Child of Greece (see below)*.

Lord Byron at Missolonghi

In January 1824 the great Philhellene poet Lord Byron arrived from Lefkáda accompanied by a doctor and nine servants. His wardrobe contained six military uniforms in various colours decorated with gold and silver braid, together with sashes, epaulettes, waistcoats and cocked hats, two gilded helmets and ten swords. More importantly he also brought funds raised by the London Greek Committee. His chief task was to unite and rally the various Greek factions. For relaxation he would paddle across the lagoon and go hunting on horseback over the flat country.
Riding home one day he was caught in a rainstorm and the chill April wind brought on a fever. His doctors resorted to bleeding but on 19 April 1824 he died. The Greeks proclaimed 21 days of mourning. His embalmed body was placed in a tin-lined case with 180 gallons of spirit in a large barrel and embarked for Zákinthos to a 37 gun salute.
His remains arrived in London on the brig *Florida* but such was his reputation he was refused burial in Westminster Abbey. It was not until 1969 that a plaque was dedicated to him in Poets' Corner.

Heroes' Garden – Within the ramparts, which were restored by King Otto, near the Sortie Gate is a pleasant garden planted with palm trees, oleanders and cypresses beneath which lie the tombs and commemorative monuments of the heroes of the War of Independence.
There is a tumulus to the nameless dead, a **statue of Byron** on the spot where his heart is buried and, on a platform *(right)*, the **tomb of Bótsaris** surmounted by a Child of Greece *(kóri tis Ellados)* reading the hero's name on a stone: the graceful white marble figure is a copy of the original sculpted in 1827 by David d'Angers which is in the National Historical Museum in Athens.

Lord Byron's House (Byron Museum) ⏲ – *Currently closed for restoration. The exhibits are on view in the local art gallery.*

EXCURSIONS

Tourlída – *6km/3.75mi south; fish restaurants and beach.* The road south beside the lagoon gives a fine view of the stagnant waters gleaming in the pearly light; this is the haunt of many sea birds attracted by the rich fishing grounds (grey mullet, eels). The fishermen's huts are built on piles beside the fish hatcheries which are reached in huge flat-bottomed boats.

Etolikó – *11km/6.75mi northwest.* Take the coast road which runs past the marshes and a salt refinery.
This picturesque little city on the lagoon reminds one of Venice. It was built in the Middle Ages on an islet commanding the entrance to an inlet and linked to the mainland by two symmetrical dykes. Miniature churches and the low houses of the fishermen and craftsmen line the network of narrow streets.
To the west at the mouth of the River **Ahelóos** the alluvion deposited by the river has created a fertile plain, the habitat of storks (many nests at Neohóri).

For adjacent sights see DELFÍ, HLEMOÚTSI, ITHÁKI, KALÁVRITA, KARPENÍSSI, KEFALONÍA, KILÍNI, MÉGA SPÍLEO, NÁFPAKTOS, PÁTRA, THÍVA, Harádra tou VOURAÏKOÚ, ZÁKINTHOS.

Michelin maps and town plans are oriented with north at the top of the page.

METÉORA★★★

Tríkala, Thessaly

Michelin map 980 fold 16

North of Kalambáka *(see below)* in the northwest corner of the Thessalian plain a group of fantastic grey rocks rises up out of the trees in the flat Piniós Valley. Perched on the top of these huge and precipitous columns of rock are the famous cenobitic monasteries known as the Metéora which means "in the air".

Unusual natural phenomenon – These towers of rock stand on the border between the Píndos massif and the Thessalian plain at the lower end of the gorges carved by the Peiiós and its tributaries in the limestone of the Píndos range. The flow of surface water has created the valley leaving the pillars of sandstone and tertiary conglomerate standing (up to 300m/984ft high) above the surrounding plain. There are some 60 of these columns of rock, a favourite haunt of vultures.

Between heaven and earth – It was in the 11C that the first hermits sought refuge in the caves of the Metéora where the solitude and broad horizons favoured the mystic way of life. When the Serbs invaded Thessaly in the 14C and brigands roamed the land, the hermits began to group together in monasteries. The first was founded by **St Athanasius** from Mount Athos, who established the Great Meteoron with nine monks on an almost inaccessible site. Others followed his example despite the considerable difficulties involved in transporting the building material to the top of the rocks by manpower or by hoist.
During the 15C and 16C the number of monasteries grew to 24 and the buildings were decorated with frescoes and icons by the great artists of the day such as **Theophanes**, a monk from Crete, who also worked on Mount Athos, and his followers. Unfortunately, rivalry between the communities and a decrease in the number of vocations led to a decline; today only five monasteries are inhabited by monks or nuns: St Nicholas', Roussánou, the Great Meteoron, Varlaám and St Stephen's. As the Metéora have become a tourist attraction, some monks and the new recruits have departed for Mount Athos or for more isolated monasteries.
Originally the only access was by means of very long ladders which could be drawn up when not in use or in a basket or net suspended on ropes from a winch which was mounted in a winching tower *(vrizoni)* above the void; according to travellers in the past the ropes were not replaced until they broke. Steps have now been cut in the rock face and there is a fine modern road serving the main monasteries.

TOUR *17km/10.5mi – about 4hr*

A tour based on Kalambáka may include the monasteries and magnificent views of the Píndos mountains and the Piniós Valley; those with limited time are advised to visit the Great Meteoron and the Varlaám monasteries.

Kalambáka – Pop 5 699. The town is the starting point for tours of the Metéora.

Mitrópoli – The 14C **cathedral** built on a hill to the north of the town *(sign)* stands on earlier foundations and is constructed of antique and early Christian materials (5C-6C AD). Inside the basilical church with a nave and two aisles and rounded apses the early-Christian elements are of special interest: marble pulpit, canopy and at the end of the nave the steps where the priests stood. The dark 16C frescoes are in the Cretan style.

From Kalambáka drive west; soon after passing through Kastráki, park the car and take the path on the left.

The Chapel of the Virgin on the "Column" of **Doúpiani** was part of the Doúpiani hermitage to which, until the 14C, the scattered hermits were attached.

★**Ágios Nikólaos** ⌚ – Although **St Nicholas' Monastery** dates from the 14C the church was built in the 16C and was decorated at that time by Theophanes the Cretan with remarkable frescoes (the Last Judgement, the Dormition of St Ephraim) which were restored in 1960.

The road skirts the foot of the rock on which stands the **Roussánou Monastery** ⌚ and reaches a T-junction. Bear left past the Varlaám Monastery *(see below)* to reach the Great Meteoron.

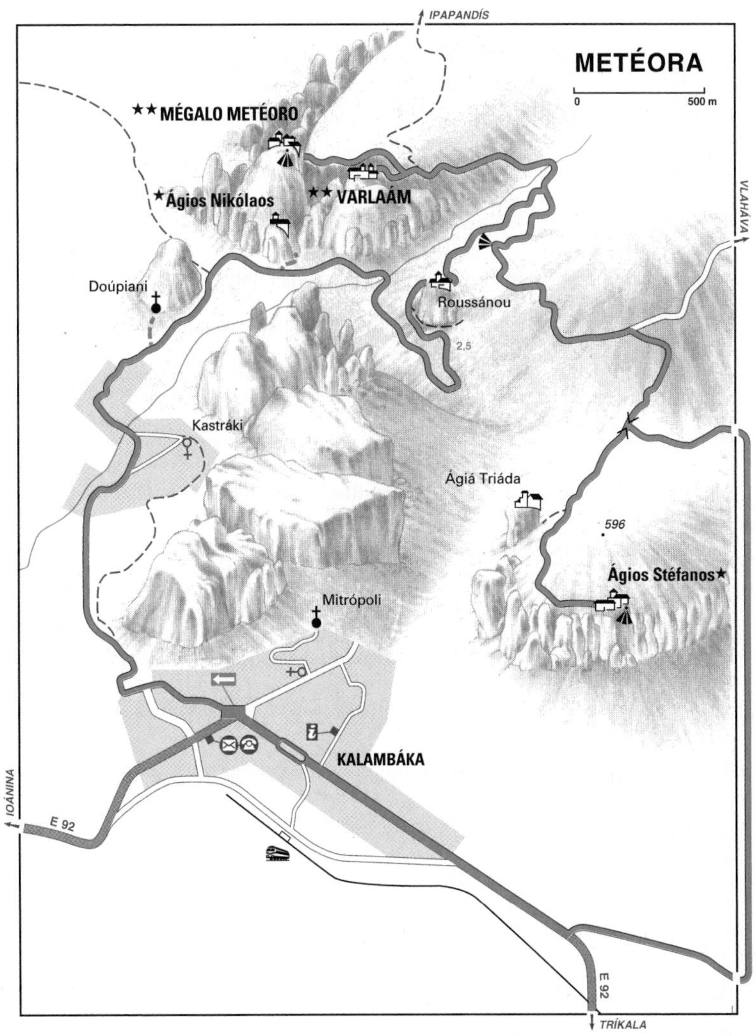

★★ **Megálo Metéoro** ⓥ – Population 6. *Access by steps cut in the rock emerging near the tower with its winch and basket.*

The **Great Meteoron Monastery** is built on a broad platform of rock *(platís líthos)* (534m/1 752ft). It was founded as the Monastery of the Transfiguration **(Metamórfossis)** in 1356 by St Athanasius and enriched with relics and works of art by his successor St Ioasaph (John Uros), a member of the ruling family in Serbia.

Church – The apse and the chancel date from the 14C and are decorated with mid-15C frescoes; the rest of the building was rebuilt in the mid 16C and consists of a huge narthex and an unusual transept built on the square cross plan with lateral apses roofed by domes, in accordance with an architectural style inherited from Mount Athos. The walls are decorated with contemporary frescoes, in an austere style, depicting the founders, St Athanasius and St Ioasaph *(west wall of the crossing)*; St Ioasaph's tomb is in the narthex. The bishop's throne, which is inlaid with mother of pearl and is a 17C work, stands in an imposing hall, divided into two aisles and roofed with domes. It now houses the Treasury: manuscripts, icons including some dating from the 14C; liturgical ornaments, reliquaries and a carved cross of St Daniel.

From the southeast of the monastery there is an impressive **view** over the other pillars of rock, particularly the one bearing the Varlaám Monastery.

★★ **Varlaám Monastery** ⓥ – A footbridge and a stairway lead up to the monastery which is perched above a ravine up which visitors and provisions used to be hoisted by the machinery in the winch tower (16C).

It was founded in 1518 by two brothers, from a rich family called Aparas from Ioánina, on the site of a 14C cenobitic hermitage established by a monk named Barlaam.

Church – All Saints' (Ágii Pándes) Church, which incorporates the original 14C chapel dedicated to the Three Hierarchs, was completed in 1544. It has a remarkable collection of **frescoes**★★. The frescoes in the narthex, which date from 1566, recall the Last Judgement and the Life of John the Baptist; the walls are covered with figures of ascetics and there are portraits of the Aparas brothers near their tomb.

The frescoes in the church proper show western influence in the realistic poses and colours; they are the work of Frango Catellano of Thebes (1548): Christ in the dome, the Dormition of the Virgin and the Crucifixion on the west wall and effigies of St John of Damascus and St Cosmas Melodus on either side of the entrance.

The 17C frescoes in the Chapel of the Three Hierarchs are well preserved and include two masterly scenes: the Dormition of St John Chrysostom and the Dormition of St Ephraim the Syrian. Also worthy of attention are the carved and gilded iconostasis (16C icon) and the inlaid furnishings.

Conventual buildings – The refectory which houses the Treasury (including an icon of the Virgin by Emmanuel Tzanés), the infirmary, the store rooms (enormous barrel holding 12 000l/2 640gal), the winepress and the tower with its winch.

Return downhill to the road junction across the river; bear left into the road which follows the slope of the hill: spectacular **view**★★ of the little **Roussánou Monastery**, rebuilt in the 16C on a bizarrely shaped rock.

Further on at the second T-junction the road on the right leads past the 15C and 17C buildings of **Holy Trinity Monastery** (Agía Triáda – illustration *p 12*) ⓥ, crowning an enormous pillar of rock, to St Stephen's Convent.

★ **Ágios Stéfanos** ⓥ – **St Stephen's Convent** is reached by a bridge spanning the chasm which separates the rock pillar from the mountain mass. It was founded in the late 15C on the site of a 12C hermitage and is now occupied by nuns. There are two churches: the older one was built in the 15C on the basilical plan and is decorated with frescoes similar to those in the Great Meteoron Monastery; the more recent is late 18C and contains a reliquary in which the head of St Charalambos is venerated.

There is a rich museum housing fine 16C and 17C icons by Emmanuel Tzanés, 17C illuminated manuscripts and 16C embroidery.

Splendid **views**★★ of the Piniós Valley and Thessaly.

For adjacent sights see LÁRISSA, Kiláda ton TÉMBON, Óros ÓLIMBOS, TRÍKALA, Óros PÍLIO, VÓLOS.

METHÓNI★★

METHONE – Messinia, Peloponnese – Population 1 173
Michelin map 980 fold 40

Methone, the watchtower of the eastern Mediterranean, stands on a pleasant **site**★ overlooking a bay protected by two islands, Sapiéndza and Shíza, which provide good inshore fishing grounds. A beach adjoining the quiet fishing harbour with several hotels and tavernas makes it a pleasant place to stay.

A desirable possession – A chance wind in 1204 blew Geoffrey de Villehardouin *(see KALAMÁTA)* into Methone harbour as he was returning from the Holy Land, but he left soon after to join William de Champlitte in the conquest of the Peloponnese.
When the conquest was complete Methone was assigned to the Venetians who called it **Modon** and held it for nearly three centuries, except for a Genoese interlude from 1354 to 1403 when the Venetian fleet took its revenge and defeated the Genoese naval force. Methone became a bishopric and earned its living by producing silk and supplying the Venetian galleys that put in on their way to Syria.
In 1500 however the Turkish army under Bayezid II captured the town after a month of bombardment. The Venetians returned in 1686 until 1715 when Methone once again fell to the Turks who held it until the 19C. In 1824 Miaoúlis *(see ÍDRA)* attacked the Ottoman fleet with fire ships and burned 25 Turkish vessels.
Finally in 1828 General Maison recaptured Methone from Ibrahim Pasha and used the troops of the French military expedition to rebuild parts of the town.

★★ **Citadel** ⌚ – The citadel was begun in the 13C on the site of an earlier fortress in a very strong position on a promontory surrounded by the sea on three sides. Further building took place in the 15C, 16C and 18C. Most of the construction is the work of the Venetians as is shown by the lions of St Mark and the carved escutcheons which adorn the building. During the Venetian occupation a whole town was squeezed round the cathedral within the fortifications but when Chateaubriand visited Methone in 1806 on his way to the Holy Land the Turks were camping in tents and makeshift buildings.
Beyond the counterscarp a bridge built by General Maison spans the moat which was covered by cross-fire from the **Bembo bastion** (15C) *(right)* and the **Loredan bastion** (1714) *(left)* which was well provided with artillery.
An outer gate (early 18C) opens into a passage against the northern rampart (13C); a vaulted approach precedes the main gate, the **Land Gate** (13C) which has Gothic arches and gives access to the open space once occupied by the medieval town: on the right stands a wall of the keep rebuilt by the Turks in the 16C; opposite is a monolithic granite column erected by the Venetians in 1494 and originally crowned by the lion of St Mark.
Follow the eastern rampart (16C-18C); on the left lies the port, on the right the confused remains of a Turkish bath, some cisterns, a powder magazine and the old Latin cathedral.

A. Arnaud /APPARENCE

Boúrdzi Tower, Methone

The **Sea Gate** on the south side of the citadel, which was rebuilt by the Turks using Venetian material (stone bearing a lion carving and the Foscolo arms), gives access to the picturesque **Boúrdzi Tower★**, which was rebuilt by the Turks in the 16C on an island of rock and linked to the citadel by a bridge; climb to the platform for a splendid **view★★** of the citadel, the harbour and the islands.
The western rampart with its five towers, which probably dates from the 13C, leads back to the keep; most of its fortifications date from the 15C but it was modernised in the 18C (firing steps for artillery). On the landward side of the moat, at the very end of the counterscarp, there is another defensive construction called a redoubt.

For adjacent sights see ITHÓMI, KALAMÁTA, KARÍTENA, KIPARISSÍA, KORÓNI, Anáktora NÉSTOROS, PÍLOS.

MÉTSOVO★★

Ioánina, Epiros – Population 2 917
Michelin map 980 folds 15 and 16 – Alt 1 160m/3 806ft

Métsovo is admirably situated in a mountain combe just below the highest road pass in Greece (alt 1 705m/5 594ft) which marks the border between Epiros *(west)* and Thessaly *(east)*. A few bears and wolves survive in the surrounding ancient forests of beech and pine trees. The little town is not only a summer resort offering the benefits of bracing mountain air but also a winter sports centre with skiing on the slopes of Mount Karakóli *(ski lift)*. Métsovo is famous for its trout, its wine and its cheese as well as for its embroidered cloth and wood carvings.

Past reflections – Métsovo, which is inhabited mainly by **Vlachs** *(see p 27)*, was already prosperous under the Turkish occupation when the town enjoyed a relative autonomy. Many important families, Greek or Vlach, lived there, occasionally receiving the klephts *(see p 27)* who were being pursued by the occupying force. Certain of the families, such as the **Avéroff** and the **Tosítsa**, who had made their fortunes growing cotton in Egypt, bequeathed large sums to their native city as well as to Athens and the Greek state, thus contributing to the development of modern Greece.
Métsovo has moreover retained a character of its own. In the steep streets, paved with stones set on edge, there are mountain ponies loaded with wood, mules carrying packs and sheep herded by shepherds with crooks. The beautiful corbelled houses are roofed with stone.
Many of the inhabitants still wear the local dress: the men in dark blue, with baggy trousers or pleated skirt *(fustanélla)* and clogs adorned with pompons *(tsaroúhia)*; the women in skirt, blouse and embroidered apron, a dark scarf on the head. On Sundays there is often traditional dancing in the square.

SIGHTS

Church of Agía Paraskeví – At the centre of Métsovo there is a vast open space shaded by huge plane trees; nearby is the Church of Agía Paraskeví which contains a rich 18C **iconostasis★** carved with flamboyant motifs.

Follow the main street and turn left into a narrow street which climbs up to the museum (sign) at the heart of the old district.

★**Moussío Laikís Téhnis** ⓥ – The museum, which is devoted to local Epirot art, is housed in the Tosítsa family residence; Michael Tosítsa (1781-1858) founded the Polytechnic in Athens.
The interior has been richly adorned with carved woodwork (particularly the ceilings); the rooms are furnished with fine carpets and embroidered textiles and decorated with gold ornaments, beaten copperwork and icons. The huge reception room is particularly impressive with its divans and its monumental samovar.

Return to the main square and take the path on the right of the Bank of Greece (sign) which leads down the slope into the Árahtos Valley to St Nicholas' Monastery (45min on foot there and back).

Pinacoteca (Art Gallery) ⓥ – Recently founded by the Tosítsa family, the gallery displays works by 19C and 20C Greek artists relating in the main to historical subjects, everyday life and socio-economic activities (craftsmen, pedlars etc).

★**Ágios Nikólaos** ⓥ – This little **Monastery of St Nicholas** has been pleasantly restored. A display of icons has been arranged in the narthex. The walls of the 14C church are painted with 16C-17C frescoes and the iconostasis is profusely decorated with gold, carving and icons.
The conventual buildings contain the monks' cells, the room belonging to the Superior *(igoúmenos)* and the secret school where the children were taught during the Turkish occupation.

For adjacent sights see ÁRTA, EFÍRA, IOÁNINA, KASSÓPI, KÉRKIRA, METÉORA, PÁRGA, TRÍKALA.

MIKÍNES★★★

MYCENAE – Argolis, Peloponnese

Michelin map 980 fold 29

Mycenae, city of the Atreids accursed of the gods, was the key to the opulent Argolid plain and occupied a wild and oppressive **site★★★** on a rocky hill ringed by barren mountains. The proud ruins of this city fortress, which dates from the second millennium BC, recall its Homeric epithet "rich in gold" and its warrior-kings, who pillaged and plundered and produced the Mycenaean civilisation.

LEGEND AND HISTORY

According to tradition Mycenae was founded by Perseus, son of Zeus and Danaë, who raised the city walls with the help of the Cyclops, giant builders who had but one eye in the middle of their forehead.

The tragedy of the Atreids – After the Perseids came the Atreids whose complicated history with its trail of vengeance and death has been told by Homer in the *Iliad* and by Aeschylus, Sophocles and Euripides in their plays. The most well known of this accursed family are:

– **Atreus**, son of Pelops *(see OLIMBÍA)*, who killed the sons of his brother Thyestes and served them to him during a banquet.

– **Menelaos**, son of Atreus and king of Sparta, whose wife **Helen** was seduced by Paris, son of Priam, King of Troy, thus provoking the Trojan War.

– **Agamemnon**, Menelaos' brother, King of Mycenae and husband of **Clytemnestra**, Helen's sister; he was the leader of the Achaians in the expedition against Troy, the king of kings who ordered the sacrifice of his daughter Iphigenia at Aulis *(see ÉVIA: Karababá Fort)* to obtain a favourable wind.

– **Aigisthos**, younger son of Thyestes who killed his uncle Atreus to avenge his father's death and became Clytemnestra's lover; she asked him to get rid of Agamemnon, just returned from Troy, and his captive **Cassandra**, Priam's daughter, known for her gloomy predictions which all refused to believe.

– **Orestes**, son of Agamemnon and Clytemnestra, who was persuaded by his sister **Electra** to kill Clytemnestra and her lover Aigisthos; he was pursued by the Furies *(see p 168)* but acquitted on the Areopagos in Athens by a jury presided over by Athena and then purified by Apollo on the *omphalos* in Delphi before ascending the throne of Mycenae; he gave his sister Electra in marriage to his faithful friend **Pylades**.

For many years these people were thought to be legendary figures. As a result of Schliemann's discoveries, historians and archeologists now think that they really existed but that their actions have been transposed by the poets, above all by **Homer**. What is certain however is that from the 16C to the 12C BC when the Achaian city was destroyed by Dorian invaders, Mycenae was the richest and most powerful state in the Mediterranean world and had close relations with Crete and even Egypt.

Excavations – By the time of Pausanias (2C AD) Mycenae was already reduced to a few overgrown ruins. Early in the 19C however the Lion Gate and the so-called Tomb of Agamemnon were known to travellers, although the heraldic aspect of the lions led to certain false assumptions: a French military expedition to the Morea in 1828 thought they were looking at a Frankish castle.

Then came **Heinrich Schliemann** (1822-90). He was a German businessman who made a fortune in the grocery trade and was obsessed with the Homeric heroes. Having retired from business at the age of 45, this brilliant amateur discovered the site of Troy on the coast of Asia Minor in 1874 while searching for King Priam's treasure.

Two years later he began to dig on the site of Mycenae in the hope of finding the tomb of Agamemnon and his retainers who were massacred by Aigisthos' assassins during a banquet. Guided by a sentence in Pausanias which said that Agamemnon had been buried within the city walls, Schliemann very soon discovered, just inside the Lion Gate, beneath a mound, the first circle of royal tombs containing 19 corpses which he thought were those of Agamemnon, Cassandra and their companions. The men wore golden face masks and golden breast plates; the women wore golden fillets, necklaces and bracelets. In 25 days a whole collection of jewellery, vases and precious items was recorded which is now the glory of the Mycenaean room in the Athens Museum. These discoveries made a great stir.

Schliemann was followed at the end of the century by two Greek scholars, Stamatákes and Tsoúntas. Extensive excavations were undertaken this century by the British School in Athens in 1920 and again in the 1950s. Restoration work was begun by the Greek Archeological School in 1951 when they also discovered the second circle of royal tombs near the tomb of Clytemnestra. Excavations are still in progress on the site within the western wall. *A building near the Tomb of the Lion is to display the objects recently excavated on the site and those which are now in the Archeological Museum in Nauplion.*

TOUR *about 3hr*

Acropolis

The hill (278m/912ft high) on which the Acropolis was built is defended to the north and south by two deep ravines. The Acropolis is triangular in shape and surrounded by ramparts (900m/2 953ft long). It housed the king, the royal family, the nobles and the palace guard. The town lay at the foot of the fortified acropolis. A few houses have been discovered below the acropolis on the left of the road.

★★ **Ramparts** – The "Cyclopean" fortifications date mostly from the 14C-13C BC; they are built of undressed stone and vary in thickness (3m–8m/10ft–26ft).

★★★ **Píli ton Leóndon** – The **Lion Gate**, which was the main entrance to the Acropolis, takes its name from the two wild animals sculpted on the huge monolithic pediment (3.90m/12ft 6in at the base, 3.30m/10ft 8in in height and 0.70m/2ft 3in in width). The animals, probably lionesses, have lost their heads which were most

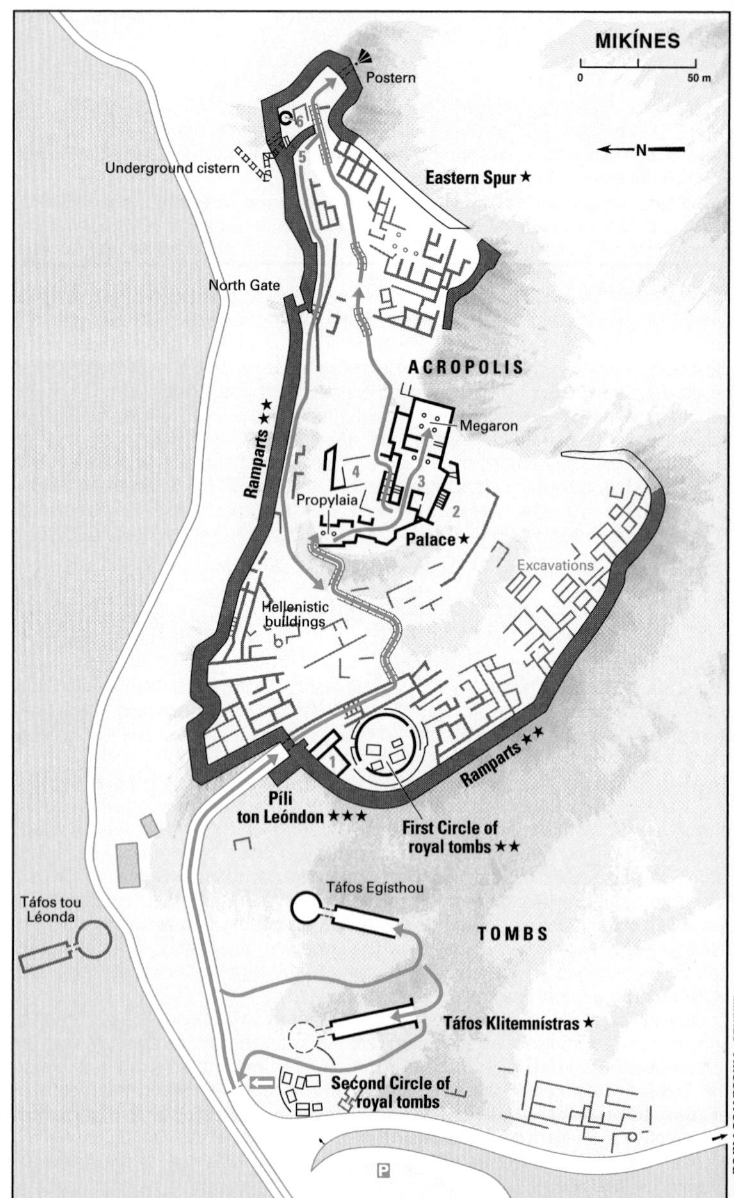

likely inlaid and facing the front; the animals are standing on either side of a central column, their front paws resting on a double altar which also supports the pillar and an entablature. This scene, which is Asiatic in inspiration, confronts the visitor from above the gateway, a symbol of Mycenaean power.

The gateway proper is flanked by two protective walls, the one on the right terminating in a tower. The entrance is 3.10m/10ft high and 2.95m/9ft 6in wide; the huge size of the constituent monolithic blocks is quite astonishing; the lintel itself measures 4.50m/nearly 15ft in length, 0.80m/over 2ft 6in in height and 1.98m/6ft 6in in depth and weighs over 20t. The wooden doors were reinforced by a bar which slotted into holes which are visible in the uprights.

Just over the threshold lay the porter's lodge *(left)* and the remains of a grain store (1) *(right)* where several carbonised grains of cereal were found in the bottom of some great jars.

★★ **First Circle of Royal Tombs** – On the right within the Lion Gate is the famous cemetery where Schliemann thought Agamemnon and his suite were buried but it is in fact much older (16C BC). Its circular outline is clearly marked by a double row of stones which formed a sort of palisade round the cemetery. It contained six shaft graves marked by *stele* decorated with low relief hunting scenes. The graves contained the bodies of 8 men, 9 women and 2 children accompanied by precious burial furnishings which are now displayed in the Athens Museum; the total weight of the golden articles reached 14kg/over 30lb.

From the First Circle of Tombs take the paved ramp, "the royal way", which leads from the imposing Lion Gate up to one of the entrances to the royal palace past an area covered by houses and depositories *(southwest)* which is still being excavated.

★ **Palace** – It dates from the 15C BC and consists of three blocks of buildings extending as far as the eastern spur of the site. The main western block contains the **megaron** which is fairly well preserved and the main stairs (2) comprising 18 steps.

The *propylaia* opened into the great courtyard (3) which was open to the sky. Beyond was a portico, a vestibule and the *megaron* itself, a royal chamber with a round hearth in the centre surrounded by four pillars (the bases are extant) supporting the roof; the floor was paved with slabs of gypsum and the walls were faced with stucco painted with decorative motifs in the Cretan style; the throne probably stood on the right.

The upper terrace of the palace has been altered by the later construction of a temple to Athena (4); only a few traces remain but there is a beautiful **view** of the site.

Visitors can either return to the Lion Gate or continue to the eastern spur of the site.

★ **Eastern Spur** – The remains of a later set of fortifications (5), dating from the 12C BC can be seen at this end of the fortress as well as an open cistern (6) from the Hellenistic period.

On the right a postern *(no access)* opens to the southeast. On the left is the entrance to an underground stair; its 99 steps bend round beneath the walls to a secret **cistern** 18m/59ft below; it was supplied with water from the Perseia spring which flowed in terracotta conduits.

Follow the inside of the north rampart to the North Gate (2.30m/7ft 6in high; 1.50m/5ft wide); the external approach is protected by a jutting section of wall from which the defenders of the citadel commanded the vulnerable side of their attackers, the right side of the body which is not protected by a shield. It is worth walking out through the gate for a few yards to get an overall view of the impressive ramparts.

Return into the citadel and take the path between the palace and the jumbled ruins of some Hellenistic buildings to regain the Lion Gate.

Tombs

About 50m/55yd from the Lion Gate.

Turn left down to the entrance to **Aigisthos' Tomb** (Táfos Egísthou) which dates from the 15C BC; the vault has fallen in.

Pass on to "Clytemnestra's Tomb".

★ **Táfos Klitemnístras** – 14C BC. A communal royal tomb beneath a dome, more recent than the shaft graves, known as **"Clytemnestra's Tomb"**. The path to the entrance (35m/38yd long and 5m/5.5yd wide) leads to a door (5.48m/18ft high) surmounted by a lintel made of enormous blocks of stone; the bases of the framing columns are still visible on either side.

The huge round funeral chamber (diameter 13.50m/44ft) is roofed with a dome *(recently reconstructed)* which reaches to 12.96m/42ft 6in above the floor. The lintel over the door is curved to follow the curve of the dome and extends on either side in a stone stringcourse.

Second Circle of Royal Tombs – 17C BC. The lefthand side of Clytemnestra's Tomb impinges on this second circle of tombs which was excavated in 1951 and is older than the circle discovered by Schliemann. Unfortunately the stone surround composed of huge blocks of limestone is in poor condition.
The second circle enclosed 24 graves, of which 14 were communal shaft graves; excavations have revealed important archeological material which is now displayed in the Athens Museum and include a remarkable rock crystal vase in the form of a duck.

Return to the car park and drive down the road to the entrance to the Treasury of Atreus (right).

Tomb of Clytemnestra, Mycenae

★★ **Treasury of Atreus or "Tomb of Agamemnon"** – 13C BC. This is the largest and the most beautiful of the nine communal beehive tombs which have been discovered to the west and southwest of the Acropolis of Mycenae. It was partially hewn out of the hillside and originally masked under a covering of earth; it is approached by a path 36m/39yd long and 6m/over 20ft wide.
The door (5.40m/nearly 18ft high) tapers towards the top and is framed by pilasters formerly preceded by two green marble half columns standing on bases which are still in position. The lintel is composed of two colossal blocks of stone: the one facing the interior is shaped to follow the curve of the dome and weighed about 120t. Resting on the lintel is a "relieving triangle" masked by a sculpted rectangular panel.
The majestic **funerary chamber** is 13.39m/44ft high and 14.60m/48ft in diameter. The skilful rows of stonework, each overlapping slightly towards the centre and cut away to form the conical vault, were ornamented with bronze rosettes and geometric motifs held in place with nails. A passage *(right)* (2.50m/over 8ft high) with another relieving triangle over the entrance, leads into a smaller rectangular chamber hollowed out of the rock; some think it was the funeral chamber of the head of the family; others that it was the treasury itself.

For adjacent sights see ARGOLÍDA, ÁRGOS, Aktí ARKADÍAS, EPÍDAVROS, ÍDRA, KÓRINTHOS, Dióriga KORÍNTHOU, LERNÍ, LOUTRÁKI, NÁFPLIO, NEMÉA, SIKIÓNA, SPÉTSES, STIMFALÍA, TÍRINTHA, TRÍPOLI.

*Admission times and charges for the sights described are listed at the end of the guide.
Every sight for which there are times and charges is identified by the symbol ⊙ in the Sights section of the guide.*

MISTRÁS★★★

MYSTRA – Lakonía, Peloponnese

Michelin map 980 north of fold 41

he ruins of Mystra occupy an exceptional **site★★★** on a steep spur of Mount Taígetos verlooking Sparta and the Evrótas (Eurotas) Valley. The Byzantine churches and nonasteries, the ruined palaces and houses testify to the former splendour of the ncient capital of the despotate of Morea.

HISTORICAL NOTES

ranco-Byzantine conflicts – The origins of Mystra seem to go back to the early 13C ut the famous fortress was not built until 1249 when William de Villehardouin *(see ALAMÁTA)* from Champagne in France, Prince of Morea and Duke of Achaia, began o construct "a superb castle, an impregnable stronghold" in the words of the *hronicle of Morea* so as to control the region of Lakonía. The site was well chosen: high bluff (621m/2037ft) commanding the Eurotas Valley and protecting it from nvasion by the Slav peoples living in the Taígetos mountains.

he Franks did not however hold Mystra for long. In 1259 **William de Villehardouin** was aptured in Macedonia at Pelagoniá by the soldiers of Michael VIII Palaiologos, the mperor of Byzantium, then reigning in Nicaea, who was to recapture Constantinople rom the Franks two years later. William was held prisoner for three years and regained is freedom only by ceding three fortresses to Michael: Monemvassía, the Great Maina nd Mystra.

nce free the Prince of Morea defeated the Byzantines near to Leondári and then noved south again into Lakonía but he was never able to recapture the fortress of Aystra below which a town was beginning to develop. Architectural elements from he abandoned Byzantine town of Lakedemonia (Sparta) were used in the buildings f the new town.

lorence of the Orient – At first Mystra was the seat of the Byzantine Governor of he province but in the 14C and 15C under the dynasties of the Kantakouzenos and alaiologos emperors it became the capital of the **despotate of Morea** which covered lmost the whole of the Peloponnese and was reserved for the younger sons or rothers of the Emperor. In this way the despots who ruled in Mystra included Manuel antakouzenos (1348-80), Theodore II Palaiologos (1407-43) and **Constantine alaiologos** (1443-49); the latter, who was crowned emperor at Mystra, died in 1453 vhile defending Constantinople against the Turks.

he despots made Mystra a centre of Hellenic politics and culture. As well as building hemselves a palace they arranged for the construction of many churches which combined the architectural formula of a cruciform plan beneath five domes with western eatures: detached belfries, apsidal chevets, extended naves, ogival arches and arcaded orches in the Cistercian style. The very skilful decoration usually took the form of rescoes instead of marbles and mosaics; the painting shows a striving for reality, novement and picturesque detail, attractive colouring and an expressive beauty which ontrasts with the hieratism of former works.

he intellectual life of Mystra was even more brilliant under the auspices of the cultivated emperors such as John VI Kantakouzenos and particularly Manuel II Palaiologos vho had spent two years in Paris.

leo-Platonic philosophy which promotes the good and the beautiful was propounded y **Manuel Chrysolorás**, "the sage of Byzantium" who had also taught in Florence in 1397 vhere he influenced the teacher Guarino da Verona and the architect Brunelleschi. n this sphere however the leading light was the humanist **Geórgios Gemistós Plethon**, the Renaissance Plato, who headed a school preaching the renewal of moral values, social eform and a religion in which Christian dogma is reinforced with the ancient myths nd the theories professed by Plato.

Plethon went to Florence in 1438 with Emperor John VIII to attend the Council which vas to prepare for the union of the Roman Catholic and Orthodox Churches; he so nspired his audience that Cosimo de' Medici decided to found an Academy of Platonism. Plethon died in Mystra in 1442 but his remains were removed in 1464 by Sigismond Malatesta, the "tyrant of Rimini" a mercenary leading an expeditionary force ent by Pope Pius II to try to drive the Turks from the Peloponnese.

Among the pupils of this great thinker one must mention **John Bessarion** (1402-72), a Greek who was trained in Mystra, spoke at the Council of Florence and was involved n the founding of the Academy of Platonism; as a Roman cardinal he preached a rusade against the Turks, failed to be elected pope and bequeathed his books to the Marciana Library in Venice.

Another Greek, **Constantine Láscaris**, a grammarian and philologist, went to Italy when he Byzantine empire fell and taught in Florence, Mantua and Milan, where in 1476 ne published *Erotemata* (questions), the first book printed entirely in Greek; he lived n Rome among Bessarion's followers and died in 1493 in Messinia (Sicily) where he neld a chair and taught Pietro Bembo. His brother, **John Láscaris** (1445-1534), was ibrarian to Lorenzo de' Medici and was appointed professor of Greek literature at the Sorbonne in Paris.

Turkish Yoke – When Mystra was surrendered to the infidels in 1460 by Demetrio Palaiologos, Emperor Constantine's brother, its churches were converted into mosque and the Despots' Palace became the residence of the Pasha.
The town however continued to thrive on the silk industry and in the 17C the inhabitants numbered 42 000.
From 1687 to 1715 Mystra was occupied by the Venetians; it was put to fire and the sword by the Russians under Count Orloff in 1770 and again by bands of Albanian ten years later; when **Chateaubriand** visited Mystra in 1806 the population had diminished to 8 000.
During the War of Independence the town was yet again pillaged and burned by the Egyptian troops of Ibrahim Pasha and afterwards it was abandoned in favour of the new town of Sparta which was founded in 1834.
The site was preserved from complete destruction by the French School of Archeology between 1896 and 1910 and was then studied by Gabriel Millet. More recently the Greeks have undertaken the restoration of monuments and frescoes.

TOUR *about 4hr (3hr excluding the castle)*

Prolific olive groves and plane trees line the road from Sparta which presents a very fine **view**★★ of Mystra, standing out like a white patch on the dark bulk of Mount Taígetos. Beyond Néa Mistrás, a pleasant flower-bedecked village *(hotel and restaurants, tavernas)*, rise the ruins of old Mystra *(restaurant Xénia)* widely scattered over the hillside.
The ancient city consisted of three distinct sections contained within their respective precincts: the castle *(kástro)* built by the de Villehardouin, the Upper Town for the aristocracy and the Lower Town where the citizens lived among the many churches. There are two entrances: one to the Lower Town through the main gate and one to the Upper Town which can be reached by taking the new road which skirts the site.

As the tour is tiring, particularly in the heat of high summer, it is best to start as early as possible.

★★1 Lower Town

The 14C defensive wall enclosed the Metropolitan Church (Cathedral), several churches and monasteries, elegant houses and craftsmen's workshops.
Enter through the little **fort** which marks the site of the old town gate and turn right towards the Metropolitan which one passes (view of the apse and belfry) in order to reach the main door.

★★**Mitrópoli** – The Metropolitan Orthodox cathedral of St Demetrios, which stands below street level, was founded c 1270 by Bishop Eugenios. The narthex was added in 1291 by the metropolitan Nikephoros who is however named as the founder of the church in an inscription on the wall of the stairway.
In the precinct there is a court with steps descending to the parvis of the cathedral; on the right a fountain decorated with the Byzantine eagle. The paving continues round the northeast side of the church into an 18C arcaded court overlooking the Evrótas Valley; the Roman sarcophagus decorated with a carving of a Bacchanalian revel and winged sphinxes was used as a basin for the Mármara Fountain *(see below)*.

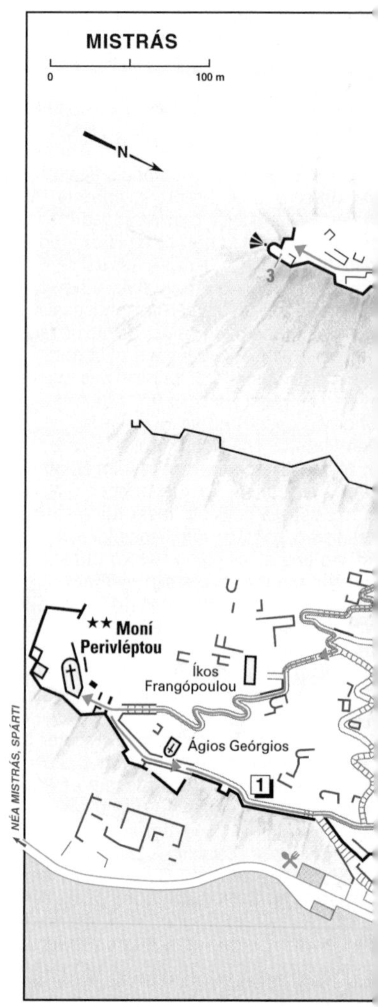

Church – It was built late in the 13C as a basilica with a central nave beneath a pitched roof and two vaulted side aisles. In the 15C Bishop Matthew reconstructed the upper part of the church on a cruciform plan with domes: in the nave the join between the 13C and 15C work is clearly visible and even accentuated by a sculpted frieze, below which are traces of earlier paintings which have been damaged.

The arcades in the nave rest on Byzantine capitals; the columns bear engraved inscriptions listing the privileges bestowed on the cathedral by the emperors. Part of the original marble paving with coloured inlay work has been preserved; set in the floor in front of the iconostasis is a stone bearing the crowned Byzantine eagle showing the place where Constantine Palaiologos is supposed to have been consecrated emperor of Byzantium in 1449. There are a few low relief sculptures (9C-11C) taken from the ruins of ancient Sparta; in the south aisle an unusual bishop's throne dating from the 17C.

The 13C-14C **frescoes**★ come from several sources; the painting on the south apse vault evokes the theme of the Preparation **(Hetoimasía)**: it shows an empty throne surmounted by the Byzantine cross symbolising the expectation of the second coming of Christ for the Last Judgement: the angels grouped on either side of the throne wear ecstatic expressions on their faces.

A Last Judgement in the narthex assembles several scenes: prominent are two admirable angels opening the records of Good and Evil. The north aisle is decorated with episodes in the martyrdom of St Demetrios. A majestic representation of the Virgin and Child fills the central apse.

Museum – *Partly closed for reorganisation.* The collection which was founded by Gabriel Millet is displayed in the old bishops' palace. Among the Byzantine sculptures are an Eagle seizing its prey (11C) and a Christ in Majesty (15C). There is

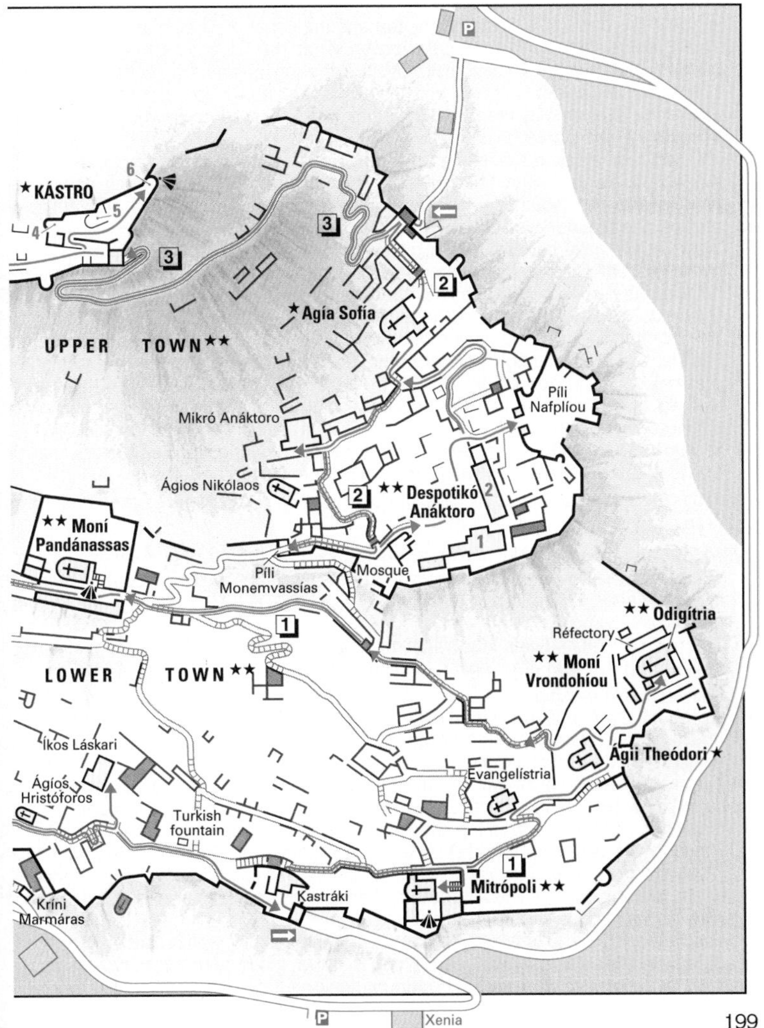

an inscription bearing the monogram of Isabeau de Lusignan, wife of Manuel Kantakouzenos and a member of the French family which had ruled in Cyprus. Further west along the street is the mortuary chapel of the **Evangelístria** (14C-15C); its well proportioned cruciform distyle structure stands in a little cemetery not far from the Brontocheion Monastery.

★★ **Moní Vrondohíou** – Within the walls of the Brontocheion Monastery are two great churches.

★ **Ágii Theódori – St Theodore's Church** was built on the cruciform plan late in the 13C; it has been heavily restored but the apse was originally faced with ceramic tiles. The dome which rests on a 16-sided tall drum is the most imposing feature both without and within where it is supported on eight pillars. The angles of the cruciform plan contain four funerary chapels, two of which *(east)* open into the arms of the transept, while the other two *(west)* open into the narthex which was added later.

★★ **Odigítria** – The **church** was dedicated to the Virgin, who shows the way, and is also known as the Afendikó (belonging to the Master) because it was built in the 14C by Pachomios, an important ecclesiastic in the Orthodox Church. Its architecture is a combination of the basilical plan with a nave and side aisles on the ground floor and the cruciform plan topped by domes in the upper storey, according to a design found only in Mystra.

The approach provides a spectacular view of the apse with triple windows, blind arches and the different roof levels. The bases and drums of columns suggest that the façade and sides of the church once boasted doorways like the Pandánassa *(see below)*. Both the church and the belfry have been restored.

The interior is decorated with remarkable **murals**★★ (14C) by several different artists. The narthex is decorated with the Miracles performed by Jesus (Healing of the Blind Man, the Samaritan at the Well, the Marriage in Cana): the flowing lines of the composition, the harmony of the colours and the introspective expressions suggest the hand of a great artist, perhaps the equal of Duccio and Giotto.

The funerary chapel *(restoration in progress)* at the far end of the narthex *(left)* contains the tombs of Pachomios, shown offering his church to the Virgin, and Theodore I Palaiologos, shown both as despot and as the monk he became at the end of his life; among the other paintings is a very well preserved Procession of Martyrs in red raiment.

The walls of a second chapel at the other end of the narthex are covered with inscriptions copied from "chrysobulls", the imperial decrees granting goods and privileges to the monastery; the vault is painted with four angelic caryatids supporting the mandorla of Christ.

Walk up the nave between the marble columns – the first on the right is capped by an elegant capital – to appreciate the luminous central space formed by the huge dome resting on pendentives, the polygonal drum, the corner domes and the *gynaecea* (galleries for women) over the narthex and side aisles.

The paintings on the ground floor, which were originally framed in coloured marble, are mostly effigies of saints; in the central apse are the saintly hieratic prelates: St Gregory of Nyssa, St Sylvester, St Basil, St John Chrysostom, St Gregory of Nazianzus etc. The brilliantly-coloured paintings in the galleries evoke the Resurrection and the Flight into Egypt; saints are portrayed on the walls *(access through the Chrysobulls Chapel)*. There are other paintings in the funerary chapels of the south aisle: the Dormition of the Virgin in the second chapel.

From the monastery precinct take the path leading uphill towards the Pandánassa Monastery.

★★ **Moní Pandánassas** – The **monastery** was founded by John Phrangopoulos, the chief minister of the Despotate, and dedicated to the Queen of the Universe *(Pandánassa)* in September 1428. It is now inhabited by a few nuns engaged in very fine embroidery work.

The main entrance leads into a narrow courtyard; on the left are the conventual cells; straight ahead are steps ascending to the church.

Church – This beautiful building is a combination of two plans: a three-aisled basilica surmounted by a six-domed cruciform design. The bell-tower and the lower part of the apses, where western Gothic influence is marked, date from the 14C, whereas the rest of the building is early 15C.

The main façade, which was originally embellished with a portico, is flanked by a superb Gothic belfry which shows French influence in the trefoil oculi, the Cistercian-style arches framing the triple arcades and the small corner towers.

Flanking the belfry on its other side is the elegant east portico roofed with four shallow domes; it is a charming place to pause and enjoy the magnificent **view**★★ of the Evrótas Valley. The southern façade is composed of three apses decorated with Gothic arches and emblazoned gables.

The first part of the interior of the church is the narthex which contains the tomb of Manuel Katzikis who died in 1445 and is shown in effigy on the wall. The church itself is decorated with **paintings**★ from various periods. The best, which are lively

and picturesque, date from the 15C: on the upper section of the central apse a majestic Virgin Platytera (with a medallion of the Birth of Christ) and an Ascension; in the left transept Christ's entry into Jerusalem (notice the small figures pulling off their cloaks); in the galleries scenes from the Life of Christ (unusual representation of Lazarus rising from the dead wrapped in a winding sheet).
Beyond the Pandánassa Church the path descends past the **house of Phrangopoulos** (Ikía Frangópoulou), which dates from 15C and has a balcony decorated with machicolations.

★★ **Moní Perivléptou** – This tiny **monastery** dates from the Frankish period (13C) but was altered in the 14C when the murals were executed.
The entrance to the precinct is an attractive arched gateway; over the arch is a low relief showing a row of fleurs-de-lys surmounted by the lions of Flanders flanking a circle containing the word *"perívleptos"* (which means "attracting attention from every side") in the form of a cross; this heraldic device and motto indicate the founder of the monastery, who was one of the first two Latin emperors of Constantinople, Baldwin of Flanders or his brother Henry.

Church – From the gateway there is a picturesque view of the church with its two external funerary chapels beyond which rises a 13C tower; the ground floor of this tower has been converted into a refectory. One is struck by the typically French look of the 13C chevet which is Romanesque with its three canted apses and the fleur-de-lys carved between two rose windows.
A door to the right of the chevet leads into the interior which is decorated with an exceptional series of 14C **murals**★★★ illustrating the New Testament and the Life of the Virgin. The harmonious composition, the expressive drawing and the variegated colouring of these scenes are as attractive as the movement of the figures and the picturesque detail:
- above the entrance door an admirable Dormition of the Virgin in which Christ is holding his mother's soul represented in the shape of a baby;
- in the central apse the Virgin in Majesty below and the Ascension above;
- in the right apse Christ sleeping, Peter's denial, Calvary;
- in the dome Christ Pantocrator surrounded by the Virgin and the Apostles; the empty throne symbolises the expectation of the Last Judgement *(Hetoimasía)*; below are the Prophets;
- on the arches framing the square base of the dome the Life of Christ including two very beautiful compositions representing the Nativity and the Baptism of Jesus.

The church is linked to the old monolithic **hermitage** which consists of a single chamber converted into a chapel and to St Catherine's Chapel, an early sanctuary surmounted by a belfry on the clifftop.
On leaving the Perívleptos Monastery take the path which passes **Ágios Geórgios**, a baronial funerary chapel dedicated to St George, and the entrance *(right)* to the Kríni **Marmáras**, which takes its name from a marble fountain, and **Ágios Hristoóforos** *(left)*, a funerary chapel dedicated to St Christopher.

Íkos Láskari – The **Lascaris House** is a fine example of a 14C patrician house which is thought to have belonged to the famous family which was related to the emperors of Byzantium and gave birth to the humanists, Constantine and John Láscaris *(see above)*. The vaulted chamber on the ground floor was probably the stables; a balcony decorated with machicolations looks out over the Eurotas Plain.

Return to the main entrance and drive up the hill to the Upper Town. Visitors without a car should walk up through the Monemvassía Gate and start at the Despots' Palace.

★★ 2 Upper Town

The Upper Town which gives access to the castle *(kástro)* is enclosed within 13C ramparts; there were two entrances: the Monemvassía Gate *(Píli Monemvassías – east)* and the Náfplio Gate *(Píli Nafplíou - west)*. Near the modern entrance from the upper car park stands Agía Sofía.

★ **Agía Sofía** – **St Sophia** was the palace church, founded in the 14C by the Despot Manuel Kantakouzenos, where the ceremonies of the Despotate were conducted and where Theodora Tocchi *(see KILÍNI)* and Cleophas Malatesta, the Italian wives of Constantine and Theodore Palaiologos, were buried.
The church is distinguished by its tall narrow proportions and by its spacious narthex which is roofed by a dome. It is flanked on two sides by porticoes and funerary chapels. Western influence is evident in the three-sided apses and in the detached bell-tower which echoes the Champagne style of architecture with its triple windows set within a round-headed arch; traces of an internal spiral staircase suggest that the tower was used as a minaret during the Turkish occupation.
In the interior beneath the dome there are fragments of the original multi-coloured marble floor. The most interesting murals are in the apse (Christ in Majesty) and in the chapel to the right (fine narrative scene of the Nativity of the Virgin).

St Sophia Church, Mystra

Mikró Anáktoro (Little Palace) – This is a huge house incorporating a corner keep with a balcony. For defensive reasons only the upper floors had windows; the vaulted ground floor was lit by loopholes.
After passing the 17C Church of St Nicholas (Ágios Nikólaos), the path reaches the **Monemvassía Gate** (Píli Monemvassías). Turn back uphill past the ruins of a mosque into the open square in front of the Despots' Palace where the market was held during the Turkish occupation.

★★ Despotikó Anáktoro – *Closed to the public for restoration.* The **Despots' Palace** consists of two wings, set nearly at a right angle to one another; the northeast wing dates from the 13C-14C, the northwest from the 15C.

Northeast wing (1) – The building at the east end dates from the 13C and was probably built either by the Franks or by the first Byzantine governors. Its structure and the pointed window arches suggest western Gothic influence; under the Despots it was probably used as a guardroom. Next in the range come two smaller buildings; the more northerly contained the kitchens serving the earlier building. The last building in this range is a great structure with several storeys (late 14C). It was designed as the residence of Manuel Kantakouzenos with six rooms on each floor and a chapel. The north façade sports an elegant porch supporting a balcony decorated with machicolations overlooking the Lakonian plain.

Northwest wing (2) – This wing consists of an imposing three storey building constructed by the Palaiologi early in the 15C.
The lowest floor which is partially underground is faced on the courtyard side by a row of round-headed arches supporting a terrace which provided access to the eight separate vaulted chambers on the middle floor. The top floor consisted of an immense hall, for receptions and entertainment (36m/118ft long by 10.50m/34ft 6in high). This chamber was lit by eight Gothic windows with stucco mouldings beneath eight round oculi and was heated by eight huge chimneys. The throne stood in the centre of the east wall in a shallow alcove.
Turn right at the south end of the wing down to the **Nauplion Gate** (13C) for a fine external view of the ramparts before returning to the modern entrance.

★ 3 Kástro (Castle)

A steep and winding path (steps) leads up from the modern entrance to the Kástro (45min on foot there and back).

The plan of the original castle with its circuit walls and towers goes back to the 13C and its founder de Villehardouin but the structure was much altered by the Byzantines, the Venetians and the Turks. William II de Villehardouin and his wife Anna Comnena *(see KALAMÁTA)* held court there in grand style surrounded by knights from Champagne, Burgundy and Flanders.
The fortress consists of two baileys. The entrance to the first is guarded by a vaulted gateway flanked by a stout square tower; the southeast corner of the bailey is marked by an underground cistern and a huge round tower (3) which gives impressive **views★★** of the ravine facing Mount Taígetos.

The inner bailey *(northwest)* contained the baronial apartments (4) *(left on entering)*, another cistern and the castle chapel (5) of which only traces remain. The ruined tower (6) on the highest point provides spectacular **views**★★ down into the many gullies in the wild slopes of Mount Taïgetos where the ancient Spartans hurled their malformed babies; in the other direction lie the ruins of Mystra, modern Sparta and the Evrótas plain.

For adjacent sights see Spílea DIROÚ, GERÁKI, GÍTHIO, ITHÓMI, KALAMÁTA, MÁNI, MEGALÓPOLI, MESSINIAKÓS Kólpos, MONEMVASSÍA, SPÁRTI.

MONEMVASSÍA★★

Lakonía, Peloponnese – Population 78

Michelin map 980 folds 41 and 42

Approaching Monemvassía can feel like reaching the world's end. This silent partially ruined medieval fortified town is half hidden in a slight depression on the southern face of a steep rock which stands just offshore creating a particularly spectacular **site**★★★.

"The only entrance" – The rock (300m/984ft high) is linked to the mainland by a narrow causeway and a bridge and takes its name from the Greek words *móni emvassía* meaning "only entrance".

Monemvassía was fortified by the Byzantines against the Slav invasions but in 1248 after a three year blockade it fell into the hands of William de Villehardouin. The Franks repaired the castle but in 1263 William was obliged to return it to Michael VIII Palaiologos as part of his ransom.

Under the Despotate of Morea *(see MISTRÁS)* the Byzantines maintained an active trading port at Monemvassía which was on the route to Constantinople. In 1460 the town passed into the hands of the Pope for four years before becoming a Venetian possession. In 1540 it was captured by the Turks who held it until 1821 except for a brief period between 1690 and 1715 when it was retaken by the Venetians. During its time as a Venetian possession, when it was known as Malvasia or Napoli di Malvasia, Monemvassía was an important trading port and port of call in the Levant. The town was protected by a fortified bridge (163m/535ft long) carried on 13 arches which could be breached in time of danger, by a castle on the top of the rock and by a circuit wall which descended from the top of the hill, swung round along the seafront and up the hill again thus enclosing the town on three sides. In those days the population numbered 30 000 and was served by about 40 churches.

Throughout the Middle Ages and on into the 19C Monemvassía exported Malmsey wine (known in French as Malvoisie as was the town too), a sweet white wine, produced mostly in the Aegean islands as well as locally, which was very popular in England. When the Duke of Clarence *(see KILÍNI)* was condemned to death by his brother Edward IV in 1477, he elected to be drowned in a butt of Malmsey wine. In 1909 the Greek poet Yánnis Rítsos *(see p 48)* was born in Monemvassía.

PRACTICAL INFORMATION

Access – In spite of being in continental Greece, Monemvassía is difficult to get to by road. It is quicker to take the hydrofoil from Piraeus which goes to Kíthira two or three times a week (Ceres Group ☎ (01) 42 80 001 in Piraeus, or (0732) 61 219 in Monemvassía).

Accommodation – The main hotels (about 15 cat A to E) and restaurants are in Géfira on the mainland. In the Kástro or Old Town 2 hotels (cat A) and furnished accommodation to let in many old houses.

Transport – Taxis from Géfira to the entrance to the Kástro (old town), where vehicles are banned; 30min on foot from Géfira to the Kástro.

★★**Kástro** – This forms the **old** or **lower town.** First there is the causeway – the "only entrance" – and the West Gate into the town which is a vaulted chicane; both it and the walls date from the Despotate but were repaired by the Venetians. Walk up the main street between the ancient houses to the main square.

Platía Dzamíou – This charming square extends southwards into a terrace graced by an 18C cannon and the observation hole of an underground cistern. On the east side stands the **Church of Christ in Chains** (Hrístos Elkomenós), a former cathedral which was founded in the 12C by the Byzantines and rebuilt late in the 17C by the Venetians; note the detached bell-tower, as in Italy, and the symbolic peacocks carved in low relief on a piece of Byzantine sculpture which has been reused in the façade. Opposite is a small local **museum** ⊙; it is housed in a late 10C building, formerly a church dedicated to St Paul, which the Turks converted into a mosque (Paleó Dzamí).

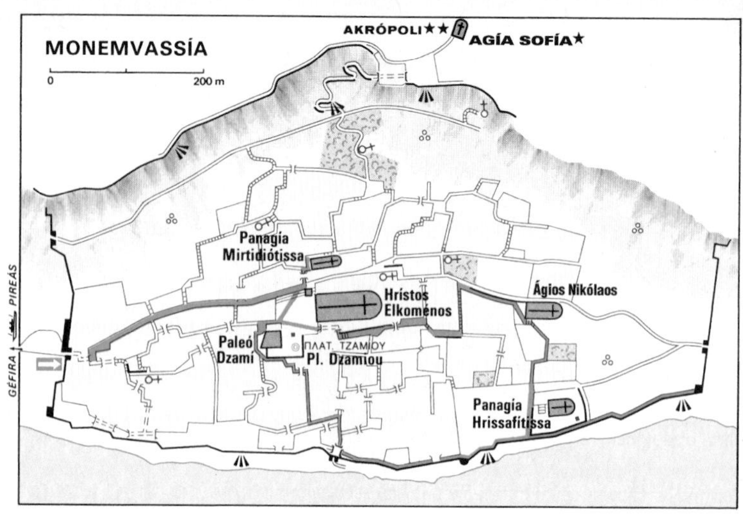

Southern Rampart – From Dzamiou square walk down to the ramparts along the seafront and follow them eastwards. There are extensive views of the sea and the Peloponnese coast south towards Cape Malea; a postern gate gives access to the rocks where it is possible to swim.

Panagía Hrissafítissa – The façade of this 16C church looks very Venetian with its framed doorway surmounted by an oculus; the open space in front was used as a parade ground. Near the ramparts stands a tiny chapel built over the "sacred spring"; it contains an icon from Chrysapha (Hrísafa) near Sparta.
It is worth pursuing the sentry walk to the corner bastion; return and descend to ground level to visit **St Nicholas'** (Ágios Nikólaos) which has a 16C Venetian doorway. Return to Dzamiou square past several Venetian houses: door and window mouldings, flamboyant recesses and broad mouthed chimneys.

Panagía Mirtidiótissa – This little church, which is up a steep rise, seems to belong to the Frankish period (13C); the façade frames a doorway surmounted by an oculus in the Venetian style. It was once a commandery belonging to the Templars and then to the Knights of St John of Jerusalem, as is shown by the sculpted escutcheon bearing the distinctive eight-pointed cross of Pierre d'Aubusson *(see RHODES: Knights of Rhodes).*

Monemvassía

A. Arnaud /APPARENCE

★★ **Akrópoli** – Originally the citadel covered a wide area, amounting almost to a town on its own; the fortifications are for the most part Venetian (16C).
Visitors who cannot climb all the way to the Citadel are advised to go half way up, if possible, for a very fine **view**★★ of the lower town.
A vaulted passage in the fortified entrance emerges into an open space; take the path leading north up the hill to the church of St Sophia.

★ **Agía Sofía** – St Sophia, the principal church of the citadel, is a large Byzantine church built on the edge of the cliff with a vertiginous **view**★★★ of the sea below. The building *(recently restored)* probably dates from the 11C (capitals, low reliefs); it may have been occupied by Cistercians for a while during the Frankish occupation and was refurbished during the Despotate of Morea (14C-15C).
The church is built to a homogenous quadrangular plan with a narthex and an impressive dome supported on squinches. There are some unusual early Byzantine capitals in shallow relief, Byzantine marble carvings over the doors in the narthex and traces of murals.
There is a rough path leading to the **highest point** on the rock overlooking the isthmus and the mountains to the west; at its eastern end the rock is shaped like the prow of a ship pointing out to sea.
Return to the main gate and follow the sentry walk westwards to reach the highest point along the circuit wall: splendid **views**★★ of the old town and the coast.
For adjacent sights see Spílea DIROÚ, GERÁKI, GÍTHIO, KALAMÁTA, KÍTHIRA, MÁNI, MESSINIAKÓS Kólpos, MISTRÁS, SPÁRTI.

NÁFPAKTOS

NAUPAKTOS – Akarnanía, Central Greece – Population 10 854
Michelin map 980 north of fold 28

This charming little city at the northwest end of the Gulf of Corinth was fortified by the Venetians in the 15C. Under its medieval name of Lepanto it recalls the famous naval battle which took place in 1571 off Missolonghi. *Pleasant beach.*

The Battle of Lepanto (7 October 1571) – The battle, the last and greatest in which oar-propelled vessels were engaged, took place in the Bay of Patras to the leeward of Oxiá Island where the Christian fleet which had sailed from Cephallonia met the Turkish fleet from Lepanto. The fleet of the Holy League was made up of contingents from the Papal States, Spain, Genoa, Naples, Malta and Venice under the command of **Don John of Austria** (1547-78), the bastard son of Charles V and then 23 years old. The Turkish fleet of Sultan Selim was commanded by Ali Pasha and consisted of 200 galleys armed, as were the Christian ships, with from 5 to 7 cannon firing forward; some of the galleys came from Egypt and Algiers. In both fleets the majority of the sailors and galley slaves were Greek.
The 12 Venetian galleys, which formed the advance guard of the Christian fleet, were led by Don John holding a crucifix aloft. They were huge ships, with a castle at either end, fitted with about 15 cannon firing laterally; they carried 750 men of whom half manned the oars. They wrought havoc among the Turkish fleet most of which was destroyed. It was a severe blow to Turkish sea power.
The battle, in which Cervantes, the author of Don Quixote, lost the use of his left hand, was the subject of many paintings by celebrated artists: Titian, Tintoretto, Veronese...; it also inspired some verses: *The Lepanto*, written by James I and printed in Edinburgh in 1591 and *Lepanto* a ballad by G K Chesterton (1911).

Harbour – The entrance to the oval basin is protected by two towers fortified with crenellations and merlons. From the parapet walk there are views of the town and the citadel half hidden in greenery and of the Peloponnese across the gulf.

Citadel – *Access from the west of the town by a narrow tarred road which climbs up through the pine trees.*
The Venetian fortress, which is well preserved, dates from the Middle Ages; its walls extend downhill to link it with the harbour; other walls built laterally divide the town into compartments, each one forming a keep.
From the top there are **views**★ of the town and the straits; to the east lies an alluvial plain created by the material deposited by the River Mórnos.
For adjacent sights see DELFÍ, HLEMOÚTSI, ITHÁKI, KALÁVRITA, KEFALONÍA, KILÍNI, MÉGA SPÍLEO, MESSOLÓNGI, PÁTRA, THÍVA, Harádra tou VOURAÏKOÚ, ZÁKINTHOS.

NÁFPLIO★★

NAUPLION – Argolis, Peloponnese – Population 11 897

Michelin map 980 fold 29

Náfplio occupies a delightful **situation★★★** on a rocky peninsula projecting into the calm waters of the Argolic Gulf. It is a charming old town dominated by the citadel Acronauplia and the powerful Venetian fort of Palamedes. Náfplio is a pleasant place to stay and an excellent centre for excursions into the Argolid. Mediterranean cruise liners often drop anchor in the sheltered roadstead and harbour.

HISTORICAL NOTES

Palamedes the inventor – Palamedes, whose father was Nauplios, the legendary founder of Nauplion and Poseidon's grandson, was looked upon as the king of the inventors by the ancient Greeks who attributed to him the invention of the order of the Greek alphabet introduced by the Phoenician Cadmos *(see THÍVA)*, lighthouses, money, weights and measures and military tactics. They also considered him to be as great a doctor as he was a distinguished astronomer.

Palamedes is said to have been at the siege of Troy and to have invented the games of dice and draughts to distract the besiegers in their long wait. He was killed by Odysseus and Diomedes who were jealous of his ingenious abilities.

The Lion of St Mark – Náfplio passed from the Byzantines to the Franks in 1247; at first it was a fief belonging to **Otto de la Roche** and the Duke of Athens before passing to the Enghien family and descending through the female line via Marie d'Enghien to her Venetian husband, Pietro Cornaro, who transferred his rights over Náfplio to Venice.

From 1388 to 1540 Náfplio was held by the Venetians who fortified the city and Boúrdzi Island. They held out against the Turks until 1540 when Turkish forces occupied the region and made Náfplio capital of Morea. The new rulers neglected the defences but in the 17C the town, together with Chios, was one of the main centres of trade with the West: silk, leather goods, wool, wax and cheeses.

In 1686 however Náfplio was recaptured by Venetian troops under **Francesco Morosini**, who also laid siege to Athens and Heraklion in Crete. For 30 years under Morosini and his successors Náfplio was involved in great activity: new fortifications particularly at the **Palamedes Fort** by French engineers, Lasalle and Levasseur, new churches (St George's and St Nicholas'), new administrative and commercial buildings (warehouses), urban development and the influx of more people from elsewhere. As the capital of Morea and the chief town of Romania, which comprised Náfplio, Árgos, Corinth and Tripoli, Náfplio then became known as **Napoli di Romania**.

This period of prosperity came to an end in 1715 with the return of the Turks whose army of 100 000 men recaptured Náfplio after a siege which cost them 8 000 lives. Pillage, massacre and deportations followed.

Náfplio capital of Greece – When the War of Independence began in 1821, the Greek fleet, including the illustrious **Bouboulína** *(see SPÉTSES)* in command of a corvette, had been blockading the harbour since the previous year. Three times the city repulsed the attackers but on 30 November 1822 **Staïkópoulos** with 350 men captured the Palamedes Fort and Náfplio was liberated from the Turks.

The city then became the centre of the struggle against the Turks. In 1827 English, French and Russian naval forces assembled offshore before attacking the Ottoman fleet at the Battle of Navarino. On 7 January 1828 **John Kapodístrias** *(see KÉRKIRA)*, the first Governor of Greece, installed his government in Náfplio and the city officially became the capital of Greece in the following year. The new administration, the foreign legations, the groups of Philhellenes, the troops and passing naval squadrons caused much excitement.

Unfortunately however bitter dissension developed among the Greeks and on 27 September 1831 Kapodistrias was assassinated on the steps of St Spiridon's Church by his political opponents who accused him of being a Russian agent. The Great Powers, England, France and Russia, turned to the son of King Ludwig I of Bavaria, **Otto of Bavaria**, who was 17 years old; his accession to the throne was ratified in 1832 by a National Assembly held in **Prónia**, the new suburb designed and commissioned by Kapodistrias.

Otto arrived in Náfplio on 18 January 1833 with his Council of Regents, 3 500 Bavarian soldiers and an embryonic court. During his stay **Kolokotrónis**, one of the chiefs of the Resistance, was condemned to death for disobedience to the established authority but the fierce soldier, the "old man of Morea", was reprieved and imprisoned only briefly in the Palamedes Fort.

In the autumn of 1834 the capital of the new kingdom was transferred to Athens. Otto's reign was marked by the construction of neo-Classical buildings with projecting balconies; the sober lines of the architecture give the city its aristocratic character. A colossal lion carved out of the rockface in Prónia commemorates the sacrifice of the Bavarian soldiers who fell in the Greek cause. There are other monuments and inscriptions recalling the heroic days of newly won independence.

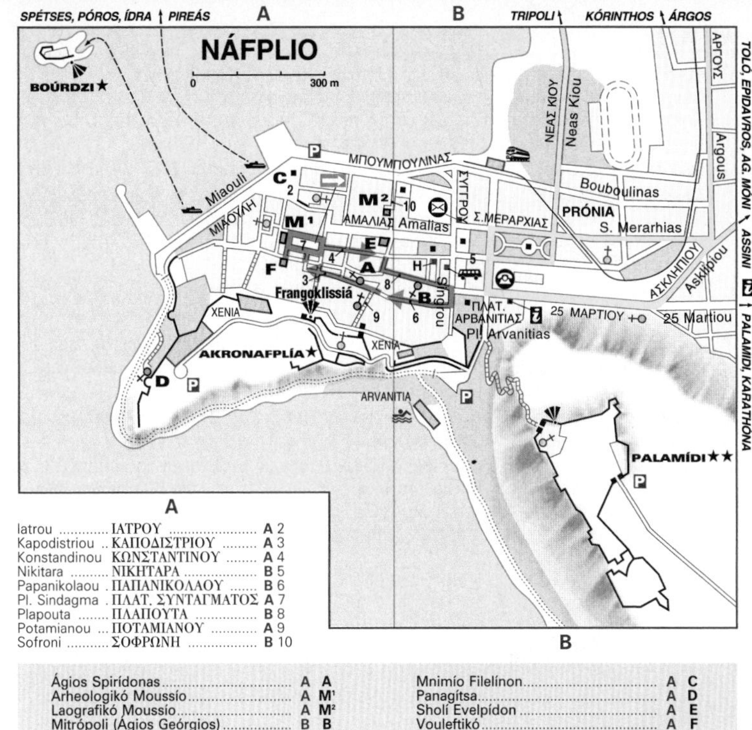

PRINCIPAL SIGHTS *1 day*

★★ Palamídi ⓥ – *Access by Leofóros 25 Martíou and the road leading to the east entrance or by 857 steps starting from Platía Arvanitiás.*

The **Palamedes Fort** was built on top of a hill, 216m/709ft above sea level. It dates from the second Venetian occupation (1686-1715) and is a powerful complex of eight bastions linked by defilades, vaults, corridors and secret passages. It is well protected by watch towers and embrasures for guns and cannon. Each bastion was designed to be self-sufficient and able to survive on its own if the neighbouring bastions were captured by the enemy.

The parapet walk provides magnificent **views** of Náfplio, the bay, the Argolid plain and the coastline of the Peloponnese.

One of the bastions, near the southeast gate, contains a splendid cistern; St Andrew's bastion enclosed a courtyard overlooked by the quarters of the Governor of the Fort and by St Andrew's Chapel which is near the cell in which Kolokotrónis was detained.

★★ Old Town – *Itinerary shown on the plan starting from Platía Síndagma.*

Platía Síndagma – This square is the centre of Náfplio and the political forum during the struggle for independence, now named after the Constitution (Síndagma). From here there is a view of Palamedes Fort on its hill.

At the west end of the square stands a naval warehouse built in 1713 by the Venetians and now converted into a museum while the cinema opposite was once a mosque.

In the southwest corner of the square, set back behind the Bank of Greece, is a flight of steps leading to another former mosque which is known by the Naupliots as the **Parliament** because it held the first meeting of the Greek National Assembly in 1822. It was also used for the session of the court which condemned Kolokotrónis, the "old man of Morea", to death in 1834.

From the centre of the east side of the square take Odós Konstandínou, a busy shopping street; turn right and left into Odós Plapoúta.

Ágios Geórgios – St George's Cathedral was built in the 16C in a mixture of styles: Byzantine domes and Venetian arcades and campanile; the interior contains the throne of King Otto.

Turn right into Leofóros Singroú and return to the old town by Odós Papanikoláou, a narrow street crossed by steep lanes leading up to the Acronauplia. One of these lanes on the left (Odós Potamianou) leads to the Frankish Church.

Frangoklissiá – A flight of steps and an attractive 13C porch lead up to the **Frankish Church** which was formerly the conventual chapel of a monastery built during the Frankish occupation. It was later converted into a mosque and then reverted to a Roman Catholic church dedicated to the Transfiguration.

Inside flanking the entrance stands a **Memorial to the Philhellenes**, who fell in the Greek War of Independence; it was erected on the initiative of a French Philhellene, Colonel Touret. Byron, Hastings and Church are among those named. Behind the high altar is the muslim prayer recess *(mihrab)*.

Return down Odós Potamianou to St Spiridon's Church near a Turkish fountain.

Ágios Spirídonas (**A E**) – **St Spiridon's** is a tiny Orthodox church built in 1702 by the Venetians. Here on the threshold two members of the Mavromichalis family from the Máni assassinated Kapodistrias, who had imprisoned one of them, **Petrobey Mavromihális** *(see MÁNI)* (picture inside the church).

Continue along Odós Kapodistríou past another Turkish fountain and return to Constitution Square.

★★**Seafront** – *About 2hr on foot.* Starting from Platía Nikitará *(northwest corner)*, take Leofóros Amalías; *no 29* (**A F**) is the house where the first school for Greek officers was founded in 1829.

Turn right into Odós Sofróni which passes the Folklore Museum before reaching the waterfront (Aktí Bouboulínas).

Harbour – It extends on both sides of Platía Iatroú, a square containing the Town Hall, St Nicholas' Church for sailors (early 18C) and the French **Philhellene Monument** (**A K**), a marble pyramid erected in 1903 "in recognition of Marshal Maison, General Fabvier, Admiral de Rigny and French soldiers and sailors...". Views of the fortified Isle of Boúrdzi.

The western waterfront (Aktí Miaoúli) which is lined by fish tavernas continues into a path which skirts the ramparts and the headland providing very fine views of the bay. Just short of the southern tip of the promontory a path *(left)* leads up to the **Chapel of the Little Virgin** (Panagítsa) (**A L**) clinging precariously to the rocky slope; during the Turkish occupation it contained one of the "secret schools".

Continue along the coastal path to Arvanitía, Náfplio's beach; then make for Platía Nikitará.

ADDITIONAL SIGHTS

★**Akronafplía (Citadel of Acronauplia)** (**A**) – *Access on foot by one of the steep lanes leading off Odós Potamianou; by car by the road from Arvanitiá which skirts the Venetian bastion where the Hotel Xenia stands.*

First a Greek (traces of polygonal construction) and then a Frankish fortress were built on Acronauplia (alt 86m/282ft). The final and major structure, which until recently housed a hospital, barracks and prisons, was built by the Venetians; it consists of several wards with the lion of St Mark over the gates.

From the walls there is a fine view down over the city, the harbour and the bay and up to the Palamedes Fort.

★**Isle of Boúrdzi** ⓥ (**A**) – During the last century the public executioner of Náfplio lived on the island. It was first fortified in 1471 by the Venetians to protect the harbour entrance and was reinforced early in the 18C; the chief defence is a strong polygonal tower topped by a gun platform.

R. Cuzin/MICHELIN

Boúrdzi Island, Náfplio

★**Laografikó Moussío** ⓥ (**A M**[2]) – The well-presented display in the Ethnographical Museum includes not only a remarkable collection of costumes from the Peloponnese but also documents concerned with life in past centuries.

Arheologikó Moussío ⓥ (**A M**[1]) – An old Venetian warehouse, built in 1713 and later used as a barracks, now houses the **Archeological Museum**; the most interesting collections are of rare neolithic pottery and Archaic art found during excavations in the Argolid: bronze cuirasses, vases decorated in an oriental style, a fresco known as "the lady of Mycenae" and some astonishing idols found at Mycenae. *Some of the finds from Mycenae are to be transferred to a new museum at Mycenae.*

EXCURSIONS

★★**Karathóna Bay and Beach** – *3km/2mi south. Access by car by the road marked Palamídi from which a secondary road branches off to the bay. Plans for a seaside resort.*
A gently curving bay protected by an island encloses a huge sandy beach backed by a wood of eucalyptus trees. From the neighbouring heights, views of Palamedes Fort and the Acronauplia.

★**Toló** – *12km/7.5mi southeast. From Náfplio take the Epídavros road; after 1.5km/1mi turn right into a narrow road (sign "Agía Moní").*

Agía Moni ⓥ – The monastery was founded in 1144 near the Kánathos Spring *(on the right below the convent)* which in mythology was supposed to return Hera to a state of virginity once a year. There is a guided tour by the monks of the 12C Byzantine church.

Return to the Epídavros road and continue for 2km/1.25mi. Turn right into the road to Toló and before reaching the coast turn left into the road to Drépano which passes a chapel near the Assíni acropolis.

Assíni (Asine) – The acropolis of the ancient city, which was mentioned by Homer in the **Iliad**, was excavated from 1922 to 1930 by Swedish archeologists among whom was the future king of Sweden, Gustave VI: remains of ramparts which are part Mycenaean and Archaic (polygonal construction) and part Hellenistic. Huge beehive tombs have yielded many Mycenaean objects.
From the top very fine **views**★★ of Toló and the citrus orchards in the coastal plain.

★**Toló** ⓥ – Toló is a pleasant seaside resort sheltered by the Assíni promontory at the end of a long sandy beach with the islands of Rómvi and Platía offshore.

Agía Triáda – *8km/5mi north. Take the Árgos road; immediately after the site of Tiryns (Tírintha) turn right into a minor road which runs through orange groves in the direction of Midéa.*

After 4km/2.5mi, on the left just before the village of Agía Triáda, is the 12C **church of the Virgin** (Kimisseos tis Theotókou) which includes elements from ancient monuments at the base and has been remodelled; it is behind a cemetery. The village was previously known as Mérbaka after Wilhelm van Moerbeke, a Fleming who was archbishop of Corinth in 1280 during the Frankish occupation and was the first to translate Aristotle.

For adjacent sights see ARGOLÍDA, ÁRGOS, Aktí ARKADÍAS, EPÍDAVROS, ÍDRA, KÓRINTHOS, Dióriga KORÍNTHOU, LERNÍ, LOUTRÁKI, MIKÍNES, NEMÉA, SIKIÓNA, SPÉTSES, STIMFALÍA, TÍRINTHA, TRÍPOLI.

NEMÉA★

Korinthía, Peloponnese
Michelin map 980 fold 29

Neméa is best known for Herakles' first "labour"; in a nearby cave Herakles surprised and strangled the fierce Nemean lion and dressed himself in its skin. The legend may have some basis in fact as there were lions in the region in the Mycenaean period (shown by representations of lion hunts on items found at Mycenae).
In the Archaic and Classical periods the Nemean Games, which were celebrated by Pindar in his odes, were one of the four great Games held in the Greek world. According to tradition they were founded by Herakles whose victory was honoured in conjunction with the glory of Nemean Zeus.
Nowadays the reputation of modern Neméa rests on its red wine, which is strong and sweet and known locally as "the blood of Herakles".

Access – *Coming from Corinth on the Corinth-Trípoli expressway, take the Neméa exit at the interchange, and about 1km/0.5mi before the town turn right (signpost). Continue for 5km/3mi and after passing through the village of Arhéa Neméa take a small road to the left (signpost not visible); the ruins are about 300m/330yd further on, hidden behind a screen of trees shading the car park.*

★**Ruins** ⏱ – The ruins lie in a valley bordered by Mount Kilíni *(west)* and the mountains of Argolis and Arcadia *(south)*.

The largest remains belonged to a huge peripteral **temple** (6 by 12 columns) built in the Doric style in the 4C BC and dedicated to Zeus. The *naós* is unusual in having Corinthian columns and a crypt. Three columns belonging to the temple are still standing and round the edge are the displaced drums of other columns. The centre of the façade is marked by a ramp; in front stood an immense sacrificial altar, narrow and elongated. Formerly a grove of sacred cypress trees ringed the sanctuary which was surrounded by buildings including nine houses *(oikoi)* on the south side built by the various states as lodgings for their representatives during the Games.

To the north there was a number of potters' ovens *(now reburied)* from the end of the 4C BC. The thermal baths from the same period *(recently laid bare and roofed over for protection)* consisted of two covered underground rooms, reached by stairs lined with columns. The room housing the baths was divided into three parts, the main part containing the swimming and stone baths. A "hotel" (20x80m/66x262ft) has also been discovered beside the main road running through the sanctuary.

South of the temple are some ancient remains which were converted by the Byzantines into a church with a semicircular apse. To the south of this, one of the 200 tombs in the cemetery has been found and reconstructed.

★★**Museum** – *Inside the site.* In the entrance hall: documents about the excavations conducted between 1880 and 1912: engravings, drawings and photographs of the site in the 19C; travellers' descriptions.

In the main gallery: rich collection of local coins (6C-3C BC), vases, sculptures, bronzes and jewellery from the Mycenean period found in the area around Neméa. In the corner of the room, a beautiful **funerary tablet** from the early 5C BC, recently found close to the site, shows a man standing beside a seated woman carved in flat relief *(on the left and at the back in relation to the entrance)*. Photographs record the excavations and locate where the objects were found. Exhibition of drawings and photographs of the ceramics depicting the athletic competitions. A model shows the site and the sanctuary as they were in the 4C BC.

In the internal courtyard there is an interesting display of architectural fragments.

Treasure of Aïdonia – This collection, which has been in the United States for a long time, should be on permanent display in the Neméa museum from March 1999. The excavations in the Aïdonia cemetery brought to light a collection of 312 precious objects of very fine quality in the Creto-Mycenean style. The treasure comprises two signet rings with wide flat stone settings, one with a picture of a chariot while the second features two women carrying flowers; three rings, two of gold and one of electrum, an alloy of gold and silver highly regarded in antiquity; seals composed of agate, haematite, glass, cornelian and steatite; gold ornaments for clothing; gold and bronze pendants; and necklaces with pearls mounted on gold, or made of other materials such as semi-precious stones, earthenware, glass or amber in a great variety of shapes.

The items represented are generally religious scenes (especially processions), but also animals.

The collection also includes pottery dating from the 15C to 13C BC, ceramic vases (mostly closed), pots, stoneware jars, cups and rhytons, as well as a large number of painted terracotta figurines from the same period but in different styles; of the Tau type (with arms crossed on the chest), of the Psi type (with arms open like wings as if in prayer) or of the Phi type (with a torso as flat as board); there are also naturalistic figurines including the **kourothrophous** (breast-feeding mother).

Stadium – *Turn left where the road from the ruins comes out, then left again at the next junction; the stadium is 100m/110yd further on, on the right, before a bend.* In the hillside 500m/550yd southeast of the Temple of Zeus, remnants of the stadium (4C BC) have been found where the Nemean Games took place. It was able to hold 40 000 spectators, being 22m/73ft wide at each end, 27m/89ft wide in the centre, and 177m/584ft long.

South of the arena, earthenware pipes (part of one is exhibited in the museum) supplied the stadium with spring water, purified in a system of basins forming an integral part of the stone gutters running round the arena. The starting line, marked with stones, is well preserved; it supported the wooden mechanism which gave the starting signal. Thirteen lanes were provided for the runners. The competitors, trainers and judges entered the stadium through a building whose interior was decorated with colonnades on three of its sides. It was here too that the athletes got ready for the competition, before entering the arena through a **vaulted passage** 36m/119ft long (c 320 BC). The names of some of the winners and young athletes are clearly legible on the walls. On 1 June 1996 the Society for the Revivial of the Nemean Games organised an international meeting with competitors taking part from 28 countries; the next one will be on 3 and 4 June 2000.

EXCURSION

Aïdónia – *7km/4.5mi from Neméa in the direction of Stimfalía. Entering the modern village, take the first road on the right, then after 300m/330yd turn right again (signpost).* The Mycenean necropolis on the little hill to the east of the modern village dates from between the 16C and 13C BC. The excavations took place from 1978 to 1980 and in 1986. The 20 tombs that were opened yielded a collection of precious objects known as the **Treasure of Aïdónia** dating from the 15C to the 13C BC. 19 of the tombs take the form of burial chambers cut out of the rock, while the 20th is a rectangular grave. Some of the tombs open onto a small adjoining room, and most are approached along a sloping corridor which comes out in a monumental façade. Many of the tombs were pillaged and the treasure was to have been sold in New York, but the Greek government took action to enable its identification and return to Greece, so that it can be now be displayed in the museum by the ruins of Neméa.

For adjacent sights see ÁRGOS, EPÍDAVROS, KALÁVRITA, KÓRINTHOS, Dióriga KORÍNTHOU, LERNÍ, LOUTRÁKI, MÉGA SPÍLEO, MIKÍNES, NÁFPLIO, SIKIÓNA, STIMFALÍA, TÍRINTHA, TRÍPOLI, Harádra tou VOURAÏKOÚ.

Anáktora NÉSTOROS★

NESTOR'S PALACE – Messinia, Peloponnese

Michelin map 980 north of fold 40

On a hill deep in the country north of Pílos (Pylos) on the road to Gargagliáni lie the foundations of the "Palace of Nestor" *(covered)*. Despite his age, King Nestor commanded a large fleet of ships at the siege of Troy; Homer praised him for his wisdom. Here in his palace Nestor received **Telemachos**, when he came to ask for news of his father Odysseus.

The site of Nestor's Palace was first explored in 1939 and then excavated from 1952 onwards by Carl Blegen, an American archeologist who is buried in the First Cemetery in Athens. The buildings, which were burnt in about 1200 BC by the Dorians, date from the Mycenaean era and were decorated with frescoes. They contained clay tablets bearing inscriptions in **Linear B** which have contributed to our understanding of the Mycenaeans' language which is the earliest known form of Greek. Near the palace many tombs have been found including several beehive tombs.

Ruins ⓥ – The ruins reveal that the palace was similar to those in Crete or the Argolid (Mycenae, Tiryns) with two storeys (traces of stairs). The entrance *(propylon)* is flanked by two archive rooms where about 1 000 clay tablets were found. On the far side of the courtyard stood the **megaron**, the royal residence, consisting of a vestibule and a large hall decorated with frescoes; at the centre was a round hearth, the throne was to the right.

On the east side of the court are the queen's apartments which include a presence chamber with a central hearth next to a bathroom containing a **bath**, the only one known to have survived from this period. Around the outside of the palace are the servants' quarters, workshops and storerooms containing utensils and numerous jars for oil or wine.

About 100m/110yd east of the palace there is a restored beehive tomb *(access from the car park by the road to Hóra)*.

Hóra – *4km/2.5mi northeast.* This town among the vineyards contains an interesting **Archeological Museum** ⓥ which displays the objects excavated in the palace and the region, especially at Peristéria *(see p 169)*: fine golden cups and jewellery from the Mycenaean period; fragments of frescoes and mosaics; mouldings of inscribed tablets.

For adjacent sights see ITHÓMI, KALAMÁTA, KIPARISSÍA, KORÓNI, MESSINIAKÓS Kólpos, METHÓNI, PÍLOS.

Arhéa OLIMBÍA★★★

OLYMPIA – Elis, Peloponnese

Michelin map 980 fold 28

The ruins of Olympia in the idyllic Alfiós Valley testify to the grandeur of the ancient sanctuary which through the Olympic Games was a symbol of Greek unity.

★★**The site** – Below the wooded slopes of **Mount Kronion** (125m/410ft – *north*) the sanctuary of Zeus shelters in a grove of trees between the Alfiós (Alpheios) and its tributary the Kládeos. Upstream the valley of the Alfiós narrows between the foothills of the mountains of Arcadia; downstream it widens out towards the Elian plain in a fertile basin surrounded by gently rolling hills. Vines, rice, cotton, cereals, olives, Aleppo pines and cypresses form a lush setting which contrasts strikingly with the brooding grandeur of the other panhellenic sanctuary, Delphi.

LEGEND AND HISTORY

In the beginning a sacred grove... – The first primitive cult centre at Olympia seems to have been a sacred grove, the Áltis, which was succeeded by a sanctuary on Mount Krónion, dedicated to **Kronos**, son of Ouranos (the Sky) and Ge or Gaia (the Earth). Kronos, the god of Time, was supplanted by his son, Zeus, and pilgrimages began to flow.

This early period is illuminated by legends; the best known is about **Pelops**, the first prince of the Peloponnese. **Oinomaos**, the ruler of the region, had been warned by an oracle that his son-in-law would depose him. He therefore declared that any pretender to the hand of his daughter Hippodameia should compete in a chariot race and the loser would be put to death... Oinomaos owned an unbeatable team of horses!

Hippodameia seemed destined to remain unwed when Pelops, an Achaian chief, son of Tantalus and father of Atreus *(see MIKÍNES)* managed to bribe the driver of the royal chariot; he lost a wheel... and the race. Pelops then killed Oinomaos, married Hippodameia and became the ruler of the Peloponnese.

The Olympic Games – According to the legend, after diverting the waters of the Alfiós to cleanse the stables of Augeas, king of Elis, **Herakles** (Hercules), son of Zeus, built a sacred precinct in the Áltis round the shrines of Pelops, Zeus and Hera. He also inaugurated competitions in athletics and gymnastics in honour of the conqueror of Oinomaos.

In fact, the institution of the Olympic Games seems to date from the 8C BC when Iphitos, King of Pisa, and Lycurgus, the Spartan law giver, decided to organise a sporting competition among the Greek peoples. These games took place regularly every four years and while they were in progress a "sacred truce" was observed at Olympia lasting one month. The games reached the height of their popularity in the 5C BC when even the more distant colonies took part.

The festivities, which included cult ceremonies and a great fair, took place in summer. The athletic contests themselves lasted for only five days but the competitors had to spend a long period at Olympia in advance training under the eye of the judges. From 150 000 to 200 000 people are thought to have been attracted to the festival.

The competitors took part in the following events: in the stadium – running, boxing, wrestling, the pancration which was a combination of wrestling and boxing, and the pentathlon comprising running, jumping, wrestling, throwing the discus and the javelin; on the race course – horse racing and chariot racing in which the owner of the team rode in the chariot with the charioteer.

The victor in each event was crowned with a wreath of olive, cut with a golden scythe from the sacred olive tree, and attended a banquet; these heroes were celebrated by poets such as

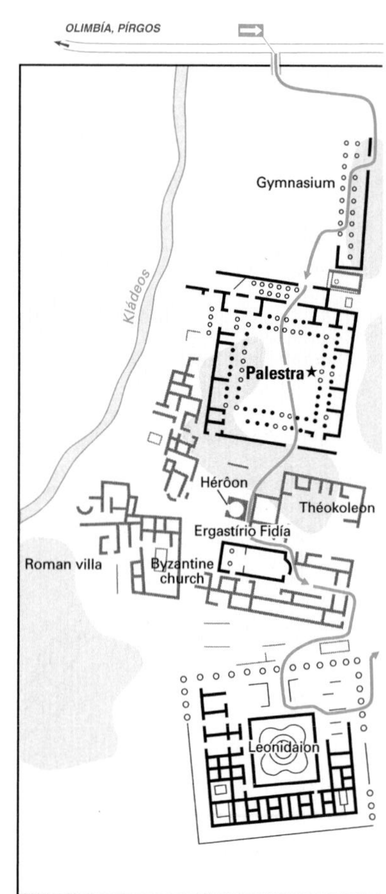

Pindar and immortalised in statues by sculptors. Their native cities often showed their pride by erecting a votive monument of a "treasury" to receive offerings in honour of the gods. The most famous laureate was **Milo of Croton** in Magna Graecia (6C BC), six times victor in the wrestling, who, it was said, could outrun race horses.

Practical Information

Access by train – from Piraeus and Athens via Patras changing at Pírgos (7hr to 8 hr).

Access by bus – from Athens changing at Pírgos (5hr 30min), 9 to 11 services daily.

Accommodation – About 20 hotels (cat A to D); 3 camp sites; youth hostel.

Grandeur and decline – The Olympian Festival thrived for several centuries and Philip of Macedon even altered the Áltis precinct to make room for a monument bearing his name, the Philippeion.

In the Roman era **Nero** supplemented the athletic contests with music and poetry competitions so that he himself could take part... he received seven prizes! In the 2C AD Hadrian and Herod Atticus carried out repairs, as they had done in other Greek sanctuaries, to houses, paths, aqueducts and *nymphaea*.

But the heart had gone out of the ceremonies; people no longer attended the games as a religious festival and then Theodosius prohibited the pagan cults; the games were held for the last time in AD 393. The statue of Zeus was sent to Constantinople where it was destroyed in a fire in AD 475. Dilapidation and destruction assisted by earthquakes, rock falls from Mount Krónion and the Alfiós floods reduced the site to ruins; eventually it was covered in a thick layer of mud (3m–4m/9ft–13ft) and the site was plundered for building material.

Rediscovery and Excavation – Although the location of the sanctuary was first raised in 1723 by Dom Montfaucon, a Parisian Benedictine, in a letter to Cardinal Querini, Archbishop of Corfu, the actual site was discovered in 1766 by Richard Chandler, an Englishman, who spent several years travelling in Greece at the expense of the

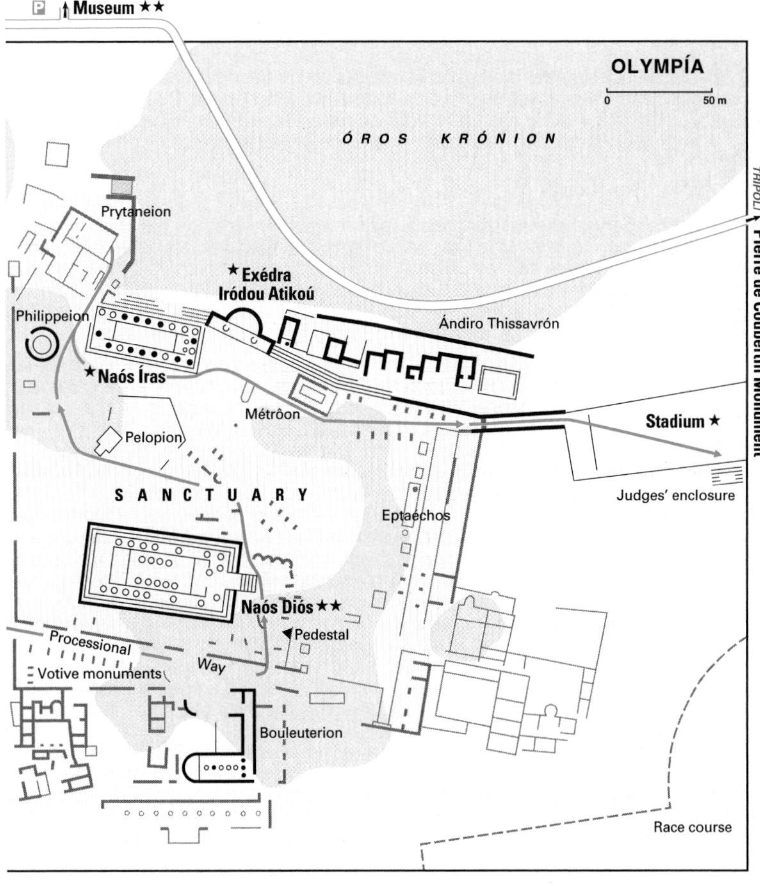

Dilettanti and published an account of all he saw. In 1768 **Winckelmann**, the German antiquary, asked the Turks for permission to make investigations but he was assassinated soon afterwards.
The first excavations were conducted by the scholars accompanying the 1828 French military expedition to the Morea; they explored the temple of Zeus in 1829 under the direction of the architect, **Abel Blouet**: three metopes and some mosaics were removed to the Louvre. Nevertheless the credit for carrying out a systematic investigation of the sanctuary goes to German archeologists, at the instigation of the historian **Ernest Curtius**; from 1875 to 1881 they spent six years excavating the sanctuary and many works of art.

★★RUINS ⏱ *Follow the route shown on the plan*

Secondary structures

First on the right through the entrance are traces of the gymnasium and then the *palestra*.

Gymnasium – It was built in the Hellenistic era (3C BC) and surrounded by covered porticoes but most of them were swept away by the flood waters of the Kládeos; only the foundations of the eastern and southern porticoes remain.

★**Palestra** – The double colonnade of the porticoes, some of which has recently been re-erected, make it possible to envisage the Hellenistic *palestra*, a sports arena (66m/216ft square). The athletes, particularly the wrestlers, trained in the courtyard and bathed or anointed themselves with oil in the surrounding rooms. South of the *palestra* lie the rather confused remains of a Roman villa and a Byzantine church which was constructed in the ruins of Pheidias' studio.

Héroon – The building, which dates from the 6C BC, consists of a single circular room, where there was an altar dedicated to an unknown hero.

Théokoleon – The residence of priests (Théokoloi) of Olympia which dates from the 4C BC.

Egastírio Fidía (Pheidias' Studio) – The excavations of 1955-58 revealed the rectangular plan of the studio which was specially built for the sculptor Pheidias to work on his statue of Zeus. A cup bearing Pheidias' name was found among the ruins.

Leonidaion – The ground plan of this huge hostelry is reasonably clear. It was built in the 4C BC by a certain Leonidas from Náxos. It consists of four ranges of rooms set round an atrium with a circular pool in the centre added by the Romans.
Follow the Roman processional way which skirts the south side of the sacred precinct enclosing the sanctuary. The pedestals on the right once supported votive monuments. Next come traces of a **bouleuterion** which dated from the 6C BC and consisted of two long chambers with an apse where the members of the council which administered the sanctuary used to hold their meetings.

Áltis (Sanctuary)

The boundary of the sacred precinct was originally traced by Herakles, or so the legend says. In the Classical period the sanctuary covered an area about 200m/656ft square and was slightly enlarged by the Romans. Over the centuries a collection of temples, altars and votive monuments accumulated.
On the right within the entrance stands a triangular pedestal which supported a Victory *(in the museum)*, an admirable statue by the sculptor Paionios.

★★**Naós Díos** – A ramp leads up to the terrace supporting the **great temple of Zeus** which was built in the 5C BC of local shell-limestone, covered with a layer of stucco. The chaotic heap of stones, the enormous drums and capitals of the columns thrown down by an earthquake in the 6C AD create a dramatic effect.
The temple was built in the Doric order and had a peristyle with six columns at either end and 13 down the sides. Its dimensions (64.12x27.66m/210x 91ft approximately) make it almost as large as the Parthenon. The pediments were decorated with sculptures *(in the museum)* illustrating the chariot race between Oinomaos and Pelops as well as the battle of the Lapiths and Centaurs; the friezes at the entrance to the *prónaos* and the *opisthódomos* were composed of 12 sculpted metopes *(in the museum)* of the Twelve Labours of Hercules *(see TÍRINTHA)*. The floor was paved with stone and mosaics, added later, some of which are still visible.
The *naós*, which consisted of a nave and two aisles, contained the famous **statue of Olympian Zeus**, one of the "Seven Wonders of the World". It was a huge chryselephantine figure (about 13.50m/44ft high) representing the king of the gods in majesty, seated on a throne of ebony and ivory, holding a sceptre surmounted by an eagle in his left hand and a Victory, also chryselephantine, in his right; his head was crowned with an olive wreath.
The majestic effigy almost reached the ceiling of the *naós* and wooden galleries were built over the side aisles to enable people to see the figure more easily.
This masterpiece has almost entirely disappeared except for a few low reliefs from the throne illustrating the murder of Niobe's children; these sculptures, which were in Rome in 17C when Van Dyck copied them, are now in the Hermitage Museum in Leningrad.

Great Temple of Zeus, Olympia

Pausanias said that when Pheidias had finished his statue he asked Zeus if he was pleased with it and a flash of lightning was followed by thunder.
A few scattered stones north of the temple mark the site of the **Pelopion**, a place of worship dedicated to Pelops; nearby were the sacred olive tree and the great altar of Zeus.

Bear left towards a spinney which hides the remains of the Philippeion.

Philippeion – One can make out the ground plan of this circular votive monument, which was built in the 4C BC in the Ionic order. It was begun by Philip of Macedon and completed by Alexander the Great.

Prytaneion – Administrative centre of the sanctuary (5C BC); the perpetual flame was kept in a sacred hearth.

★**Naós Íras (Heraion)** – A few columns have been re-erected among the remains of the imposing foundations of the **temple of Hera**.
The temple which was built in about 600 BC in the Archaic Doric order and was long and narrow (50x18.75m/164x62ft). It had six columns at either end and 16 down the sides; these columns, originally of wood, were soon replaced by others of tufa, short and stout, to support the typical Archaic capitals shaped like round cushions. The footings of the *naós* were of tufa, the walls of brick.
Within stood an effigy of Hera, of which the colossal head has been found, and one of Zeus, as well as many other statues which included the famous *Hermes* by Praxiteles.

★**Exédra of Iródou Atikoú** – This unusual Roman monument is recognisable from its semicircular shape. It was built in AD 160 by the wealthy Athenian, **Herod Atticus**, as a conduit head supplying drinking water. It was composed of two basins, the lower of which was flanked by two round fountains; a basin, architraves and columns are still extant. The *exedra* formed a sort of nymphaeum with niches containing effigies of Emperor Hadrian and the imperial family and also of Herod Atticus and his family.

Ándiron Thissavrón (Terrace of the Treasuries) – Steps lead up to the terrace which bore some dozen treasuries, of which the foundations remain, and an altar consecrated to Herakles. These treasuries were built by the cities of Greek colonies (Mégara in Attica, Gela and Selinus in Sicily, Cyrene in Africa, Byzantium etc) in the form of small Doric temples in which offerings were made to the gods.
At the foot of the terrace is a row of pedestals on which stood the bronze statues of Zeus erected out of the proceeds of the fines which were imposed on those who broke the code of the Olympic Games.

Métroon – Below the Terrace of the Treasuries there was a peripteral temple, built in the 4C BC, in the Doric order with six columns on its facade and eleven along its sides. It was dedicated first to Rhéa (Cybele); then in the Roman period, from the time of Augustus onwards, it was dedicated to the Imperial cult and statues of some of the emperors were erected there.

★Stadium

In the 3C BC a passage was built beneath the terraces to link the sanctuary to the stadium. Originally covered with vaulting, of which a small section remains, it opened on to the floor of the stadium. The starting and finishing lines are still visible; the distance between them was a *stadion* (about 194yd). The finishing line *(nearest the passage)* was marked by a *cippus*, a small low column acting as a goal or a marker round which the runners ran if the race consisted of more than one length of the stadium; the starting line was marked by several *cippi*.
The spectators, men only, were ranged on removable wooden stands mounted on the bank surrounding the stadium. It was enlarged several times until it could accommodate 20 000 people. In the middle of the south side there was a paved marble enclosure where the judges sat.
Parallel with the south side of the stadium was the **racecourse** (609x320m/667x350yd); it was destroyed in the Alfiós floods.

Eptaéchos (Poikilí) – The **Echo Portico**, erected in the 4C BC with a facade of 44 Doric columns, separated the stadium from the sanctuary. Its name was due to the resonant acoustic (a voice echoed seven times) and also to the various frescoes decorating the interior walls.

★★MUSEUM ⓥ

Around the central hall devoted to the pediments and metopes of the Temple of Zeus is a series of rooms containing objects found during the excavations arranged in chronological order. In the entrance hall there is a model of the sanctuary.

Central Hall – The sculptures of the two **pediments**★★ from the Temple of Zeus have been more or less reconstructed with pieces found on the site. The originals were carved in Parian marble (470-456 BC) in a striking and monumental style.

East Pediment – Zeus *(centre)* is presiding over the preparations for the chariot race between Oinomaos *(right)* and Pelops *(left)*; at each end is an allegorical reclining figure representing the River Alfiós *(left)* and the River Kládeos *(right)*.

West Pediment – At the centre stands a statue of Apollo (3m/nearly 10ft high); on either side are the Centaurs attending the wedding of Peirithoös, King of the Lapiths, where they drank too much and tried to carry off the women and the young men *(ephebes)* of the Lapiths. Note the plastic qualities of the figures of Apollo and Deidamia, wife of Peirithoös *(right of Apollo)*. The hall also displays the **metopes**★ from the temple frieze illustrating the Labours of Hercules *(see TÍRINTHA)*.

First Room – Mycenaean and Geometric era. A showcase *(back left)* contains an unusual Mycenaean **helmet**★ and a rare bronze horse from the 9C-8C BC.

Second Room – Archaic and Geometric era. There is a colossal **head of Hera**★ *(back right)* made of tufa, and originally painted, which was excavated in the temple of the goddess; a huge terracotta acroterion richly decorated with multi-coloured stylised motifs; an elegant bronze winged figure – a siren *(centre left)*; fine collection of helmets, numerous items of armour in bronze, helmets, shields, sollerets etc.

Third Room – Archaic era. Reconstruction of the pediments of the Treasury of Mégara showing the battle of the gods and the giants (c 520 BC), and of the Treasury of Géla in painted terracotta (c 560 BC). Note also the **battering ram**, a war machine made of bronze (mid-5C BC); on each side is the head of the animal.

Fourth Room – Archaic and Classical era. There is a remarkable terracotta group *(left)*, an acroterion from a treasury, showing **Zeus abducting Ganymede**★★ (c 470 BC); Ganymede was a handsome youth who was abducted by Zeus and taken to Mount Olympos where he became the cupbearer of the gods (note the cock in his left hand and the figures of Pegasus painted on the hem of Zeus' robe).
The **Victory**★ (5C BC) *(alcove)* has been shown by the sculptor, Paionios, at the moment of landing on earth; this figure was erected near the Temple of Zeus by the Messenians and the Naupaktians to celebrate their victory over the Spartans. There is also the helmet consecrated to Zeus by Miltiades before the Battle of Marathon, a fine head of Athena in terracotta (c 490 BC), an ear and horn of a bull in bronze dedicated to Zeus in gratitude for an Olympic victory and a little bronze horse (460 BC). Note also the ceramic items from the studio of Pheidias (440-430 BC), the wine pitcher with the inscription "I belong to Pheidias", dies and moulds for decorative motifs and a large number of tools made of bone.

Hermes by Praxiteles (Olympia Museum)

Fifth Room – Contains sculpture of the late Classical and Hellenistic periods. Fragments of marble statues, especially heads: note the fine head of Aphrodite attributed to Praxiteles, an athlete's head and a portrait of Alexander the Great. Displayed on the wall is part of the terracotta gutter from the Leonidaion (350-325 BC).

Hermes Room – The famous statue of **Hermes by Praxiteles** ★★★, a 4C BC masterpiece of Classical art in highly polished Parian marble, was found in the Temple of Hera, near to a pedestal bearing an inscription relating to the sculptor Praxiteles to whom the Hermes was also attributed by the historian Pausanias; certain scholars however assert that it is a Hellenistic or even Roman copy.
Hermes, the messenger of the gods, is carrying the infant Dionysos, son of Zeus and Semele, to entrust him to the care of the nymphs out of reach of Hera's jealousy. The perfection of the modelling and the harmony of the proportions are remarkable. Traces of colour on the lips and the hair show that the statue was originally painted.

Sixth and Seventh Rooms – Hellenistic and Roman era. The sculptures retain the Greek style, the Roman influence being restricted to the subjects and the nature of the commissions; the inscriptions on the plinths of the statues show that their creators were Greek and mainly Athenian. Among the works from the Roman period are an Antinoús (Hadrian's favourite) and a marble bull dedicated to Zeus by Regilla, Herod Atticus' wife. Accessories used by athletes.

The Revival of the Olympic Games

The revival of the Olympic Games is due to a Frenchman, **Pierre Fredy, Baron de Coubertin** (1863-1937), who had the tenacity and necessary vision to bring back to life the famous Games of antiquity, the last of which took place in AD 393.
Rejecting the military career which his family had selected for him, Baron de Coubertin devoted all his energy to promoting the importance of physical activity in education; in his view, sport is an excellent vehicle for inculcating into young people the idea of collective freedom and responsibility. Enthusiastically he dashed off thousands of articles, repeatedly pestered the authorities, undertook missions and set up sporting bodies. In June 1894 a conference was held at the Sorbonne "with the aim of the restoration of the Olympic Games", by the end of which Coubertin's cause had been won. With the aid of a public subscription and with the generous support of the Greek patron George Avéroff (1818-99), Pierre de Coubertin had the Stadium in Athens restored. On 5 April 1896 before 60 000 spectators gathered in the Panathenaic Stadium, George I, King of Greece, uttered the solemn words: "I declare open the first international Olympic Games". Since then they have been held every four years, except in time of war, and seek to help promote the universal brotherhood of man through a true sporting spirit, giving different nationalities the chance to subordinate their mutual antipathy, at least for the duration of the contests. After seeing his dream realised, Pierre de Coubertin remained President of the International Olympic Committee until 1925.
The first Winter Games did not take place until 1924 in Chamonix, France, with skiing and skating as their main focus. The Centenary Games took place in 1996 in Atlanta, Georgia, and the venue for the Summer Games in the year 2000 is Sydney, Australia.

ADDITIONAL SIGHTS

Pierre de Coubertin Monument – East of the ruins on the north side of the Trípoli road a ring of cypress trees marks the site of the mausoleum built in 1938 to contain the heart of **Baron Pierre de Coubertin**, who founded the modern Olympic Games *(see above)*.
Beside the monument stands the altar with the Olympic flame bearing the five Olympic circles, symbols of the union of the five continents of the world. At the opening of each Olympiad the sacred flame is carried from Olympia in Greece to the place where the games are to be held.

★**Museum of the Olympic Games** ⓥ – The museum was opened in 1978 in the modern town just off the main street; it contains many documents about the Games, particularly those held in Athens in 1896 and 1906.

For adjacent sights see ANDRÍTSENA, HLEMOÚTSI, ITHÓMI, KALÁVRITA, KARÍTENA, KILÍNI, KIPARISSÍA, MEGALÓPOLI, MÉGA SPÍLEO, Anáktora NÉSTOROS, PÁTRA, PÍLOS, TRÍPOLI, Harádra tou VOURAÏKOÚ.

Óros ÓLIMBOS★

Mount OLYMPOS – Thessaly and Macedonia
Michelin map 980 north of fold 17

Olympos is a huge and complex massif composed of crystalline schist. It is the highest mountain range in Greece consisting of nine peaks (exceeding 2 600m/8 530ft). It is divided into Lower Olympos in the south where the wooded slopes are easy to climb and Upper Olympos, a succession of precipices cleft by deep ravines. Despite various earlier attempts the first successful ascent was made only in 1913 by two Swiss climbers, Baud-Bovy and Boissonas.
To the ancient Greeks Olympos was a mysterious mountain, usually wreathed in clouds, situated on the northern boundary of their world; they thought it was the home of **Zeus** and the other gods, which the Giants vainly tried to rival by piling Pelion upon Óssa; these are two lesser peaks to the southeast (1 551m/4 760ft and 1 978m/6 490ft respectively). In antiquity there were lions in the forests on Lower Olympos. Excavations have revealed ancient shrines and cemeteries as well as the Hellenistic and Roman town of Dion *(see DÍO)* on the north face of Mount Olympos.

Litóhoro – Pop 6 109. This is the main town on Olympos *(hotels, youth hostels, tavernas)*.
It is also the principal base for walking and climbing in the mountains *(apply in Litóhoro or to the Alpine Clubs in Athens and Thessaloníki)*. The four major peaks (exceeding 2 800m/9 186ft) form a rocky cirque including **Mítikas** or **Pantheon** (2 917m/9 580ft) and Zeus' Throne or Crown *(stepháni)* (2 909m/9 547ft).
The peaks can be viewed by car: from Litóhoro take the road to the monastery (Moní Ágios Diónissios) and continue along a track *(suitable for motor vehicles)* to the hamlet of Priónа (about 1 000m/3 280ft).
Experienced walkers may park the car at a junction before the monastery and continue on foot to Petrostrounga *(3hr)* to the right and along the bare Skoúrta Pass to the Muses Plateau (Oropédio Moussón) *(5hr)* to the refuge of the Hellenic Alpine Club of Thessaloníki (2 750m/9 022ft). It is advisable to be accompanied by a guide before venturing to the summit.
For adjacent sights see DÍO, LÁRISSA, Kiláda ton TÉMBON, METÉORA, Óros PÍLIO, PLATAMÓNAS, TRÍKALA, VÉRIA, VÓLOS.

ORHOMENÓS

ORCHOMENOS – Boeotia, Central Greece – Population 5 525
Michelin map 980 fold 29

Orchomenos, which had been the capital of the Minyans in the prehistoric era and was rich and powerful in the Mycenaean period, was the rival of Thebes in antiquity. It is now a small country town on the edge of what was formerly a huge marsh known as **Lake Copaïs** (Kopaïda). There are traces of drainage channels dug by the Minyans. In later centuries the flooding seems to have worsened owing to earthquakes blocking the natural outlets. Modern drainage work was begun at the end of the 19C by French and Scots engineers; a network of canals was created to channel the water south towards the River Kifissós which flows into Lake Ilíki and Lake Paralímni. Over a period of years nearly 200km²/77sq mi of land was reclaimed. Until it was expropriated by the Greek Government in 1952, the estate was administered by the British Lake Copaïs Company. The land is used for animal husbandry and the cultivation of cotton, rice and cereals. Fine views of this vast, flat basin may be enjoyed from the acropolis *(below)* of ancient Orchomenos and from the fortress of Glá *(see THÍVA)* 20km/12mi to the east.

Battle of Kephisos (Kifíssos) – Near to Orchomenos, where the River Kifíssos flowed into Lake Copaïs there took place on 13 March 1311 a bloody battle which put an end to the Frankish domination of the duchies of Thebes and Athens.
The foot soldiers of the Catalan Company *(see KAVÁLA)* were drawn up on the right bank of the river and separated from the Frankish cavalry by a stretch of level ground, green but marshy. The 700 cavalry from Burgundy, Champagne and Flanders under the command of **Gautier de Brienne**, the Duke of Athens, did not notice that the ground was not firm. As they charged forward their heavy war horses sank into the quagmire. The riders were powerless to move and the light Catalan infantry had no trouble cutting them down. Only two knights escaped.

SIGHTS

The ruins of ancient Orchomenos and the Church of the Dormition of the Virgin face one another at the entrance to the modern town on the Kástro road.

Ancient ruins ⓥ – On the left of the theatre is the path leading into the **Treasury of Minyas★** (a legendary ancestor of the Minyans), a huge Mycenaean *thólos* tomb similar to the Treasury of Atreus at Mycenae; the roof has fallen in but the huge blue marble lintel is still in place over the door and the inner chamber, linked to the main tomb by a corridor, has retained part of its original ceiling.
The acropolis *(1hr on foot there and back)* gives a fine **panorama★** over Orchomenos and the Copaïc region. Remains of old walls and temples are visible along the way.

★**Kimísseos Theotókou** ⓥ – The Byzantine **Church of the Dormition of the Virgin**, which dates from the 9C, belonged to a monastery built on the site of a temple dedicated to the Graces *(charites)*, who were goddesses of Nature.
In the 13C the monastery passed to the Cistercians who altered the church and the conventual buildings, leaving their distinctive architectural mark: the open narthex in front of the church like the one at Citeaux Abbey, the porch and the triple windows; the double arched arcading along one side of the old cloisters is also typical of the Cistercian style.
Inside the church is an unusual Byzantine paved floor. There are inscriptions in Greek letters and many Byzantine stones sculpted with symbolic motifs (winged dragons, doves, lions, deer, trees of life etc) along the exterior wall.
The upper part of the transept walls and the dome have recently been restored.

For adjacent sights see ARÁHOVA, ÉVIA, DELFÍ, HERÓNIA, Drómos tou IRAKLÍ, LIVADIÁ, ÓSSIOS LOUKÁS Monastery, THERMOPÍLES, THÍVA.

ÓSSIOS LOUKÁS Monastery★★

Boeotia, Central Greece

Michelin map 980 fold 29 – Alt 490m/1 608ft

Deep in the bauxite-bearing mountains on the borders of Boeotia and Phocis stands the Monastery of Blessed Luke (Óssios Loukás). Its **position★★** is peaceful and imposing on the edge of a rounded valley beneath the green slopes (olives) of Mount Elikónas (Helicon).
The monastery was founded by a hermit, **Luke Stiris**, who died in 953 and whose tomb became the object of pilgrimages. Like the abbeys at Daphne and Orchomenos, the convent was occupied in the 13C and the 14C under the Burgundian dukes of Athens and Thebes by Cistercians who preferred an isolated site which they placed under the protection of the Virgin. The monastery was damaged by earthquakes in the 16C and the 17C and restored between 1960 and 1970; there are orthodox monks in residence. Despite its isolation in the mountains the major church is decorated with marvellous **mosaics★★** and is a masterpiece of Byzantine art.

TOUR

The monastery precinct is shaped like an irregular pentagon at the centre of which stand two churches, one for the pilgrims and one for the community. The peripheral buildings comprise the monks' cells *(north and west sides)* and a refectory *(south side)* which was rebuilt after being damaged in a bombardment in 1943.

Pass through the main entrance into the precinct to arrive in front of the pilgrims' church (Katholikon); set back on the left is the conventual church (Theotókos).

★★**Katholikon** – The huge and typical pilgrimage church was built in the 11C over the tomb of Luke the hermit.
Before examining the mosaics and frescoes in detail it is advisable to walk round the church so as to understand its architecture and decor.
From the outside the building is typically Greek with its stonework resting on a course of bricks and the windows grouped together beneath semicircular relieving arches. The church, which is preceded by a narthex, is built on the Greek-cross

Monastery Church, Óssios Loukás

plan beneath a central dome supported on pendentives and with an apse jutting from its rectangular mass, as in Agía Sophía in Constantinople. The galleries were reserved for women.

The interior décor is mostly 11C; only the murals, which replaced damaged or lost mosaics, are later (16C-17C). The visitor will marvel at the multicoloured marbles which face the walls and pillars, the jasper and porphyry in the floor, the delicate sculptures which decorate the iconostasis and the extraordinary mosaics on the ceiling, pediments and pilasters.

To examine the interior decoration start at the main door. The mosaics are set against a gold background, a typical example of the 11C hieratic style, sober and expressive, which was executed by artists from Thessaloníki and Constantinople.

Narthex (1) – Fine mosaics:
– on the pediment above the nave door, a majestic effigy of Christ preaching;
– on the pediments of the arches on either side of the central doors, the Crucifixion and the Resurrection, a scene combined with the Descent into Hell *(right)* and effigies of Helen and Constantine, who initiated the devotion to the Holy Cross;
– on the central vault, the Virgin, the Archangels Gabriel and Michael and St John the Baptist;
– in the pediments above the arches on the west side, curious figures of oriental saints;
– in the lateral recesses, the Washing of the Disciples' Feet *(north)* and Doubting Thomas *(south)*.

Dome (2) – The original mosaics were replaced by frescoes in the 16C and the 17C. In the centre is Christ Pantocrator surrounded by the Virgin, St John the Baptist and the Archangels Michael, Gabriel, Raphael and Uriel; between the windows are the sixteen prophets. The pendentives are faced with charming mosaics evoking the Nativity, the Presentation in the Temple and the Baptism of Christ.

Iconostasis – It is made of white marble and was formerly hung with four great icons (1571), the work of the famous Cretan artist, Mihális Damaskinós *(see KRÍTÍ: Cretan Renaissance)*, who taught El Greco *(stolen a few years ago and replaced with copies)*.

Chancel and Apse (3) – The mosaic in the small dome above the altar symbolises Pentecost; in the apse is the Mother of God (Meter Theou). The two mosaics facing one another in the little apse *(right)* are among the most admired of all: Daniel in the lions' den and Shadrach, Meshach and Abednego in the fiery furnace.

North transept (4) – Fine mosaic of Luke the Hermit.

Crypt – *Access from south side outside the church.* The crypt which contains the tomb of Blessed Luke dates from the 10C. The murals are 11C: note the Last Supper *(right of iconostasis)*.

★**Theotókos** – A doorway beneath a double arch leads into the monastic enclosure and the open court in front of the church.

This church is very different from its neighbour; some people think it is contemporary with Luke the Hermit, 10C; others think it is 11C.

In fact, even if Luke's oratory did stand on this spot, it seems that the present church was built or rebuilt in the 13C for the Cistercians according to the visible evidence: external porch with rib vaulting linking the church with the monastic buildings, nave and two aisles terminating in apses with flat external chevets, shape of the arches and the simplicity of the decoration.

The proportions of the narthex are admirable: the vault is supported on two columns with Corinthian capitals and the high dome rests on four granite columns with handsome carved capitals.

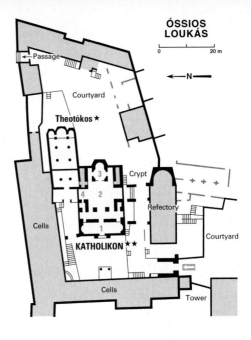

ÓSSIOS LOUKÁS

0 20 m

N

Passage

Courtyard

Theotókos ★

Crypt

Refectory

Cells

KATHOLIKON ★★

Courtyard

Cells

Tower

On leaving go round the south side of both churches into the eastern courtyard to compare the east elevations: the Byzantine pilgrims' church is massive and crowned by a powerful round dome; the conventual church soars up to an elegant octagonal lantern. The east side of the courtyard consists of another range of conventual buildings.

For adjacent sights see ARÁHOVA, ÉVIA, DELFÍ, HERÓNIA, Drómos tou IRAKLÍ, LIVADIÁ, ORHOMENÓS, THERMOPÍLES, THÍVA.

PÁRGA★★

Préveza, Epiros – Population 1 699

Michelin map 980 west of fold 15

Forests of pine trees and groves of olives and citrus fruits (citrons and particularly lemons) growing on the slopes on the Epirot coast make a green surround to Párga. It is a charming resort on a particularly attractive **site**★★; its white flower-hung houses cluster on the neck of a promontory flanked by two bays which are screened from the open sea by rocky islets and a huge gently-curving sandy beach.

Párga provides a sheltered anchorage for coastal traders and for pleasure boats *(trips to the isle of Paxí organised in season)*. From the 15C to 1797 Párga belonged to the Venetians who called it *Le Gominezze*, the anchorage. Much against the will of the inhabitants, in 1817 it was sold by the British to Ali Pasha *(see IOÁNINA)* and did not return to the Greeks until 1913.

Ionian Sea Tours, Párga ☎ (0684) 32 756 provides a service in English, French and Italian for hiring a car, renting an apartment, booking an excursion or a passage to Italy or Corfu.

Venetian Fortress – The fortress (now in ruins) was built late in the 16C and later modified. It stood on a rocky peninsula now overgrown by trees – citrus, pines and cypresses – through which there are changing **views**★★ of Párga, the bays and the islands: Panagía Island is marked by two chapels and a little fort built by the French in 1808. The Souliots *(see EFÍRA)* often found a refuge in the fortress during their struggle against Ali Pasha.

For adjacent sights see ÁRTA, EFÍRA, IOÁNINA, KASSÓPI, KÉRKIRA, LEFKÁDA, PRÉVEZA.

Use the Index to find more information about a subject mentioned in the guide people, towns, places of interest, isolated sites, historical events or natural features...

PÁTRA

PATRAS – Achaia, Peloponnese – Population 152 570

Michelin map 980 fold 28

Patras, the modern capital of the Peloponnese and Achaia, is the third largest town in Greece and the major port on the west coast. Backed by a fertile hinterland of fruit orchards and vineyards (large wine-producing firms), it is also a commercial and industrial centre (textiles, tyres) and a university town. In 1821 it was burnt by the Turks and rebuilt on a geometric plan. Its arcaded streets and shady squares and harbour breakwater, where people gather in the evening, provide a pleasant stroll. The town carnival *(see p 370)* is one of the most spectacular in Greece and the local cuisine is delicious: excellent gilt-head fish *(tsipoúres)*.

It was here that Byron first set foot on Greek soil in 1809.

A religious city – According to tradition Patras was converted to Christianity in the reign of Nero by **St Andrew**, the Apostle, who was crucified on an X-shaped cross, henceforward known as the St Andrew's cross. His tomb soon attracted many pilgrims and quarrels arose over his relics; in the 4C some were removed to Constantinople while others were carried off by St Regulus (or Rule), the Bishop of Patras, who was shipwrecked off the coast of Fife and founded St Andrews in Scotland. The head however remained in Patras where in 805 a miraculous apparition of the Apostle put to flight the bands of Slavs who were attacking the city.

The religious role of Patras grew even greater with the Frankish occupation in 1205 when the city became the seat of a powerful barony first held by William Aleman from Provence; the Latin archbishop held jurisdiction over the whole of the Peloponnese and even became a baron in 1360. For their part the dukes of Burgundy adopted St Andrew as their patron in war; the cross of Burgundy is a St Andrew's cross.

In 1408 Patras passed into the hands of the Venetians and Archbishop Pandolfo Malatesta presided over the completion of his cathedral in 1426. From 1429 to 1460 the city was ruled by the Despots of Mystra, the Palaiologi, and when Patras was captured by the Turks, Thomas Palaiologos removed St Andrew's head to Rome where it was kept in St Peter's Basilica until 1964 when it was returned to Patras.

Having returned to the Orthodox fold, the see of Patras rose to fame in 1821 when the Archbishop, Metropolitan **Germanós** gave the signal at the Monastery of Agía Lávra *(see KALÁVRITA)* for the revolt against the Turks; the latter took their revenge by setting fire to Patras which was rebuilt a few years later under the government of Kapodistrias.

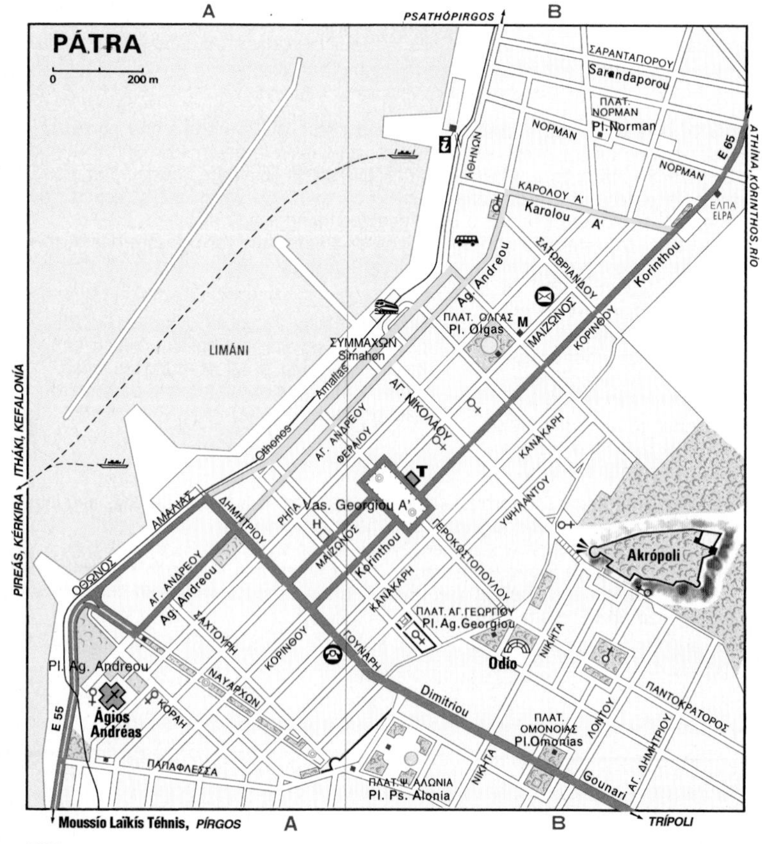

SIGHTS

Akrópoli – Early in the 9C, on the site of the ancient acropolis, the Byzantines built a fortress, including two churches, which was subsequently enlarged and remodelled by the Franks *(south and east curtain walls)*, the Venetians and the Turks. On the highest point rises the medieval **castle** defended by towers and a square keep still protected by a close-set defensive wall.
The lower ward is also reinforced by towers and a round 17C bastion which offers a beautiful **view★** of Patras and the Gulf of Patras as far as Cephallonia and Zakynthos as well as inland over the Achaian plain.

Ágios Andréas – This neo-Byzantine style **St Andrew's New Church** was completed in 1979 to receive the great pilgrimage which occurs on St Andrew's Day (30 November).
The great icons of St Andrew and of the Virgin, the "Source of Life", are to be found at the end of the nave; there is also an impressive carved wooden chandelier. St Andrew's relics are displayed at the end of the side aisle: chased gold casket containing the saint's head, which was venerated in St Peter's Rome from 1462 until 1964 when it was returned to Patras by Pope Paul VI; reliquary of St Andrew's cross, held since the 13C in the crypt of St Victor's in Marseille and sent back to Patras in 1980.

Odío – The Roman odeon (2C AD) was restored in 1960.

Moussío Laikís Téhnis ⓥ – The **Museum of Folk Art** has an interesting collection of 18C popular dress; icons, arms etc.

Municipal theatre – This elegant neo-Classical building with a loggia stands on the north side of a pleasant square; it was built in 1872 to designs by the architect Ziller.

EXCURSION

Río – *7km/4.25mi northeast; camping, ferry to Andírio, many beaches nearby.*
The **Castle of Morea** on the headland, which is matched by the Castle of Roúmeli on the northern shore, commands the narrow passage *(2km/1.25mi)* known as the Little Dardanelles which separates the Gulf of Patras from the Gulf of Corinth.
An earlier fortress built in 1499 by Sultan Bayazid II was destroyed by the Knights of Malta; the present 18C castle was built by the Venetians and strengthened by the Turks. In 1828 it was captured by the French military expedition after a siege of three weeks.
The castle (now a prison) is triangular in plan and surrounded by a moat; it has vast casemates and a bastion *(north)*; fine view over the straits.

Halandrítsa – *25km/15mi south of Patra by the road to Agía Triáda and then the road (left) to Kalávrita.* Chalandritsa is a small town, which lies deep in the hills above the coastal plain. During the Frankish occupation it was an important town, the seat of a barony which was first held by Robert de la Trémouille, whose family also held land near Kalávrita. Reminders of this period still exist in the centre of the town: a huge square tower and several Gothic churches with flat chevets and pointed vaults, of which the most typical is St Athanasius'.

For adjacent sights see HLEMOÚTSI, ITHÁKI, KALÁVRITA, KEFALONÍA, KILÍNI, MÉGA SPÍLEO, MESSOLÓNGI, NÁFPAKTOS, OLIMBÍA, Harádra tou VOURAÏKOÚ, ZÁKINTHOS.

PÉLA

PELLA – Péla, Macedonia

Michelin map 980 fold 5 – 40km/25mi northwest of Thessaloníki

The ancient city of Pella was situated in the heart of the fertile Macedonian plain on the road from Édessa to Thessaloníki. Under Philip II and Alexander the Great it was the capital of Macedon and it has not yet revealed all its secrets.

Pella, a royal city – Late in the 5C BC King Archelaos abandoned Aigai, which recent excavations suggest to be Vergína *(see VÉRIA)*, and moved to Pella where he built a splendid palace, probably in Old Pella (Paleá Péla). The palace was decorated with paintings by the famous Zeuxis (464-398 BC); here Archelaos maintained a sophisticated court, welcoming artists and men of letters, including **Euripides**, who died at Pella in 406 BC and whose play *The Bacchantes* was first performed in the town theatre. Both **Philip II of Macedon** and **Alexander the Great** were born in Pella in 382 and 356 BC respectively. Alexander, who was the son of Philip and Princess Olympia, was educated in literature as well as the military arts; one of his tutors was Aristotle, a native of Chalcidice. Pella grew to be the largest town in Macedon and was linked to the sea by a canal (22km/14mi long) but it was laid waste by the Roman Consul, Aemilius Paulus in 168 BC and never recovered.

Pella was mentioned or described by the Greek writers Herodotos, Thucydides and Xenophon and by the Roman historian Livy but it is the excavations begun in 1957 by Greek archeologists that have revealed its vast extent and its grid plan which was recommended by the architect Hippodamos of Miletus *(see ATHÍNA: Pireás)*. Remarkable Hellenistic mosaic pavements (4C-3C BC) have also been excavated; they are made of red, white and black pebbles set in frames of lead or baked clay.

Ruins ⓥ – The excavations on the north side of the road have uncovered the foundations of what must have been administrative buildings because no domestic objects have been found.

To the right lay a huge complex of buildings erected round a courtyard and an Ionic peristyle; some of the columns have been re-erected. Certain rooms were paved with mosaics: some geometric *(in situ)*, others figurative *(in the museum)*. To the left are the foundations of other buildings; the most distant are decorated with fine mosaic pavements illustrating the Abduction of Helen and of Deïanira, the battle of the Amazons and a deer hunt signed by Gnosis.

3km/2mi away, on the Pella acropolis, near to the village of ancient Pella, recent excavations have discovered more ruins including a royal residence which could be Philip V's palace. *Excavations in progress.*

Museum – Here are displayed the finds from the excavations including some superb **mosaic pavements★** (4C-3C BC): the most beautiful show Dionysos seated on a panther (the god's favourite animal) and a lion hunt in which Krateros a comrade in arms *(see DÉLFI: Temple of Apollo)* is supposed to have saved the life of Alexander the Great.

Among the other Hellenistic figures are a marble dog from a tomb, a head of Alexander, a small bronze statue of Poseidon and some attractive terracotta pieces.

For adjacent sights see AMFÍPOLI, DÍO, ÉDESSA, KASTORIÁ, LEFKÁDIA-NÁOUSSA, PLATAMÓNAS, THESSALONÍKI, VÉRIA.

Óros PÍLIO★★

Mount PELION – Magnissía, Thessaly

Michelin map 980 folds 17 and 18

Mount Pelion forms a well-wooded and well-watered promontory protecting Vólos Bay (Pagassitikós Kólpos) from the Aegean Sea. In high summer it is a haven of cool peacefulness where many people from Vólos and Athens choose to spend their holidays. Good roads and comfortable hotels add to the pleasure of visiting this charming region with its hill villages, its inviting bays and beautiful views; in winter there is good skiing.

Natural features – The mountain range is formed of schist and is marked by sheer cliffs, and deep ravines. It culminates in **Mount Pelion** (Óros Pílio) at 1 551m/5 089ft, extends north towards Mount Óssa (1 978m/6 488ft) and also south, curving west to form the Magnissía peninsula.

The relatively humid climate encourages a luxuriant growth of Mediterranean plants on the lower slopes and mountain types at altitude. Thus the olive groves (the famous Vólos olive), fruit orchards (apples, cherries, peaches...), walnut, hazel and pine trees give way higher up to forests of beeches, oaks and chestnuts.

Houses – The village centre is marked by a huge open space ***(platía)*** shaded by enormous plane trees. Owing to the abundant water sources, the houses are scattered; many are built in the traditional style with jutting upper storeys, supported on wooden corbels, and slate roofs with overhanging eaves. The local churches do not conform to the usual Orthodox style; they are rectangular, wide and low, with little apses, external galleries and detached bell-towers.

Mythology – The sense of mystery engendered by the mountain's impenetrable forests has given rise to many legends.

It was said by the ancients that during the battle between the gods and the giants *(Gigantomachía)* the latter tried to challenge Olympos by piling Pelion on Óssa.

Mount Pelion was also the remote home of **Cheiron**, the wisest of the centaurs, who played an important part in the Greek fables. Having encouraged the marriage of Peleus and Thetis, a nereid, he educated their son Achilles, one of the heroes of the Trojan War, in which Achilles died after being wounded in the heel by an arrow shot by Paris, the only vulnerable part of his body. Cheiron was also responsible for the education of Asklepios, to whom he explained the use of herbs, and of **Jason** who used timber from Pelion for the boat in which he sailed with the 50 argonauts to Colchis (Black Sea) to find the Golden Fleece.

Tour starting from Vólos *162km/100mi – about 1 day*

From Vólos (see VÓLOS) take Odós Venizélou towards Portariá (east).

Anakassiá ⓥ – In the village, which lies to the left of the road, is the **Theophilos Museum** *(park the car in the car park next to the church and walk to Odós Moussíou Theóphilou)*. The museum is installed in the "House of Kondós", a beautiful building decorated with frescoes by the great primitive painter, **Theophilos** (1873-1934), a native of Lesbos *(see LÉSVOS: Variá)* who spent part of his life in Vólos. The first floor contains scenes recalling the War of Independence.

The road continues to climb towards Portariá with a view over Vólos Bay; it passes close to **Episkopí**, a hill clothed in pines and cypresses and crowned with an old church which until 1881 was the seat of the bishop of Dimitriádi.

★**Portariá** – 650m/2 133ft. A pleasant resort in summer, cool and fresh, with a view up to Makrinítsa and down over Vólos Bay; beautiful village square with superb plane trees *(cafés, restaurants)* and characteristic houses.

From Portariá take the road (panoramic view) to Makrinítsa (3km/2mi).

★★**Makrinítsa** – 700m/2 297ft. *Park the car in the square at the entrance to the village.* Makrinítsa occupies a magnificent **site**★★ on a verdant slope facing Vólos Bay; it is pleasant to stroll through the steep and narrow streets among the splendid old houses; some of them are quite large and have been well preserved and restored.

The main **square**★★ *(platía)* is especially attractive with its fountain, its plane trees and its tiny church (18C) which has external galleries decorated with low-relief sculptures and beautiful icons within. Higher up is the former conventual Church of the Virgin (Panagía) (18C): Roman and Byzantine inscriptions on the walls.

Return to Portariá and continue to climb.

Marvellous **views**★★★ across Vólos Bay to Mount Óthris, northwards into Thessaly and south to Euboia.

Agrioléfkes (Hánia Pass) – 1 200m/3 937ft. Winter sports resort *(hotel-restaurants; ski lift)*, set in beech and chestnut woods; there is a road from here to the summit of Mount Pelion.

The road descends towards the Aegean through beech and chestnut woods before reaching the level of the orchards. *13km/8mi from the pass bear left to Zagorá.*

Zagorá – This was an important centre of Greek culture under the Turks when the Pelion region enjoyed a certain autonomy. Zagorá is a little town of houses set in orchards and gardens watered by many fountains. It was also a centre for hand-woven cloth which was exported by caïque from the port at Horeftó. The main **square** is at the top of the town near St George's Church (Ágios Geórgios) which contains a huge 18C **iconostasis**★, carved and gilded.

From Zagorá a side road plunges downhill to **Horeftó** (pop 64), a fishing village with a long beach of fine sand.

Return towards Hánia Pass; take the narrow but picturesque road to Tsangaráda.

Ágios Ioánis – Very white beach at the foot of green hills.

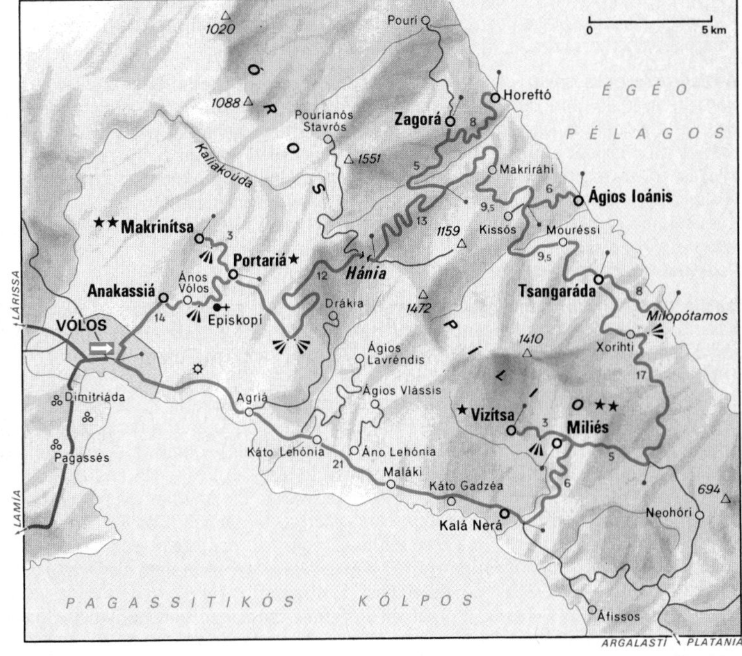

Tsangaráda – 499m/1 637ft. Peaceful resort where the houses are dispersed among the trees; the village boasts one of the oldest and largest plane trees (15m/49ft circumference) in Greece.
Nearby is **Milopótamos** which has two beaches flanked by rocks.
Just beyond Xoríhti there is a splendid **view**★★ high above the coast (Milopótamos lies immediately below) and over the Aegean Sea to Skíathos and Skópelos.
At the next junction where the road continues south to Argalastí and **Plataniá** (*36km/22mi* – beautiful sheltered beach) bear right uphill to Vizítsa.

★**Vizítsa** – Many typical old houses, some in poor condition.
Return downhill; fine **views**★★ of the peninsula and Vólos Bay.

Miliés – This is a pleasant resort, which was a centre for Greek culture under the Turks and possesses a history **library** ⓥ containing some rare volumes.
The road back to Vólos follows the line once taken by the famous Pelion railway along the shore of the bay; there are several beaches, the most popular being **Kalá Nerá**: seafront promenade lined with eucalyptus trees, large beach of fine sand. At the junction before reaching Kalá Nerá a road *(left)* branches off to the small resort of **Áfissos**.

For adjacent sights see LÁRISSA, PLATAMÓNAS, Óros ÓLIMBOS, Vóries SPORADES, Kiláda ton TÉMBON, VÓLOS.

PÍLOS★★

PYLOS Messinía, Peloponnese – Population 2 107
Michelin map 980 fold 40

Pylos, better known as **Navarino**, a name probably derived from the Avars who lived in the area from the 6C to 9C, lies on the southern shore of a majestic **bay**★★ bounded on the seaward side by the rocky ridge of the island of Sphakteria (Sfaktiría). It is endowed with a good harbour and an excellent anchorage (3x5km/2x3mi) with a varying depth of water (20m/66ft in the north to 60m/197ft in the south).
The town, which boasts a superb beach, was built in 1829 by the French military expedition to Morea and is a good base for making excursions into the southern Peloponnese. The focal point of Pylos near the port is Three Admirals Square (Platía Trion Návarhon) which is shaded by trees and bordered by arcades *(small archeological museum; cafés, tavernas)*: at the centre stands a monument to the three admirals commanding the victorious fleet at the Battle of Navarino.

A desirable possession – The strategic importance of Navarino Bay was recognised both in antiquity and the Middle Ages but in those days the town and the harbour were at the northern end of the bay at the foot of the promontory which was crowned first by an acropolis and then by a medieval castle called Port de Junch or Joncs (Port of Rushes) owing to the marshy nature of the coastline; it is now called Old Castle (Paliókastro). During the succeeding centuries the Venetians and the Turks fought for possession of this excellent anchorage; the Turks built a fortress to guard the southern approach; it is now called New Castle (Niókastro). It was captured in 1685 by the Venetian troops of Morosini.

Battle of Navarino: "an untoward event" – This was how the Duke of Wellington described the naval engagement which took place on 20 October 1827 between the allied fleet, made up of English, French and Russians, and the Turkish fleet which was at anchor in the bay.
The presence of the allied fleet was intended to intimidate **Ibrahim Pasha**, whose army, based at Navarino, was ravaging the Peloponnese, and to force the Porte to agree an armistice with the Greeks. The allied force, commanded by Admirals Codrington, de Rigny and de Heydden, consisted of 26 ships (11 English, 7 French and 8 Russian) with a total of 1 270 cannon. When they appeared at the southern entrance to the bay, a few shots fired by the nervous Turks started the action. The 82 Turkish and Egyptian ships were caught in a trap without room for manoeuvre and were annihilated despite their superior fire power (2 400 cannon) and the support of the artillery on the Niókastro; 6 000 Turks died against 174 Allies.
The Battle of Navarino created a great stir; it forced the Sultan to negotiate and paved the way for Greek independence.

Niókastro, Pylos

SIGHTS

★**Niókastro** ⓥ – *Access from the Methóni road.* This citadel which dominates the town and the anchorage was built by the Turks in the 16C on the site of an earlier structure but it was much altered in 1829 by the French who added the great cannon emplacements to the walls and the pentagonal keep with five bastions which was later converted into a prison.

A large building to the left of the entrance houses the collection of the French philhellene René Puaux: lithographs, engravings and objects closely associated with the period of the struggle for Greek independence. The former mosque *(centre)* has been converted into a church. From the southwest redoubt there are remarkable **views**★ over the bay and the island of Sphakteria; off its southern point lies an islet which bears a monument to the French who fell at Navarino and during the Expedition to Morea (1828-30). A memorial to the British sailors who died at Navarino stands on a low rock called Chelonaki (little tortoise) in the harbour.

Arheologikó Moussío ⓥ – *Odós Philéllinon.* The **Antonópoulos Archeological Museum**, which opened in 1951, has two rooms in which are gathered local finds: art objects, weapons and tools, vases and the silver- and goldsmith's work ranging from the Neolithic to the Roman era.

★**Navarino Bay** – *In the summer season boats operate from Pylos to Sphakteria and Paliókastro. Information from the harbour.*

★**Paliókastro** – *Accessible by car from Petrohori taking a bad road which goes to Voidokilia (beautiful sandy cove).* On a spur of rock near the northern approach rise the crenellated walls and towers of the **Castle of Port de Junch** which was built in 1278 by Nicolas II de St Omer, the Bailiff of Morea, on the foundations of an ancient acropolis. The castle consists of a circuit wall and a keep and commands the lagoon and the ancient port of Pylos *(bathing)*. At the foot of the cliff there is a cave with stalactites, named after King Nestor, which is linked to the castle by a second entrance higher up.

Sfaktiría (Sphakteria) – The uninhabited island of Sfaktiría (about 5km/3mi long and rising to 152m/about 500ft) is the site of several monuments raised to commemorate those who died at the Battle of Navarino (particularly the Russians) and in the cause of Greek independence (eg the grave of Paul-Marie Bonaparte: *see SPÉTSES*).

On the summit there are traces of an ancient fortress where 420 Spartans made a heroic stand against the Athenians during the Peloponnesian War (425 BC).

★**Nestor's Palace** – *14km/9mi north on the road to Hóra. See Anáktora NÉSTOROS.*

For adjacent sights see ITHÓMI, KALAMÁTA, KIPARISSÍA, KORÓNI, MESSINIAKÓS Kólpos, METHÓNI, MISTRÁS, Anáktora NÉSTOROS, SPÁRTI.

PLATAMÓNAS Castle★

Pieriá, Macedonia

Michelin map 980 north of fold 17

On a hill (200m/656ft) between the sea and Mount Olympos stands the Frankish castle of Platamónas; it occupies a commanding position at the seaward end of the Vale of Tempe *(see Kiláda ton TÉMBON)* guarding the road north to Thessaloníki.

It was begun in 1204 by the Crusaders under Boniface de Montferrat, Prince of Thessaloníki and constituted the fief of the Lombard baron, Orlando Pischia, under the name of Chytra. In the mid 13C it passed to the Byzantines and eventually to the Turks.

TOUR

Access by a footpath from the Athens-Thessaloníki road in Néa Pandeleimónas

The castle – An interesting example of medieval military architecture, consisting of three baileys. The walls of the outer rampart which was reinforced with towers varied in height (7–9m/23–30ft) and in thickness (1.20–2m/4–6ft 6in). A very narrow entry leads to a double Gothic door beneath a rounded arch which was once part of a smaller castle. Besides the keep and some officers' quarters, the fortress contained five churches; the Turks destroyed all but one which they converted into a mosque.

Two more walls defended the approach to the **keep**; the entrance was 3.50m/11ft 6in from the ground and could be reached only by ladders; note the rounded window arches, one of which is divided by a small central column.

For adjacent sights see DÍO, LÁRISSA, LEFKÁDIA-NÁOUSSA, METÉORA, Óros ÓLIMBOS, PÉLA, Kiláda ton TÉMBON, THESSALONÍKI, TRÍKALA, VÉRIA.

PÓROS★★

Saronic Gulf, Attica – Population 3 570

Michelin map 980 fold 30 – 23km²/9sq mi

Póros lies just off the east coast of the Argolid peninsula across a narrow strait which opens out at its western end into **Neorion Bay** (Órmos Neoríou) enclosed by splendid wooded hills. A canal divides the island into two parts: the major part, called **Kalavría**, is a limestone ridge rising to 390m/1 279ft; the minor is a volcanic islet called **Sfería** on which Póros Town, the main port, is situated. Its homely character and its verdant countryside (pine, olive and lemon groves) make it an agreeable place to stay or from which to make excursions to the Argolid peninsula: the lemon groves at Lemonodássos *(see ARGOLÍDA)* and the ruins at Troizen, Epidauros, Tiryns and Mycenae.

PRACTICAL INFORMATION

Access – Frequent daily services by **hydrofoil** from Piraeus (Ceres Group ☎ (01) 42 80 001 in Piraeus, (0296) 23 423 in Póros) or by **ferry** (Aktion-Préveza Consortium ☎ (01) 41 26 181 in Piraeus). It is also possible to board when these services call at Méthana (Argolid Peninsula) (☎ (0298) 92 460). From **Galatás** there is a car ferry every 30min and small boats whenever required.

Accommodation – About 15 hotels (cat B to E), especially outside the town. Many rooms in private houses in town.

Transport – Bicycle and motorcycle hire services.

Arriving by boat one has enchanting **views**★★★ of the "lake" of Póros, of the pyramid of white formed by the little town and of the green shores of the mainland, dominated to the north by the long ridge of a mountain nicknamed the "Sleeping Woman". From **Galatás** on the Argive shore there are also splendid **views**★★ of Póros Town reflected in the calm waters of the strait.

★**Póros Town** – Pop 3 605. The white cuboid houses with jasmin trailing over the trellises and courtyards, mount the slopes of the promontory towards a blue painted bell-tower; from the top there is a **view**★★ of the town, the roadstead and the hills of Troizen.

A stroll along the quay opens up a picturesque view of Galatás, the strait and the roadstead where in 1831 Miaoúlis' fire ships *(see ÍDRA)* set fire to the frigate Hellas which Kapodistrias wanted to lend to the Russian fleet to punish his rivals from Hydra. In the typical fishermen's district *(east)* the cafés and tavernas serving fish dishes are decorated with naive paintings. The old arsenal *(west)* now houses a naval school. The coast road *(turn left after crossing the canal)* runs westwards to **Russian Bay** (Órmos Rósson), a 19C Russian naval station (traces of storehouses) on a lonely site.

★Tour of Kalavría *Round trip of 15km/9.25mi*

Naós Possidóna – The road climbs up to the ruins of a **sanctuary to Poseidon** (6C BC): only the outline on the ground remains but it is on a superb site near to a little pine forest overlooking the island and the Saronic Gulf. According to legend, after **Demosthenes** was banished from Athens he took refuge in the monastery in 322 BC and later poisoned himself there. Fine **view★** over Méthana and Aegina.

★Zoodóhos Pigí Monastery ⏱ – From the temple follow the road downhill to the Monastery of the Virgin, the Source of Life, a white building set in a valley refreshed by many springs; the cloister with its noble cypress trees is open to the public; fine view of the Argolid coast extending southwest to Cape Spathí. Below the monastery there is a charming little beach *(tavernas)*.

For adjacent sights see ARGOLÍDA, ÁRGOS, Aktí ARKADÍAS, ATHÍNA, DAFNÍ, ELEFSÍNA, EPÍDAVROS, ÍDRA, LERNÍ, MIKÍNES, NÁFPLIO, SPÉTSES, TÍRINTHA.

Painted sign, Póros

D. Tuppin /PIX

PRÉVEZA

Préveza, Epiros – Population 13 341
Michelin map 980 fold 15 – Airport

’réveza, which was founded in the 3C BC by Pyrrhus, King of Epiros, guards the ntrance to the **Ambracian Gulf** (Ambrakikós Kólpos) opposite Cape Áktio (Akteion) vhere the famous naval engagement, **the battle of Actium**, took place in 31 BC: Octavian, he future Emperor Augustus, routed the fleet of his rival, Antony who was accomanied by Cleopatra, queen of Egypt, and fled to Alexandria.
'he town is now a port and seaside resort: beach, camp sites, fish tavernas, all in the hade of the pine trees to the west of the town.

★Ruins of Nikopolis (Nikópoli) ⏱ – *7km/5mi north on the Ioánina road which crosses the site; tavernas.* Nikopolis was an important Roman and Byzantine city founded in 30 BC by Octavian Augustus after his victory at Actium. Tradition says that St Paul visited the city in AD 64 and it developed into an active centre of Christianity where the future pope St Eleutherius (2C) was born. The city was destroyed by the Bulgarians in the 11C.
In 1798 the French and Souliot troops *(see EFÍRA)* who were occupying Préveza were annihilated by the forces of Ali Pasha *(see IOÁNINA)* who took 1 200 prisoners and sent them on foot to Constantinople.

City – It consists of a badly-ruined external wall dating from the time of Augustus and a huge internal Byzantine wall (6C) reinforced with towers. The main features are the museum (lion, Roman portraits), the remains of Doumetios' basilica (5C, mosaics) and Augustus' Odeon *(restored)* which from the top gives a good view of the ruined site.
The impressive traces of the **basilica of Alkyson** *(on the right of the road going towards the theatre)* were built in the 6C by a bishop of that name; it comprises an atrium, a narthex, a nave and four aisles; moulded doorframe and mosaics.

Theatre – It is built against a hillside *(beware of snakes)* and dates from the time of Augustus although it must have been altered at a later date as is shown by the brickwork. The stage is well preserved and the rows of seats are clearly traceable. Around the upper rim are the holes which held the posts to support the sun awning.

On a hill to the north of the theatre, beyond the village of Smirtoúla, are the remains of a monument commemorating the victory of Actium, which was erected by Augustus on the very site where his tent had stood during the battle.

Vónitsa – *17km/10.5mi southeast by the ferry and the gulf coast road.* From Cape Akteion, on which a temple once stood where two *kouroi* were excavated *(now in the Louvre in Paris)*, the road reaches Vónitsa *(tavernas)*. This little old town was once defended by a 17C Venetian **fortress** *(access on foot from the east side)*: glimpses of the coast and the Ambracian Gulf.

For adjacent sights see ÁRTA, EFÍRA, KASSÓPI, KÉRKIRA, LEFKÁDA, PÁRGA.

SAMOTHRÁKI

SAMOTHRACE – Evros, Thrace – Population 3 083

Michelin map 980 fold 8 – 178km²/69sq mi

The island measures 20x12km/12.5x7.5mi; from the low coastline the land rises to Mount Fengári (1 611m/5 285ft). It is a wild island, rarely visited owing to poor communications and a lack of safe harbours but there are interesting traces of the past.

PRACTICAL INFORMATION

Access by air – From Athína/Athens to Alexandroúpoli 1 to 2 services daily (continuing by boat).

Access by ferry – From Alexandroúpoli (2hr) daily service; from Kavála (3hr 45min) in summer 3 services a week; also from Ág Konstandínos (central Greece north of Euboia) via Ág Efstrátios and Límnos/Lemnos.

Accommodation – 3 hotels in Kamariótissa harbour (cat B, C, E) and Xenia hotel (cat B) in Paleopoli; few rooms in private houses in Kamariótissa and Therma.

★**Ruins of the Sanctuary of the Great Gods** ⊙ – The sanctuary, which stands on the slopes of a ravine above Paleópoli, was dedicated to two mysterious subterranean divinities, the **Kabeiroi**, highly venerated by the Ancients who underwent initiation ceremonies in the sanctuary. The first excavations were undertaken in 1863 by Champoiseau, French consul in Adrianople (now Edirne), who discovered the famous **Victory of Samothrace** *(see also RÓDOS: Acropolis)*, a masterpiece of Hellenistic art (3C BC), which is now in the Louvre in Paris.
The Anaktoron, the Hall of Princes, which dates from the 1C BC, was built of polygonal masonry and used for initiation ceremonies. The **Arsinoeion**, the largest rotunda in Greece, being over 20m/65ft in diameter, was built in about 285 BC by Arsinoë, wife of king Lysimachos of Thrace. A rectangular precinct *(témenos)* of which the foundations date from the 4C BC contained an allegorical statue of Desire by the great sculptor Skopas. The **Hieron**, an important 4C BC temple with a Doric doorway *(columns re-erected)* and an apse, was used for sacrifices.
Near the theatre, of which little remains, was the Victory fountain set in a rocky niche and decorated with the famous winged Victory, which was probably a votive monument as in Líndos; the hand was not recovered until 1950.
The Ptolemaion was erected by the king of Egypt, Ptolemy Philadelphos (280-264 BC) as a monumental gateway to the sanctuary.

Museum ⊙ – Models recall the former appearance of the main buildings in the Sanctuary of the Great Gods. The sculptures include a headless statue of Victory from the Hieron and a bust (5C BC) of **Tiresias**, the seer who was transformed into a woman for seven years and then made blind by Athena whom he had seen bathing.

For adjacent sights see KAVÁLA, LÍMNOS, THÁSSOS.

The section on Practical Information at the end of the guide lists:
local or national organisations providing additional information,
recreational sports,
thematic tours,
further reading,
events of interest to the tourist,
admission times and charges.

SIKIÓNA

SIKYON – Korinthía, Peloponnese
Michelin map 980 fold 29 – 25km/15mi west of Corinth

From Kiáto *(10km/6.25mi by car there and back)* take the small road *(sign "Ancient Sikyon")* which climbs through vineyards, groves of citrus fruits, olives and almond trees, crosses the motorway, passes through the modern village of Sikióna (Vassilikó pop 872) and reaches the ancient site.
The ruins of Sikyon on their hilltop overlooking the fertile coastal plain and the Gulf of Corinth recall an earlier ancient city which flourished in the Archaic period, particularly under the tyrant Kleisthenes who built a *thólos* and a monopteral monument at Delphi early in the 6C which were replaced in the 5C by a Treasury. The city of Sikyon then stood in the plain but it was razed to the ground in 30 BC by Demetrius Poliorketes, a king from Asia Minor, and rebuilt on the plateau: it became famous for its school of painting on wax which produced among others Pamphilos, the master of Apelles. According to Pausanias, this latter city was destroyed by an earthquake.

Ruins ⓥ – There are remains from both the Hellenistic and the Roman periods. Beyond the museum, which stands on the site of the old Roman baths, is a large theatre (3C BC) (restored) on the right built against the flank of the former acropolis. Below to the left are the foundations of a huge gymnasium (72x69m/236x226ft) on two levels bordered by porticoes and linked by a central staircase between two fountains which are clearly identifiable. The ground also shows traces of a temple, presumably dedicated to Apollo, and a senate house *(bouleuterion)*.

For adjacent sights see ÁRGOS, EPÍDAVROS, KALÁVRITA, KÓRINTHOS, Dióriga KORÍNTHOU, LOUTRÁKI, MÉGA SPÍLEO, MIKÍNES, NEMÉA, STIMFALÍA, TÍRINTHA, Harádra tou VOURAÏKOÚ.

SPÁRTI

SPARTA – Lakonía, Peloponnese – Population 13 011
Michelin map 980 north of fold 41

Although modern Sparta is built on the fertile banks of the **Evrótas** (Eurotas) at the foot of the snow-capped slopes of Mount Taígetos on the site of ancient Sparta **(Lakedaimon)**, it has nothing in common with the austere and bellicose city of antiquity which triumphed over Athens at the end of the Peloponnesian War. The modern town was developed in the reign of King Otto after 1834; it is a provincial administrative centre, the capital of Lakonía, its straight streets lined with orange trees intersecting at right angles; it is also on the route to Mystra.

HISTORICAL NOTES

An aristocratic and military state – In the Mycenaean period Sparta was part of the kingdom of Menelaos, Helen's husband. Remains from this period have been found near to Sparta, not only at the Menelaion itself (Geráki road) but also at Amíkles **(Amyklai)** (7km/4.25mi south) where there was a sanctuary to Apollo containing the tomb of Hyacinthos who was loved by Apollo. There are also the beehive tombs at Vafió **(Vapheio)** on a hill near Amíkles which have yielded the famous golden horn-shaped vessels *(rhytons)* in the Athens Museum.
Sparta was most influential however from the 9C to the 4C BC, first in the Peloponnese, which was conquered except for Árgos, and then throughout Greece.
The Greeks respected the skill of the Spartan soldiers even if they did not approve of the oligarchic constitution which had been drawn up, according to tradition, in about 900 BC by the famous lawgiver **Lycurgus**. At the head of the state were two kings, who were the military leaders, assisted by a council of 28 elders and five *ephors* who had executive power.
The population was divided into three classes: the Spartiates, the warrior class, between 5 000 and 10 000 in number, who were also land owners and holders of government posts; the Perioikoi, who were traders and artisans or farmers, free-men who paid tax; the Helots, serfs without legal status but very numerous.

Spartan way of life – The Spartiates were forbidden to work; instead they spent almost all their time in barracks, training in combat and practising an athletic war dance known as the Pyrrhic. They ate communally, living mainly on herbs and wild roots; their famous black broth, pork stewed in the animal's blood, was a banquet to them.
At 7 the boys were drafted into youth troops inured to physical exercise. They slept on the ground and were sometimes obliged to practise stealing without being caught; a well-known anecdote tells how a youth who had stolen a fox cub and hidden it beneath his tunic, preferred to let it maul him rather than reveal his booty. On reaching adulthood at the age of 20 the young Spartiates faced a series of initiation tests, the *krypteia*; they were flogged, sometimes to death, and abandoned without resources in the countryside; they proved themselves by killing any Helots who tarried out of doors after dark.

The girls also were given to strenuous exercise and shocked the other Greeks by their plunging necklines. The married women were not expected to be faithful to their husbands; their lovers were chosen with a view to procreation. It was the married women who presented the newly-graduated hoplites with their traditional shield and plumed helmet.

The Spartiates were austere and laconic soldiers but they gave up their lives without hesitation, as did **Leonidas** and his companions at Thermopylae *(see THERMOPÍLES)* in 480 BC. Their numbers diminished continually and eventually they were beaten by Epaminóndas in 371 BC at Leuktra near to Thebes *(see THÍVA)*. From then on the city declined and was supplanted by Mystra; gradually ancient Sparta was abandoned until it turned into a desert of stones.

The Spartans are generally thought to have scorned the arts but in the 6C and the 5C BC they had talented bronzesmiths who produced the statuettes which are now displayed in the museums of Sparta and Athens and also in the British Museum.

SIGHTS

Arheologikó Moussío ⓥ – *Start in the room on the right of the entrance.* The **Archeological Museum**, which is surrounded by a pleasant garden, displays the finds from local excavations, particularly Sparta and Amyklai (Amíkles): Archaic low-relief sculpture (6C BC), one of which represents Helen and Menelaos; a votive statue of the Dioscuri, Helen's brothers (5C BC); effigy of a hoplite, in marble, thought to be Leonidas (5C BC); head of Apollo or Dionysos (4C BC) discovered in 1978; Archaic bronze statuettes; terracotta masks from the sanctuary of Artemis Orthia; Roman mosaics...

Ethnikí Pinakothíki-Moussío Alexándrou Soútsos (Koumantatios Pinakothíki) ⓥ – A branch of the National Gallery in Athens, it houses a fine permanent collection of pictures by Greek and foreign painters from the 16C to the 20C.

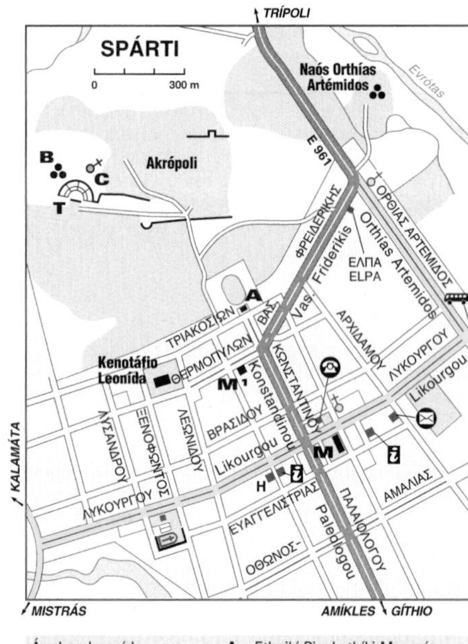

Ágalma Leonída .... A
Arheologikó Moussío .... M
Arhéo Théatro .... T
Ethnikí Pinakothíki Moussío Alexándrou Soútsou .... M¹
Naós Athinás .... B
Paliá Vizandiní Moní C

Ancient ruins – *Admission free.* Most of them date from the Hellenistic or Roman periods.

Kenotáfio Leonída – This is in fact the base of a small Hellenistic temple; Leonidas' tomb was to be found on the Acropolis. A modern statue of the hero has been erected nearby in Odós Konstandínou.

Akrópoli – The remains of the Acropolis buildings are half hidden in an olive grove on high ground north of the modern town *(sign "Ancient Sparta")*. Go through the Byzantine wall and bear left to reach the theatre which dates from the 1C BC. Above it are the foundations of a temple to Athena.

At the very top, agreeably situated among fragrant pine and eucalyptus trees next to a spring stands an old Byzantine monastery, Óssios Nikónas (10C AD).

Naós Orthías Artémidos (Sanctuary of Artemis Orthia) – The oleanders and rushes on the banks of the River Evrótas – a favourite theme with earlier writers – now screen the ruins of a temple (7C-6C) and an amphitheatre excavated by British archeologists. It was here that the ritual endurance tests of young Spartans took place: flogging and athletic dances with masks which were offered to Artemis.

EXCURSION

Zerbítsa Monastery – *12km/7.5mi to the south. Take the Gíthio road, then turn right on the road passing through Xirokámbia and follow the signs.* The monastery, usually a peaceful and enchanting place, has a beautiful 17C Byzantine church with an interior covered in frescoes of 1669, and a small museum containing an **Epitáphios** of 1539 embroidered with gold, some icons and early Christian architectural fragments.

For adjacent sights see Aktí ARKADÍAS, Spílea DIROÚ, GERÁKI, GÍTHIO, ITHÓMI, KALAMÁTA, MÁNI, MEGALÓPOLI, MESSINIAKÓS Kólpos, MISTRÁS, MONEMVASSÍA.

SPÉTSES★★

SPETSAE – Attica – Population 3 729
Michelin map 980 south of fold 30 – 22km²/9sq mi

Spetsae is popular with the Athenians who often own houses on the island.
In antiquity it was known as Pityoussa, the island of pine forests; their cool shade and the fragrant resin-scented air in summer, together with the peaceful atmosphere, are still attracting visitors to the island.
Culinary specialities are the almond cakes *(amigdalotá)* and the fish prepared in the Spetsiot manner (baked in the oven in white wine).
Like its rival Hydra, Spetsae grew rich through piracy in the Mediterranean during the 18C and 19C. The island contributed nobly to the struggle against the Turks with the vessels built in its shipyards.

Bouboulína, a Greek heroine (1771-1825) – Lascarína Pinótzis was born in prison in Constantinople, the daughter of a Hydriot captain who was condemned to death by the Turks. Her mother fled to Spetsae, where in 1788 Lascarína married Giannoutzás, a Spetsiot captain, whom she accompanied on several sea voyages but who died in 1798 when his ship was sunk by Barbary pirates. She married a second time, Boúboulis, another sailor, but he too was killed by pirates.
Her husbands' deaths made Bouboulína a rich woman; she owned shipyards and a fleet of brigs and schooners which she supplemented in 1821 with a powerful corvette, *Agamemnon*, which flew her personal colours.
Sailing at the head of her squadron, dressed in the striped Spetsiot costume and wearing a huge wimple, Admiral Bouboulína took part in the naval engagements in 1821 and 1824, participating in acts of piracy and in particular making a significant contribution to the blockade of Náfplio.
On returning to Spetsae she became involved in violent family quarrels caused by her son's seduction of a daughter of the Koutsís family. She died, a victim of the vendetta, from a gunshot wound in the head in her house in Kounoupítsa on 22 May 1825.

PRACTICAL INFORMATION

Access by sea – Several daily services by **hydrofoil** from Piraeus and Portohéli (Ceres Group ☎ (01) 42 80 001 in Piraeus, (0754) 51 543 in Portohéli; Bardakos Tourism ☎ (0298) 73 141 in Spétses) or by **ferry** (Aktion-Préveza Consortium ☎ (01) 41 26 181 in Piraeus, (0298) 74 098 in Spétses).

Accommodation – About 20 hotels in Spetsae Town and nearby (cat A to E); many rooms in private houses.

Transport – Cars are banned on the island except in the case of local people in winter; buses and taxis and bicycle and motorcycle hire services; caïques for excursions to beaches.

★★**Spétses (Spetsae Town)** – Pop 3 655. Spetsae is a spacious town, consisting of two districts round the harbour, Dápia and Paleó Limáni, as well as the upper town, Kastéli. It is pleasant to stroll past the shipowners' and sailors' houses set in their gardens. Very often the threshold is decorated with a mosaic of pebbles depicting ships, animals or marine motifs.

Dápia and Paleó Limáni – The modern port (Dápia) consists of an inlet enclosed between two jetties where caïques and motor boats are moored. The waterfront is lined by a string of administrative buildings, the harbour master's house and several tavernas. Beyond the town hall, in **Kounoupítsa**, the courtyard (unusual mosaics) of **Bouboulína's House** ⌚ can be seen. In the other direction towards Kolinariá, stands the **Méxis House** ⌚, which was built late in the 18C by Hadziyannis Mexis, a wealthy shipowner, and is now occupied by a museum devoted to the lives of great 19C Spetsiots.
Further along the coast near the lighthouse *(southeast)* lies the old port, Paleó Limáni. Its many creeks are filled with shipyards, caulking stations and moorings for the yachts and caïques which have replaced the 19C brigs.
In 1821 the first flag of independent Greece was flown from the bell-tower of **St Nicholas' Monastery** (Ágios Nikólaos). When **Paul-Marie**, the son of Lucien Bonaparte, was killed in 1827 by a pistol exploding on board the frigate *Hellas* just offshore, his body was brought to the monastery, preserved in a barrel of oil and kept in a cell for five years before being taken to Sfaktería *(see PÍLOS)*.
South of Paleó Limáni, beyond the headland, extends the rocky shore round **Agía Marína** (*tavernas*).

Kastéli – The upper town above Dápia looking across to the Argolid peninsula was fortified by the Venetians in the 16C; there are three churches, of which the largest, **Agía Triáda** (Holy Trinity) ⌚, contains a beautiful carved wood iconostasis.

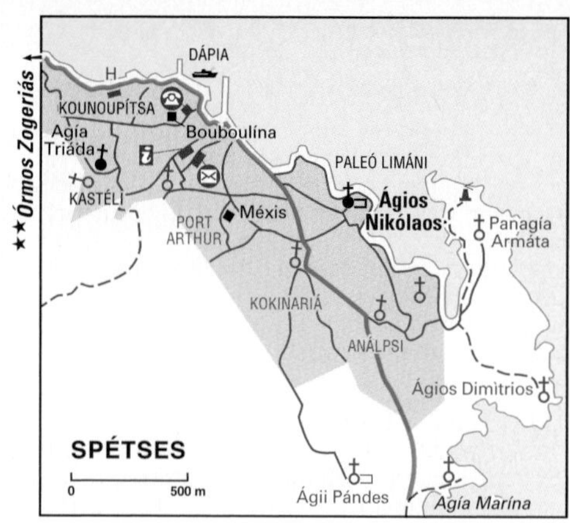

★★ Órmos Zogeriás (Zogeriá Bay) – *Take the coast road northwest (5hr on foot there and back; 2hr by bicycle there and back). There are also boats from Dápia.* The road runs past what was once a distinguished boys' school (1927-83), founded by a Spetsiot tobacco baron, **Sotírios Anárgyros**, on the lines of an English public school. Two of the English masters who taught there used their experience to write novels: *The Magus* by John Fowles and *Aleko* by Kenneth Matthews.

The road continues, cut into the hillside, through forests of Aleppo pines, round the heads of several creeks until it reaches the huge bay at Zogeriá, a beautiful site facing north up the Bay of Náfplio *(tavernas in summer)*.

Just off the southeast coast of Spetsae lies **Spetsopoúla**, an islet belonging to the shipping magnate, Stavros Niarchos, who has turned it into a game reserve and a harbour for his yachts, including the *Creole*, the largest three-master in the world.

For adjacent sights see ARGOLÍDA, ÁRGOS, Aktí ARKADÍAS, EPÍDAVROS, ÍDRA, LERNÍ, MIKÍNES, MONEMVASSÍA, NÁFPLIO, PÓROS, TÍRINTHA.

Límni STIMFALÍA★

LAKE STYMPHALOS – Korinthía, Peloponnese

Michelin map 980 fold 29 – 37km/23mi southeast of Kiáto

A good road *(sign "Stimfalía")* crosses the citrus groves in the coastal plain and then climbs the eastern foothills of Mount Kilíni overlooking the Gulf of Corinth – a fertile landscape of pine woods and vines cultivated as bushes to produce the dried grapes known as "currants". The road then descends into the huge and barren depression at the bottom of which lies Lake Stymphalos *(tavernas)*.

★The Lake – Below the acropolis of the city of Stymphalos extends an immense reed-covered marsh surrounded by a ring of dark peaks (2 000m/6 560ft); its depth and surface area vary according to the season. A touch of anguish seems to emanate from the bleak and inhospitable landscape.

A profound silence hangs over this vast tract of land which is inhabited only by rare herds of cows or flocks of sheep grazing in the custody of a herdsman swathed in a thick cloak and carrying a crook; Stymphalos is on the borders of Arcadia.

The Stymphalian Birds – The gloomy waters of Lake Stymphalos inspired fear in the ancient Greeks; according to the legend the lake was haunted by nauseating birds with huge wings which seized on passers-by, suffocating them in their grasp and killing them with their beaks before eating them. **Herakles** (Hercules) rid the region of them as the fifth of his Twelve Labours *(see TÍRINTHA)* by killing them with his arrows and then offering them to Athena.

Old Abbey of Zaraká – On the east side of the road from Kiáto are the ruins of a Cistercian monastery built in the 13C. The church was Gothic: the pillars in the nave were formed of engaged columns and the chancel was square according to the usual Cistercian practice. The cloisters were on the south side. A single tower marks the entrance to the precinct.

Kastaniá – *20km/12.5mi return from the west end of the lake.* From the lake a road winds past rocky outcrops and coniferous forests to an old mountain village; its houses are traditional with balconies and pantile roofs. It is a quiet place to spend a few days *(Hotel Xenia, tavernas)* on the slopes of **Mount Kilíni** (also Zíria) (2 376m/7 790ft) which in antiquity was supposed to be the haunt of white blackbirds.

For adjacent sights see ÁRGOS, KALÁVRITA, KÓRINTHOS, MÉGA SPÍLEO, MIKÍNES, NEMÉA, SIKIÓNA, TÍRINTHA, TRÍPOLI, Harádra tou VOURAÏKOÚ.

The key on page 4 explains the abbreviations and symbols used in the text and on the maps.

Kiláda ton TÉMBON★

Vale of TEMPE – Lárissa, Thessaly

Michelin map 980 fold 17 – 22km/14mi northeast of Lárissa

On the northern border of Thessaly the valley of the River **Piniós** narrows into a ravine, which is dark and mysterious but also verdant - clumps of plane trees, oleanders and rhododendrons. The narrow valley (5km/3mi long), once known as the "Wolf's Mouth" (Likóstomo), was caused by a seismic fracture between Olympos and Óssa; it formed a channel into which the Piniós directed its course so draining the Lárissa lake to the sea.

The laurels of Apollo – In antiquity this region was sacred to Apollo, son of Zeus and Leto. After killing the python at Delphi *(see DÉLFI: Legend and History)* he came to wash in the waters of the Piniós. There he fell in love with the nymph Daphne who was changed into a laurel tree *(dáphni)* to escape from Apollo's advances. Disappointed, Apollo gathered a sprig of the laurel and planted it at Delphi near the Kastalian spring. Every eighth year, as a token of remembrance, pilgrims went from Delphi to Tempe to gather a symbolic laurel branch.
The Vale of Tempe was much praised in antiquity for its cool freshness compared with the torrid summer climate of the Macedonian and Thessalian plains. It enchanted Emperor **Hadrian** who had it re-created by landscape architects in the grounds of his villa at Tivoli near Rome.

The Vale of Tempe

It is advisable to tour the valley by travelling upstream from east to west as most of the lay-bys are on the north (right) side of the road.

Daphne's Spring – Also known as Apollo's Spring, this is shady site, cool and restful.

Agía Paraskeví – This important place of pilgrimage dedicated to the Virgin is on the north bank of the River Piniós at the foot of an impressive cliff of rock. From the footbridge over the river there is a beautiful **view★** of the vale and the plane trees spreading their graceful arms over the water. On a rocky pinnacle are the remains of a medieval castle, one of the six fortresses which guarded the pass.

Aphrodite's Spring – It is down by the river beneath the sheltering plane trees.

Ambelákia – The town, which derives its name from its vineyards, is splendidly situated on the northwest slope of Mount Óssa at the opening of the gorge in the Vale of Tempe with an extensive view of the River Piniós basin and of the heights of Mount Olympos. It is now only a small town with a few tavernas and a tourist cooperative run by country women, which organises **lodgings** Ⓥ *(see p 366)*.
Ambelákia was once a more prosperous place with a population of 4 000. In the 17C and 18C there were thriving workshops producing silk and cotton fabrics, dyed scarlet with madder from the neighbouring plain. In 1780 these workshops combined in a cooperative for production and sales, the oldest of its type, which had commercial agents throughout Europe, particularly in France in Lyon and Rouen. Its members numbered 6 000. Unfortunately it was disbanded in 1811

T.A.P.

Interior of the Schwarz House, Ambelákia

owing to competition from British industrial manufacturers, the disruption caused by the Napoleonic wars and the heavy taxes imposed by Ali Pasha *(see IOÁNINA)*, the tyrant of Ióanina.

★ **Arhondikó Schwarz** ⓥ – This was the **residence of George Schwarz**, the head of the cooperative. It is a superb example of a typical 18C Thessalian house with projecting upper storeys, balconies and carved and turned wooden partitions. The interior has typical rounded fireplaces and is richly decorated with painted ornaments and landscapes; the offices were on the ground floor and the living rooms upstairs. There are several old houses in the village including that of George Schwarz' brother, Demetrios *(not open)*.

For adjacent sights see LÁRISSA, PLATAMÓNAS, METÉORA, TRÍKALA, Óros ÓLIMBOS, Óros PÍLIO, VÓLOS.

THÁSSOS★★

Kavála, Macedonia – Population 13 527

Michelin map 980 fold 7 – about 380km²/147sq mi

Thássos, famous in antiquity for its gold and marble, lies just off the coast of eastern Macedonia. Its wooded mountain scenery, its creeks and bathing beaches as well as its excellent hotels make it a delightful island resort for holidays.
Main beaches are at Makríamos, Alikí, Potamiá and Limenária Bay. Local specialities: fresh fish, honey and retsína. Classical drama festival in summer.

PRACTICAL INFORMATION

Access by sea – Daily services by **hydrofoil** from Kavála to Liménas, and by **ferry** from Kavála to Prínos and from Keramotí to Liménas. Information: ☎ (051) 22 37 16 in Kavála, (0591) 51 204 in Keramotí, (0593) 22 355 in Liménas, (0593) 71 290 in Prínos.

Accommodation – In Thássos-Liménas about 40 hotels (cat A to E); in Limenária about 20 hotels (cat B to E); in Skála Potamiás about 20 hotels (cat B to E), in Ormos Príniou (Prínos) about 20 hotels (cat B to E). Camp sites.

Transport – Motorcycle hire services.

From yellow gold to black gold – The island rises to the peak of Mount Ipsári or Psári (about 1 127m/3 698ft) and is composed of marble and grey-green gneiss. Ample rainfall in autumn and winter sustains the luxuriant vegetation which clothes the landscape. There are several sorts of pine tree: sea pines, Aleppo pines and Corsican pines; also cypresses, olives, oaks, chestnuts, walnuts and even poplars.
In antiquity, particularly from the 7C to the 5C BC Thássos was of considerable economic importance owing to its exports of oil and wine, of white marble and of gold and silver; the metal was used to mint money throughout the Mediterranean. In those days the inhabitants ruled part of the Macedonian coast including Kavála and Thessaloníki.
Then the island entered on a period of relative quiet until the arrival of the Romans who reactivated the production of wine and marble. In the 15C Thássos was occupied for a period by the Genoese who set up a trading post under the Gatteluzzi, the lords of Lesbos and Samothrace. Finally the Turks took over and Thássos became the personal fief of Mehmet Ali *(see KAVÁLA)* and his family from 1813 to 1902.
Interest in Thássos was renewed in 1971 when oil was discovered off-shore.

★ **Liménas (Thássos Town)** – Pop 2 600. The modern port extends westwards in a lively string of café terraces and tavernas set about with trees. The considerable traces of the ancient Greek civilisation, which the French School in Athens has been excavating since 1910, are spread over a vast area enclosed within a marble wall which dates from the 5C BC; a few of the gates are still decorated with low-relief carvings.

★ **Eastern ramparts and the acropolis** – *2hr on foot there and back.* Starting behind the long Turkish building with balconies overlooking the caïque harbour, the path runs along inside the ramparts and then climbs up above the ancient port; the outline of the old jetties can be traced beneath the water. A little way offshore lies the islet of **Thassopoúla**.
After passing the modest shipyards and the remains of a 5C paleo-Christian basilica set on a promontory, the path climbs up by the wall which is superbly constructed in places with polygonal blocks. Half way along is the **theatre**; it was built in the Hellenistic period but remodelled by the Romans as an arena for wild animal fights.

The **acropolis★** comprises three peaks in a line separated by two narrow saddles. On the first peak stood a sanctuary to Pythian Apollo which was converted into a fortress by the Genoese who reused the old material on the original foundations. The second peak, which forms a terrace, boasted a temple to Athena; the 5C foundations are still visible. At the base of the third is a small rock sanctuary dedicated to Pan; from the peak there are beautiful **views★★** of Thássos Island and the Aegean Sea as far as Samothrace.

Visitors interested in archeology should walk round the ramparts.

★ **Agorá** ⓥ – The *agorá*, which has recently been excavated, was not far from the harbour and surrounded by porticoes and studded with monuments of all sorts; it was linked to the neighbouring shrines by the Ambassadors *(Theoríes)* Passage which was decorated with low-relief sculptures (sent to the Louvre in Paris in 1864).

An anti-clockwise tour round the *agorá* takes in three porticoes: on the right of the entrance traces of the southwest portico, which dates from the Roman period and was supported by 33 Doric columns (remains of a monumental altar in south corner); then traces of the southeast portico, of the same period, of which three columns have been re-erected (at the far end the base of a monument to Glaukos set up in the 7C BC); finally traces of the "oblique" portico and a 5C paleo-Christian basilica.

Within the open space the archeologists have excavated the remains of a *thólos*, an altar dedicated to the deified Theagenes, a Thassian athlete who had been victorious in the Olympic Games, and some round stone benches *(exedrae)*.

Museum ⓥ – It displays the items found during the excavations and some interesting sculptures. Room 1 (central hall): colossal *kouros* carrying a ram (6C BC) from the acropolis and a very realistic head of Silenus (5C BC); Room 2: two 6C BC works found in the temple of Artemis, a mirror handle in bronze and an extraordinary ivory lion's head; the other rooms: an effigy of Dionysos (3C BC) from the Hellenistic period, two heads by the School of Skópas (4C BC), a low relief from a Roman altar to Cybele showing griffins devouring a doe and Roman portraits from the empire (Julius Caesar, Claudius, Hadrian).

★★Tour of the island *79km/49mi – about 3hr*

There is a good road which follows the wooded coastline not far from the shore. It passes inlets and beaches, crosses tiny coastal basins or cuts into the cliff face. Leaving Thássos-Liménas in a southeasterly direction the road first climbs to **Panagía**, the ancient capital of the island; the picturesque houses have balconies and schist roofs.

Alikí★ *(tavernas)* on the south coast is built on an attractive site on the neck of a peninsula consisting entirely of marble quarries which seem to have been abandoned only yesterday. There was an ancient city here as is proved by the remains of a double sanctuary; the edge of the hill bears traces of two paleo-Christian basilicas.

Limenária is a fishing village and a lively summer resort.

Along the west coast the road passes many fishing villages *(skála)*. If there is time make a detour to **Mariés** *(29km/18mi there and back)*, a pretty village in the traditional style.

For adjacent sights see AMFÍPOLI, FÍLIPI, HALKIDIKÍ, KAVÁLA, SAMOTHRÁKI.

THERMOPÍLES★

THERMOPYLAE – Fthiótida, Central Greece

Michelin map 980 south of fold 17 – 14km/9mi south of Lamí

The pass of Thermopylae is famous for its heroic defence by **Leonidas** and his Spartans. Hemmed in in antiquity between Mount Kalídromo *(south)* and an arm of the sea, the Maliac Gulf, the pass was the main route from Thessaly into southern Greece. In those days the pass was much narrower than it is now; the modern motorway follows the ancient shoreline. Subsequently the estuary of the River Sperhiós silted up forming a coastal plain which now produces olives and cotton.

An unequal struggle – In 480 BC, 10 years after the battle of Marathon *(see ATHÍNA)*, another Great Army of Persians led by **Xerxes**, Darius' son, crossed the Hellespont (the Dardanelles) and invaded Greece. Thus began the Second Persian War which Herodotos described in his *History*.

When the myriads of Persian soldiers (according to modern historians they numbered about 30 000) arrived at Thermopylae they found the Greeks, only 8 000, entrenched behind the Phocian wall. "Surrender your arms" cried Xerxes to Leonidas. "Come and take them" replied the Spartan commander.

The Persians attacked but for two days suffered heavy losses. Then a traitor showed them a way over the mountains so that they could turn the Greek defence and, despite the Phocian troops, take the Greeks in the rear.
When Leonidas saw what was planned, he made the bulk of the army withdraw and prepared to defend his position with 300 Spartans and 700 Thespians. He was forced to retreat to a knoll (Kolonós) under a hail of arrows to which he responded with "So much the better, we will fight in the shade". The Spartans were killed to the last man; Leonidas' body was beheaded and then crucified on the orders of Xerxes who had lost his two brothers in the engagement.
Fortunately for the Greeks the subsequent engagements at Salamis *(see ATHÍNA)* and Plataia *(see PLATEÉS)* resulted in victory and the Persians were driven out of Greece.

Leonidas' Monument – *On the north side of the road.* The monument was unveiled in 1955 by King Paul of Greece. It is constructed of white marble and decorated with low-relief sculptures of the battle; it is crowned by a bronze statue of the Spartan leader, bearing arms and wearing his helmet.
On the other side of the road is the knoll, **Kolonós**, where the Spartans took their final stand; a mausoleum has been constructed bearing an inscription:

"Go, tell the Spartans, thou who passest by,
That here obedient to their laws we lie".

Hot springs – *500m/547yd beyond the monument, on the south side of the road near a petrol station.* These sulphureous waters, which emerge at the foot of the mountain and were known in antiquity as the Baths of Herakles, have given their name to the locality; Thermopylae literally means "hot gates".

For adjacent sights see DELFÍ, Drómos tou IRAKLÍ, ÉVIA, KARPENÍSSI, Óros PÍLIO, TRÍKALA, VÓLOS.

THESSALONÍKI★★

SALONICA – Macedonia – Population 383 967 (725 785 including the suburbs)
Michelin map 980 folds 5 and 6 – Airport

Thessaloníki, the second largest town and port in Greece, is also the capital of Macedonia. It is a modern-looking town spreading up the hillside with a thriving intellectual (University: Panepistímio), commercial and industrial life. In 1997 it was named the European Capital of Culture under the auspices of the European Union.
The city is flanked on the west by an industrial zone, by a residential district on the east and on the heights to the north by an oriental quarter; the centre on the waterfront is marked by **Platía Aristotélous**, a square open to the sea. Thessaloníki's position at the head of a deep bay, its tree-lined streets, smart shops and Byzantine churches make it attractive to visitors but they should avoid the summer heat and the rigours of winter when the head of the bay sometimes freezes over.

HISTORICAL NOTES

Thessaloníki, an imperial city – Thessaloníki was founded in 315 BC on the site of the ancient town of Therme (which gave its name to the Thermaic Gulf – Thermaikós Kólpos) by Kassander, a Macedonian general *(diádochos)* who named the city after his wife Thessaloníki, sister of Alexander the Great. Under Roman rule it developed into an important port and staging post on the **Via Egnatia**, which linked Dyracchium (Durazzo in Albania) with Asia Minor and was the main highway for Roman penetration of the Levant. In 148 BC it became the capital of the Roman province of Macedonia and was an important cultural centre which was visited by Cicero when he went into exile in 58 BC.

PRACTICAL INFORMATION

Access

By air – **Thessaloníki Airport:** Information ☎ 474 113, 475 344. Airport to city centre service by buses nos 69, 72 and 73. Arrival and pickup point: Odós Egnatia. Flights to and from Athens (5 to 7 services daily), Crete, Lesbos and Rhodes. **Olympic Airways:** ☎ 230 240, ☎ 260 121-9.

By train (OSE) – Station: Odós Monastiriou ☎ 517 517-8. From Athens (about 8hr) 6 services daily.

By sea – Thessaloníki has a boat service once a week throughout the year to Piraeus, calling at Chios and Lesbos, also services to Limnos and the islands of the Sporades, Dodecanese and Cyclades. Information from the Central Harbour Office ☎ 531 505. **CERES (hydrofoils)** – Services to Moudaniá (Chalcidice) and the Sporades (Alónissos, Skópelos, Skíathos). Information ☎ 547 407 or 534 376.

By bus (KTEL) – Intercity services to Athens (7hr 30min – 10 services daily) and the main towns of Greece. Information ☎ 528 600. The buses leave from different locations according to their destinations:
– for Alexandropoúli – 31 Odós Grigoriou Koloniari ☎ 514 111.
– for Dráma – 59 Odós Ivanof ☎ 525 131.
– for Kavála – 59 Odós Langada ☎ 525 530.
– for Ioánina and Kérkira/Corfu – 19 Odós X Pizou ☎ 517 324.
– for Lárissa – 4 Odós Enotikon ☎ 544 133.
– for Halkidikí/Chalcidice – 68 Odós Karakassi ☎ 924 444; to reach the departure point take bus no 10 to Egiptou.

Events – The **Thessaloníki International Fair** is held in September, and the **Demetria**, an arts festival celebrating St Demetrios, in October. At the **Film Festival** in November both feature films and shorts are screened.

Shopping – The best streets for shops are Egnatia, Venizélou, Ermou and the very smart Leofóros Tsimiski.

Useful addresses

Greek Tourist Office (EOT) – Information: 8 Platia Aristotelous ☎ 271 888.

Post Office – Main office – 26 Odós Aristotelou.

Telephone (OTE) – 55 Vas Herakleion. Local dialling code: 031.

Greek Automobile and Touring Club (ELPA) – 228 Odós Vassillis Olgas ☎ 426 319.

British Consulate – 8 Odós Venizélou, Platia Eleftherias ☎ (031) 278 006 or 269 984; Fax 283 868.

American Consulate – 59 Leoforos Nikis ☎ (031) 24 29 05, Fax (031) 24 29 27.

Canadian Consulate – 17 Leofóros Tsimiski ☎ (031) 25 63 50.

St Paul visited Thessaloníki twice during his journeys in AD 50 and 56 and preached in the Synagogue despite the hostility of certain Jews; he also founded the church to which he addressed several Epistles.

Early in the 4C Thessaloníki became the main residence of the Emperor **Galerius** under whose edict Christians were persecuted; in 306 a Roman officer of Greek origin, St Demetrios was martyred. **Theodosius the Great** (379-395) gave official standing to the Christian religion which he had embraced during a serious illness. His conversion did not however prevent him from ordering the massacre of 7 000 Thessalonians in the circus in reprisal for the murder of one of his generals; later he repented and submitted to the penitence imposed by St Ambrose.

Under the return to order following the Barbarian invasions in the reign of the Emperor of Byzantium, **Justinian** (527-565), Thessaloníki became the second city of the Eastern Empire after Byzantium and many churches were built. St Cyril, the philosopher, future apostle of the Slavs and probable inventor of the Cyrillic alphabet, was born there in 827.

From anarchy to prosperity – After a period of uncertainty caused by dissension among the Byzantines, Thessaloníki was caught up in the capture of Constantinople by the Fourth Crusade and from 1204 to 1224 was an archbishopric and capital of a Latin kingdom of which the first king was Boniface de Montferrat.

Thessaloníki was returned to Byzantium and fell prey to anarchy until it was captured by Sultan Mourad II in 1430, who gave it the name Salonika. There followed a period of prosperity which was further enhanced by the arrival in 1492 of 20 000 Jews who had fled from Spain; they were skilled in working with wool, silk and precious stones. They formed a community of craftsmen and merchants who traded throughout Europe. They spoke Ladino, a form of Castilian written in Hebrew script, wore caftans and greatcoats trimmed with fur and by the 17C numbered about 30 000. In 1910 the Jewish community (Sephardim of Spanish origin and Romaniotes – *see p 100*) was 65 000 strong and made up nearly half the population.

Modern era – Under the Turks Thessaloníki was allowed a certain autonomy and its economy developed in the late 19C; in 1888 it was linked by railway to Central Europe and from 1897 to 1903 a new port was constructed by a French company. It was the cradle of the Young Turks who deposed Sultan Abdul Hamid in 1909 and of **Mustafa Kemal Ataturk** (1881-1938) who was the first President of the Turkish Republic; the house where he was born is in Odós Apostólou Pávlou.

In 1912 Thessaloníki was returned to Greece and reverted to its original name. During the First World War from 1915-18 it was the headquarters of the allied armies in the east and of the Greek government of National Defence under Venizélos *(see KRÍTÍ: Haniá)*. In September 1918 Greek troops joined the allies in clearing Macedonia of the enemy and advancing into Serbia and Bulgaria; those who fell in the campaign are buried in the allied military cemetery at Diavatá *(north of Thessaloníki)*.

When a large part of the city was destroyed by fire in 1917, leaving 80 000 people without shelter, it was rebuilt in concrete according to plans drawn up by the French architect Hébrard who designed the beautiful central perspective. In 1941 Thessaloníki was occupied by the Germans who deported some 50 000 Jews; monument at the beginning of Leofóros Langada *(in the direction of Kavála)*. The city suffered another disaster in 1978 when an earthquake damaged most of the monuments and caused serious harm to the churches.

Industry and commerce – Thessaloníki stands at the crossroads of the land and sea routes linking western Europe with the Levant; it has long been a trading centre which now organises an International Fair (Diethnís Ékthessi) each September. Local industry which is grouped to the west of the city has traditionally concentrated on textiles, tobacco, food (sugar, oil...) to which other activities have recently been added: an oil refinery, fertiliser factories, a steel works, a cement works etc. The traffic in the port, 50 per cent of which is hydrocarbons, is constantly increasing.

Life in Thessaloníki – Thessaloníki is the seat of the Ministry of Northern Greece as well as of the internationally famous Theatre of Northern Greece and of the Society for Macedonian Studies. There are numerous cultural events: the Greek Film Festival in late September and the art festival for the feast of St Demetrios in October.

EATING OUT

There are **patisseries** all along Leofóros Vassileos Konstandinou. The oldest patisserie in Thessaloníki, which has been selling really delicious Middle Eastern confectionery since 1908, is **Hadjis**, *50 Odós Venizélou*.

There are plenty of small restaurants – for **lunch** and **dinner** – in the bustling **Platía Navarinou** as well as in **Odós Iktinou** in the town centre. It is also worth the trouble of going out to **Panorama** in a smart suburb for its superb view.

Ouzou Melathron, *27 Odós Karipi.*

Ta Binelikia, *1-13 Odós M Kountoura, Kendrikí Agora.*

Ouzeri, *8 Odós Aristotelous – In the courtyard.*

Ouzeri Aproopto, *6 Zefxidos ☎ 241 141.*

Terrace of the Macedonia Palace Hotel, *Odós Megalou Alexandrou – Very fine view.*

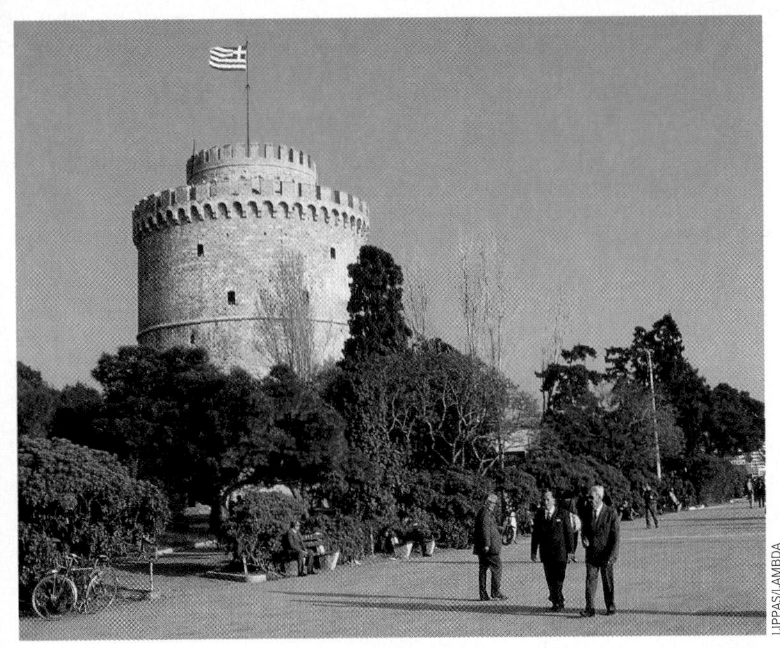
LIPPAS/LAMBDA

White Tower, Thessaloníki

The local cuisine is more heavily spiced than southern Greek food and shows more Turkish influence. The chief specialities are fish and *doner kebab* which is slices of meat layered on an upright spit revolving in front of a fire; it is carved vertically in thin slivers as it cooks. Chocolate sweets and pastries are also very popular and delicious. The main restaurants are to be found down near the seafront, while the tavernas are grouped round the central market. In the evening people gather on the terraces of the large cafés in the main square, Platía Aristotélous.

PRINCIPAL SIGHTS *half a day on foot*

Start from the main square, **Platía Aristotélous**★, a broad paved area lined with large hotels and cafés, which terminates the central axis of the city overlooking the sea. Turn left *(south)* along the **seafront**★ (Leofóros Nikis★) past restaurants and luxury boutiques: extensive views of the harbour and the bay.

★**Lefkós Pírgos** ⏱ – The **White Tower** was originally incorporated in the ramparts which surrounded the city; it stood in the southeast corner and was the main defensive element in the section fronting the sea which was pulled down in 1866. The tower was rebuilt by the Turks in the 15C and used during the following century as a prison for Janissaries, the Sultan's personal guards, who sometimes betrayed their master. Thus, when the Janissaries revolted in 1826 against Mahmoud II, he had them confined to the tower and massacred. The building became known as the Bloody Tower, an unwelcome title which the Turks decided to suppress by painting the walls with whitewash and renaming it the White Tower. The tower (35m/115ft high) is built of stones interspersed with bricks. From the top there is a view of the city and the harbour.
The tower houses a collection of **Byzantine art**★: the exhibits are well presented on five floors and relate to the town's structure in the early Christian era, Christianity in paleo-Christian times (mosaics and photos of frescoes), paleo-Christian burial practices (funerary chamber decorated with frescoes, jewellery), Byzantine art and history in Thessaloníki, Byzantine and post-Byzantine icons (Ikonomopoulou Collection). View of the town and harbour from the top of the tower.
Beyond the White Tower on the seafront stands an equestrian statue of Alexander the Great; behind it extends a park which is bordered down the east side by Odós Desperai and the Archeological Museum.

★★★**Arheologikó Moussío** ⏱ – The **Archeological Museum** houses ceramics and other objects excavated from sites in Macedonia and Thrace, but the most interesting exhibits are the treasures of ancient Macedon, recently discovered in various tombs in northern Greece.

The museum is subject to frequent reorganisation as items may be on loan for temporary exhibitions in the building or abroad; the description below is given only for guidance.

Treasures of ancient Macedon – This stunning collection of precious objects, which is housed in a specially built wing of the museum *(Room 9)*, consists mainly of offerings in bronze, silver or gold found in tombs dating from the 4C BC and the Hellenistic period, including the famous "royal tombs" at Vergína *(see VÉRIA)*.

Treasury of Síndos *(Room 1)* – Here are the objects excavated from 121 tombs (dating from the 6C-5C BC) in the cemetery at Síndos, west of Thessaloníki. The men's tombs yielded weapons, helmets of the so-called Illyrian type covered in gold leaf together with gold face masks. Several types of chariots and carts made of welded iron and small three-legged tables were also found. The women's graves produced gold jewellery showing filigree work and milling and a covered painted terracotta tomb.

Vergína Treasure *(Room 9)* – A reconstruction of the royal tomb made by Professor Andrónikos of the University of Thessaloníki is illustrated by a model and slides; the tomb, which is thought to be that of Philip II of Macedon (4C BC), consisted of a chamber and an antechamber which produced some remarkable objects.
A golden coffer *(larnax)* (over 8kg/17lb in weight) is decorated with a 12-pointed star, the emblem of the Macedonian kings *(case no 16)*; it contained the bones of a woman, a beautiful gold diadem *(displayed above)* and a cloth of gold and purple *(case no 15)* and was found in a sarcophagus in the antechamber to the tomb.
A quiver covered in gold leaf *(case no 14)* embossed with scenes from the sack of Troy vies in exquisite craftsmanship with vases in silver and polychrome ceramic, the deceased's iron armour plate *(case no 3)* decorated with golden strips and a bronze shield inlaid with gold and ivory, a funerary krater *(kálpis)* in silver and a golden necklace *(case no 19)*. Another huge golden coffer *(case no 2)*, larger and heavier (10kg/22lb), is decorated with a sixteen point star; it probably contained the bones of Philip II, whose exquisite golden crown of oak leaves is also on display. There are some very expressive carved portraits in ivory *(case no. 12)*, probably of the royal family of Macedon: Philip II with a beard, his wife Olympia and their son Alexander.

Dervéni Treasure *(Room 9)* – This is the material found in some 4C BC tombs at Dervéni *(north of Thessaloníki)*: golden jewellery (earrings, necklaces, golden crowns of ivy and myrtle leaves), vases in silver or bronze and a huge cup in bronze gilt with appliquéd figures on the neck and reliefs illustrating the life of Dionysos.

From prehistory to the Classical era *(Rooms 10 and 11)* – The ground floor is devoted to prehistoric dwellings in Macedonia from the Neolithic to the Bronze Age. Finds from excavations on the west face of Mount Olympos (the Copper Age, the Mycenaean period) are also on display. Grave goods dating from the Mycenaean and proto-geometric periods (9C BC) have been discovered in the large cemetery

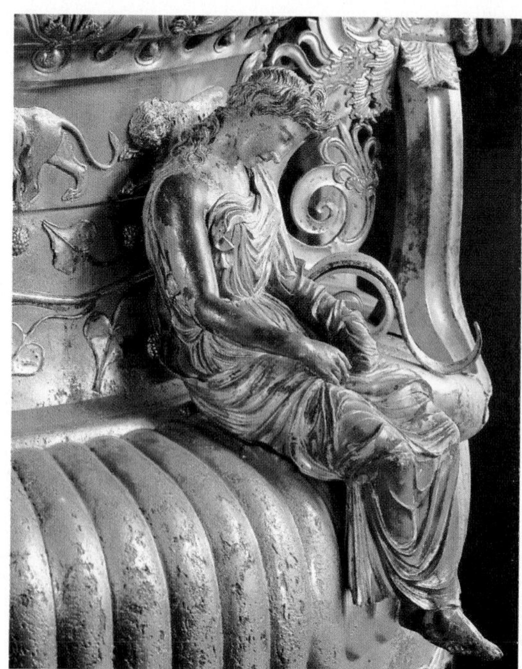

T.A.P.

Dervéni Vase, Thessaloníki

at Toróni in Chalcidice *(see HALKIDIKÍ: Sithonía Peninsula)*. Arms, vases and jewellery in copper, gold and silver have been uncovered on the site of Agía Paraskeví southeast of Thessaloníki which included 450 tombs from the 6C BC. Finds from the important Classical city of Olynthos in Chalcidice near Kassándra Bay, destroyed by Philip II in 348 BC, and from the Akanthos site (near Ierissós in eastern Chalcidice) as well as photographs of the sites are also on view.

Sculpture, glass and mosaics – These are arranged in chronological order in the hall and five other galleries *(proceed clockwise)*; a *kouros* and a *kore* without their heads, funerary reliefs *(Room 8)*, Roman copies of Muses from the Odeon *(Room 6)*, Roman portraits including one in bronze of Emperor Alexander Severus (3C) *(Room 8)*.
In Room 6 are mosaics – Ariadne and Dionysios – found in Roman villas in Thessaloníki, and a fine Roman glass collection. The 4C BC marble arch comes from Emperor Galerius' palace *(see below)*.

Proceed north (Odós Angeláki) past the International Fair ground and bear left.

Goldsmiths' Art in Ancient Greece

The purpose of Greek jewellery was not only to honour the gods and to adorn the dead – it could be given to anyone on certain specific occasions. The use of symbols of love such as Aphrodite and Eros lead us to believe that it was often given on occasions such as marriages and births.
The Greek goldsmiths used gold leaf which they cut with a chisel before pressing it against a motif standing out in relief on a support. To achieve a lace-like effect they applied filigree decoration made up of plaited or coiled gold wire, and using the granulation technique they inserted tiny balls of gold between the moulded motifs. The different parts of the piece of jewellery were assembled without any heat using rivets.
Produced not only in the cities of mainland Greece, but also in the Greek colonies of southern Italy and Asia Minor, the jewellery of the Classical era is of great beauty and shows a complete mastery of the goldsmith's art.

Moussío Vizandinoú Politismoú ⓥ – The **Museum of Byzantine Civilisation**, opened in 1994, houses a collection of Byzantine antiquities from Thessaloníki. In addition to a large number of sculptures and inscriptions, there are many fine icons including a *Virgin and Child* of 1300 and *The Wisdom of God* (early 14C), as well as embroidery, in particular the famous **Thessaloníki Epitáphios** (14C), originally used as a corporal (a cloth to cover the Communion bread and wine) and hence decorated with Eucharistic scenes framing a dead Christ.

★**Apsída Galeríou** – This **triumphal arch** was part of a monument erected in the 4C AD at the main crossroads of the Roman city in honour of Emperor Galerius. The brick pillars were faced with stone decorated with low reliefs celebrating Galerius' victories over the armies of Persia, Mesopotamia and Armenia.
The south pillar is the best preserved. On the outer face starting at the base: war scenes with elephants and a lion; a sacrifice showing Galerius *(right)* and his father-in-law Diocletian *(left)*; Galerius' triumph; Galerius addressing his soldiers. On the inside face, at the base: Mesopotamia and Armenia, represented by two women making their submission; above: Galerius in combat.

★**Rotónda** ⓥ – The building was erected in the 4C AD as a circular mausoleum for Emperor Galerius, who was not however buried within since he died far away in Sofia. In the following century, under Constantine and Theodosius the Great, the mausoleum was converted into a church by the addition of an apse to the east; the main entrance then faced south down the street lined by porticoes which led to the Arch of Galerius and the Imperial Palace.
Converted into a mosque under the Turks (minaret), the building now houses a **Lapidary Museum**. The interior was decorated with mosaics on a gold ground of which a few survive, particularly at the base of the dome where eight saintly martyrs can be seen in prayer against a background of architectural compositions.

★**Ágios Dimítrios** ⓥ – The impressive **St Demetrios' Church** marks the site of the martyrdom and tomb of St Demetrios, patron saint of Thessaloníki. After the fire in 1917 the church was totally restored to reproduce the 7C basilica which was preceded by an atrium; some of the old material (marbles, columns, mosaics) were reused. To the left are traces of Roman baths and of a minaret (the church became a mosque from 1491 to 1912).
The interior, which is surprisingly large, has a nave and four aisles lit by three rows of windows. Carved capitals crown the superb ancient columns in green, white and red marble which have been reused; their different lengths have been accommodated by mounting them on bases of the appropriate height.

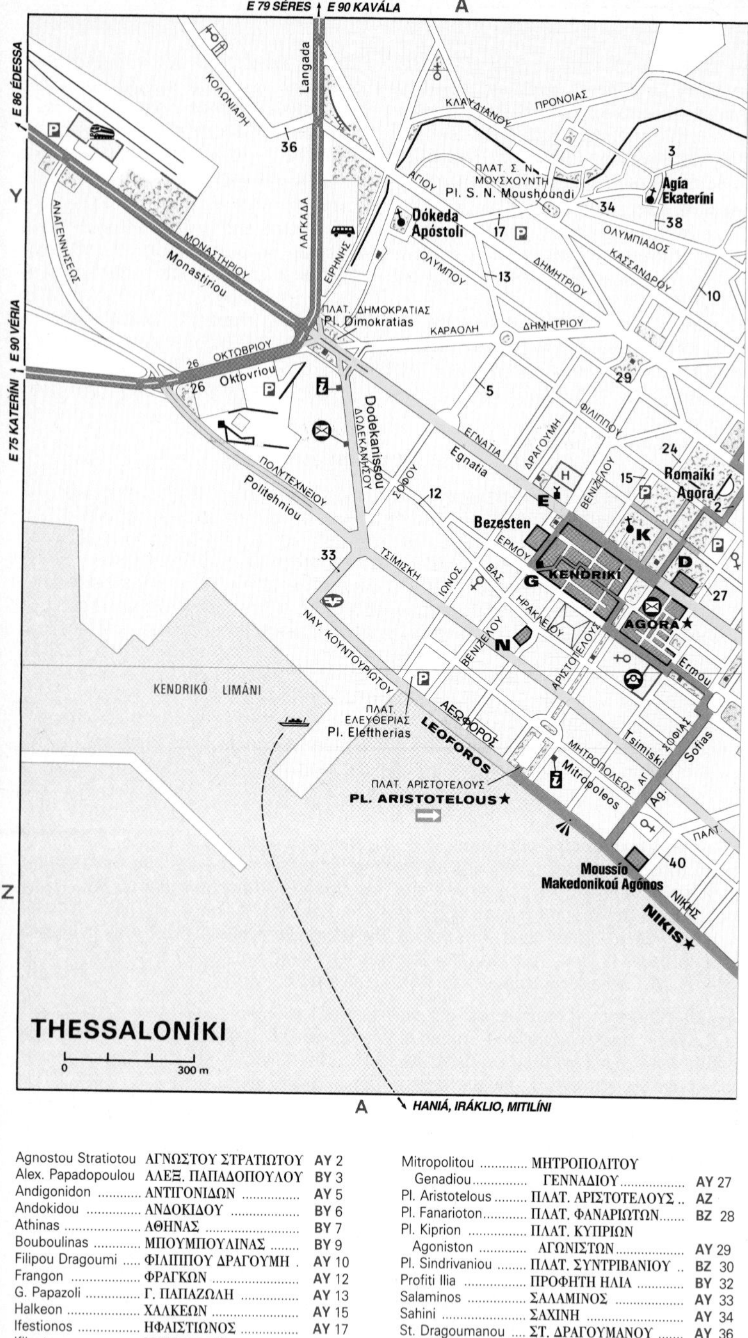

Agnostou Stratiotou	ΑΓΝΩΣΤΟΥ ΣΤΡΑΤΙΩΤΟΥ	AY 2
Alex. Papadopoulou	ΑΛΕΞ. ΠΑΠΑΔΟΠΟΥΛΟΥ	BY 3
Andigonidon	ΑΝΤΙΓΟΝΙΔΩΝ	AY 5
Andokidou	ΑΝΔΟΚΙΔΟΥ	BY 6
Athinas	ΑΘΗΝΑΣ	BY 7
Bouboulinas	ΜΠΟΥΜΠΟΥΛΙΝΑΣ	BY 9
Filipou Dragoumi	ΦΙΛΙΠΠΟΥ ΔΡΑΓΟΥΜΗ	AY 10
Frangon	ΦΡΑΓΚΩΝ	AY 12
G. Papazoli	Γ. ΠΑΠΑΖΩΛΗ	AY 13
Halkeon	ΧΑΛΚΕΩΝ	AY 15
Ifestionos	ΗΦΑΙΣΤΙΩΝΟΣ	AY 17
Ifikratous	ΙΦΙΚΡΑΤΟΥΣ	BY 19
Irodotou	ΗΡΟΔΟΤΟΥ	BY 20
Klious	ΚΛΕΙΟΥΣ	BY 23
Mak. Aminis	ΜΑΚ. ΑΜΥΝΗΣ	AY 24
Meg. Alexandrou	ΜΕΓ. ΑΛΕΞΑΝΔΡΟΥ	BZ 25
Mitropolitou Genadiou	ΜΗΤΡΟΠΟΛΙΤΟΥ ΓΕΝΝΑΔΙΟΥ	AY 27
Pl. Aristotelous	ΠΛΑΤ. ΑΡΙΣΤΟΤΕΛΟΥΣ	AZ
Pl. Fanarioton	ΠΛΑΤ. ΦΑΝΑΡΙΩΤΩΝ	BZ 28
Pl. Kiprion Agoniston	ΠΛΑΤ. ΚΥΠΡΙΩΝ ΑΓΩΝΙΣΤΩΝ	AY 29
Pl. Sindrivaniou	ΠΛΑΤ. ΣΥΝΤΡΙΒΑΝΙΟΥ	BZ 30
Profiti Ilia	ΠΡΟΦΗΤΗ ΗΛΙΑ	BY 32
Salaminos	ΣΑΛΑΜΙΝΟΣ	AY 33
Sahini	ΣΑΧΙΝΗ	AY 34
St. Dragoumanou	ΣΤ. ΔΡΑΓΟΥΜΑΝΟΥ	AY 36
Theotokopoulou	ΘΕΟΤΟΚΟΠΟΥΛΟΥ	BY 37
Tsamadou	ΤΣΑΜΑΔΟΥ	AY 38
Vas. Georgiou	ΒΑΣ. ΓΕΩΡΓΙΟΥ	BZ 39
Vogatsikou	ΒΟΓΑΤΣΙΚΟΥ	AZ 40
Zografou	ΖΩΓΡΑΦΟΥ	BY

Ágalma tou Megalexándrou	BZ	A
Ágia Ekateríni	AY	
Ágia Sofia	BZ	
Ágios Dimítrios	BY	
Ágios Nikólaos Orfanós	BY	B
Agorá	AY	
Anáktora Galeríou	BZ	C
Apsída Galeríou	BZ	
Arheologikó Moussío	BZ	
Bey Hamamí	AY	D
Bezesten	AY	
Diethni Ékthessi	BZ	
Dingirli Koulé	BY	
Dódeka Apóstoli	AY	
Hamza Bey Dzamí	AY	E
Ishak pasa Dzamí	BY	F

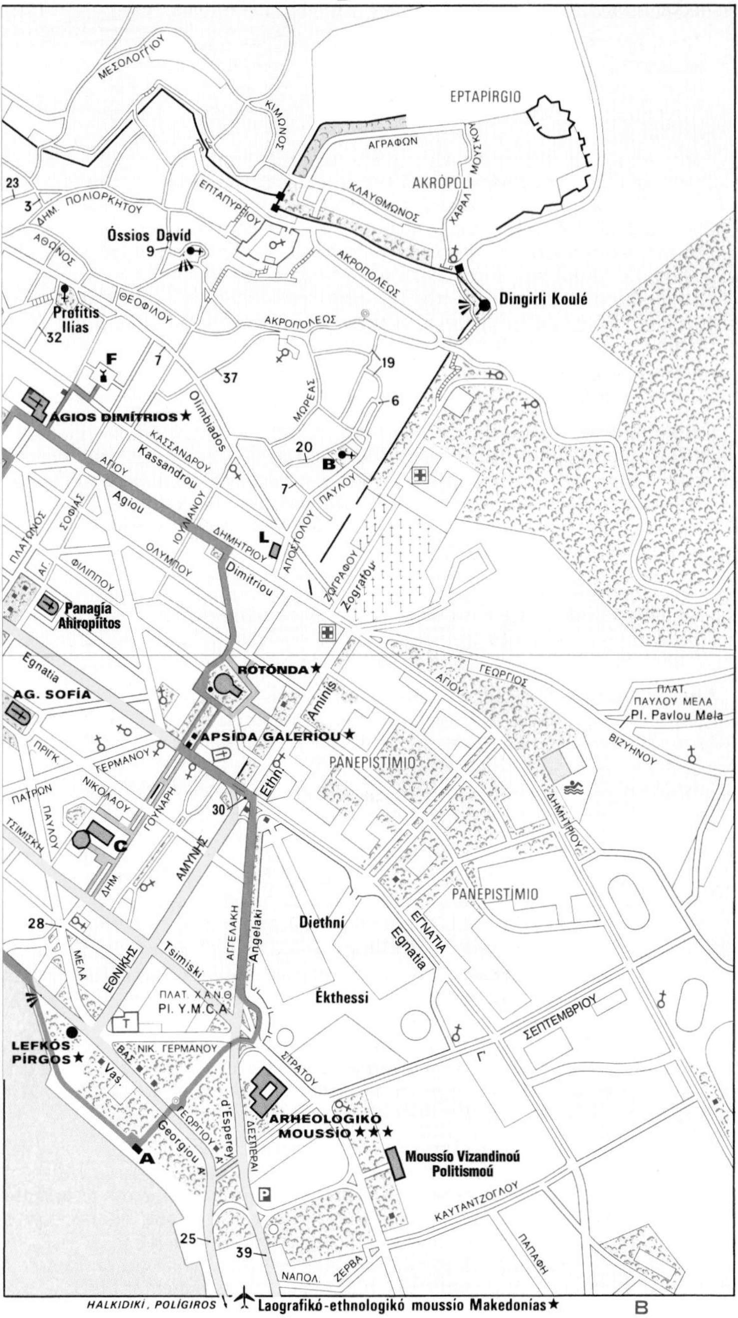

On all town plans north is at the top of the page.

Kendríki	AY	
Laografikó-ethnologikó moussío Makedonías	BZ	
Lefkós Pírgos	BZ	
Mnimío Lambráki	AY	G
Moussío Makedonikoú Agónos	AZ	
Moussío Vizandinoú Politismoú	BZ	
Óssios David	BY	
Panagía Ahiropiítos	BY	
Panagía Halkéon	AY	K
Profítis Ilías	BY	
Romaïki Agorá	AY	
Spíti génissis Kemal Ataturk	BY	L
Yahudi Hamamí	AY	N

The pillars on either side of the entrance to the apse are decorated with small 7C **mosaics★★** of very fine design and colouring – *(right pillar)* Demetrios and a deacon bearing the Gospel, Demetrios between the two founders of the church, then St Sergius; *(left pillar)* Demetrios between two children, then the Virgin and St Theodore, a later composition.

The relics of St Demetrios, which were recovered from Italy in 1980, are venerated before the iconostasis. A stairway descends from the apse *(right)* into a **crypt** (small lapidary museum) where, according to tradition, the miraculous oil which flowed from the saint's tomb beneath the high altar was collected. The semicircular marble basin surmounted by columns is probably part of the Roman bath where Demetrios was imprisoned before being martyred.

At the back of the church near the nave *(right)* there is a 15C Florentine sarcophagus. The external chapel is thought to mark the site of St Demetrios' original tomb.

From the east end of the church go up Odós Ag Nikolaou (old Turkish bath in the corner) and turn right into Odós Kassandrou and left into a small square.

Alaca Imaret – This old mosque built in 1484 by Ishak Pasha, governor of Thessaloníki under Sultan Bayazid II, was also used as a hospital *(imaret)* for the poor. Only the base of the minaret which was built in multicoloured stone *(alaca)* remains. Two large domes crown the central prayer area with two small domed rooms used as refectory and classroom on either side. A portico with its five domes flanks the building which is used for art exhibitions.

Return to St Demetrios and proceed down to the seafront.

Romaïkí Agorá – Recent excavations have uncovered traces of this Roman forum which date for the most part from the 1C AD: base of a double portico which framed the forum and also the terraces of an odeon (small theatre).

★**Bey Hamami** – This Turkish bath house, built in 1444 by Sultan Mourad II also known as Bey, is the largest in Greece. It had separate facilities for men and women. The men's section is decorated with stalactites. It remained in use as the Loutrá Parádisos (Baths of Paradise) until 1968.

Pass in front of the statue of Vénizelos (see above and KRÍTÍ: Chania) on the way to the church of Our Lady of the Coppersmiths surrounded by a garden.

Panagía Halkéon – This little brick church, which is dedicated to **Our Lady of the Coppersmiths**, was built in the 11C as the parish church of the coppersmiths and other smiths who plied their trade in the surrounding streets; it is a typical Byzantine church built on the Greek cross plan with a central dome and a façade flanked by two towers over the narthex.

The road then passes through the centre of the picturesque **Central Market★** (Kendrikí Agorá) with to the west the **Bezesten**, the old cloth market crowned by six small domes.

In the southeast corner of the market a sculpture, a woman's head and huge outstretched arms, commemorates **Lambrakis**, a member of Parliament assassinated in Thessaloníki in 1963 who was the inspiration for the film "Z" by Costa-Gavras (1968).

★**Agía Sophía** – The **Church of the Holy Wisdom**, which is probably 18C, is remarkable for its huge dimensions and its unusual design; the standard basilical plan of a nave and two aisles with galleries is combined with the Greek cross plan beneath a dome. The base of a minaret in the northwest corner recalls the fact that the church was converted into a mosque, the Agía Sofia, until 1912.

The interior displays unusual **capitals★** with acanthus leaf decorations probably taken from a 9C building. The **mosaics** (9C-10C) depict the Ascension of Christ.

ADDITIONAL SIGHTS

★**Ramparts** – The principal section of the ramparts encloses the Upper Town and the ancient acropolis where the network of streets and the terraced houses suggest an eastern bazaar. The ramparts were built late in the 4C on Hellenistic foundations and were altered in the 14C by the Byzantines and again in the 15C by the Turks who employed Venetian engineers.

Starting near the cemetery in Odós Zográphou, proceed north outside the walls; at one point there is a section built of massive pieces of stone which dates from the Hellenistic period. Higher up stands the great **Chain Tower** (Dingirlí Koulé) dating from the 15C. Before reaching it pass within the walls so as to gain entrance to the acropolis. From this side the ramparts, which have recently been restored, make a fine sight linking the two towers named after Manuel Palaiologos and Andronikos II (14C). From near the large tower the **view★** extends over the town and the bay.

Óssios David ⓥ – The church which dates from the 5C contains a well-preserved **mosaic★** of the same date representing the Vision of Ezekiel. **View** of the town from the garden.

Dódeka Apóstoli – This attractive 14C church, which is dedicated to the **Twelve Apostles**, was built on the Greek cross plan with three apses in the sanctuary, a design typical of the Palaiologos "Renaissance". The external **brickwork★** is ingeniously arranged to form decorative geometric motifs; the internal columns supporting the dome have Corinthian capitals; the mosaics and frescoes are 14C.

Ágios Nikólaos Orfanós ⓥ – *Entrance at 20 Odós Irodótou.* **St Nicholas' Church** is a charming 14C country-style church surrounded by a garden. The interior is decorated with 14C frescoes (Legend of St Nicholas, Marriage in Cana). The columns near the garden entrance belonged to a monastery.

Profítis Ilías – **Prophet Elijah's Church** is a 14C building with three apses in the elegant sanctuary; superb monolithic columns in the transept.

Panagía Ahiropíitos – It dates from the 5C but has been heavily restored: monolithic columns with Byzantine capitals; traces of mosaics. Nearby stands a small baptistry chapel. The church was named after a miraculous icon of the Virgin (Panagía Ahiropíitos, "not made by human hand") *(to the left of the entrance)*.

Anáktora Galeriou – An open space, Platía Navarínou, reveals the plan of the Imperial Roman Palace, built of brick by Galerius, which was arranged round a rectangular courtyard with porticoes.

Hamza Bey Mosque – The mosque built in 1467 for Bey Hamza's daughter was restored in 1620 after a fire. The domed prayer chamber is flanked to the west by a large portico surrounding a courtyard. The building has been converted into shops.

Yahudi Hamam – The 16C Turkish bath-house derives its name from its location in the old Jewish quarter *(Yahudi)* and now houses the flower market.

★**Laografikó-Ethnologikó Moussío Makedonías** ⓥ – *68 Odós Vassilíssis Olgas – via Odós Vas Georgíou. By bus (nos 5, 6 or 7) from Odós Mitropoleos or the White Tower; "Fleming" stop in Leoforos Megalou Alexandrou opposite the sailing club. Entrance at no 1 Odós Filipou Nikoglou. By car along Leoforos Megálou Alexándrou (one way traffic).*

This 19C mansion houses the rich collections of the **Macedonian Ethnological Museum**, which is devoted to the popular art and traditions of northern Greece. Models and photographs illustrate rural and urban architecture. Traditional costume, in particular formal dress, is presented by region: central Macedonia – also carnival costumes and photographs of the *anastenarides* (dancers who perform barefoot on hot coals, *see p 370*) – western and eastern regions and Thrace. The lifestyle of the Sarakatsani, nomadic mountain shepherds, is also depicted (costume, dwelling). There is a reconstruction of a 19C reception room. The *Karagiósis* shadow theatre and everyday life prior to the industrial era are also illustrated. The first floor is reserved for temporary exhibitions.

Moussío Makedonikoú Agónos ⓥ – The **Museum of the Macedonian Struggle** displays arms and clothing, as well as photographs of the heroes of the 1878-1912 period.

For adjacent sights see AMFÍPOLI, DÍO, ÉDESSA, HALKIDIKÍ, LEFKÁDIA-NÁOUSSA, PÉLA, PLATAMÓNAS, VÉRIA.

THÍVA

THEBES – Boeotia, Central Greece – Population 19 505

Michelin map 980 fold 30

Thebes, capital of the rich and fertile Boeotia, which was one of the most famous cities in ancient Greece, is now only a commercial centre, a busy but undistinguished town. It was rebuilt in the last century, after an earthquake, to a regular plan on the hill where the acropolis of Cadmea once stood.

MYTHOLOGY AND HISTORY

According to legend, Thebes was founded by **Cadmos**, a Phoenician, who while searching for his sister **Europa** was guided to the spot by a cow marked with a magic sign. Then **Amphion**, son of Zeus and Antiope, built the city walls, moving the enormous stones into place with the sound of his lyre. Finally Cadmos, who had married Harmonia, had a daughter Semele who became the mistress of Zeus and mother of Dionysos.

Ill-fated Oedipus – The most famous Theban, however, is Oedipus, son of Laios, King of Thebes, and Jocasta. When Laios was told by an oracle that Oedipus would kill his father and marry his mother he had him exposed on Mount Kitherónas (Kithairon)

to die of cold and hunger but some shepherds rescued the boy who was brought up by the King of Corinth in ignorance of his true parentage.
On reaching manhood Oedipus left Corinth; near Thebes he quarrelled with a man and killed him; it was Laios. At that time the Theban countryside was being terrorised by the **Sphinx**, a winged monster with a lion's body and a woman's bust, which devoured those passing by who were unable to answer the riddles it posed. Jocasta's brother, **Creon**, offered the throne of Thebes and Jocasta's hand to anyone who would rid the country of the Sphinx. Oedipus accepted the challenge and was asked "What is it that walks on four legs in the morning, on two at noon, on three in the evening ?" "Man" answered Oedipus. He was right. In vexation the Sphinx threw herself into an abyss. Oedipus became king of Thebes and married his mother, thus fulfilling the oracle's prediction.
Later, however, when Oedipus discovered the truth, he put out his eyes and Jocasta hanged herself. Oedipus left Thebes accompanied by his daughter Antigone to lead a wandering life until his death at Colona (Kolonós) near Athens.
The legend of Oedipus was the inspiration of **Sophocles'** tragedies: *Oedipus Rex* and *Oedipus at Colona.*

Proud Antigone – After Oedipus' death, Antigone returned to Thebes to be with her sister Ismene and her brothers Eteocles and Polyneices. These two quarrelled, entered into fratricidal combat and died. Their uncle Creon, the traitor, took his opportunity and seized power, forbidding Antigone to bury Polyneices who had allied himself with the seven champions of Árgos, an incident recalled by **Aeschylus** in his play *Seven against Thebes.* Oedipus' daughter defied man-made laws to follow her conscience and buried her brother before suffering her own punishment which was to be buried alive. Sophocles took this sad story as the theme of his tragedy *Antigone.*

Lucky Pindar – Thebes' moment of glory came in the 4C BC when she headed the Boeotian Confederacy and defeated Sparta at Leuktra in 371 near Plataia, initiating a period of Theban hegemony over Greece which lasted 10 years. Two men, **Epaminóndas** and Pelopidas, took the credit for reorganising the Theban army which centred on a core of crack troops, the famous **Sacred Band** composed of 300 young nobles who swore to fight together until death.
After the death of Epaminóndas at the battle of Mantineia in the Peloponnese in 362 BC, Thebes, Athens' long-time rival, declined and in 336 the city was destroyed by Alexander except for the house of Pindar the poet (518-438 BC).

Magnificent Nicholas – Thebes regained a certain importance as a commercial centre in the Byzantine period when the silk industry flourished. It also resumed its political importance in 1205 when the Crusaders occupied the region. Boeotia and Attica fell to Otho de la Roche, from Burgundy, who settled in Thebes. When he died without issue, his nephew, Guy I, inherited Athens and Attica while his niece, Bonne, received Boeotia as her dowry when she married Otho of St Omer whose descendants took the title of the Duke of Thebes. It was **Nicholas of St Omer** (1258-94) who built the castle of Cadmea and decorated it lavishly. It was captured however in 1311 and dismantled by the Catalans who defeated the Franks at the battle of Kephisos *(see ORHOMENÓS).*

★ARHEOLOGIKÓ MOUSSÍO ⊙

The **Archeological Museum** stands near a 13C **Frankish tower**, once part of the castle built by the St Omer family, at the northern entrance to Thebes. It contains Boeotian antiquities: in the room on the right of the entrance, Archaic sculptures including *(centre)* a superb 6C BC **kouros★★** from the French excavations at Ptoion (north of Thebes); in the third room funerary steles in black stone (5C BC) showing representations of warriors; in the fourth room a series of sarcophagi from the Mycenaean period (13C BC) painted with funerary scenes showing keeners, ritual ceremonies etc.

EXCURSION

Glá Fortress – *27km/17mi northwest of Thíva by E 75 towards Thessaloníki as far as Kástro. In Kástro take the road east to Lárimna for about 700m/765yd; turn right into a stony track which circles the fortress. The entrance is on the northeast side.*
The fortress of Glá, which was originally surrounded by the dull waters of Lake Copaïs (Kopaïda) *(see ORHOMENÓS)*, is composed of a rocky plateau enclosed by a perimeter wall which was built in the 14C-13C BC following the contours of the rock; it is 3km/2mi long and over 5m/16ft thick; there were four gates, the main one facing south.
Enter by the northeast gate which is flanked by square towers and turn right into a path which climbs up to the highest point on the island, 66m/217ft above the level of the marshy plain. Late in the 19C the French School of Archeology in Athens uncovered the remains of a Mycenaean type palace with two *megarons*; the stronghold has a panoramic **view** over the Copaïc Basin where rice and cotton are cultivated.

For adjacent sights see ARÁHOVA, ATHÍNA, ÉVIA, DELFÍ, HERÓNIA, KÓRINTHOS, Dióriga KORÍNTHOU, LIVADIÁ, LOUTRÁKI, ORHOMENÓS, ÓSSIOS LOUKÁS Monastery.

TÍRINTHA★★

TIRYNS – Argolis, Peloponnese

Michelin map 980 fold 29

Set on a bluff in the centre of a plain, the fortress of Tiryns is a Cyclopean structure dating from the 13C BC, a well preserved masterpiece of ancient military architecture. On every side extend the huge citrus plantations of the Argolid plain; in the neighbouring town stand the buildings of the first National School of Agriculture which was founded under Kapodistrias' government (1828-31).

The misfortunes of Amphitryon – According to legend, Tiryns was founded before Mycenae by a certain Proitos aided by Cyclops from Asia Minor. Like Mycenae it came under **Perseus'** rule; then it was governed by the son of Perseus and Andromeda, Alkaios, who was succeeded by Amphitryon.

Amphitryon, king of Tiryns, had married his cousin **Alkmene**, who was as virtuous as she was beautiful, but before consummating the union he was bound by an oath to avenge the deaths of Alkmene's brothers, who had been killed in a quarrel with the Teleboans. As a result Amphitryon went into exile in Thebes and Zeus, who was captivated by Alkmene's beauty, took advantage of Amphitryon's absence to introduce himself to Alkmene disguised as her husband.

Following her union with first a god and then a mortal Alkmene gave birth to two sons; the one, lacking in ability, was called Iphikles and took after Amphitryon while the other, brave and strong, was called **Herakles** (Hercules) and took after Zeus. As a demigod, although only 18 months old, Herakles was able to strangle the serpents sent to kill him by Hera, the jealous wife of Zeus.

Later in a fit of madness Herakles killed his children, and the Pythia at Delphi ordered him to enter the service of Eurystheus, King of Árgos, who set him the **Twelve Labours** to accomplish: to strangle the Nemean lion, to execute the many-headed hydra of Lerna, to run down the hind of Ceryneia, to capture the Erymanthian boar, to cleanse the Augean stables, to destroy the Stymphalian birds, to tame the Cretan bull, to capture the man-eating horses of King Diomedes, to obtain the girdle of the Amazon queen, to carry off the cattle of Geryon a three-headed monster, to fetch the golden apples from the Garden of the Hesperides and finally to bring back Cerberus from Hades.

In the Achaian period (13C BC) Tiryns was subject to Mycenae and under Agamemnon took part in the Trojan war. During the Dorian invasion (12C BC) it was an independent kingdom with about 15 000 inhabitants; it was frequently in conflict with its neighbour Árgos. In 468 BC the Argives captured the city and laid it waste; its role was finished.

★★ACROPOLIS

"Wall-girt Tiryns" as Homer described it, stands on a long and narrow rocky limestone bluff, only 20m/66ft above the surrounding plain, but the sea came in closer in antiquity so that its isolated position and the strength of its walls made it almost impregnable.

The ruins now visible date, for the most part, from the late 13C BC. They cover an area measuring 300x45-100m/328x49-109yd and comprise the palace on the upper level and on the lower an elliptical precinct enclosing buildings for military, religious and economic use and to house the service quarters.

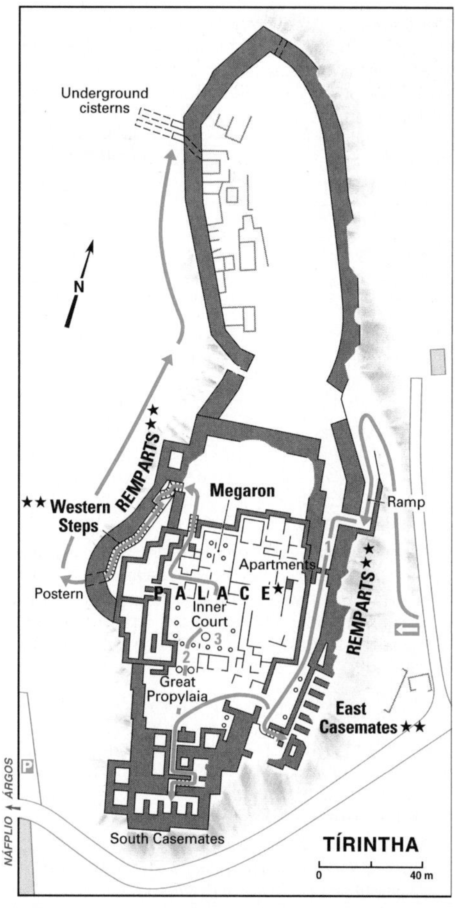

Tiryns ramparts

Fine **views** of Árgos and the Argolid, Mycenae, Nauplion and the bay.
The site has been excavated by the German School of Archeology and the acropolis has provided some frescoes *(in the Athens Museum)*, ceramics and terracottas *(in the Náfplio Museum)*.

★★ **Ramparts** – 7–10m/23–33ft wide and about 1 500m/1 640yds long, the walls reach 7.50m/25ft high in places. They were compared by Pausanias to the Pyramids and their Cyclopean structure using roughly shaped stones, up to 3.50x1.50m/11x5ft in size, is very impressive.
The ramp, which was broad enough for a chariot, leads up to the main entrance to the acropolis; an attacker advancing up the ramp would have been exposed on his righthand side (unprotected by his shield) to projectiles hurled by the defenders; the gateway, which was closed by wooden doors, was reinforced by two flanking towers.
On passing through the gateway, turn left into the passage (1) enclosed between the outer wall and the wall of the palace which is 11m/36ft high at this point; it was a real death trap; if the attackers managed to force the gate they could easily be annihilated at this point by projectiles hurled from every side.

★ **Palace** – The door to the palace is marked by a stone threshold, 4m/13ft long by 1.45m/4ft 9in wide, containing holes for hinges, and by one of the jambs containing the socket for the wooden bar which held the doors shut.
Within is the forecourt; steps *(left)* lead down to the east casemates.

★★ **East Casemates** – A narrow gallery, 30m/98ft long, with a vaulted roof, was built in the thickness of the ramparts; it had six chambers or casemates leading off it which were used by the garrison as stores or barrack rooms. The heavy blocks of stone and the gloom which reigns in these military quarters create an oppressive and timeless atmosphere.

Great Propylaia – The monumental main entrance, of which traces remain, was the forerunner of the Great Propylaia on the acropolis in Athens which was designed to the same plan: an inner and an outer porch covering a central passage. The Great Propylaia leads into the great court of the palace from which a staircase descends through a right angle to the **south casemates**, similar to those in the eastern ramparts.

Smaller Propylaia (2) – This entrance links the great court to the inner or Megaron Court.

Inner Court – Its dimensions are 20x15m/66x49ft and it was originally covered with white cement; it was enclosed on three sides by porticoes of which traces remain; at the far end rose the façade of the *megaron*. On the right within the entrance stood the royal altar (3).

Megaron – As at Mycenae the *megaron* had a porch, a vestibule, a central hearth surrounded by wooden pillars on stone bases; the king's throne stood on the right. The walls were faced with stucco and decorated with paintings in the Cretan style.

KAUFMAN/TOP

In the 7C or 6C the *megaron* was replaced by a temple to Hera; some of the foundations are visible. The royal apartments were on two floors on the north and east sides of the *megaron*.

★★**Steps and western ramparts** – A flight of 80 steps winds down inside the crescent-shaped wall to a postern gate; it is one of the most unusual features of the defences. If an attacking force had succeeded in breaching the postern gate and reaching the steps, it would have been assailed on all sides by the defenders and even if some of the attackers had managed to climb the steps they would have fallen into a sort of trap at the top. There was moreover an additional bastion protecting the heart of the acropolis.
It is worth descending the steps and going out through the postern gate to admire the western ramparts and then continuing to another postern gate further north which opens into the lower ward of the acropolis. From there it is about as far again to see the drinking water cisterns which were situated outside the ramparts but reached from within by underground passages, only recently discovered.
For adjacent sights see ARGOLÍDA, ÁRGOS, Aktí ARKADÍAS, EPÍDAVROS, LERNÍ, MIKÍNES, NÁFPLIO, TRÍPOLI.

TRÍKALA

Tríkala, Thessaly – Population 44 232
Michelin map 980 fold 16

Tríkala is an agricultural market in the fertile province of Thessaly. In antiquity it was well known for its sanctuary to Asklepios, which was the oldest in Greece. For a time under the Turkish occupation it became the capital of the province.

Old town – Containing the main churches and a picturesque bazaar, it spreads over the lower slopes of Mount Ardáni below a castle known as Fort Trikkis, a Byzantine restoration of a 4C BC original. It is a good idea to go to the top of the hill, which is a very pleasant spot with a busy café popular with tourists.

Old Mosque ⓥ – South of the town on the road to Kardítsa stands a 16C mosque with an imposing dome, the restoration of which is nearly complete; it is to house a museum.

EXCURSION

★**Stená Pórtas (Pórta Defile)** – *2km/1.25mi southwest. Take the road to Píli; beyond the village climb for about 1km/0.5mi up the south bank of the Portaïkós which rises in the Píndos range.*

★**Bridge** – The bridge, which was built in the 16C by the monk Bessarion, is narrow and high and spans the river in one impressive arch at the entrance to the pass.

Return to Pîli, cross the stream and climb up the north bank.

Soon a church appears below in a rural setting to which a group of cypress trees adds a solemn touch.

★**Sanctuary of Pórta Panagía** ⏱ – In this charming rural setting, dedicated to the **Virgin of the Gateway**, there are two distinct buildings.
The eastern church is built in the Latin style: note the dressed stone, the obvious transept, the outline of certain openings, the nave buttressed by side aisles and the remarkable chevet with an apse and smaller canted apses. In the interior the entrance to the chancel is framed by mosaics of Christ and the Virgin and Child which show a flexibility and freedom of composition not found in Byzantine hieratism.
The western church is Orthodox, designed according to the Greek cross plan beneath a dome; it was probably rebuilt in the 15C but the façade and the stone walls seem to date from the 13C and to be the work of a western mason. The 15C fresco in the interior of the dome follows the Byzantine tradition with a severe Christ accompanied by a solemn legion of saints.
The remote site, the western architectural influences and the date of construction (1283), when John I and John II Doukas, who owed allegiance to **Guy II de la Roche** *(see p 73)*, were masters of Thessaly, all suggest that this double church (13C), like the one at Óssios Loukás, belonged to a Cistercian abbey.

For adjacent sights see KARPENÍSSI, LÁRISSA, METÉORA, MÉTSOVO, PLATAMÓNAS, Óros ÓLIMBOS, Óros PÍLIO, Kiláda ton TÉMBON.

TRÍPOLI

Arkadía, Peloponnese – Population 22 429
Michelin map 980 fold 29

Trípoli is the capital of Arcadia (Arkadía) and the central point in the road network of the Peloponnese. The town is built in the centre of a high flat plain (663m/2 175ft) in the limestone massif formed by erosion and surrounded by mountains of up to 2 000m/6 560ft. The relatively high altitude means that even in summer the climate is cool and fresh; Trípoli is therefore a pleasant centre for tourists who can make excursions into the quiet and attractive countryside of the Arcadian basin which was evoked by Virgil and Poussin *(the Shepherds of Arcadia)*.
In the 18C under the name of Tripolizza, the town was the residence of the Pasha of Morea and very Turkish-looking according to Chateaubriand. It was destroyed in 1824 by Ibrahim Pasha but rebuilt: the central square is bordered by the metal awnings typical in the mountains whereas Areos Square is open and planted with gardens; the Bazaar lies to the south on the Kalamáta road. There is a small **Archeological Museum** (**Arheologikó Moussío**) ⏱ in Platía Kolokotróni.

EXCURSIONS

Tegéa – *10km/6.25mi southeast. Follow the road to Spárti for 8km/5mi; in Kerassítsa turn left (sign "Ancient Tegéa").*
Lying in the fertile plain, Tegéa was the most important city in Arcadia in antiquity; it came under Spartan domination in the 6C BC and was destroyed by barbarians in the 5C AD. It was resurrected under the name of Nikli by the Byzantines and in the 13C it was the seat of the Frankish barony of **Niclès** and of a Latin bishopric; a few miles to the south during the Frankish occupation were held the great verbena fairs which have left their mark in the name of the village Vérvena.

Paleá Episkopi – A shady park encloses the modern church which incorporates some material from the 5C paleo-Christian basilica of Nikli; elements from antiquity and from the Middle Ages.

Temple of Athena – Between 1889 and 1910 the French School of Archeology excavated the foundations of the famous **Temple of Athena Alea** (4C BC) which housed the Archaic ivory statue of the goddess and the remains of the Calydonian boar *(see MESSOLÓNGI)*. The building was designed and decorated by statues and sculptures by the great Parian sculptor, Skopas; several fragments have been found; the most beautiful, of the Calydonian hunt (Calydonian boar, head of Atalanta) are displayed in the Athens Museum, others in the little local **museum** ⏱.

Mandínia (Mantineia) – *11km/7mi north on the Olympia road; after 9km/5.5mi turn right.*
In antiquity Mantineia was a fortified city, rivalling Tegéa for control of the plain which was irrigated then and covered with crops and oak woods although it is barren today. Beneath its walls in 362 BC fell Epaminóndas, the famous Theban general *(see THÍVA)*, who was pursuing the Spartan army of Agesilaos.
The excavations *(right of the road)* by the French School of Archeology have uncovered traces of the walls (4km/2.5mi long), reinforced with towers, and the foundations of several buildings including a theatre, an *agora* and temples.

On the opposite side of the road stands a **church**★ which is dedicated to the Virgin, the Muses and Beethoven. This extraordinary building was erected between 1970 and 1978 by an American architect of Greek origin who used every possible material (marble, ashlar stone, brick, wood) aiming at a synthesis of several styles (Egyptian, Greek, Byzantine) and incorporating every imaginable sort of decoration (sculpture, frescoes, stained glass, mosaics, enamels, gold and silver work); the effect of this combination is a joy to those who appreciate Surrealism.

★**Kimísseos Theotókou** ⓥ – *27km/17mi north of Trípoli by the road to Olimbía; in Levídi take the road northeast towards Kandíla; after 2km/1.25mi turn right (sign) into the track leading to the church.*
A solitary enclosure planted with walnut trees and watered by springs surrounds the beautiful **Church of the Dormition of the Virgin**, a post-Byzantine church (17C). The interior is painted with murals which are interesting both for their picturesque detail and their pleasant colouring: scene from the Old Testament, Christ's Passion, the Dormition of the Virgin; effigies of oriental saints.

For adjacent sights see ANDRÍTSENA, ÁRGOS, Aktí ARKADÍAS, GERÁKI, KARÍTENA, LERNÍ, MEGALÓPOLI, MIKÍNES, MISTRÁS, NÁFPLIO, NEMÉA, OLIMBÍA, SPÁRTI, STIMFALÍA.

VÉRIA

Imathía, Macedonia – Population 37 858
Michelin map 980 fold 5

Véria is well sited on a spur of Mount Vérmio overlooking the Macedonian plain; it is an important fruit market (peaches, apples etc). Among the concrete buildings of this seemingly modern town, hidden in courtyards and blind alleys, are a few Macedonian houses, Byzantine and post-Byzantine churches and a mosque.
In AD 54 St Paul came from Thessaloníki to preach to the Jewish community.
The ramparts have been converted into a walk: extensive **views** over the plain.

★**Hristós** ⓥ – At the centre of the town near the main crossroads stands **Christchurch**, a Byzantine brick building recently restored. It is decorated with a remarkable collection of early 14C frescoes signed by Kaliergis: the Virgin and angels in the apse, scenes from the Life of Christ, Orthodox saints etc.

Arheologikó Moussío ⓥ – The **Archeological Museum** contains objects from various periods: prehistoric, Archaic, Hellenistic and Roman.

EXCURSION

★**Vergína and Palatítsia** – *15km/9.5mi southeast of Véria on the road to Melíki; after 12km/7.5mi turn right to the modern village of Vergína; at the end of the village turn left (sign "Royal Tombs").*

★★**Royal Tombs** ⓥ – Three huge tumulus tombs, dating from the 4C BC, have been under excavation by Professor Andrónikos since 1977. *The interior of the tombs is not open to the public.* The façade of the great central tomb, which is closed behind a door with two marble leaves, is adorned with a magnificent frieze representing a hunting scene. The interior, which consists of a vestibule and an inner chamber, has yielded a magnificent collection of funerary objects *(in the Thessaloníki Archeological Museum)* which indicate that it was the tomb of Philip II of Macedon *(see PÉLA)*. Vergína is therefore probably the site of ancient **Aigai**, which was the capital of Macedon before being superseded by Pella, and the royal burial ground.
Nearby, a smaller tomb of the same type has also proved to contain valuable artefacts. The frieze on the façade is very badly damaged; that in the vestibule, however, depicts a wonderful scene of harnessed horses engaged in a race.
Further off, a third tomb houses marvellous paintings (Persephone being carried off by Pluto), which may have been executed by the great master Nicomachos.
In 1982 the archeologists discovered the site of the theatre where Philip II was assassinated.

Vergína – Section of the great tomb

Follow the sign "To the Macedonian Tomb and to the Palace".

★**Macedonian Tomb** ⓥ – *On the left of the road.* This is a 3C *hypogeum* with an Ionic façade. The funeral chamber still contains the marble throne which shows traces of its original painted decoration.

The road reaches a platform whence a footpath climbs up to the Palatítsia.

★**Palatítsia** ⓥ – *Not open to the public.* Traces of this little palace *(palatítsia)*, which dates from the Hellenistic period, were discovered in 1861 by a French archeologist, Heuzey. An old oak tree is now growing at the centre of the terrace where the palace once stood. The buildings were altered in the Middle Ages and in the 15C were the residence of a Byzantine princess called Vergína; the palace was later destroyed by the Turks.
The plan of the ancient palace can still be traced on the ground. The rooms were arranged round a Doric peristyle courtyard; several had mosaic floors; one has been restored to reveal a pleasant décor of geometric, floral and figurative motifs.
Extensive views of the site of the ancient city and over the plain to the sea *(east)*.

For adjacent sights see DÍO, ÉDESSA, KASTORIÁ, LEFKÁDIA-NÁOUSSA, PÉLA, PLATAMÓNAS, THESSALONÍKI.

VÓLOS

Magnissía, Thessaly – Population 77 192
Michelin map 980 fold 17 – Local map see p 225

Vólos stands at the head of its vast bay (Pagassitokós Kólpos) which is almost completely cut off from the Aegean Sea by the arm of the Magnissía peninsula. It is the latest in a long line of settlements; an earlier one was ancient Iolkos, the port from which Jason *(see Óros PÍLIO)* and the Argonauts set sail in search of the Golden Fleece. Vólos is subject to frequent earthquakes, the most recent of which occurred in 1955, so that the town today looks very modern and its straight streets, laid out on the grid pattern, are lined by special "anti-quake" houses three or four storeys high. There is a pleasant promenade along the seafront bordered by hotels, cafés and restaurants. Vólos olives are famous.

Economic activity – Vólos is the third port in Greece after Piraeus and Thessaloníki. It exports the local regional products – cereals, cotton, tobacco, olives, oil, wine and fruit – and also heavy industrial manufactures – machinery and other metal products – which are transported by ship to the Middle East, particularly Syria. Vólos is also the home port for the ships serving the Northern Sporades *(see SPORÁDES)*. About 8km/5mi from the city centre there is an industrial zone with 44 factories: cement works, tanneries, textiles, cigarettes, oil etc.

★**Arheologikó Moussío** ⓥ – The **Archeological Museum** displays an astonishing series of about 300 marble funerary steles which date from the Hellenistic period. Many are painted or carved with scenes from the life of the dead person. Most were taken from the necropolis at Dimitriáda in AD 50 to reinforce the city walls, which is where they were found.
Some tombs have been reconstructed to illustrate the funerary rites and customs practised in prehistory and antiquity. There are also collections of Neolithic objects from the sites at Sésklo (4000 BC), Dimíni *(respectively 15km/9mi and 6km/4mi west of Vólos)* etc and Mycenaean vases excavated at Iolkós.

For adjacent sights see ÉVIA, LÁRISSA, METÉORA, PLATAMÓNAS, Óros ÓLIMBOS, Óros PÍLIO, Vóries SPORADES, Kiláda ton TÉMBON, THERMOPÍLES, TRÍKALA, VÓLOS.

Harádra tou VOURAÏKOÚ★★

VOURAÏKÓS GORGE – Achaia, Peloponnese
Michelin map 980 folds 28 and 29

From the heights of Mount Aroánia, which rises to 2 340m/7 677ft, the River Vouraïkós flows down into the Corinthian Gulf some 50km/30mi, to the north. Along its course it has worn a deep channel through the soft limestone rock creating a fantastic gorge, dark and narrow, through which runs a picturesque narrow-gauge railway.

★★**Rack railway from Diakoftó to Zahloroú** ⓥ – *12km/7.5mi – about 1hr.* The narrow gauge Decauville railway, which was built late in the last century between Diakoftó on the coast and Kalávrita, is a particularly bold feat of engineering. It runs for 22km/nearly 14mi along a vertiginous route – through tunnels, along

overhangs, across bridges and viaducts and on a rack in certain sections where the incline is steeper than 7%. Since 1962 diesel engines have replaced the ancient steam locomotives, which dated from 1900 and had a top speed of 35kph/22mph.
On leaving **Diakoftó** station the train crosses the foothills of Aroánia, passing through vineyards and orchards (famous for cherries), before entering the gorge between high sheer cliffs which are riddled with caves. The railway line crosses from one side to the other high above the racing torrent; the grey-green water gleams far below swirling round the blocks of stone. Here and there the austerity of the bare rock is relieved by patches of colour in the shape of oleanders and oak and plane trees growing in clumps.

Zahloroú lies on a natural terrace overlooking a narrow basin. The charming little station (Méga Spíleo) is half hidden in the trees between the rockface and the stream *(tavernas, small hotel)*. From there it is up a winding path (45min on foot or by donkey), with fine views towards Kalávrita, to the Monastery of Méga Spíleo *(see MÉGA SPÍLEO)*, which can also be reached by road.
The train continues to the terminus at Kalávrita *(see KALÁVRITA)*.

For adjacent sights see HLEMOÚTSI, KALÁVRITA, KILÍNI, MÉGA SPÍLEO, NEMÉA, PÁTRA, SIKIÓNA, STIMFALÍA.

ZÁKINTHOS★

ZAKYNTHOS – Ionian Islands – Population 32 557
Michelin map 980 fold 27 – 403km²/156sq mi

Despite being shaken by earthquakes Zakynthos is still the "Flower of the Levant" *(Fior di Levante)* praised by the Venetians for its gentle climate, its luxuriant flora, its fertile soil and the charm of its inhabitants.
The island rises in the west in a chain of limestone peaks (756m/2 480ft) and levels out to the east in a fertile plain producing olives, citrus fruits and good white wines (Delizia, Verdea). The tar deposits in the south near Kerí were used in antiquity for caulking ships.
Beaches of fine sand, particularly at **Laganás** *(hotels, tavernas)* and Argássi, attract many tourist to the south end of the island. Measures are being introduced to protect the turtles which have chosen the beaches around Laganás Bay as a breeding ground; the island is also home to the monk seal.

Cultural centre – From 1489 to 1797 Zakynthos belonged to Venice which maintained an oligarchy of nobles inscribed in a Golden Book; this was a period of intense activity.
When Crete fell to the Turks in 1669 many artists moved to Zakynthos and contributed to the Ionian School of painting which combines the Byzantine tradition and the Venetian Renaissance. Local architecture was also marked by the Venetian influence: arches and arcading and bell-towers detached from their churches.
In the late 18C and early 19C Zakynthos became a breeding ground for poets, whose work was a blend of the Hellenic and Italian cultures: **Ugo Foscolo** (1778-1827), a master of romantic Italian literature, who campaigned for the independence of Italy and died in England; **Diónysos Solomós** (1798-1857), educated in Cremona, who became the poet of Greek independence and was the author of the Greek National Anthem – *The Hymn to Liberty* – translated into English by Rudyard Kipling; **Andréas Kálvos** (1792-1867), who travelled to Zurich and London with Fóscolo and also supported the Greek struggle for independence in his poetry.
Nowadays, the poets have been succeeded by popular singers who perform the famous local barcarolles *(minóres)*.

PRACTICAL INFORMATION

Access by air – From Athens 1 to 3 services daily.

Access by boat – Daily ferry service from Kilíni (Zákinthos-Kilíni Consortium ☎ (0623) 92 385 in Kilíni, (0695) 41 500 in Zákinthos)

Accommodation – About 40 hotels in Zakynthos Town and environs (cat B to E) about 30 hotels in Laganás and environs (B to D), about 10 hotels in Alikés (A to D) and some small hotels in Vassilikós, Plános and Tragáki. Rooms in private houses in all these localities and in Gerakáki and Argássi. Camping sites.

Transport – Car, bicycle and motorcycle hire services.

Fish drying, Zakynthos

★ZÁKINTHOS TOWN

Zakynthos Town is the capital (pop 10 236) and the main port of the island. T churches, palaces and squares with their fountains and surrounding arcades, whi were built during the Venetian occupation, have made the town one of the mo picturesque in the Adriatic after Dubrovnik. Although much of the town w destroyed in an earthquake in 1953, it has been rebuilt in the Venetian style. Sc nougat *(mandoláto)* is a speciality.

★**Kástro** – The old Venetian citadel, set on a hill, 100m/361ft up, survived t earthquake and provides an extended **view**★★ of the town, the bay and the coa of the mainland from Missolonghi *(northeast)* to Pílos (Pylos-Navarino) *(southeas* and including Chlemoútsi Castle.

★**Art Museum** – *Platía Solomoú.* Many items recall old Zakynthos: model of t theatre, paintings and engravings, furniture. There is a rich collection of icons fro the 16C to the 19C by Damaskinós, Tzanés etc and religious paintings by the 1 and 18C Ionian School: massive iconostasis from the church of the Pantocrato frescoes and murals from the churches of St George in Zakynthos, St Andrew Volímes etc.

★**Kiría ton Angélon** – *Behind the Hotel Xenia.* The **Church of Our Lady of the Ang** has an elegant Venetian Renaissance façade and 17C iconostasis.

Solomós Museum – *Platía Ágiou Márkou.* Tombs of Solomós and Kálvos the ground floor; icons and souvenirs of famous citizens (portrait of Fóscolo) the first floor.

EXCURSION

★**Road from Alikés to Volímes** – *86km/53mi there and back, about 2hr plus 1 sightseeing.*
After skirting the citadel, the road runs northwest through a rural area (vineyar and country houses with gardens) before reaching **Alikés**, a sheltered seaside reso with a fine sandy beach facing Cephallonia across the sea. The road passes son salt marshes before climbing the Alikés corniche; from the top there is a **panor ma**★★ of the plain of Zakynthos to the south, of the Kyllene peninsula includir Chlemoutsi on the mainland, of the Gulf of Patras (northeast) and of Cephallor (north).
Before reaching Volímes, one can make a detour to the left to visit the **Convent Anafonítria**, occupied by an order of nuns, where St Denys, the patron saint of t island, died in 1622; medieval tower.

Volímes is an old mountain village producing carpets in the local style. To the nor lies the picturesque **Blue Grotto** accessible only by boat from Zakynthos Town.

For adjacent sights see HLEMOÚTSI, ITHÁKI, KEFALONÍA, KILÍNI, MESSOLÓNC NÁFPAKTOS, PÁTRA.

World Heritage List

In 1972 The United Nations Educational, Scientific and Cultural Organization (UNESCO) adopted a Convention for the preservation of cultural and natural sites "of outstanding universal value". To date, more than 145 States Parties are partners in the international agreement, which lists over 500 sites around the world. Each year a committee of representatives from 21 countries, assisted by non-governmental organizations (ICOMOS - International Council on Monuments and Sites; IUCN- International Union for Conservation of Nature and Natural Resources; ICCROM -International Centre for the Study of the Preservation and Restoration of Cultural Property, the Rome Centre), evaluates the proposals for new sites to be included on the list, which grows longer as new nominations are accepted and more countries sign the Convention. To be considered, a site must be nominated by the country in which it is located.

The protected cultural heritage may be monuments (buildings, sculptures, archeological structures etc) with unique historical, artistic or scientific features; groups of buildings (such as religious communities, ancient cities); or sites which are works of nature or the combined works of man and nature of exceptional beauty or human interest. A site may be a testimony to the past, whether to the stages of the earth's geological history or to the development of human cultures and creative genius. Natural sites may also represent significant ongoing ecological processes, contain superlative natural phenomena or provide a habitat for threatened species.

Signatories of the Convention pledge to cooperate to preserve and protect these sites around the world as a common heritage to be shared by all humanity.

Some of the most well-known places which the World Heritage Committee has singled out include: Australia's Great Barrier Reef (1981), the Canadian Rocky Mountain Parks (1984), The Great Wall of China (1987), the Statue of Liberty (1984), the Kremlin (1990), Mont-Saint-Michel and its Bay (France - 1979), Durham Castle and Cathedral (1986).

UNESCO World Heritage sites included in this guide are:

Temple at Bassae (Vassés)
Delphi archeological site
The Acropolis, Athens
Metéora
Mount Athos
Paleo-Christian and Byzantine monuments in Thessaloníki
Medieval city of Rhodes
Mistra
Olympia archeological site
Delos
Daphne Monastery
Óssios Loukás Monastery
Néa Moní Monastery on Chios Island
Pithagório and the Heraion on Sámos Island
Vérgina archeological site

The port and windmills, Míkonos

P. NF. Friler/HOA QUI

Eastern Islands

Kríti (Crete)

Crete is different from the other islands in the Greek archipelago. Despite the increase in tourism, particularly noticeable on the north coast, the wild grandeur of the landscape has not been spoiled and the inhabitants have retained their traditional qualities of pride, honesty and hospitality. Homer's "island of the gods" was the cradle of the Minoan civilisation which flourished in the eastern Mediterranean 2000 years before Christ. In the countryside Cretan men sometimes still wear their traditional dress: tall boots, baggy breeches and a fringed turban **(mandíli)**. On feast days they dance to the music of three-stringed lyres.

PRACTICAL INFORMATION

Climate – In winter it is mild on the coast but cold and snowy inland; the spring, usually chilly, brings a profusion of flowers (anemones, oleanders, orchids). The summer is very hot with the odd refreshing wind *(meltémi)* from the north. Autumn is marked by a more agreeable temperature and fewer tourists.

Access by air – Crete has three airports: Iráklio/Herakleion, Hanía/Chania and Sítia. The first two have daily connections with Athína/Athens (8 services to Iráklio/Herakleion, 4 to Hanía/Chania). The services to Sitía are every Saturday and Sunday. There are only very rarely international connections to these airports, and as a rule it is necessary to change at Athína/Athens when coming from other countries.

Access by boat – There are daily car ferry services from **Pireás/Piraeus** to three ports on the island. These are run at night by Minoan Lines to Iráklio/Herakleion (☎ (01) 45 11 311 for the Akti Tzelepi terminal in Pireás/Piraeus and (081) 24 50 18 for Iráklio/Herakleion), by Anek Lines S.A. to Hanía/Chania and Iráklio/Herakleion (☎ (01) 41 18 611 for Pireás/Piraeus, (0821) 27 500 for Hanía/Chania and (081) 22 24 81 for Iráklio/Herakleion), and by Cretan Ferries-Rethymniaki S.A. to Réthimno/Rethymnon (☎ (01) 42 24 844 for Pireás/Piraeus and (0831) 26 876 for Réthimno/Rethymnon). Ágios Nikólaos and Sitía have services to Pireás/Piraeus on Mondays, Wednesdays and Fridays run by L.A.N.E. (☎ (01) 42 74 009 for Pireás/Piraeus, (0843) 25 555 for Sitía and (0841) 26 465 for Ágios Nikólaos).

Accommodation – Hotels of all categories – standard hotels in towns and resort hotels mainly on the north coast. Many camping sites. Youth Hostels in Hanía/Chania, Iráklio/Herakleion, Mália and Réthimno/Rethymnon. Rooms in private houses.

Transport – Buses mainly along the north coast and from the towns to all sites and villages. Car hire service in Hanía/Chania, Réthimno/Rethymnon, Iráklio/Herakleion, Mália, Ág Nikólaos, Ierápetra and Sitía and near the resort hotels. Motorcycle hire service.

Specialities – The restaurants and tavernas, which are reasonably-priced, offer several delicious dishes such as lamb with artichokes *(arnáki me anginâres)* and, near the sea, excellent fish: swordfish *(ksifías)*, red mullet *(barboúni)*, mullet *(kéfalos)*, crayfish *(karavída)*. Cretan cheeses *(féta, graviéra, manoúri)* are well known; so also is yoghurt with honey. The local wines are full bodied with a good nose and bottled under various names: Minos, Lato, Angelo, Gortys etc but the most typical are sold in carafes in the country inns. Those who are partial to liqueurs should try *rakí* (very different from Turkish *raki*) and *tsikoudiá*, a strong and fruity *marc*.

GEOGRAPHY

Crete (8 305km²/3 200sq mi; pop 502 165) is the largest island in the Greek archipelago and the fifth largest in the Mediterranean (about 260km/162mi *(east to west)* by 12-50km/8-31mi). It is on the same latitude as Rabat (Morocco).

Physical features – Crete is composed of a limestone mountain ridge heavily eroded to form numerous inland basins, gorges, chasms and caves (over 3 000). There are three major peaks, snow-capped from November to June: Lefká Óri (White Mountains) (2 453m/8 048ft), Ida (Ídi) (2 456m/8 058ft) and Díkti (2 148m/7 047ft). The Herakleion plain *(north)* and the Messará plain *(south)* are at either end of the central depression which forms the fertile heart of Crete where the earliest Mediterranean civilisations were nurtured. The mainly flat northern coast features gulfs, bays and inlets, whereas the tall, semi-barren cliffs of the southern coast plunge sheer into the sea less than 300km/186mi from Libya.

Agriculture – Agriculture flourishes in the coastal plains, the inland basins and on the lower slopes in the valleys. Both wheat and rice are grown; irrigation enables orchards of citrus fruits to thrive beside the olives which are grown for the extraction of their oil. Vineyards tend to be concentrated in the broad valley south of Herakleion. Early vegetables, tomatoes, cucumbers, artichokes etc are grown under glass while bananas have been introduced in the Messará plain and Ierápetra. Both fruit and vegetables are exported to Piraeus and the rest of Europe. Sheep and goats are reared in the mountains.

LEGEND AND HISTORY

Minoan Crete – From about 2800 BC to 1000 BC Crete was the centre of a brilliant civilisation supposed to be of mythical origin. According to both Homer and Hesiod, Zeus was born in Crete where the nymph **Europa**, whom he had abducted, bore him three sons – **Minos**, Rhadamanthos and Sarpedon. Minos became a wise and powerful king and he started a dynasty which presided over the Minoan civilisation; archeologists have identified four broad periods.

Pre-Palace Period (c 2800-c 2000 BC) is marked by domed circular tombs which have yielded grave goods: jewellery, seals, Cycladic statuettes, pottery.

Old Palace Period (c 2000-c 1700 BC) covers the first palaces built round a central courtyard bordered by the public reception and cult rooms and the private royal apartments. Traces of such palaces have been found in Knossós, Phaistos and Mália, in legend the princely seats of Zeus' sons, Minos, Rhadamanthos and Sarpedon; mountain-top sanctuaries have also been discovered. The pottery, known as Kamáres ware, since the first examples were found in 1900 in Kamáres Cave on Mount Ida, is decorated with exuberant polychrome patterns. The island was the centre of a maritime empire, trading with Egypt and the Middle East and exporting olives, grain, vegetables and wine. In about 1700 BC an earthquake brought devastation.

New Palace Period (c 1700-c 1400 BC) is so called because new palaces were built on the sites of the earlier ones at Knossós, Phaistos, Mália and also on a fourth site at Zákros. The new palaces were larger and more richly decorated; the royal apartments in particular consisted of several floors, lit by light wells, serviced by a network of stairs and corridors and supplied with piped water. The walls are covered with low-relief sculptures or clean-lined paintings usually depicting obscure cult scenes featuring the double-headed axe or symbolic bull's horns, ritual bull-leaping events, processions and animal and, exceptionally, human sacrifices *(see KRÍTI: Arhánes)*. There are also representations of graceful priestesses presented in profile with a single eye facing straight ahead. The script current during this period, known as **Linear A**, has not yet been deciphered.
The Minoan civilisation extended beyond Crete into the Mediterranean basin and several traces of it have been found particularly on Thíra but in about 1530 BC (1630 BC according to some archeologists) a second earthquake, probably connected with the volcanic eruption on Thera, seems to have produced a tidal wave which destroyed most of the palaces, themselves rebuilt. Mycenaean influence is already evident here, and numerous tablets bearing inscriptions in **Linear B**, deciphered in 1952 by Englishmen M Ventris and J Chadwick, who showed this transcription of the Mycenaean dialect to be Greek in its oldest form, have been found at Knossós. One has to be careful however when dating the Mycenaean presence in the Minoan world and its overlapping with the new palace and post-palace periods. The latest research, still far from complete, shows various differences of opinion.

Post-Palace Period (c 1400-1100 BC) is marked by the arrival of the Mycenaeans to settle definitively in Crete (it is not known whether they used armed force for this or not), where they introduced their less refined customs, of which traces remain (tombs of warriors buried with their weapons, palaces with a *megaron*). The Mycenaeans had already been subjected to the influence of Minoan civilisation at home (through trade contacts etc). Minoan culture did not fade away overnight but persisted for some time throughout the Cretan population, before eventually being subsumed into the Greek world.

Rome and Byzantium – In 67 BC the Romans took over Crete, which with Cyrenaica formed a Roman province with its capital at Gortyn where many traces of brick buildings, temples, sculptures and mosaics from this period have been found. In AD 59 St Paul landed on the south coast at Kalí Liménes; his disciple **Titus** was later sent to convert the island to Christianity. From 395 to 1204, except for a brief Arab intervention between 824 and 961 when the city of Candia *(see IRÁKLIO)* was founded, Crete was under Byzantine rule, as the many churches demonstrate.

Under the claw of the Venetian lion – Following the Fourth Crusade in 1204 Crete was assigned to the Venetians who retained it for 400 years despite local revolts. They divided the island into four districts, Chania, Rethymnon, Sitia, and Candia (Herakleion) which was the residence of the Duke of Candia, a magistrate appointed by the Grand Council in Venice for two years. The Venetians built many fortresses on Crete and made it their main base, controlling the sea routes used by their merchant galleys trading with the Levant. Civil servants, ship owners and merchants from Venice settled in the Cretan towns; churches, loggias, houses and fountains in the Venetian style can still be seen today.

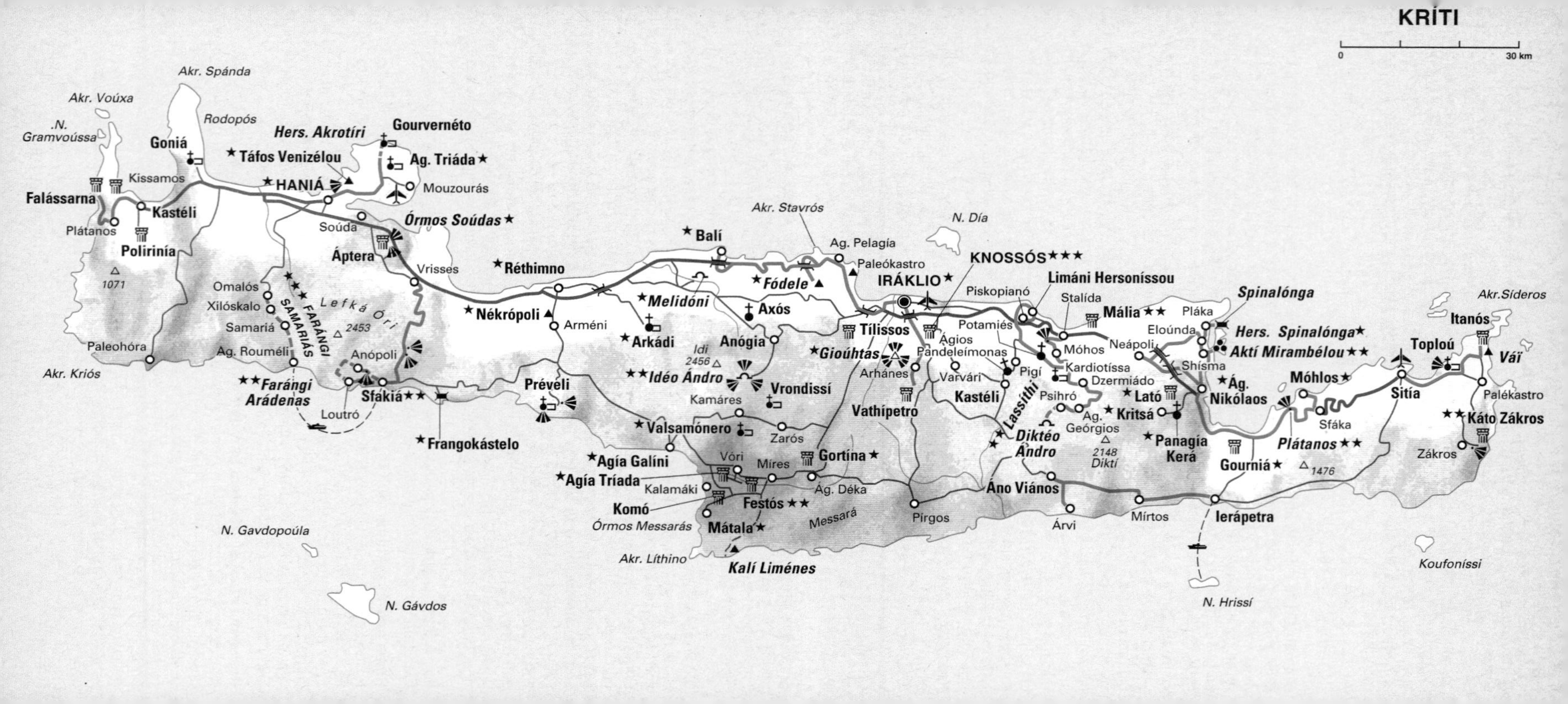

KRÍTI

0
30 km
Akr. Spánda
Akr. Voúxa
.N.
Gramvoússa
Rodopós
Goniá
Hers. Akrotíri
Gourvernéto
Táfos Venizélou
Ag. Triáda
Kissamos
HANIÁ
Mouzourás
Falássarna
Kastéli
Plátanos
Soúda
Órmos Soúdas
Polirinía
Áptera
1071
Vrisses
Réthimno
Balí
Akr. Stavrós
Ag. Pelagía
Paleókastro
N. Día
KNOSSÓS
IRÁKLIO
Omalós
Xilóskalo
FARÁNGI
SAMARIÁS
Lefká Óri
2453
Samariá
Paleohóra
Ag. Rouméli
Anópoli
Akr. Kriós
Farángi
Arádenas
Loutró
Sfákia
Frangokástelo
Nékrópoli
Arméni
Melidóni
Arkádi
Fódele
Axós
Anógia
Idí
2456
Idéo Ándro
Vrondissí
Préveli
Kamáres
Valsamónero
Zarós
Agía Galíni
Agía Tríada
Vóri
Míres
Gortína
Kalamáki
Komó
Órmos Messarás
Festós
Mátala
Ág. Déka
Messará
Akr. Líthino
Kalí Liménes
N. Gavdopoúla
N. Gávdos
Tílissos
Gioúhtas
Arhánes
Ágios
Pandeleímonas
Vathípetro
Varvári
Kastéli
Pírgos
Piskopianó
Limáni Hersonissou
Stalída
Potamiés
Mália
Móhos
Neápoli
Pigí
Kardiotíssa
Dzermiádo
Lassíthi
Psihró
Ag.
Geórgios
Diktéo
Ándro
2148
Diktí
Áno Viános
Árvi
Mírtos
Latό
Kritsá
Panagía
Kerá
Pláka
Eloúnda
Shísma
Spinalónga
Hers. Spinalónga
Aktí Mirambélou
Ág.
Nikólaos
Gourniá
Ierápetra
N. Hrissí
Móhlos
Sfáka
Plátanos
1476
Sitía
Toploú
Itanós
Akr.Síderos
Váï
Palékastro
Káto Zákros
Zákros
Koufoníssi

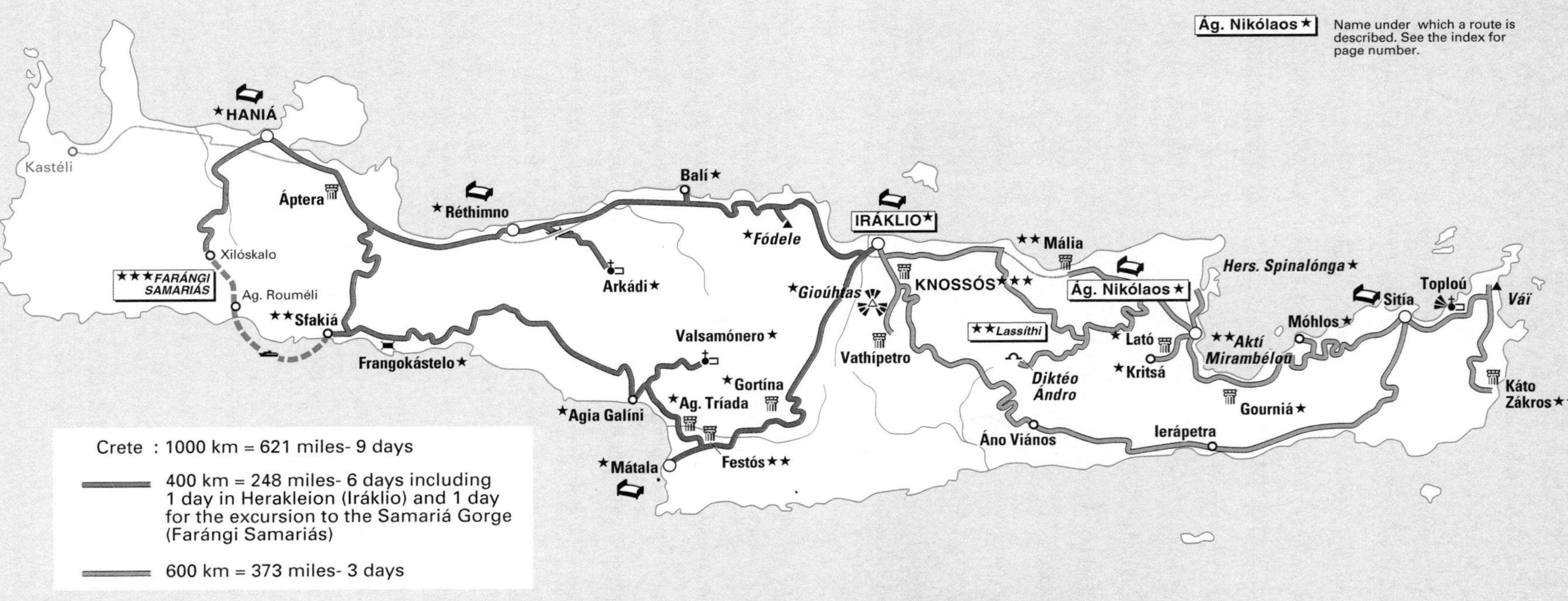
Overnight stop
Ág. Nikólaos ★
Name under which a route is described. See the index for page number.
★ HANIÁ
Kastéli
Áptera
★ Réthimno
Balí ★
Xilóskalo
★★★ FARÁNGI SAMARIÁS
Ag. Rouméli
★★ Sfakiá
Frangokástelo ★
Arkádi ★
★ Fódele
IRÁKLIO ★
★ Gioúhtas
KNOSSÓS ★★
Vathípetro
Valsamónero ★
★ Gortína
★ Ag. Tríada
★ Agia Galíni
★ Mátala
Festós ★★
★★ Mália
Ág. Nikólaos ★
Hers. Spinalónga ★
★★ Lassíthi
Diktéo Ándro
★ Lató
★ Kritsá
★★ Aktí Mirambélou
Móhlos ★
Gourniá ★
Sitía
Toplóu
Váï
Káto Zákros ★★
Áno Viános
Ierápetra
0
30 km
Crete : 1000 km = 621 miles- 9 days
400 km = 248 miles- 6 days including 1 day in Herakleion (Iráklio) and 1 day for the excursion to the Samariá Gorge (Farángi Samariás)
600 km = 373 miles- 3 days

T.A.P.

Arkádi Monastery

Finally Dominicans and Franciscans arrived preaching oecumenism: several churches (St Catherine's in Herakleion, Kritsá, Valsamónero, Toploú etc) have two naves side by side, one for the Orthodox and one for the Latin rite.

Cretan Renaissance – The fall of Constantinople to the Turks in 1453 brought Crete an influx of artists and men of letters.
Churches and monasteries were enriched with frescoes and icons by painters of the famous **Cretan School** in which the traditional Byzantine formality was softened by Italian influence, evident in the representation of volume and the arrangement of the figures: in Nativity scenes the Virgin is shown sitting or kneeling but not lying down. This school, which in the 16C migrated to Metéora and Mount Athos, reached its apogee with **Damaskinós** *(see IRÁKLIO: Agía Ekateríni)* and particularly Domenico Theotokópoulos, known as **El Greco** (1541-1614) *(see IRÁKLIO: Fódele Valley)*, a painter of icons, who emigrated first to Venice, then to Rome and finally to Spain. Later in the 17C other artists such as Emmanuel **Tzanés** settled in the Ionian islands.
The most famous works of literature were *The Sacrifice of Abraham* and the great poem *Erotókritos* by Vinkéntios Kornáros; it was based on a French work about the trials of two lovers and contained many Greek and Cretan elements.

Crete under the Turks – The Turkish occupation of Crete, which followed the capture of Herakleion *(see IRÁKLIO: The Great Siege)* in 1669, was very harsh; some Cretans had to convert to Islam while others took refuge in the mountains. Revolts erupted, particularly in 1770 under the leadership of the Sfakiot, **Daskaloyánnis** *(see SFAKIÁ)*; there were several more in the 19C. The works of the Cretan writers, Kazantzákis and Prevelakis *(see p 47)*, evoke this conflict.
Finally in 1878 Crete acquired a certain measure of autonomy under the aegis of the Great Powers and the regency of Prince George of Greece. It was thanks to the great liberal Cretan politican, Elefthérios Venizélos (1864-1936) *(see HANÍA)*, that Crete was finally attached to Greece in 1913.

Battle of Crete (1941) – After occupying mainland Greece the Germans turned their attention to Crete. In May 1941 they carried out a bold airborne operation with 500 transport aircraft and 80 gliders carrying parachutists and infantrymen. On 21 May 3 000 parachutists captured Máleme aerodrome to the west of Chania which served the Germans as a base for their penetration along the north coast of the island. The British, Australian and New Zealand troops were obliged to retreat over the White Mountains to embark at Sfakiá. It took the Germans only 10 days to capture the whole island but it cost them 6 000 of their best men.

ÁGIOS NIKÓLAOS★

Lassíthi – Population 8 093

Michelin map 980 fold 39

Ágios Nikólaos (St Nicholas) is a smart and lively resort; its white houses cover the slopes above the sparkling waters of Mirambélo Bay. It is pleasant to take an evening stroll along the quays of the lake and the fishing harbour where cafés, tavernas and restaurants spill out on to the pavement in typical Mediterranean style. The beaches and modern hotels extend along the coast to the north. Ágios Nikólaos makes a good centre from which to explore the eastern end of the island.
Local speciality: *soumáda*, a refreshing almond drink.

★**Lake Voulisméni** – Steep slopes riddled with caves encircle this pretty lake. Its water reflects the boats, cafés and shops which line the quays under the shade of tamarisk trees. Formerly it was known as "Artemis' Pool" and believed to be bottomless but in fact it is 64m/210ft deep; the channel to the sea was dug in 1870.

Arheologikó Moussío ⓥ – The **archeological museum**, which is on the road to Iráklio, contains finds from local excavations, particularly articles from the Minoan or Archaic Greek periods (Lató terracottas, jewellery from Móhlos, and a unique stone vase in the form of a triton's shell, decorated with Minoan "demons" performing libations).

EXCURSIONS

★**Hersónissos Spinalónga** (**Spinalónga Peninsula**) – *43km/27mi – about 1hr.* From Ágios Nikólaos take Odós Koundoúrou which turns into a very beautiful corniche road providing frequent **views**★★ over Mirambélo Bay. Once over a little pass the road runs down to the modern village of **Shísma** (Eloúnda – pop 1 019) which is known for its luxurious hotels. In the village turn right *(sign Oloús)* into a track suitable for vehicles which runs through onetime salt pans created by the Venetians. By two windmills the road crosses a bridge over a canal which was dug through the neck of the peninsula in 1898 by French sailors from the allied occupation forces; on the right rise the remains of ancient Oloús.

Oloús – Owing to earthquakes most of the ruins lie under the sea but an enclosure on the left beyond the bar contains traces of a paleo-Christian basilica with a fragment of 6C or 7C mosaic floor decorated with geometric motifs and fish.

Spinalónga Island – *Access by boat from Eloúnda or from the village of Pláka (5km/3mi north of Eloúnda).* A quiet and pleasant place providing a fine view of the bay. Off the northern end of the peninsula lies a rocky islet on which the Venetians built a fortress in the 16C. They held it until 1715 when it passed to the Turks.

Neápoli – *West of Eloúnda.* The village was once the home of **Pétros Filargés** (1340-1410), a Franciscan monk who became archbishop of Milan in 1402 and Pope Alexander V in 1409.

For adjacent sights see IERÁPETRA, KÁTO ZÁKROS, KRITSÁ, LASSÍTHI Plateau, MÁLIA, Kolpos MIRAMBÉLOU.

PICTOR

Ágios Nikólaos, Crete

ANÓGIA

Réthimno – Population 2 290

Michelin map 980 fold 38 – Alt 740m/2 428ft

This mountain town occupies a majestic site at the foot of **Mount Ida** (Óros Ídi), also known as Mount Psiloritis; the summit (2 456m/8 058ft) is snow-capped almost all the year. Anógia *(tavernas)* was rebuilt after being destroyed by the Germans in 1944 and is now a centre for local crafts (weaving, embroidery).

EXCURSIONS

Idéo Ándro (Idaian Cave) ⓥ – *22km/14mi south plus 30min on foot there and back.* Just before Anógia coming from Iráklio a surfaced road branches off *(left)* leading to the Nída Plateau (1 370m/4 495ft) and the Idaian Cave (1 540m/5 052ft) *(wide panorama offering superb mountain views).*

The sacred cave of Ida high on the mountain may have been the birthplace of Zeus *(see also LASSÍTHI: Diktean Cave).* During excavations at the end of the 19C Italian archeologists discovered objects dating from the 9C BC, including several decorated bronze shields which are now displayed in the museum in Herakleion.

Recent excavations by Greek archeologists have produced objects tracing the history of the cave from the Neolithic period to the 5C BC: objects made of gold, silver, pottery and rock crystal as well as small ivory pieces fashioned with skill (probably from Syria). The cave attracted pilgrims from all over the Greek world.

Axós – *6km/4mi west.* At the entrance to the village *(left)* stands **St Irene's Church** (Agía Iríni) ⓥ, a beautiful and typically Byzantine building except for the Gothic doorway in the façade. The frescoes in the interior date from the first half of the 14C and are in the style of the Palaiologos Renaissance *(see p 40).*

For adjacent sights see ARKÁDI, FESTÓS, GÓRTIS, IRÁKLIO, KNOSSÓS.

ÁPTERA

Haniá

Michelin map 980 east of fold 37

Branching off the main east-west highway is a minor road which leads up to a plateau above Soúda Bay. The **ruins** belong to a town which flourished from the 5C BC to the Byzantine period when it became a bishopric.

Ruins ⓥ

Within the fine outer walls are the remains of temples, a Roman theatre and an underground **Roman cistern**.

From the fort at the far end of the promontory there is a very fine **view**★★ of the mountain *(south)* and of **Soúda Bay**★ *(north)*, a huge natural harbour; the entrance is protected by two fortified islets which were held by the Venetians until 1715. The largest ships can anchor in Soúda Bay so that it serves both as the commercial port of Haniá *(ferries to Piraeus)* and as a strategic naval base.

For adjacent sights see HANIÁ, KASTÉLI or KÍSSAMOS, RÉTHIMNO, Farángi SAMARIÁS, SFAKIÁ, SITÍA.

ARKÁDI★

Réthimno

Michelin map 980 centre of fold 38

Arkádi Monastery *(illustration see p 264)* is one of the most impressive places in Crete as much for its site on the edge of a plateau overlooking a wild gorge as for a gloriously tragic incident in the struggle against the Turks. In 1866 some 1 000 Cretans, including many women and children, took refuge in the monastery and, after holding out in a desperate combat for two days against 12 000 Turkish soldiers, decided to blow themselves up with the powder magazine rather than yield; Gabriel, the superior of the monastery and the soul of the resistance, perished together with 829 other people.

MONASTERY ⓥ

A few monks still live in the monastery. It was founded in the 11C and its bare walls and austere exterior make it look like a fortress. A shady walk leads to the door and a vaulted passage gives access to the large courtyard in front of the church.

The church **façade** is built of golden stone and dated 1587. The Corinthian columns, the arcading and the Italian-style *oculi* give it a Renaissance look while the curves and counter-curves of the pediments add a touch of the Baroque. The convent buildings date from the 17C but have been altered since. The cellars, the kitchen, the huge refectory, the powder magazine and a small museum (displaying the sacred banner of the tragic struggle, arms from the time of the insurrection, icons, various cult objects, sacerdotal vestments, manuscripts and souvenirs of Gabriel) are open to the public.

For adjacent sights see ANÓGIA, FESTÓS, GÓRTIS, IRÁKLIO, KNOSSÓS, RÉTHIMNO, SFAKIÁ.

J. Bolland /APPARENCE

Iconostasis, Arkádi Monastery

FESTÓS★★

PHAISTOS – Iráklio

Michelin map 980 fold 38

On a spur of Mount Ida – a magnificent **site**★★ with a view of the Messará plain – stand the ruins of the Minoan palace of Phaistos which was founded by Rhadamanthos. Excavations carried out by the Italian School of Athens have identified two superimposed buildings; one dates from 2000-1650 BC and the other, which is similar in plan to the palace at Knossós, is more recent, dating from 1650-1400 BC.
Start in the North Court (traces of Hellenistic and Roman structures) (1); then go down the steps (2) which lead to the base of the Propylaia and the theatre.

SITE

Theatre – It is composed, like the one at Knossós, of straight terraces, in this case eight, facing the West Court, an open space for dancing and ritual games outside the palace. There was a little shrine (3) in the northeast corner.

Great Propylaia – A flight of steps leads up to the Propylaia, a monumental entrance consisting of a pillared hall (4). Beyond and to the left is a huge peristyle (5) surrounded by the royal apartments, to the east of which lies a range of domestic buildings where the famous "Phaistos Disk", now in the Archeological Museum in Herakleion, was discovered.

Royal Apartments – On the north side lies the King's Megaron consisting of a reception room (6) and a lustral bath (7) for ritual purification, which is down several steps; on the south side is the Queen's Megaron (8): one of the rooms has retained its original alabaster paving. A small court (9) and a corridor (10) lead into the central court.

Central Court – The vast open rectangle was flanked on the east and west sides by pillared porticoes while the north side contained the entrance to the royal apartments. As at Knossós it was probably used for displays of bull-leaping. There is a well (11) in the southwest corner.
Behind the west portico are traces of a crypt with two pillars (12) and a room surrounded by benches (13), both part of a **sanctuary**. Further along is a pillared hall (14), faced with alabaster, leading into a corridor lined with storerooms.

Storerooms – The rows of storerooms down both sides of the corridor contained supplies of cereals, oil and wine in enormous terracotta jars *(pithoi)*; in the last storeroom on the right (15) there was a device for collecting the oil which flowed from the receptacles.

Bear right to return to the entrance. Southwest of the West Court lie the ruins of the first palace which has yielded many examples of Kamáres ware.

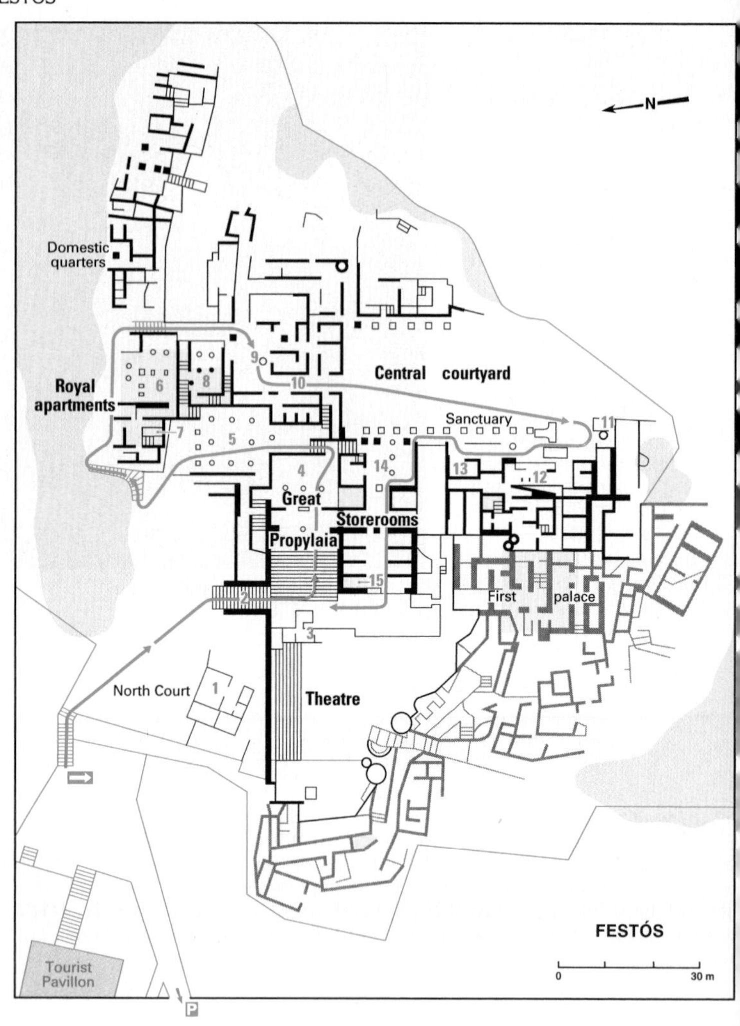

EXCURSIONS

Vóri – *4km/2.5mi north.* The **Cretan Museum of Ethnology★**, beside the church in a small town lacking any particular charm, surprises the visitor with its remarkable presentation and the quality of its collections from all over Crete.

★Agía Triáda ⏱ – *3km/2mi west.* The ruins here, as at Phaistos, occupy a fine site (its ancient name is unknown) overlooking the Messará Plain and Bay. The ruins were excavated by the Italians. To the left is a small palace; to the right and below lies a village. The local graveyard produced the famous painted sarcophagus, now in the Herakleion Museum.

The palace – It may have been the residence of a dignitary or a relative of the princes of Phaistos. Pass the grand staircase *(left)* leading up to the Altar Court and follow the paved ramp, which leads down towards the sea, past the north front of the palace; the redans are typical of Minoan architecture. This range of buildings, which was at least two storeys high (traces of stairs), comprised a central block containing the reception rooms, storerooms and the royal *megaron* with its alabaster cladding still in place. The west wing was built round small courts or light wells as living accommodation; some of the rooms have retained some of their original fittings: slate floors, benches, alabaster plaques, channels for draining off water. Further on stands St George's Church, a small 14C building decorated with delicate Byzantine sculptures, which have been re-employed.

Mycenaean Village – It was built later (1375-1100 BC) on the north side of the palace. The east side of the *agora* was bordered by a portico with shops.

Kalamáki – *6km/3.75mi southwest.* A small seaside resort lacking any particular charm, but which is likely to be further developed owing to the excellence of its beach on the wide bay of Messarás *(hotels, guest-houses, tavernas).*

Mátala Caves

★**Mátala** – *15km/9.25mi southwest.* Mátala *(hotels, tavernas)* is a little fishing village with a broad sandy beach and plenty of fresh fish. It lies in a peaceful bay almost cut off from the sea by the rocky islet blocking the entrance. According to the myth, it was here that Zeus swam ashore in the shape of a bull bearing **Europa** on his back.

Mátala is however better known for its **caves**★ which are to be found in the parallel strata of tufa on the north side of the beach. They may originally have been used as tombs but have also served as places of worship and troglodyte dwellings: benches, beds and recesses hollowed out of the stone.

Kómo – *12km/7.5mi southwest.* The ruins of a Minoan city which was probably the port of Phaistos rise above a fine sandy beach. Great buildings built of large stone blocks lining a wide paved street are visible from the fence enclosing the area. There are also traces of three temples built on the same spot and dating from the 10C BC to the 2C AD.

★**Agía Galíni** – *18km/11mi northwest.* This is a charming and very popular resort, with a picturesque harbour and many tavernas serving fish. There are boat trips to the sea caves along the coast.

Kalí Liménes – *25km/15.5mi south.* This peaceful bay where St Paul put in on his last voyage to Rome has been disfigured by oil storage tanks.

★**Valsamónero Monastery** ⓥ – *16km/10mi north to Vóri; take a minor road north to Kamáres and then east to Zarós. On the outskirts of Vorítzia turn right into an indifferent track which leads to Valsamónero (sign).*

The church of Ágios Fanoúrios which belongs to Valsamónero Monastery is in the Italian style of architecture. It has two parallel aisles preceded by a narthex. The older aisle (14C) on the left contains some remarkable **frescoes**★ (also 14C) depicting scenes from the Life of the Virgin and the saints, in particular John the Baptist; other frescoes (15C) decorate the righthand aisle and the narthex.

According to tradition, **El Greco** *(see IRÁKLIO: Fódele)* stayed in this beautifully situated monastery *(now deserted)* to study not only the frescoes but also the famous icons by Damaskinos which are now displayed in St Catherine's Church (Agía Ekateríni) in Herakleion.

For adjacent sights see ANÓGIA, ARKÁDI, GORTINA, IRÁKLIO, KNOSSÓS, RÉTHIMNO.

The towns and sights described in this guide are shown in **black lettering** *on the local maps and town plans.*

GORTÍNA★

GORTYN – Iráklio

Michelin map 980 fold 38

The impressive ruins straggling beneath the olive trees on either side of the road from Festós (Phaistos) evoke the past glory of Gortyn, capital of a Roman province and seat of the first Christian bishop of Crete.

Proud Gortyn – It was here according to legend that Zeus married Europa under the plane trees which were then granted the privilege of remaining forever green *(see above KRÍTI: Legend and History)*.
The city began to develop in the 7C BC forming an acropolis on a hill on the west bank of the little River Lethe, and it soon supplanted Phaistos as the capital of the Messará Plain. In about 500 BC a sort of civil and criminal code was drawn up regulating social relationships: the famous **Twelve Tables of Gortyn**.
Although Hannibal took refuge in Gortyn in 189 BC after being defeated by the Romans, the city nevertheless fell to the Romans in 67 BC and they made it the capital of a province comprising Crete and parts of North Africa known as Cyrenaica. As the seat of the provincial Governor the city went in for a spate of building in the 2C, particularly under Trajan, using stone from the huge quarries in the neighbouring mountains; many administrative and religious buildings were erected at this time.
Christianity took root in Gortyn in the 1C AD with the arrival of **Titus** who was sent by St Paul to convert the Cretans and became their patron saint. In AD 260 during the persecution ordered by Emperor Decius the Christian community produced its first martyrs, the Holy Ten, who are remembered in the name of a local village, **Ágii Déka** (Byzantine basilica with antique columns). In the 4C AD, following the recognition of Christianity by Emperor Constantine, Gortyn became a bishopric with jurisdiction over all the churches in Crete; richly decorated sanctuaries began to proliferate.
Gortyn was still prosperous during the Byzantine period but fell into decay after the Arab invasion in the 9C.
When the Italian monk Buondelmonti visited the city in the 15C it was in ruins but he was nonetheless impressed by its size and compared it with Florence. Excavations were first conducted in 1884 by the Italian School in Athens and continued in 1970.

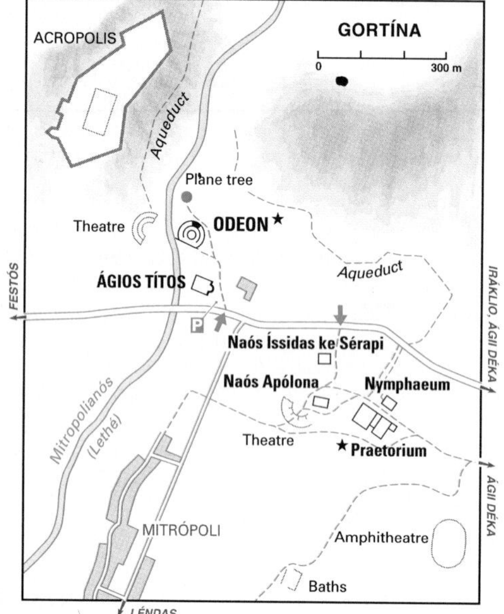

MAIN SIGHTS ⓥ *30min*

Park in the car park on the right of the road coming from Iráklio.

★**Ágios Títos (St Titus' Basilica)** – This important building, which is thought to date from the 7C, was erected on the site of Titus' martyrdom. The basilical plan of a nave and two aisles has been combined with the cruciform plan; the arms of the transept have apsidal ends. The chevet formed of three parallel apses is still standing; a few fragments of the carved decoration are on display in the Historical Museum in Herakleion.
On the north side of the basilica was an *agora*; the city had two.

★**Odeon** – The little theatre, which has been restored, consists of semicircular terraces supported by vaulting and was built early in the 2C AD under Trajan on the site of and with materials taken from an earlier rotunda *(thólos)*. Here and there lie damaged statues.
At the rear of the Odeon under the vaulting of the outer corridor are several blocks of stone taken by the Romans from the earlier building and bearing the text of the Twelve Tables of Gortyn. The Dorian letters which number 17 000 were

inscribed in about 480 BC and the lines are written alternately from left to right and right to left; the text deals with individual liberty, property, inheritance, adultery, violence etc.
Nearby stood an evergreen **plane tree** in memory, so legend would have it, of the love of Zeus and Europa *(see above)* which gave birth to Minos, Sarpedon and Rhadamanthos.

OTHER SIGHTS

Return towards Iráklio and then take the path on the right, level with the sign for Gortína.

Naós Íssidas ke Sérapi (Temple of Isis and Serapis) – The remains of a cella and a purification basin mark the site of this 2C temple which was dedicated to two Egyptian gods whose worship was widespread in the Roman world: Isis was the symbol of the universal feminine and Serapis was seen by the Romans as a manifestation of Jupiter. On the architrave is inscribed the dedication made by Flavia Phyrila and her sons.

Naós Apólona (Temple of Pythian Apollo) – Traces of a great sanctuary which dates from the Archaic period (inscriptions) but was rebuilt later; the *prónaos* is Hellenistic, the columns of the cella and the altar are Roman.

★**Praetorium (Residency)** ⓥ – Recent excavations have uncovered the impressive ruins of the praetorium, a huge building which was both the Governor's residence and the seat of the provincial administration; first built of brick in the 2C under Trajan, it was reconstructed in the 4C following an earthquake. It is possible to identify a vast chamber (basilica), the baths and the courtyard of a temple surrounded by a portico; the drums of the columns rest beside the bases. Several damaged statues have been recovered.

Nymphaeum – Opposite the praetorium is a nymphaeum which was built in the 2C as a grotto dedicated to the nymphs and converted into a fountain in the Byzantine era; it was supplied with water by an aqueduct.

EXCURSION

Vrondissí Monastery – *18km/11mi northwest to Zarós and then the road to Kamáres; about 3km/2mi beyond the village bear right into a track.* Vrondissí Monastery is situated on a terrace on the south face of Mount Ida with a magnificent view. Beneath the ancient plane trees that shade the entrance stands a beautiful **Renaissance fountain** (15C), built in marble by the Venetians; it bears the effigies of Adam and Eve.
As is often the case in Crete, the church is shared, with one aisle for the Latin rite and one for the Orthodox.

For adjacent sights see ANÓGIA, FESTÓS, IRÁKLIO, KNOSSÓS.

HANIÁ★

CHANIA – Haniá – Population 50 077
Michelin map 980 fold 37

Haniá, which is served by the port at Soúda and the airport at Akrotíri, lies in a fertile coastal basin which produces citrus fruits and potatoes. The capital of Crete until 1971, it is now a hard-working modern town, which suffered greatly in the German bombardment in 1941. Nevertheless a picturesque old district has survived round the Venetian port (Enetikó Limáni). *Beaches to the west of the town.*

★**Old town** – The old town follows the curve of the harbour which is used only by caïques and coasting vessels; it was built from the 13C onwards by the Venetians who enclosed it within a wall which was rebuilt in the 16C to the plans of the great engineer **Michele Sammicheli** *(see IRÁKLIO: Venetian Walls)*; a few segments of the wall are still standing.

Kastéli district *(East)* – In antiquity this was the site of Kydonia which was the rival of Knossós and Gortyn in the post-Minoan period. During the Venetian occupation the old district round the citadel contained the Latin cathedral, the Venetian Governor's palace, the administrative buildings (Customs, Archives), the houses of the leading citizens and the Arsenal, of which a few curious vaulted structures have survived, where the galleys were repaired.
On the quayside the former Janissaries' mosque (late 17C) now houses the tourist office.

★**Merchants' District** *(West)* – Walk along the quay (Aktí Koundouriótou) which is very busy and thronged with tavernas offering fish and seafood dishes (sea urchins). The beautiful old house *(north end)* is now a **Naval Museum** (Naftikó Moussío) ⓥ;

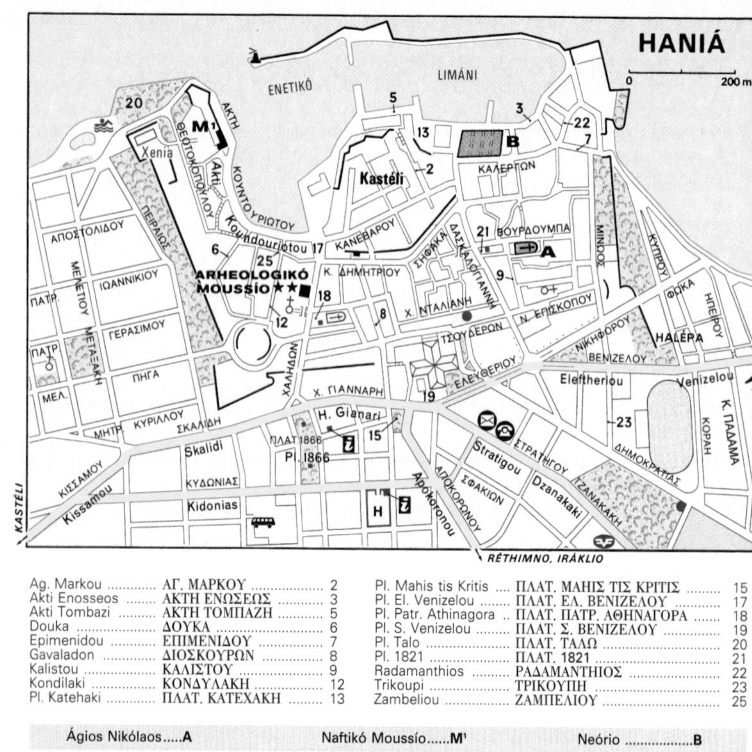

Ag. Markou	ΑΓ. ΜΑΡΚΟΥ	2	Pl. Mahis tis Kritis	ΠΛΑΤ. ΜΑΗΙΣ ΤΙΣ ΚΡΙΤΙΣ	15
Akti Enosseos	ΑΚΤΗ ΕΝΩΣΕΩΣ	3	Pl. El. Venizelou	ΠΛΑΤ. ΕΛ. ΒΕΝΙΖΕΛΟΥ	17
Akti Tombazi	ΑΚΤΗ ΤΟΜΠΑΖΗ	5	Pl. Patr. Athinagora	ΠΛΑΤ. ΠΑΤΡ. ΑΘΗΝΑΓΟΡΑ	18
Douka	ΔΟΥΚΑ	6	Pl. S. Venizelou	ΠΛΑΤ. Σ. ΒΕΝΙΖΕΛΟΥ	19
Epimenidou	ΕΠΙΜΕΝΙΔΟΥ	7	Pl. Talo	ΠΛΑΤ. ΤΑΛΩ	20
Gavaladon	ΔΙΟΣΚΟΥΡΩΝ	8	Pl. 1821	ΠΛΑΤ. 1821	21
Kalistou	ΚΑΛΙΣΤΟΥ	9	Radamanthios	ΡΑΔΑΜΑΝΘΙΟΣ	22
Kondilaki	ΚΟΝΔΥΛΑΚΗ	12	Trikoupi	ΤΡΙΚΟΥΠΗ	23
Pl. Katehaki	ΠΛΑΤ. ΚΑΤΕΧΑΚΗ	13	Zambeliou	ΖΑΜΠΕΛΙΟΥ	25

Ágios Nikólaos.....**A** Naftikó Moussío......**M¹** Neório ....**B**

the exhibits are well presented: historic documents and detailed model ships. A well documented permanent exhibition reconstructs the famous 1941 Battle of Crete.
The charming little streets behind the museum contain old Venetian houses with balconies and stone doorways sometimes ornamented with sculpted coats of arms. From time to time there is a view of the harbour between the houses.

★★**Arheologikó Moussío** ⌚ – The **Archeological Museum** is housed in an old church which was built in the 14C in the Venetian Gothic style as the conventual church of a Franciscan convent and dedicated to St Francis; it has a nave and two aisles with ogival vaulting. The Turks converted it into a mosque.
The exhibits include painted sarcophagi and ceramics from the Minoan and post-Minoan periods and Roman mosaics.
The stone exhibits are displayed in the garden beneath the palm trees and other exotic plants round a fine hexagonal Turkish fountain.

Ágios Nikólaos – **St Nicholas' Church** was built as a Dominican chapel, converted into a mosque with a minaret and became an Orthodox church in 1918; the neighbouring streets are quite picturesque.

EXCURSION

Hersónissos Akrotíri – *40km/25mi by car return.* The **Akrotíri Peninsula** which divides Soúda Bay from Chania Bay is riddled with caves.

From Haniá take the road via Halépa which is a residential district to the east; after 6km/4mi turn left towards Venizelos' Tomb.

★**Táfos Venizélou** – **Venizelos' Tomb** stands on the top of a hill named after the Prophet Elijah (Profítis Ilías) *(restaurants)*, where the Greek flag was raised by the Cretan rebels in 1897 and shot down by the navies of the Great Powers.
A great stone marks the grave of the Cretan statesman **Elefthérios Venizélos** (b 1864 Chania – d 1936 Paris); he was a lawyer and leader of the Greek liberal party who campaigned for Crete to be united with Greece and for Greece to enter the First World War on the side of the Allies *(see THESSALONÍKI: Historical Notes)*; his son Sophoclés Venizélos (1894-1964) is buried beside him. There is an extensive **view**★★ over Chania and its bay and south to the White Mountains (Lefká Óri).
Follow the signs to the Airport and at the end of the runway turn left into the road to Mouzourás and then almost immediately left again to Agía Triáda.

Agía Triáda ⓥ – *17km from Haniá.* **Holy Trinity Monastery** was founded early in the 17C by Tzangaroli, a Venetian; the church and the bell-tower are in the Italian Classical style. Its well arranged museum contains a fine collection of icons from the 16C to the 19C (in particular one of St John the Divine), sacerdotal vestments, precious cult objects (such as crosses), and manuscripts and old books connected with the history of the monastery.

Gouvernéto Monastery – *A walk (about 2hr on foot there and back or a drive of 4km/2.5mi on a partially surfaced road),* starting from Agía Triáda leads to the **monastery of St John of Gouvernéto** which was rebuilt and fortified in 1548 by the Venetians. The cave of St John the Hermit is nearby.

For adjacent sights see ÁPTERA, KASTÉLI or KÍSSAMOS, RÉTHIMNO, Farángi SAMARIÁS, SFAKIÁ, SITÍA.

IERÁPETRA

Lassíthi – Population 9 541
Michelin map 980 fold 39

There is a certain oriental feeling about Ierápetra which is the most southern town in Europe and enjoys a mild winter climate. It is a market for the agricultural products of the coastal plain: wine, oil, fruit, early vegetables and particularly tomatoes which are grown under glass throughout the year. It is also a popular resort with a long sandy beach bordered by a promenade lined with tamarisk trees and tavernas.
The port, which is devoted to fishing and coastal traffic, is not unattractive; the entrance is commanded by a 13C **fortress** with square bastions.
The old town still bears traces of the Turkish occupation: a fountain and a minaret. A **museum** ⓥ contains the finds from the prehistoric, Minoan and Roman periods, discovered in the environs of Ierápetra and from Gourniá. The coast both to the west and east of Ierápetra has been adapted to the needs of mass tourism, and the architecture is often of very poor quality.

EXCURSIONS

★**Áno Viános** – *53km/33mi west.* The road passes through heavily eroded country before reaching the verdant Mírtos Valley (oranges, bananas, vines). Beyond Péfkos a track bears left, past an imposing monument dedicated to the victims of German execution squads, down to **Árvi** *(beach, inns)*, a fishing village overlooked by a monastery of unusual construction.
Áno Viános stands on a spectacular **site**★ in a mountain cirque overlooking a great sweep of olive trees.

Hrissí Island – *Boat trip (1hr) possible (beach, fishing, sport).* A wild and beautiful island, but often overrun in summer.

For adjacent sights see ÁGIOS NIKÓLAOS, FESTÓS, GÓRTIS, IRÁKLIO, KÁTO ZÁKROS, KNOSSÓS, KRITSÁ, LASSÍTHI Plateau, Kolpos MIRAMBÉLOU.

IRÁKLIO★

HERAKLEION – Iráklio – Population 115 214
Michelin map 980 fold 39

Now the capital city and principal port of Crete, the commercial and administrative centre of the island, the medieval city of **Candia** has developed enormously since the Second World War. Nonetheless it is still surrounded by its 16C-17C ramparts and is not unattractive owing to its lively atmosphere and the contrast between port and town, broad avenues and narrow streets, modern buildings and traditional houses. It is a good base for excursions into the centre of the island.
Favourite meeting places for both locals and tourists are Platía Eleftherías (Liberty Square) and Platía El Venizélou (Venizelos Square) with their pavement cafés, book shops and newspaper kiosks, and Odós Dedálou (Daidalos Street) with its souvenir shops, local crafts (jewellery and icons), restaurants and tavernas.
It is also worth eating in the fish tavernas down by the harbour particularly in the evening; sometimes there is music performed on the Cretan lyre *(líra)*.

Historical notes – According to legend, Herakleion takes its name from Herakles (Hercules) who landed on Crete to accomplish one of his Twelve Labours *(see TÍRINTHA)*: to master the Cretan bull which was ravaging the kingdom of Minos at the instigation of Poseidon.
When Crete fell in 827 to the Arabs, they set up a fortified camp on the site of Herakleion surrounded by a ditch – El Khandak – from which the Venetians, who arrived in the 13C, derived the name Candia. Under the Venetians the city became a

commercial and military centre, the key to the rest of Crete; they erected many churches, public and private buildings and an arsenal.
The Cretans however hated the Venetians who oppressed them with heavy taxes.

Great Siege (1648-69) – In 1648 the Turks landed on Crete and laid siege to Candia. During the following 20 years they made 69 assaults on the city while the besieged carried out 89 sorties. The pressure increased in 1667 when the Grand Vizier assembled 80 000 men and the largest cannon in Europe.
As the Venetians held out under their commander **Francesco Morosini** (1619-94), who 20 years later delivered Athens from the Turks, Christendom grew concerned. Finally Louis XIV sent a naval force led by the **Duc de Beaufort**; the ships carried 6 000 soldiers. Beaufort was killed during a sortie which failed and, after losing 1 000 men, the expeditionary force withdrew. Morosini now had only 4 000 defenders and the city was under heavy bombardment; on 5 September 1669 he surrendered. About 30 000 Christians and 110 000 Muslims had died during the siege, which marked the end of Venetian sway in the eastern Mediterranean.
Under the Turkish occupation Candia gradually lost its importance to Chania which became the capital of Crete until 1971.

★★★ARHEOLOGIKÓ MOUSSÍO ⏱ *3hr*

In the shade of the garden stands a stele raised in memory of the Duc de Beaufort and his 1 000 French soldiers who fell during the siege. The **National Archeological Museum** is devoted to the Minoan civilisation discovered at the end of the last century; it is preferable to visit the museum after seeing the archeological sites of Knossós, Phaistos, Mália and Zákros.
The exhibits are arranged in chronological order and are mainly the product of the excavations complemented by reconstructions (models or watercolours) of the main palaces. The most interesting rooms are Room IV and Room VII. Please note that the positioning of the items displayed may vary according to circumstances (eg restoration or loaning of exhibits).

Room I: Neolithic and Pre-Palace Periods (5000-2000 BC). Among the funerary articles Vassilikí vases with a red decoration on a light ground *(case 6)*, alabaster and soapstone vessels, golden jewellery from Móhlos Island (west of Sitía) *(cases 7 and 17)*, seals used as signets or as lucky charms *(cases 11 and 18)*.

Rooms II and III: Old Palace Period (2000-1700 BC). Little remains of the palaces and mountain shrines of this period but excavations have produced votive offerings and a remarkable series of **Kamáres ware**: vases, amphorae, jugs with spouts, cups and goblets elegantly decorated with spirals and flowers.

In the centre of Room III in case 41 is the **Phaistos Disk**; the hieroglyphs inscribed in a spiral on the clay (not yet deciphered) are suggestive of the labyrinth of the Minotaur. Case 43 contains an astonishing bowl in Kamáres ware decorated with white flowers in relief which was found at Phaistos.

Room IV: New Palace Period (1700-1450 BC). Masterpieces of Minoan civilisation. On the left on entering *(case 50)* are the famous **snake goddesses**, faience statuettes of bare-breasted priestesses (symbols of fecundity) found in the central shrine at Knossós. Opposite *(case 51)* is a soapstone vase *(rhyton)* in the shape of a **bull's head** used for religious libations: the eye is rock crystal and the muzzle outlined with mother of pearl. Two other cases *(56 and 57)* display an extraordinary ivory **acrobat** involved in the ritual bull-leaping and a set of chessmen, made of ivory encrusted with rock crystal, blue sintered glass, gold and silver. At the far end of the room is an alabaster ritual vessel *(rhyton)* shaped like a lion's head *(case 59)*.

Room V: Late New Palace Period (1450-1400 BC). Everyday articles of porphyry (lamps, weights) and alabaster *(amphorae)*. Clay tablets with inscriptions in Linear A and B scripts.

Room VI: New and Post-Palace Periods (1450-1300 BC). Funerary objects. The group of sacred dancers and scenes from the cult of the dead in terracotta comes from a *thólos* tomb at Kamilári, southwest of Phaistos *(case 71, right)*, a libation jug *(case 80)*, gold jewellery *(cases 87 and 88, centre)*.

Room VII: New and Post-Palace Periods (1700-1300 BC). This room is one of the richest in the museum. On entering one's attention is claimed by the huge bronze double-headed axes. The first three cases display three black soapstone vessels used for ritual libations and found at Agía Triáda:
– the **Harvester Vase** *(case 94)* decorated with a procession of peasants and musicians in low relief;
– the **Chieftain Cup** *(case 95)* showing several people of whom one, a Chief or Prince, has long wavy hair; he is wearing jewellery and carries a sceptre; an official who has a sword on his shoulder makes a report;
– the **Boxer Vase** *(case 96)*, a conical vessel *(rhyton)* decorated with athletics and ritual bull-leaping scenes.

The "Parisienne"

Phaistos disk

Bull's head Rhyton

Snake goddes

Kamáres vase

Bull-leaping, Knossós

T.A.P.

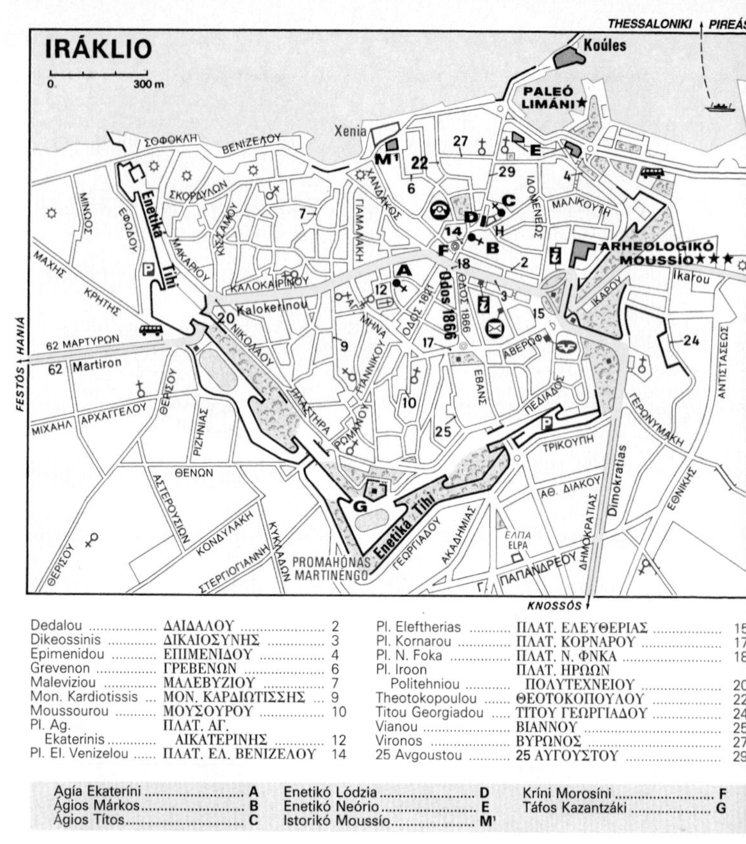

Dedalou	ΔΑΙΔΑΛΟΥ	2	Pl. Eleftherias	ΠΛΑΤ. ΕΛΕΥΘΕΡΙΑΣ	15
Dikeossinis	ΔΙΚΑΙΟΣΥΝΗΣ	3	Pl. Kornarou	ΠΛΑΤ. ΚΟΡΝΑΡΟΥ	17
Epimenidou	ΕΠΙΜΕΝΙΔΟΥ	4	Pl. N. Foka	ΠΛΑΤ. Ν. ΦΝΚΑ	18
Grevenon	ΓΡΕΒΕΝΩΝ	6	Pl. Iroon Politehniou	ΠΛΑΤ. ΗΡΩΩΝ ΠΟΛΥΤΕΧΝΕΙΟΥ	20
Maleviziou	ΜΑΛΕΒΥΖΙΟΥ	7	Theotokopoulou	ΘΕΟΤΟΚΟΠΟΥΛΟΥ	22
Mon. Kardiotissis	ΜΟΝ. ΚΑΡΔΙΩΤΙΣΣΗΣ	9	Titou Georgiadou	ΤΙΤΟΥ ΓΕΩΡΓΙΑΔΟΥ	24
Moussourou	ΜΟΥΣΟΥΡΟΥ	10	Vianou	ΒΙΑΝΝΟΥ	25
Pl. Ag. Ekaterinis	ΠΛΑΤ. ΑΓ. ΑΙΚΑΤΕΡΙΝΗΣ	12	Vironos	ΒΥΡΩΝΟΣ	27
Pl. El. Venizelou	ΠΛΑΤ. ΕΛ. ΒΕΝΙΖΕΛΟΥ	14	25 Avgoustou	25 ΑΥΓΟΥΣΤΟΥ	29

Agía Ekateríni	A	Enetikó Lódzia	D	Kríni Morosíni	F
Ágios Márkos	B	Enetikó Neório	E	Táfos Kazantzáki	G
Ágios Títos	C	Istorikó Moussío	M¹		

Note the curious bronze ingots weighing 40kg/88lb *(case 99)* and the jewellery: famous **golden pendant** composed of two foraging bees which was found at Mália *(case 101, centre of the room)*.

Rooms VIII and IX: New Palace Period (1700-1400 BC). In the first room note the objects discovered since 1962 in the palace at Zákros: ritual vases including a rock crystal *rhyton (case 109)* with pearl handles which was reconstructed by the museum workshop from a multitude of fragments and a splendid green and white stone *amphora (case 118)*.

The main exhibit in the second room is an *amphora* decorated with an octopus from Palékastro *(centre case 120)*.

Room X: Post-Palace Period (c 1400-1100 BC). The art of this period is characterized by large female figures with headdresses of birds, horns and poppies *(case 133, at the back)*.

Rooms XI and XII: Sub-Minoan and Geometric Periods (1100-650 BC). Interpenetration of the Minoan, Greek and Oriental styles. At the back of the first room *(case 148)* are female idols and a curious chariot drawn by bulls; in the second room are cinerary urns with lids and bronze objects found in a cave on Mount Ida *(case 169)*; the vase collection includes a jug *(oinochoë – case 163)* depicting an amusing scene of the lovers Theseus and Ariadne *(under restoration for an indefinite period)*.

Room XIII: Minoan sarcophagi from the Post-Palace Period (c 1400-1100 BC) often look like baths or chests.

Rooms XIV, XV, and XVI (first floor): A gallery (containing a wooden model of the palace of Knossós as it may have been in about 1400 BC) and two other rooms are devoted to Minoan frescoes from the New Palace Period, which show similarities with frescoes from the palace of Mari (Sumerian civilisation). They have been reconstructed from fragments – some parts are in relief – and show the high quality of mural painting in the palaces of this period.

One of the chief exhibits in the museum, the **Agía Triáda sarcophagus**, is to be found in the centre of Room XIV *(case 171):* the painted decoration has a funerary theme – sacrifice of a bull, priestesses pouring libations, people bearing offerings to the deceased. On the walls are the **Prince of the Lilies**, crowned with lilies and peacock feathers, a bull's head in relief and an acrobat in a bull-leaping scene – all from Knossós.

Room XV contains the famous **Parisienne**, found at Knossós and so named by Sir Arthur Evans because of the malicious charm of her expression; the small-scale but well preserved figure represents a priestess. Room XVI next door contains other well known frescoes: the Monkey collecting saffron, a dancer and "an officer of the black guard" of the sacred knots, and two remarkable frescoes called "the Olive Tree" from the palace at Knossós.
At the time this guide was being prepared, Rooms XVII, XVIII, XIX and XX were closed for an indefinite period.

OTHER SIGHTS

★**Paleó Limáni** – The **old port** is now devoted to fishing boats. Parts of the **Venetian Arsenal** are to be found at the far end of the harbour: stores, docks and in particular the hangar where the galleys were brought out of the water for caulking and repair.
The entrance to the harbour is commanded by the Koúles, the **Venetian fortress** Ⓥ still bearing the lion of St Mark; it was built in the 16C and has been recently restored. It has massive walls pierced with embrasures for cannon, a cistern, a powder magazine and casemates communicating with stores for cannon-balls. Fine views of the port and town.

Odós 1866 – In the morning the street is the scene of a lively **market**★ full of smells and colour selling local products; yoghurt and honey, herbs including dittany which is drunk as an infusion, ornamental bread rings, raisins, figs, citrus fruits, cheeses, fish and meat...
At the end of the street are two contrasting fountains: the Bembo fountain, erected by the Venetians in 1588, and a Turkish fountain converted into a street stall.

Platía El. Venizélou – This is a pleasant square reserved for pedestrians; the basin of the 17C **Morosini Fountain** is decorated with nereids, tritons and dolphins... (the upper basin, supported on lions, may come from an earlier 14C fountain).
Leading out of the southeast corner of the square is a street, also reserved for pedestrians, Odós Dedálou, where the tavernas and boutiques invite one to take a stroll.

Ágios Márkos – **St Mark's Church**, which is Italianate in style with an external portico and a nave and two aisles supported on tall columns, was the cathedral of Candia during the Venetian occupation; the Turks converted it into a mosque.
The building (14C, restored, containing some beautiful Gothic features) is now used for exhibitions, conferences and concerts.

Venetian Loggia – The reconstruction has been carried out in the style of the 17C original which was inspired by the Venetian architect, Palladio. It was here that the money changers set up their stalls and the merchants met to discuss business.

Platía Theotokopoúlou (El Greco Square) – A small green oasis with a white marble bust of the great Cretan painter.

Agía Ekateríni Ⓥ – In the 16C and 17C **St Catherine's Church** was attached to the convent of St Catherine of Sinai which organised a school; its pupils may have included El Greco *(see below)* one of whose early works was a landscape of Mount Sinai, currently on view at the Heraklion Historical Museum.
It is a shared church with two centres of worship. The one on the left, dedicated to the Holy Ten (Ágii Déka) *(see GORTÍNA)*, dates from the 13C; it has heavy ogival vaulting; the elegant Venetian façade with pilasters, tympanum and *oculus* is later, probably 15C. The other dates from the 16C; the façade and the barrel-vaulted nave lit by *oculi* reveal the influence of Italian architecture.

J. Bolland /APPARENCE

Venetian walls, Herakleion

The interior contains six remarkable **icons**★★ by **Mihális Damaskinós** who worked in Venice and the Ionian Islands from 1574 to 1582 before returning to Crete. These works, which were formerly at the Vrondissí monastery *(see GORTÍNA)* combine the traditional Byzantine formality of composition and picturesque realism with the Italian feeling for form. Compare the unusual scene of the Council of Nicaea condemning Arianism, in the Byzantine style, with the Last Supper and the Adoration of the Magi which owe much to Tintoretto.

Enetiká Tíhi (16C-17C) – The **Venetian town walls** (5km/3mi long) are reinforced by seven large bastions with lateral projections called *orillions*; they were the work of **Michele Sammicheli** (1484-1559), an architect who had designed the fortifications of Padua and Verona and came to Crete in 1538. The road running along under the walls leads to the **Martinengo Bastion** (Promahónas Martinéngo); on the top is the tomb of the great Cretan writer **Kazantzákis** (1883-1957) *(see below and p 49)*; the inscription reads: "I hope for nothing, I fear nothing, I am free".

Istorikó Moussío ⏱ – The collections of the **History Museum**, which illustrate Cretan history from the Byzantine period down to the present day, include: the one **work by El Greco**★★ in Crete, *View of Mount Sinai*, and from St Catherine's Monastery (c 1570) a reconstruction of a vaulted chapel with no side aisles, incorporating murals and frescoes typical of Cretan Byzantine art of the mid 14C and influenced by the Macedonian School, taken from the Church of the Virgin at Kardouliánou Pediáda; sculptures from St Titus' Basilica at Agía Triáda; pieces from the loggia, fountains and Venetian houses in Candia; Venetian and Turkish tomb stones; Byzantine icons; embroidery, jewellery and traditional Cretan fabrics; documents on the Battle of Crete of 1941.
Note the reconstructions of Kazantzákis' study and a 19C Cretan interior.

Ágios Títos – **St Titus' Church** was built by the Venetians in the 16C; the Turks transformed it into a mosque; it is now the Metropolitan (cathedral) church and has been completely restored.
In the narthex *(left)* is a reliquary containing St Titus' head which was returned by the Venetians in 1966.

EXCURSIONS

★★★ **Knossós** – *5km/3mi south. See KNOSSÓS.*

Kazantzákis Museum ⏱ – *At Varvári Pediádos (Mirtiá); 15km/9.5mi southeast of Iráklio.* This little museum is devoted to the life of the Greek novelist Nikos Kazantzákis *(see above and p 49)*: manuscripts of his books which have been published in 53 countries and translated into 41 languages, theatrical costumes used in presentations of his plays, photographs and some of his personal possessions.

★ **Mount Gioúhtas** – *At Vathípetro; 30km/19mi south of Iráklio. Take the road to Knossós and 5km/3mi beyond the site turn right to Arhánes.*
The road runs through a region of vineyards in which many traces of Minoan buildings have been discovered: palaces, graveyards (at Foúrni in particular), "villas"; temples where human sacrifices were occasionally made to avert an imminent or insuperable danger.
On the far side of **Arhánes**, the surfaced road comes out at a crossroads after 2km/1.25mi. Take the road on the right (passable) for 4km/2.5mi to the top of Mount Gioúhtas.

★ **Mount Gioúhtas** – In this mountain (811m/2 661ft), which has yielded a number of votive offerings from a Minoan shrine, the god Zeus is supposed to be entombed. The mountain's silhouette can indeed be said to resemble the profile of a man asleep which popular belief claims to be Zeus himself.
From the pilgrimage church at the top on the edge of a steep cliff there is a vast **panorama**★★ over Iráklio and the sea (north), Mount Díkti (east) and Mount Ídi (west).

Return to the road to Pírgos; after 2km/1.25mi turn right (sign) into a track which leads to the ruins of Vathípetro.

Vathípetro Villa – Excavations on this pleasant site have uncovered a large-scale agricultural enterprise from the Minoan period: central courtyard, stores, potter's workshop, shrine; an oil press and a winepress have been identified.

Tílissos ⏱ – *14km/8.75mi southwest; coming from Iráklio bear left on entering the village.* On the top of the hill are traces of three Minoan villas from the New Palace Period.
Near the entrance walk round the remains of Villa B *(right)* and then walk anti-clockwise round the whole of the ruins to reach the entrance to Villa C of which the northeast corner is marked by a circular cistern. Further on the right is the vestibule next to the porter's lodge: next are several rooms, some of which are still partially paved, passages and stairs.

El Greco

Born in Fódele, Crete, in 1541, El Greco (the Greek) learnt his trade on his home island, which was at that time a Venetian possession and a centre of the Greek Byzantine renaissance. At the end of 1566 he arrived in Venice, where he became a pupil of Titian. After a brief stay in Parma, he settled in Rome in 1570, and then went on to Toledo in 1577 where he lived until his death in 1614, becoming one of the great figures of Spanish painting. A complex personality, schooled in Italian techniques but still respecting the Byzantine tradition, El Greco introduced into his paintings a hieratic quality expressed in the lengthening of the silhouettes in his strikingly dramatic scenes. In developing a visionary art, he liberated his forms, using cold and contrasting colours, thus creating especially in the works of his maturity an unreal atmosphere informed with an air of mysticism. The composition of his paintings is also on two levels: heaven and earth, as El Greco saw life on earth simply as a stage on the road to life everlasting.

Beyond are the remains of Villa A; its entrance was divided by two pillars: to the right were the stores, to the left a paved corridor leading to a little court or light well surrounded by various rooms. The enormous bronze cauldrons in the Herakleion Museum were found in this villa.

★**Fódele** – *28km/30mi west. From Iráklio pass through the Chania Gate and take the new road to Réthimno.* At the end of the bay the road passes Paleókastro, a Venetian fortress, leaves the fishing village of **Agía Pelagía** *(good beaches)* on the right and then reaches the Fódele Valley.

★**Fódele Valley** – This recess in the mountainside is thought to be the birthplace of the painter Domenico Theotokópoulos, known as **El Greco** (1541-1614). Its slopes are covered with olive and carob trees; the well irrigated valley bottom is carpeted with orange and lemon groves.
On arriving in Fódele, where one can buy craft products, take the surfaced road suitable for motor traffic which fords the river, skirts a charming Byzantine church (frescoes inside) and ends in front of El Greco's father's house; it stands in a pleasant spot facing the austere grandeur of the barren mountain tops.

★**Balí** – *48 km/30mi west.* The village *(tavernas)* in a little creek offers good fishing and walking along the spectacular and rugged rocky coast; small isolated beaches.

For adjacent sights see ANÓGIA, FESTÓS, GÓRTIS, KNOSSÓS, LIMÁNI HERSONÍSSOU, MÁLIA, RÉTHIMNO.

KASTÉLI or KÍSSAMOS

Haniá – Population 2 936
Michelin map 980 fold 37

Known in antiquity as Kíssamos, Kastéli is now a market town (good quality wine, olives, early vegetables, citrus fruit) and an excursion centre *(Ferries to Kythera, the Peloponnese and Piraeus)*.
Its position in the centre of Kíssamos Bay (Kólpos Kissámou) is well sheltered by the Rodopós promontory *(east)* and by the Gramvoússa promontory *(west)*; northwest lies **Gramvoússa Islet**, which was fortified by the Venetians and held by them until the end of the 17C; it then became a pirates' retreat until the 19C.

EXCURSIONS

Falássarna – *17km/10.5mi west by the surfaced road to Plátanos. In the village turn right (after passing the sign "Plátanos") into an unsurfaced road which leads down to the sea;* fine views down over the rich coastal plain: olive groves, tomatoes under glass.
Beyond Plátanos *(7km/4.25mi)*, at the end of the track, the road reaches the ancient ruins of Falássarna *(excavations in progress)*, scattered over a lonely site on the neck of a rocky peninsula on which an acropolis once stood; the position of the harbour is still visible although it is now dry since volcanic movements have raised the level of the coastline by about 8m/26ft. Fine beach which is relatively empty.

Polirinía – *6km/3.75mi south.* Picturesque village on a bluff with a fine view of Kíssamos Bay *(30min on foot)*; traces of an ancient city founded in the 8C BC.

Goniá Monastery ⏲ – *21km/13mi northeast by the road to Chania.* The monastery of Our Lady Goniá (Moní Kirías Goniás), which is also called the Hodegetria

(Moní Odigítrias), was founded by the Venetians in 1618; since its position on the coast was of military importance it also served as a fortress and was frequently damaged and restored.
The church and the adjacent chapels contain an interesting collection of **icons**★ several of which date from the 14C: *St Paraskevi* and *St Irene*, the *Transfiguration of Jesus Christ*, and the *Merciful Mother of God* all from around 1300, as well as the very moving *Crucifixion of Christ*.
From the terrace behind the church there is a very fine **view**★ of Chania Bay.
For adjacent sights see ÁPTERA, HANIÁ, Farángi SAMARIÁS, SFAKIÁ, SITÍA.

KÁTO ZÁKROS★★

KÁTO ZÁKROS – Lassíthi
Michelin map 980 fold 40

The road from Palékastro to Zákros *(17km/10.5mi)* is not very good, but it does offer **mountain landscapes**★★ that have a wild and austere beauty.
A remote but very beautiful **site**★★ at Káto Zákros, deep in a little bay *(beach, tavernas)* on the east coast of Crete, has been excavated by Greek archeologists who have uncovered the remains of the palace of Zákros, the fourth great Minoan palace after Knossós, Phaistos and Mália. It can be reached either by an excellent road *(8km/5mi from Zákros)* or on foot *(1hr 30min walk for the last 4km/2.5mi, recommended to nature lovers; the walk starts 3.5km/2mi after leaving Zákros)*: the path runs along the side of a deep ravine, the Valley of Death, which was used in antiquity as a necropolis, with spectacular **views**★★ down into the bay.

★**Palace** ⓥ – *Entrance from the northeast.* The buildings, which were destroyed in about 1500 BC by the earthquakes accompanying the eruption of the Santoríni volcano, were arranged, as in the other Minoan palaces around a central court. On the north side was a large kitchen, the only one of its kind that has been identified with certainty; the reception rooms and place of worship lay to the west; opposite on the east were the royal apartments belonging to the sovereign and his consort and including a round basin which may have been used as a cistern; to the south stood the workshops and storerooms with an adjoining well.
The town extended south towards the sea: in those days Zákros was an important place trading with Egypt and the Orient.

For adjacent sights see ÁGIOS NIKÓLAOS, IERÁPETRA, KRITSÁ, LASSÍTHI Plateau, Kolpos MIRAMBÉLOU.

KNOSSÓS★★★

Iráklio
Michelin map 980 fold 39 – 5km/3mi south of Iráklio

The maze of corridors, passages, rooms and stairways, which make up the palace of Knossós, is one of the major sights of Crete. The palace, which was excavated and partially reconstructed by the British archeologist, Sir Arthur Evans, was the first of the Minoan palaces to be discovered and proved to be the largest.

MYTHOLOGY BASED ON HISTORY

King Minos – Knossós "the chief city of King Minos, whom great Zeus took into his confidence every nine years" (Homer), developed out of a very complicated building, the **Labyrinth** – The Palace of the Axe – since the double-headed axe was the main ritual symbol of the Minoan religion. The palace is supposed to have been designed by the cunning **Daidalos**, at Minos' request, to confine the **Minotaur**, a monster with a man's body and a bull's head, born of the unnatural union of Parsiphae, Minos' queen, and a bull.
Minos used to feed his enemies to the Minotaur and every nine years the Athenians, in retribution for the death of Minos' son at the hands of Aegeus, king of Athens, had to deliver a human sacrifice of seven youths and seven maidens. It was as part of the tribute that **Theseus** arrived from Athens and seduced Ariadne, King Minos' daughter; she gave him the thread obtained from Daidalos which Theseus unwound as he penetrated the Labyrinth and was thus able to find his way out after killing the Minotaur and escape from the palace with Ariadne *(see also NÁXOS)*.
To punish Daidalos for revealing the secret of the Labyrinth Minos had him imprisoned within the palace but Daidalos constructed some wings using birds' feathers and wax and escaped from the palace with his son **Ikaros**.
Alas for Ikaros, he flew too close to the sun which melted the wax and the unfortunate young man fell into the sea near to the present island of Ikaría (west of Sámos in the Aegean) while his father succeeded in reaching Cumae in Italy.

Excavation of the palace – The existence of Knossós had been suggested by Schliemann *(see MIKÍNES)* interpreting the Homeric epic as if it were history, as he had done for Troy and Mycenae. In 1878 a Cretan, Minos Kalokairinós, who had been the first to identify the site, had undertaken some excavations but it was the great British archeologist, **Sir Arthur Evans** (1851-1941) who began to dig in earnest in 1900 and who gained the credit for discovering the palace and making it live again.

The site of Knossós on a hill was already inhabited in the Neolithic period; in about 2000 BC a palace was built which was destroyed in 1700 BC. It was replaced by a new palace at the centre of a town with about 50 000 inhabitants; it is traces of this palace which can be seen today.

In c 1530 BC (possibly 1630 BC) an earthquake and a tidal wave, provoked, it seems, by the eruption of the volcano on Thíra (Santoríni), laid waste the new palace which was however later sacked and occupied for a short period by the Mycenaeans. It was finally destroyed by fire between 1375 and 1250 BC. Nonetheless a settlement survived in the neighbourhood and in the 4C BC Knossós was still of some importance in politics. Eventually at the end of the 3C BC it was supplanted by Gortyn *(see GORTÍNA)*.

PICTOR

Knossós Palace

PALACE RUINS ⌚ *plan see below*

Beyond the entrance gate and a statue of Sir Arthur Evans *(Ágalma Evans)*, pass through the trees into the West Court, a paved area which was probably an *agorá*. On the left are three pits for the disposal of discarded sacred objects and the base of an altar (1) in front of the entrance; behind it are the foundations of the palace about 1m/3ft high. There were no fortifications and the buildings comprised about 1 300 rooms. On the right is the West Entrance supported by a single central column of which the base remains. This entrance gave access to the **Corridor of the Procession** (2); the walls were decorated with frescoes showing a procession of people bearing offerings (Herakleion Museum).

Upper Floor – Next turn left to reach the grand entrance (3) *(propylaia)*, a pillared porch at the foot of the grand staircase to the upper floor; a section, including a copy of a fresco (bearers of offerings) has been reconstructed. The upper floor comprised a number of pillared rooms, some of which have been restored and decorated with copies of frescoes. They may have been used as reception rooms: the famous *Parisienne (see IRÁKLIO: Arheologikó Moussío)* may have formed part of the decoration.

To the west of this suite of rooms runs a long corridor serving a series of narrow storerooms piled high with provision jars *(pithoi)* some of which are still in place. To the east another staircase leads down into the central courtyard.

Central courtyard – The courtyard (60m/197ft long x 29m/95ft wide) is surrounded by the main buildings – shrines, royal apartments etc. It (or the theatre) was probably the site of the perilous acrobatic ritual bull-leaping.

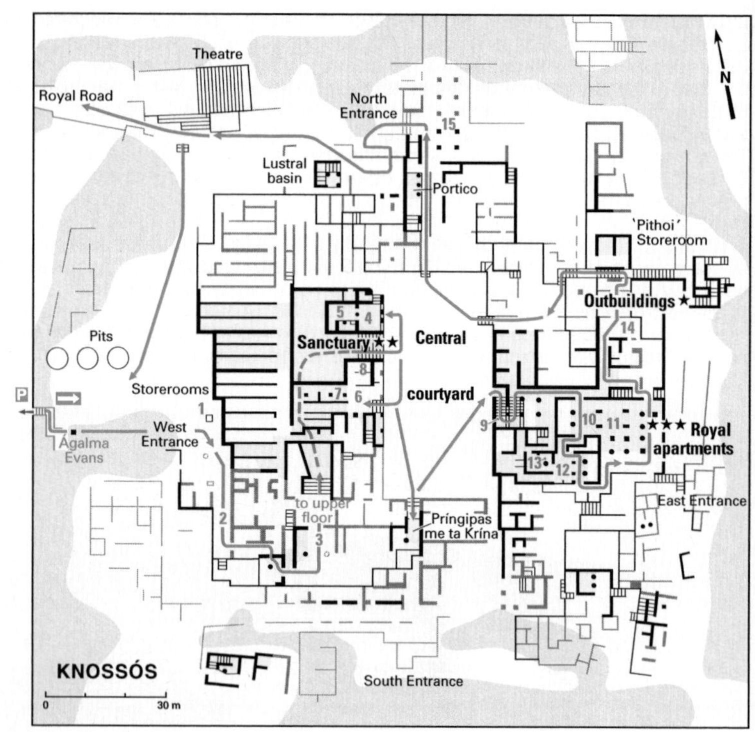

★★Sanctuary – Down the west side of the courtyard lie the rooms devoted to religious use on either side of the staircase.

On the right a vestibule (**4**), in the centre of which Evans placed a porphyry basin, leads into the "Throne Room" (**5**) which contains a bench and the alabaster throne on which the High Priestess of the Labyrinth may have sat; the Griffin Frescoes are reconstructions. Opposite the throne, steps beneath arches descend to a lustral basin.

On the left another vestibule (**6**) leads into the two "pillar crypts" (**7**) *(opposite)* where the ritual ceremonies took place (double axe heads carved on the pillars) and into the Treasury (**8**) *(right)* beneath which ritual objects were found, in particular the famous "snake goddesses" (Herakleion Museum); the sacred serpents may have been kept here.

Pringipas me ta Krína – On the south side of the courtyard, in the passage which forms the end of the Corridor of the Procession, is a copy of the **fresco of the Prince of the Lilies**; the original is displayed in the Herakleion Museum.

★★★Royal Apartments – *Closed for an indefinite period.* On the east side of the courtyard are the royal apartments, occupying four floors of rooms, two above the level of the courtyard and two below, built into the slope of the hill above the river with a view over the countryside. Here, as in other parts of the palace, there are light wells to provide the circulation of air and the partial lighting of the rooms.

A flight of steps (**9**) adjoining a light well leads to the royal apartments which are linked by a network of passages and corridors.

The first room is the Hall of the Double Axes (**10**) which may have been the Guard Room and is separated by a screen from the King's Room (**11**) which contained a wooden throne.

Queen's Chamber (**12**) – The room is lit by a light well and decorated with a copy of the Dolphin Fresco; adjoining is a tiny bathroom (**13**) with a bath made of clay. This material was also employed to make the piping which carried the palace's supply of fresh water under pressure.

From the royal apartments a covered portico, which served as a promenade (points of view) leads to the outbuildings on the north side of the palace.

★Outbuildings – There were workshops for craftsmen, stone polishers, potters (**14**) (remains of kilns), tailors, gold and silver smiths, and storerooms.

The **store** containing the *pithoi* is astonishing; these huge terracotta jars (partially reconstructed) were used to store wine, oil, grain, honey etc; this store dates from the first palace.

Return to the central courtyard and bear right down a passage which was suitable for vehicles. This lane is lined by a portico decorated with animal sculptures, including a bull, and leads to what Evans called the Customs House (15); its square pillars are thought to have supported a banqueting hall on the floor above. On the left is the north entrance to the palace; outside it *(left)* is a lustral basin.

The **Royal Road** (about 4m/4yd wide), which is paved, probably led to Katsámbas and Amnisós, the harbours to the east of Herakleion which served Knossós.

On the right of the road stands a set of terraces which are thought to belong to a sort of theatre, mentioned by Homer as the setting for ritual dances.

From there return to the west entrance.

For adjacent sights see ANÓGIA, FESTÓS, GÓRTIS, IRÁKLIO, LIMÁNI HERSONÍSSOU, MÁLIA.

KRITSÁ★

Lassíthi – Population 1 910

Michelin map 980 east of fold 39

Kritsá is a picturesque little town; its streets, arches and steps cling to the mountain slope among almond orchards overlooking Mirambélo Bay. Beneath the broad roofs and balconies craftsmen offer their wares for sale: woollen cloth, carpets, jewellery, leather boots. This was the location chosen for the film of *Christ Recrucified* based on the novel by Nikos Kazantzákis. In the summer season traditional folklore festivals (enactment of a Cretan wedding) are held.

EXCURSIONS

★**Lató Ruins** – *4km/2.5mi northeast. From Kritsá take the road to Ágios Nikólaos; by the cemetery turn left into a surfaced road (sign to Lató).*

This isolated and awesome **site**★★ has been excavated since 1967 by archeologists from the French School in Athens who have found traces of an ancient town scattered over the slopes of a sort of suspended amphitheatre.

Lató was founded in the 8C BC on a saddle between two crags, each crowned by an acropolis; the position of the *agora* is indicated by the rectangular open space at the centre of the site; there are traces of a small shrine and a cistern at its centre.

The steps on the left of the agora, which were probably used for public assemblies or games, led up to a **Prytaneion** (3C BC) where the magistrates met in a small court surrounded by a peristyle. From the northern acropolis, reached via the ruins of houses, there is an extensive view down to Ágios Nikólaos.

From the other side a path leads to a polygonal wall retaining a terrace on which stands a little **temple of Apollo** (4C-3C BC) together with an altar for sacrifices. Beyond the terrace a series of steps indicates the site of a theatre.

★**Panagía Kerá Church** ⌚ – *1km/0.5mi from Kritsá on the Ágios Nikólaos road.* A clump of cypress trees *(left)* conceals a charming white church, dedicated to the Virgin (Panagía). It was built in the 13C, at the beginning of the Venetian occupation, on a small scale but well proportioned; it has a nave and two aisles terminating in apses. The church contains a remarkable series of 14C and 15C **frescoes**★★, both sophisticated and naive, in vivid colours.

The frescoes in the right aisle depict the Life of St Anne, her husband Joachim and the Virgin Mary: note the Birth of Christ being announced to the Shepherds and the Journey to Bethlehem.

On the left wall of the nave are Herod's Banquet and the Last Supper; on the right Paradise with the Virgin and the Patriarchs, Abraham, Isaac, Jacob, receiving the souls of the blessed, and also the Massacre of the Innocents.

The frescoes in the north aisle, which date from the 15C, are dedicated to St Anthony: the most curious *(right)* shows another interpretation of Paradise, with Peter leading Eve to the gates of the Celestial City, while the Virgin is represented with the Patriarchs bearing the souls of the elect; various saints *(left)* accompany the benefactors of the church.

For adjacent sights see ÁGIOS NIKÓLAOS, IERÁPETRA, KÁTO ZÁKROS, LASSÍTHI Plateau, MÁLIA, Kolpos MIRAMBÉLOU.

The most important sights in this guide can be found on the Principal Sights map, and are described in the text. To make the most of the information, read the Introduction and consult the maps and plans, the Calendar of events and the Index.

LASSÍTHI Plateau★★

Lassíthi

Michelin map 980 fold 39

In the Díkti mountains, which rise to 2 148m/7 047ft in the south, lies the Lassíthi Plateau (800m/2 625ft), an enormous hanging basin in which rich alluvial soil has collected. The plateau is divided up into fertile fields, formerly irrigated by thousands of windmills which are gradually disappearing.

Places to stay in Dzermiádo, Áfios Geórgios and Psihró.

TOUR

★★ **Approach to the plateau by the north slope** – The road from Limáni Hersonissou winds its way up the slope through hairpin bends offering spectacular views down into the Avdoú Valley which is deep and narrow but the valley floor is carpeted with orchards and orange groves. At the entrance to **Potamiés** there stands a tiny church *(left)* built in the Venetian Gothic style; the doorway has a pointed arch; the interior is decorated with 14C frescoes. More 14C frescoes in a good state of preservation, also a "holy door" (c 1500) forming part of the iconostasis are to be found in the little 9C monastery of **Kardiótissa** *(sign)* just before the village of Kerá.

On arriving at the highest point, there is a site with a row of old corn mills, one of which is still working.

★★ **Plateau** – The unexpected expanse of the Lassíthi Plateau (12km x 6km/7.5mi x 3.5mi), hemmed in by mountains, is an attractive sight, particularly in summer if the irrigation windmills are turning. Wind power is gradually being replaced by motors which are more efficient and easier to use.

The whole plateau is involved in agriculture (cereals, potatoes, fruit) and has retained its traditional methods of working: threshing floors, draught donkeys and mules, blacksmiths and wheelwrights etc.

Skirting the plateau, one passes through the charming villages of **Dzermiádo** and **Ágios Geórgios** (craft products). In the second village there is a **Folk Museum** in an early 19C farm which reconstructs the life of the period. Further on the road reaches **Psihró** and its famous cave.

Diktéo Ándro ⓥ – *From the car park walk or ride on a mule up the steep path (30min) to the cave mouth; then walk down a steep and sometimes slippery slope; wear suitable shoes and warm clothing; the tour lasts about 30min.*

The deep and mysterious **Diktean** or **Psihró cave**, like the Idaian Cave *(see ANÓGIA)*, is supposed to have sheltered Rhea, the mother of Zeus, who was fleeing from her husband Kronos who had the annoying habit of devouring her children; thus Zeus, the master of the gods, was born in a cave, suckled by the goat Amalthea and fed by the bee Melissa.

The Diktean cave was a shrine from the Minoan period to the Archaic period and it has yielded many cult objects: altars, bronze statuettes, votive offerings, miniature double axes etc. The path descends (about 60m/197ft) past enormous rocks to a little lake. The lower section of the cave contains a variety of stalagmites and stalactites.

From the plateau take the excellent surfaced road towards Móhos and Stalída; variety of **views**★★ *looking down on Mália Bay and the north coast.*

For adjacent sights see ÁGIOS NIKÓLAOS, IERÁPETRA, KÁTO ZÁKROS, KNOSSÓS, KRITSÁ, MÁLIA, Kolpos MIRAMBÉLOU.

LIMÁNI HERSONÍSSOU

Iráklio – Population 2 638

Michelin map 980 fold 39

Limáni Hersonissou is strung out round a little bay, a sizeable seaside resort and a fishing village with many tavernas serving fish. In antiquity it was a port for Lyttos and the ancient city, which extended further west than the present one, retained its importance in the Roman period (fountain decorated with fish mosaics on the quay) and on into the beginning of the Christian era.

Paleo-Christian Basilica – On the rocky peninsula which shelters the bay to the north on a fine site overlooking the port are the foundations of a Christian basilica (6C). The ground plan can be deduced from the remains of the floor, partially decorated with wavy mosaics.

Beyond and below the church at the end of the promontory are Roman fish tanks cut into the rock at sea level.

EXCURSIONS

Piskopianó – *3km/2mi south.* This traditional village has a **Museum of Rural Life** occupying an old oil factory from the mid 19C. This *fábrika* has been open to the public since 1988 under the auspices of the History Museum in Herakleion, and houses various collections which allow one to get an idea of what life was like for a Cretan farmer in former times.

Ágios Pandeleímonas – *15km/10mi south on the road to Kastéli, just after Pigí, a road on the left leads (500m/550yd) to the church.* Hidden by trees, **St Pantaleon's Church** is an interesting building on the basilical plan with a nave and two aisles, terminating in apses. It was probably rebuilt during the Venetian period using fragments of earlier buildings (ancient capitals, Byzantine sculptures); the sanctuary is decorated with 14C frescoes and beautiful icons.

For adjacent sights see ÁGIOS NIKÓLAOS, FESTÓS, GÓRTIS, IRÁKLIO, KNOSSÓS, LASSÍTHI Plateau, MÁLIA.

MÁLIA★★

Iráklio

Michelin map 980 fold 39

3km/2mi east of the modern village of Mália *(hotels and restaurants)* a narrow road to the left *(north)* penetrates the ruins of the huge Minoan city which covers a rocky platform facing the sea.

The site was discovered by Joseph Hatzidakis and since 1921 has been excavated by the French School of Archeology. The excavations at Mália are of particular interest since the site ceased to be inhabited at the end of the second millennium BC and is not therefore cluttered with traces of later construction. The majority of the many finds made there are in the Herakleion Museum.

★★**Anáktora Malíon** ⓥ – This Minoan **palace**, which was destroyed in c 1500 BC, was smaller and less luxurious than Knossós but similar in layout, being built round an outer and central courtyard.

Outer courtyard – This court is a paved area crossed by a roadway and bordered on the east side by the foundations of the western façade of the palace. This range of buildings contained *(from right to left)* eight huge grain silos, a series of storerooms reached by a broad internal corridor, and the royal apartments.

Walk up the east side of the court towards the sea *(north)* as far as the Minoan paved road, which leads to the north entrance to the palace, past an enormous terracotta vessel *(pithos)* (1) (1.75m/nearly 6ft high) which could hold over 1 000l/220gal of oil or wine.

North entrance – First there is a vestibule (2) and then a portico supported on pillars of which the bases remain. On the left hand near a row of storerooms was another *pithos* (3). To the right lay the North Court which gave access to the royal apartments. *A corridor leads to the central courtyard.*

Central courtyard – The north and east sides are bordered by porticoes and the western range of buildings was used, as at Knossós, for religious and official activities. At the centre of the courtyard is a shallow pit for sacrifices.

The sanctuary was in the northwest corner. The royal lodge or throne room (4), which overlooked the court, is marked by a terrace in front of which lies a Byzantine

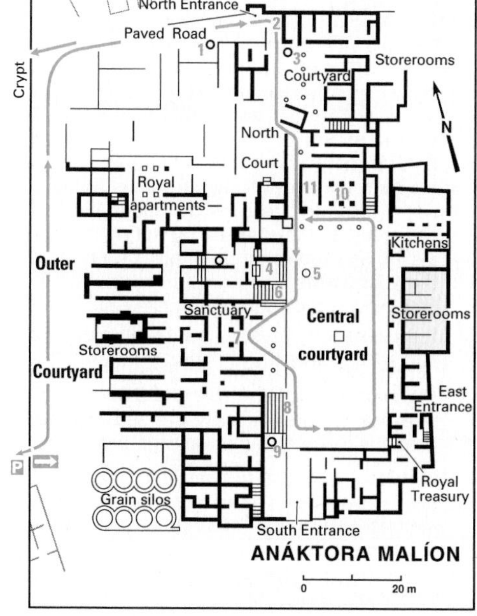

cannon-ball (5). Next are the steps of a staircase (6) which led to the upper floor, and then a cult room (7) with two square pillars engraved with the symbolic double axe.

Beyond the four monumental steps (8) in the southwest corner near the South Entrance to the palace is a circular stone table **(kérnos)** (9) which has a central hollow and many others round the circumference, where, it is thought, the faithful placed their offerings (according to another interpretation it is a gaming table). The buildings on the eastern side of the courtyard comprise the royal Treasury next to the East Entrance to the palace, followed by a range of storerooms *(not open)* which still contain drains in the floor and marble benches against the walls, on which stood jars of oil and wine. The rooms next in the range have been identified by the archeologists as the kitchens.

The north side of the court is taken up with a hall (10) with two rows of rectangular pillars, which may have been a banqueting hall; it is flanked by a vestibule (11) *(left)*.

From the precinct drive northeast.

The town – *Excavations in progress in the "mu" area, Old Palace Period.* On leaving the palace, follow the Minoan paved roadway which passes the agora *(right)* and leads to the **Hypostyle Crypt** *(see p 39)*, which was excavated after the Second World War and is protected by a roof. The steps at the end gave access to meeting rooms, still partially furnished with benches, which were probably part of the Prytaneion, where the city magistrates met. It is flanked by storerooms.

Other buildings used for religious purposes and houses, where the ground floor and basement have often survived *(not at present accessible)*, have been discovered on the outskirts of the town.

The Krysólakos (gold pit) necropolis on the north side near the sea was a royal graveyard; it contained the famous **bee pendant** now in the Herakleion Museum.

For adjacent sights see ÁGIOS NIKÓLAOS, FESTÓS, GÓRTIS, IRÁKLIO, KNOSSÓS, LASSÍTHI Plateau, LIMÁNI HERSONÍSSOU.

Kólpos MIRAMBÉLOU★★

MIRAMBÉLO BAY – Lassíthi

Michelin map 980 fold 39

From Ágios Nikólaos eastwards to Móhlos *(47km/30mi)* the road follows a well-chosen route along the magnificent rocky coast of Mirambélo Bay, first at sea level and then, after the turning to Ierápetra, slightly higher up. This road leads to or passes by many attractive inlets, some of them suitable for bathing, and offers repeated views down over the gentle curve of the shining bay dotted with headlands and islands and up to the mountains inland. The land is planted with tomatoes, beans and olive trees.

SIGHTS

★**Gourniá** ⓥ – *20km/12.5mi east of Ágios Nikólaos.* On a hill above Mirambélo Bay lie the ruins of a Minoan city, which dates from 1500-1450 BC and has been almost entirely excavated by American archeologists. The town plan is clearly visible owing to the low walls marking out the streets, lanes, squares, buildings and modest houses of the craftsmen and tradesmen.

Enter the site by the path on the east side, not far from the main road, and follow the path on the right which climbs round the ruins emerging in a paved street which bears left towards the agora and is lined with houses separated by lanes and steps; the third house on the right is particularly well preserved: it comprises a shop and rooms on the ground floor and the beginning of the stairs leading to the floor above.

Overlooking the agora stands the palace which is reached by a flight of steps.

It is possible to return to the entrance by another street running through the lower part of the city.

★★**Plátanos viewpoint** – *18km/11.25mi east of Gourniá.* From a terrace by the roadside near a café-bar there are splendid views down to Psíra Island and across Mirambélo Bay to the Spinalónga peninsula.

★**Móhlos** – *In Sfakiá turn left into a road which descends for 7km/4.25mi.* A little quay *(tavernas)* is hidden in an inlet opposite a tiny island where a mass of Minoan material was found which is now in the Herakleion Museum. A peaceful and charming spot.

For adjacent sights see ÁGIOS NIKÓLAOS, IERÁPETRA, KÁTO ZÁKROS, KRITSÁ, LASSÍTHI Plateau, MÁLIA.

RÉTHIMNO★

RETHYMNON – Réthimno – Population 23 355

Michelin map 980 fold 38

The traditional character of a Cretan town, a blend of Venetian and Turkish influences, is best preserved in this, the third largest town on the island. It is pleasant to stroll past the fish tavernas which throng the quays, through the old and narrow streets to the fortress. Crafts such as weaving and embroidery are of high quality and the Wine Festival in July attracts a big crowd.

★**Old Town** – From the main square, near the Public Garden, pass through a late 16C Venetian gate in the walls; on the right is a minaret. Turn left into Odós Ethnikis Andistasseos (National Resistance Street).

Former Nerandze Mosque ⓥ – A slim **minaret**★ set back from the street *(left)* marks the position of a domed mosque which itself replaced a 17C Venetian convent.
Further down the street are two Venetian monuments: the Loggia *(right)* and the Arimondi Fountain *(left).*

Loggia – It was built early in the 17C as an Exchange before being converted into a mosque by the Turks; it has massive pillars and rustic stonework. It now houses a library.

Roudinalexandre /DIAF

Venetian fortress, Rethymnon

Arheologikó Moussío ⓥ – The archeological museum, in an old prison, displays sculptures, bronzes, jewellery from the Minoan, Greek and Roman periods and a remarkable collection of money.

Arimondi Fountain – Three Corinthian columns mark this monumental fountain (1629).

★**Odós Thessaloníkis** – This street near the Arimondi Fountain contains several 16C-17C Venetian houses built of stone with elegant stone doorways decorated with coats of arms next to 18C-19C Turkish houses with balconies and wooden projections.

Harbour – During the Venetian occupation Malmsey wine *(see MONEMVASSÍA)* was exported from here; now the harbour is used by fishing boats and coasters. The old vaulted houses on the quayside have been converted into cafés and tavernas which open at the back into a parallel street, Odós Arkadíou. There is a fine beach southeast of the harbour.

Fortétza ⓥ **or Froúrio** – The **Venetian fortress** was built on the promontory between 1574 and 1582. The south face is reinforced with curious bastions which have an orillion (rounded projection) on one side and a redan on the other. The fortress was captured by the Turks in 1645.

The main entrance is on the east side in the angle made by the bastion. It is protected by an outwork called a barbican. Over the rusticated gateway is the Lion of St Mark. On entering follow the ramparts round to the left – views of the town and the harbour.
At the centre of the fortress stand a rectangular building which was once a prison and a domed building which was built as the Latin cathedral of St Mary of the Angels and converted into a mosque by the Turks. Elsewhere are ruined houses, stores, barracks, cisterns, powder magazines and a Byzantine chapel.

EXCURSIONS

★**Necropolis of Arméni** – *8km/5mi south towards Agía Galíni; turn right at the sign (in English) "Cemetery Late Minoan".* Nearly 200 Minoan tombs in individual chambers from the post-palace period have been found and examined. This necropolis is the most important of its period (1390 to 1200 BC) in Crete and has already provided numerous items (including sarcophagi), some of which are in the museums of Rethymnon and Chania. The size of the cemetery suggests that there must have been a large town in the vicinity.

Melidóni Cave – *30km/19mi east. First take the Iráklio road, leaving this to reach Pérama, and from there Melidóni; from the village there is a good metalled road (2km/1mi) to the cave (sign "Spileon").* This huge deep cave was the scene of a great tragedy in 1824. After an uprising against the Turks some 400 people, mainly women and children, took refuge in the cave; the Turks partially blocked the mouth with boulders and then made a fire in the restricted entrance; the people inside were asphyxiated.
From the mouth of the cave there is a fine view towards Mount Ida.

For adjacent sights see ANÓGIA, ÁPTERA, ARKÁDI, RÉTHIMNO, SFAKIÁ.

Farángi SAMARIÁS★★★

SAMARIÁ GORGE – Haniá

Michelin map 980 fold 37

In the heart of the **White Mountains** (Lefká Óri) the surface water has worn away a huge ravine (18km/11.25mi long) which runs from the Omalós Plateau down to the Libyan sea; this is the wild and sometimes awesome Samariá Gorge.

PRACTICAL INFORMATION

The walk through the gorge, which is classified as a National Park, takes 5hr to 6hr and is often hard going owing to the steep gradients *(wear stout shoes and carry a flask of water)*. It is inadvisable to undertake the walk in July or August because of the large number of tourists.
The simplest way of visiting the gorge is to join an organised all-day excursion starting from Chania, Herakleion or various other centres; reservations can be made at hotels, a tourist agency or the EOT. Walkers are transported to the top of the gorge by coach. They are collected at the lower end in Agía Rouméli by boat which docks about 1hr 30min later in Sfakiá where the coach is waiting.
Those who do not want to walk the gorge from end to end may go down as far as the viewing platform and then turn back *(30min on foot there and back)* or take the boat from Sfakiá to Agía Rouméli, walk up the gorge, as far as time and energy will allow, and then return to the shore and take the boat back to Sfakiá.

TOUR ⌚

The road up to the gorge passes over the **Omalós Plateau** (1 050m/3 445ft), a barren and austere depression surrounded by mountains; it is uninhabited and covered in snow in winter but cultivated nonetheless with cereals and potatoes and used for sheep rearing. After passing through Omalós *(tavernas)* the road ends in **Xilóskalo** on the edge of the gorge *(car park)*.
First a flight of wooden steps *(xilóskalo)* and then a twisting path descends among pine and plane trees down a steep slope to a viewing platform. There is an impressive **view**★★ of the ravine between sheer rock walls which rise to over 2 000m/6 561ft and are the refuge of the last of the local wild goats *(agrími* or *krikri)*.
The path goes on down through the woods descending rapidly to the bottom of the gorge. In a little clearing stands St Nicholas' Chapel.

KAUFMAN /TOP

Samariá Gorge

Half way down the gorge there is a handful of houses, **Samariá**, now deserted; the name of the hamlet derives from Osía María, Blessed Mary, to whom the local church was dedicated. Beyond the village is the narrowest section of the gorge where the distance between the vertical walls, which rise to 300m/984ft, is not more than 2–3m/7–10ft.

Eventually the stream bed, which is flanked by oleanders, widens out and reaches **Agía Rouméli**, known in antiquity as Tarrhia, on the edge of the Libyan Sea. From here the boats make the trip east to Sfakiá at the foot of towering rocky cliffs.

For adjacent sights see ÁPTERA, HANIÁ, KASTÉLI or KÍSSAMOS, SFAKIÁ.

SFAKIÁ★★

Haniá – Population 366
Michelin map 980 fold 37

40km/25mi south from Vrísses on the main east-west highway on the north coast.

Vrísses – A pleasant well-shaded village by a stream; it is famous for yogurt and honey *(tavernas)*.
The road south crosses the White Mountains (Lefká Óri) and then descends (1 000m/3 281ft) towards the south shore – dramatic, even vertiginous, **views**★★★ of the wild and scantily inhabited coast and the Libyan Sea.

Sfakiá (or **Hóra Sfakíon**) – This was once a considerable town with 3 000 to 4 000 inhabitants, trading with Africa. Although it is now only a small place it is still the capital of the Sfakiots, a belligerent and unyielding people, with fair hair and blue eyes, who tended sheep in the mountains and were at the root of most of the uprisings against the Venetians and Turks; in 1770 a Sfakiot called **Daskaloyánnis** (Teacher John) led a revolution against the Turks but he was defeated and flayed alive in Herakleion.
Nowadays it is a quiet resort *(Hotel Xenia, guest houses, tavernas)* beneath the ruins of a 16C Venetian fort with a picturesque little harbour and a boat service to **Agía Rouméli** at the southern end of the Samariá Gorge *(see above)*. In 1941, when British troops were evacuated from Sfakiá, 7 000 soldiers were taken off the island despite the Stuka bombardment.

EXCURSIONS

★**Frangokástelo** – *15km/9.25mi east by the coast road and an unsurfaced track; taverna.* The massive outline of the so-called Frankish castle is visible from afar; it was built in 1371 by the Venetians as a defence against pirates, Turks and insurgent Sfakiots.
It is rectangular in plan with crenellated walls and a square tower at each corner, one of which was reinforced to form the keep. Over the sea gate the lion of St Mark looks down on the remains of a deserted harbour next to a fine sandy beach. The ruined fort surveys the empty sea as if it were at the end of the world (except in high season).

Anópoli – *12km/7.5mi east.* A very steep surfaced road with splendid **views**★★; by the little abandoned village of Arádena *(after 4km/2.5mi)* just before the metal bridge which crosses the Arádena Gorge, there is a particularly **stunning view** *(signed path)*.
The **Arádena Gorge**★★ is impressive for its beauty but so far has remained off the well-trodden tourist routes. There are however a few tavernas and some hotels. The magnificent **descent** of the gorge *(6hr on foot)* is for the more energetic. It includes negotiating a rock with an amazing sheer drop (steps and a rope); part of it at least can be undertaken by any good and experienced walker.
From Loutró on the coast there is a boat service (more frequent in summer) back to Sfakiá. It is also possible to return to Sfakiá by a path running along the edge of the beach *(2hr 30min hard walking)*. There is also a bus service between Sfakiá and Anópoli.

For adjacent sights see ÁPTERA, HANIÁ, KASTÉLI or KÍSSAMOS, RÉTHIMNO, Farángi SAMARIÁS.

SITÍA

Lassíthi – Population 7 028
Michelin map 980 fold 40

Sitía *(air link with Rhodes)* is a pleasant resort on the bay of the same name, defended by the ruins of a former Venetian fortress; nevertheless the white and ochre cuboid houses give it a slightly African appearance. It is pleasant to stroll under the shade of the enormous tamarisk trees where the cafés and tavernas set out their chairs and tables.
The recently opened **Museum of Local Traditions** ⊙ is unfortunately closed most of the time. The **Archeological Museum** (Arheologikó Moussío) ⊙ displays the finds from local excavations.
Sitía is supposed to be the birthplace of Myson, one of the Seven Sages of Greece, and even today the citizens of Sitía enjoy a reputation for composure and integrity. The town earns its living by producing sultanas for export.

EXCURSIONS

Moní Toploú ⌚ – *20km/12.5mi northeast; follow the Palékastro road for 14km/8.75mi and then bear left up to the plateau.* Splendid **views★★**. **Toploú Monastery** emerges from a fold in the bare hillside; its thick walls and rare windows make it look like a fortress. It was founded in the 14C by the Venetians as Our Lady of the Cape but has been refurbished many times, particularly in the 15C and the 17C after being damaged in the uprisings against the Turks; during the Second World War it was a centre of resistance against the Germans. The monastery is the owner of nearly the whole of Cape Síderos.

A handsome Gothic door opens into the entrance court which leads into an inner court surrounded by arcades and the stairs up to the cells. The church is built in the Venetian style with pointed vaulting. It contains two very rich **icons★★** by an 18C Creto-Venetian master, Ioánnis Kornáros (Cornaro); the first one is a masterpiece showing several biblical scenes in naive and realistic detail, entitled *Thou art great, O Lord*; the second portrays *Agía Anastassia Farmakolíptera* (St Anastasia) surrounded with scenes of her martyrdom.

There is a museum (donated by T Provakatis) which has a collection of icons from the 15C to the 19C, as well as precious ecclesiastical items, rare documents, ancient editions of the gospels and parchment manuscripts. A very well presented permanent exhibition traces the history of Orthodox Christianity, with particular reference to Mount Athos and Toploú Monastery.

★**Váï Palm Grove** – *28km/17.5mi northeast.* The road continues through a barren landscape to Váï, which appears unexpectedly, looking strangely like an oasis. A palm grove *(restaurants, camping)* consisting of about 5 000 palm trees fringes a fine sandy beach.

Return to the crossroads and turn right to Itanós, 2km/1.25mi away.

Itanós – In a lonely setting on the northeast tip of Crete, where the land forms a promontory indented by wild creeks, lie traces of an ancient town which was inhabited up to the Byzantine period: sites of two acropoli, Hellenistic foundations of a terrace and remains of a large basilica.

For adjacent sights see ÁGIOS NIKÓLAOS, IERÁPETRA, KÁTO ZÁKROS, KRITSÁ, LASSÍTHI Plateau, Kolpos MIRAMBÉLOU.

C. Malraux /IMAGE BANK

Kikládes (Cyclades)★★★

The islands received their name in antiquity because they form a rough circle *(kíklos)* round the sacred island of Delos. Nowadays they attract tourists seeking the combined pleasures of transparent blue sea, constant sunshine and marvellously clear nights. The brilliant light shows a landscape rich in contrasts, both harsh and colourful, picturesque towns with windmills, chapels and immaculately white cuboid houses, rocky inlets and deserted beaches, giving the visitor the feeling of being in a different world.

PRACTICAL INFORMATION

Access

By air – Míkonos, Mílos, Náxos, Páros and Thíra/Santorini all have airports with daily flights from Athína/Athens. As the planes have a limited number of seats it is advisable to book as early as possible. Also services from Crete and Rhodes to some of the islands.

By sea – Several ferry or hydrofoil services, with varying frequency depending on the size of the island served and the possibility of changing from one route to another in certain ports:

– From Pireás/Piraeus daily in the morning (and afternoon in season) arriving the same day: to Síros, Páros, Náxos, Íos and Thíra/Santorini;

– From Pireás/Piraeus less frequent departures: the islands on the so-called "barren" route – Amorgós, Kouphoníssi, Donoússa, Iráklia, Shinoússa, Anáfi, Folégandros, Síkinos and Kímolos;

– From Pireás/Piraeus: to Kíthnos, Sérifos, Sifhnos, Mílos;

– From Lávrio (north of Cape Sounion) to Kéa and Kíthnos;

– From Rafina (east of Athens) to Ándros, Síros, Tínos, Míkonos, Páros and Náxos.

Information on boat services is available from the GNTO/EOT offices in Athens and the port authorities: Piraeus ☎ (01) 45 93 223 and 44 93 911; Lávrio ☎ (0292) 25 249; Rafína ☎ (0294) 22 300.

Accommodation

Amorgós – A small hotel at Egiali (cat C) and 2 hotels (cat C), guest houses and rooms in private houses at Katápola, Amorgós (Hóra) and Egiáli; camping site at Katápola.

Ándros – About 20 small hotels mainly in Batsí, Ándros Town (Hóra) and Gavrio (cat B to D); rooms in private houses mainly in Batsí, Ándros Town, Kórthi and Gávrio; camping sites at Gávrio.

Íos – About 30 hotels (cat B to E); rooms in private houses; 2 camping sites; the island is a very popular destination and it is sometimes difficult to find accommodation. Íos (Hóra) is very noisy at night (many night spots).

Kéa – About 6 hotels, mainly in Korissía; rooms in private houses, mainly in Korissía and Koúndouros.

Kímolos – Rooms in private houses.

Kíthnos – 3 hotels at Loutrá (cat C) and one hotel at Mérihas (cat C); rooms in private houses in the two towns and in Kanála.

Míkonos – About 70 small hotels in Mykonos Town and about 50 in the rest of the island (cat A to E); rooms in private houses (about 1 000); camping site; in high season accommodation is scarce.

Mílos – About 12 hotels (cat B to D); rooms in private houses, mainly in Adémas and Apolonia.

Náxos – About 50 small hotels (cat A to E) in Náxos Town (Hora) and areas nearby (Ág Georgios and Ág Prokópios); few simple hotels in Apólonas; many rooms in private houses in Náxos Town and near its beaches.

Páros – Over 100 hotels (cat A to E) mainly in Parikía, Náoussa and Pisso Livádi; many rooms in private houses in these areas and in Alikí and Ambelás; camping sites. In Andíparos, few hotels, many rooms in private houses and a camping site.

Sérifos – 6 to 7 small hotels (cat B, C and E) in Livadi; rooms in private houses mainly in Livádi; camping site.

Sífnos – About 6 hotels in Apolonía and Artemonas (cat B and C); 5 hotels in the harbour town of Kamáres and 4 in Platís Gialós (cat B, C and D); rooms in private houses in all villages but mainly in Apolonía, Kamáres, Platís Gialós, Fáros and in Kástro.

Síros – About 15 hotels (cat A to E) in Ermoúpoli; about 6 hotels (C and D) in Vári and also in Possidonía and Fínikas (B, C, E); rooms in private houses in Ermoúpoli, Galissá, Kíni, Possidonía and Vári. 2 camping sites.

GEOGRAPHY

The Cyclades form the largest group of islands in the Aegean Sea; there are 39 in all of which 24 are inhabited (total population 94 005); the capital is Ermoúpoli on the island of Syros. They are divided into three groups: the western Cyclades – Kéa, Kythnos, Seriphos, Siphnos, Kímolos and Melos; the central Cyclades – Syros, Páros, Náxos, Amorgós, Íos, Síkinos, Folégandros and Santoríni (also known as Thera); the northern Cyclades – Ándros, Tenos, Mykonos and Delos.
The islands are the visible part of a sunken plateau, a shelf of ancient rocks forming an extension of the Attic peninsula beneath the sea, the average level of which is between 100 and 200m/329 and 626ft below sea level. Some of them (Melos and Santoríni) have suffered volcanic eruptions. Their physical relief is clearly defined although only **Mount Náxos Días** (1 001m/3 284ft) on the island of Náxos, exceeds 1 000m in height.

Poverty offset by beauty – The Cyclades are largely arid and the poverty of their soil coupled with the infrequency of communications has led, since the beginning of this century, to heavy emigration which is now abating in the islands where tourism is developing and providing employment.
The more fertile islands produce wine, cereals, fruit and vegetables (Síros, Páros, Náxos, Thíra/Santorini); on some there is mining for iron-ore (Sérifos), manganese or sulphur (Mílos); others have quarries for marble (Páros, Tínos, Náxos), emery-stone (Náxos), pumice stone or pozzolana (Thíra/Santorini). Some, like Thíra, have so little water that extra supplies have to be imported by tanker; on such islands only a few olives, figs, carobs and oleanders are to be found in sheltered spots.

T.A.P.

Cycladic idol of a flute player (National Archeological Museum)

Local specialities – One can enjoy large prawns, squid, octopus, sword fish, red mullet, sardines and mackerel accompanied by white wines, the best of which come from Náxos, Thíra and Mílos.

Climate – The best time of the year for visiting the Cyclades is without doubt May and June: the islands are not crowded, the plants are in flower, fresh water is plentiful and the cold north wind *(meltémi)* blows only occasionally. This wind is more frequent in July and August producing white horses on the crests of the waves; the Turks called this part of the Aegean the "white sea". The wind is refreshing and often dies away at nightfall.
Ships are sometimes accompanied on their course by dolphins and flying fish.

HISTORICAL NOTES

Cycladic art and civilisation – At the end of the prehistoric era, between 3000 and 1750 BC, the islands which lay on the sea routes linking Europe to Crete and Asia Minor were involved in considerable maritime trade which encouraged the development of a brilliant civilisation; it reached its apogee between 2700 and 2300 BC. The population also engaged in agriculture, fishing and mining (obsidian and silver ore) and worked in metal, clay and marble which are still to be found in abundance in the area.
After 2300 BC the Cyclades fell into a decline as Cretan civilisation flourished *(see KRÍTI)* and spread to Santoríni and Melos. It was obliterated by the cataclysm which devastated the Aegean in about 1500 BC.
There are a number of examples of Cycladic art which derives from the islands' natural environment: extensive use of marble and pure lines.
For the period from 3000 to 2000 BC there are the famous "**idols**", female effigies, with minute heads; the pure lines are scarcely outlined in the white marble; there are also black ceramics with spiral motifs. For the following period (2000 to 1500 BC) there are the delicately drawn and brightly coloured narrative **frescoes** which were discovered on Santoríni and are related in style to the Minoan art of Crete.
In the 8C BC the islands began to enjoy a certain degree of prosperity in the orbit of Athens as is shown by a number of ruins, particularly those on Delos.

The Cycladic idols

These marble statuettes, the work of prehistoric sculptors, are mainly found on the islands of Náxos, Páros, Melos, Santoríni, Delos, Mykonos, Kéros and Syros. Nearly all female, these naked effigies are characterised by their simplified form, their frontality and their complete immobility. Some are violin-shaped, with voluptuous curves, evoking the cult of some mother goddess; most are distinguished by the abstracted form of their features and their limbs, with a head forming part of a flattened triangle on which the nose stands out in sharp relief, the arms folded on the chest and the legs tapering.
They have been found for the most part in tombs alongside the bones of the deceased, together with domestic vessels in stone, and are evidence of rituals practised by the sailors, shepherds and farmers of the Aegean. Cycladic art with its stylised forms could not fail to interest those artists at the turn of the century such as Picasso and Brancusi who were seeking new forms of artistic expression.
It is possible to get a good idea of Cycladic art by viewing the room devoted to it in the National Archeological Museum and the Museum of Cycladic Art in Athens, as well as the small museum in Náxos housed in the old ducal palace.

From the Serene Republic to the Sublime Porte – Early in the 13C, as a result of the Fourth Crusade, the Venetians established themselves in the Cyclades and the islands were handed out as fiefs to the great Venetian families. The group as a whole was placed under the sovereignty of the dukes of Naxos *(see NÁXOS)* who themselves were under the princes of Morea; Venice's interest was represented locally by a "bailiff".
The Cyclades served as ports of call on the sea route to Constantinople and flourished despite the raids carried out by Algerian pirates who forced the citizens to take refuge inland. It was at this time that Roman Catholic parishes were founded which are still thriving, particularly on the islands of Syros, Náxos, Tenos and Santoríni.
The Turks established themselves in the Archipelago by degrees, notably in 1537 and 1566 when Barbarossa captured Náxos; Tenos and Mykonos fell only in 1718. The Porte (the central office of the Ottoman government in Constantinople) allowed the islands a certain autonomy and Italian remained the official language until 1830. Similarly, under the **Capitulations** between François I and Suleiman the Magnificent, the local Roman Catholics were placed under the protection of France; missions were launched by the Capuchins in 1633 and then by the Jesuits, Lazarists, Ursulines etc who played a prominent role in the educational and social fields (schools, hospitals). In the 17C missions of a different type were launched by the English for the acquisition of antiquities which ended up in the collections of Charles I, the Duke of Buckingham and the second Earl of Arundel.
With the exception of Mykonos, the Cyclades took almost no part in the Greek War of Independence but were generous in receiving refugees from the mainland. During the First World War the islands played a strategic role on the route to the eastern front.

AMORGÓS

Population 1 632 – 124km²/48sq mi
Michelin map 980 fold 45

The island which is long and narrow has a long coastline (about 100km/62mi) with endless beaches and deserted inlets. Amorgós will appeal to those who like nature and open spaces, exploring on foot and by boat, particularly the southeast coast where the land rises in spectacular limestone cliffs.

The capital, also called Amorgós, is a typical Cycladic town. About 13km/8mi north the **Monastery of the Presentation of the Virgin** (Hozoviótissa) ⌚ occupies an impressive **position**★★ clinging to the precipitous cliff face; it was founded in 1088 by the Byzantine emperor Alexis Comnenos and owns some precious icons and manuscripts.
Excavations on the island carried out by the French School have yielded a number of Cycladic idols, some of which are now in the Louvre in Paris.
For adjacent sights see ÍOS, NÁXOS, PÁROS, THÍRA.

The most important sights in this guide can be found on the Principal Sights map, and are described in the text. To make the most of the information, read the Introduction and consult the maps and plans, the Calendar of events and the Index.

ÁNDROS

Population 8 781 – 380km²/146sq mi
Michelin map 980 folds 31 and 32

This large island is mountainous but fertile and more wooded than its neighbours; it is a pleasant summer resort, particularly popular with the Athenians, and has several beaches, the principal one being at Batsí. The **Messariá Valley**, which is parcelled out into vineyards and orchards growing figs and citrus fruits, is studded with dovecotes, square towers like those on Tenos.

Ándros (pop 1 598), the capital with its typical white cuboid houses, stands on a rocky promontory above the harbour. There are traces of a fortress built by the Venetians who occupied the island from 1207 to 1556. The chapel of the Source of Life (Zoodóhos Pigí) contains an iconostasis dating from 1717. The **Archeological Museum** (Arheologikó Moussío) ⓥ is well presented and a **Museum of Modern Art** ⓥ set up by the Goulandris Foundation includes works by the principal contemporary Greek painters and sculptors.
Elsewhere on the island there is the beautiful **site**★ of the ancient port of Palaiopolis of which few traces remain and the medieval village of Kórthio dominated by the ruins of a Venetian castle.

For adjacent sights see ATHÍNA, DÍLOS, ÉVIA, KÉA, KÍTHNOS, MÍKONOS, SÍROS, TÍNOS.

DÍLOS★★★

DELOS – Population 16 – 3km²/1sq mi
Michelin map 980 fold 32

Delos lies at the heart of the Cyclades, an island of granite and gneiss culminating in Mount Kynthos (112m/367ft). Despite its minute size, it played an important role in antiquity, both commercial and religious, when the sanctuary to Apollo attracted pilgrims and riches.
Nowadays Delos is a desolate wind-swept sea-girt place of pilgrimage for tourists only but the ruins are still imbued with a sense of mystic fervour and nostalgia.

ACCESS

From Míkonos by caïque (about 45min) in season only; several departures daily between 8.30am and 10am; return to Míkonos between 12 noon and 1pm. When the north wind is blowing the crossing can be cold and rough, so take a warm pullover and an anorak (if the sea is too rough the crossing may be cancelled). Also take a hat or scarf for the tour of the ruins (little shade) and wear comfortable, preferably closed shoes (vipers in remote grassy places and large lizards).
After rounding the northern point of Delos the boat enters the straits separating Delos from Reneia (Rínia) past two islets and moors by the West Mole which separate the sanctuary harbour (sacred port) from the commercial harbour in antiquity; if the sea is too rough the boat puts in to Goúrna Bay in the northeast of the island. The day tripper has only about 2hr 30min for visiting the ruins and climbing Mount Kynthos.

Apollo's Isle – According to legend, **Leto** whom Zeus had seduced and then abandoned wandered about the world pursued by the anger of Hera who had forbidden anyone to receive the pregnant goddess. Leto eventually found a haven on the barren island of Ortygia (Quail Land) where after nine days and nights in labour she gave birth to twins, Apollo and Artemis, at the foot of a palm tree. In recognition of this event Ortygia became known as Delos (illustrious) and the Apollo sanctuary was to become, together with the shrine at Delphi, the most important in the Greek world.
Delos was already thriving in the Mycenaean era (1400-1200 BC); traces of a palace and precious objects have been found in the course of excavations.
Delos became the capital of an **Amphictyony**, a confederation of neighbouring islands and was evoked by Homer in the *Odyssey* and the *Hymn to Apollo*; it reached its religious apogee in the 7C-6C BC, first under the Naxiots and then under the Athenians. In about 550 BC the Athenian tyrant, Peisistratos, ordered the first purification of the island so as to preserve its sacred character: no births or deaths were allowed on Delos and people near their time had to be removed to the neighbouring island of Reneia. In 478 BC, after the Persian wars, Athens united the Amphictyony and Attica in the Delian Confederacy and the Treasure, which was contributed by the participating cities, was first kept in the Apollo sanctuary before being transferred in 454 to the Acropolis in Athens. In 426 the Athenians ordered a new purification of the island and the graves and their contents were removed to a great pit on Reneia.

At the same time the Athenians lent new lustre to the sanctuary, building a new temple to Apollo and organising the famous **Delian Festival** which took place every four years in May: processions of pilgrims crowned with flowers and chanting the "paean" sacrificed oxen, took part in sacred dances, attended banquets and watched competitions in sports, music and drama. A commercial market complemented the religious festival which flourished until the 1C AD and was even enhanced by the assimilation of other cults from Egypt, Syria and Phoenicia.

Commercial and cosmopolitan centre – Despite its only average harbour, from the 4C BC onwards Delos gradually became the main port in the Aegean Sea. Its central maritime position and its sacred status, which preserved it from attack, favoured its economic development which resulted in the construction of quays, warehouses and ship yards. Delos was the principal market in the eastern Mediterranean for grain and slaves as well as the storage and redistribution centre for oil, wine and wood.
Its status as a free port which was granted by the Romans in 166 BC attracted merchants, bankers and shipping magnates from Italy, Greece, Syria and Egypt; residential districts were built for them. Early in the 1C BC the prosperity of Delos reached its zenith and the town numbered 25 000 inhabitants.
The decline of Apollo's island began with the capture and sack of Delos in 88 BC by Mithridates, King of Pontus, who rose against the Romans. Pilgrimages became less popular, depradations by pirates grew and the main shipping routes moved elsewhere. During the Venetian occupation of the Cyclades several works of art were removed to Venice and Rome. On 28 August 1628 **Sir Kenelm Digby**, who had set out from England in two ships in January of that year on a privateering expedition, "spent the day at Delos in search of antiquities"; he acquired fragments from Apollo's temple for Charles I's collection. Many other works of art ended up in the lime kilns.

Excavations – The French School of Archeology has been responsible for the exploration of the site; excavations, begun in 1872, have been carried out in parallel with those at Delphi. In 1904 with the aid of a patron, the Duc de Loubat, M Holleaux began the "great excavation" which uncovered public buildings and private houses; some have been partially reconstructed by the Greek Anastylosis Service. Work is still in progress particularly in a Hellenistic district to the north.

The modern mole, made by the spoil from the excavations, leads directly to the entrance to the archeological site. The tour outlined takes into account the time available on the island between the arrival and departure of the boat.

Ieró (Sanctuary) ⓥ

The paved open space is called the **Agorá Kombetialistón** because there freedmen and slaves honoured the Lares Compitales, Roman gods of the crossroads; remains of a monumental altar (1).

★**Sacred Way** – This was a processional road, 13m/43ft wide, used by the pilgrims to reach the sanctuary; it was lined by votive monuments, standing alone or in a semicircular recess; some of the bases are still visible.
On either side stretched two porticoes; their positions are marked on the ground by the drums of columns and pieces of architrave; the portico on the left, **Stoá Fílipou**, was built by Philip of Macedon in the 4C BC; the one on the right, **Stoá Pergámou**, was built in the same period by the kings of Pergamon, a city in Asia Minor.

Propílea – Little is left of this monumental entrance *(propyllaia)* but the numbers of pilgrims who crossed the threshold in antiquity can be judged by how much the three steps are worn away. On the right stands a marble statue of a bearded Hermes (4C BC) (2).

★**Íkos Naxíon (House of the Naxiots)** – On the right beyond the Propylaia lie the foundations of a rectangular building from the Archaic period where the religious brotherhood of Náxos used to meet. Against the north wall stands an enormous block of marble (3) which bears the following inscription in Archaic Greek letters: "I am a single block, statue and pedestal". It was the base of a **statue of Apollo** (6C BC), a colossal votive offering erected by the Naxiots, which the Venetians tried to remove; some parts of it can be seen near the sanctuary of Artemis.

Stoá Naxíon (Stoa of the Naxiots) – On the left beyond the Propylaia are traces of this 6C BC portico; in the angle stands the circular granite base (4) on which stood the famous "**palm tree of Nikias**", a colossal bronze tree, which was erected in 417 BC by the Athenian Nikias to represent the palm tree beneath which Leto had given birth to Apollo and Artemis.

★★**Témenos Apólona** – Lying south to north in the precinct are traces of three successive temples of Apollo.

The **temple of Delian Apollo** (5), a Doric building, was the largest of the three; its construction was begun by the Deliots in the 5C BC but was not completed until the 3C BC because of Athenian hostility to it.

The **Athenian temple** (c 420 BC) was also Doric (6) and the *naós (p 22)* contained seven statues set on a semicircular pedestal of black marble.

The smallest and oldest was the **Porinos temple** (7), built of hard limestone tufa, which contained an Archaic statue of Apollo and the treasure of the Delian League.

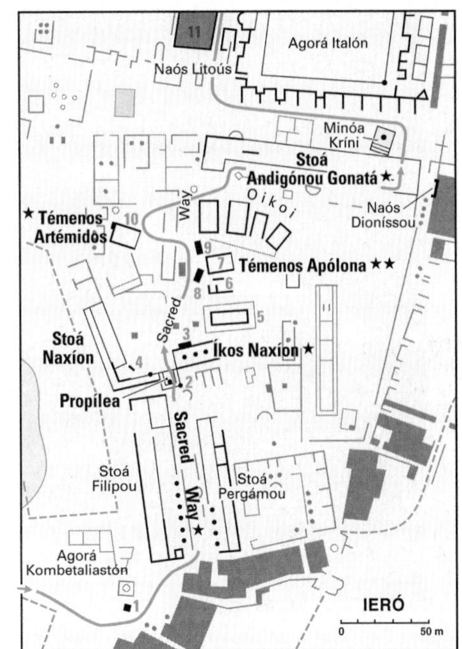

Near the Porinos temple stand two pedestals for statues; one (8) is decorated with a Doric frieze of alternating roses and bucranes (ox heads) and the other (9) in blue marble is inscribed in honour of Philetairos, first king of Pergamon. Behind the three temples and beyond are the foundations of five small buildings (6C-5C BC) ranged in an arc which were probably the meeting places **(oikoi)** of the religious brotherhoods.

★**Témenos Artémidos (Artemision)** – Set back from the Sacred Way, on the site of an ancient Mycenaean palace, are the truncated columns of the façade of the temple of Artemis, a Hellenistic building (2C BC) in the Ionic style, which had succeeded two others; digging nearby in 1946 uncovered a foundation trench, which yielded numerous Mycenaean objects *(in the museum)*.

Behind the temple of Artemis lie pieces of the colossal **Statue of Apollo**★★ (10) which was hauled this far by the Venetians in 1422; there are the torso, partially covered with curly hair, and the pelvis, which contains holes to carry a belt; one of the hands is in the local museum; one of the feet is in the British Museum.

★**Stoá Andigónou Gonatá** – The **stoa of Antigonos Gonatás** which bordered the sanctuary on the north side was 120m/394ft long and consisted of 48 Doric columns supporting a frieze of bulls' heads. It was built in the 3C BC by a Macedonian king. The ground plan shows two galleries separated by a row of columns ending in two short wings. Two rows of statues lined the façade; their bases still exist.

Behind the eastern end of the portico stands the **Minoë Fountain** *(Minóa Kríni)* which dates from the 6C BC. Nearby are the remains of the precinct wall and of a temple to Dionysos with two curious votive monuments representing a phallus.

Periohí Leóndon (Lion District)

This urban part was built in the Hellenistic period.

The path out of the sanctuary passes between the impressive remains of a granite building (11) *(left)* and the walls of the **temple of Leto** *(Naós Litoús - right)* which dates from the 6C BC and has a bench outside. East of the temple extends the **Agora of the Italians** *(Agorá Italón)* (2C BC) surrounded by a portico into which opened the cells of the Italian merchants who settled on Delos (several mosaics).

★★★**Ándiro Leóndon (Terrace of the Lions)** – Facing the Sacred Lake *(see below)* is the row of famous Archaic lions sculpted in grainy Naxian marble. Originally there were at least nine; only five remain; a sixth was removed in the 17C by the Venetians and now stands guard, with a different head, at the entrance to the Arsenal in Venice.

These stone animals have long bodies and scarcely perceptible manes; they are sitting on their haunches at different levels and give an impression of restrained power. Their hieratism and their stylised form suggest Asiatic influence.

Terrace of the Lions, Delos

Ierí Límni (Sacred Lake) – It was the habitat of the swans sacred to Apollo but was filled in in 1924 because it was a breeding ground for malarial mosquitos.

★**Ídrima Possidoniastón** – The **Institution of the Poseidoniasts** was an association of merchants and ship owners from Beirut (Lebanon) who worshipped under the aegis of Poseidon. In the peristyled court were discovered a group of Aphrodite and Pan *(now in Athens Museum)* as well as a damaged statue of the goddess Rome.

Beyond are the remains of the **House of the Diadumenos** where a Roman copy *(Athens Museum)* of the famous Diadumenos by Polykleitos was discovered.

★**Ikía Límnis** – This **Lake House** is a Hellenistic house, well-preserved (stucco and mosaics) with a charming pillared court and a cistern.

Turn south beside the Palestra by the Lake and along the eastern edge of the Sacred Lake to the Museum; on the left are the ruins of the gymnasium (3C BC) and of the stadium.

★★**Museum** – The main room contains a remarkable series of Archaic sculptures including in particular votive statues of the *kouros and kore* type; almost all the female figures were found in the sanctuary of Artemis.

Other rooms are devoted to Classical art from the 5C BC (*acroteria* figures from the temple of the Athenians), to Romano-Hellenistic sculptures found in the private houses, little bronzes, ivories and Mycenaean jewellery.

Take the path up the slopes of Mount Kynthos.

★★**Ikía Ermi** – The **House of Hermes** is named after a fine head of Hermes *(in the museum)* which was found there. It is a two-storeyed building dating from the 2C BC which was excavated and restored between 1948 and 1950 and is well preserved; the ground floor includes a vestibule, an inner courtyard bordered on three sides by a portico and a *nymphaeum*; stairs lead up to the first floor which includes a gallery and rooms leading off it.

Óros Kínthos (Mount Kynthos)

★★**Ándiro Xénon Theón** – The **Terrace of the Foreign Gods** was built in the 2C BC to take the shrines of the non-Greek divinities frequented by the many immigrants who lived on Delos.

Ieró Siriakón Theotíton – On either side of the path which was once bordered by porticoes are traces of semicircular shrines and meeting rooms, the **Shrine of the Syrian gods**. One of the porticoes enclosed a small theatre where orgiastic mysteries were celebrated in honour of Atargatis, the Syrian Aphrodite.

Ieró Egiptiakón Theotíton – The **Shrine of the Egyptian gods** contains the remains of a temple to Serapis and a temple to Isis of which the façade has been restored; in front of the latter temple stood an altar for offerings and its *naós* sheltered a statue of the goddess.

Iréon – The foundations and two columns of the façade mark the site of a little Doric temple built of marble and dedicated to Hera (6C BC); numerous cult objects *(in the museum)* were found in the *naós*.

★**Ascent of Mount Kínthos** *(45min on foot there and back)*.

Sacred Cave – This opening in the rock was covered in the Hellenistic era with enormous slabs of granite to form a shrine to Herakles.

Summit – 113m/370ft. There are traces of a sanctuary to Zeus and Athena (3C BC) and a magnificent **panorama**★★★ over Delos and the Cyclades.

Sinikía Theátrou (Theatre District)

The Theatre District was built from the 2C BC onwards to house the many foreigners who came to live on Delos. It comprised many luxurious houses built round courtyards and decorated with superb mosaic floors in lively colours.

★**Ikía Delfinión** – The central courtyard of the **House of the Dolphins** is paved with a great mosaic signed by Asklepiades of Arados. In each corner is a dolphin in harness driven by a winged Cupid; one of the dolphins has a crown in its mouth.

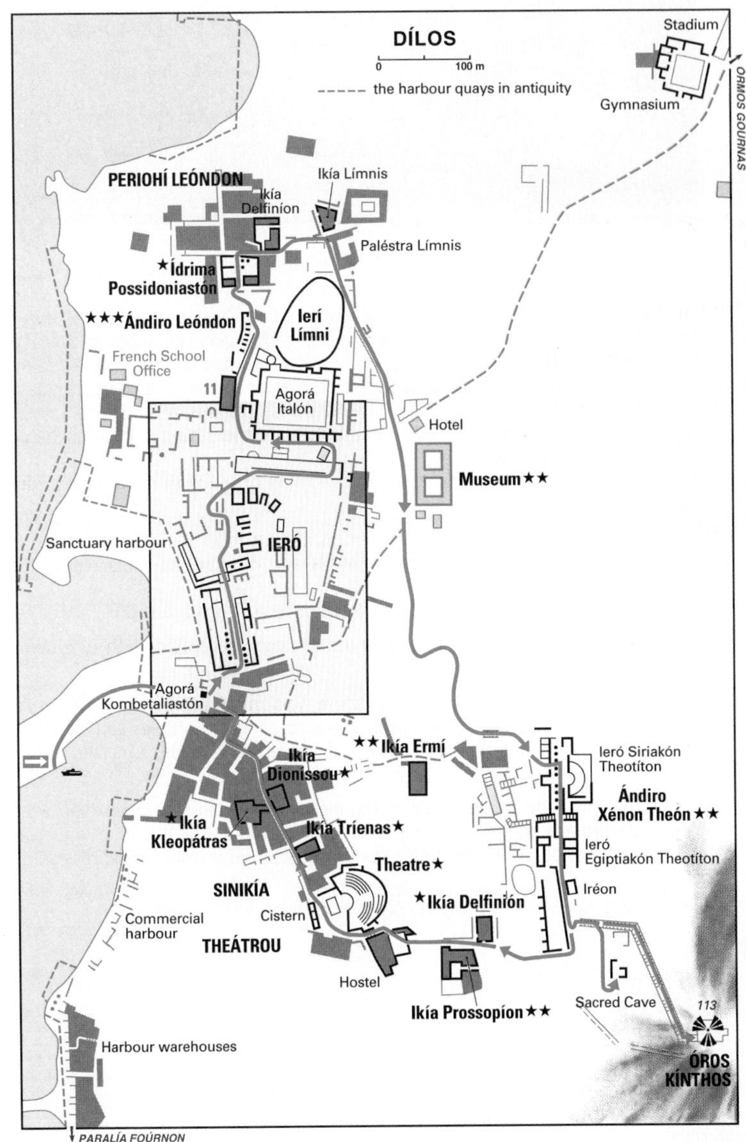

T.A.P.

Dionysos mosaic, Delos

★★**Ikía Prossopíon** – This **House of the Masks** is a huge two-storey house, recently restored, with a central courtyard surrounded with a peristyle supported on stuccoed columns. The rooms giving on to the courtyard are decorated with magnificent mosaics showing figures wearing theatre masks: a dancing Silenus and an astonishing scene in the Asiatic style showing **Dionysos** with a staff or spear *(thyrsos)* and a tambourine, dressed in a long robe and sitting on one of the panthers he subdued in India.
Continuing downhill the path passes the remains of a "**hostel**" with many rooms round a huge courtyard.

★**Theatre** – This was a majestic construction, dating from the Hellenistic era, and it is fairly well preserved, with marble walls and 43 rows of seats which could accommodate 5 000 spectators.
Opposite is a deep **cistern** with arches which once supported a roof.

★**Ikía Tríenas** – The **House of the Trident** has mosaics decorated with a trident, a dolphin entwined round an anchor and geometric motifs.

★**Ikía Kleopátras** – In the 2C BC the house was inhabited by a woman named Cleopatra and her husband Dioskourides, whose damaged effigies can be seen on the north side of the peristyled courtyard. The well still provides excellent drinking water.

★**Ikía Dioníssou** – The central motif of the mosaic in the peristyled courtyard of the **House of the Dionysos** shows Dionysos again on a panther, but this time with wings and seated astride. The panther's head is remarkable for its expression and colouring.

For adjacent sights see MÍKONOS, NÁXOS, PÁROS, SÍROS, TÍNOS.

ÍOS★

Population 1 654 – 109km^2/42sq mi
Michelin map 980 fold 44

Despite being very popular with the international young set, Íos has retained its pure Cycladic character; it is a rugged, mountainous island, rising to 713m/2 340ft on Mount Pírgos, barren and without roads, the terraced hills support a little wheat, windmills, cuboid houses and nearly 400 dazzling white chapels with domes.

The landing (Skála) with its attractive **chapel** dedicated to St Irene lies in a deep bay where the mail boat from Piraeus comes to anchor; from there the road climbs up to the main town (Hóra), hidden in a cleft from which a good beach is accessible. Further east *(2hr 30min on foot there and back)* are the ruins of the Venetian castle built by the Crispi in the 15C where the islanders used to take refuge from pirates.

According to an apocryphal Life of Homer, the blind poet died on Íos during a sea voyage and was buried on the shore.

For adjacent sights see AMORGÓS, KÍMOLOS, MÍLOS, NÁXOS, PÁROS, THÍRA.

KÉA

Population 1 245 – 131km^2/50sq mi
Michelin map 980 fold 31

Despite reasonable hotels and good beaches on the west coast (Korissía, Koúndouros), this mountainous island is little visited. In the bay of Korissía (Livádi) there are traces of a wall and the remains of the temple of Apollo Sminthios. The famous funerary *kouros* discovered on this site is in the National Museum in Athens.
To the north, not far from Vourkári, on the **St Irene (Agía Iríni) peninsula** archeologists have excavated traces of a city dating from the Minoan period (2000 BC).

A surfaced road runs up from Korissía to **Kéa★** (Hóra or Ioulída) (pop 569), the main town, which has the remains of an ancient wall, traces of the temple of Apollo and of a medieval fortress (1210), and an **Archeological Museum** (Arheologikó Moussío) ⏲. 1km/0.5mi northeast a colossal antique lion, 2.7m/9ft high, has been carved in the rock (6C BC). 6km/4mi to the north is the little port of Otzías. The same road leads to the **Monastery of Panagía Kastrianí**, the largest on the island *(it is possible to stay the night)*, built on the **site★** of Kastrí.

Taking a path leading south from Hóra, after 5km/3mi one comes to the **Monastery of Agía Marína** (16C) built around a well-preserved Hellenistic tower (4C BC). 10km/6mi from Hóra, the village of Pissés built on the site of the ancient Poiessa (some ruins remain) dominates a bay.

Proceeding from Koúndoros, a tourist village, towards the east coast and Káto Meriá, one comes to the ancient site of **Kartháia★**; partly submerged, some fortifications on the Acropolis survive, as well as foundations of three temples (to Athena, Apollo – in Doric style – and Demeter), ruins of the theatre and the aqueduct, and certain other buildings. On the return journey, 3km/2mi – 30min walk before reaching Hóra, it is worth visiting the fully restored **monastery of Agía Anna** (16C).

For adjacent sights see ATHÍNA, ÁNDROS, KÍTHNOS, SÍROS, TÍNOS.

KÍMOLOS

Population 728 – 35km^2/13.5sq mi
Michelin map 980 fold 43

Recommended to true lovers of every kind of terrain, Kímolos is the smallest of the western Cyclades. It has no hotels, no petrol pumps and no public transport.

The ferry puts in at **Psáthi**, a small fishing port, a short walk (2km/1.25mi) from **Kímolos** (pop 687), the capital of the island, a picturesque village whose houses, in two rows, form the ramparts of the old fortress. The fortifications and the three gates in them are still in excellent condition. There is an **Archeological Museum** (Arheologikó Moussío) ⏲. Worth seeing are the chapels of Agios Hrissóstomos and Evanghelístria (1608), of Agios Geórgios and of Agios Nikólaos (17C).

There are many beaches with white sand containing kimolite (chalk).

To the north *(4hr on foot there and back)* is **Paleókastro**, built from the ruins of a medieval fortress. To the northeast, **Prassá** has many hot springs. To the southeast *(2hr on foot there and back)* some graves of Phoenician origin have been preserved at **Elliniká★**. Opposite on the island of Agios Andréas (formerly a peninsula) are to be found some traces of an ancient city of 1000 BC (now submerged).

For adjacent sights see ÍOS, MÍLOS, PÁROS, SÉRIFOS, SÍFNOS, THÍRA.

KÍTHNOS

KYTHNOS – Population 1 632 – 100km²/38sq mi
Michelin map 980 fold 31

The landscape is unexciting, but since there are few tourists the island is ideal for a quiet holiday. The ferry arrives at the port of Mérihas *(west coast)*. The best beaches are near Ágios Loukas, served by a daily boat shuttle from the port from 10am to 4pm (last departure).

The main town of the island (**Hóra** or Messariá, pop 672) is typical of the Cyclades with its numerous churches, including St Saba's (Ágios Sávas), the church of the Taxiarchs, and St Nicholas (Ágios Nikólaos) (Cretan icon). 20min on foot from the village is the abandoned monastery of Panagía Níkous (Byzantine church). On the mountain there is an Aeolian village.

In the northeast, there are hot springs at Loutrá, a spa offering treatment for eczema and rheumatism. North of Loutrá *(2hr on foot there and back)* at **Cape Kéfalos★** are to be found the ruins of a medieval fortress, **Kefalókastro** or Kástro Oriás, destroyed by the Turks in 1537.

At **Vriókastro**, north of Mérihas Bay, the site of the (partially submerged) ancient capital of the island can be reached along an unsurfaced path. Opposite is an island (formerly a peninsula) on which there are ancient remains.

From Mérihas a road leads to Driopída (for Katafíki Cave, currently closed to the public for an indefinite period for improvements).

10km/6mi to the southeast is the church of **Panagía Kanála** ⏲ (1867), containing an icon with miraculous powers.

For adjacent sights see ATHÍNA, ÁNDROS, KÉA, SÉRIFOS, SÍFNOS, SÍROS, TÍNOS.

MÍKONOS★★

MYKONOS – Population 5 303 – 86 km²/33sq mi
Michelin map 980 fold 32

The granite island of Mykonos is one of the most typical of the Cyclades. It is arid with wild wind-swept coasts; the outline of its whitewashed cuboid houses is clear cut; its windmills and chapels stand out against the brilliant transparent light.

Despite its reputation as a fashionable resort, Mykonos has retained its timeless beauty. The island is the starting point for an excursion to Delos *(see DÍLOS)*.

A cradle for sailors... and a haven for pirates – In the 13C to the 14C Mykonos was a dependency of the Duchy of Náxos and ruled by the **Ghizi** of Venice; it remained in Venetian hands until the early 18C. They introduced Roman Catholicism and built the warehouses where the merchants of Venice and Marseille came for supplies.

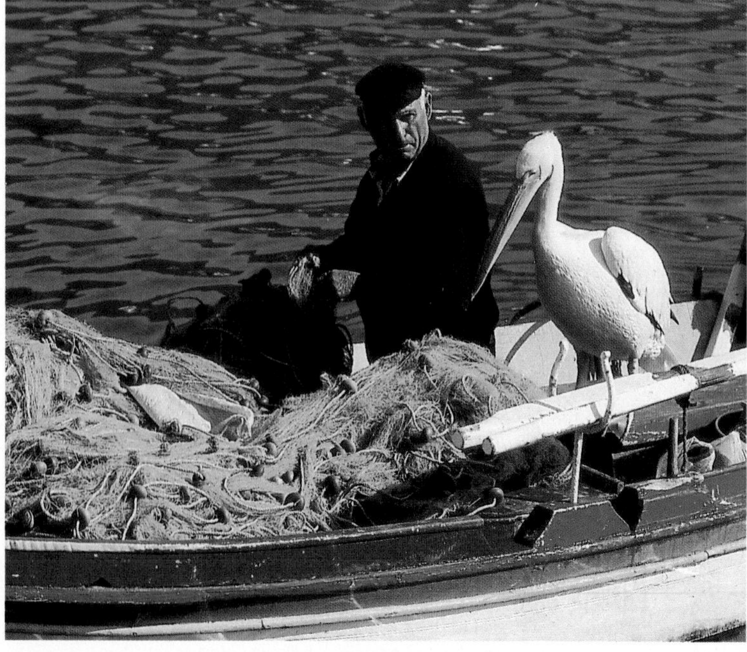

R. Mazzra/ON LOCATION

Mykonos

PRACTICAL INFORMATION

In Mykonos Town there are many tavernas, cafés and tea rooms (*amigdalotá* made from almond paste). Lively night-life; discotheques.

Transport – Cars are allowed on the island but vehicular traffic is banned in Mykonos Town. There are buses to beaches and villages, caïques to beaches, and car, bicycle and motorcycle hire services.

Beaches – The most popular beaches (fine sand) are Platís Gialós (camping) and Ágios Stéfanos which can be reached by bus. On the south coast there are many sheltered inlets which are accessible by taxi or caïque; some of them, such as Paradise and Super Paradise, are reserved for naturists. There is an excursion from Kalafáti beach (water skiing) to **Dragoníssi:** marine caves where a few seals live.

Under the Turkish occupation, which was not strictly imposed, the difficulty of landing on the island because of the prevailing winds made it an ideal refuge for pirates, both Berber and Christian, who beached their dhows in the secluded inlets.
During the War of Independence the local sailors distinguished themselves in Tombazis' fleet. The island prided itself on its heroine, **Mandó Mavrogénous**, who was young and rich, and at her own expense equipped two ships with which she repulsed about 100 Algerian Berbers who suffered 17 dead and 60 wounded. In 1823 she composed the famous *Letter to the Women of Paris* extolling the struggle for Greek freedom. She died at a great age in poverty in Páros.

★★MYKONOS TOWN (Pop 3 935)

The white buildings of Mykonos are linked by a network of narrow streets, originally intended to cut off the wind... and to frustrate pirates! Nowadays it is pleasant to wander about, always discovering new perspectives: arched or vaulted alleys, little squares shaded by an almond tree, a pepper tree or a carob tree, pathways winding between high white walls topped by hibiscus and bougainvillea. There are said to be over 300 chapels on the island, built as votive offerings by the sailors, their domes painted in lively colours. The cuboid houses, their sharp lines softened by layers of whitewash, are charming with their flower-bedecked balconies, their outside stairs, their shuttered and arched ground floors where there is sometimes the click-clack of a loom, their courtyards shaded by a vine or a fig tree. Here and there are craftsmen at work, old women talking, donkeys trotting past, street stalls and tavernas.

★★**Limáni (the harbour)** – Caïques and old tubs bump against one another as the water laps against the curved marble quays. The lively waterfront is lined by the arcades of the 18C town hall, a lonely little chapel dedicated to St Nicholas, patron saint of navigators, café terraces and craft shops as far as Mando Mavrogenous Square where a monument has been erected to the local heroine. From time to time a relative of the late lamented pelican Pétros *(see below)* will waddle into view.

★★**View of Mykonos** – A steep street, Odós Leondíou Bóni, leads up to the 16C **Boni Windmill** (Mílos˙Bóni) ⓥ which provides a splendid view of the town and the harbour, of the islands of Delos and Reneia (Rínia) *(southwest)* and also of Syros *(west)* and Tenos *(northwest)*. The sunset seen from here is particularly splendid.

★★**Old town** – Start from Mando Mavrogenous Square and walk to the Church of Agía Kiriakí which contains the most beautiful icons on Mykonos.
Continue south along **Odós Androníkou**, a very busy street with many craft workshops; turn right into Odós Enopíon Dinámeon to visit a handsome **19C house** ⓥ, richly decorated and furnished.
Next comes a charming little square, surrounded by arcades and named after three wells **(Tría Pigádia)**; the legend says that unmarried girls should drink from each of the wells so as to find a husband.
Turn right to visit the cathedral and the Roman Catholic church which bears the Ghizi coat of arms above the door. The famous pelican Petros, which died in a traffic accident in November 1985, used to parade in front of the Alexander Restaurant in the square.
Turn left to reach the promontory on which the no less famous **windmills** stand in a row; one of them is still in working order and when the wind blows miniature triangular white sails on the arms open up to catch the breeze. The interior of the mill and its mechanism may be viewed. Fine view of the town.
Return down the hill past the churches and turn left along the edge of the bay which is lined by houses with balconies and loggias projecting over the water; this is **Alefkándra**,

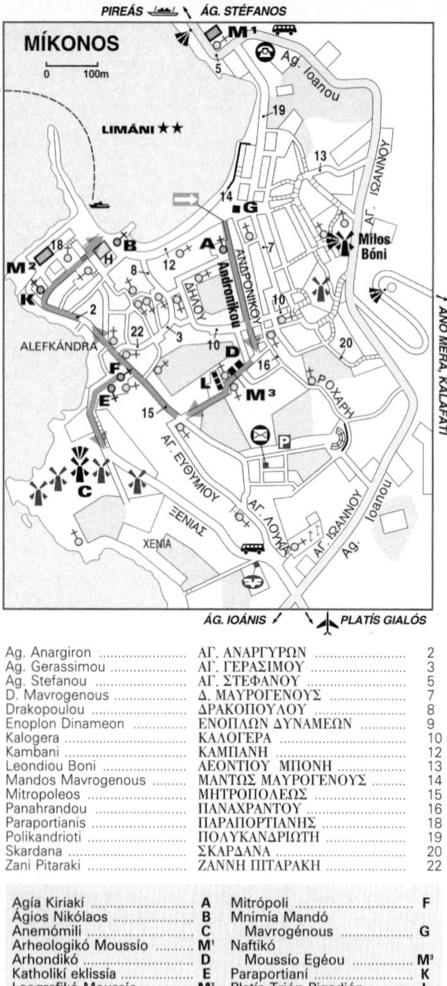

Ag. Anargiron	ΑΓ. ΑΝΑΡΓΥΡΩΝ	2
Ag. Gerassimou	ΑΓ. ΓΕΡΑΣΙΜΟΥ	3
Ag. Stefanou	ΑΓ. ΣΤΕΦΑΝΟΥ	5
D. Mavrogenous	Δ. ΜΑΥΡΟΓΕΝΟΥΣ	7
Drakopoulou	ΔΡΑΚΟΠΟΥΛΟΥ	8
Enoplon Dinameon	ΕΝΟΠΛΩΝ ΔΥΝΑΜΕΩΝ	9
Kalogera	ΚΑΛΟΓΕΡΑ	10
Kambani	ΚΑΜΠΑΝΗ	12
Leondiou Boni	ΛΕΟΝΤΙΟΥ ΜΠΟΝΗ	13
Mandos Mavrogenous	ΜΑΝΤΩΣ ΜΑΥΡΟΓΕΝΟΥΣ	14
Mitropoleos	ΜΗΤΡΟΠΟΛΕΩΣ	15
Panahrandou	ΠΑΝΑΧΡΑΝΤΟΥ	16
Paraportianis	ΠΑΡΑΠΟΡΤΙΑΝΗΣ	18
Polikandrioti	ΠΟΛΥΚΑΝΔΡΙΩΤΗ	19
Skardana	ΣΚΑΡΔΑΝΑ	20
Zani Pitaraki	ΖΑΝΝΗ ΠΙΤΑΡΑΚΗ	22

Agía Kiriakí	A	Mitrópoli	F
Ágios Nikólaos	B	Mnimía Mandó Mavrogénous	G
Anemómili	C	Naftikó Moussío Egéou	M³
Arheologikó Moussío	M¹	Paraportianí	K
Arhondikó	D	Platía Trión Pigadión	L
Katholikí eklissía	E		
Laografikó Moussío	M²		

also known as **Little Venice**. The **Paraportianí Church**, composed of four independent chapels, curiously interlocked in a geometric pattern, stands on the site of the former castle. Picturesque old alleys lead back to the town hall and the harbour.

Arheologikó Moussío ⌚ – The **Archeological Museum** displays items excavated on the island of Reneia: vases and funerary objects transferred from Delos to Reneia by the Athenians in 426 BC during the purification of Delos *(see DÍLOS)*. Unusual *amphora* (7C BC) found on Mykonos decorated with scenes from the Trojan War.

From the cliff above the museum there are remarkable **views★★** of Mykonos harbour and of the islands of Delos and Reneia.

Moussío Laikís Téhnis ⌚ – The **Museum of Folk Art** shows a traditional domestic interior.

Naftikó Moussío Egéou ⌚ – Maps, model ships, old coins and navigational instruments are attractively displayed in the **Aegean Maritime Museum**.

For adjacent sights see DÍLOS, NÁXOS, PÁROS, SÍROS, TÍNOS.

MÍLOS★

MELOS – Population 4 390 – 151km²/58sq mi
Michelin map 980 fold 43

Austere and sombre and relatively untouched by tourism, Melos, like Thíra (Santoríni), is an ancient volcano; the crater, now filled by sea water, provides a deep and safe haven which was used as a naval base by French squadrons during the Crimean War and again by the Allies in the First World War.

Riddled with mines and quarries, Melos grew rich in antiquity through the exploitation of obsidian, a hard vitreous volcanic stone which was made into axe or knife blades; later sulphur, alum and baryta were extracted. Nowadays Melos produces some good volcanic wines. There are numerous hot springs in the island.

The tribulations of the Venus de Milo – During his voyage in the Levant in 1817 the Comte de Forbin, future director of the Museums of France, had noticed that Melos was rich in antiquities but had not been able to stay long enough to investigate.

Three years later two ships put in at Melos and two officers, Vautier and the future admiral **Dumont d'Urville**, were struck by the beauty of the pieces of a marble statue which a local farmer had dug up in his field at the foot of the ancient acropolis.

They both alerted **Louis Brest**, the French Consular agent on Melos, who sent a favourable report to Pierre David, the French consul in Smyrna. The consul told the **Marquis de Rivière**, the French ambassador to the Sublime Porte in Turkey, who who had already spoken to Vautier and Dumont d'Urville when they arrived in Constantinople. In the absence of funds, he decided to acquire the statue at his own expense and sent his secretary, the **Vicomte de Marcellus**, to Melos.

The young diplomat arrived on the island on 23 May 1820 only to be informed that the statue had been loaded on to an Albanian boat bound for Turkey where it was to be offered to the Dragoman, **Prince Nikolaki Mourousi**, the Governor of the Cyclades. Marcellus

laid claim to the statue saying that Brest had acquired it first and the island chiefs gave way, although Matterer, the captain of the ship, stated in his evidence that it was carried off against the wishes of the Greeks who were beaten back by the Frenchmen. In his own account of events Marcellus explains that the statue suffered no damage once it came into his care so the arms must have been lost during the earlier moves.
Marcellus had the five pieces of the statue sewn into canvas bags, he recompensed the island chiefs, paid the farmer and set sail for Piraeus where he showed the statue to the archeologist Fauvel *(see ATHÍNA: Historical Notes)* before heading for Smyrna and Constantinople where he handed his treasure over to the Marquis de Rivière who presented it to Louis XVIII. The Melos Aphrodite, usually known as the Venus de Milo, a masterpiece of 2C BC Hellenistic art, was put on display in the Louvre.
Aphrodite, however, had her revenge. On the orders of Prince Mourousi the farmer was beaten and the island chiefs were whipped and fined 7 000 piastres; the Marquis de Rivière was never reimbursed for his expenses (30 000FF in those days); Brest had to wait six years for the post of vice-Consul which he coveted. In the end Prince Mourousi and Dumont d'Urville died violent deaths; the former was executed on the order of the Captain Pasha and the latter was killed in a railway accident at Versailles in 1842.

SIGHTS

Mílos (Pláka) – Pop 660. The capital, which has a small **museum** ⊙, is dominated by the ruins of a Frankish castle incorporating a 13C chapel surrounded by windmills; panorama over the archipelago. Louis Brest *(see above)* is buried in the Roman Catholic church.
The ancient **acropolis**, where British archeologists excavated a handsome *kouros*, now in the Athens Museum, extended down the hill towards the hamlet Klíma in the valley near where the Venus was discovered; traces of the precinct, Roman theatre, paleo-Christian **catacombs** ⊙ dating from the 3C AD.

Filakopí (Phylakope) – Excavations in the northeast of the island have uncovered traces of three superimposed cities dating from different eras: the Bronze Age, the Minoan period (c 1600 BC) and the Mycenaean (1200 BC). Their stone houses are the first indications of urbanism in the Cyclades and those built in the first period (old Cycladic) were decorated with frescoes (now in the National Archeological Museum).

★★ **Marine Caves** ⊙ – The caves, hollowed out of the volcanic rock, provided a haven for pirates and islanders in the past and are now one of the main attractions of Melos.

Papafránga Caves – *On the northeast coast, below Phylakope.* Three adjoining caves where sheltered a French priest's boats, hence the name. Fine view of the Glaronissa islands.

Glaronissa Islands – *Off the northeast coast.* Excursion by boat from Apolónia. The hexagonal basalt pillars of the cliffs (20m/65ft tall) of these volcanic islands are impressive.

Sikía Cave – *On the west coast, near the southwest tip of the island.* Excursion by boat from Adámas. Light shining through the collapsed vault turns the water a brilliant green colour in this deep cave hollowed out in the white cliff and known as the Emerald Cave.

Kléftiko – *On the south coast near the Sikiá Cave.* Excursion by boat from Adámas. The tall white cliffs jutting into the sea and pitted with caves are known as the Marine Meteors.

For adjacent sights see ÍOS, KÍMOLOS, PÁROS, SÉRIFOS, SÍFNOS, THÍRA.

NÁXOS★

Cyclades – Population 15 469 – 430km²/166sq mi
Michelin map 980 folds 32 and 44

Náxos is the largest of the Cyclades and less oriental looking than its neighbours, particularly Páros, from which it is separated by a narrow channel (only 5km/3mi wide). It is also the most attractive island with a varied landscape: rich coastal plains, verdant valleys and hills and the highest point in the archipelago, Mount Zeus (Náxos Días) (1 001m/3 284ft).
Its resources lie in the plantations of citrus fruits, olives and figs, in the fields of cereals and vegetables and in the vineyards which produce excellent white and rosé wines; its specialities are honey and a citron liqueur *(kítro)*.
The island is also very proud of its singers and dancers whose performances are appreciated throughout the whole of Greece.

Ariadne and Dionysos in Náxos – **Ariadne**, the daughter of Pasiphae and King Minos of Crete, fell madly in love with **Theseus**, son of Aegeus, helped him to overcome the Minotaur, with advice from Daedalus *(see KNOSSÓS)* and then fled with him to escape

Minos' anger. Theseus put in at Náxos on his way back to Athens but alas he left Ariadne asleep on the beach and when she woke all she could see of her faithless lover were the sails of his boat on the horizon.
Another boat arrived bearing the young **Dionysos** who as a child had been looked after by nymphs from Náxos. He was captivated by Ariadne's beauty; he married her and carried her off to Olympos.
Another version of the legend says that Ariadne died giving birth to Theseus' child.

Dukedom of the Archipelago – From 1207, when **Marco Sanudi** captured Náxos during the Fourth Crusade, until the island was taken by the Turkish pirate Barbarossa in 1566, Náxos was the seat of an important duchy administered by the Venetians. It was held by a succession of Venetian families – Sanudi, delle Carceri, Crispi – who resisted the pirate attacks by building towers or fortified houses *(pírgi, singular pírgos)*, introduced Roman Catholicism, which is still the faith of the old families on the island, and rebuilt the capital giving it the appearance which it has more or less retained to this day.

Beaches – Náxos is distinguished from the other islands in the Cyclades by the number and quality of its sandy beaches. The west coast, south of Náxos Town, has a succession of magnificent beaches lapped by turquoise waters and divided by little rocky points and sheltered coves. The most accessible beach, **Ágios Geórgios**, is immediately to the south of the town. 5km/3mi further south are two pleasant beaches, **Ágios Prokópios** and **Agía Anna** *(frequent bus service in season, numerous tavernas and rooms or studio flats)*. The latter also has a charming fishing harbour, and beyond it the huge **Pláka** *(reached on an unsurfaced road)*, which with its fine dunes, if not the most beautiful beach on Náxos, is certainly the largest. Those who want peace and quiet will like the stretch of coast to the south of the Pláka where there is a series of wilder beaches: **Mikri Vigia**, Kastraki, Aliko, **Pirgaki** and Agiassos. The village of Apólonas also has a small beach.

★HÓRA (NÁXOS TOWN)

The present town (pop 4334) is built on the site of the ancient city which was particularly flourishing during the Archaic era (7C to 6C BC); for a time the Naxiots administered the sanctuary on Delos.
Nowadays it is a picturesque little port set on a slope below the Venetian citadel. Under the arcades of the main square **(Platía)** are old cafés and tavernas where the Naxiots meet facing the pleasant view of the old harbour and the chapel of the Virgin (Panagía Mirtidiótissa) on its island. One can stroll beneath the balconies and vaults of the neighbouring streets; in Odós Ágiou Nikoumédou there are craft workshops and the house of an 18C saint, Nicomedes; some of the older men wear local costume.

VLOO

Náxos from Strongilí Portal

Strongilí Portal – It stands on Palace Island (Palátia), a circular *(strongilí)* islet north of the harbour, which is linked to the shore by a causeway where windmills once stood; the church of **St Anthony the Hermit** was built in the 15C by the Knights of St John of Jerusalem. The marble portal was the entrance to an Ionic temple to Apollo which was probably begun during the reign of the tyrant Lygdamis (6C BC) but never completed; the people called it Ariadne's Palace. Fine views of the harbour and the town. *Small beach.*

Kástro – *From the main square (Platía) take Odós Apólonos uphill.* One can still see the line of the citadel's ramparts, built in the 13C, to ward off pirate attacks. The main gate is flanked by a huge tower; under the pointed arch, marked on the stone surround *(right)* as a standard measure for the local merchants, is the Venetian metre. Within the gate is a quiet district where the streets are lined by houses built round internal courtyards with coats of arms carved above the door. These are the properties of the old Roman Catholic and aristocratic families, descended from the lords of Náxos.

Bear round to the right to reach the convent of the French Ursulines who run a school which was founded in 1672.

Beyond stands the old **ducal palace** which from 1627 housed the French College which was under the protection of the French king (escutcheon with fleur de lys and the collar of the Order of the Holy Spirit) and accepted pupils from the Roman Catholic and Orthodox churches. Now the palace houses a **museum** ⓥ displaying a fine collection of idols and Cycladic ceramics as well as a Hellenistic mosaic.

Nearby stands the **cathedral**, built in the 13C by Marco Sanudi. The interior, consisting of a nave and two aisles, contains a superb Byzantine icon on the high altar: one side shows the Virgin and Child in the presence of the benefactor, a bishop; the other shows John the Baptist; there is also a painting (17C) of the Virgin of the Rosary surrounded by members of the Sommaripa family, and Venetian funeral plaques.

EXCURSIONS

★★Tour of the island – *Round trip of 77km/48mi*

The road runs southeast across the rich coastal plain with its irrigation channels and screens of trees (market gardens, vineyards). Beyond Galanádo, Belónia tower comes into view *(right)*.

Tower and church of Belónia – The tower *(pírgos)* is a fine example of the fortified houses built by the Venetians as refuges against pirate attacks and used as country retreats in more peaceful times. It belonged to the Roman Catholic bishops of Náxos.

Beside it stands St John's (13C), a curious double church, Roman Catholic on the left and Orthodox on the right; the façade is decorated with the lion of St Mark and the interior has typically Gothic capitals with crockets.

★★**Potamiá Valley** – The road continues towards Halkí with views of the orchards, vineyards and olive groves which cover the fertile green slopes of the valley; among the trees beside the road stands the **church of Ágios Mámas** which was the seat of a bishop in the Byzantine era *(access by a track to the left 8km/5mi from Náxos Town)*; further off are the ruins of **Apáno Kástro**, a 13C Venetian fortress. In the **Tragéa Valley**, surrounded by dense olive groves and dotted with Byzantine chapels and churches, lies Halkí.

Halkí – It is a prosperous town with an interesting Byzantine parish church *(in the main street)* (9C-12C) decorated with frescoes and dedicated to the Virgin **(Panagía Protohronís)** ⓥ and a well preserved tower house, Pírgos Frangopoúlou.

Akádimi – A path to the right, opposite a new church, leads *(45min on foot return)* to a Byzantine church, the **Holy Apostles** (Ágii Apóstoli) ⓥ, half hidden among the olive trees and decorated with 13C frescoes.

Beyond Filóti there are spectacular views of the Tragéa Valley and the mountains.

Apíranthos – Apíranthos is a centre for hand-woven cloth; the narrow streets are picturesque; they contain a handsome fortified house and a small **Museum of Cycladic Idols** ⓥ.

Further on (5km/3mi) there are extensive **views**★ on either side of the road on both sides of the central ridge of the island, including the Kóronos region, which is rich in vineyards, orchards and olive groves, and marble or emery quarries.

★**Apólonas** – This charming village with a harbour and a beach nestles in a peaceful inlet. On the edge of the houses above the coast road to Náxos Town is an old marble quarry; abandoned on the edge lies a **kouros** which was roughed out in the 7C BC. The return journey to Náxos Town follows the northwest coast by a sometimes rather poor road (several towers); not far from from Náxos (3km/2mi) a steep and narrow road leads up to the **Monastery of St John Chrysostom** (Hrissóstomos) which is painted a dazzling white; **view**★ of the town of Náxos and the island of Páros across the strait.

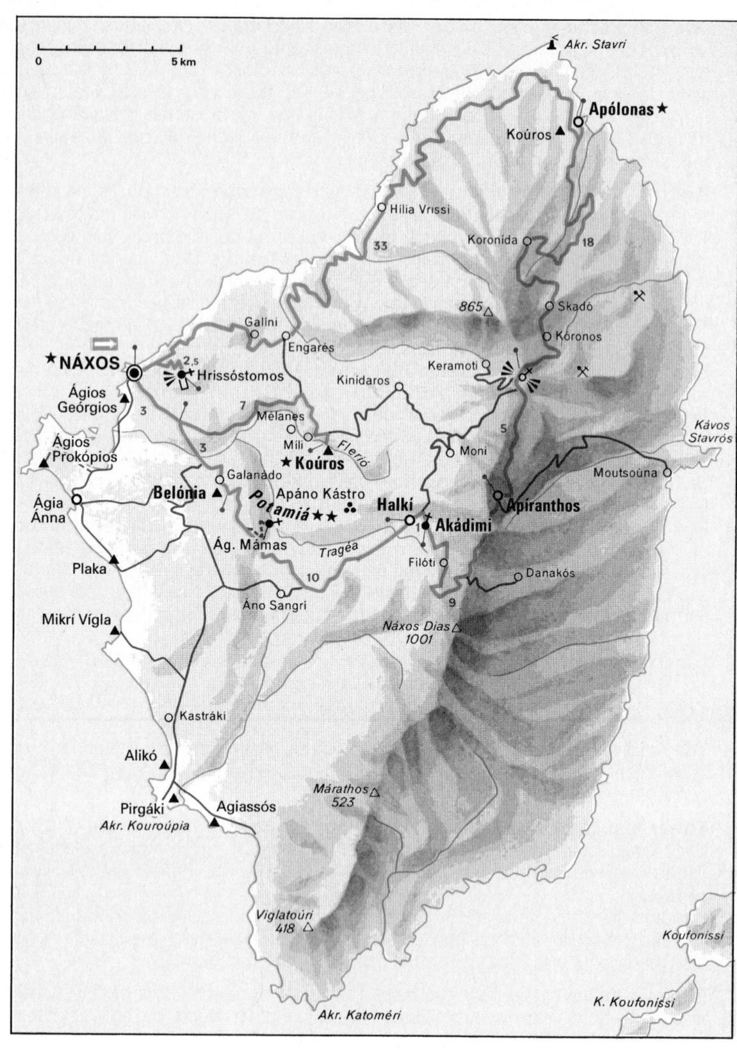

★**Flerió Kouros** – *12km/7.5mi east of Náxos Town. Take the road to Belónia. After 3km/2mi turn left and then after 1km/0.5mi left again to join the road to Míli.* Beyond Míli follow the road to **Mélanes Valley** and then the track which descends to the stream. *Park the car and continue on foot.*

The Flerió *kouros*, incomplete and abandoned like the one at Apólonas, is also smaller and more recent (6C BC); it lies in a pleasant shady garden.

For adjacent sights see DÍLOS, ÍOS, MÍKONOS, PÁROS, SÍROS, THÍRA.

PÁROS★

Population 10 470 – 196km²/75sq mi
Michelin map 980 folds 32 and 44

Famous throughout antiquity for its white marble, the island of Páros at the centre of the Cyclades has a distinct character with its white houses, its domed churches and its windmills, the most typical of which are to be found at Parikía and Léfkes.
The island has two excellent natural harbours on the west and north coasts; the terrain is hilly (rising to 771m/2 530ft on Mount Profítis Ilías) and more or less barren, although the patches of colour, many appearing in the folds of the ground, are fields of barley, vineyards, orchards and groves of olives and figs which provide the islanders with a reasonable living. The island is well known for its white and rosé wines and its citron liqueur as well as for its sardines and shellfish.
In antiquity Páros grew prosperous owing to its fine grained white marble, called lychnite which was in great demand by architects (Solomon's Temple in Jerusalem) and by sculptors (Venus de Milo, Hermes by Praxiteles).
From the 13C until it was captured by the Turks in 1537 Páros was a dependency of the Duchy of Náxos and under Venetian occupation. At the beginning of the 17C William Petty, the Earl of Arundel's chaplain, discovered the famous *Parian Chronicle* in the fortress; this was a chronological account of ancient Greek history, engraved in the 3C BC on the stone which gave the assumed date of Homer's birth. In the 17C the Capuchins founded a monastery on the site of the present Roman Catholic church. Mando Mavrogenous, the heroine from Mykonos *(see MÍKONOS)*, died destitute in 1848 in Páros.

★PARIKÍA (PÁROS TOWN)

Páros (pop 2 932), the capital of the island, has developed on the site of the ancient city. The dazzling white of the buildings is accentuated by the vivid colours of clusters of oleanders, bougainvilleas and hibiscus. It is pleasant to stroll in the maze of narrow winding streets which are crowded with shops, chapels, blue-domed churches (beautiful iconostases) and fountains, some of which date from the 18C.

Kástro – On the promontory on the site of the ancient acropolis stand the ruins of a 13C Venetian fortress; its walls incorporate some ancient fragments (marble columns, pieces of architrave). Some of these come from a temple; its foundations can be seen near the little church of St Constantine within the precinct. Beautiful view of Páros Bay.

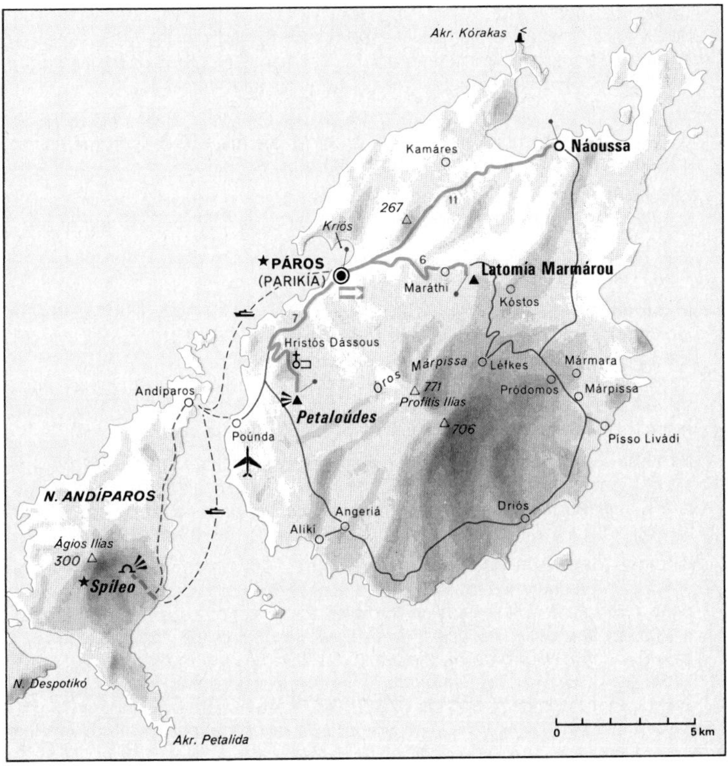

★**Panagía Ekatondapilianí** ⓥ – *At the far end of a square on the east side of the harbour.* The name (meaning "Our Lady of the Hundred Doors") may also be a corruption of *katapolianí* meaning below the town. The first church was an important Byzantine sanctuary founded by St Helen, Constantine's mother; the present building dates from the 6C only and may have been largely reconstructed in the 10C. Under the Venetians it was the Roman Catholic cathedral, probably shared with the Orthodox.

Threshing grain on Páros

An unusual narthex, with rib vaulting and apses at either end, leads into the church itself which is a combination of a basilical building with a nave and two aisles and the Greek cross plan. Inside are galleries *(gynaecea)* for the women, a rare foundation shaft *(right transept)*, a Byzantine tabernacle on the high altar and the bishop's throne *(apse)*.
St Nicholas' Chapel *(left of the chancel)* which dates from the 6C is supported on ancient columns; the iconostasis is 17C. The baptistry *(right of the church)* dates from the 6C and was designed for baptisms by total immersion.

Museum ⓥ – *Beyond and to the right of the Church of the Hundred Doors.* On display is a fragment of the *Parian Chronicle*; the main piece is in the Ashmolean Museum in Oxford. Effigy of Victory (Skópas School).

Grotto of the Nymphs – *Below Hotel Xenia and the windmill hill.* Originally dedicated to a nymph cult, the grotto was Christianised by the building of a chapel.

EXCURSIONS

Petaloúdes Valley ⓥ – *7km/4.25mi south; follow the coast road; then turn left into a road leading to the monastery of Christ in the Forest (Hristós Dássous) and the valley of the butterflies (petaloúdes).*
In spring and summer the fruit trees growing on the valley slopes are inhabited by swarms of butterflies. Visitors are requested not to disturb the butterflies. Attractive view of Andíparos; remains of a 16C Venetian castle.

Náoussa – *10km/6.5mi northeast.* Náoussa is a fishing village with picturesque alleys situated deep in a wide rugged bay where the Russian fleet spent the winter in 1770 *(several small beaches in inlets which can be reached by boat)*; down by the harbour a tower belonging to a castle built by the dukes of Náxos.

Latomía Marmárou (Marble Quarries) – *6km/3.75mi east on the slopes of Mount Márpissa. Take the road towards the attractive village of Léfkes. Beyond Maráthi turn right into a track which leads up the valley to the famous quarries. The approach is marked by abandoned buildings. Park the car near the chapel and walk 100m/110yd; pass through the low wall on the left and follow the path to the quarries.*
There are three quarries *(latomía)* side by side with steeply sloping galleries, which are sometimes slippery, and penetrate deep into the mountain since the finest and whitest marble lies very deep. There is an ancient low-relief sculpture at one of the entrances.

Andíparos Island – *Access daily in the season from Parikía by caïque which goes to the beaches and the cave; also a launch from Poúnda.*

★**Spíleo** ⏲ – The cave of Andíparos is about 165m/541ft up on the slopes of Mount Ágios Ilías. The cave is well presented and consists of a vast chamber about 90m/295ft deep (400 steps) with many concretions. At Christmas in 1673 the French Ambassador in Constantinople, the Marquis de Nointel *(see ATHÍNA: Parthenon)* arranged for midnight mass to be celebrated by the light of flaming torches; many people attended from the neighbouring island *(inscription)*. In the 19C the cave was visited by Byron and other romantic travellers.

For adjacent sights see AMORGÓS, DÍLOS, ÍOS, MÍKONOS, NÁXOS, SÉRIFOS, SÍFNOS, SÍROS, THÍRA.

SÉRIFOS

SERIPHOS – Population 1 095 – 75km²/29sq mi
Michelin map 980 fold 31

The island was famous in antiquity for its iron-ore mines which are now almost exhausted. It is typically Cycladic in its cragginess, and although popular in summer it is spared from the excesses of mass tourism.

Livádi is a pleasure port, while **Hóra**, the main town on the island with its picturesque white houses, gazes down on the **bay★** from the heights. To be seen there are the walls of a Venetian fortress, the **Church of Ágios Athanássios** (4C-5C, restored in 1820) and a **Museum of Popular Art** (Moussío Laikís Téhnis) ⏲. Its **town hall** (1907) houses an **Archeological Museum** (Arheologikó Moussío) ⏲ on the ground floor ⏲. **Beauty spot★** at the top of the hill with three churches.
To the north at **Panagía** is the Byzantine church of the same name, the oldest on the island (950 AD) and decorated with beautiful frescoes. Higher up the coast is Sikamía beach.
8 km/5mi to the northeast of Hóra is the **Monastery of the Taxiarchs★★** ⏲, the most important historic building on the island, which looks like a fortress (icon of Christ embroidered with gold from 1800, Russian chandeliers, iconostasis of carved wood and marble, bishop's throne of 1713, library containing Byzantine manuscripts). 500m/547yd further is the attractive site of the church of Panagía Skopianí.
To the south by the road to Koutálas beach stands a white tower from the Hellenistic period (Asprópirgos). The coast is indented with **numerous bays** which are difficult to reach without transport. This is undoubtedly the most attractive part of the island, well away from the crowds.

For adjacent sights see KÍMOLOS, KÍTHNOS, MÍLOS, PÁROS, SÍFNOS, SÍROS.

SÍFNOS★

SIPHNOS – Population 1 900 – 74km²/28sq mi
Michelin map 980 fold 43

On this, the most popular of the western Cyclades with tourists, the pure cuboid style of architecture peculiar to the Cyclades has survived. It was rich from the proceeds of the gold and silver mines which enabled the ancient Siphniots to build the "Treasury of Siphnos" at Delphi. The island is dotted with refuge towers and has good roads linking the main sites.

Kamáres is the port, where many potters are at work. On the road to Apolonía is the monastery **Théológos tou Moungoú** ⏲. **Apolonía**, the capital of the island since 1836 (pop 689), nestles in the amphitheatre formed by three hills. It has numerous churches: Panagía Ouranofóra, Metamórfossi tou Sotíra, Ágios Spiridonas (the island's cathedral) and Ágios Sostis, while on the main square is a **Folk Museum** (Moussío Laikís Téhnis) ⏲ . Apolonía is surrounded by typical Cycladic villages. To the south the monastery of **Profítis Ilías tou Psiloú★** ⏲, perched on a hill 680m/2 244ft high, is one of the oldest buildings on the island.

Artemónas is a picturesque little Cycladic town with windmills. It also has three remarkable churches: Ágios Konstandínos (15C), Panagía tis Ammou (renovated in 1788) and Panagía i Kóhi.

Kástro★★, the old capital of the island 3.5km/2mi from Apolónia, is a Venetian fortress and its two rows of houses formed the ramparts. It is built on the site of an ancient city of which a few traces remain, and has a fine view of the sea. The **Archeological Museum** (Arheologikó Moussío) ⏲ displays the finds from the **Agios Andréas** site on the top of a hill to the southeast of Apolónia. **Panagía Eleoússa★** (renovated in 1635) is the island's cathedral.
North of Kástro stands the church of Panagía Pouláti (1971), with a fine view. To the south on the road to **Platí Gialós** (beautiful beach) is the **monastery of Vríssi** (1614-21). Lower down are the **monastery of Panagía tou Vounoú** (1813) and

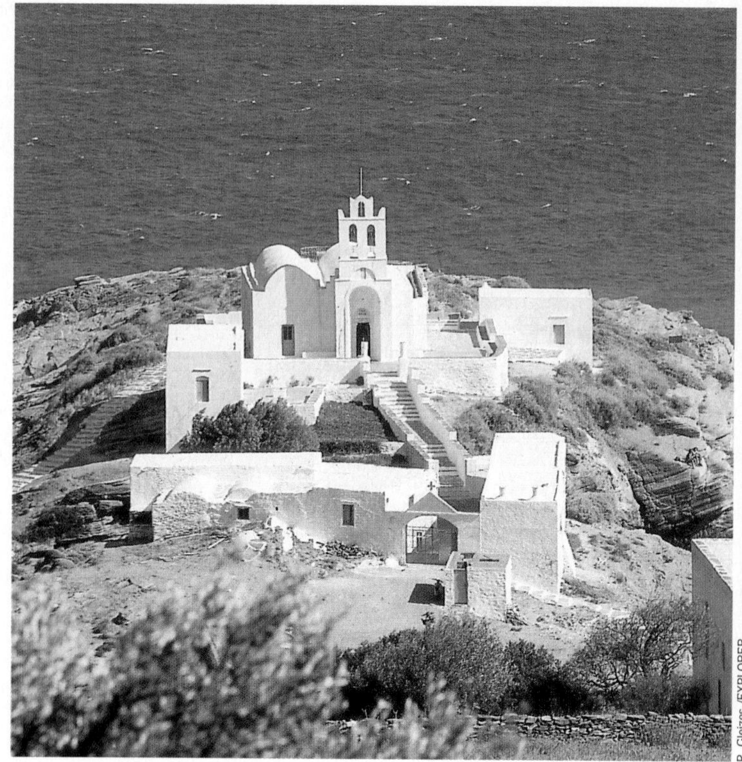
P. Gleizes/EXPLORER

Church of Hríssopigi, Sífnos

the **church of Hríssopigi** (1650), built on a rocky peninsula where a miraculous icon was discovered. This is an attractive site close to **Faros** (beautiful beach).
At **Vathi** (beautiful beach) one can see the church of the **monastery of the Taxiarchs**.
For adjacent sights see ÍOS, KÍMOLOS, MÍLOS, PÁROS, SÉRIFOS, SÍROS.

SÍROS★

SYROS – Population 26 049 – 85km²/33sq mi
Michelin map 980 fold 32

Síros enjoys a privileged position at the centre of the archipelago; its main town Ermoúpoli is the capital of the Cyclades. The island, which is steep and barren on the eastern seaboard, is green and cultivated on the opposite slope.
The vast roadstead at Ermoúpoli provides a safe and deep anchorage; in the late 19C it was the first port in Greece and is still the hub of seaborne traffic between the islands.

The Pope's Island – In the 13C the Venetian and Genoese who occupied the island sought a refuge from pirates and founded Ano Syra (Áno Síros) on the southern peak where they implanted Roman Catholicism. This version of Christianity prevailed even after 1537 when the Turks captured the island because, under the **Capitulations** agreed between François I and the Sultan, the religious institutions established by the Latins were placed under the protection of France.
The Capuchins were the first to arrive in 1633, followed by the Jesuits, the Ursulines and the Lazarists of St Vincent-de-Paul. The religious orders dispensed justice and organised schools and hospitals. In 1717 the botanist Tournefort wrote that Síros, then called **Syra**, was the most Catholic island in the archipelago with 6 000 Roman Catholic as against 12 Orthodox families. Nowadays Síros is still a Roman Catholic see.

Birth of a refugee town: Ermoúpoli – Syra had always been a focal point of the shipping routes between Athens, Constantinople, Alexandria and the other ports of the Levant and in the aftermath of Greek independence the island's importance grew. Starting in 1821 thousands of Greeks, who were driven out of Chios and other Aegean islands by the Turks, found refuge on the then uninhabited shores of Syra Bay.

Gradually a new town developed; it was placed under the patronage of Hermes, the god of Commerce, and called Hermoupolis (Ermoúpoli). Totally Greek, it grew rapidly and by 1828 it already numbered 14 000 inhabitants. At one time there was even a possibility of it becoming the capital of the newly established Greek kingdom.
In fact, Ermoúpoli flourished until the end of the century. Maritime trade, shipyards, textile workshops, tanneries, the production of wrought iron and ships' prows all enriched the cosmopolitan inhabitants. The town acquired the appearance which it has to a large extent retained: foreign architects such as Chabeau (French) and Ziller (German) contributed to the construction of public buildings, elegant houses with wrought iron balconies and the handsome villas in Vapória where the shipowners, bankers and rich merchants lived. The establishment of schools, printing presses, newspapers and even a literary circle sustained a high level of intellectual activity. A flourishing social life was expressed in the carnival, theatre or opera, concerts and balls.
The opening of the Corinth Canal in 1893 dealt Ermoúpoli a serious blow and it was supplanted by Piraeus. There was renewed activity in the port after the Second World War when Goulandris, a shipping magnate, built the Neorion floating dock.
From the entrance to the bay there is an arresting view of the **setting**★★ of the town with its white houses spread up and down the steep slopes and divided into distinct districts: on the waterfront, Ermoúpoli, built in the 19C, the administrative and commercial centre; above, on two hills divided by a valley, Áno Síros *(left)*, the old Roman Catholic town dating from the 13C and Vrondádo *(right)*, where the Orthodox live, which was built in the 19C as an offshoot of Ermoúpoli.

Ermoúpoli – Pop 13 030. The "new" town was built on a regular plan in the neo-Classical style.

The quays – The waterfront, with its cafés, shipping lines, tavernas and confectioners selling the Turkish Delight *(loukoúmi)* for which the island is famous, has a fine view of the port and the anchorage which is protected by Donkey Island (Gaidounissi).

Platía Miaoúlis – The huge square with its marble paving, its palm trees and pavement cafés is the setting for the evening stroll *(perípato or vólta)*, which is so common in Mediterranean countries, and also for concerts given in the bandstand. The neo-Classical architectural style is well in evidence in the arcades along the south side, in the majestic building designed by Ziller (1878) which is both the town hall and the law courts, and also in the library. The attractive marble theatre, a small-scale replica of the Scala in Milan, in the adjoining square was designed by Chabeau in 1862.

Nomarhía (Administrative district) – Odós Apólonos is the axis of the administrative and commercial district, which looks rather forsaken but nevertheless presents a group of solid 19C buildings: regional administrative offices, Chamber of Commerce, banks and fine mansions with balconies.
The road up to St Nicholas' Church (blue dome) passes through Vapória, a residential district with elegant villas overlooking a little bay.

Áno Síros – *Access by taxi or on foot by Odós Omírou and steps (45min return).* The road passes near the French school (St George's) which takes 160 pupils and the French hospital run by the Sisters of Charity *(right)*.
Áno Síros, the old Roman Catholic town, is criss-crossed by steep and winding streets lined by chapels (Our Lady of Carmel) and convents (Jesuits). Side by side in a square at the top of the hill are the bishop's palace and St George's Cathedral, built in the Venetian style. From the terrace there is a **view**★ down the valley between Áno Síros and Vrondádo to Ermoúpoli and the harbour.

For adjacent sights see ÁNDROS, DÍLOS, KÉA, KÍTHNOS, MÍKONOS, NÁXOS, PÁROS, SÉRIFOS, SÍFNOS, TÍNOS.

THÍRA★★★

THERA – SANTORINI – Population 9 593 – 76km²/29sq mi
(83km²/32sq mi including Thirissía and the islands)
Michelin map 980 fold 44

The island of **Thíra**, more usually known in English as **Santorini**, the southernmost of the larger Cyclades, is one of the most spectacular in the Mediterranean; it presents the awesome sight of a volcanic crater partially submerged by the sea. It is particularly impressive to approach by boat and enter the vast roadstead (10km/6.5mi in diameter) which is almost landlocked and encircles the still active cone. The blue of the water contrasts with the dark cliff face which is crowned by piles of white cubes, the houses of Ía *(north)* and Thíra, the capital.
The culinary specialities are full-bodied wines, dessert grapes, broad beans, tomatoes and fish. Water is scarce; it is collected in cisterns or brought in by boat.

A succession of disasters – Thíra has suffered many earthquakes and volcanic eruptions which have altered its configuration.

Tertiary Era – At this period Thíra was part of the Aegean continent which was composed of limestone sediment, marble and metamorphic schist. At the end of the Tertiary Era the continent sank and was covered by the sea with the exception of a few islands. Mount Profítis Ilías and the Méssa Vounó headland date from this period.

Quaternary Era – A succession of underwater eruptions and subsequent outflows of lava made the island circular so that it was called Strongilí (round).

2000-1600/1500 BC – A civilised way of life developed on the island similar to that on Crete under the Minoans *(see KRÍTI: Legend and History)*. In c 1530 BC (c 1630 BC according to some archeologists) the gases which had been building up under the lava exploded and created a huge central crater *(caldera)* which was filled by sea water rushing in through a breach in the southwest sector. A hail of ashes and slag fell on the remaining land burying entire cities (Akrotíri) while a gigantic tidal wave rolled south towards Crete.

Early 3C – mid-2C BC – While the island was being used as a naval base by the Egyptians (Ptolemaic dynasty) another earthquake in 236 created a second breach between Théra and Thirassía. In 197 an islet surfaced in the centre of the crater; it was later called Paléa Kaméni.

Christian Era – This period was marked by the appearance (1573-1711) in the flooded crater of several volcanic cones, some of which fused together in 1867, 1925 and 1928 to form Néa Kaméni. The last quake in 1956 destroyed 2 000 houses and caused 50 deaths.

The Quest for Atlantis – The first excavations on Thíra were undertaken by Ferdinand Fouqué, a geologist, who had been present at the eruption in 1867 and then proceeded to make probes on Thirassía and in the Akrotíri combe. He discovered traces of buildings and pottery and in 1869 he published an article in the *Revue des Deux-Mondes* showing that at the time of the great eruption in 1530 BC an advanced civilisation was flourishing on Thera.
A hundred years later the Greek archeologist, **Professor Marinátos**, renewed investigations in the Akrotíri combe in the hope of proving a theory he had formed before the Second World War. He had been working in Crete when he noticed volcanic deposits on land which was far removed from any volcano. He had then made the connection with the eruption in 1530 BC and put forward the idea that Minoan Crete and Thíra had belonged to the same land mass, Atlantis, where an advanced and highly civilised people had been engulfed suddenly by fire and water as Plato had described.
Marinatos' discovery of frescoes at Akrotíri similar to those found at Knossós *(see KNOSSÓS)* on Crete was proof that before 1530 BC the same type of civilisation flourished on Thíra as on Crete; this did not however prove the existence of Atlantis.

Kalliste, Thera, Santorini – After the great eruption several generations of Phoenicians occupied the island which was known as Kalliste (most beautiful). In about the 9C BC a party of Spartans arrived under the leadership of Theras, in whose honour Kalliste was named Thera. The island remained a colony or ally of Sparta and little is known about its history until the Hellenistic period when the Egyptian Ptolemies were attracted by its strategic position in the centre of the Aegean *(see below: Ancient Thera)*. Christianity took root in Thera very early; St Irene of Thessaloníki, the island's future patron, died there in 304. Following the capture of Constantinople by the Crusaders in 1204, the island passed into the hands of the Venetians for the next four hundred years and they made it a dependency of the Duchy of Náxos and then of Crete. They called it Santorini after a shrine dedicated to St Irene. The population often suffered from the rivalry between the grand Latin families and from the Turko-Venetian conflict. In this respect the period of Turkish occupation (1579-1821) was the most peaceful and prosperous. After gaining independence in the modern Greek state, the island officially resumed its ancient name of Thera (Thíra) but the majority of Greeks continue to call it Santorini.

★★FIRÁ (THÍRA TOWN) – Pop 1 524

Seen from sea level in the crater *(caldera)*, where the water is so deep (400m/1 312ft and over) that it is impossible to drop anchor, the island capital seems to perch precariously on top of the precipitous cliff (300m/984ft). The cliff face itself is of interest owing to the many layers of volcanic debris laid down after each eruption – bands of black lava, rust-coloured slag, purple grey ash, pozzolana which is sought after for making cement and at the top a light-coloured layer of pumice stone which is quarried for export.
From the landing-stage **(Skála)** a stepped path *(587 steps)* zigzags up the cliff face offering spectacular **views**★★ down into the water-filled crater; an army of mules carrying tourists wends its way up or down to the accompaniment of cries and bustle. There is also the **cable-car** ⏲.
The town, a maze of picturesque narrow streets, seems to be suspended above the sea like a balcony; from the terrace in front of the Orthodox cathedral there are splendid **views**★★★, particularly at sunset and after dark, of the sea, the vol-

canic islands (Kaménes), the crater and Thirassía Island. On the eastern side of the town a layer of lava, covered by stocky vineyards, slopes down to the Mediterranean and the island of Anáfi.

New district – This district on the north side of the town was rebuilt after the earthquake in 1956; the curved roofs are designed to resist earth tremors. This is where the Roman Catholics congregate; they have been numerous on Thíra (nearly half the population) since the Venetian occupation from 1204 to 1537. Next to the cathedral, dedicated to St John the Baptist, in the Dominican convent there is a carpet weaving workshop *(open to visitors; shop)*. The schools belonging to the Sisters of St Vincent-de-Paul and the Lazarists closed down after the catastrophe in 1956.
On the corner between the Cathedral and the Convent stands the handsome **Ghizi house** ⓥ containing a collection of furniture, engravings and ceramics.

Arheologikó Moussío ⓥ – The **Archeological Museum** houses the sculptures and ceramics from the Mycenaean to the Roman period found on the island, particularly at Ancient Thera. The museum also displays material from the excavations at Akrotíri. Another museum, devoted to prehistory is due to open near the Orthodox cathedral.

EXCURSIONS

★★★ **Boat trip in the crater** – *Departure from Firá and Ía; in Firá apply to one of the tourist agencies in the main square (bus terminal): 15min to 20min to descend on foot to the waterfront. The trip takes 2hr to 5hr according to the programme; take appropriate shoes for walking to the crater and a swimming costume.*
The view of the towering cliffs of the crater from the deck of a small boat is most impressive; the trip includes a close look at several other volcanic features. The boat stops first at **Néa Kaméni**; a tiring but not difficult walk *(30min)* over the old cinders leads to the centre of the volcano which emits wisps of sulphureous smoke: panoramic view of the outline of the original Round Island. For those who do not dally over the walk there is the possibility of a refreshing dip from the black pumice rocks.

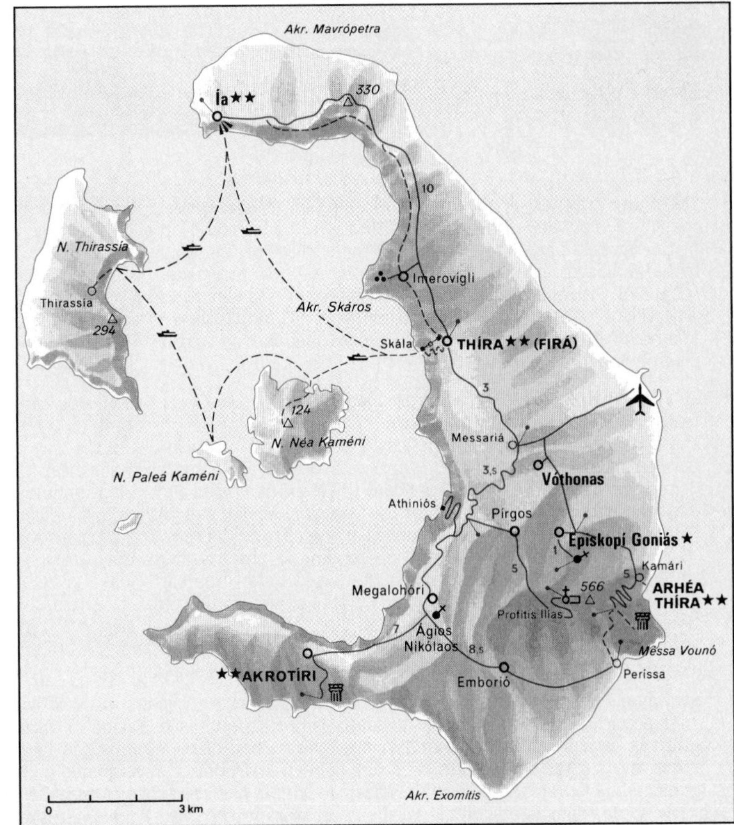

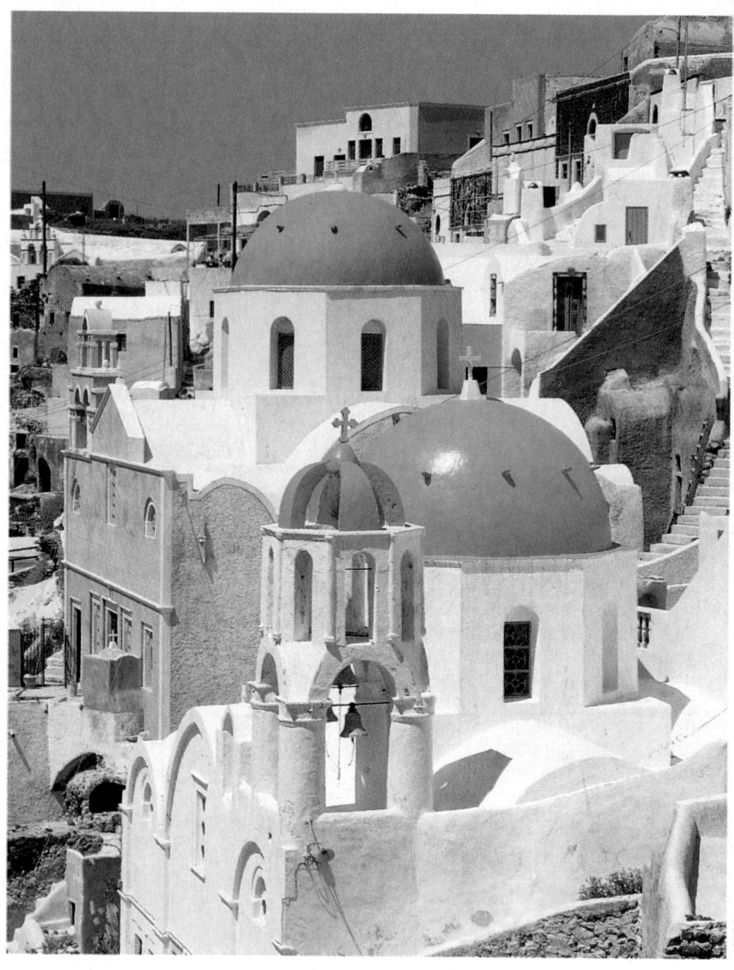

Ía, Thíra

The boat stops next at the entrance to an inlet in **Paleá Kaméni**; during the swim to the shore the water grows warmer and is coloured red by the soft volcanic mud of the inlet; bubbles of gas erupt on the surface of the sea.
At the midday break *(2.45pm Greek time)* the boat arrives at the island of **Thirassía** (pop 245) *(taverna on the beach)*. At the top of the cliff *(donkeys)* there is a quiet little village of white and blue houses *(tavernas)* and a view of the crater.
The boat returns to Firá via the Skála of Ía *(see below)* skirting the forbidding and precipitous cliffs of the crater.

★★**Ía** – *10km/6mi north. Access from Firá by bus or on foot (3hr) by the cliff-top path* (very fine views of the crater).
The new church at **Imerovígli** contains a fine **iconostasis** in carved wood, the only piece rescued from the old building which was destroyed in the earthquake in 1956. Below the village *(west)* on **Cape Skáros** traces of old walls, almost indistinguishable from the rock, indicate the site of the Venetian capital; the path is not easy.
Further north the corniche road runs near the edge of the cliffs and provides a good view east over the cultivated land descending in broad terraces down to the sea.
Ía★★, which was the main town on the island before the earthquake in 1956, is slowly restoring its damaged buildings on the slopes of the crater. Life here is more peaceful and traditional than in its rival Firá. There is a splendid **view**★★★ from the northwestern end of the village of the crescent shape of the island, the crater and the volcanoes at its centre. Small museum on merchant shipping.

★**Vóthonas; Episkopí Goniás** – *7km/4.5mi south by the Kamári road.* A narrow road *(right)*, half sunken in the ground, leads to the unusual village of **Vóthonas**, which is partially hidden in a fold in the layer of pozzolana. All that can be seen above the surrounding countryside are palm tree fronds, a few domes and the graceful bell-tower of the church. *Return to the Kamári road.* Near Méssa Goniá a track *(right)* runs south of the village of **Episkopí Goniás**★ (also Panagía Episkopís) to the **church** ⓥ, one of the most beautiful on the island. It was founded by the Byzantine emperor, Alexis Comnenos late in the 11C and the frescoes date from about 1100; re-use of ancient columns.

"Fortified" villages – *8-15km/5-9mi south of Firá.* **Pírgos**, the highest village on the island, is composed of concentric streets, the last ring of houses forming a rampart; there are several handsome neo-Classical houses and traces of a Venetian castle. Southeast of Pírgos (4km/2.5mi) stands the **Prophet Elijah Monastery** (Profítis Ilías) ⓥ which was founded in 1711; above it rises the peak of the same name, the highest point on the island (556m/1 824ft; *prohibited military area*). There is a **museum★** of religious art (icons, manuscripts, liturgical ornaments) and popular traditions.
Just beyond the village of **Megalohóri** (attractive belfry astride a street), about 500m/550yd short of the turning to Períssa, stands St Nicholas' Chapel, an unusual little building in white marble dedicated to **Ágios Nikólaos Marmarítis**; it is an ancient funerary temple (3C BC), perfectly preserved and dedicated to the goddess Basileia.
Just outside **Embório** lie the remains of a Venetian fortress which enclosed some ancient houses and the 15C Church of the Virgin.
All these villages have several churches with domes or bell-towers.

★★ARHÉA THÍRA (ANCIENT THERA) ⓥ

Access from Kamári by a concrete road winding steeply uphill; park the car at the top and take the path leading up to the ruins. There is also a footpath up from Períssa (1hr 30min of steep climbing).

Ancient Thera was founded in the 9C on a magnificent **site★★** high above the Aegean Sea. It was a considerable city in antiquity with 5 000 inhabitants and 700 cisterns and reached the height of its importance under the Egyptian Ptolemies (300-150 BC) who established a naval base in the port at Kamári (then called Oia). Ancient Thera declined under the Romans and was abandoned in the 13C.
The first section of the ruins is Byzantine (fortifications and chapels).

Témenos of Artemídoros – A Ptolemaic admiral was responsible for this sacred enclosure which has retained its altar of Concord and some inscriptions engraved in the rock walls. There are unusual sculptures representing Artemídoros, the lion of Apollo, the eagle of Zeus and the dolphin of Poseidon.

Proceed along the main street to the Agorá.

Agorá – It was divided into two parts; the first was overlooked by a temple to Dionysos at the top of a flight of steps and the second by the Royal Portico, a Roman structure of which the bases of the central colonnade can be seen. Behind the *agorá* was a residential district.
Beyond the *agorá* is the theatre *(left)* which dates from the Ptolemaic period but was repaired by the Romans; the sacred way leads to the temple of Apollo.

Temple of Apollo – It consisted of a *naós* and a *prónaos* *(see p 35)* of which the foundations remain and was preceded by a court *(right)* flanked by two chambers. Beyond lie the terrace and the gymnasium of the Ephebes.

Terrace and gymnasium of the Ephebes – On the terrace, which dates from the 6C BC, the Ephebes, young men doing their military service, engaged in naked exercises and dances, **gymnopaidia**; graffiti in their honour have been written on the rock walls.
Below the terrace at the tip of the headland are traces of the gymnasium (2C BC) where the Ephebes lived overlooking a courtyard; in the north corner of the court was a shrine dedicated to Herakles and Hermes who were venerated by the Ephebes. The baths, of which the foundations are visible, were built by the Romans.
On the way back, take the street by the theatre which climbs to the left towards the **Sanctuary of the Egyptian gods**, Isis, Serapis and Anubis which is cut out of the rock.

★EXCAVATIONS AT AKROTÍRI ⓥ

The excavations, which are roofed over, are gradually revealing a Minoan city dating from the second millennium BC which was buried when the volcano at the centre of the island erupted in 1530 BC. Many discoveries have been made including the famous frescoes which are now displayed in the National Archeological Museum in Athens.
After the eruption Akrotíri was protected and preserved by a thick layer of impervious pumice stone. Part of the city has been excavated revealing the streets and paved squares, the two-storey houses of which the stairs, doors and windows have been partially restored. The huge jars *(pithoi)* in which stores were kept have been left where they were found.
The city must have been evacuated by its inhabitants before the catastrophe because no bodies have been found.

For adjacent sights see AMORGÓS, ÍOS, KÍMOLOS, MÍLOS, NÁXOS, PÁROS.

TÍNOS

TENOS – Population 7 747 – 195km²/75sq mi
Michelin map 980 fold 32

In the Greek world Tenos is famous for pilgrimages to the miraculous icon of the Annunciation of the Virgin made on 25 March and 15 August. It is a mountainous island; its terraced slopes, on which barley and vines are grown, are often swept by the north wind *(meltémi)*.
The island is also well known for its **pigeon lofts** which number upwards of a thousand; these white towers decorated with delicate geometric patterns, often done in open-work (fine collection at **Kámbos**) were introduced during the Venetian occupation of the Cyclades in the 13C but they were still being built in the mid 19C. Scarcely less numerous are the **churches** and **chapels**, some of which contain treasures of popular art inspired by Byzantine or Venetian tradition.
Tenos was a fief of the Venetian Ghisi family in the 13C and, like Mykonos, it was the last of the Cyclades to fall to the Turks in 1718; for this reason the Roman Catholic faith is professed by nearly 50 % of the population, grouped in the centre of the island round the bishop's residence at Xinára.

Venetian pigeon lofts, Tínos

Tínos Town – Pop 3 754. Set in a broad bay, the white capital of the island is both a port and a pleasant little town, its narrow streets bustling with traders and craftsmen.

Church of Panagía Evangelístria ⓥ – A broad steeply-sloping street, which some pilgrims climb on their knees, leads up to the imposing white marble church which dominates the town. The church was built in 1823 following the discovery in 1822 by Sister Pelagia of a miraculous icon, the object of the pilgrimages which attract the sick and the faithful.
A great court enclosed by porticoes surrounds the church which is approached by a ceremonial flight of steps. On the left of the entrance in the nave is the holy icon, encrusted in jewels and hung about with countless votive offerings: hearts, legs, silver lamps, boats etc.
On the left below the church are the "caves" where the icon was discovered; a neighbouring building contains a little **Museum of Religious Art** ⓥ (icons) and an **art gallery** which displays works by local artists (Lítras, Gysis, Iacovides, **Halepás**); many are well known on the international scene.

Arheologikó Moussío ⓥ – In 1969 a building was constructed beside the approach road to the church in the style of the island pigeon lofts; among other exhibits the **Archeological Museum** houses a colossal provisions vase *(pithos)* dating from the 7C BC and found at Exómvourgo, as well as objects from the excavation of the sanctuary of Poseidon and Amphitrite.

Exómvourgo – *9km/5.5mi plus 1hr on foot return; from the Stení-Falatádos cross-roads drive to the monastery and park the car nearby; continue on foot by a fairly difficult path.*
On the hilltop (553m/1 814ft) stands Exómvourgo, a Venetian citadel built on the site of an ancient acropolis; below extended the town, also fortified, which the Venetians named Sant' Elena.

From the top **panorama**★ over the island and the northern Cyclades.

The Villages – There are about 50 villages on Tenos; they were built inland from the coast, with narrow winding streets and vaulted passages, as much for protection against the wind as against the pirates of earlier centuries. The most interesting include **Istérnia** with its two churches and **Pánormos** (or Pírgos), the home of famous painters and sculptors *(see above)*, with a beautiful beach down by the sea. The unusual **Kehrovouníou Convent**, in the northeast of the island, is a village in miniature, housing about sixty nuns.

For adjacent sights see ÁNDROS, DÍLOS, KÉA, KÍTHNOS, MÍKONOS, SÍROS.

The Dodecanese

As the name suggests (*dódeka* in Greek means 12), the Dodecanese is a group of 12 islands – Ródos (Rhodes) and Kos, the main islands, Pátmos, Léros, Kálimnos, Níssiros, Tílos, Sími, Hálki, Astypálea, Kárpathos and Kássos. The name Dodecanese was given them in 1908 when they united to rise up against the Turkish government which was trying to strengthen its hold on them. To these are added Kastelórizo (Megísti), an island off the south coast of Turkey and about 200 smaller islets. They cover altogether an area of 2 714km²/1 048sq mi, and their 163 500 inhabitants are distributed over only 27 islands.

These mountainous and picturesque islands, also known as the **Southern Sporades**, played an important role in antiquity and during the Middle Ages, when they were the advance guard of the Knights of St John facing the Turkish threat. They were occupied by the Italians in 1912 and joined the Greek State in 1947-8.

PRACTICAL INFORMATION

Access

By air – Five of the islands in the Dodecanese have airports: Karpathos, Kassos, Kos, Léros and Rhodes. The last three have daily connections with Athens (the actual number of flights varies), but have hardly any international flights, and only Rhodes-Diagoras has connections with other Greek cities (four flights weekly to Herakleion and Thessaloníki). To reach Karpathos and Kassos, it is necessary to go via Rhodes.

To get to Pátmos it is possible to take a flight to Léros and go on by sea *(see next section)*.

By sea – One or two car ferries leave Piraeus every day for Rhodes and Samos. They provide a service on the way for Astipálea, Kálimnos, Léros, Pátmos, Kos, Níssiros, Tílos and Sími, and may go on to Karpathos, but they do not call automatically at all the islands on their route so the frequency of the service is variable. Two companies run these services: Dane Sea Line-Dodekanissiaki Shipping (☎ (01) 42 93 240 in Piraeus, (0241) 77 078 in Rhodes) and G.A. Ferries (☎ (01) 41 99 100 in Piraeus, agent in Rhodes Kydon Tourist on ☎ (0241) 23 000, agent in Samos Charambalakis on ☎ (0273) 32 320).

In addition, there is also a direct service to Pátmos from Piraeus by the Nomicos Line car ferries which provide the Samos service (Akti Tzelepi terminal ☎ (01) 45 13 311 in Piraeus, Apollon Travel ☎ (0247) 31 324 in Pátmos). The daily hydrofoil service to Léros connects with the Athens-Léros flights (Apollon Travel in Pátmos as above; Kastis Travel in Léros
☎ (0247) 22 140 in Agia Marina or (0247) 22 500 in Lakó).

Accommodation

Kálimnos – Hotels and rooms in private houses.

Karpathos – Numerous small hotels (cat A to E), guest-houses and rooms in private houses.

Kos – More than 200 hotels (cat A to E), mainly in Kos Town and environs, Lámbi and Psalídi; about 30 hotels at Kardámena and Tingáki; some hotels at Kéfalos-Kamári and Mastihári. Rooms in private houses mainly at Kardámena and Kos Town; many rooms at Mastihári, Tingáki and Kéfalos. Camping site at Psalídi near Kos.

Léros – Hotels (cat B to E), mainly in Láki, and rooms in private houses. Camping site at Xirókambos.

Níssiros – Hotels and rooms in private houses in Mandráki.

Pátmos – About 25 hotels and guest-houses in Skála (cat B to D); about 10 hotels and guest-houses by Gríkou Bay. Rooms in private houses in Skála, some rooms in Hóra and other villages. Camping site in Meloi.

Ródos/Rhodes – About 300 hotels (all categories), mainly in Rhodes Town (some pensions in the old town) and nearby beaches (Lalissós/Triánda and Ixiá on the west coast and Faliráki on the east coast); some hotels in Lindos and a few in the south of the island. Rooms in private houses mainly in Rhodes and Líndos.

Sími – Some small hotels and rooms in private houses in Sími. Possibility of staying at Panormítis Monastery.

KOS★

Dodecanese – Population 26 379 – 290km²/112sq mi
Michelin map 980 fold 46

Kos is the second most important island in the Dodecanese after Rhodes. It lies northwest of the latter, close to the coast of Asia Minor near Bodrum (Halikarnassos) in Turkey. It is a fertile island, blessed with fertile countryside and a mild climate and rich in reminders of Classical Greece and the Knights of St John who held Kos from 1315 to 1522. The island (45km/28mi long by 11km/7mi wide) rises to 846m/2 776ft high. It is well supplied with rain and springs and produces cereals, vegetables, fruit such as water melons, citrus fruits and grapes; chicken farming is also common.

> **Transport**
>
> Car, bicycle and motorcycle hire services, taxis; bicycles are a useful means of transport in Kos Town which is quite large.

Kos was the birthplace of **Hippocrates**, the "Father of Medicine", in about 460 BC. He wrote several medical treatises which are the basis of the Hippocratic Oath, a sort of moral code which doctors swear to observe. Another famous native was **Apelles**, the artist who flourished in the reign of Alexander the Great (336-323 BC).

★KOS TOWN Pop 14774

Kos, which is the capital and main resort of the island, has a significant Ottoman minority. Between the harbour, Mandráki, in the bay and the majestic castle of the Knights of St John on the hill are grouped the white arcaded houses, the terraced cafés, the palm-lined walks and gardens of flowering red hibiscus which give the town its charm.

The centre of the town for tourists is **Plane Tree Square★** (Platía tou Platánou) which takes its name from the enormous plane tree (14m/46ft in girth) beneath which Hippocrates, the famous doctor, is supposed to have taught his pupils (in fact the tree is only 500 years old). Next to the tree stands a covered Turkish fountain composed of ancient materials which have been re-employed, such as the sarcophagus converted into a basin.

The **Mosque of the Loggia** (1786), on the south side of the square, has a double portico and was probably used in the past as a merchants' exchange.

★Kástro (Knights' Castle) – *Access: Over a bridge from Platía tou Platánou.* There are two concentric sets of walls with massive towers at the corners; the inner wall was built between 1450 and 1476 and the outer wall was added between 1495 and 1514 by Grand Masters Pierre d'Aubusson, Aimeri d'Amboise and Fabrizio del Carretto. The stone of which they are constructed includes pieces taken from ancient buildings, particularly the Asklepieion *(see below)*: note the Hellenistic frieze over the entrance door.

The outer wall, which was the work of Italian engineers, is reinforced at the critical points by bastions for artillery: the Carretto bastion, a round tower in the southwest corner on the left of the entrance, resembles its counterpart in Rhodes; the Aubusson tower, a polygonal structure in the northeast corner, commands the harbour entrance. The parapet walk gives a succession of picturesque views of the inner wall with its coats of arms of the Knights, the town, the harbour, the sea and Bodrum (Halikarnassos) Bay.

Agora and harbour district – *Below the Mosque of the Loggia.* In the days of the Knights of Rhodes, the medieval town adjoining the harbour was called **Lango**; it was surrounded by ramparts of which a few traces remain. The district was destroyed by an earthquake in 1933 and archeologists have conducted a systematic excavation of part of the Hellenistic and Roman city – the pavement of an *agora*, the foundations and two columns of a temple to Aphrodite, eight Corinthian columns of a *stoa* and the footings of a paleo-Christian basilica.

St John's Church, a small 15C domed building, dates from the time of the Knights.

Arheologikó Moussío – The **Archeological Museum**, which is near the old Defterdar mosque in Liberty Square (Platía Eleftherías), displays the products of excavations carried out on the island: a collection of Hellenistic and Roman sculpture including a statue of Hippocrates, another of Hygieia the goddess of Health, a figure of Mercury seated, effigies of women wearing the *peplos* and portraits.

At the centre of the courtyard is a mosaic representing Hippocrates and Asklepios.

Archeological site (west) – On either side of Odós Grigoriou south of the town, lie extensive excavations including traces of a temple of Dionysos, a colonnaded *palestra*, baths, houses decorated with **mosaics★** and frescoes and a Roman road with its original paving. The Italian archeologists reconstructed a large building surrounding a charming court *(visible through a side window)*; it was first thought to be a shrine to the Nymphs and known as the Nympheon but is in fact a latrine *(forica)*.

Casa Romana ⓥ – *On the south side of Odós Grigoriou.* A large Roman villa, uncovered in 1934, has been reconstructed. There are traces of paintings, mosaics and marble floors in the rooms surrounding the open court and the great peristyle. Further along the street a small Roman odeon has also been restored.

EXCURSIONS

★**Asklipiío** ⓥ – *4km/2.5mi south.* Four terraces cut into a hillside overlooking the Kos plain mark the site of this important sanctuary which was consecrated to Asklepios (Aesculapius), the healer and son of Apollo. It was built late in the 4C BC to commemorate the skills of Hippocrates and, like Epidauros, it was both a place of worship and a treatment centre served by eminent priest-healers, the Asklepiades, who formed a famous medical school.

To the left of the lower terrace lie the ruins of the Roman baths. The ancient monumental entrance *(propylaia)* leads up to the second terrace which was lined with porticoes enclosing the curative sulphureous waters.

At the centre of the third terrace stands a monumental altar to Asklepios, flanked *(right)* by traces of an Ionic Hellenistic temple and *(left)* by a Roman temple; the former, which was originally decorated with paintings by Apelles, son of Praxiteles (Aphrodite Anadyomene), contained the sanctuary treasury and the votive offerings of the pilgrims seeking cures. Note also the semicircular public seat *(exedra)*.

On the top terrace, on the same axis as the steps, stood the great temple of Asklepios; the black and white marble steps were part of a 2C BC Doric temple, six columns broad by eleven long. The sides and back of the terrace were bordered by porticoes.

There are magnificent **views**★★ down over the sanctuary and the surrounding woods to the town of Kos and over the sea to the Turkish coast.

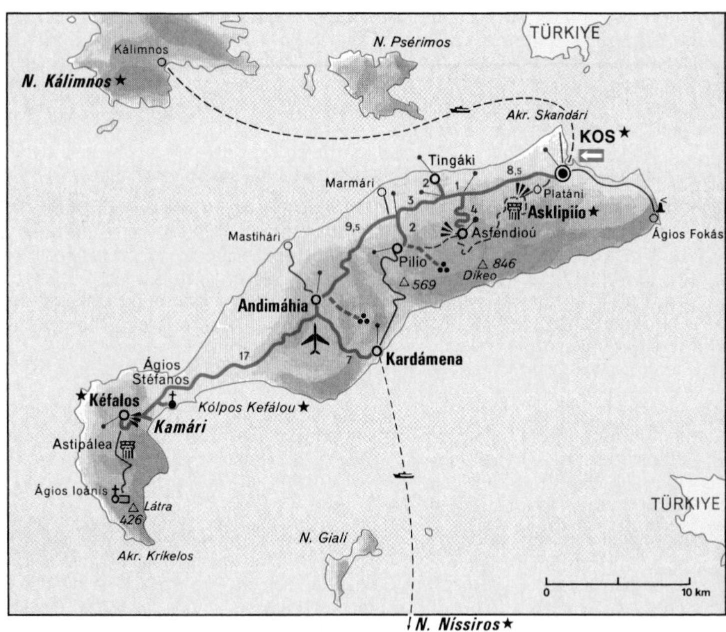

★**Road to Kéfalos** – *108km/67mi there and back.* The road runs the length of the island with side roads leading to Tingáki, a charming little port *(hotels, fish tavernas)* with a fine beach on the north coast, and to a group of villages known as Asfendioú in the hills to the south. There is an extensive **view** of the coast of Kálimnos.

Andimáhia – There is a path running south *(6km/3.75mi there and back)* to the Hospitallers' fortress, which was built to a rectangular plan and contains the ruins of churches, houses and cisterns; over the entrance are the arms of the Order and of Aimeri d'Amboise.

Kardámena – This fishing village is gradually turning into a large resort; its main attractions are a fine sandy beach and its proximity to Níssiros Island *(see OTHER ISLANDS: Níssiros)*.

Beyond the airport the road runs through a barren landscape before reaching a ridge overlooking **Kéfalos Bay**★ (Kólpos Kéfalou) with Mount Látra rising to 426m/1 398ft to the south. The road leads down to excellent sandy beaches (Hrissí Aktí – Golden or Hawaii Beach, and Parádissos – Paradise Beach).

Kamári – There is a beautiful beach near the tiny island of Ágios Nikólaos. The ruins of a paleo-Christian basilica, **Ágios Stéfanos**, rise on a rock terrace above the beach of a holiday complex *(access from the road by a public path through the complex)*. The remains of the mosaic floor are covered with sand for protection against the elements.

★ **Kéfalos** – The old village of Kéfalos lies above the ruins of its castle. From the foot of the wall there is a splendid **view**★★ over the vast Bay of Kéfalos to the east and beyond to the Resadiye Peninsula in Turkey, and to Níssiros Island in the south. From the windmill (the machinery may be viewed inside) there is an extensive view of the bay and to the north of this part of the island.

Boat trips – A stay on Kos provides the opportunity for a day trip to Kálimnos or Níssiros *(see OTHER ISLANDS)*.

For adjacent sights see PÁTMOS, RÓDOS, KÁLIMNOS, NÍSSIROS, SÍMI.

PÁTMOS★★★

Dodecanese – Population 2 665 – 34km²/13sq mi
Michelin map 980 folds 33 and 34

The tiny, arid island of Pátmos derives its extraordinary renown from its association with St John the Divine, the disciple who wrote the Apocalypse, and from the monastery built in the 11C and dedicated to St John which is an important shrine of the Orthodox Church. The houses of the capital Hora, which surround the monastery, form the finest architectural group in the Aegean.
The landscapes bathed in a bright light and the indented coastline with its numerous beaches add to Pátmos' attractions.

HISTORY AND LEGEND

Pátmos is rarely mentioned in ancient records and archeological investigation is still in the early stage. An ancient inscription kept at the monastery indicates that Orestes fleeing from the **Furies** after killing his mother *(see ATHÍNA: Areopagos and MIKÍNES)* found refuge in Pátmos. The island was later occupied by Mycenaean and Dorian settlers and then came under the Ionian rule of Miletus (now Balat) in Asia Minor. Traces of a wall on the summit of Kastéli hill are among the island's few ancient remains. A temple said to have been built by Orestes and dedicated, like the temple at Ephesus in Turkey, to **Artemis**, the mother-goddess, probably occupied the site where the monastery now stands.

St John in Pátmos – The author of the Apocalypse, by tradition identified as St John the Divine, was said to have been banished to Pátmos by the Emperor Domitian in 95 AD for preaching the Gospel at Ephesus. At the emperor's death in 97 AD John returned to Ephesus where he lived to a ripe old age. A text entitled *Voyages and Miracles of the Apostle and Evangelist St John the Divine written by his disciple Prochoros* was embraced by the Byzantine tradition and by the Christians in Pátmos. This wonderful tale is illustrated on the walls of the monastery and of many other shrines, and several places on the island are associated with the saint even today.

A troublesome period – After the founding of Constantinople and of a Christian empire, a basilica was built on the site of the razed temple to Artemis. From the 6C AD Pátmos was deserted on account of raids by Saracen pirates until the end of the 11C when Emperor **Alexis I Comnenos** ceded the island in 1080 to the monk **Christódoulos** for him to found a monastery dedicated to St John. The privileges which included exemption from all taxation and the right to charter ships, were maintained and extended over the centuries by the Byzantine emperors.
From 1089 Christodoulos and his companions built massive walls to protect the monastery from pirate and Turkish raids but as the incursions multiplied the new community had to seek temporary refuge in Euboia where Christodoulos died in 1093. The blessed monk's relics were brought back to Pátmos and pilgrims soon thronged to the island. Emperors and patriarchs donated holdings of arable land, in Crete and Asia Minor in particular, which supported the monastery. The library founded by Christodoulos enriched its collections and the monastic community produced many scholars. The buildings were maintained by Cretan workers who lived in the north of the island. At the end of the 13C the lay population resettled for protection at the base of the monastery's wall and founded the capital Hóra. Until the 16C Pátmos was occupied by the Normans, the Turks and the Crusaders but from the 14C it also suffered from the conflict between the Knights of St John of Rhodes and the increasingly powerful Ottoman Empire.

Ottoman rule – Turkish occupation which officially started in 1537 marked three hundred years of relative stability as the Turkish fleet controlled the Aegean and drove the pirates towards the western Mediterranean. The Turks did not take up residence in the small unproductive islands like Pátmos but exacted heavy taxes; the local reli-

Transport – 1 bus (to Hóra); taxis, motorcycle hire services; caïques to beaches.

gious authorities administered the island while attempting to maintain the Greek language and culture and the Orthodox religion. In the 15C refugees from Constantinople settled in Hóra and in the 17C Cretans from Candia *(see IRÁKLIO)* sought the monastery's protection. The shipping industry grew as Pátmos traded with Europe and Asia Minor; local crafts were exported. In 1659 the Venetians under Francesco Morosini *(see IRÁKLIO)* sacked the island with the exception of the monastery. In 1713 Makarios, a monk, founded the School of Pátmos near the Monastery of St John, which imparted lay and religious education; its students went on to become theologians and patriarchs and famous politicians such as Emmanuel Xanthos, one of the founders of the Filikí Etería *(see p 27)*. Although Pátmos was active in the cause of Greek independence it remained under Ottoman rule under the terms of the Treaty of Constantinople (1832) and as it was cut off from the new western-style Greek State, its prosperity declined.

Pátmos in the 20th century – Pátmos suffered the same fate as the other islands of the Dodecanese and came under Italian rule. It was finally united with Greece in 1948 *(see RÓDOS: Historical Notes)*. The development of tourism in Pátmos in recent years has not affected the great moral and spiritual influence of the Monastery of St John and religious festivals are enjoyed by the locals and the tourists alike.

★★★ÁGIOS IOÁNIS THEÓLOGOS ⓥ

Access – *By bus or taxi from Skála (to the entrance to Hóra); or on foot (about 30min) by an old mule track, a more direct route in the shade, past the cave of the Apocalypse.*

Exterior – The walls of **St John's Monastery** overshadow the white houses nestling below and dominate the island. The circuit wall was built on a polygonal plan in the 11C-12C by the Blessed Christódoulos and his successors and strengthened through the centuries; its massive canted buttresses were added in the 17C. In front of the gateway is a bastion which was converted in 1603 into the Chapel of the Holy Apostles. The terrace at the entrance affords a good **view**★ of Skála harbour.

St John's Monastery, Pátmos

Central courtyard – Beyond a dark zigzag passageway the monastery's fortress-like appearance gives way to a maze of courtyards, stairs, domed white buildings with stone arcading. The courtyard paved with black pebbles is spanned by three great arches which act as buttresses to the side buildings. At the far end on the left is a huge jar in a round cistern, previously used to store the monastery's wine.

Main church (Katholikón) – The church which stands to the left of the courtyard was completed in 1090 and is surrounded by buildings of later construction.

Exo-narthex – Two wooden beams *(símandron)* beaten to summon the monks to services hang in the gallery opening on to the courtyard. In a recess to the south is a statue of the founder Christódoulos holding the monastery in his hands.

The 17C outer narthex which incorporates columns and other fragments from a 4C basilica is decorated with 17C frescoes of the life of St John – *(above the main door)* The Resurrection of Domnos at Ephesus; *(right)* St John and Próchoros in chains; *(further on)* the Evangelist saving a young man from drowning during John's journey into exile on Pátmos; *(above the door to Christódoulos' chapel)* the magician Kynops leaps into the sea and is turned to stone by St John. The majority of the remaining frescoes were painted in the 19C.

Narthex – It was built in the 12C also with elements of the old basilica. The darkened frescoes date mainly from the 12C and 17C. The parable of the Wise and Foolish Virgins is illustrated on the narrow north wall.

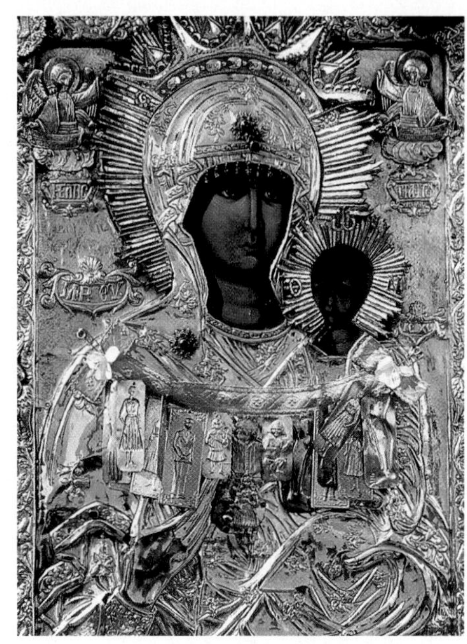

PICTOR

Processional icon, Pátmos

Chapel of the Blessed Christódoulos – It was constructed in the 16C as the final resting place of the monk's relics which are contained in an 18C wooden reliquary overlaid in silver-gilt. Its marble base was probably the original sarcophagus brought back from Euboia. A 17C iconostasis stands on the left.

Main church – The Greek cross plan church with its grey and white marble floor and central dome resting on four columns is the oldest part of the monastery; two of the columns are hidden by a heavy gilt-clad wood iconostasis (1820). Most of the frescoes on view were painted in the 19C on top of 17C murals (some are visible on the north wall); the latter probably covered Byzantine originals.

Chapel of the Virgin – *Access from the main church.* The admirable late 12C frescoes full of nobility and severity, were uncovered during restoration work carried out in 1958, under other mediocre murals dated 1745. The Byzantine frescoes include – *(behind the iconostasis)* the Virgin and Child enthroned between the Archangels Michael and Gabriel; *(on the upper level)* the Hospitality of Abraham; *(on the northern half of the vault, left of the iconostasis)* Christ and the Samaritan Woman at the well; *(lower down)* St Stephen and St James; *(on the southern half of the vault)* the Healing of the paralytic and of the blind man; *(on the upper level)* the Presentation of the Virgin in the Temple. The remaining murals depict, in the main, oriental saints and patriarchs. The chapel also contains a fine Cretan iconostasis in painted wood (1607) with an antique threshold step and a column *(left)* topped by a capital decorated with doves from the early-Christian basilica.

Old refectory – It contains two long stone tables faced with marble with niches in the bottom for the monks' cutlery. The floor comprises fragments from the ancient foundation and the early-Christian basilica. The style of the late 12C-13C frescoes on the upper west wall is more expressive than the 18C murals from the Chapel of the Virgin on the east wall *(opposite the entrance)*. The earliest murals appear on the tympanum of the north arch *(left of the entrance)* – The Apparition of Christ to the disciples by the sea of Tiberias and the Miracle of the Loaves and Fishes – the same theme was depicted in the 13C above the arch – *(above right)* Christ giving the Bread and Wine to the disciples; *(about the main pillar)* Jesus praying in the Garden of Gethsemane; *(on the north wall)* Abraham welcoming the three angels; *(above the door)* the Crucifixion and the Fainting of the Virgin. On the south wall *(right of the entrance)* an angel points out Jesus' tomb to the Holy women; the upper sections depict scenes from the second, fourth and sixth Ecumenical Councils – the Hierarchs with haloes and ceremonial robes contrast with the halo-less and simply dressed heretics; the figures hold opposing liturgical texts.

Return to the main courtyard by the vaulted passage.

The old storerooms with the monks' cells *(not open)* behind are on the left on the south side; the museum and shop are on the west side of the courtyard.

Museum – It presents the most precious articles from the monastery's library, archives and treasury *(some objects may not be on display owing to exhibitions and religious ceremonies)*.
Some 13 000 documents in the archives record its 900 year history and its relations with the Mediterranean rulers: the most precious is the charter (chrysobul) of Emperor Alexis I Comnenos ceding Pátmos to the Blessed Christodoulos.
The nucleus of the library is the donation of books brought from Asia Minor by Christodoulos. The museum's greatest treasures include 33 leaves of St Mark's Gospel, the Codex Purpureus (early 6C), written in silver lettering on purple vellum – the greater part of the manuscript is in the St Petersburg library; the Book of Job (8C) and illuminated evangelistaries (12C to 14C).
The icon collection comprises a rare 11C icon in mosaic of St Nicholas probably from Asia Minor; two 13C works – St James and the warrior saint Theodoros of Tyros; the Pantocrator and the Virgin by the 16C artist Andreas Ritzos; a round icon depicting the Kiss of the Apostles Peter and Paul; a colourful triptych by Giorgos Klotzas (16C); and St John dictating the Apocalypse to his disciple Prochoros (17C).
The treasury dates in the main from the 17C and is made up of donations from priests and patriarchs who were born or who studied in Pátmos: a 17C gold crozier decorated with enamel and precious stones offered by the Patriarch of Constantinople; a cross and medals given by Catherine II of Russia; liturgical vestments with gold and silver embroidery. The cloth squares *(epigonátia)* placed at knee level on the vestment, are used in rotation by the superior on Maundy Thursday each year for the ceremony of the washing of the feet *(niptíras)* which is held in a square in Hóra. Among the votive offerings are delicate sailing ships in silver gilt and enamel set with precious stones.
The church furnishings which were previously in the main church are displayed on the first floor.
The library of St John's Monastery is one of the oldest in the Byzantine world. It contains manuscripts, rare editions and archive documents mostly written in Greek, but also in Latin, Aramaic and several Slavonic languages. To help preserve this priceless heritage, every year since 1988, restorers from the French National Centre for Book Conservation in Arles have been invited to come and work at Pátmos. There is a vast contemporaneous programme of computerisation and microfilming of the collection which enables researchers to do their work at a distance; information technology coming to the aid of our heritage.

Terraces – *Access from the first floor in the museum or from the courtyard.* The lower terrace where stands the Chapel of the Holy Cross provides an interesting bird's-eye view of the main courtyard; the hills to the northeast of Pátmos rise beyond the merlons and crenellations and the pierced belfry with the peaks of Sámos on the horizon. From the upper terraces *(not at present accessible)* there is a panoramic view over the Aegean and the Turkish coast.

★★ HÓRA Pop 748

The white houses of Hóra (the name means principal town), which is officially called Pátmos, form a sparkling necklace around the dark fortress. The houses, which are of different sizes with the oldest probably dating back to the 16C, line a maze of steps and lanes interspersed with few squares. In times of danger storeys were built on top of the covered passageways so as to enjoy the protection of the fortified town; traces of the walls are visible in the town centre. The corbelled houses built by the refugees from Constantinople stand in the Alótina district west of the monastery. In the 17C Cretans settled in Kritiká to the east while in the 17C and the 18C the prosperous families built their mansions on the hillside to the north. High walls screen the courtyards and façades but the neo-Classical doorways decorated with carvings and mouldings, pedimented windows and, more rarely, balconies can be viewed from the street.
The **Simandrís House** ⌚ (formerly Mousoudákis House), near the Convent of the Source of Life (Zoodóhos Pigí), presents an interesting combination of the oriental tradition and the western fashion favoured in the 19C. Other mansions may sometimes be visited on application to the householders.
17C frescoes decorate the church of the **Convent of the Source of Life** (Zoodóhos Pigí) ⌚ (1607) which is surrounded by courts bright with flowers.
The town hall, a fine neo-Classical building, stands in **Lozia Square** *(Platía Lozia)*; from the square – bust of Emmanuel Xanthos *(see above)* – there is a beautiful **view★★** of the Convent of the Apocalypse on the north face of the hill and of Skála harbour.

★★★ **Panorama** – *From Hóra go east to three windmills overlooking the Gríkos road.* The area around the windmills provides admirable views of the island and the archipelago: west, Hóra and the monastery walls; on the hillside, the white cuboid buildings of the School of Pátmos rising above the Convent of the Apocalypse; below,

Skála harbour and Mérika Bay beyond the isthmus; on the horizon *(left to right from Hóra)*, the elongated shape of Ikaría and the islands of Fóurni; north, behind the hills of Pátmos, Kerketéas (1 433m/4 702ft), the tallest peak on Sámos – the island stretches practically to the Turkish coast dominated by Mount Samsum (1 229m/4 040ft); between the mainland and the northeast tip of Pátmos, the islands of Agathoníssi and Arkí; and to the south Lipsí and Léros islands.

★MONASTERY OF THE APOCALYPSE ⏲

Access ⏲ – *15min on foot by a mule track going down from Hóra or up from Skála. There is a request bus-stop near the convent.*

17C chapels and monks' cells line charming courts bedecked with flowers on the way down to St Anne's Chapel which was founded in 1090 and rebuilt in the early 18C. According to a very ancient local tradition it is in this grotto that St John had his vision of the Apocalypse and heard the great voice of God "as of a trumpet" saying "I am Alpha and Omega, the first and the last: and what thou seest, write in a book and send it unto the seven churches which are in Asia". The guide points to the three cracks in the rock vault made by the voice of God, to the place where John laid his head to rest and to the rock which served as a desk.

★SKÁLA Pop 1 442

In the old days there was little more than a collection of vaulted warehouses (now converted into cafés and shops) around the port of Pátmos as workers and merchants retreated to the safety of the upper town. Nowadays Skála is a pleasant port with simple white houses and the principal town on the island always bustling with activity. Along the quay, the Venetian arcaded building with a corner tower houses the harbour master's office, the customs, the police, an information office and the post office. Nearby are the taxi and bus stations, and the local boats which offer excursions to the beaches on Pátmos and neighbouring islands and to Léros, Kálimnos and Kos. The nearest beach is at the northern end of the port, near a red buoy marking a submerged rock; it is said to be the magus Kynops who defied St John and dived to the bottom of the sea and was turned to stone.

In addition to the excursions listed below, one-day trips to many inlets, beaches and valleys as well as monasteries may be undertaken by boat or on foot.

★★**Kastéli Hill** – *20min on foot, west of Skála.* There are traces of a Hellenistic wall and a small chapel on the hill top which offers a magnificent view of Skála harbour, Hóra, St John's Monastery and the neighbouring islands to the north and east *(see details above)*.

★**Gríkou Bay** – *By bus or boat or 45min on foot.* Traonissí Islet rises at the far end of the curving bay. Half way along is Kalíkastrou rock, honeycombed with caves which were probably occupied by hermits before the monastery was founded. *Cafés, tavernas and hotels at Gríkos.*
From Gríkos there are boat trips to the fine sandy beach of Psiliámo *(tavernas)*.

★**Kámbos and Lámbi** – *By boat or by bus to Kámbos and its beach, then about 35min on foot to Lámbi.* **Kámbos** is a large village overlooking a fertile valley with Lefkés Valley to the west. The vast and shady Kámbos **beach** *(sand and pebbles)* is very popular in summer. The windswept **Lámbi** bay *(2km/1mi north)* is famous for its coloured pebbles *(tavernas)*.

For adjacent sights see KÁLIMNOS, SÁMOS.

RÓDOS★★★

RHODES – Dodecanese – Population 98 357 – 1 400km²/540sq mi
Michelin map 980 fold 47

Close to the southwest tip of Asia Minor lies Rhodes, the island of roses. Its flower gardens and gentle climate, its beautiful buildings, its excellent beaches and tourist facilities make it attractive to visitors. Lovers of art and history will delight in evoking its glorious past, rich in souvenirs of antiquity and the Middle Ages.

GEOGRAPHICAL AND HISTORICAL NOTES

The island is long and narrow (77km/48mi x 37km/23mi) with a low straight coastline broken only in the centre. The terrain is mountainous, rising to **Mount Atáviros** (1 215m/3 986ft) and composed of limestone and schist which support a flora of conifers together with semi-tropical shrubs, red hibiscus, mauve bougainvilleas and white scented jasmin, since the average temperature in winter is 13°C/56°F. The coastal plains are devoted to the cultivation of vines, barley, figs and citrus fruits. There are good local wines, in particular *Chevaliers de Rhodes, Lindos* and *Embonas*.

The island of Helios – According to the Greek myths, Rhodes in the guise of the nymph Rhodia was given to **Helios** the sun-god, and his descendants founded the three main towns: Ialyssos (near Filérimos), Líndos and Kámiros.
In the 17C BC these three cities were already trading throughout the Middle East as far as Egypt and founding colonies in the neighbouring islands, on the coast of Asia Minor and even in Italy (Naples, Gela); the people were already engaged in the production of gold jewellery and of ceramics decorated with oriental motifs of plants and animals in stylised form. In the 6C BC the cities were wisely governed by the "tyrants" who achieved a high degree of prosperity. In 408 BC the three cities jointly founded the city of Rhodes which was not slow to supplant them.
During the 3C and the 2C BC, despite disputes with the Macedonians and the Romans, the island became the main maritime power in the eastern Mediterranean owing to its fleet and its wealth. The arts flourished, particularly a school of sculpture which became famous and exported its work far afield; eg the *Colossos of Rhodes* by Chares of Lindos (265 BC), the *Aphrodite of Rhodes*, the *Victory of Samothrace*, a masterpiece attributed to Pythekritos, and the *Laocoon* in the Vatican.

From the Cross of St John to the Cross of Savoy – The arrival in 1306 of Foulques de Villaret and his Knights of St John of Jerusalem *(see below)* brought a period of unrest which lasted until 1522. The island was the advance bastion of Christianity against the Turks and the Knights engaged in extensive building works: walls, the town and port of Rhodes, fortresses at Filérimos, Líndos, Arhángelos and Monólithos, forts to repel pirate attacks, monasteries and churches. The Provençal Gothic style was used; thus in Rhodes Town the Palace of the Grand Master recalls the Papal Palace in Avignon, St John's Church is similar to the Church of Notre Dame-des-Doms in Avignon and the gates in the ramparts are like those in Villeneuve-lès-Avignon.
The Turks *(see below)* left few traces apart from some mosques and fountains but it was during their occupation that the famous **Rhodes faience**, with its brilliant enamels, was commercialised; this consists of plates and flagons decorated with stylised oriental motifs which some historians think have been produced in Líndos since the time of the Knights of St John while others maintain that they come from Nicaea (Isnik) in Asia Minor.
In 1911 the Italians annexed Rhodes, then under Turkish rule, and in 1912 they occupied the island and the Dodecanese to protect the route to their African colonies. They attempted to impose the use of Italian and they encouraged tourism, improved the roads, constructed public buildings and hotels and restored, sometimes insensitively, the ancient monuments. Rhodes was occupied by the Germans from 1943 to 1945, then came under British rule and eventually became part of the Greek state on 7 March 1948.

OUT AND ABOUT ON RHODES

Touring – A week is time enough in which to visit the island; there are no hotels in the south but there is a road all the way round the island. It is possible to make several tours from Rhodes Town. There is little traffic but scarcely any petrol stations off the main roads. The secondary roads are sometimes in poor condition.

Transport – Frequent buses to environs of Rhodes Town and to Líndos, less frequent services to the south of the island. Car, bicycle and motorcycle hire services. Taxis. Excursions by boat in season (in particular to Líndos and Sími).

★★RÓDOS (RHODES TOWN) – Pop 42 400

This is a resort of international repute, as popular in winter as it is in summer; particularly with the Scandinavians and the Germans. The former city of the Knights of St John of Jerusalem is situated at the northeastern end of the island, facing the Turkish coast across its double harbour. There are a few ancient remains but more important is the superb medieval "City" restored by Italian architects early this century and a lively modern town, bright with flowers and tourist attractions: beaches, hotels, touring agencies, nightclubs and countless boutiques.

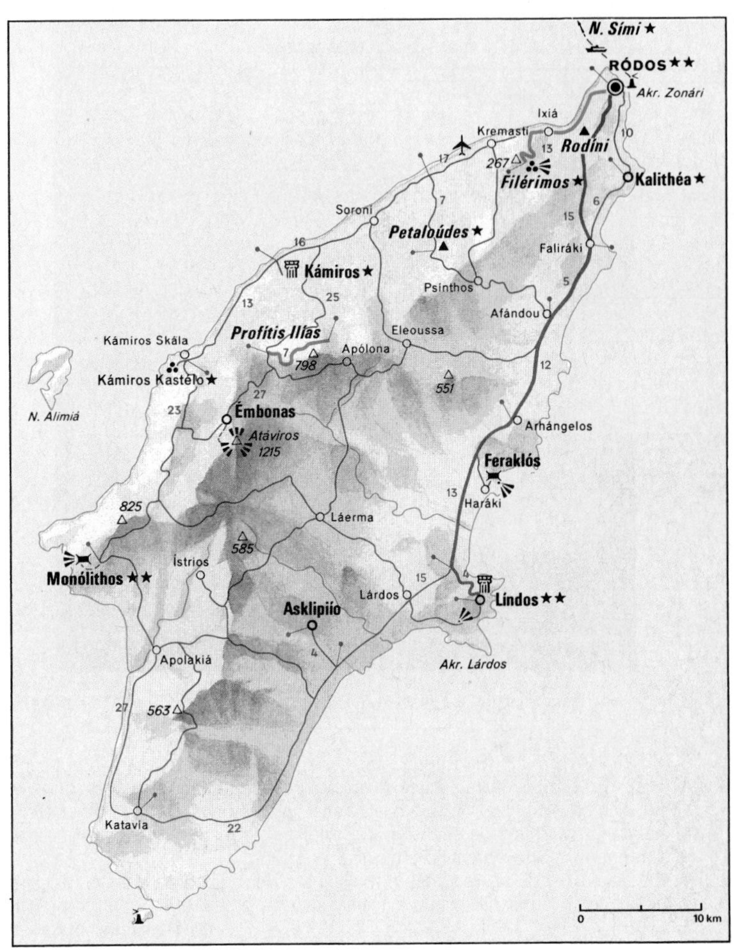

Knights of Rhodes – Founded in the 11C to protect pilgrims in the Holy Land, the order of the Hospitallers of St John of Jerusalem, was both a religious and a military body maintaining a church and a hospital in Jerusalem as well as a mighty stronghold at Acre.

After the capture of Acre by the Turks in 1291, the Knights of St John had to leave the Holy Land; they moved first to Cyprus then to Rhodes, a Genoese possession, which became their main base in their struggle against the Turks in the eastern Mediterranean.

The knights were divided into seven nations according to their **languages** – France, Provence, Auvergne, Aragon, Castille, Italy and England – each nation having its own **inn** to live in and being governed by a bailiff. The whole order, in which the French were the majority, was ruled by the Grand Master; French and Latin were the official languages. The knights took vows of poverty and chastity and were assisted by squires.

When the Knights Templar were suppressed in 1312 and their possessions and duties passed to the Hospitallers, the latter built a fleet which took part in the papal crusades. In 1331 in particular the Hospitallers signed a treaty with the French, the Italians and the Byzantine emperor against the Turks; then at the end of the 14C they joined in the naval campaign conducted by Marshal Boucicaut.

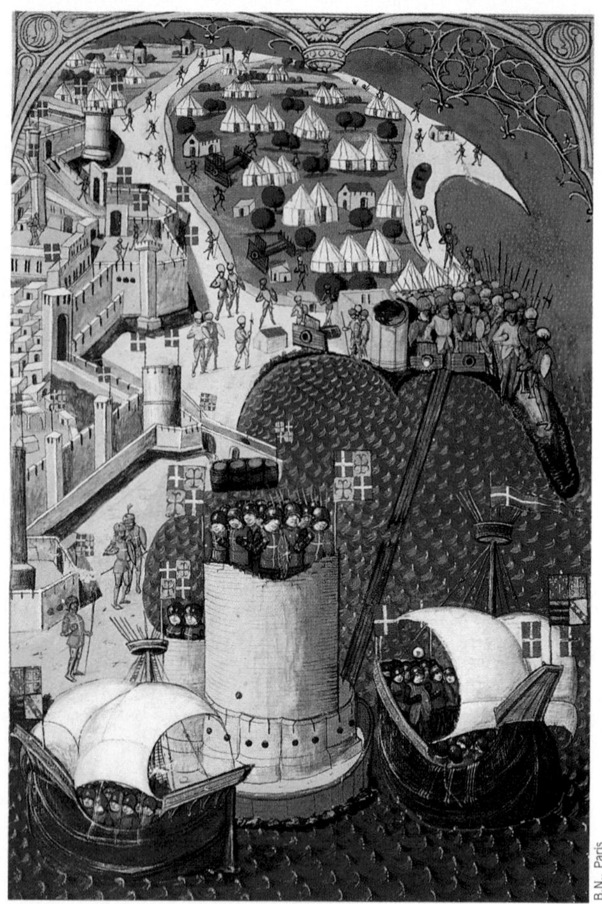

Siege of Rhodes (1480)

In 1444 and again in 1480 Rhodes was besieged by the Turks but without success. In 1482 the Grand Master, **Pierre d'Aubusson** received **Prince Djem** with great ceremony. Djem was the son of Mahomet II and unhappy rival of his brother Bayazid; he was sent to Bourganeuf, the grand priory in France of the Auvergne nation, but later removed to Italy where he died in 1495.

A third siege in 1522 proved fatal to the knights. For a good six months 650 knights and about 1 000 auxiliaries held out against an army of 100 000 Turks led by **Suleiman the Magnificent** but, despite the efforts of Pope Hadrian VI to come to their aid, the knights were obliged to surrender, betrayed by a defector. On 1 January 1523, the Grand Master, **Villiers de l'Isle-Adam** (1464-1534) and the 180 knights who had survived left Rhodes for Malta, where they eventually arrived after many peregrinations in 1530.

Specialities – Jewellery, silverware, ceramics and furs.

Entertainments – Son et Lumière in the gardens near the Palace every evening; traditional dances in the Old Town in summer every evening *(sign)*; Wine Festival in Rodíni Park during the summer season; musical entertainment in Mandráki in the evening.

★★★THE CITY

Tour 2hr 30min; plan see below; it is also worth visiting at night.

★★**Collachium (Fortress)** – The knights and their attendants lived in this part of the city which was fortified on all four sides and called Collachium; the internal wall, which no longer exists, ran parallel with Odós Sokrátous.

Enter the fortress by the Amboise Gate.

Píli Amboise (Amboise Gate) – An arched bridge over a moat approached the gate which bears the arms of the Order and those of the Grand Master, **Aimeri d'Amboise**, who caused it to be built in 1512. A vaulted entrance in the thickness of the outer wall and a narrow passage leads into the lists and thence to St Antony's Gate which opens into the Palace Square, the former outer court of the Palace; on the right once stood **St John's Chapel**, belonging to the Order, where the knights were buried and where the hand of John the Baptist, given to Pierre d'Aubusson by Sultan Bayazid, was kept for veneration.

St John's Lodge, which has ogival vaulting and was reconstructed by the Italians, was both a meeting place and a grand entrance to the Palace.

★**Paláti Megálon Magístron (Palace of the Grand Masters)** ⓥ – The Grand Masters' residence, which was built in the 14C in the northwest corner of the ramparts, more nearly resembles a fortress than a palace. In fact it acted as a supplementary line of defence since it was protected by a moat, crenelated walls and towers, a keep and three underground floors of storerooms to hold victuals and munitions. It was converted into a prison by the Turks, severely damaged by the explosion of a munition store in 1856 and restored by the Italians.
The palace is built round a central court surrounded by arcades paved with marble. The staterooms *(first floor)*, which are furnished in the Italian manner, contain a series of Hellenistic and Roman mosaics from neighbouring islands: note the Lion Hunt. The room containing a double row of columns was the chapter-house of the Order.

PICTOR

Palace of the Grand Masters, Rhodes

★★**Odós Ipotón** (Knights' Street – This is a medieval cobbled street lined by the **Inns**, 15C and 16C Gothic buildings in which the knights lived according to their native language .
The Provençal Inn *(left)* is linked by an arch to the Spanish Inn. Further down on the same side are the Chaplain's House and the chapel of the French nation (14C) with a recess containing a statue of the Virgin and Child.
Next comes the façade of the **French Inn**, the largest and most beautiful of all the inns, where Prince Djem stayed in 1482; above the tierce-point doorway is an inscription to Aimeri d'Amboise, Grand Master from 1505 to 1512.
The **Italian Inn** further down on the left bears the arms of the Italian Fabrizio del Carretto who was Grand Master from 1513 to 1521.
Knights' Street ends in Hospital Square which is flanked by St Mary's Church *(left)*, the English Inn *(east side)* and the Hospital *(right)*.

Panagía Kástrou – St Mary's Church was built in the 12C on the Greek cross plan and transformed into a Latin cathedral in the Gothic style by the Knights who fortified the east-end incorporating it into the ramparts. Subsequently the Turks turned it into a mosque. The plane tree *(right)* was used by the Turks as a gibbet.

Katálima Anglías – The **English Inn** was built in 1483 but later demolished; it was rebuilt in 1919 and bears the coat of arms of England.

★ **Nossokomío Ipotón** (and Archeological Museum) ⏱ – The impressive **Knights' Hospital** was begun in 1440 and completed under Pierre d'Aubusson, Grand Master from 1478 to 1505. Above the Gothic arch of the doorway rises the east end of the chapel bearing the arms of Jean de Lastic, Grand Master from 1437 to 1454, who bequeathed 10 000 florins to the building. Beyond the door a vaulted passageway leads into an inner court surrounded by a gallery supported on arcades; there were shops on the ground floor and rooms with fireplaces above.

The hospital proper, which was administered by a bailiff from the French nation, was reached by a staircase to the upper floor. The **Great Ward of the Sick** was divided in two and contained 32 communal beds which could accommodate about 100 sick men; the doors and ceiling are of cedar wood. Some of the knights' funerary plaques, formerly in St John's Church, are displayed here. Note the chapel entrance which is delicately carved with festoons and the alcoves where those with contagious diseases were isolated.

Next door is the former refectory communicating with the kitchens.

The building houses the **Archeological Museum** (Arheologikó Moussío) ⏱ , which contains some remarkable ancient sculpture: a 6C BC *kouros* from Kámiros; the funeral stele of Timarista to whom her daughter Krito is saying farewell (5C BC) found at Kámiros; effigy of Dionysos with a beard, Hellenistic work (2C BC); the **Aphrodite of Rhodes**, 1C BC masterpiece in the form of a small statue of the goddess rising from the waves and smoothing her hair; two small statues of Asklepios and his daughter Hygieia; a bust of the Greek poet Menander (3C BC).

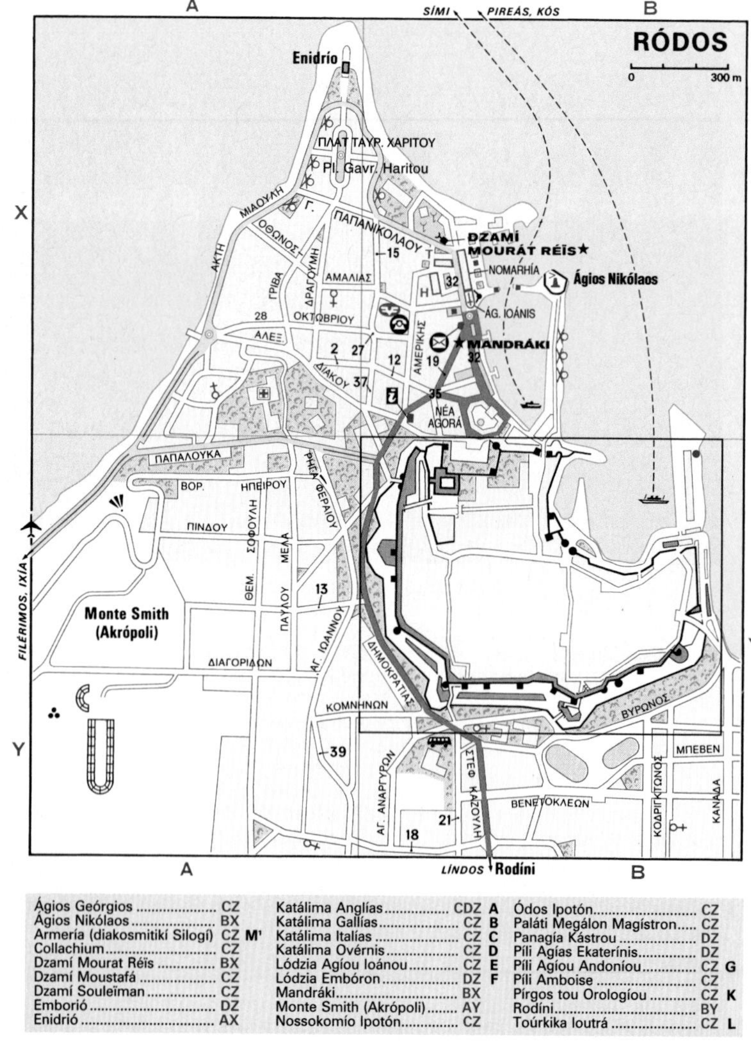

Katálima Ovérnis – Leave Hospital Square by the northwest corner, passing in front of St Mary's Church to reach Platía Alexándrou, a small square containing the **Auvergne Inn** (14C); above the Gothic doorway is an inscription dating from 1513 which mentions **Guy de Blanchefort**, nephew of Pierre d'Aubusson who was assigned to Djem while he was in Rhodes and later in Bourganeuf in France.

Pass under the arch into another square; the fountain at the centre has been created out of Byzantine baptismal fonts; on the right *(east side)* is the façade of the Auvergne Inn with an outside stair and loggia; on the left *(west side)* the former arsenal.

Arméria (Arsenal) – The main building (14C) was used as the infirmary before the construction of the Great Hospital and is adorned with the allusive arms of Roger de Pinsot, Grand Master from 1355 to 1365. One wing contains the **Museum of Decorative Arts** (Diakosmitikí Silogí) ⌚: furniture, costume and a beautiful collection of Rhodian ceramics.

Continue north to the ruins of a temple to Aphrodite and then turn right *(east)* through the Arsenal Gate (Píli Navarhíou) on to the harbour quay.

★ **Embório** (Harbour) – Now known as the Commercial Harbour, it has always been a safe anchorage. In the days of the Hospitallers the entrance was closed by an enormous chain strung between the square Naillac Tower (Pírgos Naillac), the base of which is extant, and the Mill Tower (Pírgos Mílon) named after a row of mills on the east jetty.

From the waterfront on the seaward side of the Arsenal Gate there is a fine perspective *(south)* of the ramparts with the minarets of the Turkish district in the background, and the Marine Gate in the centre.

★ **Píli Agías Ekaterínis** – The impressive **St Catherine's** (or **Marine**) **Gate** with its four machicolated towers was placed under the protection of the Virgin and Child flanked by St Peter and John the Baptist who appear on a low relief *(damaged)*; the fleur-de-Lys (the Lily of France) appears between the arms of the Order and those of Pierre d'Aubusson who caused the gate to be built in 1478.

Re-enter the town by the Marine Gate.

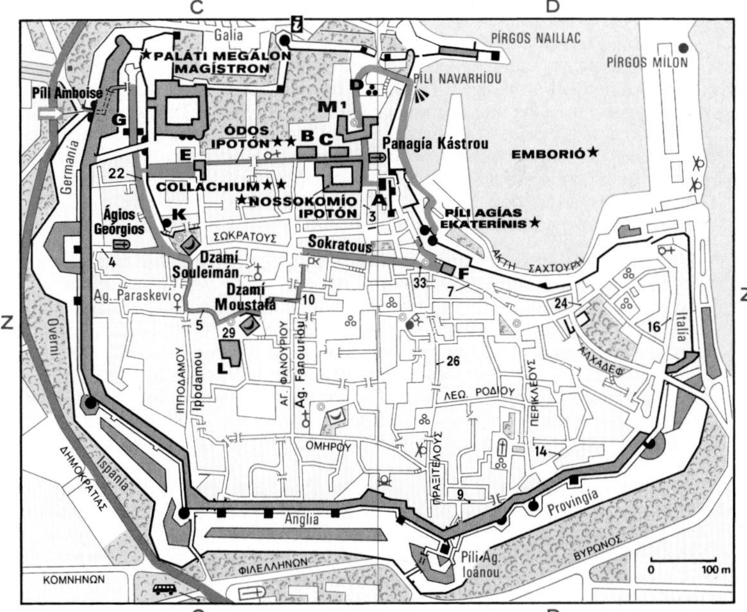

Amohostou	ΑΜΜΟΧΩΣΤΟΥ	AX 2
Apelou	ΑΠΕΛΛΟΥ	CZ 3
Apolonion	ΑΠΟΛΛΩΝΙΩΝ	CS 4
Arhelaou	ΑΡΧΕΛΑΟΥ	CZ 5
Aristotelous	ΑΡΙΣΤΟΤΕΛΟΥΣ	DZ 7
Efthimiou	ΕΥΘΥΜΙΟΥ	DZ 9
Ergiou	ΕΡΓΙΟΥ	CZ 10
G. Lambraki	Γ. ΛΑΜΠΡΑΚΗ	BX 12
Himaras	ΧΕΙΜΑΡΡΑΣ	AY 13
Ipotón	ΙΠΠΟΤΩΝ	CZ
Irinis	ΕΙΡΗΝΗΣ	DZ 14
Iroon Politehniou	ΗΡΩΩΝ ΠΟΛΥΤΕΧΝΕΙΟΥ	BX 15
Kisthiniou	ΚΙΣΘΙΝΙΟΥ	DZ 16
Kons Paleologou.	ΚΟΝΣ. ΠΑΛΑΙΟΛΟΓΟΥ	BY 18
Makariou	ΜΑΚΑΡΙΟΥ	BX 19
Meg. Konstandinou	ΜΕΓ. ΚΩΝΣΤΑΝΤΙΝΟΥ	BY 21
Orfeos	ΟΡΦΕΩΣ	CZ 22
Pindarou	ΠΙΝΔΑΡΟΥ	DZ 24
Pithagora	ΠΥΘΑΓΟΡΑ	DZ 26
Pl. Akadimias	ΠΛΑΤ. ΑΚΑΔΗΜΙΑΣ	BX 27
Pl. Arionos	ΠΛΑΤ. ΑΡΙΟΝΟΣ	CZ 29
Pl. Eleftherias	ΠΛΑΤ. /ΕΛΕΥΘΕΡΙΑΣ	BX 32
Pl. Ipokratous	ΠΛΑΤ. ΙΠΠΟΚΡΑΤΟΥΣ	DZ 33
Pl. Kiprou	ΠΛΑΤ. /ΚΥΠΡΟΥ	BX 35
Sof. Venizelou	ΣΟΦ. ΒΕΝΙΖΕΛΟΥ	BX 37
Sokratous	ΣΩΚΡΑΤΟΥΣ	CDZ
Vas. Irakliou	ΒΑΣ. ΗΡΑΚΛΕΙΟΥ	AY 39

★**Town** – Bear left through the gate into **Platía Ipokrátous** with its Turkish fountain; on the far side stands the Merchants' Loggia; behind it *(southeast)* lay the Jewish district.

Lódzia Embóron (Merchants' Loggia) – Early 16C building with an outside stairway; the ground floor was a meeting place while the upper floor was used as a court-room for hearing trade disputes. The building was initiated by Pierre d'Aubusson and completed by Aimeri d'Amboise whose arms appear on the façade and on the lintel respectively.

Turn west along Odós Sokrátous which marks the northern limit of the Turkish district.

★**Turkish district** – Busy and thriving, **Odós Sokrátous** was the main street of the Bazaar. On reaching the former Aga Mosque turn left into Odós Fanouríou, one of the oldest and most picturesque streets in the town; take the second turning on the right which leads to Platía Aríonos to see the 18C **Mustapha Mosque** (Dzamí Moustafá) and the **Turkish Baths**, which have recently been restored, a luxurious establishment dating from the time of Suleiman the Magnificent (16C).
Take Odós Arheláou and Odós Ipodámou *(northwest)* past the 15C Church of Agía Paraskeví *(left)* to reach the **Suleiman Mosque** (Dzamí Souleimán) ⓥ which was formerly the Church of the Holy Apostles and has an elegant Italian Renaissance doorway.
Turn off into Odós Apoloníon to visit **St George's Church** (Ágios Geórgios) *(no 18)*, a picturesque little 15C building, designed on a circular plan and reinforced with huge flying buttresses.
Return along Odós Apoloníon and turn left into Odós Orféos passing beneath the **Clock Tower** or belfry to return to St Anthony's Gate and Amboise Gate.

ADDITIONAL SIGHTS

★★**West and South Ramparts** ⓥ – The walls (4km/2.5mi long) already existed when the Knights arrived but they rebuilt them almost entirely and continued to strengthen them, particularly under Pierre d'Aubusson, Aimeri d'Amboise and Villiers de l'Isle-Adam. The moat was over 20m/66ft deep in places and the walls up to 5.30m/17ft thick. Large platforms were built at the base of the towers to assist in firing the cannon. The walls were divided into sections, called **boulevards**; each nation was responsible for the defence of a section.
The rampart walk runs anti-clockwise from the Amboise Gate to St John's Gate (Píli Ágiou Ioánou or Kóskinou), giving a fine view of the bastions jutting into the flower-bedecked moat and of the forest of minarets in the Turkish town. It covers four boulevards assigned respectively to Germany (Germanía), the Auvergne (Ovérni), Spain (Ispanía) and England (Anglía); the next two boulevards running east to the shore were assigned to Provence (Provingía) and Italy (Italía).
Return clockwise skirting the glacis to the Amboise Gate and beyond to the seventh boulevard, assigned to France (Galía), for a different view of the fortifications.

★**Mandráki** – Mandráki, meaning a small enclosure, is the name given to a well-protected harbour. This little harbour in Rhodes, which was in use in antiquity, is now devoted to pleasure craft and excursion boats to Líndos and Syme.
On either side of the entrance the Italians erected a column supporting two bronze deer (a buck and a doe), the symbolic animals of Rhodes. According to tradition this was originally the site of the **Colossus of Rhodes**, a bronze statue of the sun-god Helios (30m/98ft high); it was numbered among the Seven Wonders of the Ancient World and was thought to stand beside or astride the harbour entrance; it was brought down in an earthquake in 226 BC and the pieces were later put up for sale.
The east mole, which has three windmills on it, ends in **St Nicholas' Tower** (Ágios Nikólaos), a strong outer defence-work built in 1464 by Grand Master Zacosta; it was placed under the protection of St Nicholas of Bari, the patron saint of navigators, and commanded the sea approach to Rhodes. Views of the harbour and the town; *musical entertainment in the evenings.*
The northern part of the town west of Mandráki was built during the Italian period from 1912 to 1943. Liberty Square (Platía Eleftherías), a lively stretch of waterfront with pleasant gardens, is closed at the southern end by the unusual New Market (Néa Agorá), built round a central courtyard, and on the north by St John's Church (Ágios Ioánis) which was rebuilt in the Gothic style on the model of the original which stood by the Grand Masters' Palace *(see above)*. Platía Vassilíou Georgíou B, the administrative centre, is bordered by monumental buildings in the oriental Gothic style; the regional administrative offices *(Nomarhía)*, former seat of the Italian Governor, the town hall *(Dimarhío)* and the theatre.
Further north, the charming **Murad Reis Mosque**★ (Dzamí Mourát Réïs), which is named after one of Suleiman's admirals, stands in a grove of eucalyptus trees surrounded by the typical tomb stones of a Muslim cemetery; the graves of the men are distinguished by a turban, those of the women by a sort of pineapple.

Enidrío (Aquarium) ⌚ – Mediterranean marine creatures – turtles, groupers, lampreys and octopi – are presented in a reconstruction of their natural habitat.

Rodíni Park – *2km/1.25mi southeast, on the right of the road to Líndos.* Attractive physic garden, green and fresh, supplemented by a small zoo. The **Wine Festival** is held here from July to September; free wine tasting.

Akrópoli (Mount Smith) – *4km/2.5mi or 1hr 30min on foot there and back; no 5 bus from the New Market.* Several elements of the ancient city, which was founded in the 5C BC, still exist, more or less reconstructed by the Italians: the theatre (2C BC) – only the lower terrace is authentic, the stadium (2C BC) and the temple to Pythian Apollo indicated by three columns.
St Stephen's Mount is now called Mount Smith after Admiral Sir Sidney Smith of the British Navy who lived in Rhodes early in the 19C; from the top there are superb **views★★**, particularly at sunset, of the shoreline, Syme Island and the Turkish coast.

EXCURSIONS

★**Kalithéa Spa** – *East coast: 15km/9mi.* The waters which were known to the ancients and recommended by Hippocrates, are effective in the treatment of ailments of the liver and gall bladder. In 1929 the Italians built a little spa with white pavilions in the oriental style pleasantly set among the pine and palm trees but it is no longer in use. There is a charming sandy beach in a rocky inlet.

Feraklós Castle – *East coast: 37km/23mi.* Drive through the hamlet of Heráki *(taverna)* and park the car at the foot of the hill; fairly stiff climb *(45min on foot there and back)*. Only a few ruined walls now remain of what was one of the largest castles ever built by the Knights of St John but there is a very fine **view★★** of the bays on either side of the promontory; the fortress at Líndos is visible to the south.

★★**Líndos** – *East coast: 50km/31mi.* The blue sea, the white houses of the old town and the forbidding walls of the medieval fortress crowning a rise combine to make Líndos a spectacular **site★★★** where three civilisations – ancient, Byzantine and medieval Greek – have left their mark; there is a fine view of the Great Port facing north at the foot of the hill.
Líndos is a simple resort with an attractive beach in one of the sheltered bays which lie on either side of the isthmus containing the Great Port and St Paul's Port. Specialities: hand-woven cloth, ceramics. The coast nearby was used in the film *The Guns of Navarone.*

On arriving park the car in the upper car park on the right.

A maritime and religious stronghold – With its two natural harbours and its easily-defended hill, Líndos has been inhabited since the Prehistoric Era and by the 10C BC a temple to Athena had been built on the hilltop. It was in the 7C BC that colonists set out from Líndos and founded Gela in Sicily and Parthenope (now Naples) in Italy.
In the 6C BC Líndos was ruled by **Cleóbulos**, one of the many benevolent dictators in Greece. He was one of the Seven Sages of Greece and was reputed to express himself in riddles.
The cult of the gods was succeeded by Christianity. Tradition has it that St Paul landed in St Paul's Port at the end of his third missionary journey. After the Byzantines and the Genoese came the Knights Hospitaller who turned Líndos into an imposing fortress, defended by 12 Knights and a Greek garrison. When the Grand Master, **Foulques de Villaret**, was deposed in 1317 for misconduct, he took refuge in Líndos; later he was obliged to go to Avignon and defend himself before John XXII, a native of Cahors in France.

★★**Acropolis and citadel** ⌚ – *Access by a path and steps (1hr on foot or by donkey there and back).* The hilltop (116m/381ft above sea level) bears extensive traces of ancient and medieval monuments.
At the foot of the escarpment inside the first gate, there is an *exedra* (a seat in a rounded recess) hollowed out of the rock on the left and a ship's prow which bore a statue of Agesandros, the priest of Poseidon. This statue was the work of the Rhodian sculptor, Pythekritos; the *Victory of Samothrace* *(see SAMOTHRÁKI)*, which occupied a similar position, is also attributed to him.
The present **fortress** was begun under Grand Master Fulvian (1421-37) and completed under Pierre d'Aubusson (1476-1503). A long flight of steps, skirting the Governor's palace on the left, leads up to the entrance tower crowned by a bartizan. A vaulted passage emerges on the right of the old Gothic Governor's palace near to St John's Chapel consisting of three apses, a nave and two aisles marked off by the bases of pillars.

Take a second vaulted passage under the Governor's palace on the left which emerges below the acropolis.

Líndos

Early this century the site of the **acropolis** was excavated by Danish archeologists and then restored by Italians. About 20 columns mark the position of the great Doric portico *(stoa)* which was preceded by a great staircase leading up to the sanctuary entrance *(propylaia)*.
The very ancient **sanctuary to Athena Lindia**, which Pindar mentioned in one of his *Odes*, was specially venerated in antiquity because of the miracles which took place there; the temple, which housed a statue of the goddess in gold and ivory, was built above a cave inhabited by a seer of which the entrance was in the cliff face below. The traces which remain date from the 4C BC and consist of the foundations, some Doric columns and the walls of the *naós* which have been re-erected and the bases of votive statues, one of which was presented by Alexander the Great.
From the hilltop there are splendid **views★★★** of the headland and the coast; on the north side are the Great Port and Líndos beach; to the south the inlet named after St Paul who was supposed to have landed there.

★**Town** – It is pleasant to stroll through the narrow streets of the town past the white terraced houses; the most beautiful, built for the rich shipowners or sea captains in the 16C and the 17C, have pointed arches and are decorated with low reliefs of roses, plants, birds and tracery in a composite style showing both Gothic and oriental influences. Some of the internal courtyards have a black and white pebble pattern; the interiors are decorated with "Rhodes faience".
In the 19C fine houses were built in the neo-Classical style. The **Church of the Virgin** (Panagía) in the town centre, which is dated 1489-90 and bears the arms of Pierre d'Aubusson, is in fact older; the Knights restored it and added the western narthex; inside the church are a 17C iconostasis and an 18C fresco.

★**View of Líndos** – *2km/1.25mi by car return.* From the upper car park drive up a narrow unsurfaced road to a rocky peak which offers an unusual view down into St Paul's Bay *(right)*; straight ahead is the fortress dominating the ancient theatre, its terraced seating hewn out of the rock.

Asklipiío – *East coast; 65km/40mi.* Interesting village owing to its site, its old houses and its fortress. The **Church of the Dormition of the Virgin** ⓥ, which dates from the Byzantine period (1060), is decorated with fine frescoes.

★**Mount Filérimos** (267m/876ft) – *West coast; 13km/8mi by the road to Ixiá turning left in Triánda, a modern village.*
The ancient city of **Iálissos** ⓥ stood on a very fine site overlooking the coastal plain. The city was probably founded by the Phoenicians and then occupied by the Dorians and the Achaians. In the Middle Ages the Genoese laid siege to the Byzantines and were besieged in their turn by the Knights of St John; during the siege of Rhodes in 1522 Suleiman set up his headquarters on the site.

Beneath the pines and cypresses on the acropolis are the foundations of a 4C BC temple and a paleo-Christian basilica incorporating an old baptistry. The Gothic monastery, which was built by the Knights and restored by the Italians, has a quadruple church: for the Roman Catholics and the Orthodox, the Knights and relics; a miraculous image of the Virgin was kept in the church.
There is a vast **panorama★★** of the northern end of the island to be seen from the top of the Knights' fortress on the edge of the headland. St George's Chapel *(on the right on returning to the exit)*, partially underground, is decorated with 14C and 15C Gothic murals representing scenes from the New Testament and the Knights with their patron saints.
On the southern slope of the hill there stands a monumental ancient Doric fountain *(not accessible at present)*.

★Petaloúdes (Butterfly Valley) ⌚ – *West coast; 24km/15mi. Entrance signed. Restaurants.* From June to September this shady rock-strewn valley is filled with myriads of orange and black butterflies attracted by the scent emanating from the leaves of a sort of maple tree. A path climbs up the valley and is carried on wooden bridges over the narrow stream which tumbles in cascades and waterfalls. It is necessary to get quite close to the rocks and bushes where the butterflies are resting to admire their bright colours. Visitors are requested not to disturb them.

★Kámiros – *West coast; 33km/20.5mi.* In antiquity, Kámiros was one of the three great cities of Rhodes which occupied a beautiful site on a hill set back from the seashore at the heart of a fertile region covered with fig and olive groves. It was founded, so says the legend, by Althaimenes, Minos' grandson, destroyed by an earthquake in the 2C BC and rediscovered in 1859; it has been excavated by French (1863-64) and Italian archeologists.

Ruins ⌚ – Excavations have brought to light traces of Hellenistic and Roman buildings which occur in the following sequence up the hillside:
– a 3C BC sanctuary consisting of a Doric temple, approached by a flight of steps; the bases of the columns remain and one column which has been re-erected; lower down there is a semicircular seat *(exedra)*, and an area for sacrificial altars;
– an area of Hellenistic houses, several with peristyles (columns re-erected);
– an *agorá* lined by a long 3C AD portico *(stoá)* built over a 5C-6C BC cistern which was reached by two flights of steps and supplied the houses below it with water;
– a temple dedicated to Athena Kamíria dating from the 5C BC.
Near to Kámiros Skála *(13km/8mi southwest)* on a spur facing the sea are traces of **Kámiros Castle★** *(access by a poor road: 1.2km/0.75mi plus 15min on foot)* contemporary with the Knights Hospitaller; the arms of two Grand Masters – Aimeri d'Amboise and Fabrizio del Carretto – are sculpted on the outside; within is a chapel.

Profítis Ilías (Mount Elijah) (798m/2 618ft) – *West coast; 49km/30.5mi.* The mountain rises from wooded hills where herds of deer roam. A small summer resort has been built on the upper slopes among the pines and cedars and cypresses providing a peaceful cool retreat in hot and sultry weather. Beautiful views of the neighbouring peaks and along the west coast.

Émbonas – *West coast; 62km/39mi.* Émbonas, which is surrounded by famous vineyards, has kept its old-fashioned ways and women in local dress can still be seen spinning, or wearing leather boots to protect them from snakes while working in the fields. In some houses the walls are hung with **Rhodes faience**.
In Émbonas it is possible to arrange to climb **Mount Atáviros** (1 215m/3 986ft) with a guide *(6hr on foot there and back)*; from the top where a sanctuary to Zeus once stood there is a fine view.

★★Monólithos Castle – *West coast; 70km/44mi. Access by a narrow turning north of Monólithos village; sign "Froúrion".*
The Knights of Rhodes built Monólithos Castle on a spectacular **site★★** at the top of a rocky escarpment some 200m/656ft above the wild and jagged coastline. A path leads up to the fortress which contains two cisterns and a chapel; the **view** extends across the sea to Hálki Island.
For adjacent sights see KÁLIMNOS, KÁRPATHOS, NÍSSIROS, SÍMI.

*Nature lovers:
help keep rivers and streams clean,
protect the forest and mountain environment.
Leave nothing behind.*

OTHER ISLANDS

Michelin map 980 fold 46

Even if the other islands in the **Dodecanese** are less interesting from a historical or archeological point of view, they have just as much to offer where a calm and restful holiday is required or as excursions from the three islands already described. The most notable monuments on the largest of them are described below.

ACCESS

Kálimnos – Local boat services daily from Kos Town. Regular ferry service at 4pm (time: 1 hr). Hotels and rooms in private houses on Kálimnos.

Níssiros – In season boat service in the morning from Kardámena, return late afternoon. 2 hotels and rooms in private houses in Mandráki.

Sími Ferry – Operates in season, daily, departing at 9am and returning at 6pm; return trip possible same day. Some small hotels and rooms in private houses on Syme. Lodgings at the Panormitis monastery.

★**Kálimnos** ⌚ – 93km²/35sq mi. Pop 15 706. *Day excursions (3hr there and back) from Kos Town.* For centuries fishing and the sponge trade have been the mainstay of the islanders. The fishermen's departure in the spring for the North African coast and in particular their return in the autumn are marked by great festivities. The approach by boat to the bustling capital, **Póthia**, also called Kálimnos (pop 10 543), is impressive. Tall, pastel-coloured houses in the neo-Classical style lining the quays and rising up the hillside attest to an elegant lifestyle.

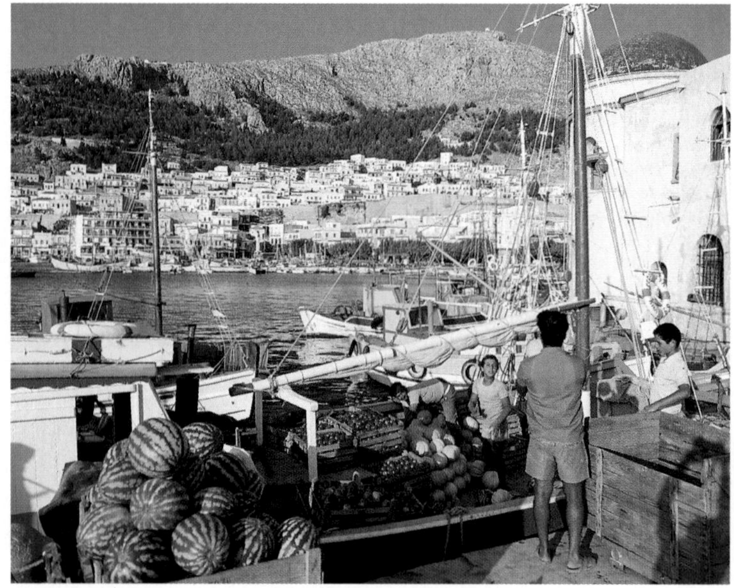

S. Tselentis /ON LOCATION

Póthia harbour, Kálimnos

A small **Archeological Museum** southeast of the town contains the remains of a temple to Apollo and finds from the island's caves. A hilltop to the northeast is crowned by three windmills dominated by the walls of a castle built by the Knights of the Order of St John of Rhodes.

Hório (2km/1mi further) is the old capital which was abandoned for Póthia in about 1840; above the town rise the ruins of a fortress where the islanders took refuge at the time of pirate raids. The island is hilly and barren except for the fertile valleys of Póthia and **Váthis** *(east)* where the orange groves and vineyards provide cool oases.

★**Níssiros** ⌚ – 37km²/14sq mi. Pop 984. *In summer day excursions by boat from Kardámena (Kos). Wear closed shoes for the excursion to the volcano.* The boat docks at **Mandráki**; the white houses are dominated by an ancient wall and a medieval castle of the Knights of St John which houses the monastery of the Panagía Spilianí and its underground church.

There is a **museum** of popular traditions in Mandráki.

The excursion bus passes through the coastal villages of Loutrá and Páli (its hot springs are sought after as a cure for arthritis and rheumatism), and reaches the central Láki plateau (4km/2.5mi long); at the edge is the vast **Stéfanos crater** formed in 1522 by a volcanic explosion. Walk down to the bottom of the crater where rise plumes of sulphureous smoke. *Refreshments near the bus stop.*

★**Sími (Syme)** ⌚ – 53km²/20sq mi. Pop 2 273. *Daily boat service from Mandráki harbour, Rhodes; all-day excursions.*
The island is barren and the inhabitants earn their living by fishing or gathering sponges. The main town has quite an air with its attractive neo-Classical houses with tiled roofs and pediments. The boats put in on the southwest coast below the 18C Panormítis Monastery *(rooms to let).*

For adjacent sights see KOS, PÁTMOS, RÓDOS.

North Aegean Islands

HÍOS★

CHIOS – Aegean Islands – Population 51 060 – 842km²/325sq mi
Michelin map 980 fold 33

The island of Chios, which lies a mere 8km/5mi off the Turkish coast, is less verdant than its neighbours, Lesbos and Sámos. The island is dominated to the north by mountains of volcanic origin – the highest point is Mount Pelinéo (1 297m/4 255 ft); the hillsides and coastal plains, which are well watered by winter rainfall, are given over to the cultivation of citrus fruit, mulberries, vines, cotton, tobacco, fruit and vegetables. In the south the Chiots traditionally grow the lentisk or **mastic** tree; its aromatic mastic or resin is used in the production of alcoholic drinks *(mastíka, rakí)*, in chewing gum and in oriental cakes, syrups and preserves.

Besides its fine beaches Chios has many attractions for visitors interested in history, Byzantine art and local traditions.

G. Grigoriou /FOTOGRAM-STONE

Rocky coast and beach, Chios

Mediterranean maritime trading centre – Chios lies on the shipping routes to Thessaloníki and Constantinople, Smyrna, Crete, Rhodes and Cyprus, the ports of the Levant and Egypt. From antiquity to the 19C the island has played a major role in the exchanges between east and west.

From the 8C BC Chios belonged to the Ionic Confederacy together with Sámos and Greek towns of Asia Minor, and it enjoyed its first cultural and economic heyday in the 6C. It was the first Greek city to engage in the slave trade. The Chios museum has few artefacts from this era but a very fine *kore* is exhibited in the Acropolis Museum in Athens. Persian invasion in 493 BC brought an end to the island's prosperity and it was then ruled more or less successfully by Athens, Macedonia and Rome. In the latter period although the island was pillaged by Verres *(see SÁMOS)* it regained a degree of prosperity.

Chios suffered centuries of neglect as pirate activity increased in the Aegean but it resumed its pivotal role after the island was included in the Christian sphere of influence which lasted four centuries. It became Venetian in 1172, then Byzantine and from 1346 to 1566 was the centre of a Genoese "empire" which incorporated Sámos, Lemnos, Lesbos, Samothrace and Thassos.

In fact in Chios the Genoese authority was delegated to a *mahone*, a financial and military body controlled by the Republic. The *mahone* of Chios, which was known as the **Giustiniani mahone** after the Genoese family which administered it, held a near monopoly of commercial traffic in the eastern Aegean. The port attracted commodities from the near East, cotton and spices, oil and soap, silk from the Caspian sea, Turkish wheat, Genoese cloth and slaves; but the two most important items of trade were the local mastic, and alum from the Phokaian mines in Anatolia, which was essential to the dyeing process and exported mainly to Bruges.

PRACTICAL INFORMATION

Access by air – From Athens 3 to 5 flights daily.

Access by boat – From Piraeus (10hr) daily except Sundays 1 to 2 services; from Lesbos (4hr) daily except Sundays; from Thessaloníki (22hr via Lesbos) weekly service; from Sámos (4hr 45min) 1 or 2 services weekly; from Kavála once a week; from Çeüsme (Turkey) in season (in principle).

Accommodation – In Chios Town, about a dozen hotels (cat B to D), hotels and guest-houses in Karfás, Kardámilia and Mestá. Traditional lodgings from GNTO/EOT in Mestá; rural lodgings in Pírgi, Olímbi and Mestá organised by the Country Women's Tourist Cooperative; information from Pírgi ☎ (0271) 72 496 or the GNTO/EOT.

Transport – Car and moped hire service in Chios Town; petrol stations are frequent in the north of the island.

Psará Island – **Access by ferry** (3hr 45min) three times per week; also caïques. **Accommodation:** hotel; also traditional lodgings from GNTO/EOT.

Despite conflicts with the Venetians and the threat of the Turks, who captured Constantinople in 1453, Chios harbour was full of shipping: Genoese brigantines, Venetian galleys, Mediterranean *tartánes* and *xebecs* and Turkish *feluccas*. Bankers, lawyers and insurance agents set up offices in the town where the great merchants had their counters and their agents.
The Turkish occupation of Chios did not damage the island's trade although Barbary pirates used it as a base; in 1681 many of them were sunk just offshore from Chios Town by a French squadron under Duquesne.
The island even retained a measure of independence; the Turks, represented by a governor, who in the early 18C was a French renegade, Count Bonneval (Achmed Pasha), demanded only allegiance and tribute. The sultan's wives were so fond of the sweet mastic gum that the peasants who cultivated lentisk trees enjoyed certain privileges including the right to ring church bells, an exceptional occurrence in the Ottoman Empire. In the 19C the Chiot ship owners had a merchant fleet to rival those of Hydra, Spetsae or Psará.

Chios Massacres – At the beginning of the War of Independence, in 1822, the island rose against the Turks at the instigation of the inhabitants of Sámos who had fled to Chios. The revolt failed and the Turks exacted a terrible vengeance which lasted five years: over 25 000 Christians were massacred or enslaved. In that same year the famous Admiral **Kanáris** retaliated by burning the Turkish flagship commanded by Kará Ali and the island was devastated in reprisal.
This cruel punishment aroused intense emotion in western Europe, particularly in France under the leadership of Chateaubriand: Delacroix's famous painting *The Massacres in Chios*, Alfred de Vigny's poem *Helena*, and Victor Hugo's verses *The Greek Child* were inspired by it.
A few years later in 1827 Colonel Fabvier, who also fought in Athens, and his Greek troops tried to take the town and besieged the castle but they had to retire finally in the face of numerous Turkish reinforcements. Chios finally became part of Greece in 1912.
The two humanists, **Adamántios Koraïs** and John **Psichári** came of families of Chiot origin, although they died in Paris in 1833 and 1929 respectively; Koraïs founded a library on the island; John Psichári is buried there *(see Literature)*.

HÍOS (CHIOS TOWN) Pop 22 894 – *about 3hr*

The small harbour town lies in a fertile coastal strip at the foot of Mount Épos and facing Asia Minor with which it maintained trade relations in the past. Although little remains of the 19C town after the dramatic events of 1822 and a big earthquake in 1881, Chios retains a certain oriental charm.
Behind the business area parallel to the quayside is **Platía Vounáki**, the town centre with its public gardens. A bronze statue of Admiral Kanáris *(see above)* stands near the cafés and on the north side of the square on the corner of Odós Martiron is a charming Turkish **fountain★** (1768); its four alcoves framed by graceful ogee arches are decorated with floral low-reliefs.

Vizandinó Moussío ⌚ – *In the old archeological museum east of Platía Vounáki.* The **Byzantine Museum** is housed in a 19C mosque which retains its minaret. In the courtyard which is lined with Turkish fountains and Venetian and French cannon are displayed fragments of early-Christian and Byzantine buildings as well as sculptures and tombstones dating from the Byzantine, Genoese and Turkish occupation. Inside is a reproduction of Delacroix's famous painting *The Massacres in Chios.*

Kástro (Citadel) – *North of the harbour and of Platía Vounáki.* The old town is still protected on three sides by ramparts built in the 14C by the Genoese on the site of a Byzantine fortress. In the Middle Ages the rich Genoese and Greek families built splendid houses there but under Ottoman rule only Turks and Jews resided in the area. Nowadays this quiet, fairly run-down quarter retains traces of its former glory.
Inside the **main gate** *(near the square)* rebuilt by the Venetians in 1694, on the right is the dark basement room of the keep where 70 local dignitaries were imprisoned in 1822 before their execution by hanging.

★**To Palatáki** (Small Palace) ⓥ – *Opposite the kástro gate.* The 15C mansion, formerly the residence of the **Giustiniani family**, overlords of Chios, houses a small collection of **Byzantine art**. A fine mosaic (5C AD) was found in the modern town; the Byzantine and post-Byzantine icons and frescoes come from churches on the island, in particular Néa Moni and the church of Panagía i Krína.

Turkish cemetery – *In a square near the Palatáki.* This tiny cemetery contains the carved tombstones of 19C Turkish notables: the tomb of Admiral Kará Ali who died in the attack launched by Kanáris.

Continue past the cemetery along Odós Navarhou Nikodimou (traces of a mosque) to Ágios Geórgios and go inside the two courtyards.

Ágios Geórgios (St George's) – In front of the church, an unusual Turkish sarcophagus pierced with holes set in the middle of a basin and covered by a large branch is the **ablution fountain** of the Eski Dzami mosque. An inscription in Turkish and French above the church doorway indicates that in 1566 the mosque replaced a Genoese church which had been built on the site of a 10C Byzantine sanctuary. The present church which has been remodelled contains ceramic wall decorations from the mosque and two columns from the Genoese church (near the iconostasis).
Continue along the street to view the remains of a Turkish bath-house on the left. Then climb up to the Kástro's corner tower to enjoy a **view** of the ramparts and of three old windmills overlooking the sea north of the town.

Koraïs Library and P Argenti Museum ⓥ – *South of the town centre, at the junction of Odós Koraïs and Odós Argendi (formerly Vassiliadou) near the cathedral.* The writer **Adamántios Koraïs**, who was born in 1743 in Smyrna from a Chiot family and spent many years in France, made a great contribution to Greece's national and cultural revival. He bequeathed his **library**, which contains over 100 000 books, to his native island. In the reading room are displayed several editions of the works of Homer who is claimed as a native of Chios. In the hall and in the stairwell there is an interesting collection of 15C–19C maps and engravings (most are facsimiles) of the town and island.
On the first floor, the costumes and decor of the Argenti family portraits evoke the gracious lifestyle of the rich Chiot families. A copy of part of Delacroix's painting and a Greek version on the same theme are on the landing. A small **Museum of Popular Art and Traditions** presents beautiful examples of local **embroidery and costumes**★.

Arheologikó Moussío ⓥ – *In Odós Mihalou, south of the harbour, near the University of the Aegean.* On display in the **Archeological Museum** are mainly the finds from excavations at Embório and Faná: fragments of Archaic vases, *korai* and architectural elements from the Temple of Apollo Phanaios as well as a collection of votive and funerary inscriptions.

EXCURSIONS

★★**Néa Moní** ⓥ – *10km/6mi west.* A superb **panoramic road** climbs the foothills of Mount Épos to the monastery which stands in a wooded valley guarded by cypress trees. It is one of the most important buildings of the Byzantine era and was founded on the spot where a miraculous icon of the Virgin had been found. It was built in the 11C by Constantine Monomachos in gratitude to the three hermits of Chios who had predicted that he would accede to the throne; it is the work of architects and painters from Constantinople.
The **church**, which is octagonal, is the best example of the architecture of the period in Greece. It was damaged by the earthquake in 1881 and the external features are now protected by a layer of plaster. The porch-belfry is a recent addition.

Interior – The large triple-domed **exonarthex** was originally faced in red marble painted with post-Byzantine frescoes; only The Last Judgement on the south wall remains. The marble floor decoration represents The Feeding of the Five Thousand. The austere figures and expressive features of the brightly coloured 11C mosaics in the narthex and the nave show great unity of style. The **esonarthex** *(coming from the exonarthex)* contains fine examples: The Raising of Lazarus *(left of the door to the nave)*; the Washing of the Feet *(left on the external wall)*; Judas' Betrayal of Christ and Christ praying in the Garden of Gethsemane on the right on the south wall. The tall dome of the **nave** and the mosaic of the Pantocrator were restored in 1900.

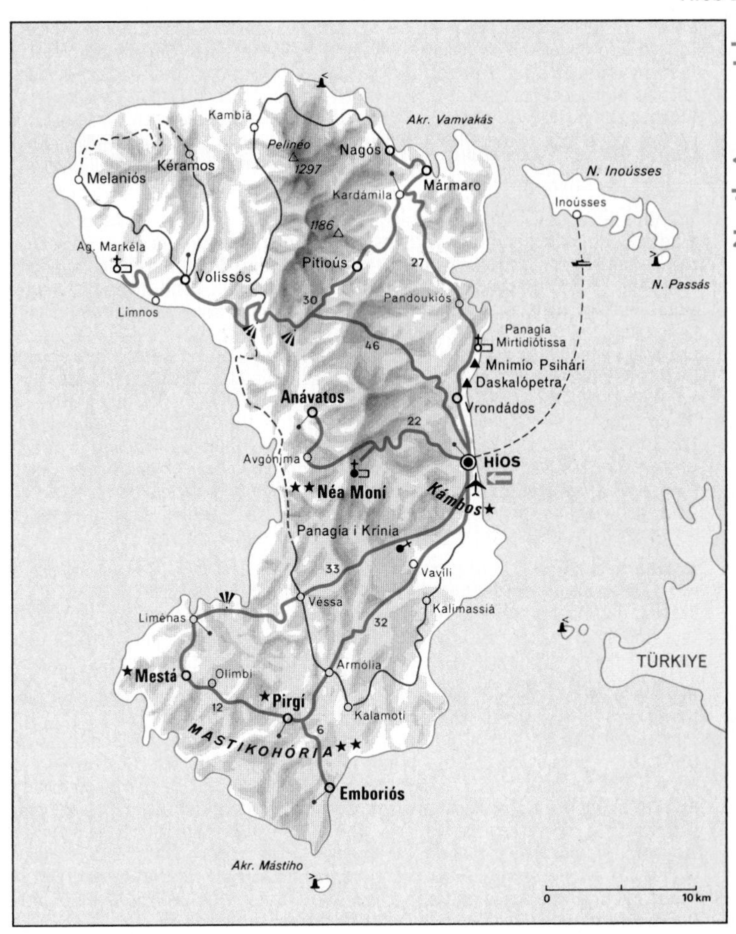

The best preserved mosaics are: in the apse, The Virgin at Prayer with the Archangels Michael and Gabriel; in the centre, to the right of the chancel *(continue clockwise)*, on the lower register John the Evangelist and above the Baptism of Christ, the Transfiguration, the Crucifixion *(above the door)*, the Descent from the Cross and the Resurrection or Descent into Hell; further down on the left, St Mark.

Anávatos – *22km/13.75mi from Chios Town (12km/7.5mi from the junction to Néa Moní).* The distant view of the village perched on a rocky spur is impressive. It was probably built to defend the east coast against the Turks; most of the inhabitants died in the 1822 massacres. Fine view of the west coast from Avgónima.

★★ **Mastikohória (Mastic villages)** – *Round tour of 89km/43mi southwest of Chios Town.* This region covers all the southern part of the island from Armólia and comprises some twenty villages dating in the main from the Genoese occupation (14C). This is where the lentisk grows; it is a bush about 2m/6ft 6in high which is cupped for its resin, **mastic**, which is collected in the early autumn. Chios is the only place where the resin solidifies naturally; annual production varies between 200 to 300t. The charming Byzantine church of the **Panagía i Krina** (12C or 13C) may be visited on the way; some of the frescoes are in To Palatáki Museum in Chios. *Access from Vavili, 1km/0.5mi on the Sklaviá road, then about 15min on foot by a track (right) through an olive grove.*

★ **Pirgí** – A tower dominates the medieval village although the walls have been razed. The geometric *sgraffito* decoration of the houses and churches is an unusual feature; the technique known as *xistá* or *skalistrá* is still in use today. A covered passage northeast of the square leads to the Church of the **Holy Apostles**★ (Ágii Apostóli, c 1200); its typically Byzantine exterior is similar to the church of Néa Moní on a smaller scale *(if the church is closed, take another alleyway to view the exterior)*. The interior is decorated with frescoes (1665). The 17C Church of the Dormition in the square contains fine carved furnishings.

Emboriós – *6km/3.5mi south of Pirgí.* There are remains of a prehistoric settlement in the coastal village which has two black pebble **beaches**.

Mestá – *Beyond the medieval village of Olímbi.* A line of fortified houses built close together forms a wall enclosing the village in five sections. *Enter by the east gate.* It is pleasant to stroll through the old lanes, which are often tortuous, and the vaulted passages. The church and the main square have replaced a defensive tower. Further along the old Byzantine **Taxiarchs Church** (Paliós Taxiárhis) contains a beautifully carved iconostasis (18C). Return to Chios Town via Liménas, Mestá's port, and the Véssa road which offers at the start extensive **views★** of the barren and indented west coast.

★**Kámbos** – A fertile plain stretching south of Chios Town (over 6km/3.75mi), is planted with lemon and orange trees and criss-crossed by a network of roads and tracks lined with high yellow walls to protect the orchards from the wind and dust. From the 15C to the 19C some 200 houses **(arhondiká)** ⌚ and mansions were built in the area by the Genoese and Greek merchants and used as summer residences. Only about 10 of the houses have survived the 19C disasters and, although some are dilapidated, they are very evocative of a bygone age. Fine porches dominated by a tower or next to a guard-house line the road to the Mastikohória. Usually, the house itself was set back from the road and built on a rise overlooking citrus groves. Some houses are occasionally open to the public: the neo-Classical **Zigomalas house** which has a fine courtyard with pebble decoration *(at the beginning of the road, on the right, about 800m/0.5mi after the bridge over the Parthenis river)*; the well preserved **Argenti house** ⌚ *(about 5km/3mi further in a parallel road to the west, Odós Argentis)*; in the courtyards shaded by pergolas are the cisterns and well with its wheel from which water was drawn for watering the trees.

Northern villages – *Round tour of 120km/74mi.* The bleak scenery at the start of the tour quickly changes as the road offers bird's-eye **views★** over the west coast. **Volissós**, dominated by a medieval fortress, has a fishing harbour at Limnos. There is a fine **beach** by the monastery of Agía Markéla (6km/3.75mi north). Continue east to **Pitioús** which like Volissós claims to be Homer's birthplace (defensive tower).

Mármaro, which lies in a deep bay, is the harbour for neighbouring Kardámila. Nagós and its environs boast the island's finest beaches.
The coast road back to Chios Town gives a view of **Inoússes** Island (pop 705). Beyond the monastery of the Virgin (Panagia Mirtidiótissa), 6km/3.75mi after Pandoukiós, a monument to John Psichári **(Mnimío Psihári)** stands below the road. Further on, above a small beach and a restaurant, is a round rock table, the famous **Daskalópetra** – the master's stone – where Homer is said to have imparted his teaching; it is probably a shrine to Cybele. In the residential suburb of **Vrondádos** which has a long maritime tradition, a small **museum** ⌚ (in the upper town, near the stadium and a large church) traces the maritime and religious past and displays the traditional arts and crafts of this prosperous region.
For adjacent sights see LÉSVOS (MITILÍNI), SÁMOS.

LÉSVOS or MITILÍNI★

LESBOS or MYTILENE – Aegean Islands
Population 105 082 – 1 630km²/629sq mi
Michelin map 980 fold 21

The Turks called Lesbos "the garden of the empire" because of its fertility; it is still sought after for its hilly wooded landscape, its huge sea inlets, the beauty of its traditional villages and its uncrowded beaches. Although there are few traces of earlier inhabitation, the Byzantines and Genoese have left some imposing fortresses and in the streets of the capital and the smaller towns there lingers a trace of the Middle East, only a few leagues away on the coast of Anatolia.
Lesbos, also known as **Mytilene**, the name of its capital, has a large population; its size makes it the third largest island in Greece after Crete and Euboia. Market gardens, fruit trees and cereals thrive on the fertile soil which also supports over 11 million olive trees, the island's most important crop. A few soap factories, several distilleries producing the best aniseed liqueur (*oúzo)* in Greece, the hot springs in the spas and a flourishing tourist sector also contribute to its economy.
In keeping with the ancient tradition, Lesbos has a lively cultural scene: several literary, dramatic, musical and artistic societies. Several of its citizens have achieved national recognition in the field of literature: Stratis Myrivilis, Ilias Venezis and the poet **Odysseus Elítis**, who was awarded a Nobel prize for literature in 1979.

Historical notes – In antiquity the island was a thriving cultural centre, particularly in the 7C and 6C BC when it nurtured the "Tyrant" Pittacos, one of the Seven Sages of Greece, Terpander, the musician and the poet Alcaeus; the famous woman poet **Sappho** *(see LEFKÁDA: Vassilikí)* was a native of Lesbos. Theophrastos, philosopher and botanist, was born in Eressós in 372 BC and it was Lesbos that Longus (2C BC) chose as the setting for his pastoral romance *Daphnis and Chloe.*

Following the division of the Roman Empire Lesbos came under the control of Byzantium. In 1354 the island was given as a dowry by Emperor John Palaiologos to his son-in-law Francesco Gattelusi from Genoa and it was administered by the Gattelusi until the Turkish conquest in 1462. Lesbos remained under Turkish occupation until 1912 and became part of the new Greek kingdom two years later. The disastrous campaign in Asia Minor in 1922 led to the influx of thousands of refugees from Anatolia and the island lost for ever its rich continental possessions.

Festivals – Religious festivals are celebrated on Lesbos with great enthusiasm and sometimes include very ancient elements. The feast of St Michael the Archangel, patron saint of the island, is celebrated on the third weekend after Easter at **Mandamádos** *(34km/21mi northwest of Mytilene)*. On Saturday afternoon a bull and several goats and sheep, decorated with flowers, are sacrificed beneath a great plane tree in the courtyard of the monastery. The spectators dip their handkerchiefs in the blood and mark their foreheads to protect themselves from illness. A service including the baptism of children is held in the church in the presence of the Archbishop; the worshippers, who come from all parts of the island, throng to kiss a very old terracotta icon of the Archangel Michael. On the following day, after more ceremonies, the meat is distributed.

A similar celebration takes place in the last week in May near the town of **Agía Paraskeví** in the centre of the island. The procession on the Saturday, where horses and mules decorated with plumes parade to the sound of music, attracts the greater crowd. The bull is sacrificed on Saturday evening and on Sunday, after the church service and the distribution of the meat, there is horse racing. The sacrifice of the bull, which the Church only tolerates, is a remnant of the ancient cult of Mithras.

The Assumption of the Virgin on 15 August is celebrated with great show particularly in **Pétra** and **Agiássos**. All these festivals are accompanied by a secular fair with stalls selling craftwork, agricultural products and other goods.

PRACTICAL INFORMATION

Access by air – From Athens 4 to 5 services daily; from Thessaloníki 1 to 2 services daily; from Lemnos 4 services a week; from Sámos and Chios 2 services a week; from Rhodes 2 services a week.

Access by ferry – From Piraeus (14hr) 1 to 2 services daily; from Chios (4hr) 6 services a week; from Thessaloníki (15hr) 1 service a week; from Kavála (12hr) via Lemnos (6hr) 2 services a week; also possible from Dikili or Ayvalik in Turkey.

Accommodation – About 75 hotels on the island, mainly at Mytilene (about 17 cat A to C) and Míthimma/Mólivos (about 10 cat A to C); many rooms in private houses; rural accommodation from the Country Women's Tourist Cooperative, information from the GNTO/EOT or in Pétra ☎ (0253) 41 238.

Transport – Car and motorcycle hire.

TOWNS AND SIGHTS *(in clockwise order from Mytilene)*

★**Mitilíni (Mytilene)** – Pop 24 953. *Small beach below the castle.* The island capital is on the east coast facing Anatolia where in the past the citizens had trading interests. The **castle** ⓥ (Kástro), which stands on a promontory projecting seawards beyond the town and thus providing two harbours, was rebuilt in the 14C by Francesco Gattelusi; some of the older construction work dates from the 6C. Above the castle gates are the arms of the Palaiologos emperors of Byzantium (a two-headed eagle), the horseshoe of the Gattelusi and Arabic inscriptions.

Behind the slightly unexpected bulk of the neo-Classical church of Ágios Thérapon is the **Byzantine Museum** (Vizandinó Moussío) ⓥ which houses precious icons (13C-17C). An attractive villa on the road to the castle houses the **Archeological Museum** (Arheologikó Moussío) ⓥ: ceramics, Greek sculptures and fragments of Roman mosaics from the "House of Menander".

The district on the isthmus between the two harbours, which was the centre of town during the Turkish occupation, has retained some fine houses, the remains of a mosque and the cathedral which contains a very fine post-Byzantine iconostasis. The **House of Lesbos** ⓥ (Lesviakó spíti) and a small **museum** a few yards further on **(The Women of Lesbos' Collection of Popular Traditions)** ⓥ contain collections of popular art and tradition.

Northwest on a pine-clad slope are the remains of a Hellenistic **theatre** ⓥ which was restored by the Romans; Pompey was so impressd by it that he had a replica built in Rome. Most of the terraces have disappeared – they were taken for building projects in the Middle Ages, in particular for the construction of the Gatteluzzi castle – but the size of the theatre (it seated 15 000 spectators) indicates the cultural importance of Lesbos in antiquity. From the upper terraces there is a fine view of the old town, the castle and the Turkish coast.

★**Variá** – *4km/2.5mi south of Mytilene.* Stratis Eleftheriadis-Teriade, famous critic and art dealer in Paris and native of Mytilene, built two museums on his property. The **Theophilos Museum** ⏱ presents 86 works by the famous naive painter Theophilos (1873-1934) who was born in Variá; the paintings are gaily coloured representations of popular scenes or incidents in Greek history. Other works by this artist are displayed in Makrinítsa, a village on Mount Pélion east of Vólos, and in the National Gallery in Athens.

On the same site under the olive trees stands the **Teriade Museum** ⏱ which contains a rich library belonging to the art dealer and engravings and lithographs coloured by Chagall, Picasso, Fernand Léger, Matisse and Giacometti. There are also paintings by Iánis Tsarouchis and other works by Theóphilos.

Plomári – *42km/26mi southwest of Mytilene.* The second largest town in the island hides its steep streets of old houses in a hollow in the cliff face which is scarcely visible from a distance. The modern seafront provides cafés and restaurants as well as a tiny beach at the west end. East of the town extends a shingle beach, Ágios Issídoros, which is very popular. Plomári is famous throughout Greece for the high quality of its anised liqueur *(oúzo).*

Agiássos – *25km/15.5mi west of Mytilene.* The wooded lower slopes of the highest peak on the island (Mount Olympos, 968m/3 235ft) frame this charming unspoilt town. A stroll up and down its shady paved streets reveals attractive cafés, fountains, sometimes a *sandoúri* (sort of cithar) player or an old woman wearing the old-fashioned full-skirted ankle-length culottes. A **Museum of Religious and Popular Art** ⏱ is attached to the church.

Vaterá – *52km/32mi west of Mytilene and south of Polihnítos.* This is the most beautiful beach on the island *(8km/5mi long). A few hotels, guest houses and tavernas.* There are traces of a paleo-Christian basilica on the Fokás headland and also east of the village.

Limónos Monastery ⏱ – *43km/27mi northwest of Mytilene.* Just beyond Kaloní in the Sígri road stand the impressive buildings of Lesbos' chief monastery. The 40 monks, whose social and educational work extends throughout the island, maintain a museum of religious and popular art.

Skála Eressoú – *90km/56mi west of Mytilene via Kaloní.* Skála Eressoú, which is the port for the larger village of Eressós, attracts many holiday-makers to its long sandy beach backed by tavernas and guest houses. **Ancient Eressós**, which was built on the slopes of a hill to the east of the village, is thought to be the birthplace of Sappho; as well as the remains of a few walls, there are two paleo-Christian basilicas decorated with mosaics and the ruins of a Genoese and a Turkish tower.

Sígri – *95km/59mi west of Mytilene via Kaloní.* This fishing village (crayfish a speciality) nestles in a little bay, guarded by a ruined Turkish fort and protected from the open sea by an island, Nissiópi. Several little beaches in the vicinity. Between Sígri and Eressós there is a **petrified forest** *(apolithoména déndra)* composed of fossilised trees which were buried under a layer of volcanic ash millions of years ago and then slowly revealed to view by erosion. The trees which are still upright reach up to 10m/33ft in height and the trunks measure about 8m/26ft round the bole. The forest spreads over a vast area but the most accessible trees are to be found on the south side of the Ándissa to Sígri road (about 7km/4mi from Ándissa).

Pétra – *60km/37mi north of Mytilene via Kaloní.* This quiet village beside its long stretch of sand was immortalised in a painting by Theophilos *(see above).* The rock which gives the village its name, is crowned by the Church of the Virgin **(Panagía Glikofiloússa)** which contains some remarkable icons; fine view of the surrounding countryside. At the centre of the village stands the **Vareldzidéna house** (Arhondikó Vareldzidéna) ⏱ with its graceful wooden balconies; the salon on the first floor is decorated with delicate paintings of the towns and fleet of the Ottoman Empire. St Nicholas' Church **(Ágios Nikólaos)** contains 15C frescoes.

★**Míthimna (Mólivos)** – *64km/40mi north of Mytilene via Kaloní.* Picturesque little town favoured by artists; beach and fishing port. The handsome houses, painted in pastel shades, climb the steep slope towards an impressive Byzantine-Genoese castle which offers views of the town and the coast.

A radioactive spring (46.8°C/124°F) beyond the beach at Eftaloú *(3km/2mi east of Míthimna)* is captured in a covered bath before warming the sea water off the shingle beach.

Thermí – *11km/7mi north of Mytilene on the coast.* Loutropóli Thermís is a popular spa; its hot waters were known in antiquity for their curative properties. In the vicinity stand some traditional residential tower houses.

South of Thermí and west of the village of Mória are traces of an impressive **Roman aqueduct**. There are traces of another near the village of Lámbou Míli on the road to Kaloní.

For adjacent sights see HÍOS, LÍMNOS, SAMOTHRÁKI, THÁSSOS.

LÍMNOS★

LEMNOS – Aegean Islands – Population 17 645 – 453km²/175sq mi
Michelin map 980 fold 20

The arid, volcanic island of Lemnos is situated midway between Mount Athos and the coast of Asia Minor, near the mouth of the Dardanelles. The principal shrines and antique sites are in the east where the fertile plains are swept by the northeasterly wind while the barren mountain chains with cultivated valleys to the west form a rugged coastline indented with bays and sandy coves. The only resort is the capital Mírina and its environs. The local specialities are fig preserve and a fruity white wine.

The fumes of brimstone – The volcanoes and sulphureous springs on the island have inspired many legends: Lemnos was the mythological home of **Hephaïstos** (Vulcan), who was cast off Mount Olympos by his angry father Zeus and landed on Lemnos. He is said to have broken his leg and to have been lame ever since. Another myth is that he was born handicapped and was thrown down from Olympos by his disappointed mother Hera. Whatever the case, the God of Fire lived on the island and toiled at his forges, the Lemnos volcanoes, and instructed the islanders in the art of metalworking. The wives of Lemnos supported Hephaïstos in his marital dispute with the unfaithful Aphrodite and refused to pay homage to the Goddess of Love, who took revenge by causing the women to exude such a foul stench that their husbands deserted them for foreign women who were being held in captivity. The neglected wives murdered all the men on the island except for King Thoas who escaped with the help of his daughter Hypsile. She became queen of a community of women only, until Jason and the Argonauts landed on Lemnos on their way to Colchis on their quest for the Golden Fleece. They stayed a few years and the island was repopulated.
During the Trojan War Philoctetes, who was companion to Heracles and inherited his arms, was abandoned on Lemnos because he had a gangrenous wound which smelt abominably. Hephaïstos and Philoctetes are said to have been cured by the famous "Lemnian earth" from Mosychlos hill (now Despóti north of Repanídi) which was still in use for its healing powers in the 19C.

Historical notes – Excavations at Polióhni in the east have revealed evidence of human settlement since the Neolithic Era (10 000–2 000 BC). The inhabitants – the Minyans and later probably Pelasgians from Anatolia – maintained close relations with Lesbos and Troy and with the Cyclades. This pre-Hellenic population who remained on the island until about the 7C BC spoke a language which has not been deciphered although it is transcribed in Greek characters. Lemnos which was repopulated by a colony from Athens, was occupied by the Persians in 513 BC and after the Persian wars remained in the main under Athenian influence. Like its neighbours it came under Macedonian and later Roman rule, then it was part of the Byzantine Empire until it was ceded to the Venetians in 1204. Until the end of the 15C the island was disputed by the Genoese, the Venetians, the Byzantines and finally the Turks. In 1476, during a Turkish attack on Kókino Castle which was held by the Venetians, a young girl by the name of Maroula won fame; her statue stands above the scant remains of the castle near the fishing village of Kótsinas north of Repanídi. Lemnos was under Turkish occupation from 1479 to 1912. During the First World War the British used the **Bay of Moudros** as a naval base from which was launched the Franco-British expedition of 1915 to the Dardanelles. The armistice between Turkey and the Allies was signed on 30 October 1918 in Moudros Bay. In 1920 Lemnos was officially united with Greece by the Treaty of Sèvres.

PRACTICAL INFORMATION

Access by air – From Athens 3 to 4 services daily; from Thessaloníki 1 service daily; from Lésvos (Mitilíni) 1 service daily.

Access by ferry – From Piraeus via Chios and Lesbos 2 services a week; from Kavála (about 5hr) en route to Ag Efstrátios 1 service a week (connecting boat for Kimi and the Sporades).

Accommodation – About 10 hotels (cat A to D) in Mírina; rooms in private houses, mainly in Mírina and a few in Plati.

Transport – Car and motorcycle hire services.

MÍRINA – Pop 4 342

The charming fishing harbour to the south offers a fine **view★** of the sheer cliffs of the rocky headland dominated by a fortress which divides Kástro Bay where the capital of Lemnos is pleasantly situated. The view is particularly spectacular on a summer's night when the ramparts are lit up. Beyond the harbour is the Turkish beach – Toúrkikos Gialós – while to the north lie the fine sandy "Greek" beach – Roméïkos Gialós – lined with cafés and restaurants, and Rihá Nerá (low tide) beach. The old town on the neck of land below the fortress has a few houses with wooden balconies.

★**Kástro (Fortress)** – The foundations of an ancient wall, on which rise the walls built on the ridge by the Venetians, the Genoese and the Turks, are the only traces of a temple to Artemis and a town called Myrina, after the wife of the mythical King Thoas *(see above)*, which stood on the jagged headland. The climb to the fortress gates *(5 to 10min from the main street)* affords good views of the harbour and the south side of the bay. Beyond the gates, a track on the left *(easy climb, about 5min)* leads to the top of the south wall *(near the flag pole)*. From this spot and from the tip of the headland *(by a path to the north)* splendid **views★★★** may be enjoyed, especially at sunset, of both sides of Kástro Bay, the indented west coast, the town and on the horizon Mount Athos (alt 2 033m/6 670ft) rising from the sea.

Arheologikó Moussío ⊙ – *Near the Hotel Kástro at Roméïkos Gialós.* The **Archeological Museum** presents the finds from the island's three main ancient sites: from Hephaistia, unusual sirens (women with the body of a bird), 6C BC sphinxes *(entrance)* and Archaic ceramics; from the Kabeiron, items dating from the 7C BC to the Roman period – the cult of the Kabeiroi, gods of fertility, celebrated at night, explains the large number of oil lamps found there; and from Polióhni objects ranging from the Neolithic Era to the end of the Bronze Age – pottery, pestles and millstones.

ENVIRONS

★★**Káspakas Bay (Ormos Káspaka)** – *11km/6.5mi north.* After the Akti Myrina Hotel and Cape Pétassos the road skirts the **Avlónas coast★** (bays and coves). The vast **bay★★** with Cape Kalógeri at the far side comes into view before the village of Káspakas nestling on the mountainside. Beyond the village a by-road runs down to the beach and hamlet of Ágios Ioánis. There are fine sandy beaches north of the bay.

Platí and Ágios Pávlos Bays – *About 10km/6mi south.* Below the mountain village of Platí stretches a large sandy **beach★** with a tiny fishing port *(south)* and a fine shady beach *(1km/0.5mi further on)*.
Return to the main road going south above Platí. Just before Thános a fine **view★** unfolds over the vast Órmos Ágios Pávlos and the bare volcanic peaks enclosing the wheat-growing plain.

West coast of Límnos

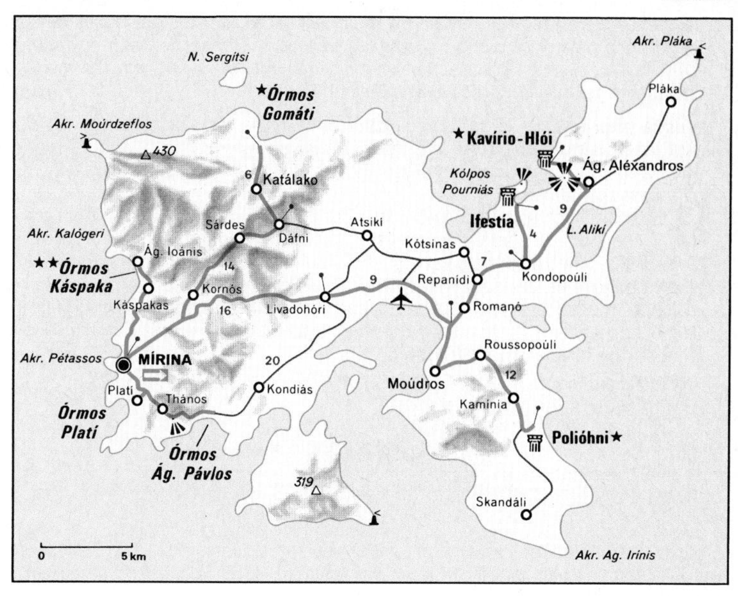

★**Gomáti Bay (Órmos Gomáti)** – *20km/12mi northeast.* This tour takes in the mountainous part of the island. *Take the airport road and after 6km/3.5mi turn left towards Kornós.* After 1.5km/1mi past Kornós bear right for Sárdes and Dáfni *(6km/3.5mi further)* overlooking the plain in the east. Then go up a road on the left to **Katálako** (pop 166 – *2km/1mi further*), a picturesque village high up on a rocky spur above which runs the road. At the end of a fertile valley (4km/2.5mi down) is Gomáti Bay (sandy beach). The air is fresh in summer (unlike on the other beaches) from the frequent northeasterly wind but the sea is rough.

ANCIENT LÍMNOS ⊙

★**Polióhni** – *37km/23mi southeast.* Past the airport take the road south to **Moúdros** (pop 973) which has one of the safest roadsteads in the Aegean *(see above)*. The British military cemetery in which stands a French monument is to the northeast of Moúdros. At the entrance to the village bear east towards Roussopoúli and proceed south to Kamínia. Beyond the village (1.5km/1mi) take a road to the left to the custodian's house. A track on the right leads to the site of Polióhni, one of the most ancient towns in Greece together with Sésklo and Dimíni near Vólos.
A 4C BC village with oval huts was replaced in the 3C BC by a fortified town built in four stages *(indicated in blue, green, red and yellow on the site)*. According to Italian archeologists who started excavating in 1930, the earliest city is more ancient than Troy in Anatolia. The site was destroyed several times by natural disasters. Finds from the later "yellow" period (2200-2100 BC) include human skeletons, pottery and gold jewellery. Settlement on a more modest scale continued until about 1275 BC, probably just before the Trojan War.
There are scant remains of the successive cities but the streets, wells and rectangular houses and wall sections are well presented and explained.
The round water tower was built before the Second World War to supply water to the archeological site which overlooks a fine beach.

★**Kavírio-Hlói (Sanctuary of the Kabeiroi)** – *41km/25.5mi northeast by the airport road. 5km/3mi past the airport bear left into a road which runs through Romanó, Repanídi and Kondopoúli (fork to Ifestía see below).* A vast lagoon lined with saltpans (Lake Alikí) comes into view on the right. *Continue for 6km/3.5mi beyond Kondopoúli and near the hamlet of Ágios Aléxandros turn left into a good track for 3km/1.75mi.* 1km/0.5mi before reaching the sanctuary climb up to the top of a hill *(indicated by a white column on the left)* to enjoy a magnificent **panorama**★ over Pourniás Bay and the barren eastern side of the island. Hephaistia *(see below)* stands on the headland in the middle of the bay to the west.
The cult of the **Kabeiroi**, the mysterious gods of the underworld said to be descended from Hephaïstos, goes back to the era of the Minyans and Pelasgians when the Lemnos shrine was more important than the one at Samothrace *(see SAMOTHRÁKI)*.
Excavations by the Italian School in the late 1930s reveal that the ruined Kabeirion in its lonely majestic **site**★ overlooking Pourniás Bay dates from a later period. Eleven columns of the south façade of a vast Hellenistic Telestrion (where the

mysteries were enacted) remain on the upper terrace. There are traces of the last period of Roman occupation on the hill beyond the Telestrion and on the south-west terrace. The earliest section of the sanctuary (8C-7C BC) on the lower level included a temple, a portico and a Telestrion.

Ifestía (Hephaistia) – *36km/22mi northeast. Take the same route as for Kavírio and just after Kondopoúli turn left into a track suitable for cars and continue for 4km/2.5mi to a sheltered bay. Park by the custodian's house and walk up to the site past the hamlet.*
Hephaistia, which was inhabited in the pre-Hellenic era and was Lemnos' principal city in the Classical period and later the seat of a Byzantine see, was deserted after a landslide. The ruins scattered on the mountainside are of little interest. A sign shows the site of an *agora* with further up a Pelasgian shrine *(partly covered)* and below to the north a small Hellenistic and Roman theatre against the hillside. From the hilltop above the sanctuary the **view**★ extends over Pourniás Bay and Kavírio-Hlói on the headland to the east.

For adjacent sights see LÉSVOS (MITILÍNI), SAMOTHRÁKI, THÁSSOS.

SÁMOS★★

Aegean Islands – Population 33 039 – 477km²/184sq mi
Michelin map 980 fold 34

A narrow strait (about 2km/1.25mi wide) separates Sámos from the Turkish coast. The hilly terrain culminating in Mount Kerketéas (1 433m/4 700ft) is green and well watered by streams and rivers. Its beaches, coves and indented coastline, together with its interesting archeological remains make Sámos a pleasant resort for a prolonged stay. Excursions to Kusadasi and to **Ephesus** (Efes) in Turkey are an added attraction. The island is well known for its sweet red Muscat wine.

A glorious dictatorship – Sámos was first known as Parthénia (Virgin) from the River Parthenió, which was known in mythology as the birthplace of the goddess, Hera.
In the Archaic period the island flourished; the people cultivated wheat, grapes and figs, produced ceramics and metals and traded widely. It reached its apogee in the middle of the 6C BC under the rule of the enlightened tyrant **Polycrates**.
He commanded a fleet of 100 ships with which he made profitable raids throughout the Aegean. He accomplished several feats of engineering: a long mole to protect the port of Sámos which he rebuilt, shipyards for construction and repair, and an underground aqueduct in a tunnel, designed by the great architect Eupalinos of Mégara, which was one of the wonders of the ancient world. On the cultural side, he welcomed men of letters at his court, such as Anacreon, the lyric poet, he rebuilt the temple of Hera and fostered a school of sculpture which was characterised by its delicate work and produced the Hera of Sámos, an Archaic votive statue which stood in the Heraion and is now in the Louvre.
Alas, Polycrates, whose good luck was proverbial, fell into a trap set by the Persians and was crucified in 522 BC. Sámos then became a Persian possession and fought on the side of the Persians at the battle of Salamis *(see ATHÍNA Excursions)* but in 479 the islanders destroyed Xerxes' fleet at **Cape Mycale** in the Sámos strait. It retained its prosperity until the Roman period but it no longer played a political role. In antiquity Sámos produced or fostered several famous men: the mathematician Pythagoras (6C BC), the sculptor Pythagoras (5C BC), the philosopher Epicurus (4C BC) and the astronomer Aristarchos (3C BC), who anticipated Copernicus and Galileo in the discovery that the earth revolves round the sun.

PRACTICAL INFORMATION

Access by air – From Athens 4 to 5 services daily (depending on the season).

Access by ferry – From Piraeus to Karlovássi and Vathí (Sámos) (10hr to 12hr) services daily (calling at Syros and Páros (occasionally) and Ikaría); from Kavála, Lemnos, Lesbos (Mytilene), Chios 1 to 2 services a week; from Rhodes, Kos, Kálimnos, Léros and Pátmos 1 to 2 services a week; from Pátmos to Pithagório (Sámos) in season daily launches; in principle from Kusudasi (Turkey) services in season.

Accommodation – About 40 hotels (cat B to E) Sámos Town and suburbs and about 40 (cat A to E) in Pithagório; about 20 hotels in Kokári (A to E) and about 10 in Ormos Marathókambou (B to D) and Karlovássi (B to D) and Iréo (B to E); many rooms in private houses all over the island.

Transport – Car and motorcycle hire services.

Modern era – Under the Byzantine Empire, Sámos fell into decline following frequent raids by Saracens, Turks, Crusaders and Venetians; the latter occupied the island several times. In 1414 the Genoese Giustiniani family, who ruled Chios, captured the island until 1475 when it was surrendered to the Turks. The population emigrated to Chios and Lesbos.

At the end of the 16C, following the promise of relative independence by a Turkish admiral, the emigrants' descendants returned to the island. In 1821, however, Sámos took an active part in the national liberation movement under Lahanas and Likourgos Logothetis. The Turkish fleet was sunk in 1824 near Pithagório. Despite the islanders' bravery *(see also HÍOS)*, under the 1830 London accord Sámos was excluded from the new Greek State but it enjoyed a great degree of autonomy under a Christian governor appointed by the Sultan. After a vote in 1912 Sámos was reunited with Greece in March 1913.

★SÁMOS TOWN – Pop 5 792

The island capital occupies an attractive **site★★** in the bay of Vathí (meaning deep). The lower town which developed round the harbour in the 19C is the business and administrative centre. In Platiá Pithagória a great marble lion stands proudly amid the palm trees, a symbol of the people's bravery. The town's only beach is at Gangos, 1km/0.5mi beyond the jetty.

★**Arheologikó Moussío** ⌚ – *Near the post office.* The **Archeological Museum** presents an outstanding collection of artefacts from the Heraion and from ancient Sámos. In gallery 1 **votive statues** (6C BC), probably of a family group, by the local artist Geneleos are displayed on a pedestal. They were found at the entrance to the Sacred Way in the Heraion; two of the statues at the centre have disappeared, another is in the Pergamum Museum in East Berlin. A marble **kouros** (4.75m/15ft high), also from the Heraion, stands in the end gallery. On the first floor in the adjoining older building are exhibited a small 4C BC **low relief** of the Chthonian Hermes (conductor of souls to Hades) and three male figures; a collection of bronzes (8C-6C BC) testifying to contacts between Sámos and the East; terracotta from Cyprus; ivories including **Perseus and Medusa** from the Peloponnese; faience birds from Egypt, 7C-6C BC wooden statuettes and figurines in an expressive primitive style. There is an ox-head shaped rhyton on the ground floor.

★**Áno Vathí** – The old town (Áno Vathí – the upper town) spreads up the hillside behind the port. Walk up Odós Smirnis from the lower town to explore the picturesque narrow and steep streets lined with Turkish corbelled houses. Chapels and fountains grace shady squares. A lovely Byzantine church, **Ágios Gianákis** with twin domes and aisles nestles in a hollow on the hillside to the east.

KAUFMAN /TOP

Sámos vineyards

EXCURSIONS

Zoodóhos Pigí Monastery ⊙ – *14km/8.5mi east there and back. From the quay by the bus station take the road skirting a rocky terrain up to Áno Vathí (sign "Vlamári").* The road leads to the fertile Kamára plateau. The **Monastery of the Source of Life** crowns a wooded hill on the Prasso headland. The church columns are probably from ancient Miletus in Asia Minor. Extensive **views**★★ of the Turkish coastline with the white houses of Kusadasi on the horizon.

On the way back, in Kamára, turn left into a small road leading to the village of Agía Zóni (1km/0.5mi).

Monastery of Agía Zóni ⊙ – The Monastery of the Holy Girdle (1695) contains late 17C frescoes and an iconostasis (1801). The church stands in a courtyard bright with flowers.

Go through the village to return to Sámos by the direct route.

Mitiliniı́ Paleontological Museum ⊙ – *New building on the edge of the village.* In the museum are displayed about 120 fossils of animals which roamed the area some 10 million years ago when Sámos was part of an Aegean mainland. Excavations near the village which began in the 19C have uncovered several fossils of the tridactyl hoofed hipparion deemed to be the ancestor of the horse.

★PITHAGÓRIO – Pop 1 405

Formerly known as **Tigani**, this popular port for fishing and pleasure boats on the southeast coast was renamed in 1955 in honour of the famous mathematician and philosopher Pythagoras. The town extends over only a small area of the site of **ancient Sámos**; its walls were over 6km/4mi long. The jetty is built on Polycrates' ancient mole. There are two small beaches on either side of the port and the Potokáki beach (5km/3mi to the west).

Logothetis Castle – It was built in the early 19C and its tall tower soars above the town. The precinct to the east contains Roman and paleo-Christian remains. There are extensive **views**★ from the coast of Cape Mycale in Turkey, Agathoníssi Island to the south and Cape Foniás to the east. In 1824 Logothetis *(see above)* built the **church of the Transfiguration** (Metamórfossis) behind the tower.

Archeological Collection ⊙ – It comprises finds from ancient Sámos and from the Heraion including a fine Archaic statue of a woman.

The next three sights are situated on the slopes of Mount Kástri.

★**Efpalínio (Eupalinos' Aqueduct)** ⊙ – *1.5km/1mi from the junction of the Sámos road.* Half way along stand the scanty ruins of an **ancient theatre**.
A small Classical structure marks the entrance to the tunnel.
According to Herodotos, the historian and geographer (5C BC), the underground aqueduct (1km/1 094yd long) hewn through the mountain was one of the three wonders of his time (the others also in Sámos are the port mole and the temple of Hera). This engineering masterpiece by Eupalinos of Mégara provided the large city of Sámos with fresh water from the Agiádes stream on the other side of the mountain near the village of Mitiliniı́. When the tunnel was completed in 524 BC after 15 years the two teams of workmen were only a few feet apart. Steep steps and a narrow vaulted passage lead to the tunnel which is about 2m/6ft wide and lit by electricity. A platform *(can be slippery)* along the canal was used as a secret means of evacuation in an emergency.

Ancient wall – The circuit wall (6.5km/4mi long) was punctuated by 35 defensive towers and extended to the mountain top. One of the best preserved sections rises about 100m/328ft west of the tunnel entrance. Other sections can be seen by the side of the road to the airport to the west, and above the road to Sámos Town on leaving Pithagório to the east.

Panagía Spilianís ⊙ – *Access by a road which climbs for 800m/0.5mi from the theatre.* The monastery of the Virgin of the

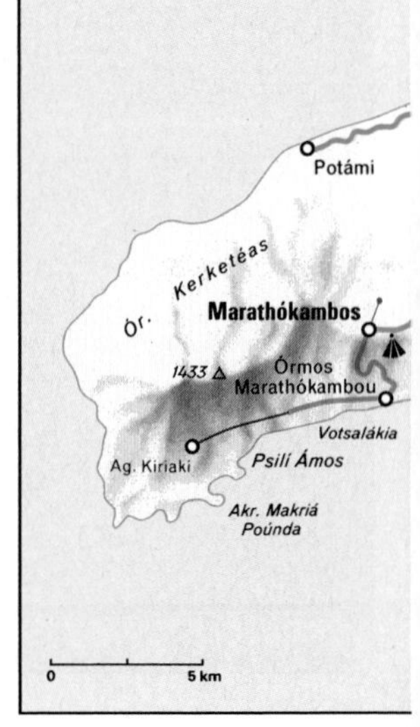

Grotto derives its name from a chapel built deep inside a vast cave where the oracle Phylo made prophecies in antiquity. Outstanding **view★** of the Pithagório plain, Cape Foniás, and Agathoníssi Island and Cape Mycale in Turkey on the horizon.

Thérma (Roman baths) ⓥ – *From Pithagório drive west.* The Romans converted a large gymnasium built in the Hellenistic period into baths which were restored and extended many times after being damaged by earthquakes. A Roman basilica was replaced in the 5C by a three-aisled Christian basilica and subsequently by a baptistry.

EXCURSIONS

★Iréo (Heraion) ⓥ – *8km/5mi to the west in Kolóna. Take the road past the airport on the left and turn left towards Pagóndas, then bear left and left again.*

Facing the sea are the meagre ruins of the celebrated shrine of Samian Hera which lie in a marshy area. As at Árgos *(see ÁRGOS)* the ancient cult of the goddess is associated with fertility. Several shrines have been built on the spot from the Bronze Age to the end of the Roman Empire; this makes it difficult to get a clear picture of the site and therefore only the main features are described below.
Walk past the foundations of the enormous **temple of Hera** which was built by Polycrates in the 6C BC to replace an earlier shrine by Roïkos (early 6C BC) destroyed by fire or by an earthquake. This new temple (108m/354ft long x 55m/180ft wide at the base) was twice the size of the Parthenon. The gigantic scale of the building can be deduced from the single standing column although it is only half its original height of 20m/65ft. The peristyle incorporated 61 columns adorned with Ionic capitals; numerous column-bases are still visible. The construction of the temple continued until the 3C BC but it was probably never completed as no traces of the roof have been found.
The Roman **exedra** (about 40m/45yd east of the column) was erected by the Samians to commemorate the two Ciceros: Quintus Tullius, the well-liked governor of the Province of Asia which included Sámos, and Marcus Tullius, the great orator who defended the Samians against the exactions of Verres, the legate, who had also plundered Sicily. Further to the left are the north wall and column-bases of a **Christian basilica** built in the 6C or 5C BC on the site of smaller Roman temples and baths. The well-preserved apse of a 16C church stands near a tree to the east. Further back, beyond a paved street, lie the remains of the **altar** dedicated to Hera built in front of the earlier temple c 560 BC and restored by the Romans; it retains remarkable friezes and a large circular pedestal which supported votive statues. Copies of statues by the Samian Geneleos *(now in the Sámos museum)* grace the original Archaic pedestal at the entrance to the **Sacred Way**, which was lined with treasuries and linked the sanctuary with the ancient town of Sámos.
A road to the left leads to the village of **Iréo**: hotels, tavernas and shady beach.

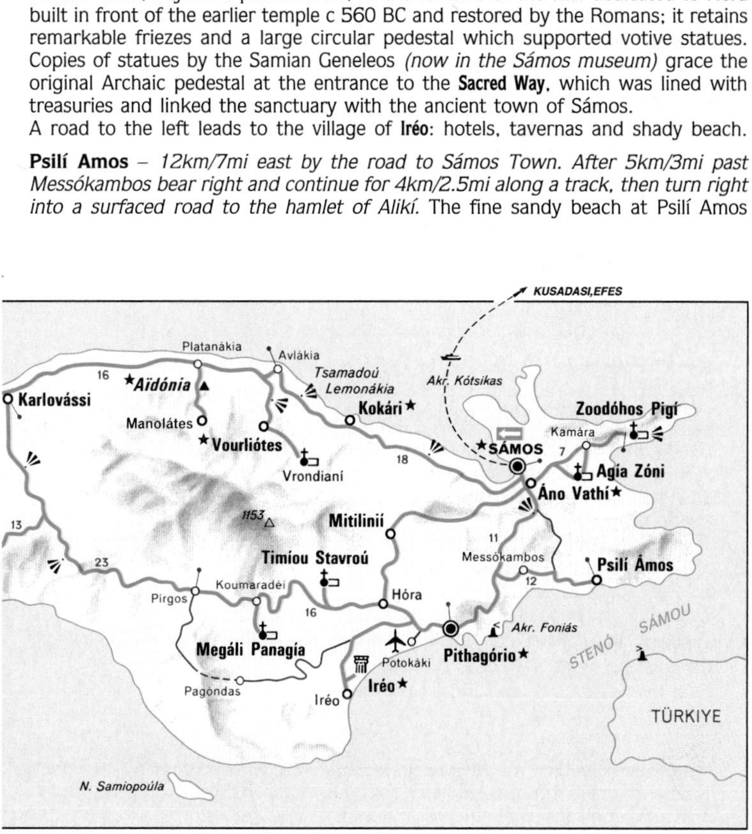

Psilí Amos – *12km/7mi east by the road to Sámos Town. After 5km/3mi past Messókambos bear right and continue for 4km/2.5mi along a track, then turn right into a surfaced road to the hamlet of Alikí.* The fine sandy beach at Psilí Amos along the Sámos strait faces Cape Mycale where a naval battle was fought against the Persians in Antiquity *(see above)*. The narrow passage (about 1 300m/4 265ft wide; 1km/0.5mi east) between Greece and Turkey is known as Eptastádios Porthmós – the Seven Stadia Channel. The white lighthouse opposite Psilí Amos is on Turkish soil on Nadra Island.

★TOUR OF THE ISLAND

132km/82mi (including 84km/52mi by the circular road)

Allow a whole day to enjoy the beaches and the cool mountain villages.

The road affords fine **vistas★** of Vathí Bay and of the Turkish coast in the distance.

★Kokári – A large fishing village and a lively resort with a rocky headland jutting out between the harbour and the pebbly beach to the west. The road then overlooks the beaches of Lemonákia and **Tsamodoú** and continues to Avlákia for a splendid **view★★** of Cape Kótsikas and of Kokári and its promontory.

★Vourliótes – 340m/1 115ft. *Beyond Avlákia bear left for 4km/2.5mi.* A wine-growing village with traditional houses. Continue 2km/1mi to the southeast to reach the **Vrondianí Monastery** (festival on 8 September), in a majestic mountain setting; it dates from 1566 and is the oldest on the island.
The road winds through the vineyards affording **views★★** of the island's coastline and of the mountains on the Turkish mainland.

★Aïdónia Gorge – Turn left after the bridge at Platanákia and drive through the valley of the fast-flowing River Aïdónia shaded by plane and chestnut trees; the occasional song of nightingales – *aïdónia* – breaks the silence. The road climbs to the flower-bedecked village of **Manolátes** overlooking the sea and the Aïdónia gorge.

Karlovássi – Muscat wine is exported from Karlovássi which is the economic centre for the western side of the island. In the past the town had several tanneries; workshops and warehouses remain near the river and by the sea. Paleó Karlovássi, overlooks the harbour area and its churches and old houses. The 11C **Church of the Transfiguration** (Metamorfóssis), which is crowned by a dome resting on four ancient columns, nestles on the mountainside near the beach at **Potámi**.

Return to Néo Karlovássi and proceed south.

There are fine **views** of the Turkish coast in the distance. Further up is the fork to Marathókambos; the ridge offers splendid vistas on both sides of the island. Continue downhill to enjoy extensive **views★★** over Marathókambos Bay: Samiopoúla on the left, the Foúrni Islands and beyond, on a fine day, the peaks of Ikaria Island.

Marathókambos – A large village rising in terraces up the mountainside. The harbour, **Órmos Marathókambou**, is also a resort *(large beach and excursions by boat to Samiopoúla and Pátmos)*. West *(2km/1mi)* lies the vast pebble beach of Votsalákia and further on *(2km/1mi)* the fine sandy beach of **Psilí Amos**.

Return to the circular road and turn right towards Pithagório.

At first the road affords lovely **views★** over Marathókambos Bay then cuts through the forest to the villages of Pirgos and Koumaradéi, famous respectively for their honey and pottery.

At the entrance of Koumaradeí, bear right into a track.

Megáli Panagía ⓥ – Founded in 1586 in a wooded valley the monastery of the Great Virgin was rebuilt in the 18C after a fire. It was again destroyed by fire in 1988 and is scheduled for restoration.

Timíou Stavroú ⓥ – The monastery of the Holy Cross founded shortly after that of Megáli Panagia after an icon of the Crucifixion was found on the spot, was extended in the 17C and rebuilt in the 19C. It is a pilgrimage centre (14 September).
The circular road passes through **Hóra**, the island's capital in the Middle Ages, and descends towards **Pithagório★** *(for description see above)*: extensive **view** over the plain and Cape Mycale. There is a fine glimpse of the harbour on the way out of Pithagório and about 9km/5.5mi further on, as the road winds down towards the capital, splendid **views★★** of Vathí Bay and of the town nestling on the hillside.

For adjacent sights see HÍOS, PÁTMOS.

This guide which is revised regularly, incorporates tourist information provided at the time of going to press. Changes are however inevitable owing to improved facilities and fluctuations in the cost of living

Vóries SPORÁDES★★

NORTHERN SPORADES – Magnissía, Thessaly

Michelin map 980 folds 18 and 19

The northern Sporades extend in a chain northwest of Évia (Euboia); there are four main islands – Skíathos, Skópelos, Alónissos and Skíros – accompanied by numerous smaller islands (*sporádes* means scattered, sporadic). The countryside is hilly and wooded, with picturesque villages of white houses cascading down the slopes to the sea, and secluded creeks with beaches ideal for bathing or under-water fishing.
The people follow their traditional way of life: raising sheep and goats, tending vines, olive groves and orchards, fishing with nets or by lamplight, boat building *(caïques)* in Skíathos and Skópelos. Local crafts still thrive: furniture, ceramics, hand-woven cloth... Fish and seafood occur frequently in the local dishes.
May and June are the most pleasant months but the islands are popular throughout the summer when they enjoy constant sunshine tempered by the north wind *(meltémi)*.

PRACTICAL INFORMATION

Access by air – From Athens to Skíathos in summer frequent services daily (in winter 3 to 6 services a week); from Athens to Skíros/Skyros in summer daily services.

Access by ferry – From Ág Konstandínos (near Kaména Voúrla in Central Greece) and from Vólos and Kímie (in Évia/Euboia) frequent services daily; also inter-island services.

Access by hydrofoil – From Ág Konstandínos, Vólos and Kími frequent services; to all islands (less frequent services from Skíros/Skyros); from Thessaloníki in season 2 to 7 services a week.

Transport – Motorcycle and bicycle hire service; caïques to beaches.

★★Skíathos. *50km²/19sq mi – Population 5 096*

Skíathos Island, which has become very fashionable, is a southern extension of the Pelion range; it is covered with pine and olive trees and rises to 438m/1 437ft. The jagged coastline creates numerous sandy creeks and a splendid lagoon bordered by **Koukounariés Beach★★**, a stretch of fine sand (over 1km/0.5mi long) backed by pine trees.

Accommodation

About 75 hotels (cat A to E) and furnished apartments; rooms in private houses; camping sites.

Daily excursions from Skíathos to Skópelos and Alónissos.

★Skíathos Town – Pop 4512. Skíathos is the capital of the island and a cosmopolitan resort in summer. It was rebuilt in 1830 on two hills overlooking a broad and sheltered roadstead; its two harbours, one for fishing boats and one for pleasure craft, are protected by an islet (Boúrdzi) which was fortified in the Middle Ages. The shady waterfront is crowded by cafés and fish tavernas. In town one can visit the house of the novelist Aléxandros Papadiamántis (1851-1911) who often wrote about Skíathos in his work.

In summer there are boat trips round the island; in passing one can admire the Blue Grotto, **Lalária** beach with its "pierced rock" and the Kástro.

★Kástro – *On the north coast; access by boat (1hr 30min) or on foot (4hr return) from Skíathos Town.*
The track passes two monasteries – Evangelístria (beautiful iconostasis of carved wood in the church) and Ágios Harálambos – before reaching the ruins of the medieval fortress (Kástro). It was the capital of the island until about 1825 and stood on a promontory, accessible only by a drawbridge. It contained 300 houses and 22 churches, two of which are well preserved: Christchurch contains a 17C carved wooden iconostasis.

★Skópelos *97km²/37sq mi – Population 4 658*

Skópelos is the most densely populated of the Sporádes and also the most fertile. It grows vines, olives, almonds and above all plums which make excellent prunes when dried in the oven.
Like Skíathos, Skópelos is well supplied with creeks and sandy beaches but it also has a traditional side and the women sometimes still wear the local dress – an embroidered skirt and a velvet bodice. Traces of the Minoans have been found, in particular the tomb of King Staphylos who may have introduced the grape *(staphíli)* to the island. Skópelos boasts some 350 churches and chapels together with about ten 17C and 18C monasteries; white buildings against the green landscape.

Accommodation

About 50 hotels (cat A to E) mainly in Skópelos Town. Rooms in private houses mainly in Skopelos and Glossa (Loutraki).

★**Skópelos Town** – Pop 2 603. It is a pleasure to stroll along the quayside by the harbour and through the narrow streets of the town; among the houses with their stone-shingled roofs are many small churches or chapels.
The medieval **castle** (Kástro) contained many houses and religious buildings. St Athanasius' Chapel was built in the 9C on the foundations of an ancient temple. From the top of the ruins there is a fine view of Skópelos and the archipelago.

Alónissos *65km²/25sq mi – Population 2 985*

The island is quite large but has few inhabitants; it has a wild landscape of woods and mountains. Fishing, shepherding and agriculture are practised. Sea caves.

Accommodation

About 10 hotels (cat B to E); rooms in private houses; camping site.

★Skíros *223km²/86sq mi – Population 2 901*

Skíros or Skyros Island is the largest of the Sporades and consists of two mountainous islets linked by an isthmus. It has a rougher, more primitive character than its neighbours.
The southern half, called **Vounó** (mountain), is barren and steep and mainly covered with holm-oak scrub although well supplied with springs in the north; it is known not only for its semi-wild herds of sheep and goats but also for its small **horses**, similar to Shetland ponies, which may date from Classical times.
The northern half of the island, called **Meroi**, is fertile and cultivated and well wooded with pine forests. The island has a strong tradition of excellent craftsmanship: carved and painted furniture, hand-woven and embroidered cloth, carpets, basketwork and ceramics. The traditional baggy blue trousers, thick black or white gaiters and distinctive Skyrian sandals *(trohádia)*, modelled on ancient sandals, are still worn by some of the older men.
Fresh fish, crustaceans and honey are plentiful. The creeks and caves along the coast invite one to explore. In summer there are excursions by road and boat.

Accommodation

6 hotels (cat B, C, E); rooms in private houses.

★**Skíros Town** – Pop 1 806. The main town, Skíros, also called Hóra, has a large sandy beach at Magaziá. Its tiny white cuboid houses more typical of the Cyclades are crowded on the inland face of a steep rock crag, spilling over into the valley and climbing up to the castle on the summit. It is a pleasure to stroll through the network of narrow alleyways and steps which pass under arches and open into courtyards. Traditionally the living room with its carved wooden furniture and its curved chimneybreast *(alóni)* bearing three rows of hooks and shelves is adorned with copper articles and porcelain plates.
An old Skyrian mansion on the northeast edge of the town houses the **Faltaïts Museum of Folk Arts**:◷ a fascinating collection of Skyrian handicrafts, both traditional and modern: jewellery, embroidery, textiles, local costumes, wood carvings, furniture, ceramics and bronze and copper household articles. Reconstruction of a local interior. Books about Skíros. Nearby is an **Archeological Museum**.◷

Kástro – The Venetian fortress was built on the old acropolis where **Achilles** *(see Óros PÍLIO: Mythology)* is supposed to have been brought up, dressed like a girl, among the daughters of King Lykomedes, so as to escape the dismal destiny which overtook him at the siege of Troy. Just below it the famous monastery of St George nestles on a ledge of rock above the town; the church dates from the 10C. There is an unusual **view**★★ over Skíros Town where the stepped roofs of the houses form a chequerboard.

Rupert Brooke Memorial and Grave – On a bastion on the northeast edge of the town *(by the museums)* stands a statue to immortal poetry in memory of Rupert Brooke (1887-1915).
The poet's grave lies in a grove of olive trees in a valley on the southern shore of the island in Trís Boúkes Bay *(1hr by road from Skíros Town or by boat from Linariá)*. When Rupert Brooke died of septicaemia on a French hospital ship in April 1915 on the eve of sailing for the Dardanelles, his last wish was to be buried on the island of Skíros.

For adjacent sights see ÉVIA, Óros PÍLIO, VÓLOS.

R.Cuzin/MICHELIN

Égina

PICTOR

Practical information

Before departure

Entry documents – A **passport** or valid **identity card** is required for a stay not exceeding three months. A visa may be required to cross Hungary.
A national driving licence is sufficient for nationals of EU member countries and for US drivers for up to 3 months but an international driving licence is necessary for other drivers.
An international **green insurance card** is compulsory.

Customs – The duty and tax free allowances on certain categories of goods – tobacco, alcohol, spirits and table wine, perfume and toilet water, and other goods – vary depending on whether the goods were obtained duty paid within the EU, as opposed to duty free, or outside the EU.
A pamphlet explaining the allowances and categories is available from HM Customs and Excise at any airport, any local office or from
– Eldon Court, 75 London Road, Reading, Berks, RG1 5BS, ☎ 0118 964 4355
The booklet ***Safe Trip Abroad*** (US$ 1.25) provides US nationals with useful information on visa requirements, customs regulations, medical care etc for international travel; available from
– ☎ (202) 512-1800; www.access.gpo.gov
The booklet ***Know Before You Go*** provides US nationals with useful information about customs regulations; available from
– Fed. Government, US Treasury (nearest office listed in phone book); ☎ 202 927 6724; www.customs.ustreas.gov

Animals – Certificates of good health and inoculation against rabies, issued in the country of origin, are required for all animals entering Greece. The certificate must be issued within a specified time limit
– for dogs not more than 12 months and not less than 6 days before arrival;
– for cats not more than 6 months and not less than 6 days before arrival.
Birds require a certificate stating that they are free from psittacosis.

Marriage – Foreign nationals not resident in Greece may marry in Greece provided that they have made the appropriate arrangements. Details available from the Greek Consulate: 1A Holland Park, London W11 3TP; ☎ 0171 221 6467.

Greek National Tourist Office (GNTO), Elinikós Organismós Tourismoú (EOT) – Information and brochures on all regions of Greece are available from the following official tourist offices:
– 4 Conduit Street, **London** W1R ODJ ☎ (0171) 734 5997; Fax (0171) 287 1369; email: EOT-Greektouristoffice@BT Internet.c
– 645 Fifth Avenue, Olympic Tower, **New York**, NY 10022 ☎ 212-421-5777; Fax 212-826-6940; email: gnto@greektourism.com
www.compulink.gr/tourism
– 611 West Sixth Street, Suite 2198, **Los Angeles**, CA 90017 ☎ 213-626-6696; Fax 213-489-9744.
– 168 North Michigan Avenue, **Chicago**, IL 60601 ☎ 312-782-1084; Fax 312-782-1091.
– 1233 rue de la Montagne, Suite 101, **Montreal**, QC H3G 1Z2 ☎ 514-871-1535; Fax 514-871-1498; email: gntomtl@aei.ca
www.aei.ca/'gntomtl
– 1300 Bay Street, **Toronto**, OT M5R 3K8 ☎ 416-968-2220; Fax 416-968-6533; email: grnto.tor@sympatico.ca
– PO Box R203, 2000, 51-57 Pitt Street, **Sydney**, NSW 2 000 ☎ 2-9241 1663, 9252 1441; Fax 3235 2174.

Local Tourist Offices – There are local tourist offices or the Tourist Police in tourist resorts and on the islands. They are generally located in the town hall and supply information on accommodation (rooms in private houses...) and transport (directions, time-tables...).
The addresses and telephone numbers of these offices are given under the appropriate heading in the chapter on Admission Times and Charges.
There are tourist information offices at **frontier posts**, at Athens International Airport (Elinikó-East) and in the following towns:

– Northern Greece	Árta	Kavála
	Igoumenítsa	Komotiní
	Ioánina	Thessaloníki/Salonica
– Central Greece	Athína/Athens	Pireás/Piraeus
	Kaména Voúrla	Platístomo (west of Lamía)
	Lamía	Thermopíles/Thermopylae
	Lárissa	Vólos
– Peloponnese	Gíthio	Pátra/Patras
	Kalamáta	
– Crete	Ágios Nikólaos	Iráklio/Herakleion
	Haniá/Chania	Réthymno/Rethymnon

– Cyclades	Síros/Syros (Ermoúpoli)	
– Dodecanese	Ródos/Rhodes	
– Ionian Islands	Kefaloniá/Cephallonia	Kérkira/Corfu
– North Aegean Islands	Mitilíni/Mytilene	Sámos

Tourist Police – The Tourist Police have posts in tourist resorts and on the islands. They speak foreign languages and are available to give assistance to tourists. They also fulfill the duties of the ordinary police.

Consulates and Embassies – Information on all Embassies and Consulates available from the Ministry of Foreign Affairs; ☎ (01) 361 1058 (8am to 2pm).

– **Australian** Embassy and Consulate, 37 Odós Soutsou, 115 21 Athína ☎ 644 7303; Fax 646 6595

– **Canadian** Embassy, 4 Odós Gennadiou, 115 21 Athína ☎ 727 3400; Fax 727 3460

– **Irish** Embassy, 7 Leofóros Vass. Kon/nou, 106 74 Athína ☎ 723 2771; Fax 724 0217

– **New Zealand** General Consulate, 24 Odós Xenias, 115 28 Athína ☎ 771 0112; Fax 777 7390

– **South African** Embassy and Consulate, 60 Leofóros Kifissias, 151 25 Maroussi ☎ 680 6645; Fax 680 6640

– **USA** Embassy and Consulate, 91 Leofóros Vass. Sophias, 115 21 Athína ☎ 721 1295; Fax 645 6282

– **UK** Embassy and Consulate, 1 Odós Ploutarchou, 106 75 Athína ☎ 723 6211; Fax 724 1872, 723 0954

Climate – The climate is more varied than one might imagine; it is continental in the north of the country and Mediterranean in the south and on the islands. The mountains are snow-capped until the late spring... even in Kríti/Crete. The rainfall on the west coast is considerably higher than on the east – 1 300mm/50.7ins in Kérkira/Corfu as opposed to 350mm/13.6ins in Athína/Athens.

Winter – The weather is severe in central and northern Greece when the north wind *(voriás)* blows. On the coast and on the islands, however, it is milder and the average temperature in January in Iráklio/Herakleion (Kríti/Crete) or Ródos/Rhodes is 12°–13°C/55°F; these are the main centres for winter tourism. The rain falls in brief but violent storms.

Spring – Despite the snow on the mountains and the occasional showers of rain, the spring flowers provide a mass of colour. May is most pleasant as, although the sea may be chilly, neither the heat nor the number of visitors is excessive.

Summer – From June to September the unchanging blue sky and the bright sunlight attract the sun and sand worshippers. In July and August the weather is very hot. In Athens and in Thessaly and Macedonia it is sultry but in southern Greece and in the Aegean islands the heat is tempered by the north wind *(meltémi)* which can blow for two or three days at a time, refreshing the air but making the sea rough.

Autumn – For some the autumn, until the end of November, is the most agreeable season. The evenings are drawing in and there are occasional rain storms but the vegetation revives, the temperatures are mild and the sea is warm.

Time – Throughout the year the time in Greece is GMT or BST + 2hr, Eastern Standard Time + 7hr. Time is usually expressed according to the 24-hour clock.

12.00	12 noon	19.00	7pm
13.00	1pm	20.00	8pm
14.00	2pm	21.00	9pm
15.00	3pm	22.00	10pm
16.00	4pm	23.00	11pm
17.00	5pm	24.00	12 midnight
18.00	6pm		

Public holidays – The following are days on which shops and public monuments may be closed. In the Orthodox Church the dates of Lent, Easter and Whitsun are fixed according to the Julian calendar and may occur from one to four weeks later than in western Europe; for the exact dates apply to the Greek Embassy or to the GNTO (EOT).

1 January	1 May
6 January (Epiphany)	Whit Sunday
1st Monday in Lent	15 August (Assumption)
25 March (Independence/National Day)	28 October (***Ohi*** Day *see p 29*)
morning of Good Friday	25 and 26 December (Christmas)
Easter Sunday and Monday	

Language – The national language is modern Greek *(see p 50)*. A knowledge of classical Greek is useful for deciphering old signs on roads and shopfronts. English is widely spoken, French and German less so. It is also courteous to be able to speak a few words in Greek.

LOCAL WAYS

Siesta – In summer the Greeks rise early and retire late at night; they usually take an afternoon nap; between 2pm and 5pm therefore visitors should refrain from making a noise.

Dress – Women in mini skirts or trousers and men or women in shorts or with bare shoulders are not admitted to monasteries. The same rule applies in principle to churches.

Gestures – Never hold out an open hand palm outwards to indicate the number five as this is considered a grave insult. A beckoning gesture with the hand is made with the fingers pointing to the ground not upwards.
The Greeks often express "No" by raising the eyes or a slight upwards nod of the head.

Water – In some areas, in particular in the Cyclades, water is very precious and should be used sparingly; the supply is sometimes cut during the day.

Toilets – In some establishments and areas with less sophisticated facilities (where the pipes are narrow) waste bins are provided for used toilet paper.

Travel and transport

TO GREECE

By air – There are daily flights by British Airways to Athína/Athens and by Olympic Airways to Athína/Athens (3hr 30min), Haniá/Chania (Kríti/Crete), Iráklio/Herakleion (Kríti/Crete), Kérkira/Corfu, Ródos/Rhodes and Thessaloníki/Salonica (3hr). *For information on arrival in Athens see p 66.*

British Airways:
65-75 Regent Street, **London** W1, ☎ (0171) 434 4770;
Tele sales (0171) 434 4617;
Reservations (0345) 222111;
Flight information Gatwick (0181) 579 2525 or (0181) 759 1818 (for non-BA flights).
1 Odós Themistokleous, 166 74 Glyfada, near Athens; Fax 89 06 510; ☎ 89 06 666 (Reservations); ☎ 96 99 318 (Lost and found).
1 Odós Mitropoleos, 546 24 Thessaliníki ☎ (031) 220 227, 221 065; Fax (031) 225 240.

Olympic Airways:
11 Conduit Street, **London**, W1R OLP ☎ (0171) 409 2400, Fax (0171) 493 0563; General enquiries and information ☎ (0171) 409 3400; Terminal 2, Heathrow Airport (0181) 759 5884 or 897 3355.
645 Fifth Avenue, **New York**, NY 10022 ☎ (212) 735 0200.
37-49 Pitt Street, Underwood House, Level 3, Suite 303, **Sydney**, NSW ☎ (02) 925 11040; Fax (02) 925 22262.
1200 McGill College Avenue, Suite 1250, **Montreal**, QC H3B 4G7 ☎ (514) 878 3891; Fax 878 4783.
80 Bloor Street West, Suite 502, **Toronto**, OT M^{5}S 2V1 ☎ (416) 964 7137; Fax (416) 920 3686.
96-199 Leofóros Singrou, 117 41 **Athens** ☎ (01) 92 69 111; Fax 92 67 154; Reservations ☎ 96 66 666; Fax 96 66 111; West Airport ☎ 93 69 111.
15 Odós Filellinon (Síndagma) ☎ 92 67 880.
2 Odós Kotopouli (Omonia) ☎ 92 67 216.
In summer there are charter flights from London and most UK provincial airports to all or some of the following destinations:

Athína/Athens (new teminal)	Míkonos/Mykonos
Kefalonía/Cephallonia	Mitilíni/Mytilene
Haniá/Chania (Kríti/Crete)	Pátra-Andravída
Kérkira/Corfu	Préveza
Iráklio/Herakleion (Kríti/Crete)	Ródos/Rhodes (Dodecanese)
Kalamáta	Sámos
Kavála	Thíra/Santorini
Kos (Dodecanese)	Skíathos (Sporades)
Lésvos/Lesbos	Thessaloníki/Salonica
Límnos/Lemnos	Zákinthos/Zakynthos

By rail – There are rail links from northern Europe to Athína/Athens changing at Munich, Cologne or Venice. For information apply to GNTO (EOT) or to **Greek Railways** (OSE), 6 Odós Sina (near the Academy), Athens, ☎ (01) 362 44 02.

By road – For travellers from Western Europe there are shipping connections between Italy and Greece:
– from Venice to Pireás/Piraeus (about 40hr) or Iráklio/Herakleion, Crete (60hr);
– from Ancona to Kérkira/Corfu or Igoumenítsa (about 24hr), to Kefalonía/Cephallonia (continuing to Pireás/Piraeus, Sámos and Kusadasi), to Pátra/Patras (about 34hr), to Iráklio/Herakleion, Crete (about 55hr);
– from Bari to Corfu or Igoumenítsa (about 12hr), Patras (19hr);
– from Brindisi to Kérkira/Corfu or Igoumenítsa (8hr to 11hr), to Itháki/Ithaca (15hr), to Kefalonía/Cephallonia (16hr), to Pátra/Patras (17 to 21hr);
– from Otranto to Kérkira/Corfu and Igoumenítsa (8hr to 11hr).
There is a daily bus service every 45min from Pátra/Patras to Athína/Athens (3hr 30min). The train service is slower and less frequent but cheaper.

WITHIN GREECE

By air – The domestic airline network is extensive. Olympic Airways, the national Greek airline, provides services from **Athína/Athens** (West terminal) and **Thessaloníki/Salonica** to about a dozen towns on the mainland and to some twenty islands. There are also various inter-island services in season.
Fares which are equal to a first class boat ticket are good value. It is advisable to book early in season as domestic services are very popular with both Greeks and tourists, particularly during Greek public holidays *(see p 361)*; also some lines operate small planes which may suffer long delays in the event of strong winds and bad weather. For further information apply to Olympic Airways *(see above)*.

By boat – Consult Michelin map 980. Most services are operated by modern ships but delays may occur in bad weather.
In general there is a daily **ferry service** from Pireás/Piraeus to the well frequented islands with a weekly or twice weekly service to the other islands. In addition to the official services, launches and caïques operate services in season between the islands.
The ships on the major routes have two, three or four classes. Normally it is all right to travel Tourist (C) class where the accommodation consists of a lounge fitted with armchairs and a bar-cafeteria, with easy access to the upper deck (usually astern) for a good view.
There are **hydrofoil services** from Pireás/Piraeus to the islands in the Saronic and Argolic Gulfs and to the east coast of the Peloponnese; also between Vólos (Thessaly), Ágios Konstandínos (southeast of Lamía), Thessaloníki/Salonica, Moundanía (Halkidíki) and the northern Sporades.

D. Hée /MICHELIN

Time-tables (which may vary from week to week, especially in mid-season) are available from Tourist Offices (GNTO/EOT) abroad and in Athens; they are published every month by the GNTO (EOT) and by:
– **Greek Travel Pages**, 6 Odós Psilla and Filellinon, 105 57 Athens ☎ (01) 324 75 11; Fax 323 3384, 324 9996, 325 4775; email: info@gtpnet.com www.gtpnet.com
The time-tables of ships operated by private companies are sometimes unreliable. The list of services on information boards on the dockside is not always exhaustive; it is advisable to enquire in the offices of the different shipping lines round the harbour.
Tickets for all trips (ferries and hydrofoils) are issued in the shipping line offices or at mobile counters on the dockside. It is sometimes necessary to book in advance for car ferries in season and for berths on night ferries (Crete and Rhodes). The ferries are likely to be crowded during Greek public holidays *(see p 361)*.
Piraeus Central Port Authority ☎ (01) 45 11 311/9.
For hydrofoil services:
– **Ceres Hydrofoil Joint Service**, 8 Akti Themistokleous, 18536 Piraeus ☎ (01) 428 0001, Fax 428 3526.

Information also available from
– **Minoan Lines**, 2 Leoforos Vass Konstantinou, 11635 Athens ☎ 751 2356, 752 0152; Fax 689 8344;
– **Magnum Travel**, 747 Green Lane, London N 21 3SA ☎ (0181) 360 5353; Fax (0181) 360 1056.

Pleasure cruising – For the hire of yachts, motor cruisers and caïques, with or without crew, apply to the GNTO (EOT). The main moorings for pleasure craft are shown on Michelin map 980.

By bus – The bus network is very extensive and the buses, some of which have air-conditioning, are a cheap and picturesque means of exploring the country as they run to even the most remote places. Information is available at all bus stations. The OSE railway company also runs bus services to the provinces.
Information on services for the Athens region and intercity connections is available from local tourist offices and the GNTO (EOT). Intercity services are run by KTEL (a group of private bus companies). In principle there are daily services with frequent express buses from Athens to the regional capitals.
The table below indicates the journey time from Athens:

Árgos	5hr	Kavála	10hr
Halkída/Chalkis	1hr 30min	Lamía	3hr 15min
Kefaloniá/Cephallonia	8hr	Monemvassía	6hr
Kérkira/Corfu	11hr	Náfplio/Nauplion	2hr 30min
Kórinthos/Corinth	1hr 30min	Olimbía/Olympia	5hr 30min
Delfí/Delphi	3hr	Pátra/Patras	3hr
Epídavros/Epidauros	2hr 30min	Spárti/Sparta	4hr
Ioánina	7hr 30min	Thíva/Thebes	1hr 30min
Kalamáta	4hr 30min	Thessaloníki/Salonica	7hr 30min

By train – The Greek railway system is not very extensive (only 2 547km/1 583 mi); the lines are shown on Michelin map 980. Fares are inexpensive; services are frequent but travel is slower than by bus. There are ordinary trains and wagon-lits organised by the Hellenic Railways Organisation (ΟΣΕ).
The northern network links Athens (Lárissa Station *for access see p 67*) to Thessaloníki/Salonica with branch lines to Halkída/Chalkis, Vólos, Tríkala and Kalambáka (Metéora), and northwest to Édessa and Kozáni; a line also runs from Thessaloníki to Alexandroúpoli and Orestiáda on the way to Istanbul in Turkey.
The southern network in the Peloponnese, which runs on a narrow gauge (982km/610mi) links Athína/Athens (Peloponnese Station *for access see p 67)* to Kalamáta via Kórinthos/Corinth, Pátra/Patras and Pírgos (branch line to Olymbía/Olympia), or via Kórinthos/Corinth, Árgos-Náfplio and Trípoli.
Some routes are very picturesque, especially the elevated section between Livadiá and Lamía (Central Greece), which includes some impressive viaducts, and the rack railway through the Vouraïkós Gorge between Diakoftó and Kalávrita (Peloponnese).
For further information from GNTO (EOT) or OSE stations *(see ATHINA and THESSALONIKI)* or
– **Greek Railways** (ΟΣΕ), 6 Odós Sina (near the Academy), Athens, ☎ (01) 362 44 02; ☎ (01) 823 7741 (booking for northern Greece); ☎ (01) 513 1601 (booking for the Peloponnese); ☎ (01) 524 0601 and 524 0646 (general information 24hr).

Taxis – Metered taxis can be hired at a taxi rank or will stop on request. Other passengers going in the same direction may share the taxi but rarely the cost. In the country, taxis **(ΑΓΟRΑΙΟΝ)** will usually pick up other fares. When paying it is advisable not to offer a high value note but to tender the right (or nearly right) amount in change.

Car and cycle hire – Car hire is fairly expensive but practical. The large car hire companies have offices in most of the tourist towns and on the islands but it is advisable to book in advance in the high season; in the smaller agencies make sure that proper insurance cover is provided. On the islands bicycles and motor scooters can be hired.
General information available from
– **Union of Greek Car Hire Enterprises**, 576 Leofóros Vouliagmenis, 164 51 Argyroupolis ☎ 99 42 850/9; Fax 99 36 654.

Motoring in Greece

Road network – Michelin map 980 covers the whole country. The Greek road network, which now consists of over 40 000km/24 850mi of roads, has improved considerably during the past 30 years. There are two motorways (tolls payable) linking Athína/Athens to Pátra/Patras and Thessaloníki/Salonica.
The other roads tend to be slow and winding owing to the terrain and relief. There are still some unsurfaced local and regional roads, at times in good condition, which carry heavy traffic including buses. Some surfaced roads are very slippery in wet weather. Roads are frequently under repair and as there are often no alternative routes delays are inevitable.
In the country extra care is required as there are numerous flocks of sheep as well as donkeys in mountain areas and slow agricultural vehicles at times with no headlights. In villages the locals tend to claim the streets as their own especially at the time of the evening stroll.

The roads are sometimes poorly signposted although many of the signs are written in Roman as well as Greek lettering; the main sights are indicated in English.

Petrol stations are frequent enough except on some mountain roads.

Highway Code – Seat belts are compulsory. In the event of illegal parking the police are empowered to remove number plates which will be returned at the police station on payment of a fine. Tourist Police ☎ 171.

The speed limit is	100 or 120 kph	on motorways
	80 kph	on trunk roads
	50 kph	in built-up areas.

Greek Automobile Touring Club (ELPA) – This organisation has about 40 offices throughout the country and runs a roadside breakdown service (OVELPA – ☎ 104) which is free to members of other national Automobile or Touring Clubs.

Where to stay

The Michelin Map 980 shows the major resorts, the places with hotels, the official camping sites, the ports with moorings and the beaches with facilities. The GNTO/EOT publishes pamphlets on the various regions of Greece with information about the resorts and accommodationl1474 including a list of hotels classified according to towns and categories (except for D and E).

Hotels – Although many hotels have been built since the 1960s, accommodation may be scarce in the high season; it is wise to reserve in advance.
Prices which include service charges and taxes vary according to category – from the luxury class down to E.
The average tourist is advised to choose B and C class hotels which are usually clean and reasonably comfortable; all rooms have facilities. B class hotels (also Luxury and A class) usually have a restaurant; C hotels rarely do. D hotels are simpler but often have rooms with facilities. D and E hotels do not serve breakfast but there are usually cafés nearby.
The Xenia Hotels are a state-run chain of hotels (usually A and B class). They are often comfortable and well-decorated and built on pleasant sites; they will also serve breakfast to non-residents.
Reception will ask for passports *(diavatíria)* and may hold them overnight.

Rooms in private houses – Outside the large towns and resorts it is common to take a room in a private house, particularly on the Aegean islands where the boats are met by householders offering rooms.
It is prudent, however, to seek accommodation through the local GNTO (EOT) office or the Tourist Office who check the rooms and make the introduction.
Standards of comfort vary but the rooms are almost always clean. Previously the accommodation was in the owner's house but some of the householders have built annexes with kitchens and other facilities; such accommodation is less picturesque but more comfortable.

S. Johnson /FOTOGRAM-STONE

Taverna terrace after dark

Rural holidays – The **Country Women's Tourist Cooperatives**, which have been set up in isolated but picturesque villages, offer visitors a wider experience of the Greek cultural heritage as well as promoting the role of country women and improving their financial independence.
The members offer rooms in private houses (there are few isolated farms in Greece) and visitors can sample home cooking or eat out in restaurants run by the local women who also offer craft products for sale. Visitors can learn local crafts or help with farm work. Rural holidays may be enjoyed in the locations listed below; information and addresses are available from the GNTO (EOT).

Ambelákia (northeast of Thessaly)
Pétra (northwest coast of Lesbos)
the Mastikohória (the "mastic villages" of Híos/Chios); ☎ (0271) 72496
Aráhova (near Delfí/Delphi)
Agios Germanós (near the Préspa Lakes in northwest Macedonia)
Marónia (south of Komotiní in Thrace).

Traditional lodgings – The GNTO (EOT) lets accommodation in renovated traditional buildings in typical settings away from the most popular locations:
– on the **mainland** at Makrinítsa, Miliés and Vizítsa on Mount Pelion (Thessaly); in the village of Pápingo (Zagoriá, Epiros), in Korishádes near Karpeníssi in Central Greece, at Areópoli and at Váthia in the Máni and in Monemvassía (Peloponnese);
– on the **islands** of Thíra/Santorini (Ía), Híos/Chios (Mestá), Psará (a small island off Chios).

Youth Hostels – There are about 20 youth hostels throughout Greece which are listed below. In Athens and Thessaloníki there are also YMCA and YWCA or XEN hostels. Holders of an International Youth Hostel Federation card should apply for a list from the International Federation or from the

Greek Youth Hostels Association, 4 Odós Dragatsaniou, Athens, ☎ 323 4107.

Delfí/Delphi
Mikínes/Mycenae
Haniá/Chania (Crete)
Iráklio/Herakleion (Crete)
Mália (Crete)
Réthimno/Rethymnon (Crete)
Thíra/Santorini (Cyclades)
Náfplio/Nauplion
Olimbía/Olympia
Pátra/Patras
Thessaloníki/Salonica

Camping – There are many official camping sites near the major towns and resorts run by the GNTO (EOT), the Greek Touring Club and private owners. Consult the Michelin map 980 and apply to the local Tourist Office or to the GNTO (EOT) which publishes an annual camping guide booklet, **Camp in Greece**, which gives a detailed description of all Greek camp sites.
Although camping outside the official sites is forbidden, it is sometimes possible with the permission of the owner of the site or of the local Tourist Office.

Spas towns – The volcanic nature of the land produces a number of hot springs, some of which have been developed as health resorts, offering a range of hydrotherapy treatments. The word *Loutrá* or *Thérma* in a place name usually signifies a spa town.

– in Central Greece – Platístomo and Loutrá Ipátis in the valley of the River Sperhiós and Loutrá Edipsoú further east on the coast of Évia;
– in the Peloponnese at Loutráki (north of Corinth) and at Loutrá Kilínis and Kaláfas on the west coast;
– at Thérma Lefkádas on Ikaría in the Aegean islands.

There are also unexploited hot springs at Thermopíles, on the north coast of Lésbos and in the crater on Thíra in the Cyclades.

Services *(see also ATHÍNA and THESSALONÍKI)*

Cost of living – It is more or less the same as in the UK. Transport costs (by bus, taxi, train, plane and boat) are relatively low.

Tipping – In principle prices are net but it is usual to round up (taxis, restaurants, tavernas) and to give a few drachmas (50-100) to porters and to the waiter *(mikró)* in a restaurant.
It would be discourteous however to give recompense for help offered spontaneously; the Greeks are a proud and hospitable people.

Currency – The currency is the drachma (drachmes in the plural); £1 = 482 Dr; US$1 = 293Dr. Travellers are advised to make enquiries at a bank about the latest regulations governing the amount of Greek currency which can be imported into Greece.

Exchange – Foreign currency, travellers' cheques and Eurocheques can be changed in banks, exchange offices and post offices at the legal rate and in hotels at a slightly lower rate.

Credit cards (particularly Visa) can be used to obtain Greek currency and in many hotels and shops. Foreign currency and travellers cheques (no credit cards) can also be exchanged at the post office.

Banking – Opening times Mondays to Fridays, 8.30am to 1.30pm. In Athens and Thessaloníki some banks open in the afternoons until 8pm (change facilities only); at the international airports the banks are open 24 hours. In Athens there are currency exchange points (open usually 9am to 9pm). In tourist resorts there are automatic cash dispensers but it is advisable to go early to avoid long delays.

Post – Post Office signs (ΕΛΤΑ) and letter boxes are yellow. Post Offices are usually open Mondays to Fridays, 7.30am to 2pm.
Stamps are sold in post offices, from automatic machines outside post offices and in newspaper kiosks.
It is also possible to change money at the post office.
Letters between Athens and London take about 3 or 4 days; postcards from more remote places are unpredictable.
There is a "Poste restante" service; the one in Athens is 100 Odós Eólou, near Omonia Square; the name and address should be written in capital letters.

Telephone (OTE) – The OTE offices are generally open all day including Saturdays (except in small towns) until late in the evening especially in the centre of large towns (10pm-midnight).
There are telephone kiosks in the streets and also at newspaper stalls *(períptera)*; some have meters from which international calls can be made. Telephone cards can be purchased from the OTE offices or in kiosks.

Domestic calls – For calls within Greece the initial 0 must be dialled.

International calls – To ring a foreign number directly from Greece dial 00 followed by the country code, the city or district code and the subscriber's number.

162	Information on calling abroad
169	Instructions for international calls (English, French and German)
161	Announcements on telephone calls abroad

International dialling codes –

6	Australia	64	New Zealand
1	Canada	44	United Kingdom
353	Ireland	1	United States of America

When telephoning Greece from abroad dial 00 30, then the city or district code (omitting the initial 0) and the subscriber's number.

Electric current – Usually 220 volts AC (50HZ). Electrical plugs have two large round prongs; an adaptor is essential.

Shopping and crafts

See also Local arts and traditions (p 52), Food and drink (p 54) and Vocabulary (p 373).

Opening times – Large stores and supermarkets are open Mondays to Saturdays, 9am to 8pm (3.30pm on Saturdays). Other shops are open Mondays, Wednesdays and Saturdays, 9am to 3pm and on Tuesdays, Thursdays and Fridays, 9am to 2pm and 5pm to 8pm. Most shops are closed on Sundays.

Export regulations – To export antiquities, icons and other works of art it is necessary to obtain an authorisation from:
– 13 Odós Polignótou, **Athens** (in Pláka between the Greek and Roman *agoras*).

Books and newspapers – In large towns and tourist centres foreign newspapers and magazines are on sale. In resorts and large towns shops sell paperbacks in English, French and German. There are English and French bookshops in Athens, Kalamáta and Thessaloníki.

Newspaper stalls *(períptera)* – They sell not only newspapers but also cigarettes, postage stamps, sweets, razor blades, sunglasses, suntan lotion, ice cream and aspirins... Often they have a telephone with a meter for long-distance or international calls.

Crafts – The **National Craft Council** runs workshops and has several shops:
– 6 Odós Ipatia, **Athens** (corner of Odós Apolonos, behind the Cathedral)
– 24a Odós Voukourestiou, **Athens** (north of Síndagma Square)
– Danília Village, **Corfu**.

There is a great variety of articles on offer throughout Greece and the quality ranges from modest to first class (even very expensive):

worry-beads *(kombolói)*
ceramics and pottery
lace
embroidered clothes and articles
bedspreads
cloth
hand-woven carpets – Volímes, Zákinthos;
long-haired rugs *(flokáti)* – from Aráhova and Thessaly
gold jewellery of ancient or modern design – jewellers such as Lalaoúnis and Zolotas have won international renown
traditional silver jewellery – from Ioánina and Macedonia
carved and turned wood
marble and onyx carvings
reproduction icons (the cheaper ones are paper images glued onto wood)
leather boots - from Crete (Krítsa and Haniá)
leather goods roughly finished but inexpensive – Athens and the islands
painted furniture - Skíros Island.

Edible specialities – Honey *(méli)*, preserves (figs or cherries), macaroons *(amigdalotá)*, almond cakes *(kourabiédes)*, pistachio nuts (*phistíkia* from Aegina), almond paste with pistachio nuts *(hálva)*, resinated wine *(retsína)*, fortified wine (Samian muscat, Mavrodaphne), liqueurs *(oúzo, rakí, mastíka)*; Plomári on Lesvos is a reputable name for oúzo.

J. Bolland /APPARENCE

Traditional fabric, Ágios Nikólaos, Crete

Help us in our constant task of keeping up-to-date.
Send your comments and suggestions to

Michelin Tyre PLC
Travel Publications
38 Clarendon Road
WATFORD, Herts
WD1 1SX
☎ 01923 415 000
Fax: 01923 415 250
Web site: www.michelin-travel.com

Recreation

With its magnificent natural features and long hours of sunshine in the summer, Greece offers many opportunities for outdoor pursuits and for special interest holidays.
The long coastline and the many islands, the forests and high mountains provide many opportunities for holidays with **outdoor themes** – water sports, bird watching, wildlife and wild flowers, painting, walking and rambling, mountain biking, skiing, climbing and mountaineering.

Archeology – The most famous archeological sites are in and around Athens, in the Peloponnese, northwest of Thessaloníki and on some of the islands. Many companies organise parties and cruises, led by experts, to tour the different sites.

National Parks – Greece has several national parks, which conserve the indigenous flora and fauna, in central and northern Greece *(from north to south)*:

Víkos-Aoós – 12 600ha/31 122 acres – north of Ioánina
Olympos – access from Vólos
Iti – near Lamía
Parnassós – 3 600ha/8 892 acres – north of Delfí/Delphi
Párnitha – 3 800ha/9 386 acres – north of Athína/Athens.

Climbing and mountaineering – Information available from:

– **Hellenic Federation of Mountaineering and Climbing**, 5 Odós Milioni, 106 73 Athína ☎ 36 45 904, 36 36 617; Fax 36 44 687.

Skiing – The ski resorts (listed below from north to south) are mostly in northern Greece; information avaialble from:

– **Hellenic Ski Federation**, 7 Odós Kar Servias, 105 63 Athína ☎ 3234 412, 32 30 182; Fax 32 30 142.

Northern Greece – Falakró (north of Dráma); Orfea Valley-Pangéo (west of Kavála); Vrontous (north of Séres); 3-5 Pigadia-Vermio and Séli (northwest of Véria); Kaimaktsalán-Voras (northeast of Flórina); Vigla Pissoderi (Flórina); Vitsi-Verno (north of Kastoria); Vasilitsa-Pindos (southwest of Grevená); Karakoli (north of Métsovo); Profitis Ilias (north of Métsovo).

Central Greece – Vrissopoules-Olympos (north of Lárissa); Agriolefkes-Pelion (east of Vólos); Timfristos-Diavolotopos (north of Karpeníssi); Kellaria-Fterolaka-Parnassos (north of Delfí).

Peloponnese – Helmos-Vathia Laka (south of Kalávrita); Menalo-Oropedio-Ostrakina (southeast of Vitína).

Water sports – The great length of the sea coast and the warm climate make holidays which concentrate on **watersports** particularly attractive. Most packages include equipment and tuition – cruising, dinghy sailing, flotilla sailing, scuba diving, windsurfing.

Calendar of events

For the exact dates apply to the tourist office.
In the Orthodox Church Lent, Easter and Whitsun are fixed according to the Julian calendar and may fall from one to four weeks later than in western Europe.

DATE and PLACE	TYPE of EVENT
6 January (Epiphany)	
Pireás/Piraeus and other ports	Blessing of the sea and immersion of a cross, retrieved by swimmers.
February-March: 8 days before the 1st Monday in Lent	
Pátra/Patras	Carnival, the most important in Greece: procession of floats.
Athína/Athens	Carnival with masks and disguises.
Skíros/Skyros	Carnival; costume procession; traditional dances.
Náoussa (Macedonia)	Carnival of the *Boúles*, masked dancers.
Monday before Lent	
Athína/Athens	Popular songs and dances near the temple of Zeus and the Pnyx Hill; kite-flying competition.
Palm Sunday and Holy Saturday	
Kérkira/Corfu	St Spiridon's procession.
Good Friday	
Throughout Greece	Procession of the Epitáfios (image of Christ).
Easter Sunday	
Throughout Greece	Midnight mass out of doors; paschal lamb feast.
Easter Tuesday	
Mégara (Attica)	Local festival: traditional dances in costume.
Easter Week	
Káristos (Euboia)	**Voriatikí** (North Wind), a men's dance.
Kálimnos	Blessing of the boats for sponge fishing.
23 April (St George's Day)	
Skála (Kefaloniá/Cephallonia)	Local festival.
Assí-Goniá (Kríti/Crete: southwest of Réthimno/Rethymnon)	Mass and popular festival; blessing of the cattle.
5-6 May	
Skinés (Kríti/Crete: south of Haniá/Chania)	Orange festival; Cretan dancing and singing.
21-23 May	
Langadás (16km/10mi northeast ... of Thessaloníki/Salonica) **and Agiá Eléni in Séres** (60km/38mi northeast of Thessaloníki/Salonica)	Ritual ceremonies (Anastenária): the *Anastenarídes*, in a trance, dance barefoot on hot coals holding icons of Constantine and Helena.
29 May	
Mistrás/Mystra (Peloponnese)	Commemoration of the death of Emperor Constantine Palaiologos on 29 May 1453 *(see MISTRÁS)*.
May	
Lésvos/Lesbos	Animal sacrifices, horse racing, dancing, religious festival *(see LÉSVOS)*.
May – September	
Athína/Athens	Dancing by the Dora Stratou company.
Mid-June – early October	
Athína/Athens	Athens Festival: Greek drama, concerts, ballet.

Saturdays and Sundays, end June – end August

Epídavros/Epidauros...................... Festival of ancient drama.

End June – September

Coastal towns................................ Nautical Week.

Mid-June – early October

Pátra/Patras.................................. Festival.

June – September

Iráklio/Heraklion (Kríti/Crete)......... Festival.

17-18 July

Vóni (Kríti/Crete: southeast of Knossós)..................... Festival of Cretan dancing and singing.

19 July

Throughout Greece........................ Pilgrimages to peaks dedicated to Elijah (Ilías).

July – August

Réthimno/Rethymnon................... Festival.

Delfí/Delphi................................... Festival of ancient drama.

Fílipi/Philippi – Thássos............... Ancient Drama Festival.

July – early September

Ródos/Rhodes............................... Wine festival: free tasting of Greek wine.

Mid-July – September

Réthimno/Rethymnon (Kríti/Crete) ... Wine festival.

August

Lefkáda/Leukas............................. Arts and folk festival.

6 August

Kérkira/Corfu................................ Procession of boats to the isle of Pondikonísi.

11 August

Kérkira/Corfu................................ St Spiridon's procession.

13-15 August

Arhánes and Neápoli (Kríti/Crete)..... Festival of popular art; wine tasting.

August – September

Pátra/Patras and Ioánina............. Wine festival.

Dodóni/Dodona............................. Performances of ancient Greek drama.

15 August

Tínos/Tenos.................................. Pilgrimage to the miraculous image of the Virgin.

Markópoulo (Kefaloniá/Cephallonia).. Procession of serpents.

Skiáthos.. Procession of the Epitáfios (image of the Virgin).

First Sunday after 15 August

Portariá (Óros Pílio/Mount Pelion)..... Representation of a traditional country wedding.

Last Sunday in August

Kritsá (Kríti/Crete).......................... Representation of a traditional country wedding.

End August – early September

Zákinthos/Zakynthos..................... International Medieval and Popular Drama Festival.

September

Thessaloníki/Salonica.................... International Fair.

October

Thessaloníki/Salonica.................... Film Festival.

14 September

Préveli .... Religious festival of the True Cross; pilgrimage.

October – November

Thessaloníki/Salonica .... St Demetrios' procession; Dimitria festival; cultural events.

8 November

Arkádi (Kríti/Crete) .... Parade and traditional dances in memory of the sacrifice of the defenders of the monastery.

30 November (St Andrew's Day)

Pátra/Patras .... Procession in honour of the patron saint of Patras.

24 and 31 December

Throughout Greece .... Children sing *Kálanda* in the streets.

PICTOR

Further Reading

See also Modern Greek Literature

ART AND ARCHEOLOGY

The Glory that was Greece, J C Stobart, revised R J Hopper, Sidgwick & Jackson.
The Architecture of Ancient Greece, William Bell Dinsmoor, Batsford 1975, 1989.
The Sea Peoples, N K Sandars, Thames & Hudson 1978.
The Mycenaean World, John Chadwick, Cambridge University Press 1976.
Writing in Gold – Byzantine Society and its Icons, R Cormack, G Philip 1985.
The Rediscovery of Greece, Fani-Maria Tsigakou, Thames & Hudson 1981.
The Victorians and Ancient Greece, Richard Jenkyns, Blackwells 1980.
Greek Inscriptions, B F Cook, British Museum Publications Ltd 1989.
Linear B and Related Scripts, J Chadwick, British Museum Publications Ltd 1987.
Cycladic Art, J Lesley Fitton, British Museum Publications Ltd 1989.
The Elgin Marbles, B F Cook, British Museum Publications Ltd 1984.
Greek Vases, D Williams, British Museum Publications Ltd 1985.

GEOGRAPHY AND HISTORY

Greece – an introduction, E M Pantelouris, Blueacre Books Glasgow 1980.
Atlas of the Greek World, Peter Levi, Phaidon Press Oxford.
A Concise History of Ancient Greece, Peter Green, Thames & Hudson 1973.
The Ancient Greeks, M I Finley, Penguin 1963.
The Spartans, L F Fitzhardinge, Thames & Hudson 1985.

The Ancient Olympic Games, J Swaddling, British Museum Publications Ltd 1980.
Crete: Its Past, Present and People, Adam Hopkins, Faber & Faber 1977.
Byzantium – An Introduction, Philip Whitting, Blackwells 1971, 1981.
The Byzantine Empire, Robert Browning, Book Club Associates 1980.
Mediaeval Greece, Nicolas Cheetham, Yale University Press 1981.
Mistra, Steven Runciman, Thames & Hudson 1980.
Britain's Greek Empire, Michael Pratt, Rex Collings 1978.
Lord Elgin and the Marbles, William St Clair, OUP 1967, 1983.
That Greece might still be free, William St Clair, OUP 1972.
Modern Greece – A short history, C M Woodhouse, Faber & Faber 1968, 1977.
The Philhellenes, C M Woodhouse, Faber & Faber 1969.
Ill Met by Moonlight, W Stanley Moss, George G Harrap 1950.
The Mountain War, Kenneth Matthews, Longman 1972.
The Greek War of Independence, C M Woodhouse, Russell & Russell 1952, 1975.
The Wound of Greece, P Sherrard, Rex Collings, 1978.

TRAVEL BOOKS; LITERATURE

The Greek Islands, Lawrence Durrell, Faber & Faber 1978.
Prospero's Cell (Corfu), Lawrence Durrell, Faber & Faber 1960.
Reflections of a Marine Venus (Rhodes), Lawrence Durrell.
Roumeli, Patrick Leigh Fermor, John Murray 1966, Penguin 1983.
Mani, Patrick Leigh Fermor, John Murray 1958, Penguin 1984.
Deep into Mani, Journey to the Southern Tip of Greece, Peter Greenhalgh & Edward Eliopoulos, Faber & Faber 1985.
The Cretan Runner, G Psychoundakis, translated by P Leigh Fermor, John Murray 1955.
Greek Myths, Robert Graves, Cassell 1955.
The Dark Crystal: Cavafy, Sikelianos, Seferis, Elytis, Gatsos, translated by Edmund Keeley and Philip Sherrard, Denis Harvey 1981.
Eleni by Nicholas Gage, Fontana-Collins 1983.
The Magus by John Fowles, Jonathan Cap 1977; 022401392-0.
Captain Corelli's Mandolin by Louis de Bernières, Minerva Fiction 1994; 9-780749-385057.

GENERAL

Greek Food, Rena Salaman, Fontana Paperbacks 1983.
Cooking the Greek Way, Anne Theoharous, Methuen Paperbacks 1979.
The Companion Guides to Mainland Greece; Southern Greece; the Greek Islands, Collins 1983.
Greece on Foot, Marc Dubin, Cordee, Leicester 1986.
The Customs and Lore of Modern Greece, Rennell Rodd, Argonaut Press, Chicago.

Vocabulary

The accent indicates the syllable which is stressed.

Numbers

1	**éna, mía**	30	**triánda**
2	**dío**	40	**saránda**
3	**tría, tris**	50	**penínda**
4	**téssera, tésseris**	60	**exínda**
5	**pénde**	70	**evdomínda**
6	**éxi**	80	**ogdónda**
7	**eptá**	90	**enenínda**
8	**októ**	100	**ekató**
9	**enéa**	101	**ekato éna (etc)**
10	**déka**	200	**diakóssia**
11	**éndeka**	300	**triakóssia**
12	**dódeka**	400	**tetrakóssia**
13	**dekatría**	500	**pendakóssia**
14	**dekatéssera**	600	**exakóssia**
15	**dekapénde**	700	**eptakóssia**
16	**dekaéxi**	800	**oktakóssia**
17	**dekaeptá**	900	**eneakóssia**
18	**dekaoktó**	1 000	**hília**
19	**dekaenéa**	2 000	**dío hiliádes**
20	**íkossi**	3 000	**trís hiliádes**
21	**íkossi éna**	5 000	**pénde hiliádes**
22	**íkossi dío**	10 000	**déka hiliádes**
23	**íkossi tría (etc)**		

General expressions

yes, no	**né, óhi**
of course, indeed	**málista**
good morning	**kaliméra**
good evening	**kalispéra**
good night	**kaliníhta**
goodbye	**adio, giá sas**
have a good trip	**kalo taxídi**
Sir, Madam	**kírie, kiría**
Miss	**despinís**
please	**parakaló**
Thank you	**evkaristó**
(very much)	**(polí)**
Excuse me	**mé sinhoríte**
sorry	**signómi**
it is...small, big	**íne... mikró, ... megálo**
beautiful	**oréo**
good, bad	**kaló, kakó**
hot, cold	**zestó, krío**
compulsory	**ipohreotikó**
forbidden	**apagorévete**
expensive, cheap	**akrivó, ftinó**
colour	**to hróma**
white	**áspro**
blue	**blé**
yellow	**kítrino**
black	**mávro**
red	**kókino**
green	**prássino**
very, much,	
too much	**pára polí**
(a) little	**lígo**
enough	**arketá**
always, never	**pándote, poté**
perhaps	**íssos**
often	**sihná**
more, less	**perissótero, ligótero**
quickly, slowly	**grígora, argá**
half	**missó**
other	**álo**
we are	**ímaste**
I have, we have	**ého, éhome**
Do you have?	**éhete?**
OK, all right	**endáxi**
What?	**ti?**
Where? When?	**pou? poté?**
Why, because	**giatí**
How much, how	**pósso, pos**
here, there	**edó, ekí**
near, far	**kondá, makriá**
with, without	**me, hóris**
from, towards	**apó, pros**
and, or	**ke, i**
not	**den**
I am a foreigner	**íme xénos (xéni)**
I do not understand	**den katalavéno**
Do you speak	**miláte**
English?	**angliká?**
French?	**galiká?**
German?	**germaniká?**
I am English	**íme anglós (anglída)**
American	**amerikanós (amerikanída)**
Scottish	**skotós (skotída)**
Irish	**irlandós (irlandída)**
Canadian	**kanadós (kanadída)**
Great Britain	**Megáli Bretanía**
England, Wales	**Anglía, Oualía**
Scotland, Ireland	**Skotía, Irlandía**
America, Canada	**Amerikí, Kanadá**
Australia,	**Afstralía,**
New Zealand	**Néa Zilandiada**
Greek, Greece	**élinas (elinída), Elás**

Time o kerós

morning	**to proí**
(until 1pm)	
mid-day	**to messiméri**
(until about 3pm)	
afternoon	**to apógevma**
(until 8pm)	
evening	**to vrádi**
(until sunset)	
night	**i níhta**
yesterday	**htes**
today	**símera**
tomorrow	**ávrio**
day after tomorrow	**methávrio**
next year	**tou hronoú**
one moment,	
just a minute	**éna leptó**
one hour	**mía óra**
(2 hours)	**(dío óres)**
one day	**mia méra**
(2 days)	**(dío méres)**
one week	**mía evdomáda**
(2 weeks) `	**(dío evdomádes)**
one month,	**éna mína**
one year	**énas hrónos**
(two years)	**(dío hrónia)**
Monday	**deftéra**
Tuesday	**tríti**
Wednesday	**tetárti**
Thursday	**pémdi**
Friday	**paraskeví**
Saturday	**sávato**
Sunday	**kiriakí**
how long?	**póssi óra?**
What time is it?	**ti óra íne?**
5 minutes past one	**mía ke pénde**
quarter past two	**dío ke tétarto**
half past three	**trís í missí**
ten past four	**tésseris pará déka**
five o'clock	**pénde i óra**
early, late	**norís, argá**

Services

Where is	**poú íne**
the lavatory?	**i toilétes?**
bank	**i trápeza**
change, exchange	**to sinálagma**
cash desk	**to tamío**
post	**to tahidromío**
letter	**to gráma**
stamp	**to gramatóssimo**
telephone, OTE	**to tiléfono OTÉ**
kiosk	**to períptero**
hospital	**to nossokomío**
health centre	**iatrikó kéndro**
doctor	**o iatrós**
chemist, pharmacy	**to farmakío**
aspirin	**aspiríni**

Tourism

ruins	**ta arhéa**
cathedral	**i mitrópoli**
castle, citadel	**to kástro (froúrio)**
church, chapel	**i eklissía**
river	**o potamós**
frescoes	**i tihografíes**
keeper	**o fílakas**
mountain	**to vounó, to óros**
mosaics	**i psifidotá**
mosque	**to dzámi**
mill	**o mílos**
museum	**to moussío**
beach	**i aktí, i paralía**
sand, shingle	**i ámos, i pétres**

cave	**to spíleo**
island(s)	**to nissí (ta nissiá)**
lake	**to límni**
sea	**i thálassa**
monastery	**i moní, to monastísi**
monument	**to mnimío**
saint	**ágios, agía**
statue	**to ágalma**
temple, shrine	**o naós, to ieró**
tower	**o pírgos**
upper town	**i akrópoli, to kástro**
view	**to théama**

Shopping

shop	**to magazí**
general store, bazaar	**to pandopolío**
grocer's shop	**to bakáliko**
bakery	**to ahtopolío (o foúrnos)**
patisserie, cake shop	**to zaharoplastío**
How much does this cost?	**pósso káni aftó?**
I don't like this	**den mou aréssi**
matches	**spírta**
cigarettes	**tsigára**
photo	**i fotografía**
film	**to film**
battery	**bataría**
gold, silver	**hrissós, assími**
tin-opener	**anihtíri konsérves**
bread	**psomí**
butter	**voútiro**
milk	**gála**
yoghurt	**iaoúrti**
honey	**méli**
jam	**marmeláda**
mineral water	**metalikó neró**
French toast	**paximadáki**
biscuit	**biskóta**
tea	**tsáï**
coffee	**kafé**
chocolate	**sokoláta**
sugar	**záhari**
the price	**i timí**

In a hotel xenodohío

Do you have a room?	**éxete éna domátio?**
with a single bed	**me éna kreváti**
with twin beds	**me dío krevátia**
with shower, bath	**me dous, bágno**
with WC	**me toilétes**
quieter	**pió íssiho**
blanket	**mía kouvérta**
passport	**to diavatírio**
identity card	**i tavtótita**
at what time?	**ti óra?**
breakfast	**to proinó?**
cup	**éna flidsáni**
key	**to klidí**

In a restaurant estiatório, tavérna

lunch, dinner	**to gévma, to dípno**
plate	**éna piáto**
spoon	**éna koutáli**
fork	**éna piroúni**
knife	**éna mahéri**
glass	**éna potíri**
bottle	**éna boukáli**
the menu	**to katálogo**
salt, pepper	**aláti, pipéri**
oil, vinegar	**ládi, xídi**
sandwich	**sansouíts**
bread	**psomí**
white (rosé) wine	**áspro (rosé) krassí**
red wine	**kókino (mávro) krassí**
resinated wine	**retsína**
beer, water	**bíra, neró**
lemonade	**lemonáda**
orangeade	**portokálada**
fruit juice	**himó froútou**
the bill	**to logariasmó**

Travelling *(see also Michelin map 980 folds 24 and 36)*

the road (to)	**o drómos (gia)**
path	**to monopáti**
good, bad condition	**káli, kakí katástassi**
dangerous	**epikíndino**
on the right	**dexiá**
on the left	**aristerá**
straight on	**efthía**
this way	**apó (e)dó**
first	**prótos**
second, third	**défteros, trítos**
up, down	**páno, káto**
in front of, behind	**embrós, písso**
kilometres	**hiliómetra**
fill up the (petrol) tank	**na to gemízete**
petrol station	**pratírio venzínis**
petrol	**venzíni**
litres	**lítra**
premium, super	**aplí, soúper**
oil	**to ládi**
Michelin tyres	**ta lastiká Messelíne**
garage	**to garáz**
battery	**i bataría**
entrance	**i íssodos**
way out	**i éxodos**
town	**i póli, i hóra (island)**
village	**to horió**
street	**i odós**
avenue	**i leofóros**
square	**i platía**
one-way	**o monódromos**
centre	**to kéndro**
market	**i agorá**
(Tourist) police	**i (touristikí) astinomía**
Tourist Office	**to grafío tou EOT (éotte)**
camping	**to kamping**
ticket	**to issitirío**
at what time leaves...?	**ti óra févgi**
at what time arrives...?	**ti óra ftáni**
where	**pou**
train	**to tréno**
bus, coach	**to leoforío**
ship	**to vapóri, plío**
caïque, boat	**to kaïki, i várka**
plane	**to aeropláno**
donkey	**to gaïdoúri**
mule	**to moulári**
(railway) station	**o (sidirodromikós) stathmós**
bus (coach) station	**o stathmós ton leoforíon**
port	**to limáni**
airport	**to aerodrómio**
station, stop	**i stássi**
terminus	**to térma**
first, last	**próto, teleftéo**
taxi	**to taxi**
car	**to avtokínito, amáxi**
bicycle	**to podílato**
moped	**motopodílato**
on foot	**me ta pódia**

Admission times and charges

The information below is given for guidance only as opening times and admission charges are liable to alteration.

Information for the islands on access (by air and sea), accommodation and transport is given for guidance only. For general information on boat services see PRACTICAL INFORMATION.

⏲ – *The symbol ⏲ after the name of a sight in the middle section of the guide indicates a sight for which admission times and charges are given in this section.*

Charges – *The prices quoted apply to individual adults with no reductions. In some cases there are reductions for students on presentation of an international student card.*

Dates – *The summer season runs approximately from mid-April to mid-October and high season from mid-June to mid-September.*

Public holidays – *See p 361. Sites, monuments and museums are usually closed on the following public holidays: 1 January, Easter Sunday, 25 March (Independence/National Day), 1 May, Good Friday (until 12 noon), 25 and 26 December.*
They are open on the remaining holidays but Sunday opening times apply.

Times – *Monasteries for which there are no visiting times are usually closed between 1pm and 5pm. The churches for which no visiting times are given are generally closed between 12.30pm and 5.30pm.*

Dress – *Informal dress is not acceptable for visits to monasteries, churches and also ancient shrines (see p 362).*

Photography – *The use of cameras is banned in some museums; in cases where photography is allowed a special ticket is required (flash photography is usually forbidden). A tax is levied on filming on archeological sites and in museums: between 7 000 and 18 000 Dr (50 % reduction for video cameras). For special conditions apply on the site.*

A

AMFIARAÍO

Access – By bus from 14 Odós Mavromateon (along Pedió Areos Park) plan of Athens, BX-CX.

Ruins – 8.30am to 3pm. 500 Dr.

ANDRÍTSENA

Temple at Vassés – Restoration in progress. All year, sunrise to sunset. 500 Dr. ☎ (0626) 22 254

ARÁHOVA

ℹ – ☎ (0267) 31 692

Óros Parnassos – For a professional guide for the climb to the top of Mount Liákoura apply in Aráhova to Mr Nikólaos Georgakos, ☎ (0267) 31 391, or at the town hall, ☎ (0267) 31 250.

ÁRGOS

Ancient ruins – Daily, summer 8am to 2.30pm, winter 8.30am to 3pm. No charge

Museum – Daily except Mondays, summer 8am to 2.30pm, winter 8.30am to 3pm. 500 Dr. ☎ (0751) 28 819.

Iréo (Argive Heraion) – Daily, summer 8am to 2.30pm, winter 8.30am to 3pm. No charge.

ÁRTA

ℹ Odós Kristali (0681) 78 551
ℹ Tourist police ☎ (0681) 33 010

Panagía Parigorítissa – Daily except Mondays, 8.30am to 3pm. 500 Dr.

Agía Theodóra (St Theodora's Church) – Daily 8am to 1pm and 5.30pm to 8pm.

Excursion

Vlacherna Monastery – Daily except Mondays, 8.30am to 3pm. 500 Dr.

ATHÍNA (Athens)

2 Odós Amérikis ☎ (01) 32 23 111; Fax 32 24 148;
Information office ☎ 33 10 562, 33 10 565
email: gnto@eexi.gr
www.eexi.gr/gnto

Akropoli (Acropolis): Site – Summer, daily, 8am to 8pm; winter, Mondays to Fridays, 8am to 4.30pm, weekends, 8am to 2.30pm. Last entry 30min before closing.

Moussío (Acropolis Museum) – Summer daily 10am to 7pm; winter, Tuesdays to Fridays, 8am to 4.30pm, Mondays, 11am to 4pm, weekends, 8am to 2.30pm. Site and museum 2 000 Dr. ☎ 32 14 172, 32 36 665, 923 87 24; Fax 92 39 023.

Théatro Dioníssou (Theatre of Dionysos) – Daily 8am (8.30am in winter) to 2.30pm. 500 Dr.

Thissío ke Agorá (Theseion and Agora) – Summer daily, 8am to 7pm; winter, daily except Mondays, 8.30am to 3pm. 1 200 Dr.

PICTOR

Theseion and Agora in Athens

Aérides – Daily 8.30am to 2.30pm. 500 Dr.

Romaikí Agorá (Roman Forum) – Daily except Mondays, 8.30am to 2.45pm. 500 Dr.

Naós Olímbiou Diós (Olympieion) – Daily except Mondays, summer 8am to 2.30pm, winter 8.30am to 3pm. 500 Dr.

Moussío Elinikís Laikís Keramikís (Museum of Traditional Greek Ceramics) – Closed temporarily for rearrangement of the collections.

Ethnikó Arheologikó Moussío (National Archeological Museum) – Summer, 8am (12.30 Mondays) to 8pm; winter, weekdays 8am (11am Mondays) to 5pm, weekends 8.30am to 3pm. 2 000 Dr. Shop. Cafeteria. ☎ 82 17 717; Fax 82 13 573.

Moussío Benáki (Benaki Museum) – Closed temporarily. ☎ 36 11 617; Fax 36 22 547.

Vizandinó Moussío (Byzantine Museum) – Daily except Mondays, 8.30am to 2.30pm (3pm in winter). 500 Dr. ☎ 72 11 027, 72 32 178; Fax 72 31 883.

Moussío Kikladikís Téhnis (Museum of Cycladic Art) – Daily except Sundays and Tuesdays, 10am to 4pm (3pm Saturdays) 1 000 Dr. ☎ 72 28 321; Fax 72 39 382.

Nomismatikó Moussío (Numismatic Museum) – Daily except Mondays, 8am to 2.30pm. ☎ 36 43 774.

Additional Sights

Moussío tis Póleos ton Athinón (City of Athens Museum) – Mondays, Wednesdays, Fridays and Saturdays, 9am to 1.30pm. 500 Dr.

Ethnikó Istorikó Moussío (National Historical Museum) – Daily except Mondays, 9am to 2pm. 500 Dr.

Keramikós (Kerameikos Cemetery) – Daily except Mondays, 8.30am to 3pm. 500 Dr. ☎ 34 63 552.

Pníka (Pnyx): Son et Lumière about the Acropolis – Early April to late October. In English every night. Duration: 45min. Tickets available just before the spectacle. For further information contact the GNTO/EOT or other tourist office. ☎ 32 27 944 and 32 23 111.

Kéndro Meletón Akropóleos (Acropolis Interpretation Centre) – Daily, summer 8.30am to 3pm, winter 9am to 2.30pm. No charge.

Moussío Elinikís Laikís Téhnis (Museum of Greek Folk Art) – Daily except Mondays, 10am to 2pm. 500 Dr.

Moussío Elinikón Moussikón Organon (Museum of Greek Folk Musical Instruments) – Tuesdays, Thursdays, Saturdays and Sundays, 10am to 2pm, Wednesdays, 12 noon to 6pm. No charge. ☎ 32 50 198, 32 54 119; Fax 32 54 129.

Evraikó Moussío tis Elládas (Jewish Museum of Greece) – Daily except Saturdays, 9am to 1pm. Closed Jewish and Greek holidays. ☎ 32 25 582 and 32 32 577.

Ethnikí Pinakothíki-Moussío Alexándros Soútsou (National Gallery and Alexander Soutzos Museum) – Daily except Tuesdays, 9am to 3pm (10am to 2pm Sundays). 1 000 Dr. ☎ 72 38 857, 72 16 560, 72 35 937; Fax 72 24 889.

Moussío Kanelopoúlou (Kanelopoulos Museum) – Daily except Mondays, summer 8am to 2.30pm, winter 8.30am to 3pm. 500 Dr. ☎ 32 12 313.

Polemikó Moussío (War Museum) – Daily except Mondays and weekends, summer 7.30am to 2pm, winter 8am to 3pm. Closed during national holidays except 25 March and 28 October. No charge. ☎ 72 90 543, 72 15 035, 72 44 464; Fax 72 45 838.

Kéndro Laikís Téhnis ke Parádossis Dimou Athinéon (Centre for Popular Art and Traditions) – September to May, daily except Sunday, Monday and Saturday afternoon, 9am to 1pm and 5pm to 9pm. No charge. ☎ 32 13 018, 32 29 031.

Moussío Kosmímatos I Lalaoúni (Lalaounis Jewellery Museum) – Daily except Tuesdays, 9am to 4pm (9pm Wednesdays). Guided tour in groups. 800 Dr. ☎ 92 21 044; Fax 92 37 358; email http:\\www.addgr.com/jewel/lalaouni

SUBURBS

Pireás (Piraeus)

ℹ Marina Zéa ☎/Fax (01) 41 81 105

Arheologikó Moussío (Archeological Museum) – Daily except Mondays, summer 8am to 2.30pm, winter 8.30am to 3pm. 500 Dr. Access by bus no 905 from the station and the main harbour. ☎ 42 15 598, 45 18 388.

Navtikó Moussío (Naval Museum) – Daily except Sundays and Mondays, summer 8.30am to 3pm, winter 9am to 12.30. Closed in August. 500 Dr. Access by bus no 904 or 905 from the station and the main harbour. ☎ 45 16 822, 45 16 264; Fax 45 16 822.

Avéroff – Saturdays and Sundays, all year, 11.am to 1pm; Mondays, Wednesdays and Fridays, June to October, 7pm to 9pm, March to May, 4pm to 7pm, November to February, 3pm to 6pm. Closed 1 to 25 August. No charge.

Kifissiá

Moussío Goulandrí Fissikís Istorías (Goulandris Museum of Natural History) – Weekends only, 9am to 2pm. Closed approximately 20 July to 15 August. 800 Dr. ☎ 80 15 870, 80 86 485; Fax 80 80 674.

Kessarianí

Monastery – Daily except Mondays, summer 8am to 2.30pm, winter 8.30am to 3pm. 800 Dr.

Excursions

Akri Soúnio (Cape Sounion)

Temple – Daily, 8am to sunset. 800 Dr. ☎ (0292) 39 363.

Peanía

Vorrés Museum – Saturdays and Sundays, 10am to 2pm; weekdays by appointment only. 1 000Dr. ☎ 66 42 520; Fax 66 45 775.

Koutoúki Cave – June to September, 10am to 5.30pm, October to May, 9am to 4.30pm. 1 500 Dr, child 800 Dr.

Vravróna (Brauron)

Sanctuary – Thursdays to Sundays, summer 8am to 2.30pm, winter 8.30am to 3pm. 500 Dr.

Moussío – Tuesdays to Sundays, same opening times as for the sanctuary. 500 Dr. (0299) 27 020.

Marathónas (Marathon)

Tímvos Marathóna (Marathon Barrow) – Summer, daily, 8am to 2.30pm; winter, daily except Mondays, 8.30am to 3pm. 400 Dr. ☎ 0294 55 155.

Tímvos Plateéon (Barrow of the Plataians) – Same opening times and ticket price as for the Marathon Barrow.

Ramnoús

Ramnoús Ruins – Summer, daily 7am to 6pm; winter, daily except Mondays, 8.30am to 3pm. 500 Dr. ☎ (0294) 63 477.

Porto Germenó

Aigosthena Fortress – Usually open. No charge.

Salamína (Salamis)

Faneroméni Monastery – Sunrise to 1pm and 5pm to sunset.

Égina (Aiginai)

☎ (0297) 23 333
Tourist Police ☎ (0297) 23 243

Cape Kolóna (Colonna) (archeological site and museum) – Summer, daily 8am to 2.30pm; winter, daily except Mondays, 8.30am to 3pm. 500 Dr. ☎ (0297) 22 248.

Paleohóra – To visit apply at least one day before to the keeper at Cape Colonna in Égina Town. Accompanied visit.

Temple of Aféa (Aphaia) – Summer, 8am to 8pm; winter, weekdays 8am to 5pm (8am to 2.30pm Saturdays and Sundays). 800 Dr. Frequent bus services from Aigina Town. ☎ (0297) 32 398.

D

DAFNÍ

Monastery – Daily except Mondays, 8.30am to 3pm. 800 Dr.

DELFÍ

ℹ Tourist Office, 27 Odós Friderikis, ☎ (0265) 82 220

Ieró Apólona (Sanctuary of Apollo) – Mondays to Fridays, 8am to 7pm (2.30pm November to March), Saturdays and Sundays, 8.30am to 2.30pm. 1 200 Dr.

Moussío – Daily, 8am to 7pm (2.30pm November to March). 1 200 Dr. ☎ (0265) 82 313.

Excursion

Galaxídi: Maritime Museum – Daily, 9.30am to 1.30pm (Mondays 9am to 1pm). 500 Dr.

T.A.P.

Siphnian Treasury frieze (Delphi Museum)

DÍO (Dion)

Excavations of the ancient town – Mondays to Fridays, 8am to 7pm (5pm winter), Saturdays and Sundays, 8.30am to 3pm. 800 Dr. ☎ (0351) 53 206.

Museum – Open Tuesdays to Fridays, 8am to 7pm (5pm winter); Saturdays and Sundays, 8.30am to 3pm, Mondays, 12.30pm to 7pm (5pm winter). 800 Dr.

Spílea DIROÚ (Dirós Caves)

Glifáda Cave – Guided tour for groups daily, 8am to 5pm (2.30pm winter). 3 500 Dr, child (under 12) 1 500 Dr. Restaurant, cafeteria.

Alepótripa Cave – Daily, 8am to 5pm (2.30pm winter). 3 500 Dr, child 1 500 Dr. **Museum:** Daily except Mondays, 8.30am to 3pm. 500 Dr.

E

ÉDESSA

Old town – 8am to 7pm (5pm winter). No charge.

EFÍRA (Ephyra)

Nekromanteion – Summer, Mondays to Fridays, 8am to 5pm, Saturdays and Sundays, 8.30am to 3pm; winter, daily 8.30am to 3pm. 500 Dr.

ELEFSÍNA (Eleusis)

Sanctuary and Museum – Daily except Mondays, 8.30am to 3pm. 500 Dr. ☎ 55 46 109.

Arhéa EPÍDAVROS (Epidauros)

Festival – End June to end August. For times (evening) and programme see leaflet produced by the EOT. Information from the Festival Office, 2 Odos Galeria Spyrou Miliou, Athens. ☎ (01) 32 34 555 or 32 23 111. Reservations on the spot at Epidauros on ☎ (753) 21 008. Excursions organised starting from Athens, Náfplio, Portohéli and the Saronic Gulf islands.

Site and museum – Daily, 8am to 8pm (6pm winter). Closed Monday morning until midday (11am winter). 1 500 Dr. ☎ (0753) 22 009.

ÉVIA

Halkída

Tourist Police ☎ (0221) 77 777, 74 459 or 75 339

Halkída: Arheologikó Moussío (Archeological Museum) – Daily except Mondays, 9am to 2.30pm (winter 2pm). 500 Dr. ☎ (0221) 25 131.

Kími: Laografikó Moussío (Museum of Popular Art) – May to October daily, 10am to 1pm and 5pm to 7pm; November to April Wednesdays 5pm to 7pm, Saturdays and Sundays 10am to 1pm. 400 Dr.

Erétria: Ancient city and museum – Daily except Mondays, summer 8am to 2.30pm, winter 8.30am to 3pm. 500 Dr. ☎ (0221) 62 206.

F – G

FÍLIPI (Phillipi)

Ruins and Museum – Daily except Mondays, summer 8am to 2.30pm, winter 8.30am to 3pm. 500 Dr.

GERÁKI

Kástro (Castle) – Daily, all day. Apply to one of the keepers of the Archeological Service in the main square.

Byzantine Churches – Same as for the castle *(see above)*.

GÍTHIO

20 Odós Vass Georgiou ☎/ Fax (0733) 24 484

Tzanetáki Tower (Historical and Archeological Museum) – Daily, 9am to 9pm (winter 5pm). 500 Dr.

H – I

HALKIDIKÍ (Chalcidice)

Petrálona

Kókines Pétres Cave – Open 9am to 6pm (4pm October to June). 1 500 Dr. child 800 Dr. ☎ (0373) 31 300. **Museum**: Open at the same times.

HLEMOÚTSI

Castle – Daily except Sundays, 8.30am to 3pm. No charge. Restoration work in progress. Theatre in July and August.

ÍDRA (Hydra)

ℹ ☎ (0298) 52 205

Monasteries of Profítis Ilías and Agía Efpraxía – Generally summer, sunrise to 1pm and 5pm to sunset.

IGOUMENÍTSA

ℹ Port ☎ (0665) 22 227

IOÁNINA

ℹ 2 Odós Nap Zerva ☎ (0651) 25 086, 28 849, 31 456; Fax 72 148
ℹ Tourist Police ☎ (0651) 25 673

Nissí Ioanínon (Island) – Ferry operates every half hour; last departure 12 midnight. It is advisable to check the opening times of the monasteries at the Tourist Office (EOT).

Monastery of Pandeleimónas – 9am to 1pm.

Monastery of Ágios Ioánnis Pródromos (St John the Baptist) – 9am to 1pm. Restoration work in progress.

Monastery of the Philanthropiní – 9am to 1pm.

Monastery of Stratigópoúlos – 9am to 1pm.

Moussío Laikís Téhnis (Folk Art Museum) – 8am (9am Saturdays and Sundays) to 3pm. 700 Dr. ☎ (0651) 20 515.

Arheologikó Moussío (Archeological Museum) – Daily except Monday, 8.30am to 3pm. 500 Dr. ☎ (0651) 33 357, 25 490.

Excursions

Pérama Cave – 8am to 7pm (5pm winter). 1 000 Dr. ☎ (0651) 81 521.

Dodóni (Dodona) ruins – Mondays to Fridays, 8am to 7pm, Saturdays and Sundays, 8.30am to 3pm. 500 Dr. ☎ (0651) 82 287.

ITHÓMI

Asklepieion – Free access.

Moussío arheologikó – Closed temporarily.

K

KALAMÁTA

ℹ Marina, Diikitirio Bldg ☎ (0721) 86 868; Fax 86 868

Kástro – Weekdays 10am to 1.30pm. Closed Saturdays and Sundays.

Museum – Daily except Mondays, summer, 8am to 2.30pm, winter, 8.30am to 3pm. 500 Dr.

KALÁVRITA

Monastery of Agía Lávra – Daily, 10am to 1pm and 4pm to 5pm. No charge.

KAMÉNA VOÚRLA

ℹ ☎ (0235) 22 053; Fax 24 727

KARPENÍSSI

Proussós Monastery – Sunrise to sunset. Accommodation at the monastery is in principle reserved for pilgrims. Access to the monastery by two steep one-way roads just before the village.

KASSÓPI

Ruins – Summer, daily, 8am to 5pm; winter, daily except Mondays, 8.30am to 3pm. 500 Dr.

KASTORIÁ

ℹ Platía Dimarhiou ☎ (0467) 24 484

Byzantine Churches – To visit apply to the keeper-guide at the Byzantine Museum near the Xenia hotel.

Vizandinó Moussío (Byzantine Museum) – Daily except Mondays, 8.30am to 6pm (3pm winter). No charge.

Museum of Folk Traditions – Apply to the tourist office for details.

Panagía Mavriótissa – Sunrise to sunset.

Excursions

Siátista: Neranzópoulou, Manoúsi and Poulkídi mansions – To visit apply to the keeper at the Neranzópoulou mansion in the main square in the upper town daily except Mondays, 8.30am to 2.30pm. No charge.

Siátista: Hatzimiháli Kanatsoúli – Private residence which can be visited.

KAVÁLA

ℹ 5 Odós Filhellinon ☎ (051) 227 409, 231 653; Fax 223 885
ℹ Platía Eleftherias ☎ (051) 222 452

Ikía Mehémet Ali – Daily except Mondays, 10am to 2pm and 5pm to 7pm.

Arheologikó Moussío (Archeological Museum) – Daily, summer 8am to 8pm (2.30pm Saturdays and Sundays), winter 9am to 3pm. 800 Dr. ☎ (051) 222 335, 224 717.

KEFALONÍA

ℹ Custom Pier, Argostoli ☎ (0671) 22 248, 24 466

Sámi: Melissáni Cave – 8.30am to 8.30pm. 800 Dr, child 400 Dr.

Sámi: Drongaráti Cave – Open (weather permitting) Easter to October, 8am to 8pm. 864 Dr, child 432 Dr.

Argostóli: Korgialénios Museum – Daily except Mondays, 9am to 3pm. 500 Dr.

Argostóli: Ágios Geórgios (St George's Castle) – Daily except Mondays, 8.30am to 7pm (3pm Sundays). No charge.

KÉRKIRA (Corfu Town)

ℹ 15 Odos Rizospaston Voulefton ☎ (0661) 37 520, 37 639, 37 640; Fax 30 298
ℹ Tourist police 4 Odós Samarzi ☎ (0661) 30 265

Cricket – Games are played daily in summer.

Paleó Froúrio (Ancient citadel) – All year, Tuesdays to Fridays, 8am to 6.30pm, Saturdays and Sundays, 8.30am to 3pm. 800 Dr.

Museum of Asiatic Art – Daily except Mondays, 8am to 2.30pm. No charge. ☎ (0661) 30 443, 23 124.

Vizandinó Moussío (Byzantine Museum) – Daily except Mondays, summer 8am to 2.30pm, winter 8.30am to 3pm. 500 Dr.

Arheologikó Moussío (Archeological Museum) – Daily except Mondays, summer 8am to 2.30pm, winter 8.30am to 3pm. 800 Dr. ☎ (0661) 30 680, 38 124.

Excursion

Argostoli ☎ (0671) 22 248; Fax 24 466

Ahílio (Achilleion) – Summer, 7.30am to 7pm; winter, 9am to 4pm. 1 000 Dr. ☎ (0661) 56 210, 56 251.

KILÍNI

Access – **by train:** from Athens and Patras or Kalamáta (changing at Kavássila between Andravída and Gastoúni). **By bus:** twice a day from Athens via Patras.

Vlacherna Monastery – Sunrise to 1pm and 5pm to sunset.

KIPARISSÍA

Peristéria Tombs – Mondays to Fridays, in principle 8am to 2pm. No charge.

KÍTHIRA (Kythera)

ℹ ☎ (0735) 31 206

Arheologikó Moussío (Archeological Museum) – Daily except Mondays, 8.30am to 2pm. ☎ (0735) 31 739.

Agía Eléssa Monastery – 7am to 9pm.

Mirthidión Monastery – 7am to 9pm.

Milopótamos: Agía Sophía – Information available on site.

KOMOTINÍ

ℹ 14 Odós Ap Souzou ☎ (0531) 70 996; Fax 70 995

KÓRINTHOS

ℹ ☎ (0741) 23 282

Moussío Vassou Petropoulou (Historical and Folk Museum) – Daily except Mondays, 8am to 1pm. ☎ (0741) 25 352.

Arhéa Kórinthos – Daily, 8am to 7pm (winter 5pm). 1 200 Dr (including the museum).

Museum – Daily, 8am to 5pm (winter 3pm). Entrance included in ticket for site. ☎ (0741) 31 207.

Akrokórinthos (Acrocorinth) – Daily, 8.30am to 7pm (winter 5pm). No charge.

Dióriga KORÍNTHOU (Corinth Canal)

Isthmian Sanctuary – Daily, 8am to 2.30pm. 500 Dr.

L

LAMÍA

ℹ 1 Platía Laou ☎ (0231) 30 065; Fax 30 066

LÁRISSA

ℹ 18 Odós Koumoundourou ☎ (041) 250 919, 534 369; Fax 250 919, 534 369

Arheologikó Moussío (Archeological Museum) – Daily except Mondays, summer 8am to 2.30pm, winter 8.30am to 3pm. No charge. ☎ (0735) 31 739.

Early Christian Basilica – Usually Mondays to Fridays, 7am to 2.30pm. Also a good view outside. No cameras allowed. Restoration in progress.

LEFKÁDA (Leukas)

Lefkáda Town: Churches – Apply to the Cathedral 8am to 1pm. ☎ (0645) 22 415.

LEFKÁDIA-NÁOUSSA

Great Tomb and Second Tomb – Daily in principle except Mondays, summer 8am to 2.30pm, winter 8.30am to 3pm. No charge. Telephone the archeological office in Náoussa beforehand on ☎ (0332) 41 121.

Lyson-Kalliklés Tomb – Closed temporarily.

LERNÍ

Prehistoric remains – 8.30am to 3pm. 500 Dr.

M

MÁNI

Areópoli: Ágios Ioánnis – If closed, apply in the morning to the town hall *(dimarhio)*.

Harouda: Church – Apply to the keeper.

Nómia: Taxiarch's Church – Key at the next house.

MEGALÓPOLI

Ruins – No charge.

MÉGA SPILEO Monastery

Access by train – From Diakoftó to Zahloroú-Méga Spíleo station (for details and times see **Harádra tou Vouraïkoú**), then climb up to the monastery on foot or by mule (45min).

Monastery – Sunrise to sunset.

MESSINIAKÓS KOLPOS (Messenian Gulf Road)

Tour of the churches – At present it is not usually possible to visit. Tourists with a genuine interest should apply in writing to the Department of Byzantine Antiquities (Eforia Vízantinon Arheotiton), 71 Odós Menelaou, Spárti (Sparta); a keeper takes visitors round by appointment. ☎ (0731) 25 363.

Messenian Gulf

MESSOLONGHI

Lord Byron's House (Byron Museum) – *Currently closed for restoration. The exhibits are on view in the local art gallery.*

METÉORA (Kalambáka)

Access by train – From Athens, Volós or Thessaloníki, changing at Paleofársalo.

Ágios Nikólaos (St Nicholas' Monastery) – Daily, summer 9am to 5.45pm. Closed in winter. ☏ (0432) 22 375.

Roussánou Monastery – Daily except Wednesdays, summer 9am to 6pm, winter 9am to 1pm and 3pm to 5pm. 500 Dr. ☏ (0432) 22 649.

Megálo Metéoro (Great Meteoron Monastery) – Daily except Tuesdays, 9am to 1pm and 3pm to 6pm (5pm in winter). 500 Dr. (0432) 22 278.

Varlaám Monastery – Daily except Fridays (and Thursdays in winter), same times as for the Mégalo Metéoro.

Agía Triáda (Holy Trinity Monastery) – Daily except Thursdays, 9am to 12.30pm and 3pm to 5pm. 500 Dr. ☏ (0432) 22 220.

Ágios Stéfanos (St Stephen's Monastery) – Daily except Mondays, 9am to 1pm and 3pm to 6pm (5pm in winter). 500 Dr. ☏ (0432) 22 279.

METHÓNI

Citadel – Daily, 8.30am to 6pm (3pm in winter). No charge. ☏ (0723) 25 363.

MÉTSOVO

Moussío Laikís Téhnis (Museum of Traditional Art) – Daily except Thursdays, 8.30am to 1pm and 4pm to 6pm (3pm to 5pm in winter). 500 Dr.

Pinacoteca (Art Gallery) – Daily except Tuesdays, 10am to 7pm (4.30pm in winter). 500 Dr.

Ágios Nikólaos (Monastery of St Nicholas) – Sunrise to sunset.

MIKÍNES (Mycenae)

Site – Daily in summer, 8am to 8pm; in winter Mondays to Fridays 8am to 5pm, Saturdays and Sundays 8.30am to 3pm. 1 500 Dr. (ticket also valid for the Treasury of Atreus). Post office in the car park. Youth hostel in the village. ☏ (0751) 66 585.

MISTRÁS (Mystra)

Site – Daily, summer 8am to 7pm, winter 8.30am to 3pm. 1 200 Dr. Museum: Daily except Mondays. Regular bus service from Sparta. ☏ (0731) 93 377.

MONEMVASSÍA

Town Hall ☏ (0732) 61 752

Paleó Dzamí (Museum) – All day usually.

N

NÁFPLIO (Nauplion)

Tourist Police ☎ (0751) 28 131

Palamídi (Palamedes Fort) – Summer, 8am to 7pm; winter, 8.30am to 2.30pm. 400 Dr. Buffet-bar in summer. ☎ (0751) 28 036.

Isle of Boúrdzi – Restoration work in progress.

Laografikó Moussío (Folk Museum) – Daily except Mondays, 9am to 2.30pm. 300 Dr. ☎ (0751) 28 379.

Arheologikó Moussío (Archeological Museum) – Daily except Mondays, 8am to 2.30pm. 500 Dr. ☎ (0751) 27 502.

Excursions

Agía Moní – Summer, sunrise to 1pm and 3pm to sunset; winter, sunrise to sunset.

Toló: Access by hydrofoil.

NEMÉA

Access – **By train:** From Piraeus, Athens, and Corinth, as well as Kalamáta and Árgos, then about 5km/3mi to the site. **By bus:** From Athens.

Ruins – Daily except Mondays, summer 8am to 2.30pm, winter 8.30am to 3pm. 500 Dr. (including museum). ☎ (0746) 22 739.

NESTOR'S PALACE

Ruins – Daily except Mondays, summer 8am to 3.30pm, winter 8.30am to 3pm. 500 Dr. ☎ (0723) 31 358.

Hóra: Archeological Museum – Daily except Mondays, 8.30am to 3pm. 500 Dr.

O

OLIMBÍA

Ruins – Summer, daily 8am to 8pm; winter, Mondays to Fridays, 8am to 5pm, Saturdays and Sundays, 8.30am to 3pm. 1 200 Dr. ☎ (0624) 22 517.

Museum – Summer, daily 8am (Mondays 12 noon) to 8pm, winter Mondays to Fridays 8am (Mondays 11am) to 5pm, Saturdays and Sundays 8.30am to 3pm. 1 200 Dr. ☎ (0624) 22 529, 22 742.

Museum of the Olympic Games – Daily, 8am to 3pm. 500 Dr. ☎ (0624) 22 544.

ORHOMENÓS

Ancient ruins – Daily except Mondays, 8.30am to 2.30pm. No charge.

Kimísseos Theotókou (Church of the Dormition of the Virgin) – Daily.

ÓSSIOS LOUKÁS

Monastery – 8am to 5.30pm (5pm winter). 800 Dr.

P

PÁTRA

🅱 26 Odós Filopimenos ☎ (061) 620 353, 621 992, 622 249; Fax 620 125

Moussío Laikís Téhnis (Museum of Popular Art) – By appointment. ☎ (061) 334 713.

PÉLA

Ruins and Museum – Summer, 8.30am (12.30am Mondays) to 7pm; winter daily except Mondays, 8.30am to 3pm. 500 Dr. ☎ (0381) 31 160, 31 278, 31 143.

Óros PILIO

Anakassiá: Theophilos Museum – Visit by appointment. ☎ (0421) 49 109

Miliés: Library – Daily except Sundays and Mondays, 8am to 2.30pm. No charge.

PÍLOS

Niókastro – Daily except Mondays, 8am to 2.30pm. 800 Dr. ☎ (0723) 22 448.

Arheologikó Moussío (Archeological Museum) – Daily except Saturdays and Sundays 8am to 2.30pm.

PLATAMÓNAS

Castle – Daily except Mondays, 8.30am to 7pm (3pm Saturdays and Sundays). No charge.

PLATISTOMO

ℹ ☎ (0236) 22 510

PÓROS

Tourist Police ☎ (0298) 22 462

Monastery of Zoodóhos Pigí (the Source of Life) – 8am to sunset.

PRÉVEZA

ℹ ☎ (0682) 27 277

Ruins of Nikopolis – Daily, 8am to 2.30pm (3pm in winter). 500 Dr. ☎ (0682) 51 317, (0684) 41 206.

S

SAMOTHRÁKI (Samothrace)

Ruins of the Sanctuary of the Great Gods – Daily except Mondays, 8.30am to 8.30pm (3.30pm in winter). 500 Dr. ☎ (0551) 41 474.

Museum – Daily except Mondays, 8.30am to 3pm. 500 Dr. ☎ (0551) 41 474.

SIKIÓNA (Sikyon)

Ruins – 8am to 6pm. No charge. **Museum**: Closed for reorganisation. ☎ (0742) 28 900.

SPÁRTI (Sparta)

Tourist Police ☎ (0731) 28 701

Arheologikó Moussío (Archeological Museum) – Daily except Mondays, summer 8am to 2.30pm, winter 8.30am to 3pm. 500 Dr. ☎ (0731) 28 575, 25 363.

Ethnikí Pinakothíki-Moussío Alexándrou Soútsos – Daily except Mondays and public holidays 9am to 3pm (Sundays 10am–2pm). 1 200 Dr; no charge Sundays.

SPÉTSES (Spetsae)

Bouboulina's House – Guided tour (45min; English). 1 000 Dr.

Méxis House – Daily except Mondays, 8.30am to 2pm. 500 Dr. ☎ (0298) 72 994.

Agía Triáda (Holy Trinity) – Apply at the house opposite the church for the keeper to be notified.

T

TÉMBI

ℹ Tourist Police, Ambelákia ☎ (014) 623 158

Lodgings in Ambelákia – Organised by the Country Women's Tourist Cooperative. ☎ (0495) 93 495 or the GNTO/EOT.

Arhondikó Schwarz (George Schwarz' House) – Daily except Mondays, 8.30am to 3pm. 500 Dr. ☎ (0495) 93 302

THÁSSOS

ℹ See Kavála

Liménas (Thássos Town)

ℹ (in summer) ☎ (0593) 23 111

Agora – 8.30am to 7.30pm (3pm winter). No charge.

Museum – Daily except Mondays 10am to 3pm. No charge. ☎ (0593) 22 180.

THERMOPÍLES

ℹ ☎ (0231) 93 301, 93 303; Fax 93 111

THESSALONÍKI

34 Odós Mitropoleos ☎ (031) 222 935, 271 888; Fax 265 504

Churches not listed below – Closed usually 12.30pm to 5pm.

Lefkós Pírgos (White Tower) – Daily except Mondays, 8am to 2.30pm. No charge. ☎ (031) 267 832.

Arheologikó Moussío (Archeological Museum) – Summer, 8am to 8pm; winter, 8.30am (11am Mondays) to 5pm, Saturdays and Sundays, 8.30am to 3pm. 1 500 Dr. Cafeteria. ☎ (031) 830 538, 831 037, 836 973.

Moussío Vizandinoú Politismoú (Museum of Byzantine Civilisation) – Daily, summer 8am (12.30pm Mondays) to 8pm; winter 8.30am to 3pm. 1 500 Dr.

Rotónda (St George's Church) – Daily except Saturdays and Sundays, 8am to 2.30pm. No charge. ☎ (031) 213 627.

Ágios Dimítrios (St Demetrios' Church) – All day. Crypt: daily except Mondays, 9am to 2.45pm. No charge. ☎ (031) 270 008.

Óssios David (Blessed David's Church) – Keeper on site.

Ágios Nikólaos Orfanós (St Nicholas' Church) – Daily except Mondays, 9am to 2.30pm. No charge.

Laografikó-ethnologikó Moussío Makedonías (Macedonian Ethnological Museum) – Closed for restoration.

Moussío Makedonikoú Agónos (Museum of the Macedonian Struggle) – Summer daily except Mondays, usually 9am (11am Saturdays and Sundays) to 2pm, also 6pm to 8pm on Wednesdays. It is however best to check. ☎ (031) 229 778.

THÍVA (Thebes)

Arheologikó Moussío (Archeological Museum) – Daily except Mondays, summer 8am to 7pm (2.30pm Saturdays and Sundays), winter 8.30am to 3pm. 500 Dr. ☎ (0262) 27 13.

TÍRINTHA (Tiryns)

Acropolis – Daily , 8am to 8pm (5pm in winter). 500 Dr. ☎ (0752) 22 657.

TRÍKALA

Old mosque – Closed temporarily for restoration. Prospective visitors should apply to the town hall ☎ (0431) 35 950.

Sanctuary of Pórta Panagia – Key available at a nearby house.

TRÍPOLI

Arheologikó Moussío (Archeological Museum) – Daily except Mondays, summer 8am to 2.30pm, winter 8.30am to 3pm. 500 Dr. ☎ (071) 24 227.

Tegéa: Museum – Daily except Mondays, summer 8am to 2.30pm, winter 8.30am to 3pm. No charge.

Excursion

Kimísseos Theotókou (Church of the Dormition of the Virgin) – To visit apply in the square in Levídi or in advance to the town hall *(dimarhio)*. ☎ (0796) 22 211.

V – Z

VÉRIA

Hristós (Church of Christ) – Daily except Mondays, 9am to 2.30pm.

Arheologikó Moussío (Archeological Museum) – Daily except Mondays, summer 8am to 2.30pm, winter 8.30am to 3pm. 500 Dr. ☎ (0331) 24 972.

Excursion

Royal Tombs – Daily, August 8am (Mondays 12.30pm) to 8pm, September 8am (Mondays 12.30pm) to 7pm, rest of the year 8.30am to 3pm. 1 200 Dr. ☎ (0331) 92 347, 830 538.

Macedonian Tomb (Romeou) – Same times and charge as for the Royal Tombs.

Palatítsia – Daily except Mondays, 8.30am to 3pm. 500 Dr. ☎ (0331) 92 347, 830 538.

VÓLOS

i Platía Riga Fereou ☎ (0421) 23 500, 36 233, 37 417; Fax 24 750 email: eotm@hol.gr

Arheologikó Moussío (Archeological Museum) – Daily except Mondays, 8.30am to 3pm. 500 Dr.

Harádra tou VOURAÏKOÚ (Vouraïkós Gorge)

Access by train – Diakoftó can be reached from Athens in about 3hr, from Corinth or Patras in about 1hr

Rack Railway – 5 departures a day from Diakoftó to Zahloroú-Méga Spíleo (50min). The train continues to Kalávrita.

ZÁKINTHOS

Tourist Police ☎ (0695) 27 367

Kástro – Summer only, 9am to 2pm. 500 Dr.

Art Museum – Daily except Mondays, 8am to 2.30pm. 800 Dr. ☎ (0695) 22 714.

Kiría ton Angélon (Our Lady of the Angels) – If closed, apply to the keeper nearby.

Solomós Museum – Daily except Mondays, 8am to 2.30pm. 800 Dr. ☎ (0695) 28 728.

Crete

ÁGIOS NIKÓLAOS

20 Marina ☎ (0841) 82 384; Fax 82 386

Arheologikó Moussío (Archeological Museum) – Daily except Mondays, summer 8am to 2pm, winter 8.30am to 3pm. 500 Dr. ☎ (0841) 24 943.

ANÓGIA

Idéo Andro (Idaian Cave) – Daily 9.30am to 4pm.

Axós: St Irene's Church – Ask for the keeper in the village square (usually in the main café).

ÁPTERA

Ruins – Daily except Mondays, 8.30am to 2pm. No charge.

ARKÁDI Monastery

Monastery – Closed 1pm to 5pm.

FESTOS (Phaistos)

Ruins – 8am to 7pm (5pm winter). 1 200 Dr. ☎ (0892) 22 615

Agía Triáda: Ruins – Daily, 9am to 3.30pm. 500 Dr.

Excursion

Valsamónero Monastery – 8.30am to 3pm.

GORTÍNA (Gortyn)

Main sights – Daily except Mondays, summer 8am to 7pm, winter 8.30am to 3pm. 500 Dr. ☎ (0892) 226 092.

Praetorium – Guided tour by the keeper except for groups. The site can be viewed from the boundary.

HANIÁ (Chania)

ℹ 40 Odós Kriari ☎ (0821) 92 943; Fax 92 624
ℹ Tourist Police, Odós Kidonías ☎ (0821) 71 111

Naftikó Moussío (Naval Museum) – Daily, 10am to 4pm (2pm November to March). 500 Dr. ☎ (0821) 26 437; Fax (0821) 27 936.

Arheologikó Moussío (Archeological Museum) – Daily except Mondays, 8.30am to 3pm. 500 Dr. ☎ (0821) 90 334; Fax 94 487.

Ágia Triáda (Holy Trinity Monastery) – Sunrise to 1pm and 5pm to sunset.

IERÁPETRA

ℹ ☎ (0842) 28 165

Museum – Daily except Mondays, 8.30am to 2.30pm. 500 Dr.

IRÁKLIO (Herakleion)

ℹ 1 Odós Xanthoudidou ☎ (081) 228 225, 228 230; Fax 226 020

Arheologikó Moussío (Archeological Museum) – Daily, summer 8am (12.30pm Mondays) to 8pm, winter 7.30am (12.30pm Mondays) to 7pm. 1 500 Dr. ☎ (081) 226 092, 224 630; Fax (081) 241 515.

Venetian Fortress – Daily except Mondays, 9am to 1pm. 1 000 Dr. ☎ (081) 246 211.

Agía Ekateríni (St Catherine's Church) – Daily except Sundays, 9am to 1.30pm; also Tuesdays, Thursdays and Fridays, 5pm to 8pm. 500 Dr. ☎ (081) 288 484; Fax (0081) 242 111.

Istorikó Moussío (History Museum) – Daily except Sundays, 9am to 5pm (2pm Saturdays). 1 000 Dr. ☎ (081) 288 484; Fax (081) 283 754.

Kazantzakis Museum – Daily except Thursdays, 9am to 1pm, Sundays 10am to 3pm. 1 000 Dr. ☎ (081) 742 451, 741 689.

Tílissos: Minoan villas – Daily except Mondays, 8am to 2.30pm. 500 Dr. ☎ (081) 226 092.

KASTÉLI/KÍSSAMOS

Goniá Monastery Church – Closed 1pm to 4pm. ☎ (081) 228 484.

PICTOR

Heraklion harbour

KÁTO ZÁKROS

Palace – Daily except Mondays, April to October 8am to 8pm, November to March 8.30am to 3pm. 500 Dr. ☎ (0841) 22 462.

KNOSSÓS

Palace Ruins – 8am to 7pm (5pm winter). 1 500 Dr. ☎ (081) 231 940.

KRITSÁ

Panagía Kerá Church – Daily except Mondays, 8.30am to 3pm. 500 Dr.

LASSÍTHI Plateau

Diktéo Ándro (Diktean Cave) – Tours up to 3pm. Telephone beforehand ☎ (0844) 31 316.

MÁLIA

Anáktora Malíon (Palace) – Daily except Mondays, summer 8am to 2.30pm, winter 8.30am to 3pm. 800 Dr. ☎ (0897) 22 462.

MIRAMBELA COAST

Gourniá – Daily except Mondays, 8.30am to 3pm. 500 Dr. ☎ (0841) 22 462.

RÉTHYMNO

ℹ Leofóros El Venizélou ☎ (0831) 29 148
ℹ Tourist Police ☎ (0831) 28 156

Former Nerandze Mosque – Closed temporarily for restoration work. Information from the tourist office.

Arheologikó Moussío (Archeological Museum) – Daily except Mondays, 8.30am to 3pm. 500 Dr. ☎ (0831) 29 975, 20 668.

Fortétza (Venetian Fortress) – 8am to 7pm. 700 Dr.

SAMARIÁ Gorge

Access – 1 May to mid-October or later (weather permitting), descent 6am to 4pm to leave time to climb out again. Caïques from Sfakiá to Ág Rouméli (accommodation available) from 1 April. In the gorge the following are strictly forbidden: smoking, playing music (radios, cassettes), camping, pets, lighting of fires and picking flowers.

SITÍA

ℹ Platía Iroon Politehniou ☎ (0843) 24 955

Museum of Local Traditions – Daily except Mondays, summer 8am to 2.30pm, winter 8.30am to 3pm. 500 Dr.

Arheologikó Moussío (Archeological Museum) – Daily except Mondays, summer 8am to 2.30pm, winter 8.30am to 3pm. 500 Dr.

Monì Toploú – Sunrise to 1pm and 5pm to sunset.

Cyclades

AMORGÓS
☎ (0285)

Hozoviótissa Monastery – Sunrise to 2pm and 5pm to sunset.

ÁNDROS
☎ (0282)

Arheologikó Moussío (Archeological Museum) – Daily except Mondays, summer 8am to 2.30pm, winter 8.30am to 3pm. 500 Dr. ☎ (0282) 23 664.

Goulandris Museum of Modern Art – Summer daily except Tuesdays, 10am to 2pm and 6pm to 8pm; winter Saturdays to Mondays, 10am to 2pm. 1 000 Dr. ☎ (0282) 22 650, 22 444.

DÍLOS

Ruins and Museum – Daily except Mondays, 8.30am to 3pm. 1 200 Dr. Only cruise passengers and visitors with their own boats can remain until 3pm. The 4 rooms in the hotel are generally reserved for archeologists. ☎ (0289) 22 259.

ÍOS
☎ (0286)

KÉA
ℹ ☎ (0288) 31 256

Arheologikó Moussío (Archeological Museum) – Daily except Mondays, 8.30am to 3pm. No charge. ☎ (0288) 22 079.

KÍMOLOS
☎ (0287)

Arheologikó Moussío (Archeological Museum) – Tuesdays and Saturdays, 9.30am to 12 noon but often closed.

KÍTHNOS
☎ (0281)

Panagía Kanála Church – Open all day. Keeper in attendance.

MÍKONOS
ℹ Town Hall ☎ (0289) 22 201, 23 990, Fax 22 229

Mílos Bóni (Boni Windmill) – Interior may be viewed. ☎ (0289) 22 246. Agricultural Museum (nearby): All year 4pm to 8pm.

19C House (Lena) – April to October, 6pm (7pm Sundays) to 9pm. No charge.

Arheologikó Moussío (Archeological Museum) – Daily except Mondays, summer 8am to 2.30pm, winter 8.30am to 3pm. 500 Dr. ☎ (0289) 22 325.

Míkonos harbour

Moussío Laikís Téhnis (Museum of Folk Art) – April to mid-October, daily except Sundays, 2.30pm (4.30pm on Saturdays) to 9.30pm. No charge.

Naftikó Moussío Egéou (Aegean Maritime Museum) – April to October, 10.30am to 1pm and 6.30pm to 9pm. 200 Dr. Caïque *Evangelistria* (1939): June to October, same times. ☎ (0289) 22 700.

MÍLOS ☎ (0287)

Mílos-Pláka: Museum – Daily except Mondays, summer 8am to 2.30pm, winter 8.30am to 3pm. 500 Dr. ☎ (0287) 21 292.

Catacombs – Daily except Mondays, summer 8am to 8pm, winter 8.30am to 1pm.

Marine Caves – Regular excursions in summer organized by fishermen in Adámas and Apolónia.

NÁXOS ☎ (0285)

Náxos Town: Museum – Daily except Mondays, summer 8am to 2.30pm, winter 8.30am to 3pm. 500 Dr. ☎ (0285) 22 725.

Halkí: Panagía Protothronís – To visit apply to the keeper, Mr Kostas Cherouvim in Halkí. ☎ (0285) 31 361.

Akádimi: Ágii Apóstoli (Church of the Holy Apostles) – Same as for the Panagía Protothronís *(see above)*.

Apíranthos: Museum – 8.30am to 2pm. No charge.

PÁROS Tourist Office in Parikía in the mill beside the harbour ☎ (0284) 22 079

Panagía Ekatondapilianí (Church of the "Hundred Doors") – 7am to 1pm and 5pm to 10pm (8pm in winter).

Museum – Daily except Mondays, 8am to 2.30pm. 500 Dr.

Petaloúdes Valley (Butterfly Valley) – Summer only 9am to 8pm. 400 Dr. By bus *no* 3 (and 10min on foot) or donkey from Parikía.

Andíparos: Spíleo (cave) – May to October, 11am to 5pm. 500 Dr. Caïques from Paríkia, buses and donkeys from Andíparos village. Donkeys up to the cave.

SÉRIFOS ☎ (0281)

Moussío Laikís Téhnis (Museum of Traditional Art) – Daily except Mondays, 5pm to 8pm. No charge.

Arheologikó Moussío (Archeological Museum) – Daily except Mondays, 9am to 1pm. No charge.

Taxiarchs Monastery – 9.30am to 1pm and 5.30pm to 7.30pm. It is advisable to telephone in advance as there is only one monk in residence. ☎ (0281) 51 027.

SÍFNOS Kamáres ☎ (0284) 31 977, 31 345

Theologós tou Moungou Monastery – Only one keeper to give guided tour. 9.30am to 1.30pm and 5.30pm to 7pm.

Apolonia: Moussío Laikís Téhnis (Folk Museum) – Daily, summer 9.30am to 2pm and 5pm to 11pm, winter 10am to 2pm and 6.30pm to 10pm.

Profítis Ilías tou Psilou Monastery – At all times. Keeper in permanent attendance. Great Festival of St Elijah 19 July.

Kastro: Arheologikó Moussío (Archeological Museum) – Daily except Mondays, 10am to 2pm.

SÍROS ℹ 10 Odós Dodekanissou ☎ (0281) 86 725; Fax 82 375

THÍRA (Santorini) ☎ (0286)

Access from Skála to Firá (Thíra) – 800 Dr. By cable-car or by mule.

Firá (Thíra Town): Ghizi House – May to September, 10am to 1.30pm and 5pm to 8pm; October, 10.30am to 4pm. Closed November to April. 500 Dr.

Firá (Thíra Town): Arheologikó Moussío (Archeological Museum) – Daily except Mondays, 8.30am to 3pm. 800 Dr. ☎ (0286) 22 217.

Episkopí Goniás: Church – May to September, 9am to 1pm and 4pm to 8pm; in winter, when keeper is absent, apply to Fíra cathedral. ☎ (0286) 22 260.

Profítis Ilías: Monastery – May to September, 9am to 1pm; otherwise apply to Fíra Cathedral *(see above)*.

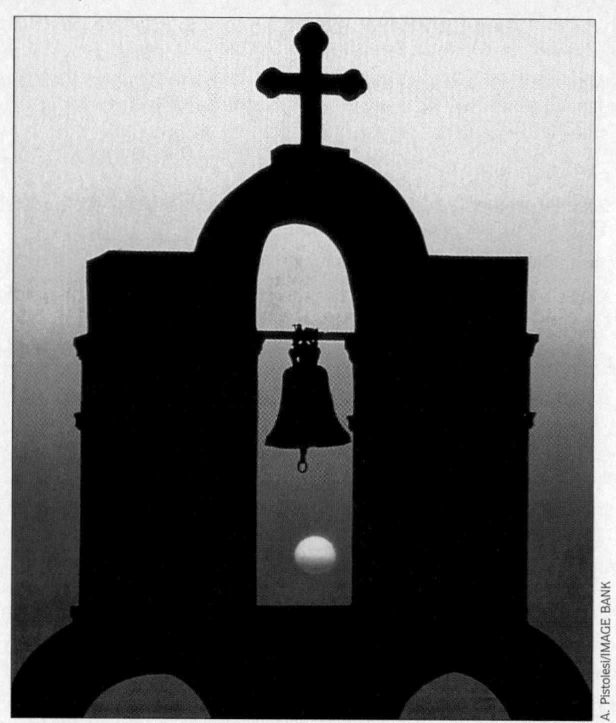
A. Pistolesi/IMAGE BANK

Sunset on Thíra

Arhéa Thíra (Ancient Thera): **Ruins** – Daily except Mondays, 8.30am to 3pm. No charge. ☎ (0286) 23 217.

Akrotíri: Excavations – Daily except Mondays, 8.30am to 3pm. 1 200 Dr. ☎ (0286) 81 366.

TÍNOS

ℹ ☎ (0283) 23 733, 22 234, Fax 23 513

Church of Panagía Evangelístria – 7am to 8pm (5pm October to May). No charge.

Museum of Religious Art and Art Gallery – Daily, 8.30am to 8.30pm (3pm October to May). No charge.

Arheologikó Moussío (Archeological Museum) – Daily except Mondays, 8.30am to 3pm. 500 Dr. ☎ (0283) 22 670.

The Dodecanese

KOS

2 Akti Miaouli ☎ (0242) 29 200; Fax 29 201

Kástro (Knights' Castle) – Summer, daily except Mondays, 8am to 2pm. 800 Dr. ☎ (0242) 28 326.

Arheologikó Moussío (Archeological Museum) – Daily except Mondays, 8am to 2.30pm. 800 Dr.

Archeological site (west) ⓥ – No charge. ☎ (0242) 28 326.

Casa romana – Daily except Mondays, 8am to 2pm. 500 Dr.

Asklipiío (Asklepieion) – Daily except Mondays, 8am to 7.30pm (2pm Saturdays and Sundays). 800 Dr.

PÁTMOS

ℹ ☎ (0247) 31 666, 31 158

Ágios Ioánis Theológos (St John's Monastery) – In principle, Mondays, Wednesdays, Fridays and Saturdays 8am to 2pm, Tuesdays and Thursdays 8am to 1.30pm and 4pm to 6pm, Sundays 10am to 12 noon and 4pm to 6pm. Opening times may vary at the request of travel agents or depending on docking times of cruise ships. 1 000 Dr. ☎ (0247) 21 954.

Simandris House – Summer daily, 9am to 2pm and 5pm to 8pm. 500 Dr.

Convent of Zoodóhos Pigí (The Source of Life) – Sunrise to sunset. Closed during siesta.

Monastery of the Apocalypse – Same as for St John's Monastery.

PICTOR

Pátmos

RÓDOS

Corner of Odós Arhiepiskopu Makariou and Odós Papagou
☎ (0241) 23 255, 23 655, 27 466; Fax 26 955
email: eot-rodos@otenet.gr

Ródos Town

"Son et Lumière" (in the gardens of the Palace of the Grand Masters) – April to October, daily except Sundays (in English), Wednesdays and Sundays (in French).

Paláti Megálon Magístron (Palace of the Grand Masters) – Daily except Mondays, 8.30am to 6.30pm (5pm in winter, 3pm Saturdays and Sundays). 1 200 Dr. ☎ (0241) 21 954.

Nossokomío Ipotón (Knights' Hospital) – Daily except Mondays 8am to 8pm, Mondays 12.30pm to 7pm. 1 200 Dr.

Arheologikó Moussío (Archeological Museum) – Daily except Mondays, 8am to 8pm (3pm Saturdays and Sundays). 800 Dr.

Diakosmitikí Silogí (Museum of Decorative Arts) – Daily except Mondays, 8.30am to 3pm. 600 Dr.

Dzamí Souleïmán (Suleiman Mosque) – Closed temporarily for restoration work.

West and South Ramparts – Tuesdays and Saturdays, 2.45pm. 1 200 Dr.

Enidrío (Aquarium) – 9am to 9pm. 600 Dr.

Excursions

☎ (0244) 31 428

Líndos: Acropolis and fortress – Daily, 8.30am (12.30am Mondays) to 7.30pm (7pm Mondays). 1 200 Dr.

Asklipiío: Church of the Dormition of the Virgin – Only for services.

Mount Filérimos: Iálissos – Daily, Tuesdays to Fridays 8am to 8pm (3pm in winter), other days 8am to 2.30pm. 800 Dr.

Petaloúdes – May to September 8am to 6pm. 600 Dr. from July to mid-September, 300 Dr. in May, June and second half of September.

Kámiros: Ruins – Daily except Mondays, 8am to 8pm (3pm in winter, 2.30pm Saturdays and Sundays). 400 Dr.

KÁLIMNOS

☎ (0243) 29 310

NISSIROS

☎ (0242)

SÍMI

☎ (0241)

North Aegean Islands

HÍOS (Chios)

🅸 Chios town ☎ (0271) 24 217

Híos Town

Vizandinó Moussío (Byzantine Museum) – Daily except Mondays, 9am to 1pm. 500 Dr. ☎ (0271) 26 866.

To Palatáki (Giustiniani Museum) – Daily except Mondays, 9am to 1pm. 500 Dr. ☎ (0271) 22 819

Koraïs Library and P Argenti Museum – Daily except Sundays, 8am to 1.30pm (12 noon Saturdays); also Monday and Thursday evenings 5pm to 8pm. Library no charge. Museum: 400 Dr.

Arheologikó Moussío (Archeological Museum) – Closed temporarily. ☎ (0271) 44 239; Fax (0271) 20 745.

Excursions

Néa Moní – Sunrise to 1pm and 4pm to sunset.

Kámbos: Arhondiká – Most houses are still inhabited and are not open regularly. Visiting is at the owner's discretion. *Groups not admitted to any of the houses.*

Kámbos: Argenti House – To visit apply by phone to the tourist office ☎ (0271) 24 217.

Vrondádos Museum – July and August, Wednesdays and Saturdays 6pm to 8pm; otherwise by appointment. Apply to Mr Liadis, ☎ (0271) 92 608 or 93 440.

LÉSVOS (Lesbos)/MITILÍNI

🅸 6 Odós T Aristarhou ☎ (0251) 42 511, 42 513
at Mitilíni harbour ☎ (0251) 28 199
Airport ☎ (0252) 61 279; Fax 42 512
Northern Aegean Tourist office ☎ 42 511, 42 513, Fax 42 512

Mitilíni (Mytilene): Kástro (Castle) – Daily except Mondays, summer 8am to 2.30pm, winter 8.30am to 3pm. 500 Dr.

Mitilíni (Mytilene): Vizandinó Moussío (Byzantine Museum) – Easter to September or October, daily except Sundays, 9am to 1pm. 400 Dr. ☎ (0251) 27 130.

Mitilíni (Mytilene): Arheologikó Moussío (Archeological Museum) – Daily except Mondays, summer 8am to 2.30pm, winter 8.30am to 3pm. 500 Dr. ☎ (0251) 28 032; Fax (0251) 20 745.

F. TONDEUR

Octopus drying

Mitilíni (Mytilene): Lesviakó spíti (House of Lesbos) – By appointment only; apply on the day or 1 or 2 days in advance to Mrs Vlahou. ☎ (0251) 28 550.

Mitilíni (Mytilene): Women of Lesbos' Collection of Popular Traditions – same applies as for the House of Lesbos.

Mitilíni (Mytilene): Hellenistic Theatre – Daily except Mondays, summer 8am to 2.30pm, winter 8.30am to 3pm. No charge.

Variá: Theophilos Museum – Daily, summer 9am to 2pm and 5.30pm to 8pm, winter 9.30am to 2.30pm. 500 Dr. ☎ (0253) 41 644.

Variá: Teriade Museum – Daily except Mondays, May to September 9am to 2pm and 5pm to 8pm; October to April, 9am to 5pm. 500 Dr.

Agiássos: Museum of Religious and Popular Art – Daily, summer 8am to 8pm, winter 9am to 2pm. 100 Dr.

Limónos Monastery – Sunrise to sunset. Closed summer 1pm to 5pm, except for group tours by appointment.

Pétra: Arhondikó Vareldzidéna (Vareldzidéna House) – Daily except Mondays, 8.30am to 3pm. No charge. ☎ (0253) 41 510.

LÍMNOS (Lemnos)

ℹ ☎ (0254) 22 996

Mírina: Arheologikó Moussío (Archeological Museum) – Daily except Mondays, summer 8am to 2.30pm, winter 8.30am to 3pm. 500 Dr. ☎ (0251) 22 087, 42 589; Fax (0251) 20 745.

Ancient Límnos – Daily except Mondays, summer 9am to 2.30pm, winter 8.30am to 3pm. No charge.

SÁMOS

☎ (0273) 27 980 or 28 582
EOT ☎ (0273) 28 533 or 28 530

Sámos Town

ℹ 4 Odós 25 March ☎ (0273) 28 530

Arheologikó Moussío (Archeological Museum) – Daily except Mondays, summer 8am to 2.30pm, winter 8.30am to 3pm. 800 Dr. ☎ (0273) 27 469.

Zoodóhos Pigí (Source of Life Monastery) – Sunrise to 1pm and 4pm to sunset.

Agía Zóni (Holy Girdle Monastery) – 9am to 1pm and 5pm to sunset.

Mitilíni: Palaeontological Museum – April to October 9am to 2pm. 500 Dr.

Pithagório

ℹ ☎ (0273) 61 333 or 61 389

Archeological Collection – Daily except Mondays, 8.30am to 2pm. No charge. ☎/Fax (0273) 61 400.

Efpalínio (Eupalinos' Aqueduct) – Daily except Mondays, 8.15am to 2pm. 500 Dr. ☎ (0273) 61 400.

Monastery of Panagía Spilianís – Sunrise to sunset.

Thérma (Roman Baths) – Daily except Mondays 10.30am to 2.30pm. No charge.

Iréo (Heraion) – Daily except Mondays, 8am to 2.30pm. 800 Dr. ☎ (0273) 61 177.

Monastery of Megáli Panagía – From June to September 10am to 2.30pm.

Monastery of Timíou Stavroú – 9am to noon and 5pm to 8pm (4pm to sunset November to April).

SKÍROS

Faltaïts Museum of Folk Arts – Summer only, 10am to 1pm and 5.30pm to 9pm. No charge. ☎ (0222) 91 327.

Arheologikó Moussío (Archeological Museum) – Daily except Mondays, summer 8am to 2.30pm, winter 8.30am to 3pm. 500 Dr.

Index

Herakleion *Crete* .... Towns, sights, ruins and tourist regions.
Achilles, témenos .... Mythological and historical people or specialist terms explained in the text.

The spelling used is either a phonetic transcription from demotic Greek (with stress accents) or reflects the Greek spelling; variants are common.

A

B

C

D

E

F

G

H

I – J

K

L

M

N – O

P

R

S

T

U – V

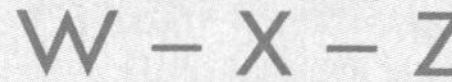